75

INSIGHT

second edition

INSIGHT

A Rhetoric Reader

Edited by

Emil Hurtik
San Diego Mesa College

Robert E. Yarber
Consulting Editor

J. B. LIPPINCOTT COMPANY
Philadelphia

New York   Toronto

Library of Congress Cataloging in Publication Data

Hurtik, Emil, comp.
    Insight: a rhetoric reader.

    1.   English language – Rhetoric.   2.   College
readers.   I.   Yarber, Robert E., joint comp.
II.   Title.
PE1417.H82 1973   808'.04275   72-10873
ISBN 0-397-47274-9

Preface

Since the First Edition of INSIGHT was published three years ago, many users have kindly offered suggestions for changes and improvement. All of these comments have been carefully weighed; in whole or in part most have been incorporated in this new edition. However, because classroom experience has proved its effectiveness, the structure and organization of the original edition has been retained.

Approximately 20% of the selections that appeared in the First Edition have been replaced by new pieces that are better suited to the rhetorical division in which they appear, or that are clearly more pertinent to the needs of today's students. A few essays from long ago, such as those of Swift and Johnson, have been added in response to specific requests.

Thus the balance between the old and the new, the traditional and the cutting edge, conservative and radical, serious and ironic, has not been disturbed. Within each rhetorical division essays are arranged to increase the level of complexity as the student progresses; examples of student themes included as part of the apparatus are designed to simplify the instructor's task of tailoring assignments to fit the limitations of composition classes.

Exercises at the end of each essay are organized so that questions begin with specific items and continue to more general topics involving vocabulary, rhetoric and theme. Additional topics and suggestions for writing assignments are designed to range from simple to relatively complex, encouraging the novice writer to increase gradually the length and difficulty of his responses.

I would like to express my thanks and appreciation to my esteemed colleague and editorial consultant for J. B. Lippincott Company, Robert E. Yarber, who assisted with sound judgment and welcome counsel through all stages of preparation of the manuscript. I am also indebted to my daughter Karla, who served as critic and contributor out of the experience of her own college years, and to Val Rementer, of J. B. Lippincott Company, whose conscientious editing helped to make my task easier than it might otherwise have been.

Rhetorical
Table of Contents

Part One: Narrative
Eldridge Cleaver: *A Day in Folsom Prison*   1
George Orwell: *A Hanging*   9
Anonymous: *Dialogue Across the Gap*   15
Henry David Thoreau: *Where I Lived, and What I Lived For*   22
Gary Snyder: *The Wilderness*   30
Student Example: *Educational Breakthrough*   35

Part Two: Description
Herbert Gold: *Death in Miami Beach*   37
Francis Bacon: *Idols of the Mind*   40
Henry David Thoreau: *The Woodchuck*   43
LeRoi Jones (Imamu Amiri Baraka): *The City of Harlem*   46
Student Example: *View from a Circus*   52

Part Three: Comparison and Contrast
Isaac Asimov: *The Slowly Moving Finger*   55
Margaret Mead: *One Vote for This Age of Anxiety*   66
John Lukacs: *It's Halfway to 1984*   71
Jacob Bronowski: *Science, the Destroyer or Creator?*   81
Avrum Ben-Avi: *Zen Buddhism*   91
Louis J. Halle: *The Language of Statesmen*   100
Kamuti Kiteme: *What is Our Name in Africa?*   106
Student Example: *Crippled Christians*   114

Part Four: Analogy
Julian Huxley: *The Crowded World*   117
Tom Wolfe: *O Rotten Gotham—Sliding Down into the Behavioral
Sink*   126
Leonard I. Stein: *Male and Female: The Doctor-Nurse Game*   138
Student Example: *Britain's Flammable Potato Paddy*   149

Part Five: Definition

Scientific American: *What Is Death?*   153
Eric Berne: *Games*   155
Germaine Greer: *from* THE FEMALE EUNUCH   ✓   165
Ashley Montagu: *On Tribalism Today*   176
Kenneth MacCorquodale: *Behaviorism is a Humanism*   185
Student Example: *What is the Establishment?*   189

Part Six: Classification

Michael V. Kuttnauer: *Logic and Logical Fallacies*   191
Max Black: *Principles of Really Sound Thinking*   221
Samuel Johnson: *Roarers, Whisperers, and Moderators*   226
Hans Selye: *Personality Types*   231
Aldous Huxley: *Who Are You?*   242
Robert Brinckerhoff: *Freudianism, Behaviorism, and Humanism*   258
Rubin Carson: *The Transcendental, Ecological, Proletarian,
   Romantic, Radical Chic, Unisexual, Hot Pants, Paramilitary,
   Nude Los Angeles Woman*   263
Student Example: *Three Faces of Youth*   267

Part Seven: Analysis and Process

Joseph C. Pattison: *How to Write an "F" Paper*   270
Richard K. Redfern: *A Brief Lexicon of Jargon for Those Who Want
   to Speak and Write Verbosely and Vaguely*   273
Kenneth L. Pike: *No Empty Universe*   278
Joan W. Moore and Ralph Guzman: *The Mexican-Americans:
   New Wind from the Southwest*   282
Jan Ehrenwald: *The Occult*   289
Melvin Maddocks: *The Limitations of Language*   296
Eugene Rabinowitch: *Student Rebellion: The Aimless Revolution?*   301
John Taylor: *The Shadow of the Mind*   309
Adrian Dove: *Soul Story*   316
Student Example: *Thorns under the Flowers*   325

Part Eight: Reports and Abstracts

Philip B. Gove: *Preface to* WEBSTER'S THIRD NEW INTERNATIONAL
   DICTIONARY   327
Elizabeth McGough: *Body Language . . . It Tells on You*   337
Dexter K. Strong: *Hair: The Long and the Short of It*   341
Edward J. Moody: *Urban Witches*   352
Donald W. Hastings and Glenn M. Vernon: *Ambiguous Language
   as a Strategy for Individual Action*   365

Part Nine: Arguments and Persuasion

John Milton: *In Defense of Books from* AREOPAGITICA   370
Celia Hubbard: *Missing the Yellow Submarine*   372

John Donne: *Meditation* XVII *from* DEVOTIONS UPON EMERGENT
    OCCASIONS   377
Jonathan Swift: *A Modest Proposal*   380
Karla Hurtik: *One-Track Liberation?*   389
McGeorge Bundy: *The Corrosiveness of Prejudice*   394
John D. Rockefeller, III: *The Youth Revolution: A Positive
    Response*   399
Robert Kasanoff: *Right to Lie?*   407
Robert M. Hutchins: *Limits of Dissent*   411
Philip Wylie: *Generation of Zeros*   414
Mervyn Cadwallader: *Marriage as a Wretched Institution*   420
Ashley Montagu: *The Natural Superiority of Women*   429
Thomas Hobbes: *Of the Natural Condition of Mankind as
    Concerning Their Felicity and Misery*   439
W. T. Stace: *Man Against Darkness*   444
Charles E. Wyzanski, Jr.: *On Civil Disobedience*   457
Paul Ehrlich: *Eco-Catastrophe*   464
A. J. Ayer: *The Elimination of Metaphysics*   478
Shirley Chisholm: *Needed: Equal Educational Opportunity for All*   486
Student Example: *The Los Angelization of the World: A Cultural
    Tragedy*   490

Part Ten: Reviews
George Frazier: *A Sense of Style*   493
Herbert Gold: *Richard Brautigan Mystifies Gently*   498
Ronald Hilton: *Ten Commandments for the New Behavioral
    Science—A Case Study*   502
Stefan Kanfer: *Holden Today: Still in the Rye*   507
Student Example: *The Use and Significance of Dark/Light Imagery
    in Joseph Conrad's* HEART OF DARKNESS   514

Part Eleven: Letters and Miscellany
Frederick S. Perls: *An Editorial: I Am What I Am—No Instant Joy*   517
Henry F. Ottinger: *In Short, Why Did the Class Fail?*   521
John F. Kennedy: *Inaugural Address*   526
Dwight D. Eisenhower: *The Dangers of a Military-Industrial
    Complex*   530
Malcolm X: *Letter from Mecca*   536
Douglas M. Davis: *An Interview with Peter De Vries*   541
John C. Pollard: *An Open Letter to New Students on the Subject
    of Substances, Both Natural and Synthetic, That Have the
    Property of Getting You in Trouble, of Various Sorts*   550
Anonymous: *Desiderata*   558
Student Example: *Bopping Down Memory Lane*   559

Glossary   562

Thematic Table of Contents

Youth and Conflicts

Anonymous: *Dialogue Across the Gap*   15
Eugene Rabinowitch: *Student Rebellion: The Aimless Revolution?*   301
John D. Rockefeller, III: *The Youth Revolution: A Positive Response*   399
Henry F. Ottinger: *In Short, Why Did the Class Fail?*   521
John C. Pollard: *An Open Letter to New Students on the Subject of Substances, Both Natural and Synthetic, That Have the Property of Getting You in Trouble, of Various Sorts*   550
Student Example: *Three Faces of Youth*   267
Student Example: *Thorns under the Flowers*   325

Men vs. Women

Leonard I. Stein: *Male and Female: The Doctor-Nurse Game*   138
Germaine Greer: *from* THE FEMALE EUNUCH   165
Karla Hurtik: *One-Track Liberation?*   389
Ashley Montagu: *The Natural Superiority of Women*   429

Psychology, Personality, and Identity

Henry David Thoreau: *The Woodchuck*   43
Margaret Mead: *One Vote for This Age of Anxiety*   66
Eric Berne: *Games*   155
Hans Selye: *Personality Types*   231
Aldous Huxley: *Who Are You?*   242
Elizabeth McGough: *Body Language . . . It Tells on You*   337
Frederick S. Perls: *An Editorial: I Am What I Am—No Instant Joy*   517
Student Example: *Bopping Down Memory Lane*   559

Art and Culture

Gary Snyder: *The Wilderness*   30
LeRoi Jones (Imamu Amiri Baraka): *The City of Harlem*   46

Adrian Dove: *Soul Story*   316

Dexter K. Strong: *Hair: The Long and the Short of It*   341

John Milton: *In Defense of Books from* AREOPAGITICA   370

McGeorge Bundy: *The Corrosiveness of Prejudice*   394

Philip Wylie: *Generation of Zeros*   414

Mervyn Cadwallader: *Marriage as a Wretched Institution*   420

Herbert Gold: *Richard Brautigan Mystifies Gently*   498

Douglas M. Davis: *An Interview with Peter De Vries*   541

Student Example: *The Los Angelization of the World: A Cultural
Tragedy*   490

Government, Politics, and Sociology

Eldridge Cleaver: *A Day in Folsom Prison*   1

Kamuti Kiteme: *What is Our Name in Africa?*   106

John Lukacs: *It's Halfway to 1984*   71

Ashley Montagu: *On Tribalism Today*   176

Joan W. Moore and Ralph Guzman: *The Mexican-Americans:
New Wind from the Southwest*   282

Shirley Chisholm: *Needed: Equal Educational Opportunity for All*   486

Dwight D. Eisenhower: *The Dangers of a Military-Industrial
Complex*   530

Malcolm X: *Letter from Mecca*   536

Student Example: *View from a Circus*   52

Student Example: *Britain's Flammable Potato Paddy*   149

Student Example: *What is the Establishment?*   189

Religion, Philosophy, and the Occult

Francis Bacon: *Idols of the Mind*   40

Avrum Ben-Avi: *Zen Buddhism*   91

Kenneth L. Pike: *No Empty Universe*   278

Jan Ehrenwald: *The Occult*   289

Edward J. Moody: *Urban Witches*   352

Celia Hubbard: *Missing the Yellow Submarine*   372

John Donne: *Meditation* XVII *from* DEVOTIONS UPON EMERGENT
OCCASIONS   377

Thomas Hobbes: *Of the Natural Condition of Mankind as
Concerning Their Felicity and Misery*   439

W. T. Stace: *Man Against Darkness*   444

A. J. Ayer: *The Elimination of Metaphysics*   478

Student Example: *Crippled Christians*   114

Student Example: *The Use and Significance of Dark/Light Imagery
in Joseph Conrad's* HEART OF DARKNESS   514

Population, Pollution, and Ecology

Julian Huxley: *The Crowded World*   117

Tom Wolfe: *O Rotten Gotham — Sliding Down into the Behavioral Sink*   126
Paul Ehrlich: *Eco-Catastrophe*   464

Law and Order
Robert Kasanoff: *Right to Lie?*   407
Robert M. Hutchins: *Limits of Dissent*   411
Charles E. Wyzanski, Jr.: *On Civil Disobedience*   457

Science and Semantics
Isaac Asimov: *The Slowly Moving Finger*   55
Jacob Bronowski: *Science, the Destroyer or Creator?*   81
Louis J. Halle: *The Language of Statesmen*   100
Kenneth MacCorquodale: *Behaviorism is a Humanism*   185
Michael V. Kuttnauer: *Logic and Logical Fallacies*   191
Robert Brinckerhoff: *Freudianism, Behaviorism, and Humanism*   258
Richard K. Redfern: *A Brief Lexicon of Jargon for Those Who Want to Speak and Write Verbosely and Vaguely*   273
Melvin Maddocks: *The Limitations of Language*   296
John Taylor: *The Shadow of the Mind*   309
Philip B. Gove: *Preface to* WEBSTER'S THIRD NEW INTERNATIONAL DICTIONARY   327
Donald W. Hastings and Glenn M. Vernon: *Ambiguous Language as a Strategy for Individual Action*   365

Humor and Satire
Max Black: *Principles of Really Sound Thinking*   221
Samuel Johnson: *Roarers, Whisperers, and Moderators*   226
Rubin Carson: *The Transcendental, Ecological, Proletarian, Romantic, Radical Chic, Unisexual, Hot Pants, Paramilitary, Nude Los Angeles Woman*   263
Joseph C. Pattison: *How to Write an "F" Paper*   270
Jonathan Swift: *A Modest Proposal*   380
George Frazier: *A Sense of Style*   493
Ronald Hilton: *Ten Commandments for the New Behavioral Science — A Case Study*   502
Student Example: *Educational Breakthrough*   35

Values: Eternal and Short-time
George Orwell: *A Hanging*   9
Henry David Thoreau: *Where I Lived, and What I Lived For*   22
Herbert Gold: *Death in Miami Beach*   37
Scientific American: *What Is Death?*   153
Stefan Kanfer: *Holden Today: Still in the Rye*   507
John F. Kennedy: *Inaugural Address*   526
Anonymous: *Desiderata*   558

Part One:
Narrative

Eldridge Cleaver

A Day in Folsom Prison

My day begins officially at 7:00, when all inmates are required to get   1
out of bed and stand before their cell doors to be counted by guards who
walk along the tier saying, "1, 2, 3 . . ." However, I never remain in bed
until 7. I'm usually up by 5:30. The first thing I do is make up my bed.
Then I pick up all my books, newspapers, etc., off the floor of my cell and
spread them over my bed to clear the floor for calisthenics. In my cell,
I have a little stool on which I lay a large plywood board, about 2½ by
3 feet, which I use as a typing and writing table. At night, I load this
makeshift table down with books and papers, and when I read at night I
spill things all over the floor. When I leave my cell, I set this board,
loaded down, on my bed, so that if a guard comes into my cell to search
it, he will not knock the board off the stool, as has happened before. Still
in the nude, the way I sleep, I go through my routine: kneebends, butterflies, touching my toes, squats, windmills. I continue for about half an
hour.

Sometimes, if I have something I want to write or type so that I can   2
mail it that morning, I forgo my calisthenics. But this is unusual. (We are
required, if we want our mail to go out on a certain day, to have it in the
mailbox by about 8:00. When we leave our cells at 7:30 to go to breakfast, we pass right by the mailbox and drop in our mail on the way to
mess hall.)

Usually, by the time I finish my calisthenics, the trustee (we call him   3
tiertender, or keyman) comes by and fills my little bucket with hot water.
We don't have hot running water ourselves. Each cell has a small sink
with a coldwater tap, a bed, a locker, a shelf or two along the wall, and
a commode. The trustee has a big bucket, with a long spout like the ones
people use to water their flowers, only without the sprinkler. He pokes

the spout through the bars and pours you about a gallon of hot water. My cell door doesn't have bars on it; it is a solid slab of steel with fifty-eight holes in it about the size of a half dollar, and a slot in the center, at eye level, about an inch wide and five inches long. The trustee sticks the spout through one of the little holes and pours my hot water, and in the evenings the guard slides my mail in to me through the slot. Through the same slot the convicts pass newspapers, books, candy, and cigarettes to one another.

When the guard has mail for me he stops at the cell door and calls my   4
name, and I recite my number—A-29498—to verify that I am the right Cleaver. When I get mail I avert my eyes so I can't see who it's from. Then I sit down on my bed and peep at it real slowly, like a poker player peeping at his cards. I can feel when I've got a letter from you, and when I peep up on your name on the envelope I let out a big yell. It's like having four aces. But if the letter is not from you, it's like having two deuces, a three, a four, and a five, all in scrambled suits. A bum kick. Nothing. What is worse is when the guard passes my door without pausing. I can hear his keys jingling. If he stops at my door the keys sound like Christmas bells ringing, but if he keeps going they just sound like—keys.

I live in the honor block. In the other blocks, the fronts of the cells   5
consist of nothing but bars. When I first moved into the honor block, I didn't like it at all. The cells seemed made for a dungeon. The heavy steel doors slammed shut with a clang of finality that chilled my soul. The first time that door closed on me I had the same wild, hysterical sensation I'd felt years ago at San Quentin when they first locked me in solitary. For the briefest moment I felt like yelling out for help, and it seemed that in no circumstances would I be able to endure that cell. All in that split second I felt like calling out to the guards, pleading with them to let me out of the cell, begging them to let me go, promising them that I would be a good boy in the future.

But just as quickly as the feeling came, it went, dissolved, and I felt at   6
peace with myself. I felt that I could endure anything, everything, even the test of being broken on the rack. I've been in every type of cell they have in the prisons of California, and the door to my present cell seems the most cruel and ugly of all. However, I have grown to like this door. When I go out of my cell, I can hardly wait to get back in, to slam that cumbersome door, and hear the sharp click as the trustee snaps the lock behind me. The trustees keep the keys to the cells of the honor block all day, relinquishing them at night, and to get into your cell, all you have to do is round up the trustee in charge of your tier. Once inside my cell, I feel safe: I don't have to watch the other convicts any more or the guards in the gun towers. If you live in a cell with nothing but bars on the front,

you cannot afford to relax; someone can walk along the tier and throw a Molotov cocktail in on you before you know it, something I've seen happen in San Quentin. Whenever I live in one of those barred cells, I keep a blanket within easy reach in case of emergency, to smother a fire if need be. Paranoia? Yes, but it's the least one can do for oneself. In my present cell, with its impregnable door, I don't worry about sabotage—although if someone wanted to badly enough, they could figure something out.

Well . . . after I've finished my calisthenics and the hot water has arrived, I take me a bird (jailbird) bath in the little sink. It's usually about 6:00 by then. From then until 7:30, when we are let out for breakfast, I clean up my cell and try to catch a little news over the radio. Radio?— each cell has a pair of earphones!—with only two channels on it. The programs are monitored from the radio room. The radio schedule is made up by the radio committee, of which I am a member. *7*

At 7:30, breakfast. From the mess hall, every day except Saturday, my day off, I go straight to the bakery, change into my white working clothes, and that's me until about noon. From noon, I am "free" until 3:20, the evening mandatory lockup, when we are required, again, to stand before our cell doors and be counted. There is another count at 6:30 P.M.—three times every day without fail. *8*

When I'm through working in the bakery, I have the choice of (1) going to my cell; (2) staying in the dining room to watch TV; (3) going down to the library; or (4) going out to the yard to walk around, sit in the sun, lift weights, play some funny game—like checkers, chess, marbles, horseshoes, handball, baseball, shuffle board, beating on the punching bag, basketball, talk, TV, paddle-tennis, watching the other convicts who are watching other convicts. When I first came to Folsom, I was astonished to see the old grizzled cons playing marbles. The marble players of Folsom are legendary throughout the prison system: I first heard about them years ago. There is a sense of ultimate defeat about them. Some guy might boast about how he is going to get out next time and stay out, and someone will put him down by saying he'll soon be back, playing marbles like a hasbeen, a neverwas, blasted back into childhood by a crushing defeat to his final dream. The marble players have the game down to an art, and they play all day long, fanatically absorbed in what they are doing. *9*

If I have a cell partner who knows the game, I play him chess now and then, maybe a game each night. I have a chess set of my own and sometimes when I feel like doing nothing else, I take out a little envelope in which I keep a collection of chess problems clipped from newspapers, and run off one or two. But I have never been able to give all my time to *10* one of these games. I am seldom able to play a game of chess out on the yard. Whenever I go out on the yard these days, I'm usually on my way to the library.

On the yard there is a little shack off to one corner which is the office   *11* of the Inmates Advisory Council (IAC). Sometimes I visit the shack to shoot the bull and get the latest drawings (news). And sometimes I go out to the weightlifting area, strip down to a pair of trunks, and push a little iron for a while and soak up the sun.

At 3:20, lockup. Stand for count. After count, off to the evening meal.   *12* Back to the cell. Stand for count at 6:30. After the 6:30 count, we are all let out of our cells, one tier at a time, for showers, to exchange dirty socks and towels for clean ones, a haircut, then back to the cell. I duck this crush by taking my showers in the bakery. At night, I only go to exchange my linen. In the honor block, we are allowed to come out after the 6:30 count every Saturday, Sunday, and Wednesday night to watch TV until 10:00, before we are locked up for the night. The only time I went out for TV was to dig the broads on Shindig and Hollywood-A-Go-Go, but those programs don't come on anymore. We recently got the rule changed so that, on TV nights, those in the honor block can type until 10:00. It used to be that no typing was allowed after 8:00. I am very pleased to be able to get in that extra typing time: I can write you more letters.

On Thursday I go out of my cell after the 6:30 count to attend the   *13* weekly IAC meetings. These meetings adjourn promptly at 9:00. On Saturday mornings, my off day, I usually attend the meetings of the Gavel Club, but this past Saturday I was in the middle of my last letter to you and I stole away to my cell. I enjoyed it so much that I am tempted to put the Gavel Club down, but I hope that I don't because that's where I'm gaining some valuable experience and technique in public speaking.

On the average I spend approximately seventeen hours a day in my   *14* cell. I enjoy the solitude. The only drawback is that I am unable to get the type of reading material I want, and there is hardly anyone with a level head to talk to.

There are quite a few guys here who write. Seems that every convict   *15* wants to. Some of them have managed to sell a piece here and there. They have a writers' workshop which meets in the library under the wing of our librarian. I've never had a desire to belong to this workshop, partly because of my dislike for the attitude of the librarian and partly because of the phony, funny-style convicts. Mostly, I suppose, it's because the members of the workshop are all white and all sick when it comes to color. They're not all sick, but they're not for real. They're fair-weather types, not even as lukewarm as good white liberals, and they conform to the Mississippi atmosphere prevalent here in Folsom. Blacks and whites do not fraternize together in comfort here. Harry Golden's concept of vertical integration and horizontal segregation about covers it. The whites want to talk with you out on the yard or at work, standing up, but they shun you when it comes to sitting down. For instance, when we line up for chow, the lines leading into the mess halls are integrated. But once inside the mess hall, blacks sit at tables by themselves and whites sit with themselves or with the Mexicans.

There's this one Jewish stud out of New York who fell out of Frisco. *16* He thinks he is another Lenny Bruce. In point of fact he is funny and very glib, and I dig rapping (talking) with him. He's a hype but he is very down with the current scéne. Says that he lived in North Beach and all that, and that he has this chick who writes him who is a member of the DuBois Club in Frisco. Well, this cat is well read and we exchange reading material. He says that at home he has every copy of *The Realist* published up to the time of his fall. *The Evergreen Review* kills him. We communicate pretty well and I know that stud is not a racist, but he is a conformist — which in my book is worse, more dangerous, than an out-and-out foe. The other day we were talking about the Free Speech Movement. He was reading a book by Paul Goodman, *Growing Up Absurd,* which he had with him. We were very hung up talking and then it was time for lunch. We got in line and continued our conversation. He was trying to convince me that the whole FSM was predicated on the writings of Paul Goodman, and that he had heard, with his own ears, Mario Savio say as much. Then all of a sudden I noticed this cat grow leery and start looking all around. He made me nervous. I thought maybe someone was trying to sneak up on us with a knife or something. When he kept doing this, I asked him what was the matter with him. He turned real red and said that he "just remembered" that he had to talk to another fellow. I dug right away what the kick was, so I said, "later," and he split. I'm used to such scenes, having a 400-year heritage of learning to roll with that type of punch. I saw him in the mess hall looking very pushed out of shape. I had to laugh at him. I felt that he was probably thinking that if the whites put the blacks in the gas chambers they might grab him too if he was with me. That thought tickled me a little as I watched him peeping around like a ferret. One of his points of indignation is that, he says, he will never forgive Israel for kidnapping and killing Eichmann, and he gets mad at me because I take Israel's side, just to keep the conversation alive. Too much agreement kills a chat. What really bugs him is when I say that there are many blacks who, if they were in the position, would do a little rounding up of the Eichmann types in America. A few days later he told me, "You saw through me the other day, didn't you?"

"I see through you every day," I told him. He looked as if he expected *17* or wanted me to hit him or something. I told him that he was good for nothing but to be somebody's jailhouse wife and he laughed, then launched into a Lenny Bruce-type monologue.

My own reaction is to have as little as possible to do with the whites.   *18*
I have no respect for a duck who runs up to me on the yard all buddy-buddy, and then feels obliged not to sit down with me. It's not that I'm dying to sit with him either, but there is a principle involved which cuts me deeply.

Talk about hypocrisy: you should see the library. We are allowed to   *19*
order, from the state library, only non-fiction and law books. Of the law books, we can only order books containing court opinion. We can get any decision of the California District Court of Appeals, the California Supreme Court, the U.S. District Courts, the Circuit Courts, and the U.S. Supreme Court. But books of an explanatory nature are prohibited. Many convicts who do not have lawyers are forced to act *in propria persona*. They do all right. But it would be much easier if they could get books that showed them how properly to plead their cause, how to prepare their petitions and briefs. This is a perpetual sore point with the Folsom Prison Bar Association, as we call ourselves.

All of the novels one *needs* to read are unavailable, and the librarian   *20*
won't let you send for them. I asked him once if he had read a certain book.

"Oh, yes!" he exclaimed.   *21*

"What did you think of it?" I asked.   *22*

"Absolutely marvelous!" he said.   *23*

"How about letting me send to the state library for it?" I asked.   *24*

"No."   *25*

Books that one wants to read — so bad that it is a taste in the mouth,   *26*
like Calvin C. Hernton's *Sex and Racism in America* — he won't let you have.

"The warden says 'no sex,'" is his perpetual squelch.   *27*

There is a book written by a New York judge which gives case histories   *28*
of prostitutes. The authors explore why white prostitutes, some of them from the deepest South, had Negroes for pimps, and I wanted to reread it.

"No sex," said the librarian. He is indifferent to the fact that it is a   *29*
matter of life and death to me! I don't know how he justifies this because you can go over to the inmate canteen and buy all the prurient pot-boiling anti-literature that has ever been written. But everything that "is happening" today is verboten. I've been dying to read Norman Mailer's *An American Dream,* but that too is prohibited. You can have *Reader's Digest,* but *Playboy?* — not a chance. I have long wanted to file suit in Federal Court for the right to receive *Playboy* magazine. Do you think

Hugh Hefner would finance such an action? I think some very nice ideas would be liberated.

The library does have a selection of very solid material, things done ³⁰ from ten years ago all the way back to the Bible. But it is unsatisfactory to a stud who is trying to function in the last half of the twentieth century. Go down there and try to find Hemingway, Mailer, Camus, Sartre, Baldwin, Henry Miller, Terry Southern, Julain Mayfield, Bellow, William Burroughs, Allen Ginsberg, Herbert Gold, Robert Glover, J. O. Killens, etc.—no action. They also have this sick thing going when it comes to books by and about Negroes. Robert F. Williams' book, *Negroes with Guns,* is not allowed any more. I ordered it from the state library before it was too popular around here. I devoured it and let a few friends read it, before the librarian dug it and put it on the blacklist. Once I ordered two books from the inmate canteen with my own money. When they arrived here from the company, the librarian impounded them, placing them on my "property" the same as they did my notebooks.

I want to devote my time to reading and writing, with everything else ³¹ secondary, but I can't do that in prison. I have to keep my eyes open at all times or I won't make it. There is always some madness going on, and whether you like it or not you're involved. There is no choice in the matter: you cannot sit and wait for things to come to you. So I engage in all kinds of petty intrigue which I've found necessary to survival. It consumes a lot of time and energy. But it is necessary.

QUESTIONS AND EXERCISES

Vocabulary

1. Define or explain each of the following terms:

calisthenics (2)	monologue (17)
paranoia (6)	hypocrisy (19)
impregnable (6)	*in propria persona* (19)
sabotage (6)	prurient (28)
prevalent (15)	

2. What is the level of diction of each of the following?

stud (16)	split (16)
rapping (16)	bugs (16)
dug (16)	pimp (27)
kick (16)	verboten (28)

3. What is the name of the product of the following process?
   Inmates Advisory Council = IAC
   Congress Of Racial Equality = CORE

Rhetoric

4. What figure of speech is each of the following:
   "like a poker player peeping at his card" (4)
   "like Christmas bells ringing" (4)
   "like having two deuces, a three, a four, and a five, all in scrambled suits" (4)
   "as lukewarm as good white liberals" (15)
   "peeping around like a ferret" (16)
5. What rhetorical device is used in each of the following excerpts?
   "poker player peeping" (4)
   "prurient pot-boiling" (28)
6. To what literary figures does Cleaver allude?
7. What qualities do these writers have in common?
8. In what ways does Cleaver try to give the reader the feeling of prison life?

Theme

9. Although the main emphasis of this essay is the description of a day in Folsom Prison, Cleaver includes bits of narrative and attitudes about other topics. Find an example of one of his attitudes.
10. What does Cleaver want to do most while in prison?
11. What emotions does Cleaver's essay evoke in you? Are they the same ones that he experienced?

Topics and Assignments for Composition

1. In one sentence describe Cleaver's attitude toward the life in prison.
2. In a 200 to 300 word paragraph analyze Cleaver's style.
3. Describe a place that you know well; limit your description to one well-developed paragraph.
4. Write a composition in which you emulate Cleaver's technique of giving many concrete details and examples to create an emotional impact upon the reader.
5. Most people in a college environment have never been in prison, even as visitors. However most students have visited unpleasant places. Write an essay describing the worst place that you have ever visited. Try to project the emotions that you experienced using details, illustrations, examples, and images.

George Orwell

A Hanging

It was in Burma, a sodden morning of the rains. A sickly light, like yellow tinfoil, was slanting over the high walls into the jail yard. We were waiting outside the condemned cells, a row of sheds fronted with double bars, like small animal cages. Each cell measured about ten feet by ten and was quite bare within except for a plank bed and a pot for drinking water. In some of them brown, silent men were squatting at the inner bars, with their blankets draped round them. These were the condemned men, due to be hanged within the next week or two. *1*

One prisoner had been brought out of his cell. He was a Hindu, a puny wisp of a man, with a shaven head and vague liquid eyes. He had a thick sprouting moustache, absurdly too big for his body, rather like the moustache of a comic man on the films. Six tall Indian warders were guarding him and getting him ready for the gallows. Two of them stood by with rifles and fixed bayonets, while the others handcuffed him, passed a chain through his handcuffs and fixed it to their belts, and lashed his arms tight to his sides. They crowded very close about him, with their hands always on him in a careful, caressing grip, as though all the while feeling him to make sure he was there. It was like men handling a fish which is still alive and may jump back into the water. But he stood quite unresisting, yielding his arms limply to the ropes, as though he hardly noticed what was happening. *2*

Eight o'clock struck and a bugle call, desolately thin in the wet air, floated from the distant barracks. The superintendent of the jail, who was standing apart from the rest of us, moodily prodding the gravel with his stick, raised his head at the sound. He was an army doctor, with a grey toothbrush moustache and a gruff voice. "For God's sake hurry up, *3*

Francis," he said irritably. "The man ought to have been dead by this time. Aren't you ready yet?"

Francis, the head jailer, a fat Dravidian in a white drill suit and gold   *4*
spectacles, waved his black hand. "Yes sir, yes sir," he bubbled. "All iss satisfactorily prepared. The hangman iss waiting. We shall proceed."

"Well, quick march, then. The prisoners can't get their breakfast till   *5*
this job's over."

We set out for the gallows. Two warders marched on either side of the   *6*
prisoner, with their rifles at the slope; two others marched close against him, gripping him by arm and shoulder, as though at once pushing and supporting him. The rest of us, magistrates and the like, followed behind. Suddenly, when we had gone ten yards, the procession stopped short without any order or warning. A dreadful thing had happened—a dog, come goodness knows whence, had appeared in the yard. It came bounding among us with a loud volley of barks and leapt round us wagging its whole body, wild with glee at finding so many human beings together. It was a large wooly dog, half Airdale, half pariah. For a moment it pranced round us, and then, before anyone could stop it, it had made a dash for the prisoner, and jumping up tried to lick his face. Everybody stood aghast, too taken aback even to grab the dog.

"Who let that bloody brute in here?" said the superintendent angrily.   *7*
"Catch it, someone!"

A warder detached from the escort, charged clumsily after the dog, but   *8*
it danced and gambolled just out of reach, taking everything as part of the game. A young Eurasian jailer picked up a handful of gravel and tried to stone the dog away, but it dodged the stones and came after us again. Its yaps echoed from the jail walls. The prisoner, in the grasp of the two warders, looked on incuriously, as though this was another formality of the hanging. It was several minutes before someone managed to catch the dog. Then we put my handkerchief through its collar and moved off once more, with the dog still straining and whimpering.

It was about forty yards to the gallows. I watched the bare brown back   *9*
of the prisoner marching in front of me. He walked clumsily with his bound arms, but quite steadily, with that bobbing gait of the Indian who never straightens his knees. At each step his muscles slid neatly into place, the lock of hair on his scalp danced up and down, his feet printed themselves on the wet gravel. And once, in spite of the men who gripped him by each shoulder, he stepped lightly aside to avoid a puddle on the path.

It is curious, but till that moment I have never realized what it means   *10*
to destroy a healthy, conscious man. When I saw the prisoner step aside

to avoid the puddle I saw the mystery, the unspeakable wrongness, of cutting a life short when it is in full tide. This man was not dying, he was alive just as we are alive. All the organs of his body were working— bowels digesting food, skin renewing itself, nails growing, tissues form- ing—all toiling away in solemn foolery. His nails would still be growing when he stood on the drop, when he was falling through the air with a tenth-of-a-second to live. His eyes saw the yellow gravel and the grey walls, and his brain still remembered, foresaw, reasoned—even about puddles. He and we were a party of men walking together, seeing, hear- ing, feeling, understanding the same world; and in two minutes, with a sudden snap, one of us would be gone—one mind less, one world less.

The gallows stood in a small yard, separate from the main grounds of *11* the prison, and overgrown with tall prickly weeds. It was a brick erection like three sides of a shed, with planking on top, and above that two beams and a crossbar with the rope dangling. The hangman, a grey-haired con- vict in the white uniform of the prison, was waiting beside his machine. He greeted us with a servile crouch as we entered. At a word from Fran- cis the two warders, gripping the prisoner more closely than ever, half led, half pushed him to the gallows and helped him clumsily up the ladder. Then the hangman climbed up and fixed the rope round the prisoner's neck.

We stood waiting, five yards away. The warders had formed in a rough *12* circle round the gallows. And then, when the noose was fixed, the pris- oner began crying out to his god. It was a high, reiterated cry of "Ram! Ram! Ram! Ram!" not urgent and fearful like a prayer or cry for help, but steady, rhythmical, almost like the tolling of a bell. The dog answered the sound with a whine. The hangman, still standing on the gallows, pro- duced a small cotton bag like a flour bag and drew it down over the pris- oner's face. But the sound, muffled by the cloth, still persisted, over and over again: "Ram! Ram! Ram! Ram! Ram!"

The hangman climbed down and stood ready, holding the lever. Min- *13* utes seemed to pass. The steady, muffled crying from the prisoner went on and on, "Ram! Ram! Ram!" never faltering for an instant. The super- intendent, his head on his chest, was slowly poking the ground with his stick; perhaps he was counting the cries, allowing the prisoner a fixed number—fifty, perhaps, or a hundred. Everyone had changed colour. The Indians had gone grey like bad coffee, and one or two of the bayonets were wavering. We looked at the lashed, hooded man on the drop, and listened to his cries—each cry another second of life; the same thought was in all our minds: oh, kill him quickly, get it over, stop that abominable noise!

Suddenly the superintendent made up his mind. Throwing up his head *14*
he made a swift motion with his stick. "Chalo!" he shouted almost
fiercely.

There was a clanking noise, and then dead silence. The prisoner had *15*
vanished, and the rope was twisting on itself. I let go of the dog, and it
galloped immediately to the back of the gallows; but when it got there it
stopped short, barked, and then retreated into a corner of the yard, where
it stood among the weeds, looking timorously out at us. We went round
the gallows to inspect the prisoner's body. He was dangling with his toes
pointed straight downwards, very slowly revolving, as dead as a stone.

The superintendent reached out with his stick and poked the bare *16*
brown body; it oscillated slightly. "*He's* all right," said the superintendent. He backed out from under the gallows, and blew out a deep
breath. The moody look had gone out of his face quite suddenly. He
glanced at his wrist-watch. "Eight minutes past eight. Well, that's all for
this morning, thank God."

The warders unfixed bayonets and marched away. The dog, sobered *17*
and conscious of having misbehaved itself, slipped after them. We walked
out of the gallows yard, past the condemned cells with their waiting prisoners, into the big central yard of the prison. The convicts, under the
command of warders armed with lathis, were already receiving their
breakfast. They squatted in long rows, each man holding a tin pannikin,
while two warders with buckets marched round ladling out rice; it seemed
quite a homely, jolly scene, after the hanging. An enormous relief had
come upon us now that the job was done. One felt an impulse to sing, to
break into a run, to snigger. All at once everyone began chattering gaily.

The Eurasian boy walking beside me nodded towards the way we had *18*
come, with a knowing smile: "Do you know, sir, our friend (he meant the
dead man) when he heard his appeal had been dismissed, he pissed on
the floor of his cell. From fright. Kindly take one of my cigarettes, sir.
Do you not admire my new silver case, sir? From the boxwallah, two
rupees eight annas. Classy European style."

Several people laughed—at what, nobody seemed certain. *19*

Francis was walking by the superintendent, talking garrulously: "Well, *20*
sir, all hass passed off with the utmost satisfactoriness. It was all finished
—flick! like that. It iss not always so—oah, no! I have known cases where
the doctor wass obliged to go beneath the gallows and pull the prisoner's
legs to ensure decease. Most disagreeable!"

"Wriggling about, eh? That's bad," said the superintendent. *21*

"Ach, sir, it iss worse when they become refractory! One man, I recall, *22*
clung to the bars of hiss cage when we went to take him out. You will

scarcely credit, sir, that it took six warders to dislodge him, three pulling at each leg. We reasoned with him, 'My dear fellow,' we said, 'think of all the pain and trouble you are causing to us!' But no, he would not listen! Ach, he wass very troublesome!"

I found that I was laughing quite loudly. Everyone was laughing. Even   23
the superintendent grinned in a tolerant way. "You'd better all come out and have a drink," he said quite genially. "I've got a bottle of whisky in the car. We could do with it."

We went through the big double gates of the prison into the road. "Pull-   24
ing at his legs!" exclaimed a Burmese magistrate suddenly, and burst into a loud chuckling. We all began laughing again. At that moment Francis' anecdote seemed extraordinarily funny. We all had a drink together, native and European alike, quite amicably. The dead man was a hundred yards away.

QUESTIONS AND EXERCISES

Vocabulary

1. Define or explain each of the following terms:

Dravidian (4)	lathis (17)
pariah (6)	pannikin (17)
gambolled (8)	Eurasian (18)
Ram (12)	boxwallah (18)
abominable (13)	garrulously (20)
Chalo (14)	refractory (22)
timorously (15)	

Rhetoric

2. Almost every reader will experience an emotional reaction upon reading Orwell's "A Hanging." Why?
3. Comment on the originality and appropriateness of the following figures of speech:

"like yellow tinfoil" (1)	"like bad coffee" (13)
"like men handling a fish" (2)	"as dead as a stone" (15)

4. What does *verisimilitude* mean? Does Orwell achieve it in his description?
5. Give several examples of concrete images.
6. Find several examples of Orwell's rather dry irony.
   Example: paragraph 9, "he stepped aside to avoid a puddle" = irony: a man about to die avoiding a trivial annoyance.

Theme

7. At what point does Orwell shift from a cool, detached observer to an emotionally involved participant?
8. How does the dog's treatment of the prisoner serve as a comment on man's values?
9. Explain the magistrate's reactions after the hanging.
10. What is the implication of the phrase "one world less" in paragraph 11?
11. Comment on the significance of the final sentence in paragraph 24.

Topics and Assignments for Composition

1. Write a one sentence summary of the essay.
2. Write a short paragraph on Orwell's use of irony.
3. In one paragraph discuss the effectiveness of Orwell's language.
4. Write a short essay on the conflict between law and human values.
5. Write an essay in which you point out the psychology and function of humor in human relationships. What examples of humor did you find in the article? Why do you think the humor was there?

Anonymous

Dialogue Across the Gap

Echoes of a bugle-blown "retreat" racketed from venerable red brick   *1*
buildings around the grassy campus. ROTC cadets, led by graduating
officers parading their commission for the first time, passed in review
under the fond eyes of parents and sweethearts gathered on the New
England campus for the bittersweet rites of spring. After retreat, among
the many khaki-clad lieutenants, a lone naval ensign in dress whites
mingled with the throng which slowly dissipated and left me alone with
my only son.

That ensign's uniform with its deliberately antiquated choker collar,   *2*
its vulnerable but impeccable whiteness, scornful of the grimy world outside the senior service, filled me with nostalgia for my youth. For five
years I had worn that uniform and a glimpse of it under the emotional
conditions of my son's graduation brought back the plunging bridge of
my destroyer, gale-driven spume, snapping pennants and crashing guns.
Once again a ragged circle of rockets soared forward in a lazy arch and
dropped a lethal girdle around an enemy submarine. Once again for a
moment I was one of my country's young lions.

But that uniform which had stirred me so deeply was not worn by my   *3*
son. Nor was he garbed in the khaki of the ROTC graduate. He wore a
pair of corduroy trousers and a nylon windbreaker, his only insignia a
pin with the curious four-pronged symbol that internationally marks the
peacenik and looks so incongruously like an intercontinental ballistic
missile in its gantry.

My son had not come to the quadrangle as part of the martial review,   *4*
but for a counterdemonstration, a ceremony rejecting the military and
pledging resistance to conscription, even unto the penitentiary.

Reprinted from VISTA, copyright © 1968 by the United Nations Association.

The reasons for the anonymity of this article are, upon reading, obvious. It is
a very personal report by one of America's most respected writers.

Perhaps 45 or 50 students and spectators sat on the library steps and   *5*
strained to hear almost inaudible speeches by graduating seniors, leaders
of the resistance. A half dozen faculty members sat behind the speakers,
facing the audience. Apparently daunted by the penitentiary sentence that
threatened Dr. Benjamin Spock and Chaplain Coffin, they let the kids do
all the counselling against conscription. (Their timid prudence gave me
a hint of why the young have almost deified the sexagenarian but gallantly
imprudent doctor.)

After the pomp of the military, the peace demonstration had a de-   *6*
pressingly grubby air. The spokesman of the group wore a wispy pale
moustache that did little to virilize the epicene effect of girlishly plump
breasts bulging under a knit jersey blouse. But he was the hero of the
meeting, for he alone had had the courage to turn in his draft card and
court prison for his beliefs. A few protesters, my son most prominent
among them, had the scrubbed good looks of the typical vitamin-enriched
American bourgeois of the "less than 30" generation. But a disturbing
few affected the eccentric coiffures, bizarre clothing, and somnambulant
manner my generation associates with sloth, alienation, anarchy. Hippies,
in a word.

The protesters signed a formal statement swearing to refuse military   *7*
service so long as the Vietnam war lasts. Protest leaders handed the document to a faculty member for filing in the school's archives. The ceremony
ended with a little song of self-conscious defiance and a tentative showing by a few of the two-fingered victory salute borrowed by peaceniks
from that redoubtable warrior Winston Churchill.

That night the futility of the gesture and the hideous retribution the   *8*
youngsters were courting disturbed my sleep. The bravely-worded petition itself was already lost in the vast archival deposits of almost 200
years. The only person of authority who had noted the counterdemonstration was a sinister photographer who had recorded the act of signing by
each protester.

On the drive with my son through New England to New York next day,   *9*
Jack handled the wheel with the nerve-wracking ease of sharp young
reflexes, casually negotiating hairbreadth escapes from disaster. Worse,
he flipped on the radio and jerked his head happily to hard rock rhythms
that bashed my brain to a throbbing pulp. But I held my peace.

Flashing red lights and a tangle of stalled cars forced us to creep by a   *10*
station wagon with motor pushed to the rear seat and front tires almost
touching the rear axel. On the pavement lay a still form covered by a
blanket.

"What a stupid way to die," I hinted.   *11*

"Why? He was on a peaceful mission and knew where he was going.   *12*

It beats getting killed while you burn down a village you never heard of and call yourself a hero."

The callousness, the indifference to the death he had just witnessed, the arrogant assumption of superior morality by this featherless nestling made me explode. (I had myself shelled villages with Oriental names and had indeed felt heroic doing it.)   *13*

"What the hell do you know about war? You young punks pontificate about war but you've never heard a shot fired in anger. You knock the Establishment as murderously inept and you can't even organize a campus demonstration that isn't a pitiful and dangerous farce. The only thing you accomplish is to get yourselves thrown into the penitentiary and break your mothers' hearts. Let those other dismal asses go to jail. For you, I won't have it. I forbid it."   *14*

The car slowed, Jack's eyes narrowed and his breathing became rapid and shallow, his ordinarily vapid good looks coarsened and hardened.   *15*

"Now I have to say it. I did more than graduate yesterday. I grew up.   *16*

"You have accused me of bullying my mother and sister and I have never given you the obvious answer. If I am a bully, I come by it honestly. You have reminded me almost daily that you are smarter and tougher than I am. And I have been a good boy and taken it in silence. Doesn't it tell you something that the only distinction I made in school was in track, a sport you always scorned. You never even knew I was good till I won the state 440 dash championship—then everybody thought you had run the race to hear you tell about it.   *17*

"But I am 22 now, a graduate of a prestigious college, which was your dream for me, but with only a mediocre record which was my sorry thanks to you. But it was my record not ours. I'll get my butt kicked all over the place, but it is my butt. I remain your most loving admirer, but I am a grown man."   *18*

He broke off and resumed speed, breathing heavily. I sat silent and numb. Amidst the green pastures of the Berkshires, the dreaded confrontation had come between the old bull and the young bull. I wanted to tiptoe away from the encounter with this frightening young bull for fear of losing.   *19*

He continued.   *20*

"If I put on that uniform you admire so much, I'd wear it as Daddy's Boy and hate you and myself every second I wore it."   *21*

Then I wanted to tiptoe away from the encounter for fear of winning.   *22*

At a pleasant maple-shady village, the car slowed to zigzag through a volunteer fire company recoiling hoses after fighting a blaze at a gas station. I saw again the apocalyptic vision of a year ago when I flew at 33,000 feet over Da Nang and witnessed at one glance dozens of smoking   *23* fires spread over miles of tormented Vietnam. At the marine base below, brave men had been pushing sorties into the bush to battle, marines every bit as brave as the tigers I had known and respected at Iwo.

"Why do you despise the uniform, son? I wore it with pride. It hurts   24
me enough that you won't wear it, but it crushes me that you spit on it."

"I don't despise the uniform. I just won't wear it during this war. Your   25
war was easy. Hitler was a monster; the Japanese attacked us wantonly. Even I would have fought that one. But this war stinks. And the young people, the ones who have to do the fighting, at least the ones who think a little, despise the war and loathe the old people who got us into it and now want us to die getting them out of it so they can toast the victory and have a good cry putting wreaths on our graves."

"The young ensign who got his commission yesterday looked pretty   26
gung ho to me."

"He'll look pretty gung ho three years from now too, and not a scar on   27
his body. The son-of-a-bitch signed every hawk manifesto on the campus and called us protesters every kind of traitorous faggot his little bird brain could remember. But the big bad hero is going to spend his three years as a Navy officer in a graduate school on a deferment from the armed forces —a privilege we protesters can't get from our draft boards. That's the kind of uniformed hero that really gives us protesters the bellyache.

"We got it on the underground this June that at Dartmouth six of the   28
nine ROTC officers who refused to sign an anti-war advertisement paid for by other officer graduates have bugged out of active service by taking graduate school deferments. A much higher percentage of the officer protesters quietly accepted active duty without bugging out—the idiots. Now what are *they* proving—killing people in a war they have publicly called immoral and illegal. They're worse than John Wayne's asinine commandos. At least the Green Berets believe in their horrors."

"How can you say we are fighting in Vietnam illegally? We went there   29
by request of a government invoking a legal defense treaty."

"But that government existed only because we blocked the general   30
elections promised by the Geneva agreements that ended the French Indo-China war. We set up that corrupt Diem government against the will of the people, armed it against the Geneva agreement, sent the first foreign soldiers into the country, bombed a nation which hasn't attacked us—and now we show innocent bewilderment when lots of folks call us aggressors."

The verdant Berkshires had levelled near the seacoast and the highway   31
ran a gauntlet of neon and glass front monstrosities that effectively hid what vestiges of New England charm had survived mid-century progress. The sun was low, so I proposed a cocktail and snack before bucking the

expressway traffic near the city. Jack's track training habits hung on and he settled for a malted, but he sat through two of my martinis. The juke box banged out a stupefying rock number and we had to shout to be heard.

"I know lots of the kids in here," Jack said. "Most of them are sailors   *32* on weekend liberty from the base up the coast."

"Why are they all in civilian clothes?"   *33*

"My God, they shuck that monkey suit the second the whistle blows."   *34*

"But in my day a uniform in a bar was good for a dozen free drinks   *35* from old-timers like me."

"You've really got to forget that old-fashioned jazz, Dad. No old-   *36* timers are buying young people anything these days but a splendidly murderous M-16 and a one-way ticket to the Far East. Your generation is scared to death of my people, in or out of uniform. In your hearts you know we are raging about the corner you've backed us into—and you're scared of us. You have poured something like 30 billion dollars a year into a stupid brush fire halfway around the world, and our schools rot away for lack of money to hire good teachers, children grow up stupid and runty from lack of protein, our cities fall apart for lack of leaders who give a damn. Our life every day looks more squalid here at home while we puke up fountains of dollars for the warlords of Asia. You'd *better* be scared of us.

"Look around the bar. Not one black face. One out of five Americans   *37* in combat is black. When that black man finally steps on a pongi stick and dies of gangrene, he can't be buried in a white cemetery back home. If he does make it back alive, he can't get a job because you can't park cars with only one leg. And if he miraculously makes it back in one piece, he'll be as welcome in this bar as a toad in a punchbowl."

That day's papers had carried headlines about more blind fury in some   *38* black urban pesthole somewhere—nobody even remarks the exact location any more so long as it is comfortable miles away.

"The President says we are fighting in Vietnam so we won't have to   *39* fight in California. Man, we already are fighting in California. Watts, remember? The black population of this country is almost exactly as large as the Vietnamese population. And the blacks are here, all around us. And they are just as angry as the Viet Cong. And they are just as tough and mean. How much more of this stupidity of saving Vietnam at the expense of Harlem do you think they are going to put up with? And when that guerilla war starts for real, there is not enough napalm to stop it. For one thing, one-fifth of the army is going to leave us for the other side—and it won't be the sissy fifth leaving."

We left the bar and bulled our way into the citybound crowd on the   *40* interstate highway. Within minutes we were zipping by the squalor of Spanish Harlem. I looked down into teeming streets and through grimy windows into the unlovely flats of the urban poor.

"I can't deny the justice of much of what you say, son. But don't go to the penitentiary. That's too ugly. Run off to Sweden or Canada—I'll pay the freight—but don't go to jail."   *41*

"You still don't understand. Running away is truly a sign of despair for the country. Leaving America, knowing you'll never see it again, does verge on treason. I am patriotic and still hope for my country. If I must go to jail, I hope my sacrifice will help jolt this nation back to sanity. If enough of America's smartest young men choose five years in a Federal pen rather than military service, maybe even the American Legion will dimly suspect something is grievously wrong."   *42*

"Isn't there something you can do besides volunteering for jail?"   *43*

"Sure, and we're doing it. We're working for the country in Vista or the Peace Corps. We're badgering our congressmen with mail and demonstrations. We're fighting for the rights of Negroes and the poor. We're sharing our little money with the American Civil Liberties Union to keep at least one agency working on the side of law and order for everybody— not just for the suburban fat cat. And we flatly refuse to delegate the right to make our moral decisions to a ranch hand who happens to live in the White House. So here we are back at the jailhouse door again."   *44*

"Well, at least you live in a country where you have the right to dissent."   *45*

"Ha! Go tell that to Dr. Spock."   *46*

"He was convicted for conspiring against the Selective Service Act."   *47*

"Even you don't believe that and I'll prove it to you. You are a professional writer and you use every experience as grist for your mill. I know you're going to write up this encounter with me. But because you are afraid the draft board will nail me with a punitive induction for publicly dissenting, you won't dare sign your name."   *48*

He's right.   *49*

QUESTIONS AND EXERCISES

Vocabulary

1. Define or explain each of the following terms:

dialogue	virilize (6)
anonymity	epicene (6)
dissipated (1)	bizarre (6)
antiquated (2)	somnambulant (6)

impeccable (2)	farce (14)
spume (2)	vapid (15)
lethal (2)	prestigious (18)
incongruously (3)	mediocre (18)
gantry (3)	apocalyptic (23)
sexagenarian (5)	gung ho (26)
impudent (5)	asinine (28)

2. What level of usage is each of the following words?

peacenik (3)	punks (14)
hippies (6)	bugged out (28)

3. Give the history behind each of these words:

lethal (2)	establishment (14)
gantry (3)	apocalyptic (23)

Rhetoric

4. Find an example of a simile in paragraph 37.
5. Find an example of irony in paragraph 42.
6. What is the meaning of the allusion: "Run off to Sweden or Canada" in paragraph 41?
7. What unusual quality of style results from the use of the dialogue?

Theme

8. Which of the participants in the dialogue seems to change more in his attitude as the dialogue progresses?
9. With whom did you side in the argument? Why?

Topics and Assignments for Composition

1. In one sentence summaries, outline each of the positions in the dialogue.
2. In one paragraph discuss the psychological give-and-take between father and son.
3. Write a 300 word essay in which you analyze the logic of either of the positions in the dialogue.
4. Write a short dialogue between persons who have a personal relationship. Have them discuss a controversial subject that often ends in heated, emotional argument.
5. Write a 500-word essay about the generation gap.

Henry David Thoreau

Where I Lived, and What I Lived For

I went to the woods because I wished to live deliberately, to front only 1
the essential facts of life, and see if I could not learn what it had to teach,
and not, when I came to die, discover that I had not lived. I did not wish
to live what was not life, living is so dear; nor did I wish to practise resignation, unless it was quite necessary. I wanted to live deep and suck out
all the marrow of life, to live so sturdily and Spartan-like as to put to rout
all that was not life, to cut a broad swath and shave close, to drive life into
a corner, and reduce it to its lowest terms, and, if it proved to be mean,
why then to get the whole and genuine meanness of it, and publish its
meanness to the world; or if it were sublime, to know it by experience,
and be able to give a true account of it in my next excursion. For most
men, it appears to me, are in a strange uncertainty about it, whether it is
of the devil or of God, and have *somewhat hastily* concluded that it is the
chief end of man here to "glorify God and enjoy him forever."

Still we live meanly, like ants; though the fable tells us that we were 2
long ago changed into men; like pygmies we fight with cranes; it is error
upon error, and clout upon clout, and our best virtue has for its occasion
a superfluous and evitable wretchedness. Our life is frittered away by
detail. An honest man has hardly need to count more than his ten fingers,
or in extreme cases he may add his ten toes, and lump the rest. Simplicity,
simplicity, simplicity! I say, let your affairs be as two or three, and not a
hundred or a thousand; instead of a million count half a dozen, and keep
your accounts on your thumb-nail. In the midst of this chopping sea of
civilized life, such are the clouds and storms and quicksands and thousand-and-one items to be allowed for, that a man has to live, if he would
not founder and go to the bottom and not make his port at all, by dead
reckoning, and he must be a great calculator indeed who succeeds. Simplify, simplify. Instead of three meals a day, if it be necessary eat but
one; instead of a hundred dishes, five; and reduce other things in proportion. Our life is like a German Confederacy, made up of petty states, with

its boundary forever fluctuating, so that even a German cannot tell you how it is bounded at any moment. The nation itself, with all its so-called internal improvements, which, by the way are all external and superficial, is just such an unwieldy and overgrown establishment, cluttered with furniture and tripped up by its own traps, ruined by luxury and heedless expense, by want of calculation and a worthy aim, as the million households in the lands; and the only cure for it, as for them, is in a rigid economy, a stern and more than Spartan simplicity of life and elevation of purpose. It lives too fast. Men think that it is essential that the *Nation* have commerce, and export ice, and talk through a telegraph, and ride thirty miles an hour, without a doubt, whether *they* do or not; but whether we should live like baboons or like men, is a little uncertain. If we do not get out sleepers, and forge rails, and devote days and nights to the work, but go to tinkering upon our *lives* to improve *them*, who will build railroads? And if railroads are not built, how shall we get to heaven in season? But if we stay at home and mind our business, who will want railroads? We do not ride on the railroad; it rides upon us. Did you ever think what those sleepers are that underlie the railroad? Each one is a man, an Irishman, or a Yankee man. The rails are laid on them, and they are covered with sand, and the cars run smoothly over them. They are sound sleepers, I assure you. And every few years a new lot is laid down and run over; so that, if some have the pleasure of riding on a rail, others have the misfortune to be ridden upon. And when they run over a man that is walking in his sleep, a supernumerary sleeper in the wrong position, and wake him up, they suddenly stop the cars, and make a hue and cry about it, as if this were an exception. I am glad to know that it takes a gang of men for every five miles to keep the sleepers down and level in their beds as it is, for this is a sign that they may sometimes get up again.

Why should we live with such hurry and waste of life? We are determined to be starved before we are hungry. Men say that a stitch in time saves nine, and so they take a thousand stitches to-day to save nine to-morrow. As for *work,* we haven't any of any consequence. We have the Saint Vitus' dance, and cannot possibly keep our heads still. If I should only give a few pulls at the parish bell-rope, as for a fire, that is, without setting the bell, there is hardly a man on his farm in the outskirts of Concord, notwithstanding that press of engagements which was his excuse so many times this morning, nor a boy, nor a woman, I might almost say, but would foresake all and follow that sound, not mainly to save property from the flames, but, if we will confess the truth, much more to see it burn, since burn it must, and we, be it known, did not set it on fire,—or to see it put out, and have a hand in it, if that is done as handsomely; yes, even if it were the parish church itself. Hardly a man takes a half-hour's nap after dinner, but when he wakes he holds up his head and asks, "What's the news?" as if the rest of mankind had stood his sentinels. Some give directions to be waked every half-hour, doubtless for no other purpose; and then, to pay for it, they tell what they have dreamed. After a night's sleep the news is as indispensable as the breakfast. "Pray tell me anything new that has happened to a man anywhere on this globe," — and he reads it over his coffee and rolls, that a man has had his eyes gouged out this morning on the Wachito River; never dreaming the while that he lives in the dark unfathomed mammoth cave of this world, and has but the rudiment of an eye himself.

For my part, I could easily do without the post-office. I think that there   *4* are very few important communications made through it. To speak critically, I never received more than one or two letters in my life — I wrote this some years ago — that were worth the postage. The penny-post is, commonly, an institution through which you seriously offer a man that penny for his thoughts which is so often safely offered in jest. And I am sure that I never read any memorable news in a newspaper. If we read of one man robbed, or murdered, or killed by accident, or one house burned, or one vessel wrecked, or one steamboat blown up, or one cow run over on the Western Railroad, or one mad dog killed, or one lot of grasshoppers in the winter, — we never need read of another. One is enough. If you are acquainted with the principle, what do you care for a myriad instances and applications? To a philosopher all *news,* as it is called, is gossip, and they who edit and read it are old women over their tea. Yet not a few are greedy after this gossip. There was such a rush, as I hear, the other day at one of the offices to learn the foreign news by the last arrival, that several large squares of plate glass belonging to the establishment were broken by the pressure, — news which I seriously think a ready wit might write a twelvemonth, or twelve years, beforehand with sufficient accuracy. As for Spain, for instance, if you know how to throw in Don Carlos and the Infanta, and Don Pedro and Seville and Granada, from time to time in the right proportions, — they may have changed the names a little since I saw the papers, — and serve up a bull-fight when other entertainments fail, it will be true to the letter, and give us as good an idea of the exact state or ruin of things in Spain as the most succinct and lucid reports under this head in the newspapers: and as for England, almost the last significant scrap of news from that quarter was the revolution of 1649; and if you have learned the history of her crops for an average year, you never need attend to that thing again, unless your speculations are of a merely pecuniary character. If one may judge who rarely looks into the newspapers, nothing new does ever happen in foreign parts, a French revolution not excepted.

What news! how much more important to know what that is which ⁵
was never old! "Kieou-he-yu (great dignitary of the state of Wei) sent a
man to Khoung-tseu to know his news. Khoung-tseu caused the messenger to be seated near him, and questioned him in these terms: What is
your master doing? The messenger answered with respect: My master
desires to diminish the number of his faults, but he cannot come to the
end of them. The messenger being gone, the philosopher remarked: What
a worthy messenger! What a worthy messenger!" The preacher, instead
of vexing the ears of drowsy farmers on their day of rest at the end of the
week,—for Sunday is the fit conclusion of an ill-spent week, and not the
fresh and brave beginning of a new one,—with this one other draggle-tail
of a sermon, should shout with thundering voice, "Pause! Avast! Why
so seeming fast, but deadly slow?"

Shams and delusions are esteemed for soundless truths, while reality ⁶
is fabulous. If men would steadily observe realities only, and not allow
themselves to be deluded, life, to compare it with such things as we know,
would be like a fairy tale and the Arabian Nights' Entertainments. If we
respected only what is inevitable and has a right to be, music and poetry
would resound along the streets. When we are unhurried and wise, we
perceive that only great and worthy things have any permanent and absolute existence, that petty fears and petty pleasures are but the shadow
of the reality. This is always exhilarating and sublime. By closing the
eyes and slumbering, and consenting to be deceived by shows, men establish and confirm their daily life of routine and habit everywhere, which
still is built on purely illusory foundations. Children, who play life, discern its true law and relations more clearly than men, who fail to live it
worthily, but who think that they are wiser by experience, that is, by
failure. I have read in a Hindoo book, that "there was a king's son, who,
being expelled in infancy from his native city, was brought up by a
forester, and, growing up to maturity in that state, imagined himself to
belong to the barbarous race with which he lived. One of his father's
ministers having discovered him, revealed to him what he was, and the
misconception of his character was removed, and he knew himself to be
a prince. So soul," continues the Hindoo philosopher, "from the circumstances in which it is placed, mistakes its own character, until the
truth is revealed to it by some holy teacher, and then it knows itself to
be *Brahme*." I perceive that we inhabitants of New England live this
mean life that we do because our vision does not penetrate the surface
of things. We think that that *is* which *appears* to be. If a man should walk
through this town and see only the reality, where, think you, would the
"Mill-dam" go to? If he should give us an account of the realities he
beheld there, we should not recognize the place in his description. Look

at the meeting-house, or a court-house, or a jail, or a shop, or a dwelling-house, and say what that thing really is before a true gaze, and they would all go to pieces in your account of them. Men esteem truth remote, in the outskirts of the system, behind the farthest star, before Adam and after the last man. In eternity there is indeed something true and sublime. But all these times and places and occasions are now and here. God himself culminates in the present moment, and will never be more divine in the lapse of all the ages. And we are enabled to apprehend at all what is sublime and noble only by the perpetual instilling and drenching of the reality that surrounds us. The universe constantly and obediently answers to our conceptions; whether we travel fast or slow, the track is laid for us. Let us spend our lives in conceiving then. The poet or the artist never yet had so fair and noble a design but some of his posterity at least could accomplish it.

Let us spend one day as deliberately as Nature, and not be thrown off the track by every nutshell and mosquito's wing that falls on the rails. Let us rise early and fast, or breakfast, gently and without perturbation; let company come and let company go, let the bells ring and the children cry,—determined to make a day of it. Why should we knock under and go with the stream? Let us not be upset and overwhelmed in that terrible rapid and whirlpool called a dinner, situated in the meridian shallows. Weather this danger and you are safe, for the rest of the way is down hill. With unrelaxed nerves, with morning vigor, sail by it, looking another way, tied to the mast like Ulysses. If the engine whistles, let it whistle till it is hoarse for its pains. If the bell rings, why should we run? We will consider what kind of music they are like. Let us settle ourselves, and work and wedge our feet downward through the mud and slush of opinion, and prejudice, and tradition, and delusion, and appearance, that alluvion which covers the globe, through Paris and London, through New York and Boston and Concord, through Church and State, through poetry and philosophy and religion, till we come to a hard bottom and rocks in place, which we can call *reality,* and say, This is, and no mistake; and then begin, having a *point d'appui,* below freshet and frost and fire, a place where you might found a wall or a state, or set a lamp-post safely, or perhaps a gauge, not a Nilometer, but a Realometer, that future ages might know how deep a feshet of shams and appearances had gathered from time to time. If you stand right fronting and face to face to a fact, you will see the sun glimmer on both its surfaces, as if it were a cimeter, and feel its sweet edge dividing you through the heart and marrow, and so you will happily conclude your mortal career. Be it life or death, we crave only reality. If we are really dying, let us hear the rattle in our throats and feel cold in the extremities; if we are alive, let us go about our business.

Time is but the stream I go a-fishing in. I drink at it; but while I drink   8
I see the sandy bottom and detect how shallow it is. Its thin current
slides away, but eternity remains. I would drink deeper; fish in the sky,
whose bottom is pebbly with stars. I cannot count one. I know not the
first letter of the alphabet. I have always been regretting that I was not
as wise as the day I was born. The intellect is a cleaver; it discerns and
rifts its way into the secret of things. I do not wish to be any more busy
with my hands than is necessary. My head is hands and feet. I feel all my
best faculties concentrated in it. My instinct tells me that my head is an
organ for burrowing, as some creatures use their snout and fore paws, and
with it I would mine and burrow my way through these hills. I think that
the richest vein is somewhere hereabouts; so by the divining-rod and thin
rising vapors I judge; and here I will begin to mine.

QUESTIONS AND EXERCISES

Vocabulary

1. Define or explain each of the following terms:

sublime (1)	culminates (6)
sleepers (2)	perturbation (7)
supernumerary (3)	meridian (7)
rudiment (3)	freshet (7)
myriad (4)	*point d'appui* (7)
succinct (4)	Nilometer (7)
lucid (4)	Realometer (7)
pecuniary (4)	cimeter (7)
illusory (6)	alluvion (7)

2. Identify or explain the allusions in the following terms:

German Confederacy (2)	Ulysses (7)
Spartan (1)	revolution of 1649 (4)
Saint Vitus' dance (3)	divining rod (8)

Rhetoric

3. Make a list of words from this essay that appeal to the sense and consequently create images. Some of these words will be incorporated
into figures of speech as well, but for this exercise consider only the
words as graphic, concrete, image-creating entities.
Example: live *meanly* (2)
  thumb nail (2)
  clouds and storms and quicksands (2)

4. Thoreau used rhetorical devices and figures of speech extensively.

Identify the following:

"I wanted to live deep and suck out all the marrow of life . . ." (1)

"to drive life into a corner" (1)

"like pygmies we fight with cranes" (2)

"An honest man has hardly need to count more than his ten fingers, or in extreme cases he may add his ten toes" (2)

"keep your accounts on your thumb nail" (2)

"In the midst of this chopping sea of civilized life, such are the clouds and storms and quicksands and thousand-and-one items to be allowed for, that a man has to live, if he would not founder and go to the bottom and not make his part at all, by dead reckoning, and he must be a great calculator indeed who succeeds." (2)

"They are sound sleepers, I assure you." (2)

"We are determined to be starved before we are hungry." (3)

"Let us spend one day as deliberately as Nature, and not be thrown off the track by every nutshell and mosquito's wing that falls on the rails." (7)

"Time is but the stream I go a-fishing in." (8)

"The intellect is a cleaver." (8)

"My head is hands and feet." (8)

5. What gives paragraph 8 unity and coherence?
6. Find a paragraph that is an example of an extended metaphor.
7. How does Thoreau make his transitions between paragraphs?

Theme

8. What is the theme of this essay?
9. Why is Thoreau called a transcendentalist? Find examples of transcendentalism in this essay.
10. Comment on Thoreau's knowledge of history and philosophy. Give examples from the essay which support your opinion.
11. Do Thoreau's comments on the hurry and waste of life still pertain today?
12. Comment on Thoreau's statement concerning newspapers in paragraph 4: "One is enough." Is his attitude possible for the average man today?
13. What is the reality that Thoreau is searching for in paragraph 7?

Topics and Assignments for Composition

1. Imitate one of Thoreau's sentences in which he talks about concrete things but suggests philosophical overtones.
   Examples: "Time is but the stream I go a-fishing in."
   "Life is but a sleep I go dreaming in."

2. Write a paragraph in which you comment on one of the time wasters of contemporary life (television, for example).
3. Write an essay analyzing the fascination Thoreau holds for many contemporary alienated thinkers.
4. Develop a thesis in which you compare Thoreau's philosophy to some aspect of contemporary oriental (Zen), mystical (Buddhism), or alienated (Existentialism) philosophy.

Gary Snyder

The Wilderness

I am a poet. My teachers are other poets, American Indians, and a few Buddhist priests in Japan. The reason I am here is because I wish to bring a voice from the wilderness, my constituency. I wish to be a spokesman for a realm that is not usually represented either in intellectual chambers or in the chambers of government. *1*

I was climbing Glacier Peak in the Cascades of Washington several years ago, on one of the clearest days I had ever seen. When we reached the summit of Glacier Peak we could see almost to the Selkirks in Canada. We could see south far beyond the Columbia River to Mount Hood and Mount Jefferson. And, of course, we could see Mount Adams and Mount Rainier. We could see across Puget Sound to the ranges of the Olympic Mountains. My companion, who is not a poet, said: "You mean, there is a senator for all this?" *2*

Unfortunately, there isn't a senator for all that. And I would like to think of a new definition of humanism and a new definition of democracy that would include the nonhuman, that would have representation from those spheres. This is what I think we mean by an ecological conscience. *3*

I don't like Western culture because I think it has much in it that is inherently wrong and that is at the root of the environmental crisis that is not recent; it is very ancient; it has been building up for a millennium. There are many things in Western culture that are admirable. But a culture that alienates itself from the very ground of its own being—from the wilderness outside (that is to say, wild nature, the wild, self-contained, self-informing eco-systems) and from that other wilderness, the wilderness within—is doomed to a very destructive behavior, ultimately perhaps self-destructive behavior. *4*

The West is not the only culture that carries these destructive seeds. 5
China had effectively deforested itself by 1000 A.D. India had effectively
deforested itself by 800 A.D. The soils of the Middle East were ruined
even earlier. The forests that once covered the mountains of Yugoslavia
were stripped to build the Roman fleet, and those mountains have looked
like Utah ever since. The soils of southern Italy and Sicily were ruined
by latifundia slave-labor farming in the Roman Empire. The soils of the
Atlantic seaboard in the United States were effectively ruined before
the American Revolution because of the one-crop (tobacco) farming. So
the same forces have been at work in East and West.

You would not think a poet would get involved in these things. But 6
the voice that speaks to me as a poet, what Westerners have called the
Muse, is the voice of nature herself, whom the ancient poets called the
great goddess, the Magna Mater. I regard that voice as a very real entity.
At the root of the problem where our civilization goes wrong is the mistaken belief that nature is something less than authentic, that nature is
not as alive as man is, or as intelligent, that in a sense it is dead, and that
animals are of so low an order of intelligence and feeling, we need not
take their feelings into account.

A line is drawn between primitive peoples and civilized peoples. I 7
think there is a wisdom in the worldview of primitive peoples that we
have to refer ourselves to, and learn from. If we are on the verge of post-
civilization, then our next step must take account of the primitive worldview which has traditionally and intelligently tried to open and keep open
lines of communication with the forces of nature. You cannot communicate with the forces of nature in the laboratory. One of the problems is
that we simply do not know much about primitive people and primitive
cultures. If we can tentatively accommodate the possibility that nature
has a degree of authenticity and intelligence that requires that we look
at it more sensitively, then we can move to the next step. "Intelligence"
is not really the right word. The ecologist Eugene Odum uses the term
"biomass."

Life-biomass, he says, is stored information; living matter is stored 8
information in the cells and in the genes. He believes there is more information of a higher order of sophistication and complexity stored in a few
square yards of forest than there is in all the libraries of mankind. Obviously, that is a different order of information. It is the information of the
universe we live in. It is the information that has been flowing for millions
of years. In this total information context, man may not be necessarily
the highest or most interesting product.

Perhaps one of its most interesting experiments at the point of evolu- 9
tion, if we can talk about evolution in this way, is not man but a high

degree of biological diversity and sophistication opening to more and more possibilities. Plants are at the bottom of the food chain; they do the primary energy transformation that makes all the life-forms possible. So perhaps plant life is what the ancients meant by the great goddess. Since plants support the other life-forms, they became the "people" of the land. And the land—a country—is a region within which the interactions of water, air, and soil and the underlying geology and the overlying (maybe stratospheric) wind conditions all go to create both the microclimates and the large climactic patterns that make a whole sphere or realm of life possible. The people in that realm include animals, humans, and a variety of wild life.

What we must find a way to do, then, is incorporate the other people— *10* what the Sioux Indians called the creeping people, and the standing people, and the flying people, and the swimming people—into the councils of government. This isn't as difficult as you might think. If we don't do it, they will revolt against us. They will submit nonnegotiable demands about our stay on the earth. We are beginning to get nonnegotiable demands right now from the air, the water, the soil.

I would like to expand on what I mean by representation here at the *11* Center from these other fields, these other societies, these other communities. Ecologists talk about the ecology of oak communities, or pine communities. They *are* communities. This institute—this Center—is of the order of a kiva of elders. Its function is to maintain and transmit the lore of the tribe on the highest levels. If it were doing its job completely, it would have a cycle of ceremonies geared to the seasons, geared perhaps to the migrations of the fish and to the phases of the moon. It would be able to instruct in what rituals you follow when a child is born, when someone reaches puberty, when someone gets married, when someone dies. But, as you know, in these fragmented times, one council cannot perform all these functions at one time. Still it would be understood that a council of elders, the caretakers of the lore of the culture, would open themselves to representation from other life-forms. Historically this has been done through art. The paintings of bison and bears in the caves of southern France were of that order. The animals were speaking through the people and making their point. And when, in the dances of the Pueblo Indians and other peoples, certain individuals became seized, as it were, by the spirit of the deer, and danced as a deer would dance, or danced the dance of the corn maidens, or impersonated the squash blossom, they were no longer speaking for humanity, they were taking it on themselves to interpret, through their humanity, what these other life-forms were. That is about all we know so far concerning the possibilities of incorporating spokesmanship for the rest of life in our democratic society.

Let me describe how a friend of mine from the Santo Domingo Pueblo *12* hunts. He is twenty-seven years old. The Pueblo Indians, and I think probably most of the other Indians of the Southwest, begin their hunt, first, by purifying themselves. They take emetics, a sweat bath, and perhaps avoid their wife for a few days. They also try not to think certain thoughts. They go out hunting in an attitude of humility. They make sure that they need to hunt, that they are not hunting without necessity. Then they improvise a song while they are in the mountains. They sing aloud or hum to themselves while they are walking along. It is a song to the deer, asking the deer to be willing to die for them. They usually still-hunt, taking a place alongside a trail. The feeling is that you are not hunting the deer, the deer is coming to you; you make yourself available for the deer that will present itself to you, that has given itself to you. Then you shoot it. After you shoot it, you cut the head off and place the head facing east. You sprinkle corn meal in front of the mouth of the deer, and you pray to the deer, asking it to forgive you for having killed it, to understand that we all need to eat, and to please make a good report to the other deer spirits that he has been treated well. One finds this way of handling things and animals in all primitive cultures.

QUESTIONS AND EXERCISES

Vocabulary

1. Define or explain each of the following terms:
   humanism (3)   latifundia (5)
   ecological (3)   life-biomass (8)
   millennium (4)

Rhetoric

2. Find three allusions to other cultures and explain their relevance to the central point of the essay.
3. The essay begins with description and ends with narrative. What effect on style do these rhetorical techniques have?
4. What other stylistic effects do you find?

Theme

5. What is the thesis of the essay?
6. What proof does Snyder give to support his position?
7. How does Snyder's essay bring together the disparate elements of our times?
8. How does Snyder interpret evolution?

9. Show that Snyder indulges in the "pathetic fallacy" (the practice of assigning human feelings and emotions to animals).
10. Do plants and inanimate objects have feelings and intelligence? Explain.
11. Find evidence in the essay that Snyder is a poet.
12. Are there ideas in the essay that may be useful in freeing man from his present dilemmas?
13. Why does Snyder dislike Western culture?

Topics and Assignments for Composition

1. Describe Snyder's philosophy of life.
2. Write an essay supporting or rejecting Snyder's major points.
3. Choose a label for Snyder's views and defend the choice. Possible labels are romantic, naturalist, primitivist, escapist, etc.
4. Write an essay in which you analyze one of the problems Snyder presents.

Student Example

Educational Breakthrough

Though I graduated from high school only a short while ago, I am surprised how little I remember of what went on there, how little impressed me or registered in my mind at all. My high school memories are a jumble of stuffy, box-like classrooms, boring assignments, failures in gym, and teachers, with few exceptions, characterized only by varying degrees of mediocrity. I escaped from this unending dullness through daydreams, which always seemed to be more interesting than anything happening in class.

I did much of this daydreaming in Senior English Lit., very possibly the most uninspiring class ever devised. The teacher, Mrs. Johnson, constantly strove to outdo herself in creating trite assignments and dull discussions. The class was conducted on a level highly suitable for delinquent seventh graders; absolute quiet and order were maintained at all times. In discussions and written assignments, it was perfectly permissible to disagree with the teacher's viewpoint, as long as you were willing to accept a low "B" or a "C." Most students quickly learned Mrs. Johnson's likes and dislikes.

The class was divided between nonparticipants, who couldn't care less and showed it, and participants, who looked eager and sincere and who always contributed to class discussions. I was a nonparticipant, but got along by looking interested. The boy who sat in front of me was definitely a nonparticipant, as well as being the only interesting thing about English Lit. He was unusual, with his very long dark hair, sideburns almost reaching his jaw, and his dark eyes. He wore flared jeans with strips of braid around the cuffs, topped by long tunic shirts, unusual for our conservative school. He spent the class periods reading or looking out the window. Sometimes he looked at the teacher with an ironic, amused half-smile. Understandably, he was not one of Mrs. Johnson's favorites; she seldom called on him and usually ignored him completely. One day she did ask him to contribute, something she probably still regrets.

The class was discussing the student revolt, a topic which was in the news almost every day that year. A class discussion usually meant a dialogue between Mrs. Johnson and her favorite participants, all of whom said exactly what she wanted to hear. A wholesome-looking blond boy, a member of the student council, the staff of the school paper, and the trash pick-up committee, talked about the inability of student radicals to create constructive programs while Mrs. Johnson smiled approvingly. The discussion began to lag. A few students contributed while others yawned, gazed out the window, or did their homework. Mrs. Johnson began calling on people. She looked in my direction, and I was afraid I would be next; but instead she asked Steve Graham, the boy in front of me, what he thought about the student revolt.

Steve put down the copy of "Avant Garde" he had been reading, looking annoyed at the interruption. He sighed loudly and asked her to repeat the question.

"I asked for a comment, a positive, concrete statement concerning the subject we have been discussing for the past fifteen minutes. Well, some of us have been discussing it. I presume the rest of you have more interesting things to do." Mrs. Johnson glared at Steve.

"Yes, I guess some of us do. I don't know anything about student revolt, I'm afraid," he said politely, dismissing the matter and returning to his magazine.

"Well, I'm certain you have something to contribute. Just anything positive. How about a brief summation of the violent aspects of the student revolt?" Mrs. Johnson was demonstrating her ability to remain cool and in control of a rapidly deteriorating situation.

"A summation of the violent aspects of the student revolt? All right, if that's what you want." Steve looked totally bored and indifferent, like someone forced to humor a small child. He picked up the fat gray *Literature of England* book from his desk and threw it through the window. The glass shattered and fell onto the floor in little pieces. Everyone stopped doing homework and yawning and turned around to stare. Steve calmly sat down and resumed his reading. Mrs. Johnson, having lost her cool control of the situation, began hunting for referrals or passes to the office. She apparently could not find any and simply sat down, looking lost and helpless. The room was completely silent and no one moved, except the boy on the trash pick-up committee, who, having recovered from the initial shock, decided to carry out his duties and began picking up the glass.

Order soon prevailed again in English Lit. Steve was transferred to another class, and Mrs. Johnson began to regain some of her shattered confidence in her teaching methods. Having provided the only memorable incident of my high school career, the class once more became just another hour of daydreaming.

Part Two:
Description

Herbert Gold

Death in Miami Beach

The state of madness can be defined partly as an extreme of isolation *1*
of one human being from everyone else. It provides a model for dying.
Only an intermittent and fragmentary awareness of others interrupts the
black folding of the layers of self upon each other—this also defines the
state of that dilemma known as "mental health."

There is a false madness induced by the accidents of isolation which *2*
prisoners, travelers, and the very ill may sometimes experience without
giving up their return ticket. Surely you out there all know what I mean
from your own troubles and painful decisions. To say that it is false madness does not soften its extremity. The mask of existence fits harshly on
your skin, but it is in fact your only skin; and when harshly your skin is
peeled off—beneath it you are naked and your naked isolation is no joy
to you.

During a period of work on a long job of writing in the winter of 1958, *3*
I deliberately withdrew myself from all those who knew my name and
traveled by automobile in slow stages through the deep South to Miami
Beach, Key West, Havana, and finally back up toward Detroit. No one
asked me to write a novel, no one asked me to go away; but I did anyway.
I was tempted by the prospect of dreaming through my story amid a
pleasant chaos of sun and sea, all other responsibilities suspended, and
so I arranged it for myself.

Work is very fine, but after the day's work, isolation, silence, and death *4*
seemed to follow me through the zazzy carnival of Miami, the casual
resort indolence of Key West, and the smoky, blistered elegance of a
tourist's Havana. In Havana, from the rooftop of the Ambos 'Mundos
Hotel, I could see Batista's police loafing with their weapons in front of

public buildings; occasionally there were bombs; once a body happened to be left in the street and people hurried by as if they knew nothing, nothing, nothing at all but the next step before them.

At Key West, a few days before Christmas, I visited the turtle slaugh-   5
terhouse. It is one of the few tourist attractions on this spot of island, "North Havana," raised far out into the sea off the coast of Florida. Visitors take their kiddies by the hand and lead them to see the nice turtles.

Before being killed and canned, the turtles swim in dense kraals, bump-   6
ing each other in the murky water, armor clashing, dully lurching against the high pens. Later, trussed on a plank dock, they lie unblinking in the sun, their flippers pierced and tied. The tough leather of their skin does not disguise their present helplessness and pain. They wear thick, sun-hardened accumulations of blood at their wounds. Barbados turtles, as large as children, they belong to a species which has been eliminated locally by ardent harvesting of the waters near Key West, but the commercial tradition still brings them here to be slaughtered. Crucified like thieves, they breathe in little sighs, they gulp, they wait.

At a further stage, in the room where the actual slaughtering occurs,   7
the butchers stride through gore in heavy boots. The visitor must proceed on a catwalk; a misstep will plunge him into a slow river of entrails and blood. Because it was near Christmastime, the owners of the plant had installed a speaker system for musical divertissement of the butchers, and while the turtles dried under the sun or lay exposed to the butchers' knives, Christmas bells tolled out, electronically amplified, "God Rest Ye Merry, Gentlemen," or the Bing Crosby recording of *"Adeste Fideles."*

These commercial details are not intended to support a special plea on   8
behalf of the humane harvesting of Barbados turtles. In fact, let me grant that I sought out this scene and visited the abattoir without having any proper business there at all: merely curiosity and the need to confirm my imagination about it. I should be judged for vulgarity by the man who chooses out of purity not to follow me, not by the man I saw lurking outside, with a face ravaged by the horrified fascination which makes it impossible for him to visit his dreams. What had I done which he could not permit himself? Was I filthied, was I weakened by pleasure but obscurely nourished, was I fed on coveted turtle joys after trampling in turtle blood? Had I asked permission from the butcher and plied a knife with my own hands on the belly of one of the slow, unblinking, dragon-headed, ancient sea-beasts? And did it arch its graceful dragon neck in reproach as I stabbed? He stared at me like a jealous lover, imagining my wickedness, rabid and hopeless, wanting to bury his head in the reek on my hands.

Most of us turn from the vision of death only out of weakness, and this   9
is no turning from death. Serve up your turtle steak, gourmet friend, with
no protest from me; I'll eat at your table. ("A nice rendition," one gentleman said of Bing Crosby to his wife. Turtle is tasty, somewhat gamy meat.
Protein nourishes the brain — brings oxygen and freedom.)

QUESTIONS AND EXERCISES

Vocabulary

1. Define or explain the following terms:
   dilemma (1)   divertissement (3)
   abattoir (8)   "Adeste Fideles" (7)
   gourmet (9)   vulgarity (8)
   gamy (9)

Rhetoric

2. How does the author link paragraph 2 to paragraph 1?
3. What words does Gold use that evoke emotional responses?
4. Comment on the figure of speech at the end of paragraph 8.
5. What does Gold mean by the phrase ". . . which makes it possible
   for him to visit his dreams"? (8)
6. What is the touch of irony in paragraph 9?
7. Is Gold too flippant in his description in "Death in Miami Beach"?

Theme

8. What do you think was Gold's purpose in this description?
9. What is the overall topic?
10. Do you think that Gold is a sentimentalist?
11. How does Gold exhibit his emotional honesty to the reader?

Topics and Assignments for Composition

1. Write a sentence using an unusual or unexpected simile.
2. Write a short paragraph that has an ironic end (see paragraphs 7
   and 9).
3. Describe an event that is loaded with emotional potential but maintains an objectivity or aloofness toward the impact of the situation
   (a doctor at an operation, a traffic officer at a fatal accident, a judge
   sentencing a prisoner).

Francis Bacon

Idols of the Mind

The *Idols* and false notions which have already preoccupied the human 1
understanding, and are deeply rooted in it, not only so beset men's minds,
that they become difficult of access, but even when access is obtained,
will again meet and trouble us in the instauration of the sciences, unless
mankind, when forewarned, guard themselves with all possible care
against them.

Four species of *Idols* beset the human mind: to which (for distinction's 2
sake) we have assigned names: calling the first *Idols of the Tribe;* the
second *Idols of the Den;* the third *Idols of the Market;* the fourth *Idols
of the Theater.*

The formation of notions and axioms on the foundations of true *in-* 3
duction, is the only fitting remedy, by which we can ward off and expel
these *Idols.* It is however of great service to point them out. For the doctrine of *Idols* bears the same relation to the *interpretation of nature,* as
that of the confutation of sophisms does to common logic.

The *Idols of the Tribe* are inherent in human nature, and the very tribe 4
or race of man. For man's sense is falsely asserted to be the standard of
things. On the contrary, all the perceptions, both of the senses and the
mind, bear reference to man, and not to the universe, and the human mind
resembles those uneven mirrors, which impart their own properties to
different objects, from which rays are emitted, and distort and disfigure
them.

The *Idols of the Den* are those of each individual. For every body (in 5
addition to the errors common to the race of man) has his own individual
den or cavern, which intercepts and corrupts the light of nature; either
from his own peculiar and singular disposition, or from his education and
intercourse with others, or from his reading, and the authority acquired
by those whom he reverences and admires, or from a different impression
produced on the mind, as it happens to be preoccupied and predisposed,
or equable and tranquil, and the like: so that the spirit of man (according

to its several dispositions) is variable, confused, and as it were actuated by chance; and Heraclitus said well that men search for knowledge in lesser worlds and not in the greater or common world.

There are also *Idols* formed by the reciprocal intercourse and society 6
of man with man, which we call *Idols of the Market*, from the commerce and association of men with each other. For men converse by means of language; but words are formed at the will of the generality; and there arises from a bad and unapt formation of words a wonderful obstruction to the mind. Nor can the definitions and explanations, with which learned men are wont to guard and protect themselves in some instances, afford a complete remedy: words still manifestly force the understanding, throw everything into confusion, and lead mankind into vain and innumerable controversies and fallacies.

Lastly, there are *Idols* which have crept into men's minds from the 7
various dogmas of peculiar systems of philosophy, and also from the perverted rules of demonstration, and these we denominate *Idols of the Theater*. For we regard all the systems of philosophy hitherto received or imagined, as so many plays brought out and performed, creating fictitious and theatrical worlds. Nor do we speak only of the present systems, or of the philosophy and sects of the ancients, since numerous other plays of a similar nature can be still composed and made to agree with each other, the causes of the most opposite errors being generally the same. Nor, again, do we allude merely to the general systems, but also to many elements and axioms of sciences, which have become inveterate by tradition, implicit credence and neglect. We must, however, discuss each species of *Idols* more fully and distinctly in order to guard the human understanding against them.

QUESTIONS AND EXERCISES

Vocabulary

1. Define or explain each of the following terms:

idols (1)	meted (5)
instauration (1)	perturbation (5)
axioms (3)	consort (6)
induction (3)	wont (6)
sophisms (3)	dogmas (7)

Rhetoric

2. Who was Heraclitus?
3. Exactly what is Bacon classifying?

4. How many categories does Bacon set up?
5. Why do some of Bacon's phrases seem archaic?

Theme

6. Compare Bacon's classifications with some contemporary system of classification about the same general topic.
7. What evidence of inductive logic do you see in Bacon's essay? Of deductive logic?
8. Bacon is often admired for his thought and style. Is there a relationship between the two?

Topics and Assignments for Composition

1. In a short paragraph evaluate Bacon's classifications.
2. Set up your own classification scheme for people. In a short essay discuss your classifications and give examples and illustrations, as does Bacon.
3. Discuss the validity of making classifications about man. What academic disciplines use classification systems? What is the value of classification? Have some unifying devices to tie your observations into a coherent essay. Notice Bacon's transitions: paragraph 6, "There are also . . ." and paragraph 7, "Lastly, there are . . ."

Henry David Thoreau

The Woodchuck

April 16, 1852

As I turned round the corner of Hubbard's Grove, saw a woodchuck, the first of the season, in the middle of the field, six or seven rods from the fence which bounds the wood, and twenty rods distant. I ran along the fence and cut him off, or rather overtook him, though he started at the same time. When I was only a rod and a half off, he stopped, and I did the same; then he ran again, and I ran up within three feet of him, when he stopped again, the fence being between us. I squatted down and surveyed him at my leisure. His eyes were dull black and rather inobvious, with a faint chestnut iris, with but little expression and that more of resignation than of anger. The general aspect as a coarse grayish brown, a sort of grisel. A lighter brown next the skin, then black or very dark brown and tipped with whitish rather loosely. The head between a squirrel and a bear, flat on the top and dark brown, and darker still or black on the tip of the nose. The whiskers black, two inches long. The ears very small and roundish, set far back and nearly buried in the fur. Black feet, with long and slender claws for digging. It appeared to tremble, or perhance shivered with cold. When I moved, it gritted its teeth quite loud, sometimes striking the under jaw against the other chatteringly, sometimes grinding one jaw on the other, yet as if more from instinct than anger. Whichever way I turned, that way it headed. I took a twig a foot long and touched its snout, at which it started forward and bit the stick, lessening the distance between us to two feet, and still it held all the ground it gained. I played with it tenderly awhile with the stick, trying to open its gritting jaws. Ever its long incisors, two above and two below, were presented. But I thought it would go to sleep if I stayed long enough. It did not sit upright as sometimes, but *standing* on its fore feet with its head down, *i.e.* half sitting, half standing. We sat looking at one another about half an hour, till we began to feel mesmeric influences. When I was tired, I moved away, wishing to see him run, but I could not start him. He would not stir as long as I was looking at him or could see him. I walked round him; he turned as fast and fronted me still. I sat down by his side within a foot. I talked to him *quasi* forest lingo, babytalk, at any rate in a conciliatory tone, and thought that I had some influence on him. He gritted his teeth less. I chewed checkerberry leaves and presented them to his nose at last without a grit; though I saw that by so much gritting of the teeth he had worn them rapidly and they were covered with a fine white powder, which, if you measured it thus, would have made his anger terrible. He did not mind any noise I might make. With a little stick I lifted one of his paws to examine it, and held it up at pleasure. I turned him over to see what color he was beneath (darker or more purely brown), though he turned himself back again sooner than I could have wished. His tail was also all brown, though not very dark, rat-tail like, with loose hairs standing out on all sides like a caterpillar brush. He had a rather mild look. I spoke to him kindly. I reached checkerberry leaves to his mouth. I stretched my hands over him, though he turned up his head and still gritted a little. I laid my hand on him, but immediately took it off again, instinct not being wholly overcome. If I had had a few fresh bean leaves, thus in advance of the season, I am sure I should have tamed him completely. It was a frizzly tail. His is a humble, terrestrial color like the partridge's, well concealed where dead wiry grass rises above darker brown or chestnut dead leaves,—a modest color. If I had had some food, I should have ended with stroking him at my leisure. Could easily have wrapped him in my handkerchief. He was not fat nor particularly lean. I finally had to leave him without seeing him move from the place. A large, clumsy, burrowing squirrel. *Arctomys,* bearmouse. I respect him as one of the natives. He lies there, by his color and habits so naturalized amid the dry leaves, the withered grass, and the bushes. A sound nap, too, he has enjoyed in his native fields, the past winter. I think I might learn some wisdom of him. His ancestors have lived here longer than mine. He is more thoroughly acclimated and naturalized than I. Bean leaves the red man raised for him, but he can do without them.

QUESTIONS AND EXERCISES

Vocabulary

1. Define or explain each of the following terms:

rod	conciliatory
iris	checkerberry
grisel	terrestrial
mesmeric	*arctomys*
quasi	lingo
acclimated	

Rhetoric

2. What effect is achieved by including such diverse terms as *arctomys* and bearmouse?
3. First locate, and then defend, attack, or explain the use of two sentence fragments in a succession towards the end of the selection.
4. What is the unifying method of organization in this paragraph? Notice one of the rhetorical problems you are confronting: this paragraph is approximately 700 words long and your beginning themes rarely exceed 500 words. What conclusions can be drawn from these two facts?
5. Thoreau uses several complex sentences with the subordinate clause introducing the sentence. Find one of these.
6. What is the tone of this selection?
7. This excerpt is taken from *The Journals.* What effect might this observation have on the style of the selection?

Theme

8. Thoreau has the reputation of being deceptively simple in his writing. What does such a claim mean? Find an example of this observation in the selection.
9. Explain the sentences "I think I might learn some wisdom of him. His ancestors have lived here longer than mine. He is more thoroughly acclimated and naturalized than I."
10. What does Thoreau mean by the word "naturalized"? Is he being deliberately ambiguous?

Topics and Assignments for Composition

1. Copy one of Thoreau's sentences and imitate it with a sentence of your own.
2. Choose one of the longer sentences from the essay and in one paragraph analyze one of the following aspects: meaning, style, grammar or figurative language.
3. Write a journal entry in which description of a thing, animal, process or person is emphasized rather than the narrative.
4. If you are familiar with the poetry of Robert Frost, make a comparison of Frost's "Mending Wall" and Thoreau's "The Woodchuck."

LeRoi Jones (Imamu Amiri Baraka)

The City of Harlem

In a very real sense, Harlem is the capital of Black America. And   *1*
America has always been divided into black and white, and the substance of the division is social, economic, and cultural. But even the name
Harlem, now, means simply Negroes (even though some other peoples
live there too). The identification is international as well: even in Belize,
the capital of predominantly Negro British Honduras, there are vendors
who decorate their carts with flowers and the names or pictures of Negro
culture heroes associated with Harlem like Sugar Ray Robinson. Some
of the vendors even wear t-shirts that say "Harlem, U.S.A." and they
speak about it as a black Paris. In Havana a young Afro-Cuban begged
me to tell him about the "big leg ladies" of Lenox Avenue, hoping, too,
that I could provide some way for him to get to that mystic and romantic
place.

There are, I suppose, contained within the central mythology of   *2*
Harlem, almost as many versions of its glamour, and its despair, as there
are places with people to make them up. (In one meaning of the name,
Harlem is simply a place white cab drivers will not go.) And Harlem
means not only Negroes, but, of course, whatever other associations
one might connect with them. So in one breath Harlem will be the
pleasure-happy center of the universe, full of loud, hippy mamas in electric colors and their fast, slick-head papas, all of them twisting and grin-
ning in the streets in a kind of existential joyousness that never permits
of sadness or responsibility. But in another breath this same place will
be the gathering place for every crippling human vice, and the black men
there simply victims of their own peculiar kind of sloth and childishness.
But perhaps these are not such different versions after all; chances are
both these stereotypes come from the same kinds of minds.

But Harlem, as it is, as it exists for its people, as an actual place where   *3*
actual humans live—that is a very different thing. Though, to be sure,
Harlem is a place—a city really—where almost anything any person
could think of to say goes on, probably does go on, or has gone on, but
like any other city, it must escape *any* blank generalization simply because it is alive, and changing each second with each breath any of its
citizens take.

When Africans first got to New York, or New Amsterdam as the Dutch   *4*
called it, they lived in the farthest downtown portions of the city, near
what is now called The Bowery. Later, they shifted, and were shifted,
as their numbers grew, to the section known as Greenwich Village. The
Civil War Draft Riots in 1863 accounted for the next move by New
York's growing Negro population.

After this violence (a few million dollars' worth of property was   *5*
destroyed, and a Negro orphanage was burned to the ground) a great
many Negroes moved across the river into Brooklyn. But many others
moved farther uptown to an area just above what was known as Hell's
Kitchen. The new Negro ghetto was known as Black Bohemia, and later,
after the success of an all black regiment in the Spanish-American war,
this section was called San Juan Hill. And even in the twenties when
most Negroes had made their move even further uptown to Harlem,
San Juan Hill was still a teeming branch office of black night life.

Three sections along the east side of Manhattan, The Tenderloin,   *6*
Black Bohemia, and San Juan Hill or The Jungle featured all kinds of
"sporting houses," cabarets, "dancing classes," afterhours gin mills,
as well as the Gumbo Suppers, Fish Fries, Egg Nog Parties, Chitterlin'
Struts, and Pigfoot Hops, before the Negroes moved still farther uptown.

The actual move into what is now Harlem was caused by quite a few   *7*
factors, but there are a few that were particularly important as catalysts.
First, locally, there were more race riots around the turn of the century
between the white poor (as always) and the Negroes. Also, the Black
Bohemia section was by now extremely overcrowded, swelled as it was
by the influx of Negroes from all over the city. The section was a notorious red light district (but then there have only been two occupations a
black woman could go into in America without too much trouble: the
other was domestic help) and the overcrowding made worse by the moral
squalor that poverty encourages meant that the growing local black population had to go somewhere. The immigrant groups living on both sides
of the black ghetto fought in the streets to keep their own ghettos autonomous and pure, and the Negro had to go elsewhere.

At this time, just about the turn of the century, Harlem (an area which   *8*
the first Africans had helped connect with the rest of the Dutch city by

clearing a narrow road—Broadway—up into the woods of Nieuw Haarlem) was still a kind of semi-suburban area, populated, for the most part, by many of the city's wealthiest families. The elaborate estates of the eighteenth century, built by men like Alexander Hamilton and Roger Morris, were still being lived in, but by the descendants of wealthy merchants (The Hamilton house still stands near Morningside Heights, as an historic landmark called The Grange. The Morris house, which was once lived in by Aaron Burr, is known as The Jumel House, and it still stands at the northern part of Harlem, near the Polo Grounds, as a museum run by the D.A.R. George Washington used it as his headquarters for a while during the Revolutionary War.) So there was still the quiet elegance of the nineteenth century brownstones and spacious apartment buildings, the wide drives, rolling greens, and huge-trunked trees.

What made the area open up to Negroes was the progress that America   9
has always been proud of—an elevated railway went up in the nineties, and the very rich left immediately and the near rich very soon after. Saint Philips Church, after having its old site bought up by a railroad company, bought a large piece of property, with large apartment buildings, in the center of Harlem, and, baby, the panic was on. Rich and famous Negroes moved into the vacated luxury houses very soon after, including the area now known as "Strivers Row," which was made up of almost one hundred brick mansions designed by Stanford White. The panic was definitely on—but still only locally.

What really turned that quiet suburb into "Black Paris," was the   10
coming of the First World War and the mass exodus of Negroes from the South to large urban centers. At the turn of the century most Negroes still lived in the South and were agricultural laborers, but the entrance of America into the War, and the desperate call for cheap unskilled labor, served to start thousands of Negroes scrambling North. The flow of immigrants from Europe had all but ceased by 1914, and the industrialists knew immediately where to turn. They even sent recruiters down into the South to entice the Negroes north. In 1900 the Negro population of New York City was 60,000; by 1920 it was 152,467; by 1930 it was 327,706. And most of these moved, of course, uptown.

It was this mass exodus during the early part of the century that was   11
responsible for most of the black cities of the North—the huge Negro sections of New York, Chicago, Philadelphia, Detroit, etc. It was also responsible for what these sections would very shortly become, as the masses of Southern Negroes piled into their new Jordans, thinking to have a go at an innocent America.

The twenties are legend because they mark America's sudden insane   12
entrance into the 20th century. The war had brought about a certain in-

ternationalism and prosperity (even, relatively speaking, for Negroes).
During the twenties Harlem was the mecca of the good time and in many
ways even came to symbolize the era called the Jazz Age. Delirious
white people made the trip uptown to hear Negro musicians and singers,
and watch Negro dancers, and even Negro intellectuals. It was, I suppose, the black man's debut into the most sophisticated part of America.
The old darkies of the plantation were suddenly all over the North, and
making a whole lot of noise.

There were nightclubs in Harlem that catered only to white audiences,   13
but with the best Negro entertainers. White intellectuals made frequent
trips to Harlem, not only to find out about a newly emerging black America, but to party with an international set of swinging bodies. It was the
era of Ellington at The Cotton Club for the sensual, and The New Negro
for the intellectual. Everyone spoke optimistically of the Negro Renaissance, and The New Negro, as if, somehow, the old Negro wasn't good
enough. Harlem sparkled then, at least externally, and it took the depression to dull that sparkle, and the long lines of unemployed Negroes
and the longer lines at the soup kitchens and bread queues brought reality
down hard on old and New Negroes alike. So the tourist trade diminished,
and colorful Harlem became just a social liability for the white man, and
an open air jail for the black.

The cold depression thirties, coupled with the decay of old buildings   14
and ancient neighborhoods, and, of course, the seeming inability of the
"free enterprise" system to provide either jobs or hope for a great many
black people in the city of Harlem, have served to make this city another
kind of symbol. For many Negroes, whether they live in Harlem or not,
the city is simply a symbol of naked oppression. You can walk along
125th Street any evening and meet about one hundred uniformed policemen, who are there, someone will tell you, to protect the people from
themselves.

For many Negroes Harlem is a place one escapes from, and lives in   15
shame about for the rest of his life. But this is one of the weirdest things
about the American experience, that it can oppress a man, almost suck
his life away, and then make him so ashamed that he was among the
oppressed rather than the oppressors, that he will never offer any protest.

The legitimate cultural tradition of the Negro in Harlem (and America)   16
is one of wild happiness, usually at some black man's own invention—
of speech, of dress, of gait, the sudden twist of a musical phrase, the
warmness or hurt of someone's voice. But that culture is also one of
hatred and despair. Harlem must contain all of this and be capable of
producing all of these emotions.

People line the streets in summer—on the corners or hanging out the   17 windows — or head for other streets in winter. Vendors go by slowly . . . and crowds of people from movies or church. (Saturday afternoons, warm or cold, 125th is jammed with shoppers and walkers, and the record stores scream through loudspeakers at the street.) Young girls, doctors, pimps, detectives, preachers, drummers, accountants, gamblers, labor organizers, postmen, wives, Muslims, junkies, the employed, and the unemployed: all going someplace — an endless stream of Americans, whose singularity in America is that they are black and can never honestly enter into the lunatic asylum of white America.

Harlem for this reason is a community of nonconformists, since any *18* black American, simply by virtue of his blackness, is weird, a nonconformist in this society. A community of nonconformists, not an artists' colony — though blind "ministers" still wander sometimes along 137th Street, whispering along the strings of their guitars — but a colony of old-line Americans, who can hold out, even if it is a great deal of the time in misery and ignorance, but still hold out, against the hypocrisy and sterility of big-time America, and still try to make their own lives, simply because of their color, but by now, not so simply, because that color now does serve to identify people in America whose feelings about it are not broadcast every day on television.

QUESTIONS AND EXERCISES

Vocabulary

1. Define or explain each of the following terms:

mythology (2)	catalysts (7)
existential (2)	exodus (10)
stereotypes (2)	

2. What special problems of vocabulary are present in this essay?

Rhetoric

3. The essay abounds with allusions. List five of them and explain their significance to the essay.
4. LeRoi Jones has created many phrases that, because of their figurative nature, add a very poignant meaning to the literal one. Find several such phrases as ". . . Harlem became just a social liability for the white man, and an open air jail for the black."
5. Discuss Jones' use of examples and illustrations. What do they do for the quality of the description?
6. What are some of the other characteristics of Jones' style?
7. Find examples of paradoxes in the essay.

Theme

8. What stereotypes does Jones analyze?
9. Discuss the sociological, economic, and cultural elements in the essay.
10. What are the implicit themes that Jones develops from an essay that is basically descriptive?

Topics and Assignments for Composition

1. Choose a representative excerpt from the essay and write an analysis of the sensory details and images that are present.
2. Pick an area analogous to Harlem with which you are familiar and write a descriptive essay similar to Jones'.
3. Write an essay about one of the elements in "The City of Harlem" in which you develop your own analytic or thematic insights.
4. Discuss the relationship between a writer's experiences, beliefs, culture, and the influence of these elements on his style. Use Jones as one of your examples and choose any other authors from the text for further examples.

Student Example

View from a Circus

Weak, watery, late-afternoon sunshine filters gently and ineffectually through a mildly suffocating haze of dirt, dust, damp heat, car and bus exhaust. The monotonous growl of traffic blends with the sounds of people flowing in and out of Piccadilly Circus Underground Station. The garish neon cinema, theater, and advertising signs, which make Piccadilly look like a Disneyland version of Las Vegas at night, are not yet turned on, so one's attention is focused on the swirling mass of traffic and people.

Piccadilly Circus is the junction of six main, and several very small, central London streets. Though orderly by Continental standards, this chaotic little circular road is remarkable for its rate of near accidents. Self-important, bright-red double-decker buses, and white ones covered with brown gingerbread men advertising a kind of bread (and adding immeasurably to the trippy Disneyland aura of the place), jostle for position with determined little Minis, graceful polished taxis, sleek Jags, majestic Rolls, huge fume-belching trucks, and an endless variety of other vehicles of all sizes, shapes, colors, and nationalities. This struggle for supremacy is temporarily halted by the authority of the traffic light, which signals the Piccadilly pedestrians that for a few precious moments they have command. And they make full use of it, purposefully pushing and shoving each other as they scurry toward their destinations.

The people, like their wheeled counterparts, come in all varieties, creating a sort of international shoving match: the subtly aggressive British versus robust Scandinavians and Germans, sly-looking Southern Europeans, coldly aloof Indians, and confused Americans.

Crossing from Eros, the cherub dominating the central paved area of the Circus, to Lord Kitchener's Valet, a pop boutique/souvenir shop on Shaftesbury Avenue, one has the opportunity to be poked in the eye by a spiky black umbrella, deftly wielded by a pinstriped businessman haughtily summoning a taxi, and to be nearly crushed under the taxi itself, which is getting an early start on the amber light. (London traffic lights show amber before green, enabling motorists to run down more easily crossing pedestrians and bicyclists.)

Lord Kitchener's is a dark, noisy, open-fronted shop selling all kinds of London souvenirs, as well as the customary records, posters, T-shirts, incense, and so on. The usual two-dimensional images of Raquel Welch, Peter Fonda, Brigitte Bardot, Steve McQueen, Mick Jagger, Jimmy Hendrix, and the Who preside over the scene. Loud, distorted sound, vaguely resembling Black Sabbath ritual music, floats under the arcade opposite the boutique and over the heads of the people disappearing into one of the many entrances to the station, possibly even reaching the icy polished elegance of Barclay's Bank, Piccadilly Branch.

Inside Lord Kitchener's, tired, bored salesgirls face an onslaught of purchasers. A large, quarrelling Italian family buys its quota of plastic palace guards, pop dishtowels, Union Jack alarm clocks, and a couple of Tom Jones posters. A group of young uniformed Americans—jeans, heavy shoes, jackets, and backpacks—examine change and maps, arguing over how to get to the Haymarket, the street containing American Express. Two freaks, obviously not tourists, are quietly and efficiently filling a large shopping bag with posters, selecting the ones they want and rejecting others. No one seems to notice.

Outside the boutique, the haze seems to have yellowed and thickened, enveloping the impatient motorists and pedestrians alike in a squalid swirl of authentic London air. A half-dozen sturdy, authoritative-looking policemen, are persistently removing young longhaired tourists from the steps of Eros, which are supposed to be kept clear. The fountains that splash over the steps to achieve this objective, to prevent the heart of Britain, the symbol of civilized culture, from "looking like a decaying Roman ruin being blatantly defiled by its invaders," in the words of one MP, are not working, being either broken or turned off.

One more red light and the Haymarket entrance to the underground is at hand. Among the crowd waiting for the light to change is a dark young man with generous sideburns and moustache, who is wearing a tight, shiny Italian suit. He murmers mildly obscene suggestions in a heavy accent at various girls. A couple of scruffy, unsteady old men lean against the railing, talking softly to each other or to themselves. Everyone else, carefully ignoring the deviants, stands stiff, posed, elbows at the ready to make his way through the mass of bodies.

Finally the light changes, and everyone rushes to the Haymarket entrance, brushing past ranks of hollow-eyed junkies, sprawled on the steps; harried businessmen and lady shoppers in large floppy hats trying to hail taxis; hot-panted, giggling dollybirds with heavily lashed, insipid faces; bewildered tourists with two or three maps and at least as many cameras, hunting for street signs; and groovy pushers in Oz T-shirts, velvet pants, and suede boots, looking for gullible young Americans or Europeans on whom they can unload their inferior, overpriced acid and speed. Once inside the station there's a stampede over the grimy, tiled floors, past the rows of out-of-order telephones and ticket machines, the wooden Edwardian ticket office and the dazed, mechanical-looking ticket collectors, down to the dark, stuffy caverns of train-catching. It is a nice place to visit, occasionally.

Part Three:

Comparison and Contrast

Isaac Asimov

The Slowly Moving Finger

Alas, the evidences of mortality are all about us; the other day our little *1* parakeet died. As nearly as we could make out, it was a trifle over five years old, and we had always taken the best care of it. We had fed it, watered it, kept its cage clean, allowed it to leave the cage and fly about the house, taught it a small but disreputable vocabulary, permitted it to ride about on our shoulders and eat at will from dishes at the table. In short, we encouraged it to think of itself as one of us humans.

But alas, its aging process remained that of a parakeet. During its last *2* year, it slowly grew morose and sullen; mentioned its improper words but rarely; took to walking rather than flying. And finally it died. And, of course, a similar process is taking place within me.

This thought makes me petulant. Each year I break my own previous *3* record and enter new high ground as far as age is concerned, and it is remarkably cold comfort to think that everyone else is doing exactly the same thing.

The fact of the matter is that I resent growing old. In my time I was a *4* kind of mild infant prodigy—you know, the kind that teaches himself to read before he is five and enters college at fifteen and is writing for publication at eighteen and all like that there. As you might expect, I came in for frequent curious inspection as a sort of ludicrous freak, and I invariably interpreted this inspection as admiration and loved it.

But such behavior carries its own punishment, for the moving finger *5* writes, as Edward Fitzgerald said Omar Khayyam said, and having writ, moves on. And what that means is that the bright, young, bouncy, effervescent infant prodigy becomes a flabby, paunchy, bleary, middle-aged non-prodigy, and age sits twice as heavily on such as these.

It happens quite often that some huge, hulking, raw-boned fellow,   6
cheeks bristling with black stubble, comes to me and says in his bass
voice, "I've been reading you ever since I learned to read; and I've collected all the stuff you wrote *before* I learned to read and I've read that,
too." My impulse then is to hit him a stiff right cross to the side of the
jaw, and I might do so if only I were quite sure he would respect my age
and not hit back.

So I see nothing for it but to find a way of looking at the bright side, if   7
any exists . . .

How long do organisms live anyway? We can only guess. Statistics   8
on the subject have been carefully kept only in the last century or so,
and then only for Homo sapiens, and then only in the more "advanced"
parts of the world.

So most of what is said about longevity consists of quite rough esti-   9
mates. But then, if everyone is guessing, I can guess, too; and as light-
heartedly as the next person, you can bet.

In the first place, what do we mean by length of life? There are several   10
ways of looking at this, and one is to consider the actual length of time
(on the average) that actual organisms live under actual conditions. This
is the "life expectancy."

One thing we can be certain of is that life expectancy is quite trifling   11
for all kinds of creatures. If a codfish or an oyster produces millions or
billions of eggs and only one or two happen to produce young that are
still alive at the end of the first year, then the average life expectancy
of all the coddish or oysterish youngsters can be measured in weeks, or
possibly even days. I imagine that thousands upon thousands of them live
no more than minutes.

Matters are not so extreme among birds and mammals where there is a   12
certain amount of infant care, but I'll bet relatively few of the smaller
ones live out a single year.

From the cold-blooded view of species survival, this is quite enough,   13
however. Once a creature has reached sexual maturity, and contributed
to the birth of a litter of young which it sees through to puberty or near-
puberty, it has done its bit for species survival and can go its way. If it
survives and produces additional litters, well and good, but it doesn't
have to.

There is, obviously, considerable survival value in reaching sexual   14
maturity as early as possible, so that there is time to produce the next
generation before the first is gone. Meadow mice reach puberty in three
weeks and can bear their first litter six weeks after birth. Even an animal
as large as a horse or cow reaches the age of puberty after one year, and
the largest whales reach puberty at two. Some large land animals can af-

ford to be slower about it. Bears are adolescent only at six and elephants only at ten.

The large carnivores can expect to live a number of years, if only be-   15
cause they have relatively few enemies (always excepting man) and need not expect to be anyone's dinner. The largest herbivores, such as elephants and hippopotami, are also safe; while smaller ones such as baboons and water buffaloes achieve a certain safety by traveling in herds.

Early man falls into this category. He lived in small herds and he cared   16
for his young. He had, at the very least, primitive clubs and eventually gained the use of fire. The average man, therefore, could look forward to a number of years of life. Even so, with undernourishment, disease, the hazards of the chase, and the cruelty of man to man, life was short by modern standards. Naturally, there was a limit to how short life could be. If men didn't live long enough, on the average, to replace themselves, the race would die out. However, I should guess that in a primitive society a life expectancy of 18 would be ample for species survival. And I rather suspect that the actual life expectancy of man in the Stone Age was not much greater.

As mankind developed agriculture and as he domesticated animals, he   17
gained a more dependable food supply. As he learned to dwell within walled cities and to live under a rule of law, he gained greater security against human enemies from without and within. Naturally, life expectancy rose somewhat. In fact, it doubled.

However, throughout ancient and medieval times, I doubt that life   18
expectancy ever reached 40. In medieval England, the life expectancy is estimated to have been 35, so that if you did reach the age of 40 you were a revered sage. What with early marriage and early childbirth, you were undoubtedly a grandfather, too.

This situation still existed into the twentieth century in some parts of   19
the world. In India, for instance, as of 1950, the life expectancy was about 32; In Egypt, as of 1938, it was 36; in Mexico, as of 1940, it was 38.

The next great step was medical advance, which brought infection and   20
disease under control. Consider the United States. In 1850, life expectancy for American white males was 38.3 (not too much different from the situation in medieval England or ancient Rome). By 1900, however, after Pasteur and Koch had done their work, it was up to 48.2; then 56.3 in 1920; 60.6 in 1930; 62.8 in 1940; 66.3 in 1950; 67.3 in 1959; and 67.8 in 1961.

All through, females had a bit the better of it (being the tougher sex).   21
In 1850, they averaged two years longer life than males; and by 1961, the edge had risen to nearly seven years. Non-whites in the United States

don't do quite as well — not for any inborn reason, I'm sure, but because they generally occupy a position lower on the economic scale. They run some seven years behind whites in life expectancy. (And if anyone wonders why Negroes are restless these days, there's seven years of life apiece that they have coming to them. That might do as a starter.)

Even if we restrict ourselves to whites, the United States does not hold   22
the record in life expectancy. I rather think Norway and Sweden do. The latest figures I can find (the middle 1950s) give Scandinavian males a life expectancy of 71, and females one of 74.

This change in life expectancy has introduced certain changes in social   23
custom. In past centuries, the old man was a rare phenomenon — an unusual respository of long memories and a sure guide to ancient traditions. Old age was revered, and in some societies where life expectancy is still low and old men still exceptional, old age is still revered.

It might also be feared. Until the nineteenth century there were par-   24
ticular hazards to childbirth, and few women survived the process very often (puerperal fever and all that). Old women were therefore even rarer than old men, and with their wrinkled cheeks and toothless gums were strange and frightening phenomena. The witch mania of early modern times may have been a last expression of that.

Nowadays, old men and women are very common and the extremes of   25
both good and evil are spared them. Perhaps that's just as well.

One might suppose, what with the steady rise in life expectancy in the   26
more advanced portions of the globe, that we need merely hold on another century to find men routinely living a century and half. Unfortunately, this is not so. Unless there is a remarkable biological breakthrough in geriatrics, we have gone just about as far as we can go in raising the life expectancy.

I once read an allegory that has haunted me all my adult life. I can't   27
repeat it word for word; I wish I could. But it goes something like this. Death is an archer and life is a bridge. Children begin to cross the bridge gaily, skipping along and growing older, while Death shoots at them. His aim is miserable at first, and only an occasional child is transfixed and falls off the bridge into the cloud-enshrouded mists below. But as the crowd moves farther along, Death's aim improves and the numbers thin. Finally, when Death aims at the aged who totter nearly to the end of the bridge, his aim is perfect and he never misses. And not one man ever gets across the bridge to see what lies on the other side.

This remains true despite all the advances in social structure and medi-   28
cal science throughout history. Death's aim has worsened through early and middle life, but those last perfectly aimed arrows are the arrows of old age, and even now they never miss. All we have done to wipe out war,

famine, and disease has been to allow more people the chance of experiencing old age. When life expectancy was 35, perhaps one in a hundred reached old age; nowadays nearly half the population reaches it — but it is the same old old age. Death gets us all, and with every scrap of his ancient efficiency.

In short, putting life expectancy to one side, there is a "specific age" *29* which is our most common time of death from inside, without any outside push at all; the age at which we would die even if we avoided accident, escaped disease, and took every care of ourselves.

Three thousand years ago, the psalmist testified as to the specific age *30* of man (Ps. 90:10), saying: "The days of our years are threescore years and ten; and if by reason of strength they be fourscore years, yet is their strength labor and sorrow; for it is soon cut off, and we fly away."

And so it is today; three millennia of civilization and three centuries of *31* science have not changed it. The commonest time of death by old age lies between 70 and 80.

But that is just the commonest time. We don't all die on our 75th birth- *32* day; some of us do better, and it is undoubtedly the hope of each one of us that we ourselves, personally, will be one of those who will do better. So what we have our eye on is not the specific age but the maximum age we can reach.

Every species of multicellular creature has a specific age and a maxi- *33* mum age; and of the species that have been studied to any degree at all, the maximum age would seem to be between 50 and 100 per cent longer than the specific age. Thus, the maximum age for man is considered to be about 115.

There have been reports of older men, to be sure. The most famous is *34* the case of Thomas Parr ("Old Parr"), who was supposed to have been born in 1481 in England and to have died in 1635 at the age of 154. The claim is not believed to be authentic (some think it was a put-up job involving three generations of the Parr family), nor are any other claims of the sort. The Soviet Union reports numerous centenarians in the Caucasus, but all were born in a region and at a time when records were not kept. The old man's age rests only upon his own word, therefore, and ancients are notorious for a tendency to lengthen their years. Indeed, we can make it a rule, almost, that the poorer the recording of vital statistics in a particular region, the older the centenarians claim to be.

In 1948, an English woman named Isabella Shepheard died at the re- *35* ported age of 115. She was the last survivor, within the British Isles, from the period before the compulsory registration of births, so one couldn't be certain to the year. Still, she could not have been younger by more than a couple of years. In 1814, a French Canadian named Pierre

Joubert died and he, apparently, had reliable records to show that he was born in 1701, so that he died at 113.

Let's accept 115 as man's maximum age, then, and ask whether we *36* have a good reason to complain about this. How does the figure stack up against maximum ages for other types of living organisms?

If we compare plants with animals, there is no question that plants *37* bear off the palm of victory. Not all plants generally, to be sure. To quote the Bible again (Ps. 103: 15-16), "As for man his days are as grass: as a flower of the field, so he flourisheth. For the wind passeth over it, and it is gone; and the place thereof shall know it no more."

This is a spine-tingling simile representing the evanescence of human *38* life, but what if the psalmist had said that as for man his days are as the oak tree; or better still, as the giant sequoia? Specimens of the latter are believed to be over three thousand years old, and no maximum age is known for them.

However, I don't suppose any of us wants long life at the cost of being *39* a tree. Trees live long, but they live slowly, passively, and in terribly, terribly dull fashion. Let's see what we can do with animals.

Very simple animals do surprisingly well and there are reports of sea- *40* anemones, corals, and such-like creatures passing the half-century mark, and even some tales (not very reliable) of centenarians among them. Among more elaborate invertebrates, lobsters may reach an age of 50 and clams one of 30. But I think we can pass invertebrates, too. There is no reliable tale of a complex invertebrate living to be 100 and even if giant squids, let us say, did so, we don't want to be giant squids.

What about vertebrates? Here we have legends, particularly about fish. *41* Some tell us that fish never grow old but live and grow forever, not dying till they are killed. Individual fish are reported with ages of several centuries. Unfortunately, none of this can be confirmed. The oldest age reported for a fish by a reputable observer is that of a lake sturgeon which is supposed to be well over a century old, going by a count of the rings on the spiny ray of its pectoral fin.

Among amphibia the record holder is the giant salamander, which may *42* reach an age of 50. Reptiles are better. Snakes may reach an age of 30 and crocodiles may attain 60, but it is the turtles that hold the record for the animal kingdom. Even small turtles may reach the century mark, and at least one larger turtle is known, with reasonable certainty, to have lived 152 years. It may be that the large Galapagos turtles can attain an age of 200.

But then turtles live slowly and dully, too. Not as slowly as plants, but *43* too slowly for us. In fact, there are only two classes of living creatures that live intensely and at peak level at all times, thanks to their warm blood, and these are the birds and the mammals. (Some mammals cheat a little and hibernate through the winter and probably extend their life span in that manner.) We might envy a tiger or an eagle if they lived a long, long time and even—as the shades of old age closed in—wish we could trade places with them. But do they live a long, long time?

Of the two classes, birds on the whole do rather better than mammals *44* as far as maximum age is concerned. A pigeon can live as long as a lion and a herring gull as long as a hippopotamus. In fact, we have long-life legends about some birds, such as parrots and swans, which are supposed to pass the century mark with ease.

Any devotee of the Dr. Dolittle stories (weren't you?) must remember *45* Polynesia, the parrot, who was in her third century. Then there is Tennyson's poem *Tithonus,* about that mythical character who was granted immortality but, through an oversight, not freed from the incubus of old age so that he grew older and older and was finally, out of pity, turned into a grasshopper. Tennyson has him lament that death comes to all but him. He begins by pointing out that men and the plants of the field die, and his fourth line is an early climax, going, "And after many a summer dies the swan." In 1939, Aldous Huxley used the line as a title for a book that dealt with the striving for physical immortality.

However, as usual, these stories remain stories. The oldest confirmed *46* age reached by a parrot is 73, and I imagine that swans do not do much better. An age of 115 has been reported for carrion crows and for some vultures, but this is with a pronounced question mark.

Mammals interest us most, naturally, since we are mammals, so let me *47* list the maximum ages for some mammalian types. (I realize, of course, that the word "rat" or "deer" covers dozens of species, each with its own aging pattern, but I can't help that. Let's say the typical rat or the typical deer.)

Elephant	77	Cat	20
Whale	60	Pig	20
Hippopotamus	49	Dog	18
Donkey	46	Goat	17
Gorilla	45	Sheep	16
Horse	40	Kangaroo	16
Chimpanzee	39	Bat	15
Zebra	38	Rabbit	15
Lion	35	Squirrel	15
Bear	34	Fox	14
Cow	30	Guinea Pig	7
Monkey	29	Rat	4
Deer	25	Mouse	3
Seal	25	Shrew	2

The maximum age, be it remembered, is reached only by exceptional *48* individuals. While an occasional rabbit may make 15, for instance, the average rabbit would die of old age before it was 10 and might have an actual life expectancy of only 2 or 3 years.

In general, among all groups of organisms sharing a common plan of *49* structure, the large ones live longer than the small. Among plants, the giant sequoia tree lives longer than the daisy. Among animals, the giant sturgeon lives longer than the herring, the giant salamander lives longer than the frog, the giant alligator lives longer than the lizard, the vulture lives longer than the sparrow, and the elephant lives longer than the shrew.

Indeed, in mammals particularly, there seems to be a strong correla- *50* tion between longevity and size. There are exceptions, to be sure — some startling ones. For instance, whales are extraordinarily short-lived for their size. The age of 60 I have given is quite exceptional. Most cetaceans are doing very well indeed if they reach 30. This may be because life in the water, with the continuous loss of heat and the never-ending necessity of swimming, shortens life.

But much more astonishing is the fact that man has a longer life than *51* any other mammal — much longer than the elephant or even than the closely allied gorilla. When a human centenarian dies, of all the animals in the world alive on the day that he was born, the only ones that remain alive on the day of his death (as far as we know) are a few sluggish turtles, an occasional vulture or sturgeon, and a number of other human cente-narians. Not one non-human mammal that came into this world with him has remained. All, without exception (as far as we know), are dead.

If you think this is remarkable, wait! It is more remarkable than you *52* suspect.

The smaller the mammal, the faster the rate of its metabolism; the more *53* rapidly, so to speak, it lives. We might well suppose that while a small mammal doesn't live as long as a large one, it lives more rapidly and more intensely. In some subjective manner, the small mammal might be viewed as living just as long in terms of sensation as does the more sluggish large mammal. As concrete evidence of this difference in metabolism among mammals, consider the heartbeat rate. The following table lists some rough figures for the average number of heartbeats per minute in different types of mammal.

Shrew	1000	Sheep	75
Mouse	550	Man	72
Rat	430	Cow	60
Rabbit	150	Lion	45

Cat	130	Horse	38
Dog	95	Elephant	30
Pig	75	Whale	17

For the fourteen types of animals listed we have the heartbeat rate *54* (approximate) and the maximum age (approximate), and by appropriate multiplications, we can determine the maximum age of each type of creature, not in years but in total heartbeats. The result follows:

Shrew	1,050,000,000
Mouse	950,000,000
Rat	900,000,000
Rabbit	1,150,000,000
Cat	1,350,000,000
Dog	900,000,000
Pig	800,000,000
Sheep	600,000,000
Lion	830,000,000
Horse	800,000,000
Cow	950,000,000
Elephant	1,200,000,000
Whale	630,000,000

Allowing for the approximate nature of all my figures, I look at this *55* final table through squinting eyes from a distance and come to the following conclusion: A mammal can, at best, live for about a billion heartbeats and when those are done, it is done.

But you'll notice that I have left man out of the table. That's because I *56* want to treat him separately. He lives at the proper speed for his size. His heartbeat rate is about that of other animals, of similar weight. It is faster than the heartbeat of larger animals, slower than the heartbeat of smaller animals. Yet his maximum age is 115 years, and that means his maximum number of heartbeats is about 4,350,000,000.

An occasional man can live for over 4 billion heartbeats! In fact, the *57* life expectancy of the American male these days is 2.5 billion heartbeats. Any man who passes the quarter-century mark has gone beyond the billionth heartbeat mark and is still young, with the prime of life ahead.

Why? It is not just that we live longer than other mammals. Measured *58* in heartbeats, we live *four times as long! Why??*

Upon what meat doth this, our species, feed, that we are grown so *59* great? Not even our closest non-human relatives match us in this. If we assume the chimpanzee to have our heartbeat rate and the gorilla to have a slightly slower one, each lives for a maximum of about 1.5 billion heart-beats, which isn't very much out of line for mammals generally. How then do we make it to 4 billion?

What secret in our hearts makes those organs work so much better and last so much longer than any other mammalian heart in existence? Why does the moving finger write so slowly for us, and for us only?   60

Frankly, I don't know, but whatever the answer, I am comforted. If I were a member of any other mammalian species my heart would be stilled long years since, for it has gone well past its billionth beat. (Well, a *little* past.)   61

But since I am Homo sapiens, my wonderful heart beats even yet with all its old fire; and speeds up in proper fashion at all times when it should speed up, with a verve and efficiency that I find completely satisfying.   62

Why, when I stop to think of it, I am a young fellow, a child, an infant prodigy. I am a member of the most unusual species on earth, in longevity as well as brain power, and I laugh at birthdays.   63

(Let's see now. How many years to 115?)   64

QUESTIONS AND EXERCISES

Vocabulary

1. Define or explain each of the following terms:

petulant (3)	multicellular (33)
Homo sapiens (8)	centenarians (40)
carnivores (15)	invertebrates (40)
herbivores (15)	devotee (45)
puerperal (24)	incubus (45)
geriatrics (26)	carrion (46)
allegory (27)	cetaceans (50)
millennia (31)	metabolism (53)

Rhetoric

2. Asimov cleverly weaves the allusion to Edward Fitzgerald's *Omar Khayyam* into the title of the essay. Find another such allusion.

3. What does the length of the paragraphs do for the tone and pace of this essay?

4. "As for man his days are as grass: as a flower of the field, so he flourisheth. For the wind passeth over it, and it is gone; and the place thereof shall know it no more." (37) Discuss the figurative language in this quotation. In paragraph 38 Asimov says that it is a simile. Is he correct?

5. In paragraph 27 Asimov uses an allegory to illustrate a truism. In a phrase or two summarize the meaning of the allegory.
6. Is Asimov's final sentence trite? Defend your answer. What is the name for this rhetorical device?

Theme

7. Comment on Asimov's use of statistics. Why are they interesting? Why are they effective?
8. Why is man statistically superior to the other animals described?
9. Do you think that Asimov is religious? Why?
10. Does Asimov use comparison and contrast exclusively as a pattern of development? What is the implication of your answer?
11. What assumption does Asimov make about the nature of man and of man's relationship to animals?

Topics and Assignments for Composition

1. From your previous reading, theater attendance, or movie going, write several phrases or sentences of popular wisdom that might serve as titles for essays. For example: "Faint heart never won fair lady" may become "Faint Hearts, Fair Ladies."
2. Make up a short allegory to illustrate a truth about the human condition.
3. In an essay, use statistics to compare and/or contrast some complicated relationships.
4. Write an analysis of several book titles that are based on other literary works. Examples: *For Whom the Bell Tolls*
Brave New World

Margaret Mead

One Vote for This Age of Anxiety

When critics wish to repudiate the world in which we live today, one of   *1*
their familiar ways of doing it is to castigate modern man because anxiety
is his chief problem. This, they say, in W. H. Auden's phrase, is the age of
anxiety. This is what we have arrived at with it, our vaunted progress, our
great technological advances, our great wealth—everyone goes about
with a burden of anxiety so enormous that, in the end, our stomachs and
our arteries and our skins express the tension under which we live. Americans who have lived in Europe come back to comment on our favorite
farewell which, instead of the old goodbye (God be with you), is now
"Take it easy," each American admonishing the other not to break down
from the tension and strain of modern life.

Whenever an age is characterized by a phrase, it is presumably in con-   *2*
trast to other ages. If we are the age of anxiety, what were other ages?
And here the critics and carpers do a very amusing thing. First, they give
us lists of the opposites of anxiety: security, trust, self-confidence, self-
direction. Then without much further discussion, they let us assume that
other ages, other periods of history, were somehow the ages of trust or
confident direction.

The savage who, on his South Sea island, simply sat and let bread fruit   *3*
fall into his lap, the simple peasant, at one with the fields he ploughed and
the beasts he tended, the craftsman busy with his tools and lost in the
fulfillment of the instinct of workmanship—these are the counter-images
conjured up by descriptions of the strain under which men live today. But
no one who lived in those days has returned to testify how paradisaical
they really were.

Certainly if we observe and question the savages or simple peasants in   *4*
the world today, we find something quite different. The untouched savage
in the middle of New Guinea isn't anxious; he is seriously and continu-

ally *frightened*—of black magic, of enemies with spears who may kill him or his wives and children at any moment, while they stoop to drink from a spring, or climb a palm tree for a coconut. He goes warily, day and night, taut and fearful.

As for the peasant populations of a great part of the world, they aren't   5
so much anxious as hungry. They aren't anxious about whether they will get a salary raise, or which of the three colleges of their choice they will be admitted to, or whether to buy a Ford or Cadillac, or whether the kind of TV set they want is too expensive. They are hungry, cold and, in many parts of the world, they dread that local warfare, bandits, political coups may endanger their homes, their meager livelihoods and their lives. But surely they are not anxious.

For anxiety, as we have come to use it to describe our characteristic   6
state of mind, can be contrasted with the active fear of hunger, loss, violence and death. Anxiety is the appropriate emotion when the immediate personal terror—of a volcano, an arrow, the sorcerer's spell, a stab in the back and other calamities, all directed against one's self—disappears.

This is not to say that there isn't plenty to worry about in our world of   7
today. The explosion of a bomb in the streets of a city whose name no one had ever heard before may set in motion forces which end up ruining one's carefully planned education in law school, half a world away. But there is still not the personal, immediate, active sense of impending disaster that the savage knows. There is rather the vague anxiety, the sense that the future is unmanageable.

The kind of world that produces anxiety is actually a world of relative   8
safety, a world in which no one feels that he himself is facing sudden death. Possibly sudden death may strike a certain number of unidentified other people—but not him. The anxiety exists as an uneasy state of mind, in which one has a feeling that something unspecified and undeterminable may go wrong. If the world seems to be going well, this produces anxiety —for good times may end. If the world is going badly—it may get worse. Anxiety tends to be without locus; the anxious person doesn't know whether to blame himself or other people. He isn't sure whether it is 1956 or the Administration or a change in climate or the atom bomb that is to blame for this undefined sense of unease.

It is clear that we have developed a society which depends on having   9
the *right* amount of anxiety to make it work. Psychiatrists have been heard to say, "He didn't have enough anxiety to get well," indicating that, while we agree that too much anxiety is inimical to mental health, we have come to rely on anxiety to push and prod us into seeing a doctor about a symptom which may indicate cancer, into checking up on that old life insurance policy which may have out-of-date clauses in it, into having

a conference with Billy's teacher even though his report card looks all right.

People who are anxious enough keep their car insurance up, have the brakes checked, don't take a second drink when they have to drive, are careful where they go and with whom they drive on holidays. People who are too anxious either refuse to go into cars at all—and so complicate the ordinary course of life—or drive so tensely and overcautiously that they help cause accidents. People who aren't anxious enough take chance after chance, which increases the terrible death toll of the roads.   10

On balance, our age of anxiety represents a large advance over savage and peasant cultures. Out of a productive system of technology drawing upon enormous resources, we have created a nation in which anxiety has replaced terror and despair, for all except the severely disturbed. The specter of hunger means something only to those Americans who can identify themselves with the millions of hungry people on other continents. The specter of terror may still be roused in some by a knock at the door in a few parts of the South, or in those who have just escaped from a totalitarian regime or who have kin still behind the Curtains.   11

But in this twilight world which is neither at peace nor at war, and where there is insurance against certain immediate, down-right, personal disasters, for most Americans there remains only anxiety over what may happen, might happen, could happen.   12

This is the world out of which grows the hope, for the first time in history, of a society where there will be freedom from want and freedom from fear. Our very anxiety is born of our knowledge of what is now possible for each and for all. The number of people who consult psychiatrists today is not, as is sometimes felt, a symptom of increasing mental ill health, but rather the precursor of a world in which the hope of genuine mental health will be open to everyone, a world in which no individual feels that he needs be hopelessly brokenhearted, a failure, a menace to others or a traitor to himself.   13

But if, then, our anxieties are actually signs of hope, why is there such a voice of discontent abroad in the land? I think this comes perhaps because our anxiety exists without an accompanying recognition of the tragedy which will always be inherent in human life, however well we build our world. We may banish hunger, and fear of sorcery, violence or secret police; we may bring up children who have learned to trust life and who have the spontaneity and curiosity necessary to devise ways of making trips to the moon; we cannot—as we have tried to do—banish death itself.   14

Americans who stem from generations which left their old people behind and never closed their parents' eyelids in death, and who have   15 experienced the additional distance from death provided by two world wars fought far from our shores are today pushing away from them both a recognition of death and a recognition of the tremendous significance—for the future—of the way we live our lives. Acceptance of the inevitability of death, which, when faced, can give dignity to life, and acceptance of our inescapable role in the modern world, might transmute our anxiety about making the right choices, taking the right precautions, and the right risks into the sterner stuff of responsibility, which ennobles the whole face rather than furrowing the forehead with the little anxious wrinkles of worry.

Worry in an empty context means that men die daily little deaths. But good anxiety—not about the things that were left undone long ago, that return to haunt and harry men's minds, but active, vivid anxiety about what must be done and that quickly—binds men to life with an intense concern.   *16*

This is still a world in which too many of the wrong things happen somewhere. But this is a world in which we now have the means to make a great many more of the right things happen everywhere. For Americans, the generalization which a Swedish social scientist made about our attitudes on race relations is true in many other fields: anticipated change which we feel is right and necessary but difficult makes us unduly anxious and apprehensive, but such change, once consummated, brings a glow of relief. We are still a people who—in the literal sense—believe in making good.   *17*

QUESTIONS AND EXERCISES

Vocabulary

1. Define or explain:

admonishing (1)	locus (8)
castigate (1)	inimical (9)
instinct (3)	specter (11)
counter-images (3)	totalitarian (11)
conjured (3)	precursor (13)
paradisaical (3)	transmute (15)
warily (4)	harry (16)
sorcerer (6)	consummated (17)

Rhetoric

2. Why does Margaret Mead allude to New Guinea?
3. What is one of Miss Mead's favorite ways of making transitions between paragraphs?

Theme

4. Who is W. H. Auden? Why is he mentioned at the very beginning of the essay?
5. According to the author, what is the function of anxiety in our society?
6. Paragraph 15 is almost an essay within an essay. In longer essays writers often indulge in a few digressions that may touch upon the main subject in only a general way. What is the observation about American life presented in this digression?

Topics and Assignments for Composition

1. In one sentence summarize the thesis of "One Vote for this Age of Anxiety."
2. Agree or disagree with the factual statements presented in paragraph 15, and comment on the value judgments expressed in the paragraph.
3. Develop an essay in which you emulate Miss Mead's direct way of stating a thesis in the title and then persuading the reader to go along with her. The catch, however, is to pick the less popular side of the controversy.

John Lukacs

It's Halfway to 1984

We are now halfway to 1984. George Orwell, the author of "1984," finished his book in 1948. That was 18 years ago, and it is not more than another 18 years before that ominous date rolls around.

It is *ominous,* in every sense of that antique adjective. There is reason to believe that 18 years from now thousands of people will experience a feeling of uneasiness, perhaps a light little shudder of trepidation, as they first encounter that new year's numerals in print. In the English-speaking world, at least, "1984" has become a household term, suggesting some kind of inhuman totalitarian nightmare. And since millions who have not read the book now recognize the term, it is reasonable to assume that both the theme of the title and the book have corresponded to an emerging consciousness among many people in the otherwise progressive-minded English-speaking democracies, to the effect that things are *not* getting better all the time—no, not at all.

The plot of "1984" is well-known but it may be useful to sum it up briefly. By 1984 most of the world has been divided by three superstates —Oceania, Eurasia and Eastasia. They are perpetually at war with one another, but no one of them is completely able to subdue the others. This state of war enables the rulers of these states (the ruler of Oceania being Big Brother) to keep their peoples both ignorant and submissive. This is achieved by totalitarian and technical methods, by the absoluteness of one-party rule and by a kind of censorship that controls not only the behavior but even the thinking process of individuals. The hero of "1984," Winston Smith, born in 1945 (both the date and the first name are significant), is a simple party member and a functionary of the Ministry of Truth in London, which is the chief city of Airstrip One, for that is what Britain became after she had been absorbed by the United States to form Oceania. (Continental Europe, having been absorbed by the Soviet Union, had become Eurasia.)

Winston is a weak and forlorn intellectual who, however, is sickened   4
not only by the dreary living conditions in 1984 but by the prevalence of
official lying and the almost complete absence of personal privacy. One
day he stumbles into a love affair, which in itself is a dangerous thing since
the party punishes illicit relationships severely. Winston experiences
happiness and a sense of personal fulfillment, especially as Julia shares
his hatred of the existing system.

There is a high official in the Ministry of Truth, O'Brien, whom Win-   5
ston instinctively trusts. He and Julia confide in O'Brien. They are deceived. All along, O'Brien has set a trap for them: they are arrested in
their secret little room. They are tortured. Winston, despite his strong
residue of convictions, not only confesses to everything imaginable, but
in the end, faced by an especially horrible torture, he even betrays Julia.
He is finally released; he is a completely broken man; he has even come
to believe in the almightiness and goodness of Big Brother.

But it is not this plot, it is rather Orwell's description of everyday life in   6
1984 that is the principal matter of the novel and, one may suppose, the
principal matter of interest to its readers. Life in 1984 is a mixture of
horror and dreariness. What is horrible is not so much war as the shrivel-
ing of personal freedoms and privacy with the planners of the superstate
controlling vast portions of once-independent lives. What is dreary is that
within these totalitarian conditions the living standards of masses of
people in what were once civilized and prosperous countries are reduced:
Food and drink are little better than standardized slop: mass entertainments are primitive and vulgar; personal property has virtually disappeared.

One of the profound differences between "1984" and Aldous Huxley's   7
"Brave New World" (published in 1932, the latter still had many of the
marks of the light-headed twenties; its philosophy compared with that of
"1984" is a rather irresponsible *jeu d'esprit*) lies in Orwell's view of the
past rather than of the future. Looking back from 1984, conditions in the
early, capitalistic portion of the 20th century seem romantic and almost
idyllic to Winston Smith, so much so that on a solemn occasion he offers
a toast "to the past." Unemployment, revolutions, Fascism and, to some
extent, even Nazism and Communism are lesser evils than what is going
on in Oceania in 1984, since by that time the rulers of the state have per-
fected brainwashing and thought-control to the point that the memories
of entire generations, and hence their opinions about the past have been
eliminated.

This, of course, does not happen overnight: It is a brutal but gradual   8
development. In "1984," Orwell set the decisive turning point in the
middle sixties, "the period of the leaders of the Revolution were wiped

out once and for all. By 1970 none of them was left, except Big Brother himself."

Let us keep in mind that "1984" is the work of a novelist and not of a   *9*
prophet; Orwell ought not be criticized simply because some of his visions have not been borne out. On the other hand, Orwell was concerned in the late forties with certain tendencies of evil portent; and "1984" was a publishing success because around 1950, for great numbers of people, the picture of a society such as he described was not merely fantastic but to some extent plausible.

It is still plausible today, but not quite in the way in which Orwell   *10*
envisaged the future 18 years ago. Halfway to 1984 we can say, fortunately, that most of Orwell's visions have proved wrong. It is true that the United States, the Soviet Union and China correspond to some extent to the superpowers Oceania, Eurasia and Eastasia. But the United States has not annexed Britain, the Soviet Union has fallen far short of conquering all of Europe, and even China does not extend much beyond her traditional boundaries.

What is more important, the superpowers are not at war with one an-   *11*
other. It is true that during the so-called cold war between the United States and the Soviet Union many of the practices of traditional and civilized diplomacy were abandoned; but the cold war has given place to something like a cold peace between these two superpowers. Even the dreadful and ominous war in Asia is marked by the reluctance of the United States and China directly to attack each other.

Orwell proved correct in saying that "war . . . is no longer the des-   *12*
perate, annihilating struggle that it was in the early decades of the 20th century. It is a warfare of limited aims between combatants who are unable to destroy one another. . . ." Yet Orwell was interested principally not in international but internal developments. For example, in "1984" the peoples of Oceania are isolated; travel is forbidden except for a small minority of the élite; and the press is controlled to the extent that no meaningful information from the outside world is available to the public.

But now, halfway to 1984, the opposite has been happening. It is not   *13*
warfare but torrents of automobiles and mass tourism that threaten to destroy entire landscapes and cityscapes; great amounts of information are available to us about an undigestible variety of matters; and at times it seems that the cultural traditions of great Western nations are endangered less by the persistence of isolationism than by a phony internationalism drummed up by a kind of pervasive publicity that drowns out the once truer music of the arts.

Also, in the world of "1984" most people are ill-fed, badly clothed, run-   *14*
down. But this, too, has not happened. Now, halfway to 1984, almost

everywhere in the world, living standards have risen, and the danger is not, as Orwell envisaged it, that entire generations of once-prosperous countries will no longer know such things as wine, oranges, lemons and chocolate; it is, rather, that our traditional tastes and table habits may be washed away by a flood of frozen and synthetic foods of every possible kind, available to us every hour of the day.

The reasons why Orwell's visions of 1984 have been wrong seem to be   *15* bound up with the time and the circumstances of the book's conception. About the circumstances Orwell himself was supposed to have said that "1984" "wouldn't have been so gloomy if I had not been so ill." He wrote most of the book in self-imposed isolation on a rain-shrouded Scottish island, finishing it in an English country hospital in late 1948. Shortly thereafter, he was moved to a hospital in London, where in January, 1950, he died. As for the time of writing, in the late nineteen-forties Orwell's imagination succumbed, at least in part, to the temptation of conceiving the future as an increasingly acute continuation of what seems to be going on at the present. (In one of his earlier essays, Orwell had criticized the American writer James Burnham for this very fault.) Around 1949, when most intellectuals had come around to recognizing that Stalin's tyranny was hardly better than Hitler's, many of them concluded that it is in the nature of totalitarianism to become more and more tyrannical as time goes on. Indeed, some of them established their reputations by the ponderous books they produced on this theme. (Hannah Arendt's "The Origins of Totalitarianism" is an example.) Yet only a few years later, events in Eastern Europe and in Russia showed that history is unpredictable and that the projections of intellectuals are often oversimplified. But this Orwell did not live to see.

He foresaw the horrible features of 1984 as the consequences of totali-   *16* tarianism, of political tyranny, of the despotism of a dictator. But halfway to 1984 we can see, for example, that the era of totalitarian dictatorship is sliding away, into the past. Even the Soviet Union seems to be moving in the direction of what one may call "post-totalitarian"; all over Eastern Europe (though not yet in Asia) we can perceive regimes that, though dictatorial, are no longer totalitarian. The danger for us is, rather, the obverse: the possibility of totalitarian democracy.

Totalitarian democracy? The words seem paradoxical; our eyes and   *17* ears are unaccustomed to the sight and the sound of them in combination. Yet I believe that we ought to accustom our imaginations to the possibility of a democratic society in which universal popular suffrage exists while freedom of speech, press and assembly are hardly more than theoretical possibilities for the individual, whose life and ideas, whose rights to privacy, to family autonomy and to durable possessions are regimented by government and rigidly molded by mass production and by mass communications.

Let me, at this point, fall back on a personal illustration. For a long time the term "1984" evoked, to me, the image of a police state of the Eastern European type. But when I think of 1984 now, the image that swims into my mind is that of a gigantic shopping center and industrial complex—something like the one which has been erected a few miles from where I live in eastern Pennsylvania.   *18*

The undulating rural landscape around Valley Forge, with its bright dots of houses and its crossroads, has been transformed. There is now the eerie vastness of the General Electric Space Center whose square edifices spread across hundreds of acres. Beyond it stand other flat windowless blocks of buildings—the King of Prussia shopping center, around the trembling edges of which bulldozers roar from morning to night, boring their brutal tracks into the clayey soil which they must churn to mud before it can be covered by concrete. The predominant material is concrete, horizontal and vertical concrete. Twice a day, thousands of people pour into and out of this compound, in a tremendous metallic flow. But no one lives there. At night and on Sundays, these hundreds of acres resemble a deserted airport, with a few automobiles clustering here and there, or slowly cruising on one of the airstrips, occasionally peered at by uniformed guards. Why fly to the moon? Stand on a cold January night in the middle of a parking lot in a large shopping center in the American North. It is a man-made moonscape. This is how the moon will look after our Herculean efforts, after we reach it, colonize it, pour concrete over it.   *19*

This is how 1984 looks to me, in the middle of the sixties, but I know and feel that this view is neither solitary nor unusual. There are millions of Americans who, passing a similar space-age complex of buildings, will say "1984," covering up their resignation with a thin coat of defensive humor. What strikes us is not just the ugliness of the buildings but something else, something that is not so much the reaction of middle-aged earth-men against brave new worlds as it is the expression of a feeling which is, alas, close to the Orwellian nightmare vision: a sense of impersonality together with a sense of powerlessness.   *20*

The impersonality is there, in the hugeness of the organization and in the anonymous myriads of the interchangeable human beings who make up most of their personnel. The powerlessness is the feeling which I share with so many of my neighbors—that we cannot stop what in America is called the March of Progress, the cement trucks coming toward us any day from across the hill; the knowledge that our voices, our votes, our appeals, our petitions amount to near-nothing at a time when people   *21* have become accustomed to accepting the decisions of planners, experts and faraway powerful agencies. It is a sickening inward feeling that the essence of self-government is becoming more and more meaningless at the very time when the outward and legal forms of democracy are still kept up.

Let us not fool ourselves: Now, halfway to 1984, with all of the recent   22
advances of civil rights, with all of the recent juridical extensions of con-stitutional freedoms, we *are* facing the erosion of privacy, of property and — yes — even of liberty. This has nothing to do with the Communist Conspiracy or with Ambitious Government Bureaucrats — that is where our New Conservatives go wrong. It has nothing to do with Creeping Socialism. It has very much to do with Booming Technology. The dan-gers which our modern societies in the West, and particularly the United States, face now, halfway to 1984, are often new kinds of dangers, grow-ing out of newly developing conditions. What ought to concern us is the rootlessness of a modern, technological, impersonal society, with inter-changeable jobs and interchangeable people, on all levels of education.

We ought to dwell less on the possibility of unemployment arising out   23
of automation, in a society which, after all, feels obligated to produce full employment; rather, we ought to consider the growing purposeless-ness of occupations in a society where by now more people are employed in administration than in production. And in such a society we ought to prattle less about the need for more "creative leisure" when the problem is that work becomes less and less creative. We ought to worry not about the insufficient availability of products but about the increasing imper-manence of possessions. We ought to think deeply not so much about the growth of the public sectors of the public economy at the expense of pri-vate enterprise (which, at any rate, is no longer very "private"), but rather, about the cancerous growth of the public sectors of our existence at the expense of the private autonomy of our personal lives.

We ought to concern ourselves less with the depreciation of money and   24
more with the depreciation of language; with the breakdown of interior, even more than with the state of exterior, communications — or, in other words, with the increasing practices of Orwell's Doubletalk and Double-think, and with their growing promotion not so much by political tyrannies as by all kinds of techniques, in the name of Progress.

I cannot — and perhaps, I need not — explain or illustrate these concerns   25
in greater detail. They are, in any event, 1966 concerns about the future, not 1984 ones. Still, while many of the phantoms that haunted Orwell's readers 18 years ago have not materialized, the public currency of the term 1984 has lost none of its poignancy. The tone of our literature, in-deed of our entire cultural atmosphere, is far more pessimistic than it

was 18 years ago. "Alienation" and "hopelessness" are no longer Central European words; they are very American. This broad, and often near-nihilistic, cultural apathy and despair is relatively new on the American (and also on the British) scene. Its existence suggests that, despite the errors of Orwell's visions, the nightmare quality of "1984" continues to obsess our imagination, and not merely as the sickly titillation of a horror story. It haunts millions who fear that life may become an Orwellian nightmare even without the political tyranny that Orwell had predicted.

"It is by his political writings," Bertrand Russell once wrote, "that   26
Orwell will be remembered." If this is so—and at this moment, halfway to 1984, it still seems so—he will be remembered for the wrong reasons, and one can only hope that the slow corrective tides of public opinion in the long run will redress the balance.

Orwell was not so much concerned with the degeneration of justice as   27
with the degeneration of truth. For Orwell, both in the beginning and in the end was The Word. This is true of "1984," too, which had three levels. On the top level there is the "plot," the love affair of Winston and Julia, which is really flat and inconsequential. On the second level there is the political vision which, as we have seen, sometimes holds up, sometimes not. It is the third level, of what is happening to words and to print, to speech and to truth in 1984, which agitated Orwell the most. Indeed, this spare and economical writer chose to end the novel "1984" by adding an appendix for "The Principles of Newspeak." Orwell was frightened less by the prospects of censorship than by the potential falsification of history, and by the mechanization of speech.

The first of these protracted practices would mean that the only pos-   28
sible basis for a comparison with conditions other than the present would disappear; the second, that the degeneration of traditional language would lead to a new kind of mechanical talk and print which would destroy the meaning of private communications between persons. This prospect haunted Orwell throughout the last 12 years of his life. Some of his best essays dealt with this theme of falsifications of truth—even more than totalitarianism, this was his main concern. As long as people can talk to one another meaningfully, as long as they have private beliefs, as long as people retain some of the qualities of Winston Smith's mother (she had not been an "unusual woman, still less an intelligent one; and yet she had possessed a kind of nobility, a kind of purity, simply because the standards she obeyed were private ones. Her feelings were her own, and could not be altered from the outside . . ."), tyranny was vulnerable; it could not become total.

Orwell was wrong in believing that the development of science was   29
incompatible with totalitarianism (by 1984, "science, in the old sense has

almost ceased to exist. In Newspeak there is no word for science"). As we have seen, he foresaw a decay of technology ("the fields are cultivated by horse-ploughs while books are written by machinery"). This is not what has happened; now, halfway to 1984, the fields are cultivated by bull-dozers while books are written by machine-men. But Orwell was right in drawing attention to Doublethink, "the power of holding two contra-dictory beliefs in one's mind simultaneously, and accepting both of them," and to the desperate prospects of Doubletalk, of the degeneration of standards of language through varieties of supermodern jargon, prac-ticed by political pitchmen as well as by professional intellectuals. There is reason to believe that, were he alive today, Orwell would have modified his views on the nature of the totalitarian menace; and that, at the same time, he would be appalled by many of the present standards and prac-tices in mass communications, literature and publishing, even in the West, and perhaps especially in the United States.

In short, the 1984 that we ought to fear is now, in 1966, different from   30
the 1948 version. Politically speaking, Tocqueville saw further in the eighteen-thirties than Orwell in the nineteen-forties. The despotism which democratic nations had to fear, Tocqueville wrote, would be different from tyranny: "It would be more extensive and more mild; it would de-grade men without tormenting them. . . . The same principle of equality which facilitates despotism tempers its rigor." In an eloquent passage Tocqueville described some of the features of such a society: Above the milling crowds "stands an immense and tutelary power, which takes upon itself alone to secure their gratifications and to watch over their fate. That power is absolute, minute, regular, provident and mild. . . ." But when such a government, no matter how provident and mild, becomes om-nipotent, "what remains but to spare [people] all the care of thinking and all the trouble of living?"

Orwell's writing is as timely as Tocqueville's not when he is concerned   31
with forms of poetry but when he is concerned with evil communication. In this regard the motives of this English Socialist were not at all different from the noble exhortation with which Tocqueville closed one of his chapters in "Democracy in America": "Let us, then, look forward to the future with that salutary fear which makes men keep watch and ward for freedom, not with that faint and idle terror which depresses and enervates the heart." Present and future readers of "1984" may well keep this dis-tinction in mind.

Newspeak

In George Orwell's "1984," standard English (Oldspeak) has been re-placed by Newspeak, "a language designed to diminish the range of thought." Below is a sample "1984" lexicon:

bellyfeel — Blind, enthusiastic acceptance.

blackwhite — Contradiction of plain facts. (Also used to mean a loyal willingness to say that black is white when discipline demands it.)

crimestop — Faculty of stopping short at the threshold of a dangerous thought.

crimethink — Thoughtcrime.

doublethink — Power of holding two contradictory beliefs simultaneously, and accepting both.

duckspeak — To quack like a duck; implies praise if opinions quacked are orthodox ones.

goodsex — Normal intercourse between man and wife for the sole purpose of begetting children, and without physical pleasure on the part of the woman.

goodthinkful — Orthodox.

joycamp — Forced-labor camp.

Minipax — Ministry of Peace — i.e., Ministry of War.

oldthink — Wickedness and decadence.

prolefeed — Entertainment and news.

QUESTIONS AND EXERCISES

Vocabulary

1. Define or explain each of the following terms:

ominous (1)	alienation (25)
trepidation (2)	near-nihilistic (25)
idyllic (7)	tutelary (30)
portent (9)	omnipotent (30)
paradoxical (17)	polity (31)
myriads (21)	exhortations (31)
poignancy (25)	enervates (31)

2. Explain or identify the allusions to each of the following:

   Aldous Huxley (7)
   Bertrand Russell (26)
   de Tocqueville (30)

Rhetoric

3. Outline briefly the organization of the essay. What two items are compared and contrasted?

4. How does the title of the essay function as a device for unity and coherence? How many times was a variation of it mentioned in the essay itself?
5. What are the weaknesses in the organization of this essay?
6. What is the effect of introducing a new authority (de Tocqueville) in paragraph 30? Are his ideas sufficiently explained?

Theme

7. What is Lukacs' main thesis? What are the subordinate theses?
8. In what ways was Orwell's blueprint for *1984* correct? In what ways was he wrong?
9. What does Lukacs say we have to fear? Discuss his examples. Would most Americans agree with him about the shopping centers? Why are shopping centers and the other things that he thinks to be so bad so very successful? Why is Lukacs an enemy of the "March of Progress"?
10. What is ironic and paradoxical about a totalitarian democracy?
11. Discuss the problem of alienation, impersonality, hugeness and anonymity of life to which Lukacs objects. Do you agree with him?
12. Which do you think is the bigger problem: unemployment due to automation or the purposelessness of many occupations?

Topics and Assignments for Composition

1. Make up a few examples of Newspeak that reflect aspects of our society that bother you.
2. Write a paragraph refuting one of Lukacs' main points.
3. Write an essay using the rhetorical pattern of comparison and contrast as your organization.
4. If you have read any two of the following: *1984, Brave New World, Leviathan, Utopia, Republic,* or *Walden II,* write an essay comparing and/or contrasting the different attitudes towards men and their governments.

Jacob Bronowski

Science, the Destroyer or Creator?

We all know the story of the sorcerer's apprentice; or *Frankenstein*   *1*
which Mary Shelley wrote in competition with her husband and Byron;
or some other story of the same kind out of the macabre invention of the
nineteenth century. In these stories, someone who has special powers
over nature conjures or creates a stick or a machine to do his work for
him; and then finds that he cannot take back the life he has given it. The
mindless monster overwhelms him; and what began as an invention to do
the housework ends by destroying the master with the house.

These stories have become the epitome of our own fears. We have   *2*
been inventing machines at a growing pace now for about three hundred
years. This is a short span even in our recorded history, and it is not a
thousandth part of our history as men. In that short moment of time we
have found a remarkable insight into the workings of nature. We have
used it to make ourselves far more flexible in our adaptation to the outside world than any other animal has ever been. We can survive in cli-
mates which even germs find difficult. We can grow our own food and
meat. We can travel overland and we can tunnel and swim and fly, all in
the one body. More important than any of these, we have come nearest
to the dream which Lamarck had, that animals might inherit the skills
which their parents learnt. We have discovered the means to record our
experience so that others may live it again.

The history of other animal species shows that the most successful in   *3*
the struggle for survival have been those which were most adaptable to
changes in their world. We have made ourselves by means of our tools
beyond all measure more adaptable than any other species, living or extinct; and we continue to do so with gathering speed. Yet today we are
afraid of our own shadow in the nine o'clock news; and we wonder
whether we shall survive so over-specialised a creature as the Pekinese.

Reprinted by permission of the publishers from Jacob Bronowski, THE COM-
MON SENSE OF SCIENCE, Cambridge, Mass.: Harvard University Press.

Everyone likes to blame his sense of defeat on someone else; and for   4
some time scientists have been a favourite scapegoat. I want to look at
their responsibility, and for that matter at everybody's, rather more
closely. They do have a special responsibility; do not let us argue that
out of existence; but it is a complicated one, and it is not the whole
responsibility. For example, science obviously is not responsible for the
readiness of people, who do not take their private quarrels beyond the
stage of insult, to carry their public quarrels to the point of war. Many
animals fight for their needs, and some for their mere greeds, to the point
of death. Bucks fight for females, and birds fight for their territories. The
fighting habits of man are odd because he displays them only in groups.
But they were not supplied by scientists. On the contrary, science has
helped to end several kinds of group murder, such as witch hunting and
the taboos of the early nineteenth century against disinfecting hospitals.

Neither is science responsible for the existence of groups which be-   5
lieve themselves to be in competition: for the existence above all of
nations. And the threat of war today is always a national threat. Some
bone of contention and competition is identified with a national need:
Fiume or the Polish Corridor or the dignity of the Austrian Empire; and
in the end nations are willing to organise and to invite the death of citizens on both sides in order to reach these collective aims. Science did
not create the nations; on the contrary, it has helped to soften those strong
national idiosyncrasies which it seems necessary to exploit if war is to
be made with enthusiasm. And wars are not made by *any* traditional
groups: they are made by highly organised societies, they are made by
nations. Most of us have seen Yorkshiremen invade Old Trafford, and
a bloody nose or two if the day was thirsty. But no Yorkshireman would
have grown pale if he had been told that Lancashire had the atomic bomb.

The sense of doom in us today is not a fear of science; it is a fear of   6
war. And the causes of war were not created by science; they do not differ
in kind from the known causes of the War of Jenkins' Ear or the Wars of
the Roses, which were carried on with only the most modest scientific
aids. No, science has not invented war; but it has turned it into a very
different thing. The people who distrust it are not wrong. The man in the
pub who says "It'll wipe out the world," the woman in the queue who
says "It isn't natural"—they do not express themselves very well; but
what they are trying to say does make sense. Science has enlarged the
mechanism of war, and it has distorted it. It has done this in at least two
ways.

First, science has obviously multiplied the power of the warmakers.   7
The weapons of the moment can kill more people more secretly and more
unpleasantly than those of the past. This progress, as for want of another

word I must call it—this progress has been going on for some time; and for some time it has been said, of each new weapon, that it is so destructive or so horrible that it will frighten people into their wits, and force the nations to give up war for lack of cannon fodder. This hope has never been fulfilled, and I know no one who takes refuge in it today. The acts of men and women are not dictated by such simple compulsions; and they themselves do not stand in any simple relation to the decisions of the nations which they compose. Grapeshot and TNT and gas have not helped to outlaw war; and I see no sign that the hydrogen bomb or a whiff of bacteria will be more successful in making men wise by compulsion.

Secondly, science at the same time has given the nations quite new   8
occasions for falling out. I do not mean such simple objectives as someone else's uranium mine, or a Pacific Island which happens to be knee-deep in organic fertilizer. I do not even mean merely another nation's factories and her skilled population. These are all parts of the surplus above our simple needs which they themselves help to create and which gives our civilization its character. And war in our world battens on this surplus. This is the object of the greed of nations, and this also gives them the leisure to train and the means to arm for war. At bottom, we have remained individually too greedy to distribute our surplus, and collectively too stupid to pile it up in any more useful form than the traditional mountains of arms. Science can claim to have created the surplus in our societies, and we know from the working day and the working diet how greatly it has increased it in the last two hundred years. Science has created the surplus. Now put this year's budget beside the budget of 1750, anywhere in the world, and you will see what we are doing with it.

I myself think there is a third dimension which science has added to   9
modern war. It has created war nerves and the war of nerves. I am not thinking about the technical conditions for a war of nerves: the camera man and the radio and the massed display of strength. I am thinking of the climate in which this stage lightning flickers and is made to seem real. The last twenty years have given us a frightening show of these mental states. There is a division in the mind of each of us, that has become plain, between the man and the brute; and the rift can be opened, the man submerged, with a cynical simplicity, with the meanest tools of envy and frustration, which in my boyhood would have been thought inconceivable in a civilised society. I shall come back to this cleavage in our minds, for it is much more than an item in a list of war crimes. But it is an item. It helps to create the conditions for disaster. And I think that science has contributed to it. Science; the fact that science is there, mysterious, powerful; the fact that most people are impressed by it but ignorant and

helpless—all this seems to me to have contributed to the division in our minds. And scientists cannot escape the responsibility for this. They have enjoyed acting the mysterious stranger, the powerful voice without emotion, the expert and the god. They have failed to make themselves comfortable in the talk of people in the street; no one taught them the knack, of course, but they were not keen to learn. And now they find the distance which they enjoyed has turned to distrust, and the awe has turned to fear; and people who are by no means fools really believe that we should be better off without science.

These are the indictments which scientists cannot escape. Of course, they are often badly phrased, so that scientists can side-step them with generalities about the common responsibility, and who voted the credits for atomic research anyway; which are perfectly just, but not at all relevant. That is not the heart of the matter; and the people in queues and pubs are humbly groping for the heart. They are not good at saying things and they do not give model answers to interviewers. But when we say "We've forgotten what's right," when they say "We're not fit to handle such things," what is in their minds is perfectly true. Science and society are out of joint. Science has given to no one in particular a power which no one in particular knows how to use. Why do not scientists invent something sensible? Wives say it every time they stub their toe on the waste bin, and husbands say it whenever a fuse blows. Why is it the business of no one in particular to stop fitting science for death and to begin fitting it into our lives? We will agree that warlike science is no more than a by-product of a warlike society. Science has merely provided the means, for good or for bad; and society has seized it for bad. But what are we going to do about it?   10

The first thing to do, it seems to me, is to treat this as a scientific question: by which I mean as a practical and sensible question, which deserves a factual approach and a reasoned answer. Now that I have apologised on behalf of scientists, and this on a scale which some of them will certainly think too ample, let us cut out what usually happens to the argument at this point, the rush of recriminations. The scientists are conscious of their mistakes; and I do not want to discuss the mistakes of non-scientists—although they have made a great many—except those which we all must begin to make good.   11

I have said that a scientific answer must be practical as well as sensible. This really rules out at once the panaceas which also tend to run the argument into a blind alley at this stage; the panaceas which say summarily "Get rid of them." Naturally, it does not seem to me to be sensible to get rid of scientists; but in any case, it plainly is not practical. And whatever we do with our own scientists, it very plainly is not practical   12 to get rid of the scientists of rival nations; because if there existed the conditions for agreement among nations on this far-reaching scheme, then the conditions for war would already have disappeared. If there existed the conditions for international agreement, say to suspend all scientific research, or to abandon warlike research, or in any other way to forgo science as an instrument of nationalism—if such agreements could be reached, then they would already be superfluous; because the conditions for war would already have disappeared. So, however we might sigh for Samuel Butler's panacea in *Erewhon,* simply to give up all machines, there is no point in talking about it. I believe it would be a disaster for mankind like the coming of the Dark Ages. But there is no point in arguing this. It just is not practical, nationally or internationally.

There are no panaceas at all; and we had better face that. There is   *13* nothing that we can do overnight, in a week or a month, which can straighten by a laying on of hands the ancient distortion of our society. Do not let us fancy that any one of us out of the blue will concoct that stirring letter to *The Times* which will change the black mood of history— and the instructions to diplomats. Putting scientists in the Cabinet will not do that, and women in the War Office will not, nor will bishops in the Privy Council. There are no panaceas. We are the heirs to a tradition which has left science and society out of step. The man in the street is right: we have never learnt to handle such things. Nothing will do but that we learn. But learning is not done in a year. Our ultimate survival is in our own hands. Our survival while we are learning is a much chancier thing. We had better be realistic about that.

Meanwhile we had better settle down to work for our ultimate survival;   *14* and we had better start now. We have seen that the diagnosis has turned out to be not very difficult. Science and our social habits are out of step. And the cure is no deeper either. We must learn to match them. And there is no way of learning this unless we learn to understand *both.*

Of the two, of course, the one which is strange is science. I have al-   *15* ready blamed the scientist for that. He has been the monk of our age, timid, thwarted, anxious to be asked to help; and with a secret ambition to play the Grey Eminence. Through years of childhood poverty he dreamt of this. Scientific skill was a blue door beckoning to him, which would open into the society of dignitaries of state. But the private motives of scientists are not the trend of science. The trend of science is made by the needs of society: navigation before the eighteenth century, manufac- ture thereafter; and in our age I believe the liberation of personality. Whatever the part which scientists like to act, or for that matter which painters like to dress, science shares the aims of our society just as art does. The difficulties of understanding either are not fundamental; they are difficulties only of language. To grow familiar with the large ideas of science calls for patience and an effort of attention; and I hope I have shown that it repays them.

For two hundred years, these ideas have been applied to technical needs; and they have made our world anew, triumphantly, from top to toe. Our shoes are tanned and stitched, our clothes are spun and dyed and woven, we are lighted and carried and doctored by means which were unknown to neat Mr. Pope at Twickenham in 1740. We may not think that is much to put against the eighty thousand dead in Hiroshima, or we may. We may not think it recompenses us for the absence of any Mr. Pope from Twickenham today, we may even hold it responsible. It is certainly not a spiritual achievement. But it has not yet tried to be. It has applied its ideas monotonously to shoeleather and bicycle bells. And it has made a superb job of them. Compare its record in its own field with that of any other ideas of the same age: Burke's ideas of the imagination, or Bentham's on government, or Adam Smith on political economy. If any ideas have a claim to be called creative, because they have created something, then certainly it is the ideas of science.

We may think that all that science has created is comfort; and it certainly has done that — the very word "comfortable" in the modern sense dates from the Industrial Revolution. But have we always stopped to think what science has done not to our mode of living but to our life? We talk about research for death, the threat of war and the number of civilians who get killed. But have we always weighed this against the increase in our own life span? Let us do a small sum. The number of people killed in Great Britain in six years of war by German bombs, flying bombs, and V2's was sixty thousand. They were an average lot of people, which means that on an average they lost half their expectation of life. Quite an easy long division shows that the effect of this in our population of fifty million people was to shorten the average span of life by less than one thenth of one per cent. This is considerably less than a fortnight. Put this on the debt side. And on the credit side, we know that in the last hundred years the average span of life in England has increased by twenty years. That is the price of science, take it or leave it — a fortnight for twenty years of life. And these twenty years have been created by applying to daily life, to clothing and bedding, to hygiene and infection, to birth and death, the simple ideas of science — the fundamental ideas I have been talking about: order, cause, and chance. If any ideas have a claim to be called creative, because they have created life, it is the ideas of science.

We have not neglected these ideas altogether in our social organisation. But, it is a point I have made several times, we have got hopelessly behind with them. The idea of order is now old enough to have reached at least our filing cabinets. The idea of cause and effect has entered our habits, until it has become the new *a priori* in the making of administrative plans. The difficulty is to dislodge it, now that it is hardening into a scholastic formula. For the idea which has given a new vigour to science in our generation is larger than the machinery of cause and effect. It stipulates no special mechanism between the present and the future. It is content to predict the future, without insisting that the computation must follow the steps of causal law. I have called this the idea of chance, because its method is statistical, and because it recognises that every prediction carries with it its own measurable uncertainty. A good prediction is one which defines its area of uncertainty; a bad prediction ignores it. And at bottom this is no more than the return to the essentially empirical, the experimental nature of science. Science is a great many things, and I have called them a great many names; but in the end they all return to this: science is the acceptance of what works and the rejection of what does not. That needs more courage than we might think.

It needs more courage than we have ever found when we have faced   *19* our worldly problems. This is how society has lost touch with science: because it has hesitated to judge itself by the same impersonal code of what works and what does not. We have clung to Adam Smith and Burke, or we have agitated for Plato or Aquinas, through wars and famine, through rising and falling birth-rates, and through libraries of learned argument. And in the end, our eyes have always wandered from the birth-rate to the argument: from the birth-rate to what we have wanted to believe. Here is the crux of what I have been saying. Here is our ultimate hope of saving ourselves from extinction. We must learn to understand that the content of all knowledge is empirical; that its test is whether it works; and we must learn to act on that understanding in the world as well as in the laboratory.

This is the message of science: our ideas must be realistic, flexible,   *20* unbigoted—they must be human, they must create their own authority. If any ideas have a claim to be called creative, because they have liberated that creative impulse, it is the ideas of science.

This is not only a material code. On the contrary, my hope is that it   *21* may heal the spiritual cleft which two wars have uncovered. I have seen in my lifetime an abyss open in the human mind: a gulf between the endeavour to be man, and the relish in being brute. The scientist has indeed had a hand in this, and every other specialist too, with his prim detachment and his oracular airs. But of course, the large strain which has opened this fault is social. We have made men live in two halves, a Sunday half and a workday half. We have ordered them to love their neighbour and to turn the other cheek, in a society which has constantly compelled them to shoulder their neighbour aside and to turn their backs. So we have created a savage sense of failure which, as we know now to our cost, can be tapped with an ease which is frightening; and which can thrust up, with explosive force, a symbol to repeat to an unhappy people its most degrading dream.

Can science heal the neurotic flaw in us? If science cannot, then *22* nothing can. Let us stop pretending. There is no cure in high moral precepts. We have preached them too long to men who are forced to live how they can: *that* makes the strain which they have not been able to bear. We need an ethic which is moral *and* which works. It is often said that science has destroyed our values and put nothing in their place. What has really happened of course is that science has shown in harsh relief the division between our values and our world. We have not begun to let science get into our heads; where then was it supposed to create these values? We have used it as a machine without will, the conjured spirit to do the chores. I believe that science can create values: and will create them precisely as literature does, by looking into the human personality; by discovering what divides it and what cements it. That is how great writers have explored man, and this whether they themselves as men have been driven by the anguish in *Gulliver's Travels* or the sympathy in *Moll Flanders*. The insight of science is not different from that of the arts. Science will create values, I believe, and discover virtues, when it looks into man; when it explores what makes him man and not an animal, and what makes his societies human and not animal packs.

I believe that we can reach this unity in our culture. I began this book *23* by recalling that nations in their great ages have not been great in art or science, but in art and science. Rembrandt was the contemporary of Huygens and Spinoza. At that very time, Isaac Newton walked with Dryden and Christopher Wren. We know that ours is a remarkable age of science. It is for us to use it to broaden and to liberate our culture. These are the marks of science: that it is open for all to hear, and all are free to speak their minds in it. They are marks of the world at its best, and the human spirit at its most challenging.

QUESTIONS AND EXERCISES

Vocabulary

1. Define or explain each of the following terms:

macabre (1)	*a priori* (18)
conjures (1)	stipulates (18)

epitome (2)

idiosyncrasies (5)

cynical (9)

panacea (13)

empirical (18)

cleft (21)

oracular (21)

2. Identify or explain the importance of the following allusions:

Lamarck (2)	empirical (18)
scapegoat (4)	stipulates (18)
War of Jenkins' Ear (6)	Plato (19)
Wars of the Roses (6)	Aquinas (19)
queues (10)	*Gulliver's Travels* (22)
Dark Ages (12)	*Moll Flanders* (22)
Grey Eminence (15)	Rembrandt (23)
Mr. Pope (16)	Spinoza (23)
Burke (16)	Newton (23)
Bentham (16)	Dryden (23)
Adam Smith (16)	Christopher Wren (23)
Industrial Revolution (17)	

Rhetoric

3. How does Bronowski achieve unity in this essay?
4. How is the theme in paragraph 1 developed?
5. What transitional devices are used in paragraphs 7, 8, and 9?
6. Discuss the use of figurative language in paragraph 21. Why do you think a scientist feels he needs to use figurative language?
7. What is the function of the title?

Theme

8. Much of the essay is a peroration for the thesis itself. Why does Bronowski have a long introduction?
9. What is the crux of the article? In what paragraph do you find it stated?
10. In paragraph 22 Bronowski mentions a neurotic flaw in us. What is this neurotic flaw?
11. Give a few examples of high moral precepts that have not been a cure for our problems. Why does he refrain from giving a few examples of his own?
12. In paragraph 22 what analogy does he make between science and the arts?
13. What, if any, are the flaws in Bronowski's arguments? How, for example, will science create values?
14. Can one accept Bronowski's analysis of the climate of opinions without accepting his conclusions?

Topics and Assignments for Composition

1. Outline in a series of short sentences the pattern of Bronowski's argument.
2. In an organized paragraph present a basis for a system of ethics based on Bronowski's position.
3. In an organized essay take one of the following positions:
   a. Accept Bronowski's position and support it in your own fashion with your own arguments.
   b. Defend high moral precepts as the necessary bases for the kind of world you would like to live in.
   c. Science is the source of most of the world's ills.

Avrum Ben-Avi

Zen Buddhism

One of the prime difficulties in approaching Zen Buddhism lies in the conception of mysticism, which, in the Western world, is often associated with the abstract, the mysterious, or the occult. This is contrary to the position taken by Suzuki* who writes, "Taking it all in all, Zen is emphatically a matter of personal experience; if anything may be called radical empirical, it is Zen. No amount of reading, no amount of teaching, no amount of contemplation will ever make one a Zen master." This section is concerned with those central qualities inherent in the teaching of Zen which are significantly related to the psychotherapeutic process. Thus, rather than attempt to compare the two systems of thought with regard to practices, goals, or efficiency, it would seem more useful to consider what there is about this Eastern discipline that might be of interest to the Western psychiatrist or psychologist.

The introduction of Buddhism to China is estimated to have occurred around A.D. 520, the Chinese influence making it less abstract and intellectual and more directly linked in life's experience. As Watts points out, ". . . it made Buddhism a possible way of life for human beings, for people with families with everyday work to do, and with normal instincts and passions." Basho, a Zen poet, said Zen is "the everyday mind," and Zen has continued to be rooted in the here, the now, the available, and the concrete. It was taught that the intellectual, analytic, discursive, and rational ways of man were, in fact, hurdles to be overcome in the course of enlightenment. "Ummon (Yun-men) once appeared in the pulpit, and said, 'In this school of Zen no words are needed; what, then, is the ulti-

From AMERICAN HANDBOOK OF PSYCHIATRY edited by Silvano Arieti, Volume II © 1959 by Basic Books, Inc., Publishers, New York.

* Dr. Daisetz Teitaro Suzuki has, for the past fifty of his eighty-seven years, been engaged in the study and interpretation of Eastern and Western mysticism. He has, in the course of his work, become the foremost authority and interpreter of Zen Buddhism to the Western world.

mate essence of Zen teaching?' It was Hui-neng the sixth patriarch, considered the Chinese founder of Zen, whose teaching set the mood and direction for the developments of Zen. It is in his teachings that one finds the clearly stated conceptions that have drawn the attention and interest of workers in the field of psychiatry. According to Hui-neng, Zen was the "seeing into one's own Nature." Suzuki comments, "This is the most significant phrase ever coined in the development of Zen." Categorically, Hui-neng taught, "we talk of seeing into our own Nature, and not of practicing dhyana (meditation) or obtaining liberation." He insisted that what was central to Zen practice was that intuitive understanding—rooted in the individual's life experience and everyday work rather than in intellection or quiet contemplation—was the promise of enlightenment. It is this central conception so basic to our own work that has touched the curiosity and excited the imagination of C. G. Jung, Karen Horney, and Erich Fromm, among others, to know the Zen experience. The Zen experience has been characterized by Jung as follows: "One has the feeling of touching upon a true secret, not something that has been imagined or pretended, this is not a case of mystifying secrecy, but rather an experience that baffles all language."

In addition to the qualities of immediacy and concreteness mentioned, other features of Zen which are important are intensity, dedication, overwhelming tension, and the radicalism or abruptness of the experience. The intensity and radicalness are seen in the manner of the pursuit of an idea or a principle, pushing it, extending it, and coming at last to some sense of an ultimate understanding of it. For example, we talk of relatedness, empathy, or intuition. In fact, one of the basic tenets of psychoanalysis has to do with the notion that, in order to know the other, one must first know oneself. This can be modified or extended; I know you to the extent that I know myself—or I know you only as I know myself. Zen however goes beyond these conceptions. They do not deal merely in knowing or in the quantitative terms expressed above. For them it is a simple concrete statement, "I am myself, I am you, you are me. We are a unity." The intensity and the dedication with which Zen is approached is seen in the use of the Koan. The Koan is a rather brief, simply stated, but baffling question to which there is no logical or intellectual solution. The recipient of the Koan is entirely devoted to its solution, regardless of his other activities. Rather than "regardless of his other activities," it would be more accurate to say, "through his devotion to his current and immediate experience." The solution may come to him whether he is actually in the meditation hall or out in the yard chopping wood. This does not mean that he thinks about the Koan as he chops wood but that the insight into the Koan is more likely to be available at a time when he is completely involved in the task at hand. It is the thoroughgoing quality of the experience rather than the nature of the activity which can yield up the secret. The student may work on a single Koan for many years, and often does. The solution of the Koan is directed at bringing the person into touch with ultimate reality. The following are two traditional Koans:

> What are your original features which you have even prior to your birth?
> What is the sound of one hand clapping?

Now, what is interesting is that some of the same Koans have been used for centuries, yet previously acceptable answers are not adequate for the new student. The answer or truth must come from the individual himself, from his own life's experience. The need for the personalized experience of the solution to a personal problem is clearly related to the psychotherapeutic process. Although in Zen there is no apparent direct study of the disciple's personal history, the answer must be uniquely his, or it is not acceptable to the master. A solution based upon something learned, a reasonable formulation or generalization will not do. The limitations and possible irrelevance of the intellectualized formulation of a neurotic problem are equally recognized and discouraged by the psychoanalyst. The Koan is actually a method to demonstrate to the disciple the limitations of the intellect. Suzuki says, "The worst enemy of Zen experience, at least in the beginning, is the intellect . . . The discriminating intellect must be cut short if Zen consciousness is to unfold itself." "A penetrating insight is born of the inner depths of consciousness, as the source of a new life has been tapped, and with it the Koan yields up its secrets."

The tension, abruptness, and radical qualities of Zen are most clearly exemplified by the satori. Antecedent to satori is a feeling of overwhelming tension; one feels cornered like a rat, or as if hanging from a precipice by one's teeth, needing to say but a word to be saved. Then, with the abruptness of an explosion, the essence of one's entire life is thereafter changed. Suzuki says:

> Satori as the Zen experience must be concerned with the entirety of life. For what Zen proposes to do is the revolution, and the revaluation as well, of oneself as a spiritual unity. . . . Satori may be defined as an intuitive looking into the nature of things in contradistinction to the analytical or logical understanding of it. Practically, it means the unfolding of a new world hitherto unperceived in the confusion of a dualistically-trained mind.

Of particular interest is the nature of the collaboration between the   5
master and the disciple in the course of this overwhelming experience.
There is a true sense that this is a mutually shared, significant experience.
As Suzuki puts it, "when the Koans are understood, the master's state of
mind is understood, which is satori and without which Zen is a sealed
book." Personal accounts of those working with Zen masters substantiate this feeling. The degree of responsibility assumed by the master, as
well as the commitment on the part of the disciple, are both characterized
by an intensity and devotion which, I believe, is rarely found in our work.
A Zen master said, "There are three factors making for success in the
study of Zen: (1) great faith, (2) great resolution, and (3) great spirit of
inquiry. When any one of these is lacking it is like a cauldron with a
broken leg, it limps."

Now Zen disclaims being a religion, a philosophy, or a science, yet in   6
characteristic fashion would probably turn around and say that it included
them all. This is not merely perverse. Zen is essentially an attempt to
solve the human problem of life. This is actually at the root of serious
work in the field of philosophy, science, and religion, as it is equally at
the root of the life of any man who seriously contemplates his own existence. For example, each school of psychoanalysis, or at least each of
the individuals who formulated the significant theories of human behavior, was really grappling with the problem of the nature of man rather
than being concerned with explanations for particular aspects of pathology. Then we have what may be a universal danger, where a philosophy,
an idea, or a method, once vital and energetic, becomes institutionalized.
With the transmission through generations of teachers, there seems to be
a tendency toward a serious constriction of the scope of thought. What is
transmitted are the ritualistic practices rather than the originally vibrant
spirit. Zen has consciously tried to block this trend in its own history.
The defense against the setting in of an institutionalized rigidity is inherent in the insistence upon an experience in Zen which goes beyond
mere knowledge. This, incidentally, is also attempted in psychoanalytic
training in the requirement for both the personal and supervisory analytic
experience. To the extent that if either or both of these two training experiences are restricted to the transmittal of information and knowledge,
they fail. In analytic work we have also tried to sustain the more basic
conceptions by not necessarily accepting as the major consideration in
the therapy the presenting complaint or symptomatology of the patient.
This is also the basis for not accepting as unqualified criteria of analytic
success the alleviation of symptoms, or the so-called social adjustment.
Implicit in this is what we are talking about, that there is something about
the person's life of great significance with which we have as yet not come

to grips. We still lack, however, as far as psychological theories are concerned, a clear statement or understanding of the precise nature of the
essential quality of human life. Zen has been described as essentially an
attempt to solve *the* human dilemma, and this certainly needs clarification. This dilemma, according to Zen, is that man exists in this world as
both the subject and object of his experience and that this dichotomy must
be abolished if he is to achieve his ultimate nature. Suzuki puts it this way:

> According to the philosophy of Zen, we are too much a slave to
> the conventional way of thinking, which is dualistic through and
> through. . . . Zen, however, upsets this scheme of thought and sub-
> stitutes a new one in which there exists no logic, no dualistic arrange-
> ment of ideas. We believe in dualism chiefly because of our tradi-
> tional training.

Now the notion of a person being in a state of absolute oneness is not   7
entirely foreign to us in the field of psychology and psychiatry. It is known
that this is the experience of the infant before he distinguishes himself
from the world around him. This is certainly also a frequent occurrence
in dreams as well as in certain psychotic states. But here we come to a
critical point for the Westerner in dealing with Zen. One way to rid ourselves of the unfamiliar and disquieting notions of Zen is to relegate this
kind of experience to one of the following: It is a regression to an infantile
level of development, a state of advanced autism, or an extreme experience of autosuggestion. There is another way with which we can deal
with Zen experience, and that is to try to bridge the gap with what is more
familiar in our own lives. These we categorize as "intuitive" or "empha-
tic." That is, it is not too strange for us to feel into and be one with another
person. This we grasp. In fact, it is a quality and a talent that we cherish
and in our lives strive toward and at rare moments share, if even in a
fleeting fashion, with another person. For many of us it is these rare and
transitory moments that hold for us even in our Western mode the essence of living and loving. Yet the oneness with the inanimate object is
also not entirely remote, since there is the occasional experience of
"going out of ourselves" which we may have momentarily when an exciting painting or a magnificent landscape makes impact upon us or we
on it. It is not suggested that the above is Zen. To do so would be a second
convenient way to dismiss the vitality of the experience; that is, to put it
in the position of "it's the same as what we mean when we say so and so,
but they just use different words." We, in this field, are only too familiar
with this as an obscuring and diffusing gambit. These illustrations with
which we are familiar are given to indicate that it is possible for people

with our Western background to try seriously to learn Zen rather than dismiss it as something completely beyond us, as a pathological state, or even simply as nonsense.

In summarizing, there are certain points which are of interest for psy-   *8* chotherapists:

The essence of Zen Buddhism consists in acquiring a new viewpoint   *9* on life and things generally, and this is rooted in one's penetrating understanding of one's self.

There are in its teaching and method an urgency, devotion, and radical   *10* quality which are known to be significant if one is to change one's life.

The changes are not brought about by one person doing something to   *11* another. One seeks, and with the help of another — although essentially by his dedication to himself — resolves his dilemma.

The solution is in one's self — "If you wish to seek the Buddha, you   *12* ought to see into your own nature."

The essence of whatever it is called, change, illumination, or growth,   *13* must be rooted in the immediate, the concrete experience of the individual rather than based on an intellectual or abstract formulation.

The problems in living of any single person constitute his unique at-   *14* tempt to solve the perplexities of human existence. He cannot, however, solve his own unique problem by ignoring that it arises by virtue of his being human. That is, his difficulties in living are simply his own way of expressing the human dilemma.

What seems to be close to the heart of the matter is this. If psycho-   *15* therapy or psychoanalysis is to look toward dealing with the essential human problem rather than what might be the person's unique way of contending with the problem, that is, his pathology, there is a need to become expert in living rather than expert in the problems of living. In fact, one might doubt whether one could really be an expert in the problems of living without being an expert in living.

One last Zen quote: "When there is enough faith there is enough doubt   *16* which is the great spirit of inquiry, and when there is a great spirit of inquiry there is an illumination."

In presenting a brief statement of Zen it is possible for misconceptions   *17* to be encouraged. For example, rather than present Zen as antiintellectual or antiscientific, there is, rather, an intention to indicate the specification of the limitation of the intellectual and scientific approaches to experience. Much of what is uniquely human in man's history as well as in a particular person's life falls outside these realms. This is simply because intellect and knowledge do not encompass the totality of man's being. To delimit the relevant data of the psychotherapeutic inquiry to these fields is justifiable neither by evaluating the sources of most of the advances in this field nor by referring to daily clinical practice. The major explanation for the resistance to expanding the sources of relevant data rests in the human condition. It is much easier "to learn about something," than to "become someone." The scientist may remain constant, unchanging, objective, and aloof; he acquires additional data and knowledge, but he himself is not necessarily affected. His function is to assemble the data, then control or predict the future course of events relevant to such data. The mystic or humanistic investigator has, however, as his primary source of observation, himself. His goal is not to "know about" but to "become." It is true that the intellect is a significant agent for "becoming," but it is certainly not the sole or most powerful source of change. Herein lies the gap between the exclusively "scientific" investigator and the mystic or humanistic researcher. In psychotherapeutic work these may produce two very divergent attitudes. The scientist manipulates and alters the subject; in the mystical condition there is a mutually experienced adventure. The significant changes in the patient cannot take place unless there is a significant experience on the part of the therapist, although the avowed purpose of the collaboration is change in the patient. The more rewarding and genuine the change in the patient's life, the more certain has the impact upon the therapist's life been, not merely in terms of knowledge but in his own way of life.

QUESTIONS AND EXERCISES

Vocabulary

1. Define or explain each of the following terms:

mysticism (1)	Koan (3)
occult (1)	satori (4)
radical (1)	criteria (6)
empirical (1)	dualism (6)
psychotherapeutic (1)	psychotic (7)
discursive (2)	autism (7)
intuitive (2)	intuitive (7)
empathy (3)	emphatic (7)
tenets (3)	gambit (7)
disciple (3)	

2. Identify each of the following individuals:

Suzuki (1)	Karen Horney (2)
Basho (2)	Eric Fromm (2)
C. G. Jung (2)	

Rhetoric

3. In the essay there are several attempts to compare one thing with another. Although psychiatry claims to be a science, and Zen claims to be non-religion, non-science, non-philosophy, and non-communicable, both the psychiatrist, Ben-Avi, and the Zen Buddhist, Suzuki, resort to figurative language when they wish to communicate. They tell what something is *like*. What figure of speech is each of the following?

   "one feels cornered like a rat, or as if hanging from a precipice by by one's teeth needing to say but a word to be saved." (4)

   "when the Koans are understood, the master's state of mind is understood, which is satori and without which Zen is a sealed book" (5)

   "When any one of these is lacking it is like a cauldron with a broken leg, it limps." (5)

   "We, in this field, are only too familiar with this as an obscuring and diffusing gambit." (7)

   "What seems to be close to the heart of the matter is this." (15)

   "When there is enough faith there is enough doubt which is the great spirit of inquiry, and when there is a great spirit of inquiry, there is an illumination." (16)

   "and that is to try to bridge the gap" (7)

4. Find several examples of short definitions, acknowledging that the entire essay may be an extended definition of Zen.

   Examples:

   "Zen is emphatically a matter of personal experience . . ." (1)

   "Zen is essentially an attempt to solve the human problem of life." (6)

5. Discuss the organization of the essay.

   For example, paragraph 1 = introduction and statement of purpose

   paragraph 2 = history of Zen

6. Make a list of some of the transitional devices used by the author. Are they sufficient in effecting the shift?

7. What is the tone of the essay?

8. What are the major characteristics of the style?

Theme

9. What audience did the author have in mind?

10. This essay has two purposes: one is to give an extended definition of Zen and the other is to compare and contrast Zen to psychoanalysis and psychotherapy. In what way does Ben-Avi succeed in accomplishing his purposes? Are there any weaknesses in his presentations?

11. What seems to be the major contradition in Zen?
12. Why has Zen captured the imagination of many American writers of fiction during the 1950s and 1960s?
13. Why is a Zen master like a psychiatrist?
14. What comparisons do you find between Zen and existentialism?
15. What comparisons do you find between Zen and the current drug mystique?
16. Ben-Avi makes some concluding distinctions in paragraph 17. What are the implications of his distinction between the "scientific" investigator and the mystic of humanistic researcher? Which side does he choose?

Topics and Assignments for Composition

1. Write several sentences summarizing the similarities between Zen and psychiatry.
2. Make up a few Koans.
3. Write a paragraph of extended definition about one of the following items: Zen, mysticism, "the human problem of life," Western dualism, psychotherapy.
4. Write a 500 word essay on one of the following topics:
     The Conflict of Western and Eastern Thought
     The Relationship Between Zen and Japanese Art
     The Haiku: A Vehicle for Zen
     The Beat Generation and Zen Buddhism
     The Difference Between Science and Mysticism
     The Metaphors of Mysticism
     The Zen of Watts, Barrett, and Suzuki
     Zen in Archery, Gardens, and Poetry

Louis J. Halle

The Language of Statesmen

If we have in our minds a sharper distinction between poetry and prose *1*
than exists in fact, it is because we are misled by the difference between
the appearance on paper of what is presented as the one and what as the
other. At its best, prose has always verged on poetry, and in our own
day especially, what is presented as poetry may be utterly prosaic. A
composition that appears as prose may, in fact, represent poetry better
than another that appears as poetry. No one questions that the following
is poetry, although cast in the typographic form of prose.

> Yea, though I walk through the valley
> of the shadow of death, I will fear no
> evil: for thou art with me; thy rod and
> thy staff they comfort me. . . .

If, then, we rid our minds of a categorical distinction based on superficial form only, we are in a position to resolve a common paradox pertaining to the language of statesmanship.

Lincoln's Gettysburg Address is not notable for the substance of what *2*
is said in it, which is commonplace. Why, then, should it rank among the
greatest utterances of statesmanship? Why should it remain unforgettable
when utterances of other American presidents, far richer in content,
have been quickly forgotten? The answer is that, like the Twenty-third
Psalm, it is a poem.

To appreciate this one must read it aloud, even if soundlessly, as an *3*
actor reads Shakespeare to himself. The Twenty-third Psalm and the
Gettysburg Address are poems not so much on account of any images
they contain as on account of their music: their rhythms, their beat, the
echo of their phrases; the symmetry of passages that rise, each one, from

Reprinted by permission of the author.

the level of its beginning only to return to it again, as a passage in music takes flight from the keynote only to conclude, like a bird, by coming to rest on it again.

The theme of the Address is dedication, the dedication of a national   *4*
cemetery and the word "dedicate" is repeated like an incantation, gaining in power and meaning at each repetition.

"The world will little note nor long remember what we say here, but it   *5*
can never forget what they did here." This has equilibrium as well as rhythm, for it is statement and response.

The large rhythm of the phrases in the Twenty-third Psalm tends to be   *6*
triple:

> He maketh me to lie down in green pastures:
> he leadeth me beside the still waters.
> He restoreth my soul. . . .

And again:

> Thou preparest a table before me
>   in the presence of mine enemies:
> thou anointest my head with oil:
> my cup runneth over.

The second set of diminishing phrases echoes the first. In the Gettysburg Address the rhythm is primarily duple, secondarily triple, the two rhythms setting each other off, as in so much of Bach's music.

Certainly Lincoln was not consciously practicing the principles of   *7*
poetics when he composed what he referred to as "a few appropriate remarks." Presumably, because his mind had been formed so largely on the King James Bible, his language fell into certain rhythms naturally. So one who does nothing but read sonnets will at last find himself speaking, naturally and unconsciously, in iambic pentameters.

Evidence of this is that Lincoln's private letters have, in greater or   *8*
lesser degree, the same elements of poetry as his public utterances. His letter of August 22, 1862, to Horace Greeley is an example. After its opening statement ("I have just read yours of the 19th, addressed to my-self through the New York 'Tribune.' "), it goes on:

> If there be in it any statements or assumptions of fact which I may
> know to be erroneous, I do not, now and here, controvert them. If
> there be in it any inferences which I may believe to be falsely drawn,
> I do not, now and here, argue against them. If there be perceptible in

it an impatient and dictatorial tone, I waive it in deference to an old friend whose heart I have always supposed to be right.

All the rest of the letter (which at one point falls into a rhyme in keeping with the context) has the same rhythmical quality, the same beat. The style was the man, and therefore it was consistent throughout his writings. *9*

Here is Walter Pater's famous description of Leonardo's *Mona Lisa:* *10*

She is older than the rocks among which she sits; like the vampire, she has been dead many times, and learned the secrets of the grave; and has been a diver in deep seas, and keeps their fallen day about her; and trafficked for strange webs with Eastern merchants: and, as Leda, was the mother of Helen of Troy, and, as Saint Anne, the mother of Mary; and all this has been to her but as the sound of lyres flutes, and lives only in the delicacy with which it has moulded the changing lineaments, and tinged the eyelids and the hands.

William Butler Yeats, in his *Oxford Book of Modern Verse,* presents this as a poem, having broken it up into lines of varying length for the purpose.

The question arises whether the elements of poetry to which I have drawn attention have any fundamental importance, whether they are more than the mere ornamentation of language, the serious purpose of which is not to produce pleasant sounds but to say something. *11*

Would it not be extraordinary if the judgment of the centuries on what constituted great utterance had consistently gone to mere ornament? Would it not be extraordinary if this judgment were wrong in preferring the Gettysburg Address, as empty of substance as it is, to the forgotten address of February 22, 1947, in which Secretary of State Marshall, aware that the United States faced one of the greatest crises in world history, summoned the American people to adopt a higher standpoint and a more magnanimous attitude than in the past, and on that basis at last to shoulder their worldwide responsibilities — but summoned them to do this in language that would hardly have served for an argument in favor of raising the postman's salary? Surely such judgment is not wrong, and poetry is not something that is merely added to the substance of language like the icing on a cake. *12*

Having argued that what passes for prose may be poetry, I am tempted to make the further argument that language itself is poetry. At least there is a sense in which it is. Again I go to music for an analogy. The difference between noise, on the one hand, and musical tone, on the other, is that the former represents chaos and the latter order. Noise represents chaos *13* because there is no regularity in the frequency of its vibrations, while musical tone represents order because its vibrations are rhythmical, occurring at fixed intervals. Language is logic, and logic, too, represents order as opposed to chaos. So language as logic is related to sound as music. Each is confined by rule, whether the rule of fixed intervals or the rule of logical sequence.

My premise is that mankind in its present condition, its evolution uncompleted, is suspended between the aboriginal chaos, above which it has risen some way, and a higher order of which it still perceives only glimmers. Each one of us, at least with part of his being, aspires to the higher order and is drawn to it. Therefore, when we organize ourselves into societies, it is not only for the sake of greater physical security and economic advantage; it is also for the sake of realizing a nobler life than is possible for wild animals rooting in the woods. The Athenians of the fifth century B. C. did not give their devotion to Athens merely because it sheltered them behind a stone wall and allowed them to make a living. They did so as well—indeed they did so primarily—because it represented the order epitomized in the Parthenon, in the statues of Phidias, and in the religious dramas performed at the foot of the Acropolis. Certainly the patriotism that caused Americans to break with the England of George III was based on the vision of a higher life that seemed already on the way to realization in our new national society.

If this is so, then political leadership is failing in its role if it confines itself to the problems of physical security and the economy. Abraham Lincoln, even while exercizing the leadership of one side in a civil war that was being fought with savage partisanship, rose above the partisanship to the vision of a national union, embracing both sides alike, that had to redeem a sordid past, the guilt of which both shared, and thereby to attain a state of grace. All this he made explicit, while the war was still being fought, in the poem that we know as his Second Inaugural Address. With little change, parts of it might be included among the psalms.

In the present stage of our development, I say, we men are uneasily suspended between a sordid chaos and the sublime order of which we have intimations. It is the function of poets—as of painters, sculptors, and musicians—to catch these intimations and enshrine them for us in the forms of language or of the graphic arts. This is also the function of political leadership at the highest level, a function that can be discharged only in what an early poet called "wingéd words."

The elements of a higher order, which our greatest leaders enshrine in language, are not represented only by such attitudes as those of compassion and magnanimity that we may think of as constituting the content of the Second Inaugural Address. They are also represented by the rhythmic forms into which inspired language falls, by the shapes its phrases take, and by the harmony of its sounds. At the highest level, then, as perhaps at the lowest too, thought and language are inseparable. The greatest political leadership has always expressed itself in poetry, under whatever guise. That is why the Gettysburg Address, while saying so little, still says so much.

QUESTIONS AND EXERCISES

Vocabulary

1. Define or explain each of the following terms:
   duple (6)   epitomized (14)
   iambic pentameters (7)   explicit (15)

Rhetoric

2. Notice the rhetorical questions in paragraph 2. What are the advantages of using them?
3. The simile in paragraph 3 is one of many figures of speech used. Why is figurative language particularly called for in this essay?
4. Explain the meaning of the last sentence in paragraph 12. Why is it difficult to understand?
5. Halle makes several comparisons and contrasts; list two of them.
6. Analyze the structure of paragraph 14. Why is it like a miniature self-contained essay?
7. How does Halle use repetition, echo words, and other devices to unify his essay. Check especially "chaos," "order," "sordid," and "sublime" in paragraphs 13, 14, and 16

Theme

8. How does Halle merge "sound and sense" in his essay?
9. Where does his thesis become evident?
10. Is his method of development inductive or deductive? Explain.
11. Do you accept his premise that statesmen should be poets?
12. Are thought and language inseparable?
13. Explain the meaning of the paradox in the last sentence, "That is why the 'Gettysburg Address,' while saying so little, still says so much."
14. Does Halle's thesis about poetry and language make sense to you? Be prepared to attack or defend it.
15. Are there extensions of Halle's ideas that may lead to undesirable

ends, that is, poetic language used by a demagogue to sway masses to evil goals? Remember Plato would have kept the poet out of his ideal republic for just such a reason.

Topics and Assignments for Composition

1. Write a paragraph making an extended comparison between two historical happenings.
2. Write a short essay using some of the rhetorical principles found in this essay.
3. Select a well-known speech that has moved people to act, and analyze it in light of Halle's premises. Churchill, Roosevelt, and Kennedy made such speeches.
4. What are the premises and assumptions of this essay? Are they logically consistent and valid and empirically verifiable? In light of your analysis, defend or attack them.

Kamuti Kiteme

What is Our Name in Africa?

Part I: What is Our Name in Africa, According to Europeans?

Themes:

1. When it rains heavily on a lion, people mistake it for a monkey.
2. A man who has never seen the new moon before, calls the stars the moon.
3. Since you think you are cleverer than everybody else, let us see you lick your own back.

—African Proverbs

4. Here's a very slender and weak pole; but it touches the earth and the heaven simultaneously.

—African Riddle

Long before Europeans went to Africa, they talked about the "Dark Continent". We are told that it was like darkness because Europe knew very little about it. Later, the term "dark" was used to refer to the black peoples of Africa.

Then strange things began to happen. Europeans ignored African people's ethnic identities. Instead, we were collectively called Negroes (negroes?). As far back as 1443 (the date when Europeans terrorized friendly Africans and took the first cargo of slaves to Portugal—an event which was later blessed by The Pope, (believe it or not), we have evidence that they referred to Africans as negroes or negro Moors.

And to separate us into "different black colors", colonial education taught us that "negro" only meant the very dark people in Central and Western Africa. The "lighter" ones in the North, East and Southern

Reprinted by permission of publisher from *Negro History Bulletin*, April 1972. Copyright © by the Association for the Study of Negro Life and History.

Africa were *not* actually negroes; but Bantus, Semites, Hamites and Nilotes.

The racist derivative of negro — nigger to be exact — is just as ancient.   *4* Our research shows that it was first used all over Africa by Europeans who went to trade in slaves; and to police and exploit their spheres of influence (a euphemism for colonies). For example, Cecil Rhodes (the man who hallucinated about a universal British Empire, beginning with the conquest of the entire Continent of Africa) once declared: "I prefer land to niggers".

The most innocent of all the words that Europeans corrupted was (and   *5* still is) "native". To get it from the horse's mouth, Webster (U.S.A.) defines native as ". . . belonging to a particular place by birth . . ." Chambers (Britain) tells us that it is ". . . belonging naturally, or innate . . ." However, European customary usage has given this word other meanings and implications. The distortion is so thorough that "native" now means something like "a childish, naked savage". Hence, when Europeans talk of the "natives" in Africa, New Guinea, and the Amazon, they mean a quite different thing from the "natives" in Scandinavia, Hungary, or Moscow. By the same token, Europeans born and brought up in Africa never call themselves "natives" of Africa. The term is exclusively used to refer to Africans.

The same "savage" meaning of of "native" was widely publicized in   *6* European news media, text books and films. The most notorious of the films being "Tarzan" — a white man who always conquered "spear-throwing savage natives" (and their chiefs) with his bare hands. Little did the white world know that the film was made in the U.S.A.; and that the "star" himself had never been to Africa. We hasten to point out that "Tarzan" and other Tarzan-type films, are still shown by some TV stations; and that the "star" has had a somewhat similar production from South East Asia entitled (hush!) "The Man From Africa"!

Just recently, a member of our team gave a speech in a mid-western   *7* U.S.A. town. The speaker deliberately talked about natives in southern France, northern England and the suburbs of Washington, D.C. Immediately the audience started blushing. Some had uncontrollable outbursts, yelling that the speaker was being rude because there were no "natives" in those areas!

Other terms misused by Europeans are "tribe" and "tribesmen". J. S.   *8* Mbiti, one of Africa's leading scholars, emphatically suggests in his book, *African Religions and Philosophies,* that "tribe" has been so abused that African peoples should abandon it and, instead, use African "ethnic groups" or "societies"; or else use the African names such as the Yoruba or the Zulu peoples. We support this thesis.

Take, for a classic analogy, typical European tribal groupings as we   9
find in Iceland, Scotland, Switzerland (three languages), Wales, Belgium
(two or more languages or dialects), Norther Ireland (two religions), New
York City (five main ethnic groups) and Quebec (English and French
tribes). They tell us that these people are nationals of their respective
countries. In numbers, there are some African ethnic groups which are
much, much larger than these European tribes. But, in our case, Africans
remain tribesmen; and *not* nationals of their countries. We object to the
implied difference in meaning because we feel it has a taint of racist
snobbishness.

As far as the two cultures were concerned, Europeans entered Africa   10
armed with the myth of cultural superiority. They despised, rejected or ignored African cultural institutions, beliefs and values. That which was
not European was automatically called "savage", "uncivilized", "primitive", "wild", "stupid", "uncultured" and "uncouth". Thus, Europeans
have consistently described our people by attaching these obnoxious
adjectives before our names, religions, customs, art, music, dance, and
nearly all other cultural styles of life.

Our religions, for example, are supposed to be mere superstition and   11
animism (worshipping spirits). Some go as far as saying that we had no
religions at all—that is to say, we were pagans. In Southern Africa the
Boers (European settlers) use Kaffir (kafiri in Arabic) which means "pagan or a person without religion, good manners and civilization". Whenever we refused to embrace the European religion, we were unchristian
and, therefore, doomed to a miserable afterlife in hell because of our sins.
They called our doctors witches (witch-doctors?). Our general way of
life was primitive, in other words, different from Europeans! Ridiculous
as it may sound, even "jungle" has come to mean a "primitive forest".
These days we hear of forests in Europe and North America; and of
jungles in Africa and other tropical areas.

As in the Western Hemisphere, being 100% white was the only recog-   12
nized determinant of excellence and, therefore, acceptance by Europeans. Africans of the so-called mixed heritage had more privileges than
the dark ones. For the lighter a man was, the more elements of the ideal
color he possessed—white. Despite the privileges, the "mixed" people
were classified as "mulattoes", "half-castes" or "colored". Most of free
Africa has changed this situation, usually without bloody revenge against
Europeans. In Southern Africa, however, customs and laws dictate that
the racist hierarchy is God's rule, and that it shall be maintained. But one
exception to God's rule exists—the Japanese are white and, therefore,
European.

Speaking of Europeans in Africa, those who emigrated there genera-   13 tions ago, not only refuse to be called natives of Africa, but also continue to refer to themselves as Europeans. We think it is silly and misleading that some writers call them white Africans (because they were born there); while, on the other hand, they stubbornly insist that they have always been Europeans living in Africa (because they are white). Nor do we see any sense in talking about black Africans (because Africans are black). Do we ever speak of white Frenchmen or white Europeans?

One thing is certain, though. First and foremost, we are nothing else *14* but African peoples.

Part II: What is Our Name, in Africa, according to Africans?

Themes:

1. It is foolish for a man to become so angry at his head, that he wears his hat on his buttocks.
2. If a crocodile deserts the water, he will find himself on a spear.
3. An axe can never grow a beard.

—African Proverbs

4. It bears fruit which cannot be picked; but when the fruit falls by itself, it cannot be gathered either.

—African Riddle

Among the traditional African peoples, a man's name was a precious *15* possession. The name's meaning, history and connotations were taken very seriously. In some societies, a name of a person, or of a people, was only second to religion in terms of total spiritual involvement, security, identification and ethnic pride. The concept of "name-pride" was so strong that there were several conflicts between individuals caused by simply referring to a person by a wrong name—let alone a bad name. It was particularly offensive to tell a person that he belonged to ethnic group Y, instead of his own group X. For all practical purposes, the "offense" literally meant depriving the individual of his own heritage, ancestral identification, his history, his culture, beliefs, pride and hope for the future. Thus, the offended individual would go as far as fighting physically to force his opponent to retract the curse of calling him a different or wrong name. At times, such incidents developed into full-scale interethnic wars to defend the sanctity of "*the NAME*".

The importance of names to traditional African societies is further dem- *16* onstrated by the unusually elaborate, ceremonial and ritualistic customs in naming babies. Very often, it is an occasion witnessed and celebrated by everyone in the community. In some societies the first son is automatically named after his grandfather; and the first daughter after her grandmother. But, usually, before the baby has its first cry and breath, no one talks about its name. It is said that a human name should never be given to a non-born human; others say pre-naming (or guessing the sex before birth) can cause bad omen, which will kill the child—leaving a precious name without an heir. This belief makes some societies wait for weeks before they name babies—the idea being to make sure that the baby will survive and, hopefully, perpetuate the name, as well as what it represents for him and for his people.

As far as our research has shown, all traditional African names have   17
meanings. The meanings take different forms. Examples: A child is named after his grandfather because the child's father has in turn "begotten" his father, and hence the ancestral line remains unbroken. In this case, all three men—grandfather, father and grandson—become fathers, each bearing equal responsibilities for the clan's procreation and livelihood.

They also utilize the entire physical and metaphysical phenomena   18
which surround them; and which influence their daily lives. Thus children are named after God, stars, animals, rain, rivers, trees, mountains, air, wind, water, grass, sky, days, nights, months, years, time of day, oceans, lakes and spirits. Specifically, a child named in the morning may be called "MORNING", or "BORN-IN-THE-MORNING". A child named "HYENA" may mean he "looked like a hyena" when he was born; or that a hyena terrorized the community during the time he was born.

Names can also take the forms of intangible concepts such as evil and   19
good; beauty and ugliness; kind and cruel; success and failure; peace and war; cowardly and brave; cold and hot.

In all the above instances, the "ugly" or "aggressive" names are re-   20
served for men; and the "courteous", "kind" and "friendly" names are for women. Thus a man may be named "TIGER"; while a woman is given a name of a harmless animal like "CAT". Similarly, rarely are women called "UGLY", "CRUEL", or "EVIL". Only men can be ugly, cruel and evil.

Parents and relatives gave children all these names because they loved   21
them. In this sense, names did *not* make children ugly or beautiful. Rather, the implied societal meaning, history and custom superseded the literal translation of names.

These, then, were some of our names—and what they stood for—   22
before the advent of Europeans.

European missionaries brought with them Biblical names; and Euro-   23 peans, as a group, introduced their surnames. The missionaries insisted that we could never be real Christians unless we dropped our "primitive names" and adopted Christian names. The African-born members in our research team have all witnessed adult Africans being baptized; and forced to drop their childhood names in preference for European God's names. The tremendous ignorance among our people regarding these "civilized names" is illustrated by a true story about a woman — just before she was immersed in the water for baptism somewhere in Africa.

European priest: I baptize you in the name of the Father, the Son and   24
the Holy Ghost.

African woman: Yes, Sir.   25

Priest: What holy name do you choose?   26

Woman: Call me Peter, Sir.   27

Priest: My God, that's a man's name.   28

Woman: Call me Solomon, Sir.   29

Priest: That's a man's name, too.   30

Woman: But, Sir, they all appear in the Bible which you always read   31
to us.

Priest: The primitive devil still possesses you. Go home and learn   32
your catechism; and come for baptism next year.

Woman: Yes, Sir, please pray for me. I need God's forgiveness be-   33
cause I've misused His holy names.

Those who knew the difference between Esther and Solomon, or Mary   34
and Peter, qualified for baptism. Thereafter they forsook their satanic names — the African names. All their children were given Christian names. The tragic result was that a Solomon would, for example, name his son John, and his daughter Mary. And so the children became John Solomon and Mary Solomon; thus obliterating African names altogether.

Worse still, African Christians took European (Christian?) surnames.   35
Even anti-Christian Africans adopted European and Christian names because they were "more civilized". Again, the results? We find all over Africa names like Peggy, Barbara, Smith, Jackson, Bella, Jim, David, John, Esther, Washington, Stanley, Cynthia, Wilson, Ann, Elizabeth, George, Francis(es), Wellington, Jacob, Shem, Ham, Japheth and Sally. A glance at some of the names of our heroes and leaders in Africa, the diplomatic corps, authors, athletes, intellectuals and people from all walks of life, reveals an embarrassing conglomeration of European and Biblical names. A cruel paradox indeed, when we consider that some African peoples on the other side of the Atlantic are making remarkable efforts to search for (and to resume) African names.

Another method was to "civilize names" by Europeanizing them   36
through transliteration. With all due respect, the name Houphouet-

Boigny is actually a Francophile derivation of Ufwe Bwanyi. Thousands of less well-known examples exist all over our Old Continent.

Some of our people went even further. Take, for instance, ABUNGANA   *37* son of CHEMITA. In the Irish-Scottish tradition, he would call himself ABUNGANA *MAC*HEMITA. Following some of the Nordic customs, he would be ABUNGANA CHEMITA*SON*. This poor man might also use more Europeanized spelling like ABHUNNGANY, ABUNGERNER, CHEMYTIER and CHEMETAH.

On the brighter side, however, some of our people (mostly those who   *38* were educated in Europe and the U.S.A.) have abandoned these slave names. Most of free Africa has changed colonial names of countries and cities into African names. Examples: GHANA (Gold Coast), ZAMBIA (Northern Rhodesia), KINSHASA (Leopoldville), KISANGANI (Stanleyville). And why not? How many European missionaries and settlers have adopted our names? How many European and Biblical names can we find in the Indian subcontinent which was colonized like Africa? Talk about Japan — economically the most European of all Asian countries — how many Japanese Jims and Lisas and Johns do we hear of?

The Biblical mythology has a good lesson for us. Noah's sons were   *39* Shem, Ham (supposedly the black guy) and Japheth. After they left the ark, which, they say, saved mankind, animals and birds from a universally devastating flood, Noah got drunk, and lay down naked. The bad "black" son saw his father's nude body; and told his brothers about it. The two good brothers ("non-black") covered their father's body (with their faces turned the other way) so as to avoid looking at him. When he recovered from his drunkenness, and found out that Ham (father of Canaan) had seen him without a stitch on his body, he said, "Cursed be Canaan; a slave of slaves shall he be to his brothers. Blessed by the Lord may God be Shem; and let Canaan be his slave". (Genesis 7, 8 and 9:18-27)

The parallel drawn by this mythology greatly concerns all of us. But   *40* its ugly truth will persist until we unequivocally tell the sons of Shem and Japheth (in word and deed) that we are not their parrot-like slaves expected to ape their names, and to abandon our own.

QUESTIONS AND EXERCISES

Vocabulary

1. Define or explain each of the following terms:

ethnic (2)	myth (10)
euphemism (4)	metaphysical phenomena (18)

analogy (9)   obliterating (34)
dialects (9)   paradox (35)
racist (9)

2. What are some of the problems of translating words from one language to another?
3. Discuss the meanings of the word *native*.
4. Discuss the semantic distinctions in paragraph 10.

Rhetoric

5. How is the essay organized? Pay particular attention to the "Part I" and "Part II" distinctions.
6. What is the function of the proverbs and riddles that introduce each part?
7. Comment on Dr. Kiteme's extensive use of examples, illustrations, and specific allusions.
8. What is the effect of the anecdote that begins in paragraph 23?

Theme

9. What has Dr. Kiteme established about the relationship of language and racism? Language and culture? Culture and racism?
10. How has Dr. Kiteme demonstrated that the problem of erasing racism cannot be accomplished by mere surface acceptance of slogans?
11. Why does Dr. Kiteme end the essay with an example based upon the Bible?

Topics and Assignments for Composition

1. Utilizing Dr. Kiteme's rhetorical techniques, analyze a few terms that he does not cover in his essay, showing the nature, history, and current status of terms that suggest racism.
2. Write an original essay about names using Dr. Kiteme's thesis and Shakespeare's "What's in a name" quotation as starting points.
3. Write an essay analyzing the semantic processes of "pejorative" and "honorific" shifts in the meaning of words. Give several examples and illustrations.
4. Write an essay in which you apply Dr. Kiteme's analysis to give insight into a specific, difficult racial problem that confronts us.

Student Example

Crippled Christians

The burning question about the Jesus movement at this stage is: will it go the way of yesterday's fads, the Bibles and crosses joining the cast-off Davy Crockett caps, hula hoops, Beatle magazines, and roach clips, or will it develop a significance that will transcend the glowing Jesus watches and other gimmicks surrounding it? Like all the other trends of American youth culture, the Jesus revolution is so tangled up in its own publicity and commercialism that its motivations are obscured by all the jargon and glitter. But one thing that is clear about the movement is that it reflects, and to an extent satisfies, the need to believe and get involved in something new and positive. During the late sixties the facades supporting many of the old myths and values—God, country, Mother, material success, puritanism—were pulled down, revealing dust and decay. And several new ideas emerged, new concepts of behavior and alternative values and lifestyles.

One change that had immediate and widespread impact was drug use: an astonishing number of kids, from junior high school age up, went absolutely berserk, as if they had found a new god. But a couple of years later, when the craze had taken its toll, a large number of casualties were left. Some kids were simply unlucky or a little too daring; the majority just weren't bright enough to realize that the exciting new god was tarnished and false; and others who did were too bored or desperate to care. Thus, it's not surprising that many of the Jesus converts are drawn from this group. The movement offers a path to young casualties of all kinds, and the drug-damaged are among the more visible members of a group of mentally, physically, and emotionally crippled young, confused and beaten by shortcomings and contradictions within their society, their families, and themselves. For some of them the Jesus movement offers a way out by providing a ready-made set of beliefs, relatively clear values and objectives, and a well-defined code of behavior.

In addition, the necessity of coming to terms with our complex, bewildering, and sometimes impossible society while exploring and developing individual identity and purpose is a goal as difficult to achieve as it is vital if the young are to sustain any kind of existence that goes beyond mere physical survival. For some who are struggling to make it on their own, involvement in such an all-enveloping movement simplifies the process by unifying their loyalties and aspirations and by providing a framework from which the individual relates to society, and within which he relates to himself.

But, the Jesus movement is simply not powerful or cohesive enough to exert that much influence on all of its adherents' lives. Nevertheless, in a society as pluralistic as ours, where everything is open to doubt and questioning, there are a lot of disillusioned, disappointed, and disgusted young people. Unable to evaluate things adequately for themselves, or to eke out a sense of personal direction and significance from the wilderness of alternative ideas and stances, betrayed and battered by what they consider the hypocrisy and restrictiveness of traditional values as well as their own failure to handle the permissiveness of the new, they are ripe for something which offers a fresh start and definite beliefs, guidelines for behavior and thought, and, perhaps most important, genuine friendliness, sincerity, and interest. And there is no doubt that dedicated, hard-core Jesus freaks are sincere in wanting to help, comfort, and save their converts.

Therefore, it would seem that any movement which gives formerly jaded, kick-seeking kids such purpose should be praised rather than condemned. Certainly it has helped steer a number of wandering and confused sheep onto what seems a secure path; but the danger is that this path merely leads to another dead end, the trap of false security and blind belief. Having so much faith in one particular concept inevitably leads to some degree of rigidity of thinking, intolerance, smugness, and superiority. Is it better to flounder, confused, and self-critical, in the chaos of noncommitment and doubt, or to gain reassurance and concrete belief at the expense of flexibility, open-mindedness, and intellectual honesty? Most of the potential Jesus converts are those who haven't the ability and individualism to make it independently; they need something to rely upon which doesn't require them to think for themselves and which offers more beneficial long-term results than other mass activities like drugtaking did.

Realization of the shortcomings of the Jesus movement may take somewhat longer than it did for drug use. Unlike drugs, a Jesus overdose is unlikely to cause dangerous medical or legal side effects. But the eventual psychological withdrawal may be even more damaging to the personality. Judging by past experience, the Jesus craze will probably continue until another major antidote to the pain and panic of trying to cope with the alternatives and pressures of our culture is found. That the Jesus cult is flourishing at all is in itself a very telling comment on the sort of confusion that culture produces.

Part Four:
Analogy

Julian Huxley

The Crowded World

Population has at last made the grade and emerged as a World Prob- *1*
lem. Unfortunately, most of those who speak or write about the problem
persist in thinking of it in terms of a race between human numbers and
world resources, especially of food—a kind of competition between
production and reproduction. The neo-Malthusians, supported by progressive opinion in the Western World and by leading figures in most
Asian countries, produce volumes of alarming statistics about the world
population explosion and the urgent need for birth-control, while the
anti-Malthusians, supported by the two ideological blocs of Catholicism
and Communism, produce equal volumes of hopeful statistics, or perhaps
one should say of wishful estimates, purporting to show how the problem
can be solved by science, by the exploitation of the Amazon or the Arctic,
by better distribution, or even by shipping our surplus population to
other planets.

Certainly, the statistics are important. The major fact emerging from *2*
them is that there really *is* a population explosion. During the millennia
of man's early history, world population increased steadily but very
slowly, so that by the end of the seventeenth century it had barely topped
the half-billion mark. But then, as a result of the great explorations during
and after the Renaissance, and still more of the rise of natural science and
technology at the end of the seventeenth century, the process was stepped
up, so that by the beginning of the present century world population
stood at about $1\frac{1}{2}$ billion, and its compound interest rate of increase had
itself increased from under $\frac{1}{2}$ of 1 per cent in 1650 to nearly 1 per cent
(and we all know what big results can flow from even a small increase in
compound interest rates).

But the real explosion is a twentieth-century phenomenon, due pri- *3*
marily to the spectacular developments in medicine and hygiene, which

Reprinted by permission of A. D. Peters & Co.

have drastically cut down death-rates without any corresponding reduction in birth-rates – death-control without birth-control. The compound interest rate of increase meanwhile crept, or rather leapt, up and up, from under 1 per cent in 1900 to 1½ per cent at mid-century, and nearly 1¾ per cent today; and it will certainly go on increasing for some decades more. This means that the *rate* of human doubling has itself been doubled within the past 80 years. World population has more than doubled since 1900 to reach about 2¾ billion today; and it will certainly reach well over 5½ billion, probably 6 billion, and possibly nearly 7 billion by the year 2000.

Coming down to details, Britons will be jolted by the fact that the net   *4* increase of world population amounts to about 150,000 every 24 hours, or the equivalent of a good-sized New Town every day – Hemel Hempstead yesterday, Harlow today, Crawley tomorrow, and so on through the weeks and months; while Americans will be startled out of any complacency they may have possessed by the fact that this is the equivalent of 10 baseball teams, complete with coach, every minute of every day and night. Such facts make the idea of interplanetary disposal of the earth's surplus population merely ridiculous.

It is also salutary to be reminded that the number of human beings alive   *5* in A.D. 1999 – within the lifetime of many now living – will be about double that of those alive today; that some populations, like that of Barbados, are growing at a rate of over 3 per cent compound interest per annum, which means doubling in less than 20 years; that in an underdeveloped but already densely populated country like India, successful industrialization will be impossible unless the birth-rate is cut to about half within the next 30 or 40 years, for otherwise the capital and the trained man- and woman-power needed to give the country a stable industrial economy will be swallowed up in feeding, housing, educating, and servicing the excess population; that religious opposition to population-control is strongest and most effective in regions like Latin America, where population-increase is most rampant; that there is no provision for international study and research on population-control as there is on atomic energy, on the world's arid zones, on brain function, or on oceanography; that there is already an alarming (and increasing) shortage of available water-supplies, high-grade mineral resources, and educational facilities, even in industrially advanced countries like the U.S.A.; that the annual increase of Communist China's population is 13 million, more than the equivalent of a new Sweden and a new Denmark every year; or that the World Health Organization has twice been prevented by Roman Catholic pressure from even considering population-density as a factor in the world's health.

But in the broad view the most important thing about the population   6
explosion is that it is making everyone — or rather everyone capable of
serious thought — think seriously about the future of our human species
on our human planet.

The Middle Ages were brought to an end by a major revolution in   7
thought and belief, which stimulated the growth of science and the
secularization of life at the expense of significance in art and religion,
generated the industrial-technological revolution, with its stress on economics and quantitative production at the expense of significance in
quality, human values and fulfilment, and culminated in what we are
pleased to call the Atomic Age, with two World Wars behind it, the
threat of annihilation before it, and an ideological split at its core.

Actually our modern age merits the adjective atomistic rather than   8
atomic. Further, it will soon become very unmodern. For we are on the
threshold of another major revolution, involving a new pattern of thought
and a new approach to human destiny and its practical problems. It will
usher in a new phase of human history, which I like to call the Evolutionary Age, because it envisages man as both product and agent of the
evolutionary process on this planet.

The new approach is beginning to take effect in two rather distinct   9
fields, of ecology and ideology, and is generating two parallel but linked
currents of thought and action, that may be called the Ecological Revolution and the Humanist Revolution.

The population explosion is giving a powerful impetus to both these   10
revolutionary currents. Ecology is the science of relational adjustment —
the balanced relations of living organisms with their environment and
with each other. It started botanically in a rather modest way as a study
of plant communities in different habitats; went on to the fruitful idea of
the ecological succession of different plant communities in a given habitat, leading up to an optimum climax community — mixed forest in the
humid tropics, rich grassland on the prairies; was extended to take in
animal communities, and so to the illuminating concepts of food-chains
and adaptive niches; and finally, though rather grudgingly, was still
further enlarged to include human as well as biological ecology.

The population explosion has brought us up against a number of tough   11
ecological facts. Man is at last pressing hard on his spatial environment —
there is little leeway left for his colonization of new areas of the world's
surface. He is pressing hard on his resources, notably nonrenewable but
also renewable resources. As Professor Harrison Brown has so frighten-
ingly made clear in his book, *The Challenge of Man's Future,* ever-
increasing consumption by an ever-increasing number of human beings
will lead in a very few generations to the exhaustion of all easily exploit-

able fossil and high-grade mineral ores, to the taking up of all first-rate agricultural land, and so to the invasion of more and more second-rate marginal land for agriculture. In fact, we are well on our way to ruining our material habitat. But we are beginning to ruin our own spiritual and mental habitat also. Not content with destroying or squandering our resources of material things, we are beginning to destroy the resources of true enjoyment — spiritual, aesthetic, intellectual, emotional. We are spreading great masses of human habitation over the face of the land, neither cities nor suburbs nor towns nor villages, just a vast mass of urban sprawl or subtopia. And to escape from this, people are spilling out farther and farther into the wilder parts and so destroying them. And we are making our cities so big as to be monstrous, so big that they are becoming impossible to live in. Just as there is a maximum possible size for an efficient land animal — you can't have a land animal more than about twice as large as an elephant — so there is a maximum possible efficient size for a city. London, New York, and Tokyo have already got beyond that size.

In spite of all that science and technology can do, world food-production is not keeping up with world population, and the gap between the haves and the have-nots of this world is widening instead of being narrowed. *12*

Meanwhile everywhere, though especially in the so-called Free Enterprise areas of the world, economic practice (and sometimes economic theory) is concerned not primarily with increased production, still less with a truly balanced economy, but with exploitation of resources in the interests of maximized and indiscriminate consumption, even if this involves present waste and future shortage. *13*

Clearly this self-defeating, self-destroying process must be stopped. The population explosion has helped to take our economic blinkers off and has shown us the gross and increasing imbalance between the world's human population and its material resources. Unless we quickly set about achieving some sort of balance between reproduction and production, we shall be dooming our grandchildren and all their descendants, through thousands upon thousands of monotonous generations, to an extremely unpleasant and unsatisfactory existence, overworked and undernourished, overcrowded and unfulfilled. *14*

To stop the process means planned conservation in place of reckless exploitation, regulation and control of human numbers, as well as of industrial and technological enterprise, in place of uninhibited expansion. And this means an ecological approach. Ecology will become the basic science of the new age, with physics and chemistry and technology as its hand-maidens, not its masters. The aim will be to achieve a balanced rela- *15* tion between man and nature, an equilibrium between human needs and world resources.

The Humanist Revolution, on the other hand, is destined to supersede *16* the current pattern of ideas and beliefs about nature (Including human nature) and man's place and role in it, with a new vision of reality more in harmony with man's present knowledge and circumstances. This new pattern of ideas can be called humanist, since it is focused on man as a product of natural evolution, not on the vast inanimate cosmos, nor on a God or gods, nor on some unchanging spiritual Absolute. For humanism in this sense, man's duty and destiny is to be the spearhead and creative agent of the overall evolutionary process on this planet.

The explosive growth of scientific and historical knowledge in the past *17* hundred years, especially about biological and human evolution, coupled with the rise of rationalist criticism of established theologies and ancient philosophies, had cleared the ground for this revolution in thought and executed some of the necessary demolition work. But now the population explosion poses the world with the fundamental question of human destiny — *What are people for?* Surely people do not exist just to provide bomb-fodder for an atomic bonfire, or religion-fodder for rival churches, or cannon-fodder for rival nations, or disease-fodder for rival parasities, or labour-fodder for rival economic systems, or ideology-fodder for rival political systems, or even consumer-fodder for profit-making systems. It cannot be their aim just to eat, drink and be merry, and to hell with posterity. Nor merely to prepare for some rather shadowy afterlife. It cannot be their destiny to exist in ever larger megalopolitan sprawls, cut off from contact with nature and from the sense of human community and condemned to increasing frustration, noise, mechanical routine, traffic congestion and endless commuting; nor to live out their undernourished lives in some squalid Asian or African village.

When we try to think in more general terms it is clear that the dominant *18* aim of human destiny cannot be anything so banal as just maximum quantity, whether of human beings, machines, works of art, consumer goods, political power, or anything else. Man's dominant aim must be increase in quality — quality of human personality, of achievement, of works of art and craftsmanship, of inner experience, of quality of life and living in general.

"Fulfilment" is probably the embracing word: more fulfilment and less *19* frustration for more human beings. We want more varied and fuller achievement in human societies, as against drabness and shrinkage. We want more variety as against monotony. We want more enjoyment and less suffering. We want more beauty and less ugliness. We want more adventure and disciplined freedom, as against routine and slavishness. We want more knowledge, more interest, more wonder, as against ignorance and apathy.

We want more sense of participation in something enduring and worth-   20
while, some embracing project, as against a competitive rat-race, whether with the Russians or our neighbours on the next street. In the most general terms, we want more transcendence of self in the fruitful development of personality: and we want more human dignity not only as against human degradation, but as against more self-imprisonment in the human ego or more escapism. But the inordinate growth of human numbers bars the way to any such desirable revolution, and produces increasing frustration instead of greater fulfilment.

There are many urgent special problems which the population explo-   21
sion is raising—how to provide the increasing numbers of human beings with their basic quotas of food and shelter, raw materials and energy, health and education, with opportunities for adventure and meditation, for contact with nature and with art, for useful work and fruitful leisure; how to prevent frustration exploding into violence or subsiding into apathy; how to avoid unplanned chaos on the one hand and over-organized authoritarianism on the other.

Behind them all, the long-term general problem remains. Before the   22
human species can settle down to any constructive planning of his future on earth (which, let us remember, is likely to be many times longer than his past, to be reckoned in hundreds of millions of years instead of the hundreds of thousands of his prehistory or the mere millennia of History), it must clear the world's decks for action. If man is not to become the planet's cancer instead of its partner and guide, the threatening plethora of the unborn must be for ever banished from the scene.

Above all we need a world population policy—not at some unspecified   23
date in the future, but now. The time has now come to think seriously about population policy. We want every country to have a population policy, just as it has an economic policy or a foreign policy. We want the United Nations to have a population policy. We want all the international agencies of the U.N. to have a population policy.

When I say a population policy, I don't mean that anybody is going to   24
tell every woman how many children she may have, any more than a country which has an economic policy will say how much money an individual businessman is allowed to make and exactly how he should do it. It means that you recognize population as a major problem of national life, that you have a general aim in regard to it, and that you try to devise methods for realizing this aim. And if you have an international population policy, again it doesn't mean dictating to backward countries, or

anything of that sort; it means not depriving them of the right (which I should assert is a fundamental human right) to scientific information on birth-control, and it means help in regulating and controlling their increase and planning their families.

Its first aim must be to cut down the present excessive rate of increase   25
to manageable proportions: once this is done we can think about planning for an optimum size of world population—which will almost certainly prove to be less than its present total. Meanwhile we, the people of all nations, through the U.N. and its Agencies, through our own national policies and institutions, and through private Foundations, can help those courageous countries which have already launched a population policy of their own, or want to do so, by freely giving advice and assistance and by promoting research on the largest scale.

When it comes to United Nations agencies, one of the great scandals of   26
the present century is that owing to pressure, mainly from Roman Catholic countries, the World Health Organization has not been allowed even to consider the effects of population density on health. It is essential and urgent that this should be reversed.

There is great frustration in the minds of medical men all over the   27
world, especially those interested in international affairs, who, at the cost of much devoted labour, have succeeded in giving people information on how to control or avoid disease. Malaria in Ceylon is a striking example. As a result of all this wonderful scientific effort and goodwill, population has exploded, and new diseases, new frustrations, new miseries are arising. Meanwhile medical men are not allowed to try to cope with these new troubles on an international scale—and indeed sometimes not even on a national scale. It is an astonishing and depressing fact that even in the advanced and civilized U.S.A. there are two States in which the giving of birth-control information on medical grounds even by non-Catholic doctors to non-Catholic patients, is illegal.

In conclusion I would simply like to go back to where I started and   28
repeat that we must look at the whole question of population increase not merely as an immediate problem to be dealt with *ad hoc*. We must look at it in the light of the new vision of human destiny which human science and learning has revealed to us. We must look at it in the light of the glorious possibilities that are still latent in man, not merely in the light of the obvious fact that the world could be made a little better than it is. We must also look at it in the light of the appalling possibilities for evil and misery that still hang over the future of evolving man.

This vision of the possibilities of wonder and more fruitful fulfilment on   29
the one hand as against frustration and increasing misery and regimentation on the other is the twentieth-century equivalent of the traditional

Christian view of salvation as against damnation. I would indeed say that this new point of view that we are reaching, the vision of evolutionary humanism, is essentially a religious one, and that we can and should devote ourselves with truly religious devotion to the cause of ensuring greater fulfilment for the human race in its future destiny. And this involves a furious and concerted attack on the problem of population; for the control of population is, I am quite certain, a prerequisite for any radical improvement in the human lot.

We do indeed need a World Population Policy. We have learnt how to control the forces of outer nature. If we fail to control the forces of our own reproduction, the human race will be sunk in a flood of struggling people, and we, its present representatives, will be conniving at its future disaster. *30*

QUESTIONS AND EXERCISES

Vocabulary

1. Define or explain the following terms:

millennia (2)	megalopolitan (17)
phenomenon (3)	banal (18)
per annum (5)	slavishness (19)
ecology (9)	ego (20)
ideology (9)	apathy (21)
optimum (10)	plethora (22)
niches (10)	*ad hoc* (28)
aesthetic (11)	prerequisite (29)
cosmos (16)	conniving (30)
supersede (16)	

Rhetoric

2. How does Huxley define each of the following:

Middle Ages (7)	Ecological Revolution (9)
Atomic Age (7)	Humanistic Revolution (9)
Evolutionary Age (8)	

3. Identify or explain the allusion or meaning of the following:

neo-Malthusians	Renaissance
anti-Malthusians	

4. Huxley's sentences are often complicated. Note, for example, the structure of the final sentence in paragraph 10. What kind of sentence is it? How many words does it contain? What makes it difficult to understand?

5. At the beginning of many paragraphs, Huxley uses transitional devices or links to tie the paragraph to the previous one. Find five such devices and if possible give them a label describing their function. Example: paragraph 24, "population policy" — repetition.
6. What rhetorical technique does Huxley use in paragraph 19?
7. Find an example of figurative language in paragraph 22.

Theme

8. What is the main population problem in the world today? Is Huxley's opinion the usual one?
9. It is often suggested that students put their thesis in the first paragraph. Is the main thesis of this essay found there? Why not?
10. Huxley asks the question — *What are people for?* What answer does he give?
11. What is one of his proposed solutions to the problems he has posed?
12. If you have trouble understanding the thesis, re-read paragraphs 28, 29 and 30. Huxley repeats and summarizes his essay here. He uses three paragraphs (approximately 250 words, half a freshman composition) to repeat his main points. In a short essay a concluding sentence might suffice. Write a concluding sentence of your own that Huxley might have used as a summary statement in a shorter essay.

Topics and Assignments for Composition

1. Write an imitation of the sentence discussed in question 4 above. You may use any topic for your sentence.
2. Write a paragraph-long answer to the question *What are people for?*
3. Write a 500-word essay on one of today's major world problems: war, over-population, morality, nationalism, racism, automation, pollution, etc.

Tom Wolfe

O Rotten Gotham — Sliding Down into the Behavioral Sink

I just spent two days with Edward T. Hall, an anthropologist, watching *1*
thousands of my fellow New Yorkers short-circuiting themselves into
hot little twitching death balls with jolts of their own adrenalin. Dr. Hall
says it is overcrowding that does it. Overcrowding gets the adrenalin
going, and the adrenalin gets them hyped up. And here they are, hyped
up, turning bilious, nephritic, queer, autistic, sadistic, barren, batty,
sloppy, hot-in-the-pants, chancred-on-the-flankers leering, puling,
numb — the usual in New York, in other words, and God knows what else.
Dr. Hall has the theory that overcrowding has already thrown New York
into a state of behavioral sink. Behavioral sink is a term from ethology,
which is the study of how animals relate to their environment. Among
animals, the sink winds up with a "population collapse" or "massive
die-off." O rotten Gotham.

It got to be easy to look at New Yorkers as animals, especially looking *2*
down from some place like a balcony at Grand Central at the rush hour
Friday afternoon. The floor was filled with the poor white humans, running around, dodging, blinking their eyes, making a sound like a pen full
of starlings or rats or something.

"Listen to them skid," says Dr. Hall. *3*

He was right. The poor old etiolate animals were out there skidding on *4*
their rubber soles. You could hear it once he pointed it out. They stop
short to keep from hitting somebody or because they are disoriented and
they suddenly stop and look around, and they skid on their rubber-sole
shoes, and a screech goes up. They pour out onto the floor down the

escalators from the Pan-Am Building, from 42nd Street, from Lexington Avenue, up out of subways, down into subways, railroad trains, up into helicopters—

"You can also hear the helicopters all the way down here," says Dr. Hall. The sound of the helicopters using the roof of the Pan-Am Building nearly fifty stories up beats right through. "If it weren't for this ceiling"— he is referring to the very high ceiling in Grand Central—"this place would be unbearable with this kind of crowding. And yet they'll probably never 'waste' space like this again."

They screech! And the adrenal glands in all those poor white animals enlarge, micrometer by micrometer, to the size of cantaloupes. Dr. Hall pulls a Minox camera out of a holster he has on his belt and starts shooting away at the human scurry. The Sink!

Dr. Hall has the Minox up to his eye—he is a slender man, calm, 52 years old, young-looking, an anthropologist who has worked with Navajos, Hopis, Spanish-Americans, Negroes, Trukese. He was the most important anthropologist in the government during the crucial years of the foreign aid program, the 1950's. He directed both the Point Four training program and the Human Relations Area Files. He wrote *The Silent Language* and *The Hidden Dimension,* two books that are picking up the kind of "underground" following his friend Marshall McLuhan started picking up about five years ago. He teaches at the Illinois Institute of Technology, lives with his wife, Mildred, in a high-ceilinged town house on one of the last great residential streets in downtown Chicago, Astor Street; has a grown son and daughter, loves good food, good wine, the relaxed, civilized life—but comes to New York with a Minox at his eye to record—perfect!—The Sink.

We really got down in there by walking down into the Lexington Avenue line subway stop under Grand Central. We inhaled those nice big fluffy fumes of human sweat, urine, effluvia, and sebaceous secretions. One old female human was already stroked out on the upper level, on a stretcher, with two policemen standing by. The other humans barely looked at her. They rushed into line. They bellied each other, haunch to paunch, down the stairs. Human heads shone through the gratings. The species North European tried to create bubbles of space around themselves, about a foot and a half in diameter—

"See, he's reacting against the line," says Dr. Hall.

—but the species Mediterranean presses on in. The hell with bubbles of space. The species North European resents that, this male human behind him presses forward toward the booth . . . *breathing* on him, he's disgusted, he pulls out of the line entirely, the species Mediterranean resents him for resenting it, and neither of them realizes what the hell they are getting irritable about exactly. And in all of them the old adrenals grow another micrometer.

Dr. Hall whips out the Minox. Too perfect! The bottom of The Sink.   *11*

It is the sheer overcrowding, such as occurs in the business sections of   *12* Manhattan five days a week and in Harlem, Bedford-Stuyvesant, southeast Bronx every day—sheer overcrowding is converting New Yorkers into animals in a sink pen. Dr. Hall's argument runs as follows: all animals, including birds, seem to have a built-in, inherited requirement to have a certain amount of territory, space, to lead their lives in. Even if they have all the food they need, and there are no predatory animals threatening them, they cannot tolerate crowding beyond a certain point. No more than two hundred wild Norway rats can survive on a quarter acre of ground, for example, even when they are given all the food they can eat. They just die off.

But why? To find out, ethologists have run experiments on all sorts of   *13* animals, from stickleback crabs to Sika deer. In one major experiment, an ethologist named John Calhoun put some domesticated white Norway rats in a pen with four sections to it, connected by ramps. Calhoun knew from previous experiments that the rats tend to split up into groups of ten to twelve and that the pen, therefore, would hold forty to forty-eight rats comfortably, assuming they formed four equal groups. He allowed them to reproduce until there were eighty rats, balanced between male and female, but did not let it get any more crowded. He kept them supplied with plenty of food, water, and nesting materials. In other words, all their more obvious needs were taken care of. A less obvious need—space— was not. To the human eye, the pen did not even look especially crowded. But to the rats, it was crowded beyond endurance.

The entire colony was soon plunged into a profound behavioral sink.   *14* "The sink," said Calhoun, "is the outcome of any behavioral process that collects animals together in unusually great numbers. The unhealthy connotations of the term are not accidental: a behavioral sink does act to aggravate all forms of pathology that can be found within a group."

For a start, long before the rat population reached eighty, a status   *15* hierarchy had developed in the pen. Two dominant male rats took over the two end sections, acquired harems of eight to ten females each, and forced the rest of the rats into the two middle pens. All the overcrowding took place in the middle pens. That was where the "sink" hit. The aristocrat rats at the ends grew bigger, sleeker, healthier, and more secure the whole time.

In The Sink, meanwhile, nest building, courting, sex behavior, repro-   *16* duction, social organization, health—all of it went to pieces. Normally, Norway rats have a mating ritual in which the male chases the female, the female ducks down into a burrow and sticks her head up to watch the male. He performs a little dance outside the burrow, then she comes out, and he mounts her, usually for a few seconds. When The Sink set in, however, no more than three males – the dominant males in the middle sections – kept up the old customs. The rest tried everything from satyrism to homosexuality or else gave up on sex altogether. Some of the subordinate males spent all their time chasing females. Three or four might chase one female at the same time, and instead of stopping at the burrow entrance for the ritual, they would charge right in. Once mounted, they would hold on for minutes instead of the usual seconds.

Homosexuality rose sharply. So did bisexuality. Some males would mount anything – males, females, babies, senescent rats, anything. Still other males dropped sexual activity altogether, wouldn't fight and, in fact, would hardly move except when the other rats slept. Occasionally a female from the aristocrat rats' harems would come over the ramps and into the middle sections to sample life in The Sink. When she had had enough, she would run back up the ramp. Sink males would give chase up to the top of the ramp, which is to say, to the very edge of the aristocratic preserve. But one glance from one of the king rats would stop them cold and they would return to The Sink.   *17*

The slumming females from the harems had their adventures and then returned to a placid, healthy life. Females in The Sink, however, were ravaged, physically and psychologically. Pregnant rats had trouble continuing pregnancy. The rate of miscarriages increased significantly, and females started dying from tumors and other disorders of the mammary glands, sex organs, uterus, ovaries, and Fallopian tubes. Typically, their kidneys, livers, and adrenals were also enlarged or diseased or showed other signs associated with stress.   *18*

Child-rearing became totally disorganized. The females lost the interest or the stamina to build nests and did not keep them up if they did build them. In the general filth and confusion, they would not put themselves out to save offspring they were momentarily separated from. Frantic, even sadistic competition among the males was going on all around them and rendering their lives chaotic. The males began unprovoked and senseless assaults upon one another, often in the form of tail-biting. Ordinarily, rats will suppress this kind of behavior when it crops up. In The Sink, male rats gave up all policing and just looked out for themselves. The "pecking order" among males in The Sink was never stable. Normally, male rats set up a three-class structure. Under the pressure of overcrowding, however, they broke up into all sorts of unstable subclasses, cliques, packs – and constantly pushed, probed, explored, tested one another's power. Anyone was fair game, except for the aristocrats in the end pens.   *19*

Calhoun kept the population down to eighty, so that the next stage,   *20*
"population collapse" or "massive die-off," did not occur. But the autopsies showed that the pattern—as in the diseases among the female rats—was already there.

The classic study of die-off was John J. Christian's study of Sika deer   *21*
on James Island in the Chesapeake Bay, west of Cambridge, Maryland. Four or five of the deer had been released on the island, which was 280 acres and uninhabited, in 1916. By 1955 they had bred freely into a herd of 280 to 300. The population density was only about one deer per acre at this point, but Christian knew that this was already too high for the Sikas' inborn space requirements, and something would give before long. For two years the number of deer remained 280 to 300. But suddenly, in 1958, over half the deer died; 161 carcasses were recovered. In 1959 more deer died and the population steadied at about 80.

In two years, two-thirds of the herd had died. Why? It was not starva-   *22*
tion. In fact, all the deer collected were in excellent condition, with well-developed muscles, shining coats, and fat deposits between the muscles. In practically all the deer, however, the adrenal glands had enlarged by 50 percent. Christian concluded that the die-off was due to "shock following severe metabolic disturbance, probably as a result of.prolonged adrenocortical hyperactivity. . . . There was no evidence of infection, starvation, or other obvious cause to explain the mass mortality." In other words, the constant stress of overpopulation, plus the normal stress of the cold of the winter, had kept the adrenalin flowing so constantly in the deer that their systems were depleted of blood sugar and they died of shock.

Well, the white humans are still skidding and darting across the floor   *23*
of Grand Central. Dr. Hall listens a moment longer to the skidding and the darting noises, and then says, "You know, I've been on commuter trains here after everyone has been through one of these rushes, and I'll tell you, there is enough acid flowing in the stomachs in every car to dissolve the rails underneath."

Just a little invisible acid bath for the linings to round off the day. The   *24*
ulcers the acids cause, of course, are the one disease people have already been taught to associate with the stress of city life. But overcrowding, as Dr. Hall sees it, raises a lot more hell with the body than just ulcers. In everyday life in New York—just the usual, getting to work, working in massively congested areas like 42nd Street between Fifth Avenue and Lexington, especially now that the Pan-Am Building is set in there, working in cubicles such as those in the editorial offices at Time-Life, Inc., which Dr. Hall cites as typical of New York's poor handling of space, working in cubicles with low ceilings and, often, no access to a window,

while construction crews all over Manhattan drive everybody up the
Masonite wall with air-pressure generators with noises up to the boil-a-
brain decibel levels, then rushing to get home, piling into subways and
trains, fighting for time and for space, the usual day in New York—the
whole now-normal thing keeps shooting jolts of adrenalin into the body,
breaking down the body's defenses and winding up with the work-a-
daddy human animal stroked out at the breakfast table with his head
apoplexed like a cauliflower out of his $6.95 semispread Pima-cotton
shirt, and nosed over into a plate of No-Kloresto egg substitute, signing
off with the black thrombosis, cancer, kidney, liver, or stomach failure,
and the adrenals ooze to a halt, the size of eggplants in July.

One of the people whose work Dr. Hall is interested in on this score is   25
Rene Dubos at the Rockefeller Institute. Dubos's work indicates that
specific organisms, such as the tuberculosis bacillus or a pneumonia virus,
can seldom be considered "the cause" of a disease. The germ or virus,
apparently, has to work in combination with other things that have already broken the body down in some way—such as the old adrenal hyperactivity. Dr. Hall would like to see some autopsy studies made to record
the size of adrenal glands in New York, especially of people crowded into
slums and people who go through the full rush-hour-work-rush-hour
cycle every day. He is afraid that until there is some clinical, statistical
data on how overcrowding actually ravages the human body, no one will
be willing to do anything about it. Even in so obvious a thing as air pollution, the pattern is familiar. Until people can actually see the smoke or
smell the sulphur or feel the sting in their eyes, politicians will not get
excited about it, even though it is well known that many of the lethal substances polluting the air are invisible and odorless. For one thing, most
politicians are like the aristocrat rats. They are insulated from The Sink
by practically sultanic buffers—limousines, chauffeurs, secretaries, aides-
de-camp, doormen, shuttered houses, high-floor apartments. They almost
never ride subways, fight rush hours, much less live in the slums or work
in the Pan-Am Building.

We took a cab from Grand Central to go up to Harlem, and by 48th   26
Street we were already socked into one of those great, total traffic jams
on First Avenue on Friday afternoon. Dr. Hall motions for me to survey
the scene, and there they all are, humans, male and female, behind the
glass of their automobile windows, soundlessly going through the torture
of their own adrenalin jolts. This male over here contracts his jaw muscles
so hard that they bunch up into a great cheese Danish pattern. He twists
his lips, he bleeds from the eyeballs, he shouts . . . soundlessly behind
glass . . . the fat corrugates on the back of his neck, his whole body shakes
as he pounds the heel of his hand into the steering wheel. The female

human in the car ahead of him whips her head around, she bares her teeth, she screams . . . soundlessly behind glass . . . she throws her hands up in the air, Whaddya expect me—Yah, yuh stupid—and they all sit there, trapped in their own congestion, bleeding hate all over each other, shorting out the ganglia and—goddam it—

Dr. Hall sits back and watches it all. This is it! The Sink! And where is   27
everybody's wandering boy?

Dr. Hall says, "We need a study in which drivers who go through   28
these rush hours every day would wear GSR bands."

GSR?   29

"Galvanic skin response. It measures the electric potential of the skin,   30
which is a function of sweating. If a person gets highly nervous, his palms begin to sweat. It is an index of tension. There are some other fairly simple devices that would record respiration and pulse. I think everybody who goes through this kind of experience all the time should take his own pulse—not literally—but just be aware of what's happening to him. You can usually tell when stress is beginning to get you physically."

In testing people crowded into New York's slums, Dr. Hall would like   31
to take it one step further—gather information on the plasma hydrocortisone level in the blood or the corticosteroids in the urine. Both have been demonstrated to be reliable indicators of stress, and testing procedures are simple.

The slums—we finally made it up to East Harlem. We drove into 101st   32
Street, and there was a new, avant-garde little church building, the Church of the Ephiphany, which Dr. Hall liked—and, next to it, a pile of rubble where a row of buildings had been torn down, and from the back windows of the tenements beyond several people were busy "airmailing," throwing garbage out the window, into the rubble, beer cans, red shreds, the No-Money-Down Eames roller stand for a TV set, all flying through the air onto the scaggy sump. We drove around some more in Harlem, and a sequence was repeated, trash, buildings falling down, buildings torn down, rubble, scaggy sumps or, suddenly, a cluster of high-rise apartment projects, with fences around the grass.

"You know what this city looks like?" Dr. Hall said. "It looks bombed   33
out. I used to live at Broadway and 124th Street back in 1946 when I was studying at Columbia. I can't tell you how much Harlem has changed in twenty years. It looks bombed out. It's broken down. People who live in New York get used to it and don't realize how filthy the city has become. The whole thing is typical of a behaviorial sink. So is something like the Kitty Genovese case—a girl raped and murdered in the courtyard of an apartment complex and forty or fifty people look on from their apartments and nobody even calls the police. That kind of apathy and

anomie is typical of the general psychological deterioration of The Sink."

He looked at the high-rise housing projects and found them mainly *34* testimony to how little planners know about humans' basic animal requirements for space.

"Even on the simplest terms," he said, "it is pointless to build one of *35* these blocks much over five stories high. Suppose a family lives on the fifteenth floor. The mother will be completely cut off from her children if they are playing down below, because the elevators are constantly broken in these projects, and it often takes half an hour, literally half an hour, to get the elevator if it is running. That's very common. A mother in that situation is just as much a victim of overcrowding as if she were back in the tenement block. Some Negro leaders have a bitter joke about how the white man is solving the slum problem by stacking Negroes up vertically, and there is a lot to that."

For one thing, says Dr. Hall, planners have no idea of the different *36* space requirements of people from different cultures, such as Negroes and Puerto Ricans. They are all treated as if they were minute, compact middle-class whites. As with the Sika deer, who are overcrowded at one per acre, overcrowding is a relative thing for the human animal, as well. Each species has its own feeling for space. The feeling may be "subjective," but it is quite real.

Dr. Hall's theories on space and territory are based on the same infor- *37* mation, gathered by biologists, ethologists, and anthropologists, chiefly, as Robert Ardrey's. Ardrey has written two well-publicized books, *African Genesis* and *The Territorial Imperative*. *Life* magazine ran big excerpts from *The Territorial Imperative*, all about how the drive to acquire territory and property and add to it and achieve status is built into all animals, including man, over thousands of centuries of genetic history, etc., and is a more powerful drive than sex. *Life*'s big display prompted Marshall McLuhan to crack, "They see this as a great historic justification for free enterprise and Republicanism. If the birds do it and the stickleback crabs do it, then it's right for man." To people like Hall and McLuhan, and Ardrey, for that matter, the right or wrong of it is irrelevant. The only thing they find inexcusable is the kind of thinking, by influential people, that isn't even aware of all this. Such as the thinking of most city planners.

"The planners always show you a bird's-eye view of what they are *38* doing," he said. "You've seen those scale models. Everyone stands around the table and looks down and says that's great. It never occurs to anyone that they are taking a bird's-eye view. In the end, these projects do turn out fine, when viewed from an airplane."

As an anthropologist, Dr. Hall has to shake his head every time he *39* hears planners talking about fully integrated housing projects for the year 1980 or 1990, as if by then all cultural groups will have the same feeling for space and will live placidly side by side, happy as the happy burghers who plan all the good clean bird's-eye views. According to his findings, the very fact that every cultural group does have its own peculiar, unspoken feeling for space is what is responsible for much of the uneasiness one group feels around the other.

It is like the North European and the Mediterranean in the subway line. *40* The North European, without ever realizing it, tries to keep a bubble of space around himself, and the moment a stranger invades that sphere, he feels threatened. Mediterranean peoples tend to come from cultures where everyone is much more involved physically, publicly, with one another on a day-to-day basis and feels no uneasiness about mixing it up in public, but may have very different ideas about space inside the home. Even Negroes brought up in America have a different vocabulary of space and gesture from the North European Americans who, historically, have been their models, according to Dr. Hall. The failure of Negroes and whites to communicate well often boils down to things like this: some white will be interviewing a Negro for a job; the Negro's culture has taught him to show somebody you are interested by looking right at him and listening intently to what he has to say. But the species North European requires something more. He expects his listener to nod from time to time, as if to say, "Yes, keep going." If he doesn't get this nodding, he feels anxious, for fear the listener doesn't agree with him or has switched off. The Negro may learn that the white expects this sort of thing, but he isn't used to the precise kind of nodding that is customary, and so he may start overresponding, nodding like mad, and at this point the North European is liable to think he has some kind of stupid Uncle Tom on his hands, and the guy still doesn't get the job.

The whole handling of space in New York is so chaotic, says Dr. Hall, *41* that even middle-class housing now seems to be based on the bird's-eye models for slum project. He took a look at the big Park West Village development, set up originally to provide housing in Manhattan for families in the middle-income range, and found its handling of space very much like a slum project with slightly larger balconies. He felt the time has come to start subsidizing the middle class in New York on its own terms — namely, the kind of truly "human" spaces that still remain in brownstones.

"I think New York City should seriously consider a program of en- *42* couraging the middle-class development of an area like Chelsea, which is already starting to come up. People are beginning to renovate houses there on their own, and I think if the city would subsidize that sort of thing with tax reliefs and so forth, you would be amazed at what would result. What New York needs is a string of minor successes in the housing field, just to show everyone it can be done, and I think the middle class can still do that for you. The alternative is to keep on doing what you're doing now, trying to lift a very large lower class up by main force almost and finding it a very slow and discouraging process."

"But before deciding how to redesign space in New York," he said, *43* "people must first simply realize how severe the problem already is. And the handwriting is already on the wall."

"A study published in 1962," he said, "surveyed a representative *44* sample of people living in New York slums and found only 18 percent of them free from emotional symptoms. Thirty-eight percent were in need of psychiatric help, and 23 percent were seriously disturbed or incapacitated. Now, this study was published in 1962, which means the work probably went on from 1955 to 1960. There is no telling how bad it is now. In a behavioral sink, crises can develop rapidly."

Dr. Hall would like to see a large-scale study similar to that undertaken *45* by two sociopsychologists, Chombart de Lauwe and his wife, in a French working-class town. They found a direct relationship between crowding and general breakdown. In families where people were crowded into the apartment so that there was less than 86 to 108 square feet per person, social and physical disorders doubled. That would mean that for four people the smallest floor space they could tolerate would be an apartment, say, 12 by 30 feet.

What would one find in Harlem? "It is fairly obvious," Dr. Hall wrote *46* in *The Hidden Dimension,* "that the American Negroes and people of Spanish culture who are flocking to our cities are being very seriously stressed. Not only are they in a setting that does not fit them, but they have passed the limits of their own tolerance of stress. The United States is faced with the fact that two of its creative and sensitive peoples are in the process of being destroyed and like Samson could bring down the structure that houses us all."

Dr. Hall goes out to the airport, to go back to Chicago, and I am com- *47* ing back in a cab, along the East River Drive. It is four in the afternoon, but already the damned drive is clogging up. There is a 1959 Oldsmobile just to the right of me. There are about eight people in there, a lot of popeyed silhouettes against a leopard-skin dashboard, leopard-skin seats —and the driver is classic. He has a mustache, sideburns down to his jaw socket, and a tattoo on his forearm with a Rossetti painting of Jane Burden Morris with her hair long. All right; it is even touching, like a postcard photo of the main drag in San Pedro, California. But suddenly Sideburns guns it and cuts in front of my cab so that my driver has to hit the brakes, and then hardly 100 feet ahead Sideburns hits a wall of traffic himself and has to hit his brakes, and then it happens. A stuffed white Angora animal, a dog, no, it's a Pekingese cat, is mounted in his rear window—as soon as he hits the brakes its *eyes* light up, Nighttown pink. To keep from ramming him, my driver has to hit the brakes again, too, and so here I am, out in an insane, jammed-up expressway at four in the afternoon, shuddering to a stop while a stuffed Pekingese grows bigger and bigger and brighter in the eyeballs directly in front of me. Jolt! Night-town pink! Hey—that's me the adrenalin is hitting, *I* am this white human sitting in a projectile heading amid a mass of clotted humans toward a white Angora stuffed goddam leopard-dash Pekingese freaking cat—kill that damned Angora—Jolt!—got me—another micrometer on the old adrenals—

QUESTIONS AND EXERCISES

Vocabulary

1. Define or explain each of the following terms:

anthropologist (1)	sadistic (1)
hyped up (1)	ethology (1)
nephritic (1)	etiolate (4)
autistic (1)	satyrism (16)

Rhetoric

2. Make a list of the names of places and persons alluded to in the essay. Are there too many allusions? What effect do all these references have on Wolfe's style?
3. Notice the first sentence in the first paragraph. What figure of speech do you find?
4. Paragraph 4 begins a long series of reverse personifications, turning humans into animals. It begins an analogy that continues for the entire essay. What is the tone of this analogy?
5. Wolfe places direct quotations of scientific language in juxtaposition with his breathless, journalistic prose. What is the effect on his style?
6. Notice the short sketch of Dr. Hall in paragraph 7. Find another such description.
7. Paragraphs 24, 26, and 32 contain very graphic descriptions. What aspects of language are used for these effects?
8. Find the hyperbole in paragraphs 23 and 24.
9. Wolfe uses dashes and hyphens profusely. Why?
10. Find examples of diction that most college level dictionaries label nonstandard. Justify Wolfe's use of these terms.

11. What changes would have to be made in the essay to submit it for publication in a journal of anthropology?

Theme

12. Method and idea merge in "Sliding Down the Behavioral Sink." Explain the figurative and literal meaning of the title.
13. What is the meaning of the analogy that Wolfe develops in this essay?
14. Give our society's equivalents to the inhabitants of the animal behavioral sink.
    Example: politicians = super-rats
15. What is the effect of the stress of overpopulation?
16. What should our society do about high-rise apartments, tenements, ghettos, and other examples of over-crowding if it accepts the findings of the scientists noted?
17. What life styles seem to be a result of the behavioral sink analogy?
18. In the 19th century Huxley explained science to the less educated classes of England. How does Wolfe's essay perform a similar function?
19. Discuss the meaning of body language and the cultural differences mentioned in paragraph 40.
20. What contemporary thinkers and ideas does Wolfe mention in his essay? Are you aware of them?

Topics and Assignments for Composition

1. Write a description of some public figure you know in the terse, colorful manner used by Wolfe in paragraph 7.
2. Write a paragraph describing a scene in which you imitate Wolfe's descriptions in paragraphs 24, 26, and 32.
3. Choose a paragraph representative of the style of this essay and write an analysis of its stylistic elements.
4. Write an essay analyzing what the behavioral sink theory means for American civilization.
5. Conduct research to substantiate or refute the theory expounded by Hall. Write a report of your research.

Leonard I. Stein

Male and Female:
The Doctor-Nurse Game

The relationship between the doctor and the nurse is a very special one.   *1*
There are few professions where the degree of mutual respect and cooperation between co-workers is as intense as that between the doctor
and nurse. Superficially, the stereotype of this relationship has been
dramatized in many novels and television serials. When, however, it is
observed carefully in an interactional framework, the relationship takes
on a new dimension and has a special quality which fits a game model.
The underlying attitudes which demand that this game be played are unfortunate. These attitudes create serious obstacles in the path of meaningful communications between physicians and nonmedical professional
groups.

The physician traditionally and appropriately has total responsibility   *2*
for making the decisions regarding the management of his patients' treatment. To guide his decisions he considers data gleaned from several
sources. He acquires a complete medical history, performs a thorough
physical examination, interprets laboratory findings, and at times, obtains
recommendations from physician-consultants. Another important factor
in his decision-making are the recommendations he receives from the
nurse. The interaction between doctor and nurse through which these
recommendations are communicated and received is unique and interesting.

The Game

One rarely hears a nurse say, "Doctor I would recommend that you   *3*
order a retention enema for Mrs. Brown." A physician, upon hearing a

Reprinted with permission from *Archives of General Psychiatry* 16 (June
1967), pp. 699-703. Copyright 1967, American Medical Association.

recommendation of that nature, would gape in amazement at the effrontery of the nurse. The nurse, upon hearing the statement, would look over her shoulder to see who said it, hardly believing the words actually came from her own mouth. Nevertheless, if one observes closely, nurses make recommendations of more import every hour and physicians willingly and respectfully consider them. If the nurse is to make a suggestion without appearing insolent and the doctor is to seriously consider that suggestion, their interaction must not violate the rules of the game.

Object of the game. The object of the game is as follows: the nurse is   *4*
to be bold, have initiative, and be responsible for making significant recommendations, while at the same time she must appear passive. This must be done in such a manner so as to make her recommendations appear to be initiated by the physician.

Both participants must be acutely sensitive to each other's nonverbal   *5*
and cryptic verbal communications. A slight lowering of the head, a minor shifting of position in the chair, or a seemingly nonrelevant comment concerning an event which occurred eight months ago must be interpreted as a powerful message. The game requires the nimbleness of a high wire acrobat, and if either participant slips the game can be shattered; the penalties for frequent failure are apt to be severe.

Rules of the game. The cardinal rule of the game is that open disagree-   *6*
ment between the players must be avoided at all costs. Thus, the nurse must communicate her recommendations without appearing to be making a recommendation statement. The physician, in requesting a recommendation from a nurse, must do so without appearing to be asking for it. Utilization of this technique keeps anyone from committing themselves to a position before a sub rosa agreement on that position has already been established. In that way open disagreement is avoided. The greater the significance of the recommendation, the more subtly the game must be played.

To convey a subtle example of the game with all its nuances would   *7*
require the talents of a literary artist. Lacking these talents, let me give you the following example which is unsubtle, but happens frequently. The medical resident on hospital call is awakened by telephone at 1:00 A.M. because a patient on a ward, not his own, has not been able to fall asleep. Dr. Jones answers the telephone and the dialogue goes like this:

> This is Dr. Jones.
> (An open and direct communication.)
> Dr. Jones, this is Miss Smith on 2W—Mrs. Brown, who learned today of her father's death, is unable to fall asleep.
> (This message has two levels. Openly, it describes a set of circum-

stances, a woman who is unable to sleep and who that morning received word of her father's death. Less openly, but just as directly, it is a diagnostic and recommendation statement; i.e., Mrs. Brown is unable to sleep because of her grief, and she should be given a sedative. Dr. Jones, accepting the diagnostic statement and replying to the recommendation statement, answers.)

What sleeping medication has been helpful to Mrs. Brown in the past?

(Dr. Jones, not knowing the patient, is asking for a recommendation from the nurse, who does know the patient, about what sleeping medication should be prescribed. Note, however, his question does not appear to be asking her for a recommendation. Miss Smith replies.)

Pentobarbital mg 100 was quite effective night before last.

(A disguised recommendation statement. Dr. Jones replies with a note of authority in his voice.)

Pentobarbital mg 100 before bedtime as needed for sleep; got it?

(Miss Smith ends the conversation with the tone of a grateful supplicant.)

Yes, I have, and thank you very much doctor.

The above is an example of a successfully played doctor-nurse game. **8** The nurse made appropriate recommendations which were accepted by the physician and were helpful to the patient. The game was successful because the cardinal rule was not violated. The nurse was able to make her recommendation without appearing to, and the physician was able to ask for recommendations without conspicuously asking for them.

The scoring system. Inherent in any game are penalties and rewards **9** for the players. In game theory the doctor-nurse game fits the nonzero sum game model. It is not like chess, where the players compete with each other and whatever one player loses the other wins. Rather, it is the kind of game in which the rewards and punishments are shared by both players. If they play the game successfully they both win rewards, and if they are unskilled and the game is played badly, they both suffer the penalty.

The most obvious reward from the well-played game is a doctor-nurse **10** team that operates efficiently. The physician is able to utilize the nurse as a valuable consultant, and the nurse gains self-esteem and professional satisfaction from her job. The less obvious rewards are no less important. A successful game creates a doctor-nurse alliance; through this alliance the physician gains the respect and admiration of the nursing service. He can be confident that his nursing staff will smooth the path for getting his work done. His charts will be organized and waiting for him when he arrives, the ruffled feathers of patients and relatives will have been smoothed down, and his pet routines will be happily followed, and he will be helped in a thousand and one other ways.

The doctor-nurse alliance sheds its light on the nurse as well. She gains *11* a reputation for being a "damn good nurse." She is respected by everyone and appropriately enjoys her position. When physicians discuss the nursing staff it would not be unusual for her name to be mentioned with respect and admiration. Their esteem for a good nurse is no less than their esteem for a good doctor.

The penalties for a game failure, on the other hand, can be severe. The *12* physician who is an unskilled gamesman and fails to recognize the nurses' subtle recommendation messages is tolerated as a "clod." If, however, he interprets these messages as insolence and strongly indicates he does not wish to tolerate suggestions from nurses, he creates a rocky path for his travels. The old truism "If the nurse is your ally you've got it made, and if she has it in for you, be prepared for misery" takes on lifesized proportions. He receives three times as many phone calls after midnight than his colleagues. Nurses will not accept his telephone orders because "telephone orders are against the rules." Somehow, this rule gets suspended for the skilled players. Soon he becomes like Joe Bfstplk in the "Li'l Abner" comic strip. No matter where he goes, a black cloud constantly hovers over his head.

The unskilled gamesman nurse also pays heavily. The nurse who does *13* not view her role as that of consultant, and therefore does not attempt to communicate recommendations, is perceived as a dullard and is mercifully allowed to fade into the woodwork.

The nurse who does see herself as a consultant but refuses to follow *14* the rules of the game in making her recommendations has hell to pay. The outspoken nurse is labeled a "bitch" by the surgeon. The psychiatrist describes her as unconsciously suffering from penis envy and her behavior is the acting out of her hostility towards men. Loosely translated, the psychiatrist is saying she is a bitch. The employment of the unbright outspoken nurse is soon terminated. The outspoken bright nurse whose recommendations are worthwhile remains employed. She is, however, constantly reminded in a hundred ways that she is not loved.

Genesis of the Game

To understand how the game evolved, we must comprehend the nature *15* of the doctors' and nurses' training which shaped the attitudes necessary for the game.

Medical student training. The medical student in his freshman year   *16*
studies as if possessed. In the anatomy class he learns every groove and
prominence on the bones of the skeleton as if life depended on it. As a
matter of fact, he literally believes just that. He not infrequently says,
"I've got to learn it exactly; a life may depend on me knowing that." A
consequence of this attitude, which is carefully nurtured throughout medical school, is the development of a phobia: the overdetermined fear of
making a mistake. The development of this fear is quite understandable.
The burden the physician must carry is at times almost unbearable. He
feels responsible in a very personal way for the lives of his patients.
When a man dies leaving young children and a widow, the doctor carries
some of her grief and despair inside himself; and when a child dies, some
of him dies too. He sees himself as a warrior against death and disease.
When he loses a battle, through no fault of his own, he nevertheless feels
pangs of guilt, and he relentlessly searches himself to see if there might
have been a way to alter the outcome. For the physician a mistake leading
to a serious consequence is intolerable, and any mistake reminds him of
his vulnerability. There is little wonder that he becomes phobic. The classical way in which phobias are managed is to avoid the source of the fear.
Since it is impossible to avoid making some mistakes in an active practice
of medicine, a substitute defensive maneuver is employed. The physician
develops the belief that he is omnipotent and omniscient, and therefore
incapable of making mistakes. This belief allows the phobic physician to
actively engage in his practice rather than avoid it. The fear of committing
an error in a critical field like medicine is unavoidable and appropriately
realistic. The physician, however, must learn to live with the fear rather
than handle it defensively through a posture of omnipotence. This defense
markedly interferes with his interpersonal professional relationships.

Physicians, of course, deny feelings of omnipotence. The evidence,   *17*
however, renders their denials to whispers in the wind. The slightest mistake inflicts a large narcissistic wound. Depending on his underlying personality structure the physician may obsess for days about it, quickly
rationalize it away, or deny it. The guilt produced is unusually exaggerated and the incident is handled defensively. The ways in which physicians enhance and support each other's defenses when an error is made
could be the topic of another paper. The feeling of omnipotence becomes
generalized to other areas of his life. A report of the Federal Aviation
Agency (FAA), as quoted in *Time Magazine* (August 5, 1966), states
that in 1964 and 1965 physicians had a fatal-accident rate four times as
high as the average for all other private pilots. Major causes of the high
death rate were risk-taking attitudes and judgments. Almost all of the
accidents occurred on pleasure trips, and were therefore not necessary

risks to get to a patient needing emergency care. The trouble, suggested an FAA official, is that too many doctors fly with "the feeling that they are omnipotent." Thus, the extremes to which the physician may go in preserving his self-concept of omnipotence may threaten his own life. This overdetermined preservation of omnipotence is indicative of its brittleness and its underlying foundation of fear or failure.

The physician finds himself trapped in a paradox. He fervently wants *18* to give his patient the best possible medical care, and being open to the nurses' recommendations helps him accomplish this. On the other hand, accepting advice from nonphysicians is highly threatening to his omnipotence. The solution for the paradox is to receive sub rosa recommendations and make them appear to be initiated by himself. In short, he must learn to play the doctor-nurse game.

Some physicians never learn to play the game. Most learn in their in- *19* ternship, and a perceptive few learn during their clerkships in medical school. Medical students frequently complain that the nursing staff treats them as if they had just completed a junior Red Cross first-aid class instead of two years of intensive medical training. Interviewing nurses in a training hospital sheds considerable light on this phenomenon. In their words they said,

> A few students just seem to be with it, they are able to understand what you are trying to tell them, and they are a pleasure to work with; most, however, pretend to know everything and refused to listen to anything we have to say and I guess we do give them a rough time.

In essence, they are saying that those students who quickly learn the game are rewarded, and those that do not are punished.

Most physicians learn to play the game after they have weathered a *20* few experiences like the one described below. On the first day of his internship, the physician and nurse were making rounds. They stopped at the bed of a fifty-two-year-old woman who, after complimenting the young doctor on his appearance, complained to him of her problem with constipation. After several minutes of listening to her detailed description of peculiar diets, family home remedies, and special exercises that had helped her constipation in the past, the nurse politely interrupted the patient. She told her the doctor would take care of the problem and that he had to move on because there were other patients waiting to see him. The young doctor gave the nurse a stern look, turned toward the patient, and kindly told her he would order an enema for her that very afternoon. As they left the bedside, the nurse told him the patient had had a normal bowel movement every day for the past week and that in the twenty-three days the patient had been in the hospital she had never once passed up an opportunity to complain of her constipation. She quickly added that *if* the doctor wanted to order an enema, the patient would certainly receive one. After hearing this report the intern's mouth fell open and the wheels began turning in his head. He remembered the nurse's comment to the patient that "the doctor had to move on," and it occurred to him that perhaps she was really giving him a message. This experience and a few more like it, and the young doctor learns to listen for the subtle recommendations the nurses make.

Nursing student training. Unlike the medical student who usually learns   21
to play the game after he finishes medical school, the nursing student begins to learn it early in her training. Throughout her education she is trained to play the doctor-nurse game.

Student nurses are taught how to relate to physicians. They are told   22
he has infinitely more knowledge than they, and thus he should be shown the utmost respect. In addition, it was not many years ago when nurses were instructed to stand whenever a physician entered a room. When he would come in for a conference the nurse was expected to offer him her chair, and when both entered a room the nurse would open the door for him and allow him to enter first. Although these practices are no longer rigidly adhered to, the premise upon which they were based is still promulgated. One nurse described that premise as, "He's God almighty and your job is to wait on him."

To inculcate subservience and inhibit deviancy, nursing schools, for   23
the most part, are tightly run, disciplined institutions. Certainly there is great variation among nursing schools, and there is little question that the trend is toward giving students more autonomy. However, in too many schools this trend has not gone far enough, and the climate remains restrictive. The student's schedule is firmly controlled and there is very little free time. Classroom hours, study hours, mealtime, and bedtime with lights out are rigidly enforced. In some schools meaningless chores are assigned, such as cleaning bedsprings with cotton applicators. The relationship between student and instructor continues this military flavor. Often their relationship is more like that between recruit and drill sergeant than between student and teacher. Open dialogue is inhibited by attitudes of strict black and white, with few, if any, shades of gray. Straying from the rigidly outlined path is sure to result in disciplinary action.

The inevitable result of these practices is to instill in the student nurse   24
a fear of independent action. This inhibition of independent action is most marked when relating to physicians. One of the students' greatest fears is making a blunder while assisting a physician and being publicly

ridiculed by him. This is really more a reflection of the nature of their training than the prevalence of abusive physicians. The fear of being humiliated for a blunder while assisting in a procedure is generalized to the fear of humiliation for making any independent act in relating to a physician, especially the act of making a direct recommendation. Every nurse interviewed felt that making a suggestion to a physician was equivalent to insulting and belittling him. It was tantamount to questioning his medical knowledge and insinuating he did not know his business. In light of her image of the physician as an omniscient and punitive figure, the questioning of his knowledge would be unthinkable.

The student, however, is also given messages quite contrary to the 25 ones described above. She is continually told that she is an invaluable aid to the physician in the treatment of the patient. She is told that she must help him in every way possible, and she is imbued with a strong sense of responsibility for the care of her patient. Thus she, like the physician, is caught in a paradox. The first set of messages implies that the physician is omniscient and that any recommendation she might make would be insulting to him and leave her open to ridicule. The second set of messages implies that she is an important asset to him, has much to contribute, and is duty-bound to make those contributions. Thus, when her good sense tells her a recommendation would be helpful to him she is not allowed to communicate it directly, nor is she allowed not to communicate it. The way out of the bind is to use the doctor-nurse game and communicate the recommendation without appearing to do so.

Forces Preserving the Game

Upon observing the indirect interactional system which is the heart of 26 the doctor-nurse game, one must ask the question, "Why does this inefficient mode of communication continue to exist?" The forces mitigating against change are powerful.

Rewards and punishments. The doctor-nurse game has a powerful in- 27 nate self-perpetuating force—its system of rewards and punishments. One potent method of shaping behavior is to reward one set of behavioral patterns and to punish patterns which deviate from it. As described earlier, the rewards given for a well-played game and the punishments meted out to unskilled players are impressive. This system alone would be sufficient to keep the game flourishing. The game, however, has additional forces.

The strength of the set. It is well recognized that sets are hard to break. 28 A powerful attitudinal set is the nurse's perception that making a suggestion to a physician is equivalent to insulting and belittling him. An example of where attempts are regularly made to break this set is seen on psychiatric treatment wards operating on a therapeutic community model. This model requires open and direct communication between members of the team. Psychiatrists working in these settings expend a great deal of energy in urging for and rewarding openness before direct patterns of communication become established. The rigidity of the resistance to break this set is impressive. If the physician himself is a prisoner of a set and therefore does not actively try to destroy it, change is near impossible.

The need for leadership. Lack of leadership and structure in any or-   *29* ganization produces anxiety in its members. As the importance of the organization's mission increases, the demand by its members for leadership commensurately increases. In our culture human life is near the top of our hierarchy of values, and organizations which deal with human lives, such as law and medicine, are very rigidly structured. Certainly some of this is necessary for the systematic management of the task. The excessive degree of rigidity, however, is demanded by its members for their own psychic comfort rather than for its utility in efficiently carrying out its mission. The game lends support to this thesis. Indirect communication is an inefficient mode of transmitting information. However, it effectively supports and protects a rigid organizational structure with the physician in clear authority. Maintaining an omnipotent leader provides the other members with a great sense of security.

Sexual roles. Another influence perpetuating the doctor-nurse game   *30* is the sexual identity of the players. Doctors are predominately men and nurses are almost exclusively women. There are elements of the game which reinforce the stereotyped roles of male dominance and female passivity. Some nursing instructors explicitly tell their students that their femininity is an important asset to be used when relating to physicians.

The Community

The doctor and nurse have a shared history and thus have been able to   *31* work out their game so that it operates more efficiently than one would expect in an indirect system. Major difficulty arises, however, when the physician works closely with other disciplines which are not normally considered part of the medical sphere. With expanding medical horizons encompassing cooperation with sociologists, engineers, anthropologists, computer analysts, etc., continued expectation of a doctor-nurselike interaction by the physician is disastrous. The sociologist, for example, is not willing to play that kind of game. When his direct communications are rebuffed the relationship breaks down.

The major disadvantage of a doctor-nurselike game is its inhibitory   *32*
effect on open dialogue which is stifling and anti-intellectual. The game is
basically a transactional neurosis, and both professions would enhance
themselves by taking steps to change the attitudes which breed the
game. . . .

QUESTIONS AND EXERCISES

Vocabulary

1. Define or explain each of the following terms:

stereotypes (1)	paradox (18)
nuances (7)	inculcate (23)
cardinal (8)	omniscient (24)
phobias (16)	interactional (26)
omnipotence (17)	mitigating (26)

2. What is the plural of "phenomenon"?

Rhetoric

3. Why is "bitch" put in quotation marks at one point and not at another
   in paragraph 14?
4. What is the name of the process that uses the first letters of words to
   form a word as in paragraph 17 where Federal Aviation Agency becomes FAA?
5. Explain the level of diction of "how to relate to" in paragraphs 22,
   24, and 30.
6. Find the simile in paragraph 12. What other rhetorical device is involved?
7. Discuss the figurative language in paragraph 23, "Open dialogue is
   inhibited by attitudes of strict black and white, with few, if any,
   shades of gray."
8. Discuss the tone and style of this essay. How does the style fit the
   substance?

Theme

9. Define the meaning of "game" as it is used in this essay.
10. What is the advantage of using the game model to explain a real life
    situation? Are there any disadvantages?
11. What does this presentation do to the image of the doctor?
12. Are the games doctors and nurses play necessary? Do all profes-
    sions have analogous games?
13. Does the image of psychiatrists emerge as one of "super" doctors?

Explain and illustrate your answer with evidence from the text. Who analyzes the analyzers?

14. What insights does this analysis give the layman about the practice of medicine?

Topics and Assignments for Composition

1. Write a definition of "game" as it is used in psychology.
2. Write an essay in which you analyze a "game" in some other discipline than medicine.
3. Write an essay in which you make an analogy between games and life.
4. Research the origins of the game theory of transactional psychology and write an objective report of your findings.

Student Example

Britain's Flammable Potato Paddy

The age-old, Anglo-Irish, Protestant-Catholic struggle, which has flared up again during the past three years and has caused increased violence, bloodshed, and destruction in the first half of 1972, can justifiably be called Britain's Vietnam. Of course, there are vital differences between the two conflicts which must be stressed at the outset. First, the historical relationships are clearly different. Because of Ireland's size and geographical closeness to Britain, the two have strong cultural, economic, and political ties. Thus, Britain, unlike the United States, is not intervening in a distant conflict; the disputed territory is legally British.

Second, in terms of men and munitions, the fighting in Northern Ireland is being conducted on a significantly smaller scale than the war in Vietnam. There are no battlefields as such, for the Ulster struggle consists of guerilla acts of sabotage and civil disobedience (e.g., the refusal of councilhouse tenants to pay rent), against the legal, political, and social repression of a sizable segment of the population. This repression is backed effectively by the clubs, guns, and internment camps of the police and the British army. But Britain is not attempting to gain control of any territory. Officially, British troops are in Northern Ireland to keep peace, not to wage war. While obviously not completely true, this explanation can be substantiated in many ways: the British army's role is more like that of the National Guard sent in to control a big urban riot than that of the American army in Vietnam; it is not required to fight large battles, but to contain rebellion and in some cases to serve as a buffer in a limited area.

Third, Vietnam and Ulster differ greatly in their international political significance as well as in the ideological and power struggles involved. Vietnam involves, directly or indirectly, the power, prestige, and national interests of the two superpowers, plus China, the largest Asian power, and several other Asian countries, whose forms of government and future directions will be greatly influenced by its outcome. It involves the traditional Cold War Communism vs. Capitalism struggle, and the newer battle for supremacy in Asia, complicated by the growing power and presence of China. And it has caused irreparable internal and external damage to the most powerful, and once the most influential country in the world. On the other hand, the struggle in Northern Ireland is of almost miniscule impact and long-range significance, except for Britain, Ireland, and those of Irish descent living abroad. But even here, unless there are relatives or friends directly involved, the interest is likely to be cursory and laced with confusion (as demonstrated by the lack of rapport between fiery Socialist Bernadette Devlin and the predominately Middle-American Irish she went to America to solicit money from).

Although mostly superficial, the similarities can now be examined more clearly. There is the British army, playing the American role. The Protestant loyalists, some of whom are quite wealthy, are the equivalent of the South Vietnamese. The Catholics, about 40 percent of the population, play the role of the peasants. The role of the poor Protestants in relation to Catholics might be described as the traditional one of poor whites vs. blacks in the American South. The IRA, in its various forms, resembles the Vietcong and is the villain in British eyes, while the Republic of Ireland assuming the combined roles of North Vietnam, Russia, and China, is the barely out-of-sight heavy. As in Vietnam, issues, factions, and individuals are divided and confused. Many people are apathetic, just wanting to go on living as best they can, hoping for peace and order. The issues of religious freedom and freedom from oppression parallel those of Communism and freedom from oppression in Vietnam. The Catholics want legal, economic, political, educational, and social equality, and freedom from the rule of wealthy Protestant factory and land owners. Protestants are trying to maintain their real or imagined positions of superiority. Violence and repression are growing on all sides.

The British attitudes toward the Irish conflict, particularly as expressed by the government and political leaders, and reflected in and fostered by the media, are remarkably similar to American attitudes toward Vietnam in the mid-sixties. There is the insistence that "we are just keeping order, supporting the legitimate, elected government." This insistence can be seen in the vitriolic outbursts against the "IRA killers, butchers, etc.;" the emotional rhetoric about "supporting our boys;" and the coloration of news, designed to present the army as trying to do a difficult job in impossible circumstances and succeeding remarkably well, and anyone who opposes it as anarchists, murderers, and Communists (because of the discovery of Czech arms intended for Ulster).

If the Irish hate the British as oppressors, the British seem to have an ingrained dislike for the Irish who are more stereotyped than any other immigrant group in Britain. Attitudes range from colonialistic paternalism to a deep contempt which seems rooted in a strong belief in their inherent inferiority. Just as Americans saw the North Vietnamese as subhuman creatures who didn't really count for anything, reflected in the "We're over here to kill Gooks" philosophy, British feelings toward the Irish are perhaps best expressed by the shouts of "Fenian bastards" which apparently come readily from the mouths of British soldiers, particularly when no newsmen and photographers are close at hand.

Another interesting aspect of the British attitude toward the Ulster situation is the almost universal agreement that, while the British government and army may not be entirely right in all instances, they are certainly not wrong. While many support direct control of Ulster from London, less power in the hands of the Protestants, more British civilian surveillance and involvement, release or immediate trial of those interned, and a stepped-up program of reforms, hardly anyone in government, media, or any other public position will come out and say that the British are wrong and should withdraw from Ulster. Labor MP's, liberal newspapers, and other moderate and liberal voices in Britain are all strangely reluctant to play a dovish role. In fact, many are surprisingly hawkish. The general public is seemingly apathetic.

There is also a growing feeling, as there was in America in the mid-sixties, that the war is getting larger and more complicated every day, that Britain will eventually have to reverse her stand dramatically and either get out quickly, or pay the price of sticking to her commitments. The latter course will result in more and more deaths, as well as more money spent on the military, spending which Britain can ill afford with the current rise in unemployment and prices.

Because the scale of the war in Ulster is still very small compared to Vietnam, the "guns or butter" economic issue is not applicable to the British situation at present. Neither has the war been used successfully to obscure internal problems or to postpone necessary political changes and social improvements. And it has not had the devastating psychological effect on Britain that Vietnam has had on America. Nevertheless, a few acts such as the discovery of Czech arms intended for use by the IRA, IRA bombing attacks, and recent bombings within London itself (initially attributed to the IRA, but now suspected to be the work of local anarchists) have created a reaction of defensive righteousness within Britain, an insistence that the country is being threatened. (Whether by the Communists, anarchists, or the IRA, is unclear.) The public has the feeling that somehow Britain, her honor, integrity, and her institutions, are under possible attack.

Adopted and spread by the more sensationalist press and, to an extent, by television and the "responsible" press, this feeling is widely believed. It could, if carried to its logical conclusion, be used to justify additional legal and political repression, for there are several separate revolutionary groups in Britain which share a mistrust of and disbelief in the British government, establishment, and ruling class. These groups—workers, blacks, and anarchists—are the least likely to support the war in Ulster, and the most likely to shake things up inside Britain.

Thus Britain, frightened by slowly stirring unrest within segments of her own population, necessary changes which are occurring constantly, and the even more bewildering fluctuations of the outside world within which she is struggling to maintain her past dignity and to define her present role, seems to be using the Ulster situation to somehow prove herself, to show that she is capable of maintaining order and commanding respect. It seems likely that pursuing her present policy may yield the opposite effect.

Part Five:
Definition

Scientific American

What Is Death?

The traditional criteria for death are cessation of respiration and heart   *1*
action, but modern medical technology can keep a patient breathing and
his blood circulating long after his brain has died. Now a special Harvard
University committee has recommended that brain death, or irreversible
coma, be considered a definition of death and has drawn up a set of guidelines for determining when there is no discernible activity of the central
nervous system. The 13-man committee, drawn from the faculties of
medicine, public health, law, arts and sciences and divinity, was headed
by Henry K. Beecher of the Harvard Medical School. Its report was published in the *Journal of the American Medical Association.*

According to the committee a permanently nonfunctioning brain is   *2*
characterized by certain clinical signs. One is unreceptiveness and un-
responsiveness of the patient to any external stimuli or inner needs.
Another is lack of any spontaneous muscular movement or any unassisted
breathing — or effort to breathe — over a period of at least an hour. Finally,
there are no reflexes: the pupil of the eye is fixed and dilated even in the
presence of a bright light, there is no swallowing or yawning and usually
no stretch reflex. These clinical signs constitute primary evidence of
brain death; electroencephalograms should be considered secondary because they may show spurious waves. A "flat" brain-wave pattern, according to the report, constitutes confirmation of brain death.

The final determination of death through irreversible coma should be   *3*
made only when the clinical and encephalographic tests have been repeated at least 24 hours after the initial tests. The determination should
be made by the physician in charge; it is "unsound and undesirable" to
have the family make the decision. Then the family should be informed.
"At this point death is to be declared and *then* the respirator turned off."

The decision, the committee noted, "should be made by physicians not involved in any later effort to transplant organs or tissue from the deceased individual."

QUESTIONS AND EXERCISES

Vocabulary

1. Define or explain the following terms:

    criteria (1)   electroencephalograms (2)
    coma (1)   spurious (2)
    dilated (2)

Rhetoric

2. Would an educated layman have trouble understanding any of the concepts in the essay?
3. What is the tone of the essay? Why?
4. Explain the use of quotations in this essay.

Theme

5. Why is the definition of death a problem today?
6. Why was the committee that drafted the recommendation composed of faculty members from medicine, public health, law, arts and sciences, and divinity?
7. Discuss concepts of death found in different cultures and different eras.

Topics and Assignments for Composition

1. In your own words define "death."
2. Pick spokesmen from different occupations and define death in a way which would be appropriate to each occupation.
    Examples: Logician: Death is the absence of life.
              Poet: Death is a little like taking a long trip.
4. Write a parody of this essay. Instead of being serious and solemn about a serious subject, be either serious about a trivial subject or trivial about a serious subject.
5. Write an essay in which you develop the thesis that technology and science have made many terms and concepts obsolete. Suggest solutions to the problems you pose.

Eric Berne

Games

Definition

A game is an ongoing series of complementary ulterior transactions *1*
progressing to a well-defined, predictable outcome. Descriptively it is a
recurring set of transactions, often repetitious, superficially plausible,
with a concealed motivation; or, more colloquially, a series of moves with
a snare, or "gimmick." Games are clearly differentiated from procedures,
rituals, and pastimes by two chief characteristics: (1) their ulterior quality
and (2) the payoff. Procedures may be successful, rituals effective, and
pastimes profitable, but all of them are by definition candid; they may involve contest, but not conflict, and the ending may be sensational, but it
is not dramatic. Every game, on the other hand, is basically dishonest, and
the outcome has a dramatic, as distinct from merely exciting, quality.

It remains to distinguish games from the one remaining type of social *2*
action which so far has not been discussed. An *operation* is a simple
transaction or set of transactions undertaken for a specific, stated purpose. If someone frankly asks for reassurance and gets it, that is an operation. If someone asks for reassurance, and after it is given turns it in some
way to the disadvantage of the giver, that is a game. Superficially, then,
a game looks like a set of operations, but after the payoff it becomes apparent that these "operations" were really *maneuvers;* not honest requests but moves in the game.

In the "insurance game," for example, no matter what the agent ap- *3*
pears to be doing in conversation, if he is a hard player he is really looking
for or working on a prospect. What he is after, if he is worth his salt, is
to "make a killing." The same applies to "the real estate game," "the
pajama game" and similar occupations. Hence at a social gathering, while
a salesman is engaged in pastimes, particularly variants of "Balance

Sheet," his congenial participation may conceal a series of skillful maneuvers designed to elicit the kind of information he is professionally interested in. There are dozens of trade journals devoted to improving commercial maneuvers, and which give accounts of outstanding players and games (interesting operators who make unusually big deals). Transactionally speaking, these are merely variants of *Sports Illustrated, Chess World,* and other sports magazines.

As far as angular transactions are concerned—games which are con-   4
sciously planned with professional precision under Adult control to yield
the maximum gains—the big "con games" which flourished in the early
1900's are hard to surpass for detailed practical planning and psychological virtuosity.

What we are concerned with here, however, are the unconscious games   5
played by innocent people engaged in duplex transactions of which they
are not fully aware, and which form the most important aspect of social
life all over the world. Because of their dynamic qualities, games are easy
to distinguish from mere static *attitudes,* which arise from taking a position.

The use of the word "game" should not be misleading. As explained in   6
the introduction, it does not necessarily imply fun or even enjoyment.
Many salesmen do not consider their work fun, as Arthur Miller made
clear in his play, *The Death of a Salesman.* And there may be no lack
of seriousness. Football games nowadays are taken very seriously, but
no more so than such transactional games as "Alcoholic" or "Third-
Degree Rapo."

The same applies to the word "play," as anyone who has "played"   7
hard poker or "played" the stock market over a long period can testify.
The possible seriousness of games and play, and the possibly serious
results, are well known to anthropologists. The most complex game that
ever existed, that of "Courtier" as described so well by Stendhal in *The
Charterhouse of Parma,* was deadly serious. The grimmest of all, of
course, is "War."

A Typical Game

The most common game played between spouses is colloquially called   8
"If It Weren't For You," and this will be used to illustrate the characteristics of games in general.

Mrs. White complained that her husband severely restricted her social   9
activities, so that she had never learned to dance. Due to changes in her
attitude brought about by psychiatric treatment, her husband became less
sure of himself and more indulgent. Mrs. White was then free to enlarge

the scope of her activities. She signed up for dancing classes, and then discovered to her despair that she had a morbid fear of dance floors and had to abandon this project.

This unfortunate adventure, along with similar ones, laid bare some *10* important aspects of the structure of her marriage. Out of her many suitors she had picked a domineering man for a husband. She was then in a position to complain that she could do all sorts of things "if it weren't for you." Many of her women friends also had domineering husbands, and when they met for their morning coffee, they spent a good deal of time playing "If It Weren't For Him."

As it turned out, however, contrary to her complaints, her husband was *11* performing a very real service for her by forbidding her to do something she was deeply afraid of, and by preventing her, in fact, from even becoming aware of her fears. This was one reason her Child had shrewdly chosen such a husband.

But there was more to it than that. His prohibitions and her complaints *12* frequently led to quarrels, so that their sex life was seriously impaired. And because of his feelings of guilt, he frequently brought her gifts which might not otherwise have been forthcoming; certainly when he gave her more freedom, his gifts diminished in lavishness and frequency. She and her husband had little in common besides their household worries and the children, so that their quarrels stood out as important events; it was mainly on these occasions that they had anything but the most casual conversations. At any rate, her married life had proved one thing to her that she had always maintained: that all men were mean and tyrannical. As it turned out, this attitude was related to some daydreams of being sexually abused which had plagued her in earlier years.

There are various ways of describing this game in general terms. It is *13* apparent that it belongs in the large field of *social dynamics*. The basic fact is that by marrying, Mr. and Mrs. White have an opportunity to communicate with each other, and such an opportunity may be called *social contact*. The fact that they use this opportunity makes their household a social aggregation, as contrasted with a New York subway train, for example, where people are in spatial contact but rarely avail themselves of the opportunity and so form a dis-social aggregation. The influence the Whites exert on each other's behavior and responses constitutes *social action*. Various disciplines would investigate such social action from different points of view. Since we are here concerned with the personal histories and psychodynamics of the individuals involved, the present approach is one aspect of *social psychiatry;* some implicit or explicit judgment is passed on the "healthiness" of the games studied. This is somewhat different from the more neutral and less committed attitudes of sociology and social psychology. Psychiatry reserves the right to say, "Just a moment!" which the other disciplines do not. Transactional analysis is a branch of social psychiatry, and game analysis is a special aspect of transactional analysis.

Practical game analysis deals with special cases as they appear in   *14* specific situations. Theoretical game analysis attempts to abstract and generalize the characteristics of various games, so that they can be recognized independently of their momentary verbal content and their cultural matrix. The theoretical analysis of "If It Weren't For You," Marital Type, for example, should state the characteristics of that game in such a way that it can be recognized just as easily in a New Guinea jungle village as in a Manhattan penthouse, whether it is concerned with a nuptial party or with the financial problems of getting a fishing rod for the grandchildren; and regardless of how bluntly or subtly the moves are made, according to the permissible degrees of frankness between husband and wife. The *prevalence* of the game in a given society is a matter for sociology and anthropology. Game analysis, as a part of social psychiatry, is only interested in describing the game when it does occur, regardless of how often that may be. This distinction is not complete, but it is analogous to the distinction between public health and internal medicine; the first is interested in the prevalence of malaria, while the latter studies cases of malaria as they come up, in the jungle or in Manhattan.

At the present time the scheme given below has been found the most   *15* useful one for theoretical game analysis. No doubt it will be improved as further knowledge accumulates. The first requisite is to recognize that a certain sequence of maneuvers meets the criteria of a game. As many samples as possible of the game are then collected. The significant features of the collection are isolated. Certain aspects emerge as essential. These are then classified under headings which are designed to be as meaningful and instructive as possible in the current state of knowledge. The analysis is undertaken from the point of view of the one who is "it" —in this case, Mrs. White.

Thesis. This is a general description of the game, including the imme-   *16* diate sequence of events (the social level) and information about their psychological background, evolution and significance (the psychological level). In the case of "If It Weren't For You" Marital Type, the details already given will serve. For the sake of brevity, this game will henceforth be referred to as IWFY.

Antithesis. The presumption that a certain sequence constitutes a game   *17* is tentative until it has been existentially validated. This validation is carried out by a refusal to play or by undercutting the payoff. The one who is "it" will then make more intense efforts to continue the game. In the face of adamant refusal to play or a successful undercutting he will then lapse into a state called "despair," which in some respects resembles a depression, but is different in significant ways. It is more acute and contains elements of frustration and bewilderment. It may be manifested, for example, by the onset of perplexed weeping. In a successful therapeutic situation this may soon be replaced by humorous laughter, implying an Adult realization: "There I go again!" Thus despair is a concern of the Adult, while in depression it is the Child who has the executive power. Hopefulness, enthusiasm or a lively interest in one's surroundings is the opposite of depression; laughter is the opposite of despair. Hence the enjoyable quality of therapeutic game analysis. The antithesis to IWFY is permissiveness. As long as the husband is prohibitive, the game can proceed. If instead of saying "Don't you dare!" he says "Go ahead!" the underlying phobias are unmasked, and the wife can no longer turn on him, as demonstrated in Mrs. White's case.

For clear understanding of a game, the antithesis should be known and its effectiveness demonstrated in practice. *18*

Aim. This states simply the general purpose of the game. Sometimes there are alternatives. The aim of IWFY may be stated as either reassurance ("It's not that I'm afraid, it's that he won't let me") or vindication ("It's not that I'm not trying, it's that he holds me back"). The reassuring function is easier to clarify and is more in accord with the security needs of the wife; therefore IWFY is most simply regarded as having the aim of reassurance. *19*

Roles. As previously noted, ego states are not roles but phenomena. Therefore ego states and roles have to be distinguished in a formal description. Games may be described as two-handed, three-handed, many-handed, etc., according to the number of roles offered. Sometimes the ego state of each player corresponds to his role, sometimes it does not. *20*

IWFY is a two-handed game and calls for a restricted wife and a domineering husband. The wife may play her role either as a prudent Adult ("It's best that I do as he says") or as a petulant Child. The domineering husband may preserve an Adult ego state ("It's best that you do as I say") or slip into a Parental one ("You'd better do what I say"). *21*

Dynamics. There are alternatives in stating the psychodynamic driving forces behind each case of a game. It is usually possible, however, to pick out a single psychodynamic concept which usefully, aptly and meaningfully epitomizes the situation. Thus IWFY is best described as deriving from phobic sources. *22*

Examples. Since the childhood origins of a game, or its infantile prototypes, are instructive to study, it is worth-while to search for such cognates in making a formal description. It happens that IWFY is just *23* as frequently played by little children as by grown-ups, so the childhood version is the same as the later one. with the actual parent substituted for the restricting husband.

Transactional Paradigm. The transactional analysis of a typical situa- 24 tion is presented, giving both the social and psychological levels of a revealing ulterior transaction. In its most dramatic form, IWFY at the social level is a Parent-Child game.

> Mr. White: "You stay home and take care of the house."
> Mrs. White: "If it weren't for you, I could be out having fun."

At the psychological level (the ulterior marriage contract) the relationship is Child-Child, and quite different.

> Mr. White: "You must always be here when I get home. I'm terrified of desertion."
> Mrs. White: "I will be if you help me avoid phobic situations."

The two levels are illustrated below.

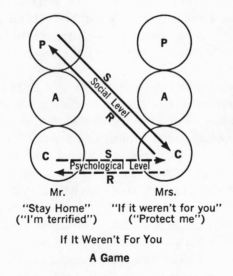

Mr.   Mrs.

"Stay Home"   "If it weren't for you"
("I'm terrified")   ("Protect me")

If It Weren't For You
A Game

Moves. The moves of a game correspond roughly to the strokes in a 25 ritual. As in any game, the players become increasingly adept with practice. Wasteful moves are eliminated, and more and more purpose is condensed into each move. "Beautiful friendships" are often based on the fact that the players complement each other with great economy and satisfaction, so that there is a maximum yield with a minimum effort from the games they play with each other. Certain intermediate, precautionary or concessional moves can be elided, giving a high degree of elegance to the relationship. The effort saved on defensive maneuvers can be devoted to ornamental flourishes instead, to the delight of both parties and sometimes of the onlookers as well. The student observes that there is a minimum number of moves essential to the progress of the game, and these can be stated in the protocol. Individual players will embellish or multiply these basic moves according to their needs, talents or desires. The framework for IWFY is as follows:

(1) Instruction-Compliance ("You stay home" — "All right").

(2) Instruction-Protest ("You stay home again" — "If it weren't for you").

Advantages. The general advantages of a game consist in its stabilizing (homeostatic) functions. Biological homeostasis is promoted by the stroking, and psychological stability is reinforced by the confirmation of position. As has already been noted, stroking may take various forms, so that the *biological advantage* of a game may be stated in tactile terms. Thus the husband's role in IWFY is reminiscent of a backhanded slap (quite different in effect from a palmar slap, which is a direct humiliation), and the wife's response is something like a petulant kick in the shins. Hence the biological gain from IWFY is derived from belligerence-petulance exchanges: a distressing but apparently effective way to maintain the health of nervous tissues.

Confirmation of the wife's position — "All men are tyrants" — is the *existential advantage*. This position is a reaction to the need to surrender that is inherent in the phobias, a demonstration of the coherent structure which underlies all games. The expanded statement would be: "If I went out alone in a crowd, I would be overcome by the temptation to surrender; at home I don't surrender: he forces me, which proves that all men are tyrants." Hence this game is commonly played by women who suffer from feelings of unreality, which signifies their difficulty in keeping the Adult in charge in situations of strong temptation. The detailed elucidation of these mechanisms belongs to psychoanalysis rather than game analysis. In game analysis the end product is the chief concern.

Internal psychological advantage of a game is its direct effect on the psychic economy (libido). In IWFY the socially acceptable surrender to the husband's authority keeps the woman from experiencing neurotic fears. At the same time it satisfies masochistic needs, if they exist, using masochism not in the sense of self-abnegation but with its classical meaning of sexual excitement in situations of deprivation, humiliation or pain. That is, it excites her to be deprived and dominated.

External psychological advantage is the avoidance of the feared situation by playing the game. This is especially obvious in IWFY, where it is the outstanding motivation: by complying with the husband's strictures, the wife avoids the public situations which she fears.

Internal social advantage is designated by the name of the game as it   *30* is played in the individual's intimate circle. By her compliance, the wife gains the privilege of saying "If it weren't for you." This helps to structure the time she must spend with her husband; in the case of Mrs. White, this need for structure was especially strong because of the lack of other common interests, especially before the arrival of their offspring and after the children were grown. In between, the game was played less intensively and less frequently, because the children performed their usual function of structuring time for their parents, and also provided an even more widely accepted version of IWFY, the busy-housewife variation. The fact that young mothers in America often really are very busy does not change the analysis of this variation. Game analysis only attempts to answer this question without prejudice: given that a young woman is busy, how does she go about exploiting her busyness in order to get some compensation for it?

External social advantage is designated by the use made of the situa-   *31* tion in outside social contacts. In the case of the game "If It Weren't For You," which is what the wife says to her husband, there is a transformation into the pastime "If It Weren't For Him" when she meets with her friends over morning coffee. Again, the influence of games in the selection of social companions is shown. The new neighbor who is invited for morning coffee is being invited to play "If It Weren't For Him." If she plays, well and good, she will soon be a bosom friend of the old-timers, other things being equal. If she refuses to play and insists on taking a charitable view of her husband, she will not last long. Her situation will be the same as if she kept refusing to drink at cocktail parties — in most circles, she would gradually be dropped from the guest lists.

This completes the analysis of the formal features of IWFY. In order to   *32* clarify the procedure further, the analysis of "Why Don't You — Yes But," which is the most common game played at social gatherings, committee meetings and psychotherapy groups the world over, should be consulted.

QUESTIONS AND EXERCISES

Vocabulary

1. Define or explain each of the following terms:
       complementary (1)   cognates (23)

ulterior (1)   paradigm (24)
transactions (1)   elided (25)
maneuvers (2)   protocol (25)
morbid (9)   homeostatic (26)
dynamics (13)   tactile (26)
implicit (13)   palmar (26)
explicit (13)   petulant (26)
matrix (14)   elucidation (27)
criteria (15)   libido (28)
adamant (17)   masochistic (28)
phobias (17)   self-abnegation (28)
epitomizes (22)   strictures (29)
prototypes (23)

2. From what academic discipline are most of the technical terms taken?

Rhetoric

3. What is unusual about the tone of this essay? What elements contribute to this tone?
4. The overall pattern of this excerpt is, of course, the definition of games. What specific techniques are used to accomplish the major goal?
5. Comment on the logic of presentation; that is, does the author keep in mind the feedback that he might normally expect from the reader?

Theme

6. What kinds of games does Berne mention in his analysis? Is war a game?
7. What assumptions about human nature does Berne make?
8. The tenets of what school of psychology are utilized in the presentation? With what other positions are you familiar?
9. Why do you think *The Games People Play* was on the best-seller list even though it is a book about psychiatry?
10. What elements of satire do you think are present in this selection? Do you think a psychiatrist should be satirical and sarcastic?
11. What is rationalization? Find an example of rationalizing in "Games."

Topics and Assignments for Composition

1. In a paraphrase of Berne's language, define a game.
2. In a paragraph comment on the effectiveness of Berne's examples and illustrations.
3. Write an autobiographical sketch in which you present and analyze games that you have played. Assume Berne's definition of game.

4. Compare or contrast Berne's analysis of human motivation and conduct with the position of a more conventional analysis of human conduct as illustrated by Norman Vincent Peale or Reverend Billy Graham.

5. Write a parody of Berne's presentation. Find copies of various college humor magazines or James Thurber for examples of parody.

Germaine Greer

from The Female Eunuch

The Stereotype

In that mysterious dimension where the body meets the soul the
stereotype is born and has her being. She is more body than soul, more
soul than mind. To her belongs all that is beautiful, even the very word
beauty itself. All that exists, exists to beautify her. The sun shines only
to burnish her skin and gild her hair; the wind blows only to whip up the
color in her cheeks; the sea strives to bathe her; flowers die gladly so that
her skin may luxuriate in their essence. She is the crown of creation, the
masterpiece. The depths of the sea are ransacked for pearl and coral to
deck her; the bowels of the earth are laid open that she might wear gold,
sapphires, diamonds and rubies. Baby seals are battered with staves,
unborn lambs ripped from their mothers' wombs, millions of moles,
muskrats, squirrels, minks, ermines, foxes, beavers, chinchillas, ocelots,
lynxes, and other small and lovely creatures die untimely deaths that
she might have furs. Egrets, ostriches and peacocks, butterflies and
beetles yield her their plumage. Men risk their lives hunting leopards
for her coats, and crocodiles for her handbags and shoes. Millions of
silkworms offer her their yellow labors; even the seamstresses roll seams
and whip lace by hand, so that she might be clad in the best that money
can buy.

The men of our civilization have stripped themselves of the fineries
of the earth so that they might work more freely to plunder the universe
for treasures to deck my lady in. New raw materials, new processes,
new machines are all brought into her service. My lady must therefore
be the chief spender as well as the chief symbol of spending ability and
monetary success. While her mate toils in his factory, she totters about
the smartest streets and plushiest hotels with his fortune upon her back

and bosom, fingers and wrists, continuing that essential expenditure in his house which is her frame and her setting, enjoying that silken idleness which is the necessary condition of maintaining her mate's prestige and her qualification to demonstrate it. Once upon a time only the aristocratic lady could lay claim to the title of crown of creation: only her hands were white enough, her feet tiny enough, her waist narrow enough, her hair long and golden enough; but every well-to-do burgher's wife set herself up to ape my lady and to follow fashion, until my lady was forced to set herself out like a gilded doll overlaid with monstrous rubies and pearls like pigeon's eggs. Nowadays the Queen of England still considers it part of her royal female role to sport as much of the family jewelry as she can manage at any one time on all public occasions, although the male monarchs have escaped such showcase duty, which devolves exclusively upon their wives.

At the same time as woman was becoming the showcase for wealth and caste, while men were slipping into relative anonymity and "handsome is as handsome does," she was emerging as the central emblem of western art. For the Greeks the male and female body had beauty of a human, not necessarily a sexual, kind; indeed they may have marginally favored the young male form as the most powerful and perfectly proportioned. Likewise the Romans showed no bias towards the depiction of femininity in their predominantly monumental art. In the Renaissance the female form began to predominate, not only as the mother in the predominant emblem of *madonna col bambino,* but as an aesthetic study in herself. At first naked female forms took their chances in crowd scenes or diptychs of Adam and Eve, but gradually Venus claims ascendancy, Mary Magdalene ceases to be wizened and emaciated, and becomes nubile and ecstatic, portraits of anonymous young women, chosen only for their prettiness, begin to appear, are gradually disrobed, and renamed Flora or Primavera. Painters begin to paint their own wives and mistresses and royal consorts as voluptuous beauties, divesting them of their clothes if desirable, but not of their jewelry. Susanna keeps her bracelets on in the bath, and Hélène Fourment keeps ahold of her fur as well!

What happened to women in painting happened to her in poetry as well. Her beauty was celebrated in terms of the riches which clustered around her: her hair was gold wires, her brow ivory, her lips ruby, her teeth gates of pearl, her breasts alabaster veined with lapis lazuli, her eyes as black as jet. The fragility of her loveliness was emphasized by the inevitable comparisons with the rose, and she was urged to employ her beauty in love-making before it withered on the stem. She was for consumption; other sorts of imagery spoke of her in terms of cherries and cream, lips as sweet as honey and skin white as milk, breasts like cream uncrudded, hard as apples. Some celebrations yearned over her finery as well, her lawn more transparent than morning mist, her lace as delicate as gossamer, the baubles that she toyed with and the favors that she gave. Even now we find the thriller hero describing his classy dames' elegant suits, cheeky hats, well-chosen accessories and foot-wear; the imagery no longer dwells on jewels and flowers but the con-sumer emphasis is the same. The mousy secretary blossoms into the feminine stereotype when she reddens her lips, lets down her hair, and puts on something frilly.

Nowadays women are not expected, unless they are Paola di Liegi 5 or Jackie Onassis, and then only on gala occasions, to appear with a king's ransom deployed upon their bodies, but they are required to look ex-pensive, fashionable, well-groomed, and not to be seen in the same dress twice. If the duty of the few may have become less onerous, it has also become the duty of the many. The stereotype marshals an army of serv-ants. She is supplied with cosmetics, underwear, foundation garments, stockings, wigs, postiches and hairdressing as well as her outer garments, her jewels and furs. The effect is to be built up layer by layer, and it is expensive. Splendor has given way to fit, line and cut. The spirit of com-petition must be kept up, as more and more women struggle towards the top drawer, so that the fashion industry can rely upon an expanding market. Poorer women fake it, ape it, pick up on the fashions a season too late, use crude effects, mistaking the line, the sheen, the gloss of the high-class article for a garish simulacrum. The business is so complex that it must be handled by an expert. The paragons of the stereotype must be dressed, coifed and painted by the experts and the style-setters, although they may be encouraged to give heart to the housewives studying their lives in pulp magazines by claiming a lifelong fidelity to their own hair and soap and water. The boast is more usually discouraging than other-wise, unfortunately.

As long as she is young and personable, every woman may cherish 6 the dream that she may leap up the social ladder and dim the sheen of luxury by sheer natural loveliness; the few examples of such a feat are kept before the eye of the public. Fired with hope, optimism and ambition, young women study the latest forms of the stereotype, set out in *Vogue*, *Nova*, *Queen* and other glossies, where the mannequins stare from among the advertisements for fabulous real estate, furs and jewels. Nowadays the uniformity of the year's fashions is severely affected by the emergence of the pert female designers who direct their appeal to the working girl, emphasizing variety, comfort, and simple, striking effects. There is no longer a single face of the year: even Twiggy has had to withdraw into marketing and rationed personal appearances, while the Shrimp works mostly in New York. Nevertheless the stereotype is still supreme. She has simply allowed herself a little more variation.

The stereotype is the Eternal Feminine. She is the Sexual Object   7 sought by all men, and by all women. She is of neither sex, for she has herself no sex at all. Her value is solely attested by the demand she excites in others. All she must contribute is her existence. She need achieve nothing, for she is the reward of achievement. She need never give positive evidence of her moral character because virtue is assumed from her loveliness, and her passivity. If any man who has no right to her be found with her she will not be punished, for she is morally neuter. The matter is solely one of male rivalry. Innocently she may drive men to madness and war. The more trouble she can cause, the more her stocks go up, for possession of her means more the more demand she excites. Nobody wants a girl whose beauty is imperceptible to all but him; and so men welcome the stereotype because it directs their taste into the most commonly recognized areas of value, although they may protest because some aspects of it do not tally with their fetishes. There is scope in the stereotype's variety for most fetishes. The leg man may follow miniskirts, the tit man can encourage see-through blouses and plunging necklines, although the man who likes fat women may feel constrained to enjoy them in secret. There are stringent limits to the variations on the stereotype, for nothing must interfere with her function as sex object. She may wear leather, as long as she cannot actually handle a motorbike: she may wear rubber, but it ought not to indicate that she is an expert diver or waterskier. If she wears athletic clothes the purpose is to underline her unathleticism. She may sit astride a horse, looking soft and curvy, but she must not crouch over its neck with her rump in the air.

Because she is the emblem of spending ability and the chief spender,   8 she is also the most effective seller of this world's goods. Every survey ever held has shown that the image of an attractive woman is the most effective advertising gimmick. She may sit astride the mudguard of a new car, or step into it ablaze with jewels; she may lie at a man's feet stroking his new socks; she may hold the petrol pump in a challenging pose, or dance through woodland glades in slow motion in all the glory of a new shampoo; whatever she does her image sells. The gynolatry of our civilization is written large upon its face, upon hoardings, cinema screens, television, newspapers, magazines, tins, packets, cartons, bottles, all consecrated to the reigning deity, the female fetish. Her dominion must not be thought to entail the rule of women, for she is not a woman. Her glossy lips and mat complexion, her unfocused eyes and flawless fingers, her extraordinary hair all floating and shining, curling and gleaming, reveal the inhuman triumph of cosmetics, lighting, focusing and printing, cropping and composition. She sleeps unruffled, her lips red and juicy and closed, her eyes as crisp and black as if new painted, and her false lashes immaculately curled. Even when she washes her face with a new and creamier toilet soap her expression is as tranquil and vacant and her paint as flawless as ever. If ever she should appear tousled and troubled, her features are miraculously smoothed to their proper veneer by a new washing powder or a bouillon cube. For she is a doll: weeping, pouting or smiling, running or reclining, she is a doll. She is an idol, formed of the concatenation of lines and masses, signifying the lineaments of satisfied impotence.

Her essential quality is castratedness. She absolutely must be young, her body hairless, her flesh buoyant, and *she must not have a sexual organ*. No musculature must distort the smoothness of the lines of her body, although she may be painfully slender or warmly cuddly. Her expression must betray no hint of humor, curiosity or intelligence, although it may signify hauteur to an extent that is actually absurd, or smoldering lust, very feebly signified by drooping eyes and a sullen mouth (for the stereotype's lust equals irrational submission), or, most commonly, vivacity and idiot happiness. Seeing that the world despoils itself for this creature's benefit, she must be happy; the entire structure would topple if she were not. So the image of woman appears plastered on every surface imaginable, smiling interminably. An apple pie evokes a glance of tender beatitude, a washing machine causes hilarity, a cheap box of chocolates brings forth meltingly joyous gratitude, a Coke is the cause of a rictus of unutterable brilliance, even a new stick-on bandage is saluted by a smirk of satisfaction. A real woman licks her lips and opens her mouth and flashes her teeth when photographers appear: *she* must arrive at the premiere of her husband's film in a paroxysm of delight, or his success might be murmured about. The occupational hazard of being a Playboy Bunny is the aching facial muscles brought on by the obligatory smiles.

So what is the beef? Maybe I couldn't make it. Maybe I don't have a pretty smile, good teeth, nice tits, long legs, a cheeky arse, a sexy voice. Maybe I don't know how to handle men and increase my market value, so that the rewards due to the feminine will accrue to me. Then again, maybe I'm sick of the masquerade. I'm sick of pretending eternal youth. I'm sick of belying my own intelligence, my own will, my own sex. I'm sick of peering at the world through false eyelashes, so everything I see is mixed with a shadow of bought hairs; I'm sick of weighting my head with a dead mane, unable to move my neck freely, terrified of rain, of wind, of dancing too vigorously in case I sweat into my lacquered curls. I'm sick of the Powder Room. I'm sick of pretending that some fatuous male's self-important pronouncements are the objects of my undivided attention, I'm sick of going to films and plays when someone else wants to, and sick of having no opinions of my own about either. I'm sick of being a transvestite. I refuse to be a female impersonator. I am a woman, not a castrate. . . .

Energy

Energy is the power that drives every human being. It is not lost by exertion but maintained by it, for it is a faculty of the psyche. It is driven to perverted manifestations by curbs and checks. Like the motive force that drives the car along the highway, when it meets with an obstacle it turns to destructive force and shakes its source to pieces. It is not too hard to point out to the averagely perceptive human being that women have plenty of the destructive kind of energy, but far fewer people can see that women's destructiveness is creativity turned in upon itself by constant frustration. Nervous diseases, painful menstruation, unwanted pregnancies, accidents of all kinds, are all evidence of women's energy destroying them. It extends beyond them wreaking havoc with the personalities and achievements of others, especially their husbands and their children. That is not to say that women must hate all their relatives, but that if children are presented to women as a duty and marriage as an inescapable yoke, then the more energy they have the more they will fret and chafe, tearing themselves and their dependants to pieces. When children are falsely presented to women as their only significant contribution, the proper expression of their creativity and their lives' work, the children and their mothers suffer for it. 11

Although many people will see the justice of this description of the perversion of female energy, they will not so easily see that the solution does not lie in offering adult women other alternatives besides home and children and all that. The adult woman has already established a pattern of perversity in the expression of her desires and motives which ought to fit her for the distorted version of motherhood: it will not disappear if she is allowed alternatives. Any substituted aim is likely to be followed in a "feminine" way, that is, servilely, dishonestly, inefficiently, inconsistently. In most cases women are not offered a genuine alternative to repressive duties and responsibilities: most would happily give up unskilled labor in a factory or the tedium of office work for the more 12 "natural" tedium of a modern household, because their energies are so thwarted by the usual kinds of female work that they imagine even housework would be a preferable alternative. Women who are offered education are offered a genuine alternative, insofar as they are offered genuine education, a rare commodity in these days of universal induction. And yet, when they were offered education at first, the result was not the creation of an instant race of superwomen. This is one contemporary's account of the first female undergraduates, and university teachers will recognize a familiar phenomenon:

> At lectures women students are models of attention and industry; perhaps they even apply themselves too much to carrying home in black and white what they have heard. They generally occupy the front seats because they enter their names early and then because they arrive early, well before the beginning of the lectures. Only this fact is noticeable, that often they merely give a superficial glance at the preparations that the professor passes around; sometimes they even pass them on to their neighbors without even looking at them; a longer examination would hinder their taking notes.

What this rather prejudiced observer noticed is real enough: the girls *13* were diligent, even too diligent, but their efforts were expended on mistaken goals. They were anxious to please, to pick up everything that they were told, but the preparations handed around by the lecturer were the real subject of the lecture, and in that they were not interested at all. Their energy is all expended on conforming with disciplinary and other requirements, not in gratifying their own curiosity about the subject that they are studying, and so most of it is misdirected into meaningless assiduity. This phenomenon is still very common among female students, who are forming a large proportion of the arts intake at universities, and dominating the teaching profession as a result. The process is clearly one of diminishing returns: the servile induce servility to teach the servile, in a realm where the unknown ought to be continually assailed with all the human faculties; education cannot be, and has never been, a matter of obedience. It is not surprising then that women seldom make the scientific advances, but rather serve men as laboratory assistants, working under direction: it is merely a continuation of the same phenomenon that we observed in their undergraduate days. By the time they have come to apply for entrance to a university the pattern of their useless deflection of energy is already set. In the very great majority of cases they have not retained enough drive to desire to qualify themselves any further; the minority who go to university do so too often as a response to guidance and pressure from their mistresses at school, still not knowing what the real point is, still not interested in developing their own potential, at most hoping for a good degree and a qualification to join the Cinderella profession of teaching. The degree of satisfaction gained by women following this pattern is very slight; we are not surprised to find that many of them think of even their professional life either as a stop-gap or an indirect qualification for marriage.

All the blanket objections to women in professions may be understood   14
as ways of stating this basic situation. They appear to be the judgments of prejudice, and, insofar as they adduce no other cause than sex, we must admit that they are. However, unless feminists admit that the phenomena described by critics of women's performance in industry, offices, schoolrooms, trade unions and in the arts and sciences are real, they must fail to identify the problem, and therefore to solve it. It is true that opportunities have been made available to women far beyond their desires to use them. It is also true that the women who avail themselves of opportunities too often do so in a feminine, filial, servile fashion. It must be understood that it will not suffice to encourage women to use an initiative that they have not got, just as it is useless to revile them for not having it. We must endeavor to understand how it is that women's energy is systematically deflected from birth to puberty, so that when they come to maturity they have only fitful resource and creativity.

In speaking of energy, I have had to use terms like resource, applica-   15
tion, initiative, ambition, desire, motive, terms which have a masculine ring, because they convey marginal meanings which are incompatible with femininity. It is often falsely assumed, even by feminists, that sexuality is the enemy of the female who really wants to develop these aspects of her personality, and this is perhaps the most misleading aspect of movements like the National Organization of Women. It was not the insistence upon her sex that weakened the American woman student's desire to make something of her education, but the insistence upon a *passive* sexual *role*. In fact the chief instrument in the deflection and perversion of female energy is the denial of female sexuality for the substitution of femininity or sexlessness. For, no matter which theory of the energy of personality we accept, it is inseparable from sexuality. McDougall called it *élan vital,* Jung and Reich called it libido, Janet called it tension, Head called it vigilance, Flügel called it orectic energy. All the terms amount to the same thing. One of the errors in the traditional theory is that it presupposes a sort of capitalist system of energy, as a kind of substance which must be wisely invested and not spent all at once. In fact, as we

ought to know from the concept of energy we have derived from physics, energy cannot be lost but only converted or deflected. Freud saw that repression employs energy which might otherwise be expressed in creative action: what happens to the female is that her energy is deflected by the denial of her sexuality into a continuous and eventually irreversible system of repression. The women students expended as much energy taking notes and being early and attentive to lectures as their male counterparts did in exploring the subject: in the laboratory they expended it by dropping things and asking silly questions, fussing and fumbling. Male energy is contoured and deformed too, but in a different way, so that it becomes aggression and competitiveness. The female's fate is to become deformed and debilitated by the destructive action of energy upon the self, because she is deprived of scope and contacts with external reality upon which to exercise herself.

The acts of sex are themselves forms of inquiry, as the old euphemism 16 "carnal knowledge" makes clear: it is exactly the element of quest in her sexuality which the female is taught to deny. She is not only taught to deny it in her sexual contacts, but (for in some subliminal way the connection is understood) in all her contacts, from infancy onward, so that when she becomes aware of her sex the pattern has sufficient force of inertia to prevail over new forms of desire and curiosity. This is the condition which is meant by the term *female eunuch.* In traditional psychological theory, which is after all only another way of describing and rationalizing the status quo, the desexualization of women is illustrated in the Freudian theory of the female sex as lacking a sexual organ. Freud may have not intended his formulations to have been taken as statements of natural laws, but merely as coherent descriptions of contingent facts in a new and valuably revealing terminology; nevertheless he did say:

> Indeed, if we were able to give a more definite connotation to the concept of "masculine" and "feminine," it would also be possible to maintain that libido is invariably and necessarily of a masculine nature, whether it occurs in men or women, and irrespectively of whether its object is a man or a woman.

If we are to insist on the contingency of feminine characteristics as the 17 product of conditioning, we will have to argue that the masculine-feminine polarity is actual enough, but not necessary. We will have to reject the polarity of definite terms, which are always artificial, and strive for the freedom to move within indefinite terms. On these grounds we can, indeed we must, reject femininity as meaning *without libido,* and therefore incomplete, subhuman, a cultural reduction of human possibilities, and rely upon the indefinite term female, which retains the possibility of female libido. . . .

QUESTIONS AND EXERCISES

Vocabulary

1. Define or explain each of the following terms:

    eunuch   hauteur (9)
    stereotype   rictus (9)
    caste (3)   fatuous (10)
    gala (5)   transvestite (10)
    paragon (5)   assiduity (13)
    neuter (7)   adduce (14)
    fetishes (7)   euphemism (16)
    gynolatry (8)   subliminal (16)
    concatenation (8)

Rhetoric

2. What is the allusion in ". . . she was urged to employ her beauty in love-making before it withered on the stem."? (4)
3. Why could the following statement be a paradox? "Her essential quality is castratedness."
4. What level of diction is "So what is the beef"? (10)
5. What rhetorical device is used in paragraph 10?
6. Find the simile in paragraph 11.
7. Analyze the rhetoric in: "The female's fate is to be deformed and debilitated by the destructive action of energy upon the self, because she is deprived of scope and contacts with external reality upon which to exercise herself." (15)
8. Why is "carnal knowledge" euphemistic?
9. Why is the title an oxymoron?

Theme

10. Summarize Greer's definition of female eunuch (16).
11. Was Freud a male chauvinist? Explain. (16)
12. Is there any logical flaw in Greer's argument?
13. Discuss the range of subjects which are used to support the case Greer makes.
14. Point out any appeals to emotion that are made.
15. What is most convincing about her presentation? Least convincing?

Topics and Assignments for Composition

1. Pick a stereotype with which you are familiar and write a short explanation of the cause of it.
2. Write an essay in which you attempt to destroy a stereotype.
3. Research briefly Freud's attitude toward and relationship with women. Write a short objective report of your research.

Ashley Montagu

On Tribalism Today

Tribalism is the practice of the belief that one's own tribe is better than   *1*
or superior to the tribes of others. It is a belief which is supported and
reinforced by sacred rites and secular rituals, serving to identify the member with the group in peace, and to unify the whole tribe in times of stress
or conflict. Not all human populations are tribes, and not all tribes consider themselves to be better than or superior to other peoples.

With their highly elaborated techniques for scapegoating and their   *2*
remarkable ability for rationalization, the civilized peoples of the world
have scornfully relegated tribalism to "primitive" peoples, while considering themselves wholly exempt from such "barbarism."

The truth, however, is that the societies in which tribalism flourishes in   *3*
its most dangerously developed forms are the societies which are among
the most technologically highly developed nations in the world. In no
"primitive" societies are such tribalistic excesses of belief and conduct
practised as among the great nations of the western world, and in civilized
nations generally, whether of the western world, the Middle East or the
Far East. The tribal gods of civilized peoples are among the most vicious,
and upon a scale surpassing all others, the most destructive in the world.

Tribalism is not the less tribalism when it is called "nationalism," or   *4*
when the weakminded and brainwashed join together to make up in
quantity what they lack in quality, and call it "patriotism," that last
refuge, as Dr. Samuel Johnson described it, of the scoundrel.

Tribalism by elevating one's own group above that of others essentially   *5*
represents a denial of the humanity of others. It produces isolationism,
clannishness, and the rejection of "outsiders." It emphasizes differences
in ways such that difference becomes identified with inferiority. It makes
a virtue of exclusiveness and institutionalizes ethnocentrism and xeno-

"On Tribalism Today" by Ashley Montagu. In VISTA, November-December
1968 and reprinted with permission.

phobia. It creates and reenforces the anxieties of the weak and the insecure by providing them with the rationalizations which, in a sort of self-fulfilling prophecy, make tribalism their main defense against the malignant and evil spirits which are alleged to lurk everywhere, and which threaten the tribesman's existence.

In such an atmosphere the tribal gods not only require the ceremonial   6
and ritual incantations of allegiance, but they must also be propitiated by the offerance, every so often, of sacrificial victims. The witch doctors, in the form of such demagogues as the late Senator Joseph McCarthy, as well as the official and unofficial bodies of inquisitors, have no difficulty in fastening upon their victims. The method is much the same as that which was set out for the use of witch-hunters in that notorious handbook on the subject, the *Malleus Maleficarum,* 1490. To the question "Why a greater number of witches are found in the fragile feminine sex than among men," the answer was as simple as it was succinct. Said the authorities, "It is indeed a fact that it were idle to contradict, since it is accredited by actual experience, apart from the testimony of credible witnesses" (Question 6, Part I).

The accusation is sufficient evidence for the tribalist. The evil he per   7
ceives in the "other" represents his own insecurities and bad conscience projected upon the "other." Exclusion or elimination of the other who, by his very being, and in ways which are all the more dangerous because they cannot be formulated, threaten one's own existence and that of one's tribal blood brothers.

In our own time we have witnessed some of the horrible consequences   8
of tribalism among civilized nations. The pseudo-philosopher of The Third Reich, Alfred Rosenberg, described the tribalistic spirit of the "Herrenvolk" in words to which no member of the most primitive tribalistic societies could take exception. Said Rosenberg, "A nation is constituted by the predominance of a definite character formed by its blood, language, geographical environment, and the sense of a united political destiny. These last constituents are not, however, definitive; the decisive element in a nation is its blood. In the first awakening of a people, great poets and heroes disclose themselves to us as the incorporation of the eternal values of a particular blood soul. I believe that this recognition of the profound significance of blood is now mysteriously encircling our planet, irresistibly gripping one nation after another" (*Vossiche Zeitung,* 3 September 1933).

The rites, regalia, rituals, giant flag-bedecked rallies, marches, patriotic   9
music, and all the paraphernalia designed to produce the amalgamation of each in the blood brotherhood of the tribe, was only too tragically effective in Hitler's Germany. This Voodoo possession that turned so many

Germans into indescribable monsters, in the name of the "Fatherland," constitutes perhaps the most frightful example of the ghastliness to which tribalism can lead.

In Africa, in which so many new independent nations have come into   *10* being, tribalism is rife. The tragedy of the Congo, and the genocidal war of Nigeria against the Ibo of Biafra are terrible object lessons in the *schrecklichkeit* of contemporary tribalism.

The tribalism of the whites in South Africa and the whites of Rhodesia   *11* has become a way of life for whole populations. Here, the whites have, by force of arms, elected themselves the "Superior Race," and have relegated all nonwhites to the substatus of the "Inferior Race." Racism is, of course, a form of tribalism.

It is here very necessary to make the point that not all tribes are   *12* tribalistic. The Bushmen of South Africa, the Australian aborigines, and the Pueblo Indians, for example, were each constituted of a number of tribes, but they did not engage in intertribal hostilities or in superpatriot displays of ferocity.

Tribalism exists when a people or a group elevates itself or distin-   *13* guishes itself in such a manner that it declares all others "off-limits," rigidly enforcing its exclusiveness, and by saber-rattling and jingoism warning all others of the dire consequences to them of any infringements of their rights. The tribalistic psychosis was perfectly enshrined in that patriotic ditty, so popular during the heyday of the British Empire:

> We don't want to fight
> But By Jingo if we do,
> We've got the ships,
> We've got the men,
> We've got the money, too.

Very few tribes have ever achieved the tribalism of the British during   *14* the height of the British Empire. It is significant that with the deliberate breakup of the Empire the British have become among the least tribalistic of peoples. There is, perhaps, a lesson to be learned here: When the tribal gods decay, and their power to whip the people up into a patriotic frenzy is lost, the people are content to live at peace with themselves and with their neighbors.

It is usually a small but powerful group, with not the least interest in   *15* peace, but with a hunger for power, who are responsible for beating the tribal drums and arousing the people to the proper pitch of excitement, of patriotic fervor, that is, to tribalistic mania.

Perhaps the most tribalistic people in the world today is the American.   *16*

Americans have more tribal gods to worship and more holidays during which to burn incense before their shrines than any other people in the western world, and probably any people anywhere in the contemporary world. With the bogeymen of the Russian and Chinese communists to bedevil them, Americans are now more tribalistic than ever, so that any opportunistic self-seeking demagogue can whip them up to the most calamitously destructive behavior. Vietnam, it may be safely predicted, will no more prove a lesson to Americans in the futility and wickedness of tribalism than will the next contrived assault upon "our external enemies."

The tragedy of tribalism is that it is not the creation of external enemies 17 but of internal enemies, of tribal "leaders," "fuehrers," who have generally achieved their position of "leadership" by means not genuinely designed to present the people with a fair choice. The result is "leaders" who achieve power by the abuse of power, and continue to abuse that power upon an even larger scale once they are in office.

Witch-doctors sometimes have this power thrust upon them, as among 18 the Chukchee of Siberia who, often unwillingly, qualify for the office of Shaman by the development of some hysteroid form of behavior. Others seek such power out. In any event, the frequent history of such witch-doctors, whether in "primitive" or in civilized societies (when they are called "Statesmen") is that however corrupt they may have been before achieving office, they tend to become further corrupted by the power that is placed in their hands.

Tribalism is just what such "leaders" batten on. One has only to read 19 Hitler's *Mein Kampf*, reeking as it does from every page with cynical contempt for the masses, to wonder what it is that makes those who believe in "group solidarity" thirst to abdicate their will to that of a "leader."

Erich Fromm gave the most cogent answer to that question years ago 20 in his seminal book, *Escape From Freedom*. Those who are afraid of freedom, who are unprepared to accept responsibilities, would much rather have someone else assume those responsibilities for them, would much rather lean on a group as a rod, and draw the strength that they individually lack vicariously from membership in the group. Hence, the popularity of such groups as the American Legion, Veterans of Foreign Wars, Masons, Rotarians, Daughters of the American Revolution, and innumerable others of a similar sort.

Whatever the external causes the "joiners" adopt tribalism, in one or 21 other of its forms, as a means of fortifying themselves. They may be the "superiors" who reject the "others," or they may be the "inferiors" who feel rejected. In either case they will often feel forced to elevate their separateness into a shrine at which they can worship their tribal gods.

An example of tribalism into which people are sometimes forced by the   *22*
exclusiveness and discrimination that has been practised against them is
provided by the recent history of the American Negro. Indeed, many
American Negroes have now come to reject that description of themselves, and prefer to be called, and call themselves, Afro-Americans.
They regard the term "Negro" as a pejorative one. That term, in their
view, fails to make sufficient reference to the tribal origins of Blacks.
Hence, in reaction to white exclusivism, which has prevented them from
becoming full Americans, they propose to return to their African past as
something with which they can genuinely identify. Hence, the prolifera-
tion of courses on African history, African art, African languages,
African hairdress, and African attire, all being offered as means of accomplishing what American whites have for the most part denied the American Blacks: a self-image they can respect, and a cultural background to
which they can look with pride, and from which they can go forward as a
separate but equal tribe within the United States

Desirable as all these things are, and important as I for one regard the   *23*
teaching of African history *to all students,* and understandable as the
American Negro's development of an interest in his cultural origins may
be, that interest seems to me to have been generated by and for the wrong
reasons. What that reaction represents is little more than a counter-
reaction to the tribalism of the white. This seems to me a tragic folly. By
all means let us have the fullest teaching of all things African. As an
anthropologist I can vouch for both the value and the quality of African
culture, but let no one make the mistake of assuming that the resort to
tribalism on the part of the American Negro is going to solve anyone's
problems, any more than tribalism anywhere in the world has solved any
problem.

Surely, the proper approach in the contemporary world to the solution   *24*
of the problems of group misunderstanding and group conflict is not
separatism and the creation of barriers, but the breaking down of the
sense of tribalism, of separateness, of barriers; not the creation of new
nations, but the creation of new commonwealths of nations with the ideals
of amity, not the enmity, of nations in view, until the objective is achieved
of a genuinely functioning United Nations.

The followers of Martin Luther King carried signs which stated simply,   *25*
"I am a man." Not a black man, not a white man, not a lodge man, not a
separate man—just a man. *That,* being a man, is responsibility enough.
And the question of questions is not whether this people is better than
others, or that the member of such and such a group is better than the
member of other groups, but whether the individual in any and every

group, by virtue of the fact that he is a man, has a right to his birthright: the optimum fulfillment of his potentialities as a human being.

If, as there are, many tribalists who not only refuse to grant, but do everything in their power to abort, the right to human development of millions of their fellow men, counter-tribalism is not going to cure them of *their* tribalism; it is much more likely to solidify it and make it more intransigent. It is true that it is difficult and disheartening to talk to so many deaf ears for so long with so little result, and not lose patience, and it is perhaps too easy for us who are not Negroes to talk of patience. How long is "patience"? Nevertheless, it is necessary for those of us who believe that tribalism is evil and the wrong approach to what is called "the race problem" or "the Negro problem" to make the case against tribalism unequivocally clear. 26

There is neither a "race" nor a "Negro" problem, but there very definitely is a white man problem, and he, the white man, is the Negro's problem. Until the problem of white tribalism is solved we shall make no significant progress in human relations, in so-called "race relations." The "white man" problem will not be solved by affording him an even more defined and delimited segregate as a whetstone upon which to sharpen his wits for further scapegoating. 27

It is also true that one of the few things that the white man understands is physical force. This precisely is the reason why the white man should not be provided with any further opportunities for the exercise of that dreadful understanding. 28

It should be abundantly clear from the long, and particularly the recent, history of tribalism that it constitutes a highly destructive form of group behavior which in the contemporary world should receive every possible kind of discouragement. The brainwashed flag-waving patriot, as a consequence of repeated conditionings, is automatically bathed in a broth of glandular secretions and stimulated to neuro-muscular reactions at the very sight of "the flag" or upon hearing any of the tribal anthems. He will react in the same way when "the honor" of his tribe is challenged, and will think of such neuro-humoral reactions as "love of country," or whatever other substitute for thinking with which he may be inclined to react. The tribalist may genuinely believe that he loves his country, and therein lies the great danger of such beliefs, for in the name of "love of country" he may do his country irreparable harm. 29

Man may not learn from history, nonetheless it is evident to some that in the recent history of mankind, at any rate, it has been the tribalistic mentality that has created so much havoc in the world. The English "Hang the Kaiser," the German "Gott Strafe England," the English "A Land Fit For Heroes," the American "The World Made Safe for Democ- 30 racy,"—all tribalistic shibboleths of the First World War, not one of which was realized, and only for the most part the contraries were established, haunt the memories of those who lived through that unspeakable and wholly unnecessary slaughter of the innocents.

The fabricated atrocity stories were of the most evil and malignant kind. In the Second World War the fabrications became the terrible realities. The tribesmen came to believe the lies their leaders had indoctrinated them with, and given the opportunity avenged themselves upon the unspeakable enemy that could be guilty of such crimes. *31*

The tribalistic psychosis is such that it readies the tribalistically conditioned mind to receive without critical examination any statement which calls upon it for instantaneous tribalistic reaction. The critic, indeed, under such conditions is considered suspect, disloyal, and anathema. During World War I Bertrand Russell was jailed for protesting the lies with which the tribal leaders of England were deceiving the British public. During recent days he has been ridiculed and condemned for initiating an international examination of the guilt of Mr. Johnson in connection with the war in Vietnam. The tribalists, of course, would far prefer that nothing at all were said upon such matters if it cannot be put in supportive tribalistic language. It matters not that Russell, in every position he adopted and courageously stood by in spite of the barking of all the dogs of St. Ernulphus, during the First and Second World Wars, and in connection with the Vietnam war, was invariably right. His views were in opposition to those of the tribalists, and he therefore had to be repudiated and chastized. *32*

I cite the case of Bertrand Russell because he is indisputably one of the great benefactors of humanity. He stands as representative of many others of perhaps lesser fame, who have often been made to suffer ever greater injustices and indignities than those visited by the tribalists upon Russell. *33*

The beat of the tribal drums is recognized for what it is by those who have retained their ability to think for themselves. They decline to yield to the hypnotic effect of the martial clamor, to fall in and march with the herd. It is a kind of independence of spirit the world stands much in need of. While there are today more individuals of this genre than ever before, we need to produce more of them if we are ever to be rid of the spirit of tribalism. How may this be accomplished? Principally, I would answer, through education in the schools. *34*

But how is such education to be introduced into the schools? Are not schools among the most tribalistic of institutions as they are today constituted? They are, indeed, and as long as they continue to be organized *35* as they are and motivated by their present value-system, there is little hope to be expected from this quarter.

Where, then, is the requisite education to come from? I think it must *36* continue to come where it has always come from, namely, from such teachers outside the schools as Bertrand Russell, Martin Luther King, Albert Schweitzer, and those who write and speak on social, political, international, and related problems; those, in short, who freely discuss the tribalism of our day, and what, if anything, can be done about it. They are the people who essentially clarify the issues, and thus make it possible for the individual to judge them on their merits, and to arrive at his own decisions of conscience in regard to them.

Everything should be done to encourage freedom of debate and discus- *37* sion in the schools and the colleges, and, indeed, everywhere possible.

If we can secure a sufficiently wide discussion on tribalism, that will, *38* I believe, more than anything else, open the understanding of people to its dangers, and constitute, at least, a first step in the right direction.

QUESTIONS AND EXERCISES

Vocabulary

1. Define or explain each of the following terms:

tribalism (1)	psychosis (13)
rites (1)	hysteroid (18)
scapegoating (2)	batten (19)
rationalization (2)	cynical (19)
ethnocentrism (5)	seminal (20)
xenophobia (5)	pejorative (22)
incantation (6)	proliferation (22)
propitiated (6)	anthropologist (23)
demagogues (6)	amity (24)
succinct (6)	enmity (24)
regalia (9)	optimum (25)
paraphernalia (9)	intransigent (26)
amalgamation (9)	neuro-muscular (29)
genocidal (10)	havoc (30)
aborigines (12)	anathema (32)

2. Identify or explain each of the following terms or people:

Dr. Samuel Johnson (4)	*schrecklichkeit* (10)
Senator Joseph McCarthy (6)	jingoism (13)

Malleus Maleficarum (6)   "feuhrers" (17)
"Herrenvolk" (8)   Bertrand Russell (32)
Voodoo (9)   St. Ernulphus (32)

Rhetoric

3. What is the main unifying theme in this essay?
4. Most of the paragraphs are shorter than one would expect for an article of this nature. What is a plausible explanation for the shorter paragraph?
5. The total essay is developed by a combination of techniques, the dominant ones being definition, example, illustration, and analysis. Further, the individual paragraphs are developed by a variety of techniques. Comment on the method of development in any three paragraphs.
6. Find the example of a hyperbole in paragraph 28.
7. In paragraph 29 Montagu indulges in a possible mild invective. Find the example and decide whether it is, in fact, invective or a factual description. How does one resolve such a question?

Theme

8. What methods of definition can you identify in this essay (synonym, example and illustration, analysis, etc.)?
9. What types of definitions can you identify in the essay (formal, dictionary, stipulative, persuasive, etc.)?
10. Some of Montagu's opinions are revealed by implication rather than by direct statement. Find several of these implied opinions.

Topics and Assignments for Composition

1. In a sentence for each, define "tribalism" by synonym, example, and analysis.
2. Using a combination of methods and types of definitions, write a paragraph in which you develop an extended definition of tribalism.
3. Choose an abstract idea such as honesty, justice, Americanism, or loyalty, and in a paragraph develop a persuasive or stipulative, extended definition.
4. Write an essay using the overall unifying technique of definition.

Kenneth MacCorquodale

Behaviorism is a Humanism

Behaviorism is simply the application of the methods of experimental   *1*
science to the behavior of organisms, an application that was inevitable
once the tremendous power of these methods became evident in the
explanation and ordering of physical, chemical, astronomical, and non-
behavioral puzzles. The methods of science give us decision rules for
distinguishing between fact and convenient fiction in nature, especially
insofar as we are concerned with causality. This characteristic com-
mends the methods of scientific observation and reasoning to the student of behavior, whose subject matter is, by long heritage, overridden
with curiosity-assuaging but utterly untestable lore. To forbid the application of science to the facts of behavior will have to be done by fiat,
not reason. Because the voice of science is itself impeccably rational,
insistently reasonable, and forever self-correcting, it cannot be deduced
out of existence. Science may be unwelcome in the domain of human
behavior but it is reasonable all the same.

Forbidding by fiat may, of course, be based upon an understandable   *2*
first-blush feeling that it is somehow bad form, dehumanizing, and disrespectful to man to look for him in the orderly, deterministic universe
of other things in nature—or to speak of any man-in-person as an instance
of man-in-general. But the rationality and origins of man's discomfort are
somewhat puzzling. Simply looking at a man, especially with the detachment and distance of science, and reporting only what can be seen, does
not alter him in any way. It does not detract from his essence, nor deny
his uniqueness, nor destroy his integrity. The scientist cannot place man's
behavior securely within the natural order—he can only look for it there.
Man's distaste at finding himself so located is probably something he
will simply have to get used to, since it seems unlikely that he can talk

This article first appeared in THE HUMANIST March/April 1971 and is
reprinted by permission of the publisher.

his way out of it. In light of this, it is interesting that the timing of the renaissance of the third revolution of psychology coincides nicely with the rise of an impressively effective behaviorist alternative. Anguish and rage at *Walden Two* have been predicated on a respectful (and justified) suspicion that the principles that were to run this utopia, including operant conditioning, would indeed work—and that someone might just do it. The true disbeliever, however, would greet the attempt with glee, not fear, confidently anticipating its *coup de grace*.

When science discovers and enumerates the variables that control   *3* man's behavior, man does not lose his autonomy and freedom; at worst, he discovers that they had unsuspected limits. Yet he loses nothing he once had. The limits are those imposed by the laws of nature, not the laws of scientists. No scientist can actually create control, he can only reveal it.

Even so, behaviorism is not a doctrine of man's helplessness in a de-   *4* terministic world. Quite the contrary, once the variables that affect behavior are firmly identified in scientific laws, man is free at last to alter his fate—the course of his history, mind you, not his inner essence—by, literally, exercising control in manipulating the variables that are already affecting his behavior for better or for worse. He does not choose behavior directly, nor does he tinker with the machine. He controls the input, arranging for some inputs to occur and preventing others. He is free to choose rationally and effectively, just as Dostoevsky's underground man, seemingly a realist and a good behaviorist, chose to stick his tongue out—*but only on the sly!* On sober second thought, the underground man sided with Thomas Huxley after all; neither of them favored outright caprice and randomness of choice.

One apparent consequence of applying the methods of science to man's   *5* behavior is that such an application analytically disassembles the behavior and seems to destroy or ignore man's wholeness or self in doing so. In actual practice, however, although the behaviorist does indeed analyze, he does not leave man in pieces. He analyzes in order to discover and conceptualize the components and origins of behavior as an organized whole. Selves—as detached, unique, whole essences—are not, on the other hand, susceptible to scientific analysis and therefore require that some other method of inquiry be applied by scholars with other goals.

Above all, behaviorism is not really a bleak conspiracy to delimit man's   *6* choice and freedom by artificial constraint, any more than physics is a conspiracy against atoms. When poor, belabored Watson said he wanted to "control man's reactions," he was proposing not to apply psychology against man, but only to test the accuracy of his science. He did not want to make beggars and thieves; he wanted to see if it could be done. The decision to apply science, for or against, is not a scientific one, nor is it a part of the science applied. This is surely elementary and needs no further argument.

The variables that affect behavior, if left uncontrolled, may work mischievously and cruelly against man. The true authoritarian personality is the one who says: "Don't teach, don't touch, don't tinker. Let man choose, badly and stupidly and in ignorance, and live miserably. He is so gloriously free to do so. Let him." The question is, Is man free *not* to do so? Behaviorism, by locating the means of self-control outside of behavior, where they are accessible and manageable, gives man this choice. That is hardly inhumane, and hardly disrespectful of man's dignity.

It is somewhat poignant and paradoxical then that the behavioral scientist, surely a "human person," is exhorted, in the name of a doctrine that emphasizes freedom, choice, and personal respect, to desist at once —especially since the behaviorist sees the product of his own inquiry contributing precisely to man's freedom, choice, and self-respect. As a scientist, the behaviorist is himself in the humanistic traditions of inquiry, reason, and understanding. But oddly, now he is—and seemingly only for the behavioral nonce—the black sheep of the family.

QUESTIONS AND EXERCISES

Vocabulary

1. Define or explain each of the following terms:

behaviorism (1)	*coup de grace* (2)
causality (1)	caprice (4)
assuaging (1)	paradoxical (8)
fiat (2)	poignant (8)
utopia (2)	humanistic (8)

Rhetoric

2. What does the allusion to *Walden Two* signify?
3. Is there an allusion in the phrase "the true disbeliever"?
4. Point out the figure of speech in paragraph 4.
5. Who was Watson? (6)
6. What is the figure of speech found in the last sentence of the essay?

Theme

7. Explain the significance of the sentence, "No scientist can actually create control, he can only reveal it."

8. Explain the meaning of the quotation, "The true authoritarian personality is the one who says; 'Don't teach, don't touch, don't tinker. Let man choose, badly and stupidly and in ignorance, and live miserably. He is so gloriously free to do so. Let him.' " (7)
9. Against whom is MacCorquodale defending behaviorism?
10. What is the tradition of humanism?
11. In general, what is the conflict between behaviorism and humanism?

Topics and Assignments for Composition

1. In a paragraph, explain why behaviorism is a humanism.
2. In a short essay defend behaviorism against the charge that it destroys man's freedom to alter his fate.
3. Choose one of the alternatives to behaviorism and write an essay showing the advantages it has in helping man to alter his fate.
4. Research the relationship of science and behaviorism and report your findings objectively.

Student Example

What is the Establishment?

In the past few years the word Establishment, meaning the existing power structure and authority, has been used almost to the point of meaninglessness. Black power advocates and members of other minorities rail against the white racist Establishment. Student radicals want to destroy the Establishment, so-called hippies want to drop out of it, political activists, young and old, want to reform it. Military men blame it for Vietnam and other world troubles, as do war protestors. Law enforcement officials deplore its permissive attitude, rebellious churchmen, educators and students castigate it for encouraging conformity and callousness. George Wallace and Eldridge Cleaver agree that it has caused America's problems and hatreds and that it must be fought.

It seems highly unlikely that all of these people have the same idea of what the Establishment is. Nevertheless, a very general definition is necessary and possible to attempt after giving some consideration to the derivation, history, and general use of this term. First heard in England in the fifties, the Establishment referred to the British power structure: Parliament, the Prime Minister and the cabinet, the Queen and royal family, the established political parties, the courts, the military, the civil service, the financial and business Establishment, the church, Oxbridge, the unions, the nobility and all established traditions and institutions, particularly those involving the upper classes.

In the sixties the word came into general use in America, where its meaning changed somewhat. American society, generally more pluralistic and less unified than that of Great Britain, has never really had an Establishment that everyone would define as such. Basically, the American Establishment consists of three general power areas, political, economic, and social or cultural. The Political Establishment may be further divided into federal, state, and local areas of authority. Political power is vested in the President, Congress, and the courts, the civil service, political parties, and political interest groups. The military, basically under the control of governmental authorities, may be classified as a political element. All agencies, bureaus and organizations under federal control may be labeled part of the Political Establishment. State and local political authority and institutions (such as schools) over which they exercise control can also be grouped in this area.

The Economic Establishment includes major companies, businesses, corporations and financial centers. The Social or Cultural Establishment is much harder to define and is open to subjective evaluation. Usually it is agreed that major religious groups, important national organizations and powerful institutions fall into this category, although these labels are general enough to include almost anything. In addition, there are many smaller divisions, including the Literary, Educational and Artistic Establishments.

The preceding definition is comprehensive enough to cover a variety of individual interpretations. To many, the Establishment is a derogatory term used to describe a source of real or imagined oppression. Thus, the young, the black, the poor whites, the intellectuals, the left, the right, and all other minorities are protesting against what they determine to be the Establishment. To a young black man, for example, the Establishment may mean whites and Uncle Toms. To a white Southerner, it may mean Washington bureaucrats, intellectuals and Northern liberals. To a young white revolutionary, it is all existing political authority while to his college professor it is the military-industrial complex.

This diversity of definitions, aided by popular double-talk such as the Revolutionary Establishment, has made the term ambiguous, emotional and virtually useless in modern American society. It has come to mean anything powerful which one opposes, a sinister, omnipotent, almost mythical evil which must be eradicated at all costs. Clearly, it has become a catch-all phrase, stretched far beyond its original meaning. In contemporary America, the Establishment is a bland, general term which can and does mean almost anything.

Part Six:
Classification

Michael V. Kuttnauer

Logic and Logical Fallacies

Formal Logic

The Categorical Syllogism. Logic deals with arguments, good and bad. *1*
Consider the following:

> Petting is harmful to young people. It is harmful because it is a
> kind of sex act, and sex is harmful to youngsters.

This is an example of an argument. Whether it is good or bad argumentation we have yet to see, but it is an argument. It is so because it is an
inference; it has *premises* and a *conclusion.* The premises are:

> Sex is harmful to youngsters, and
> Petting is a kind of sex act.

The conclusion is:

> (Therefore) Petting is harmful to young people.

It qualifies as an argument because the conclusion is *supported* by the
premises; that is, we are asked to accept the conclusion "because (and
only because) of" the premises. Indeed, had the conclusion been asserted
alone, without the premises, it would have been appropriate to ask, "*Why*
is petting harmful to young people?" But this question really amounts
to asking, "Where is the evidence for saying that petting is bad?" or, to
use the technical language of logic, "Where are the premises that support
your claim that petting is bad?"

In sum, an argument is the process of inferring one statement (the con- *2*

Reprinted by permission of the author.

clusion) where the conclusion "follows from" or "is supported by" those premises.

Arguments are of two kinds, deductive and inductive. The differences between them are not easy to summarize briefly, but we may say now that deductive arguments support their conclusions with *necessity* – if the premises are true, that is to say, then the conclusion *must necessarily* be true – but that inductive arguments do not do so – even if the premises of an inductive argument are true, the conclusion might be false. A valid deductive argument violates none of the inference rules (see paragraph 18); it supports its conclusion with "necessity;" its premises assert in themselves what the conclusion asserts. This is not so for inductive arguments. Validity, to put it another way, describes a purely formal relationship between the premises of a deductive argument and its conclusion; *valid* means merely that the argument *form* is an acceptable one. Validity itself guarantees nothing whatever about the truth of the conclusion. In our petting example, for instance, although the truth of the conclusion may be suspect, the argument form is acceptable, is valid. But we can say that the conclusion can be false even though the argument is valid if we remember that the conclusion of a valid deductive argument "must" necessarily be true only if the premises are true. In the special event that the argument form is valid, and also the premises are true, then the argument is said to be *sound*.

Statements in standard form.

Statements, for the purposes of syllogistic logic, refer to "classes," or "sets." And classes are designated by "*terms*." There are two terms in every statement that is in *standard form* – a subject term (often indicated by the letter S), and a predicate term (P).

Standard form statements, then, assert a relationship between the subject class and the predicate class. But a relationship between two classes can hold for *all* the members or only *some* of the members of the subject class: thus the logical *quantifiers* ("all," "no," and "some") say that either "all" or only "some" of the members of the subject class have a certain relationship to the predicate class. The person who asserts that petting is harmful must mean one of two things – either that *all* petting is harmful, or that *some* petting is harmful.

The nature of this relationship between the subject and predicate classes, moreover, is that of *inclusion* or *exclusion*. To say that all S are P is to say that "all S are *included within* P;" to say that some S are P is to say that "some S are *included within* P." (All members of the class of acts of petting are included within the class of things harmful to young people; or some members of the class of acts of petting are included within the class of things harmful to young people.)

But statements can assert not only that all or some members of the subject class are *included within* the predicate class, but also that all or some of the members of the subject class are *excluded from* the predicate class. To convey this notion of exclusion, we must use the negative verb form, "are not," or for the universal negative statement "No ... are ...." The affirmative verb form (the verb form is called the *copula*) is simply, "are."   7

Summary: For the purposes of syllogistic logic, each statement in standard form must include "two expressions intended to indicate the two classes that constitute its subject matter — its 'terms,' subject (S) and predicate (P) — a quantifier (Q) indicating a quantity, universal or particular; a copula (C), indicating whether the relationship asserted is affirmative or negative." (*Logic,* D. B. Terrell, p. 25). Every logical statement can then be diagrammed thus: (Q)(S)(C)(P).   8

Having so defined logical statements, we can now say that statements conforming to the above-mentioned requirements are statements in *standard form,* and we can now identify the four kinds of statement in standard form: 9

NAME	QUANTITY	QUALITY	FORM
A	Universal	Affirmative	All S are P
E	Universal	Negative	No S are P
I	Particular	Affirmative	Some S are P
O	Particular	Negative	Some S are not P

Statements in categorical syllogisms must be in standard form, i.e., must be either an A, E, I, or O statement.

In deciding whether arguments are valid or not, we will need to know, among other things, whether the terms of the statements are *distributed* or not. There is an easy formula for making this discovery: the subjects of universal statements and the predicates of negative statements are distributed. For a term to be distributed in a statement means that the statement in which the term occurs tells us something about all the members of that class for which the term stands (tells us, that is, that all the members of that class are included in or excluded from the other class in the statement). Thus, in the statement "All acts of petting are harmful" the subject term, "acts of petting," is distributed, because it is the subject of a universal affirmative statement; and, again, this means that the statement tells us something about *all* acts of petting (that is, in this case, all of them are included within the class of acts harmful to youngsters).   10

"Ronald Reagan is Governor of California" is a kind of statement   *11*
which does not appear to be one of the four types of statement in standard
form mentioned above. The statement is a *singular* statement; it is so
because its subject term is a singular term, i.e., a term which refers to a
specified individual (instead of referring to a class). For the important
purposes of distribution singular statements are regarded as universal
statements. This is because their subject is, in fact, "distributed." The
singular statement certainly refers to *all* the members of the class designated by the subject term, even though, as obvious in our sample singular
statement, there is in the "class" of Ronald Reagan, only one member. To
exemplify the translation that would make this clear, "Ronald Reagan is
Governor of California" may be translated, "All things equal to Ronald
Reagan are things which are Governor of California."

Immediate inference.

Immediate inference allows us to change the form of a statement, but   *12*
to derive another statement that means exactly the same – i.e., that asserts the same class relationship.

An inference is *immediate* when its conclusion is derived from only a   *13*
single premise. The first principle of immediate inference is *conversion*.
Conversion, which can be used *only* on E and I statements, involves reversing the position of the subject and predicate terms. Thus, the "converse" of "No professors are fair graders" is "No fair graders are professors." And the converse of "Some acts of petting are bad" is "Some
bad things are acts of petting." To try to convert the A or O statements is
fallacious. It does not follow necessarily that "All mortal things are men"
merely because (as is true) "All men are mortal." Nor would it be logically correct to infer "Some Californians are not Americans" from the
statement "Some Americans are not Californians."

Obversion is in some ways like the principle of double negation. To   *14*
negate and negate again is of course to derive exactly the same thing. In
obversion, a statement in standard form means exactly the same if the
quality of the entire statement is negated, and then the quality of the
predicate term is negated. If, for example, "All men are mortal," then,
surely, "No men are immortal." Similarly, if "Some women are tempt-
resses," then it is also the case – indeed, it is quite the same statement –
that "Some women are not non-temptresses." In each example the move
from the first statement to the second is an instance of the immediate inference procedure of obversion, the process of negating first the entire
statement and then the predicate, thus deriving a statement which means
the same, but is expressed somewhat differently.

In using obversion one must be careful to supply the *contradictory*[1] of   *15*
the predicate term. If, instead of the contradictory of the predicate term,
a mere contrary is substituted, then true obversion will not have been accomplished, and the inference will not be valid.

Contradiction insists that from the truth value of any statement ("truth   *16*
value" refers to the fact that statements are either "true" or "false") the
opposite truth value can be inferred for another statement with the same
terms, opposite quantity, and opposite quality. Thus, for example, if
"Some bears are gentle," then by contradiction, it must be false that "No
bears are gentle." (If Some S are P is true, then, by contradiction, No S
are P is false.)

Limitation allows that the universal quantifier can be replaced with the   *17*
particular quantifier. For example, if "All coeds are promiscuous," then
"Some coeds are promiscuous." (Limitation is often helpful when used
in conjunction with conversion. We can infer from "All brides are beautiful," "Some beautiful things are brides." The intermediate step, of course,
was to infer that "Some brides are beautiful," and then to apply conversion.)

The practical utilization of these principles of immediate inference   *18*
depends upon a rule for applying them. That rule is as follows: Any statement can be replaced by a statement logically equivalent to it. Logical
equivalence is discovered for the purposes of this development by using
one of the four principles of immediate inference discussed. (Limitation
does not yield strict logical equivalence, since the more limited statement cannot be substituted for the more general one.) More precisely,
any statement can be replaced in any relationship by a statement produced from it by applying the principles of conversion, obversion, contradiction, or limitation.

The syllogism.

A syllogism is a deductive argument with three statements in standard   *19*
statement form—each statement being either A, E, I or O, having two
premises and one conclusion. A syllogism includes three terms, each
occurring twice. The predicate term of the conclusion is called the *major* term, and the subject term the *minor* term. Thus, the premise having
the major term is the *major premise,* and the premise having the minor

[1] Two terms are *contradictory* when they are both exclusive and exhaustive.
Thus, "apples" and "nonapples" are contradictories. But two terms are only
contraries when they are exclusive of one another, but are not also exhaustive
of all possibilities. The terms "blue" and "red" are contraries (nothing can be
both at the same time), but they are not exhaustive (since there are possibilities
other than they).

term is the *minor premise*. It is traditional and convenient for the major premise to be put first, the minor premise second and the conclusion — prefaced with "Therefore" (or an equivalent thereof) — last. The term which occurs in both premises is called the *middle* term.

Rules of the syllogism: *20*

Rules of Quality.
1. There can be only one negative premise.
2. If there is a negative premise, the conclusion must be negative; if there is a negative conclusion, one premise must be negative.
Rules of Distribution.
1. The middle term must be distributed at least once.
2. If a term is distributed in the conclusion, it must be distributed in the premise in which it occurs.

The rules of the syllogism are most important because it is they to   *21* which we must turn when we want to know if any particular syllogism is valid or not. When, that is to say, the question of the validity of a syllogistic argument arises, the answer is found simply by referring to the inference rules of the syllogism. If none of the rules is violated, then the syllogism is valid; if one or more of the rules is violated, then the syllogism is invalid.

To exemplify the employment of the rules, let us take the original pet-   *22* ting argument:

Petting is harmful to young people. It is harmful because it is a kind of sex act, and sex is harmful to youngsters.

The first requirement is to distinguish the premises from the conclusion: we know that a conclusion is asserted "because of" something else, and that that something else is/are the premises. Thus, "Petting is harmful to young people" is the conclusion, and "Sex is harmful to young people," and "Petting is a kind of sex act" are the premises.

But these statements are not yet in standard form. Remembering the   *23* requirements of standard form — (Q)(S)(C)(P) — we translate the first premise, "All sex acts are acts harmful to young people." For the second premise we get, "All acts of petting are sex acts." The conclusion is rendered: "All acts of petting are acts harmful to young people." But now that the syllogism is in standard form, we can proceed to test its validity with the inference rules. The first rule of quality is not violated: there is *no* negative premise. The second rule of quality is not violated, again because of the fact that there is no negative premise. The first rule of distribution is not violated: the middle term, "sex acts," is distributed in at least one of its occurrences, namely, in the major premise. The second rule of quality is not violated: the term "acts of petting," the subject of the conclusion, is distributed in the conclusion, being the subject of a universal statement, and is also distributed in the premise in which it occurs, the minor, for the same reason. But if none of the rules of the syllogism is violated, then the syllogism is valid. None is. Therefore, the syllogism is valid.

Two types of syllogism — enthymemes and sorites.

An *enthymeme* is an incomplete syllogism. In ordinary discourse people often reason syllogistically, but also often fail to state explicitly one of the premises or the conclusion. If someone says, "All criminals are lawbreakers, aren't they. Well, then, all criminals are wicked," he has actually failed to state the major premise of the syllogism, namely, "All lawbreakers are wicked." This premise is clearly *implied,* but not stated explicitly.   *24*

The unstated part can also be the conclusion. Innuendo often is accomplished enthymemetically. For example: one woman, anxious to insult another woman of whom she is quite jealous, might say, "Wearing too much expensive jewelry is certainly offensive; and you *are* wearing too much expensive jewelry." The implied conclusion is obvious; and because it is only implied, the argument is an enthymeme. Where the missing premise is the major, the enthymeme is said to be first order; where the minor, second order; where the conclusion is not stated, third order.   *25*

Occasionally we run across an argument in which the evidence offered in support of the conclusion consists of *more* than two premises. We know immediately that it is not a categorical syllogism for just that reason, of course. We cannot therefore test the validity of the argument by the rules of the syllogism (paragraph 20). But we may be able to so test the argument if we can show that it actually consists of more than one syllogism: then we can test each of the syllogisms separately, seeing which if any are valid.   *26*

Consider the following sorites: *27*

All racial prejudices are harmful to human beings.
All things harmful to human beings are morally wrong.
All morally wrong acts are national liabilities.
All national liabilities are unpatriotic.
Therefore, All racial prejudices are unpatriotic.

Although not a syllogism in standard form—one having two premises and one conclusion—the *sorites* can be treated as a chain of syllogisms in which the conclusion of one syllogism becomes a premise of the next one. In our example, the conclusions of each of the syllogisms except the last are unexpressed; but, as we have learned from considering the enthymeme, it is sometimes necessary to *supply* an implied statement in order to bring out the validity of an argument; and that is what is required here. A sorite, then, is actually a series of syllogisms in which the conclusion of one is a premise in the next, where all the conclusions except the last one are unexpressed, and in which the premises are so arranged that any two successive ones contain a common term.

The enthymeme and the sorites help to clarify a crucially important 28 fact; one should not think that because either some argument is not in standard syllogistic form, or some statements in it are not in standard statement form, that it is not, therefore, a syllogism capable of being evaluated by the rules of the categorical syllogism. We can "translate" many arguments that are not yet in standard syllogistic form into that form.

Nor are the enthymeme and the sorites the only kinds of arguments that 29 can be rendered into standard syllogistic form. Practically any argument or statement can be so rendered; and, more importantly for the purposes of doing logic, all arguments and statements *must* be so rendered if the logician is to evaluate the argument's validity. Until the argument is in standard form, there is just no way to decided if it is valid. If I argue that "Eskimos are lazy; therefore, Eskimos deserve to be poor," a logician will respond that there is just no way to know whether this argument is valid or not. It must first be put into standard form. We must know, that is:

1. What the missing premise is: it is probably "All lazy people are people who deserve to be poor."
2. What the quantifier of the first premise is: It would have to be, in order to make the argument valid, "All."
3. We need to change the verb "deserve" in the conclusion to "are" —the only acceptable verb in standard statement form—and we must then express the predicate by the term, "People who deserve to be poor."

Now, with two premises and one conclusion, the argument is a standard syllogism, and with appropriate verb form and appropriate quantifiers, the statements are in standard form. Only now can the argument finally be evaluated by the four rules of the categorical syllogism. One might now say that the original argument about Eskimos has been "translated" into standard syllogistic and standard statement form.

The Hypothetical Syllogism. The hypothetical syllogism differs from the   *30* categorical syllogism in that at least one of its three statements is *hypothetical*. A statement is hypothetical when it asserts that "If" something is the case "then" something else is the case. The person who claimed that petting was harmful might have chosen a hypothetical syllogism, rather than a categorical one. He might, for example, have argued:

> If petting is a kind of sex act, then petting is harmful to youngsters. Surely, petting is a kind of sex act; after all, petting involves kissing and touching various parts of the body, and doing those things is pretty clearly a kind of sex act. Thus, petting is harmful to youngsters.

Notice that the hypothetical syllogism is in some ways more modest   *31* than the categorical syllogism: it says—at least in the premise(s) that is *hypothetical*—only that "if" something is the case, "then" something else is the case. In the syllogism above, the minor premise does assert that that first something *is* the case; and, thus, the conclusion asserts that that second something is the case. Traditionally, the statement following "If" in a hypothetical statement is called the *antecedent* statement, and the statement following "then" the *consequent* statement. Together, the antecedent and consequent make a *hypothetical* statement.

The hypothetical syllogism about petting is a *mixed* hypothetical syl-   *32* logism (named *modus ponens*) because it has a hypothetical statement and two categorical statements. But there is also a *pure* hypothetical syllogism, in which all three of the statements are hypothetical. One might find a prosecuting attorney demanding that the defendant be punished as a criminal, and that he not be held blameless for having committed his crime as some psychologists suggest:

> If all men are creatures having free will, then all men are creatures morally responsible for their actions. If all men are creatures morally responsible for their actions, then all men are creatures blameable for their wrong actions. Therefore, if all men are creatures having free will, then all men are creatures blameable for their wrong actions.

Often, of course, one will not be content to settle for a hypothetical *33*
conclusion. Often one will try to prove the antecedent of the conclusion
to be true, thus proving the consequent true also. The prosecutor might
be expected to be very interested in showing that all men *are* creatures
of free will; if this is so, then it will be true that they are blameable for
their wrong actions. And this is just what he really wants to show. But
showing that the antecedent of the conclusion is true is not at all necessary for showing that the pure hypothetical syllogism is *valid:* the argument as such only claims that

> If All A are B, then All C are D.
> If All C are D, then All E are F.

Therefore, if All A are B, then All E are F. The validity of the hypo- *34*
thetical arguments is easier to see if, instead of diagramming the statements by using capital letters we use p and q to stand for the subject and
predicate terms of the statement, thereby diagramming the pure hypothetical syllogism as follows:

> If p, then q.
> If q, then r.
> Therefore, if p, then r.

where p, q, and r stand for the respective categorical statements of the
argument.

We can now identify each of the three valid types of hypothetical *35*
syllogism:

The pure hypothetical syllogism.

As the discussion has indicated, this syllogism contains three hypo- *36*
thetical statements. It asserts that if one statement implies another, and
that other still another, then the first statement implies the third.

The mixed hypothetical syllogism.

The mixed hypothetical syllogism has two varieties, *modus ponens* *37*
and *modus tollens,* each containing only one hypothetical statement:
1. *Modus ponens* asserts in its hypothetical statement that if something,
then something else. The second premise is categorical, asserting the
antecedent. The conclusion asserts the consequent. The hypothetical
argument above which concluded that petting is harmful to youngsters
is *modus ponens.* The argument form is:

If p, then q
P
Therefore, q.

2. *Modus tollens,* rather than affirming in its second premise, denies. It denies the consequent of the hypothetical statement. It concludes by denying the antecedent of the hypothetical statement. For example:

If petting is harmless, then some kinds of sex are harmless.
It is not the case that some kinds of sex are harmless.
Therefore, petting is not harmless.

This argument form insists that if any statement is false, then any statement that implies it is also false. The argument form is easily seen in the following diagram:

If p, then q
not q
Therefore, not p.

If a hypothetical statement is true, then to deny the consequent (in the second premise) allows us to deny the antecedent (in the conclusion). As another example, imagine a frustrated spinster refuting a suitor who is protesting that he really loves her:

If you loved me, then you would marry me.
You won't marry me.
Therefore, you don't love me.

The disjunctive syllogism. A syllogism is *disjunctive* when one of its   *38*
premises is a disjunction, that is, two statements separated by the word
"or." Each of the two varieties of disjunctive syllogisms has a disjunctive premise, followed by a categorical premise, followed by a categorical conclusion.

Modus ponendo tollens.

Modus ponendo tollens has, as its second premise, an affirmative state-   *39*
ment (as *tollendo ponens* has, as its second premise, a negative statement.)
The second premise, that is to say, affirms one of the disjuncts of the first (disjunctive) premise, and then the conclusion denies the other disjunct.

An example of *ponendo tollens* might occur in a courtroom situation, where a man who has killed another man is being evaluated as to his sanity. If the psychiatrists decide that he is insane, he will be found guilty of first-degree murder (for he has admitted the killing) and will likely be sentenced to death. The disjunctive premise of the argument might look like this:

Either Jones is legally insane, or he is guilty. The argument can be completed when the psychiatrists make their decision as to his sanity, and thus supply the second premise. Let us suppose they decide that he is insane. Then the second premise will be:
Jones is legally insane
But now the conclusion is: Therefore, Jones is not guilty.

The conclusion of *ponendo tollens* denies one of the disjuncts; and does so by affirming the other disjunct in the second premise. The meaning of this disjunctive syllogism can be understood as follows: "p or q, but not p and q." The two disjuncts, to put it another way, are, in *ponendo tollens,* mutually exclusive: if the one holds, then the other does not.

Modus tollendo ponens.

In *tollendo ponens,* the two disjuncts are not mutually exclusive: the intent of this argument can be understood as meaning, "p or q, and *possibly* (but not necessarily), p and q." We surely want to insist that there is a difference between an *exclusive* disjunction and an inclusive disjunction—as *ponendo tollens* was exclusive, so *tollendo ponens* is inclusive. It leaves open the possibility that both of the disjuncts hold, although the conclusion affirms only one of them. For example; suppose a customer to be angry that the car he has just purchased is not running. He says: "Either I will write a letter to the dealer or I will go personally to him to complain." If he decides to go personally to complain, then it does not follow that he will not also write a letter. But if he firmly decides that he will not write (feeling, perhaps, that such letters are not taken seriously by car dealers), it does follow that he will go personally to the dealer to complain.

Unlike the example of *ponendo tollens,* these two alternatives—either p (writing the letter) or q (going personally) are not mutually exclusive. The minor premise was "not q." Thus, the valid conclusion is, of course, "p." *Tollendo ponens* only insists that if the disjunction is true, *at least one* of the disjuncts must be true; it does not demand, further, as does *ponendo tollens,* that the other must be false.

Inductive Logic

Inductive logic is importantly different from deductive logic. Perhaps *42*
the most significant difference is that in inductive logic the material truth
of the conclusion is all-important. A good inductive argument is good because its conclusion is very likely "true." A good deductive argument is
good because its conclusion means the same as its premises — whether
they are true or false.

Some of the other differences are these: the conclusion of an induction *43*
asserts more than the premises themselves. The conclusion of an induction is never certain; at best, it is highly probable. Although, therefore,
all the premises of an induction are known to be true, it is still possible
that the conclusion is false. This cannot be the case in a valid deductive
argument, because the conclusion of a valid deduction merely makes explicit the meaning of the premises and their logical relations. Because
it does, it could not happen that the premises could be true and the conclusion — which means the same as those premises — false.

Good deductive arguments are valid: the logical or class relationships *44*
asserted in the conclusion are the same as those asserted in the premises.
The *truth* of the conclusion is not a criterion of the validity of the argument. But the truth of the conclusion is a criterion for evaluating inductive
arguments. Inductive arguments — even good ones — are not valid, since
their conclusions always assert more than their premises; but some are
better than others, and the mark of a good induction is the truth of the
conclusion. The more likely it is that the conclusion is *true,* the *better*
the induction.

Inductive generalization. When a physicist at Cape Kennedy is asked *45*
to comfort a visiting Senator who is worried that the latest rocket may fail
to get off the pad, thus wasting millions of taxpayer dollars, he may assert
an inductive conclusion about actions and reactions. He may say, for
example:

> "All actions, Senator, are such that they have equal and opposite
> reactions. Thus, when we ignite this rocket's motors and get action,
> we *will* get reaction which will propel the vehicle upward." This
> claim, he might continue, "is the product of many observations, each
> of which reported that a particular action had an equal and opposite
> reaction. When many such claims have been verified, we scientists
> claim that the relationship holds not merely in the finite number of
> cases we or other scientists have actually witnessed, but, rather, in
> 'all' cases."

"But," the Senator may protest, "I don't really care about what has happened in the past—what I want to know is what will happen tomorrow when you ignite the engines in *this* rocket!"

"We will get the expected reaction," replies the physicist.

"How do you *know?*" asks the worried Senator.

The Senator's question is perhaps not unfair. It does make sense to   46
ask how our scientific generalizations are known to be true. How can we know anything about all of the members of some class, when there are members of that class we have not observed? We know that many inductive generalizations are poor, and this should remind us both to be careful, and, even before that, to know the *criteria* which distinguish good inductive arguments from bad.

The crucial criterion for distinguishing good inductive generalizations   47
from bad ones is the *fair* or *representative* nature of the sample of the class referred to by the generalization. We will be entitled to assert that "all" the members of the class have the characteristic of interest ("reactions" in this case) if the members of the sample are the same or nearly the same as the other members of the class. If they differ in important respects, then what we know about some of them may not necessarily apply to those that are unknown. But, if a verifying instance (an action, followed by an equal and opposite reaction) is representative of all possible instances, then whatever it shows about one member of a class also likely holds for all members of that class. This likelihood is increased the *more* confirming observations there are.

The criteria of a representative sample are three: 1. The degree of   48
positive analogy among the observed cases; 2. The degree of negative analogy among the observed cases; 3. The number of observed cases. An inductive argument will be a good one when the observed cases which   ·
constitute the premises of the argument are quite similar, in relevant respects, to the unobserved cases; when they are dissimilar in relevant respects; and when the number of such observed cases is reasonably large. The premises that support the generalization that "All actions are such that they have equal and opposite reactions" would seem to satisfy these three requirements: the equal and opposite reactions that follow actions of stagecoaches, internal combustion engines, the flight of baseballs, etc., etc., are very similar to *all* actions; they differ in few *relevant* respects; and the number of such observations is very large. Therefore, it would seem reasonable to regard the conclusion about "all" actions having reactions as well supported by the premises.

On the other hand, consider the inductive conclusion, "All grizzly   49
bears are friendly." Suppose we ask the person who asserts this generali-

zation to defend it. If he replies that he has observed ten grizzlys, we will call the sample too *small*. If he has observed 1,000 grizzly bears, and all of those – all the bears in his "sample" – are friendly, we might still suspect that his induction is not representative, and, if so, then we will have shown that the conclusion is *not* to be regarded as true. Suppose that he has taken his sample in Yellowstone Park. The grizzlys there are partially domesticated, accustomed to eating food that humans eat, and to being handled and fed by children. Even if these bears are friendly, it does not follow that all grizzlys are, because this sample is select, not representative at all. These bears are importantly different from most of the grizzlys that there are: grizzlys outside the park are just not the same. Even if the third criterion of a representative sample has been satisfied, and, perhaps, the first as well – the sample was large, and the grizzlys do have many characteristics in common with all grizzlys – the second criterion has not been met – there is a relevant *negative* analogy between these bears and the other grizzly bears in North America, specifically, that most grizzlys are not at all domesticated, do not eat human food, and are not used to being handled by children. Thus, even if all of the bears of the sample have the characteristic of friendliness, it does not follow, because the sample of bears is not representative, that all grizzly bears are friendly.

Causal induction. We often are interested in knowing the "cause" of   *50* something. We want to know the causes of urban disorders, cancer, and juvenile delinquency. Many of our causal claims are unwarranted: people used to think that disease was caused by malicious demons and that toads caused warts. Sometimes the causal controversies are bitter: People argue vehemently over whether Hoover was the cause of the Depression, and whether a Communist conspiracy is the cause of urban disorders in America.

Causal claims share in common with inductive generalizations certain   *51* features: they are supported by particular observations in the premises; the conclusion is never certain, but only probable; and it is possible for the premises to be true, and the conclusion false.

1. The method of agreement. If there is an effect the cause of which   *52* we want to discover, then that cause, to be the cause, must occur all of the times the effect is observed to occur.

2. The method of difference. If we suspect a causal connection be-   *53* tween two phenomena, then if we experimentally remove the one suspected to be the cause, the effect should not appear. If smoking is the cause of lung cancer, then if smoking is eliminated, lung cancer should also disappear. If the suspected cause is suppressed, and the effect ap-

pears anyway, then the suspected cause may no longer be regarded as the cause. Additionally, if the effect does not materialize, any factor that is present then cannot be its cause.

3. The method of concomitant variation. If a factor is present in all *54* those cases where the effect is present (agreement) and only those cases (difference), then the more closely it varies in degree with that other factor, the more likely that it is the *cause* of that other factor. If flame is the cause of the water's boiling, then as the flame is increased, the water should boil more rapidly. Even if flame were present in all cases of boiling, and even if water didn't boil when flame was not present, if increases in flame were not followed by increases in the rapidity of boiling, the causal claim would be therefore suspect.

In summary, causal induction is the attempt to show that C is the cause *55* of E. Mill's methods allow us to affirm or deny that C is the cause of E. They do so by saying that if two factors are present together and absent together, and if they vary in degree together, then the one (C) is the cause of the other (E). On the other hand, no factor can be regarded as the cause of the other if it is present when the other is absent, or absent when the other is present, or if its variations in degree are not correlated with variations in degree in the other.

Fallacies

Formal fallacies. Having insisted that formal logic is mainly the study *56* of inferences, and having said, moreover, that some of these inferences that people make are valid and others invalid, it remains to list some of the different kinds of invalid inferences, the logical *fallacies,* so that the reader can *expose* them for what they are in the writing and speeches of others, and also so that the reader can *avoid* them in his own writing and speaking.

Formal fallacies are probably the easiest to classify and discover. They *57* all exhibit a violation of one or more of the inference rules that comprise formal logic. The rules of logic are like the rules of games, or the rules of moral conduct, or any other kind of rules. If in a baseball game, a player who has been removed from the game tries to bat, the umpire will explain that this is a violation of the rules. If a seventeen-year-old attempts to cast a vote for president in a national election, the registrar of voters will explain the "rule" which prohibits this. If a person argues that "All professors are educated; all dictators are educated; therefore, all professors are dictators," a logician will point out that a "rule" of the syllogism (the first rule of distribution) has been violated in that argument.

There are four inference rules for the syllogism. To know that a formal *58* fallacy has been committed, to know that a syllogistic inference is *invalid,* one need know *only* these rules, and apply them to any given syllogism.

Material fallacies. Material fallacies are here divided into two kinds, fal- *59* lacies of *equivocation,* and fallacies of *presumption.* The latter category has two subcategories, fallacies of *petitio,* and *irrelevance.* All material fallacies are fallacious in that the conclusion does not really follow from the premises, because (equivocation) the premises are ambiguous and therefore do not necessarily assert what the conclusion asserts, or (petitio) because the premises presume as proved the very point that the conclusion assumes as proved, or (irrelevance) because the premises assume as proved something which — even if true — in no way supports the conclusion of the argument.

Fallacies of equivocation.

Fallacies of equivocation are ambiguous. Ambiguity occurs when a *60* language item — either a statement, or a single term or phrase — has more than one meaning, and, in the argument in which it is used, the language item can mean either one.[2] One of the interpretations, that is, is implied in the premises, but the other is implied in the conclusion. There is more than one plausible meaning, and we are in real doubt as to which is *the* meaning in that context.

Two types of ambiguity — sentential and term.

In sentential ambiguity, the whole sentence is ambiguous. A sentence *61* by itself, of course, cannot commit a fallacy; only an argument can do that. Thus, for a fallacy to be committed, the writer or speaker must draw an inference using an ambiguous sentence. The most famous type of sentential ambiguity is the *amphiboly.*

Consider the following example of amphiboly: *62*

Upon entering a National Forest site which includes campsites, a family, wanting to spend a week camping, sees the following sign:

---

[2] But not both. This qualification must be added to exempt, for example, poems from being criticized as ambiguous. Poems often exploit the multiple meanings of statements and terms; but when the context is poetry, and the intent of the writer is to delight his reader with them, it will not be ambiguity. Fallacies of ambiguity, by contrast, are fallacious because they occur in *rational* discourse and are therefore likely to mislead.

SET UP CAMP. The sign is probably amphibolous because it is not clear just which of the two possible meanings is here intended: one possible meaning is that the sign names a type of camp, i.e., that the phrase SET UP is an adjective modifying a type of camp and SET UP CAMP is a *name* of a kind of camp. It could be a kind of camp that is already prepared, already "set up" by the park rangers, and which is very different from those kinds of campsites which are not at all prepared (which may have, for example, no stoves, no cut wood, no toilet facilities, etc.). On the other hand, SET UP *may*—it is certainly *plausible*—be an infinitive verb, it may be a command to the people who are entering the park to go ahead and begin making their camp, even if the ranger is not there yet to take the money and explain the rules. Sentential ambiguity occurs when it is not clear what part of speech a term is. One easy way to eliminate this kind of ambiguity, of course, is to make clear just which part of speech the phrase SET UP is supposed to be. In this example, a hyphen inserted between "set" and "up" would certainly eliminate the ambiguity, if the phrase is intended to be an adjective and not an infinitive verb.

63   Amphiboly itself is not a logical fallacy. But one can imagine cases where an amphibolous statement is used in the premises of an argument. Had the ranger, for example, attempted to fine the above family for preparing a campsite without authorization, on the grounds that the sign was merely a name of a kind of camp, then the family could say that the sign was amphibolous, and that the ranger's argument ("The sign merely named the camp type; but you wrongly set up your camp.") was fallacious on that account.

64   The point is this: we cannot allow any inference to follow validly from a premise when that premise is unclear as to its exact meaning. If it is unclear, then we must call invalid any inference drawn from it (until such time as the ambiguity is rectified).

65   Term ambiguity is the type of ambiguity arising when a single word or phrase is used in more than one sense. Term ambiguity exhibits the fact of a term or phrase having more than one meaning. As such, this would not constitute a fallacy. The fallacy begins when an ambiguous term is used in an argument. Then, when it appears in both the premises and conclusion, we charge that a fallacy has been committed because we know that there is no *necessary* connection between premises and conclusion, and there is none precisely because there is in the context no specified single meaning for the term that is ambiguous. Consider the following:

I find beating children desirable. Therefore, my beating children *is* desirable.

The reason we would say that some sort of fallacy has been committed here is that the word "desirable" has more than one meaning possible in its two occurrences; and, moreover, has, it would seem, *both* of these meanings exploited in the argument. The first meaning of "desirable" refers to what anyone happens to desire. Thus, French Apple Pie, Steinbeck and chess are "desirable" (for *me,* anyway). But there is another very different meaning of "desirable," viz., "that which is *worthy* of desire." Thus, following the second meaning, we can say things like "Smallpox vaccination is desirable," where we do *not* mean that anyone actually desires smallpox vaccination (we can safely assume that most people do not desire it as such), but, rather, that smallpox vaccination is in some sense, "good," or "worthy of desire," or, better "likely to be beneficial."

But surely any argument that has a term like "desirable" is fallacious 66 if it does not endorse one or the other of the possible meanings of the term (and, by implication, exclude the other) before it proceeds to draw a conclusion which includes that term. This is so because we just do not know—unless it is somehow clarified in advance—just which of the two possible meanings are intended, and if one is plausible in the conclusion, but another equally plausible in the premises, then we must say that the argument is invalid, is "fallacious," because the ambiguous premises do not necessitate any single conclusion.

There are four varieties of fallacies of term ambiguity: composition, 67 division, accident, and converse accident:

1. Like the other fallacies of term ambiguity *composition* suffers from 68 the fact that one of its terms is susceptible of one interpretation in the premises, but another in the conclusion, and, additionally, no clarification as to which interpretation ought to be made is given. For example:

> The Los Angeles Lakers are great players—it is difficult to imagine better men than Jerry West, Gail Goodrich, and Wilt Chamberlain. Therefore, the Los Angeles Lakers are a great basketball team.

The problem here is that the term "Los Angeles Lakers" has two different senses. In the premise it refers to the individual members themselves. It is likely true that, *as individuals,* these "Lakers" are great players. But the term, in the conclusion, refers to the whole team *as a unit.* And it is not necessarily true that the whole team as a team has the quality that some of the parts have. The fallacy occurs when a term like "Los Angeles Lakers" has more than one sense, but is used in an argument which ignores these distinct senses, and which proceeds as if there were but one clear sense in both occurrences of that term.

2. *Division* is the reverse of composition. It is exemplified as follows: *69*

> The United States Army is fighting an immoral war in Vietnam. Corporal Jones is U.S. Army; I guess he is immoral, then.

Surely we do not want to say that because some whole can be described in some way that, therefore, every part of that whole also necessarily can be thus described. Like division, composition exhibits the fallacy of ignoring two importantly different sense of a given term. "United States Army" refers to the whole army taken together in the premise. But it refers to individual members of that whole in the conclusion. There is no necessary connection between a whole having certain characteristics and each of its parts having those characteristics; we will be fooled only if we fail to point out that the term has different senses in its different occurrences.

3. *Accident* occurs when a characteristic which is accidental is treated   *70* as if it were essential. For example, suppose an insurance adjustor from the Slashrate Insurance Company were to say the following to a customer who had just wrecked his car:

> Sorry, Mr. Brown. Slashrate will not reimburse you for your car. The application that you filled out for us five years ago says that your car is blue, but this wreck in front of me is red. Therefore, because this wreck is not yours, we will not pay.

Now if Brown has studied the fallacies of equivocation he can say, "Wait! You are committing the fallacy of accident. You are assuming that because my car had a given characteristic in one context, that it must have that same characteristic in all contexts, or not be the same car. But that is absurd. Surely characteristics such as color are 'accidental,' not 'essential' at all. And, if so, then some or all of these 'accidental' characteristics can change, and yet the thing can still be the same thing."

The ambiguity in this argument is in the verb. "Is," the singular form   *71* of the verb "to be," has two different senses in this argument. When the adjustor, in the premise, says "your car is blue," he is using "is" as a verb indicating *predication* (just as it is used in standard form categorical statements). But when, in the conclusion, he says "This (car) is not yours," he is using 'is' as a verb indicating *identity*.[3] This we must call fallacious.

[3] A fairly reliable clue as to which sense of the verb "to be" is intended is the kind of predicate term which follows it: general or class terms follow the verb of predication; singular terms, e.g., "your car," follow the verb of identity.

4. The fallacy of *converse accident* is the opposite of *accident:* a char-   *72*
acteristic which is really essential is treated in one of its occurrences as
if it were quite accidental. A famous Supreme Court decision seems to
have committed this fallacy.

In the case of Plessy v. Ferguson the plaintiff, Plessy, argued that seg-   *73*
regation of Negroes by law was unconstitutional because it deprived
Negroes of equal treatment before the law, inasmuch as it necessarily
relegated them to an inferior position. The Court disagreed:

> (Plessy) necessarily assumes that if, as has been more than once the
> case, and is not unlikely to be so again, the colored race should be-
> come the dominant power in the state legislature, and should enact
> a law in precisely similar terms, it would thereby relegate the white
> race to an inferior position. We imagine that the white race, at least,
> would not acquiesce in this assumption.

If we try to put this argument into standard form, we might get something
like the following:

> All segregation statues are laws which merely require separation of
> the races.
> Some laws which merely require separation of the races are not laws
> which impute racial inferiority.

But the Court's argument seems to turn on an ambiguous term, namely,
"segregation statutes." The Court argues that segregation statutes
directed against whites would not impute racial inferiority, and concludes
that, therefore, segregation statutes *directed against blacks* would not,
either.

But, surely, the meanings given the history of the Negro in America   *74*
are importantly different. But if the meanings of the two terms are really
quite different, and if we are to regard the argument form—as the Court
doubtless did—as valid (the fallacy is not formal, does not consist in
having four terms instead of the allowable three), then the fallacy must
consist in an ambiguity, viz., the ambiguity of the term "segregation
statutes." And, in converse accident, the ambiguity consists in the fact
that a part of the meaning of the term "directed against blacks"—is considered as quite accidental, when, in fact, it would appear essential. The
specific kind of segregation statute—segregation "directed against
blacks"—is treated by the Court as if it were not at all essential to the
meaning expressed in the conclusion; and yet it *is*.

Fallacies of presumption—petitio principii.

Petitio principii has three varieties. Each suffers the same defect: each   75
somehow takes for granted what it is supposed to prove. They will thus
be unlike the other class of presumptive fallacies—the fallacies of irrelevance—in that the latter do not take for granted what they are purporting
to prove, but, rather, have conclusions which are not logically connected
at all with their premises.

1. The first variety of the fallacies of petitio is called *begging the ques-*   76
tion. It consists in "proving" a conclusion by assuming that very conclusion in the premises of the argument. For example:

A: I question whether the ABM system is really a good idea.
B: But the system is essential to the national defense.
A: Why do you say that?
B: Why? Because this system is vital to our security.

Clearly, the fallacy here consists in the fact that the conclusion to be
proved is proved by asserting the same statement in the premises. If we
allow this argument to be "sound" then people can "prove" their points
merely by *repeating* them!

Vicious circle is like begging the question, but with an additional move.   77
Should one's opponent not be satisfied with a question-begging premise
offered in support of a conclusion, then that premise itself might be de-
fended. But the defense of that premise is just the repeating of the conclusion. The technique is sneaky, and often, perhaps, successful, but
hardly logically satisfactory.

A: Adultery is wrong.
B: How do you know this to be true?
A: The Bible says so.
B: How do you know the Bible is right?
A: Surely any book that condemns adultery must be right.

2. The fallacy of the *false question* is a favorite device of trial lawyers.   78
In trying to embarrass and thus discredit the testimony of an unfriendly
witness a lawyer might open the questioning with, "Are you still a practicing homosexual?" Or, perhaps, someone might ask, "Why do all redheads have bad tempers?" The question is "false" in the sense that it
presumes that all redheads *do* have bad tempers (as the lawyer presumed
that the man was really a homosexual). But, often, that is the whole
point. One is not entitled to assume that redheads do have bad tempers
without detailed *proof.* Indeed, we suspect that if testing were done on

this issue, the result would be that not all redheads have bad tempers. Therefore, no one is entitled to assume—as is done in the argument above—that something is the case without evidence. If, as is the case in these examples, there is no evidence, then it is fallacious to conclude that the question asked justifies the conclusion wanted.

3. *Black and white* is committed when one assumes that two alterna-   79
tives are mutually exclusive or jointly exhaustive, when, in fact, they are not.

Let us first consider the mistake of assuming that the two alternatives   80
really are mutually exclusive, as when the parent angrily says to the child who is not eating his supper, "Either you eat that food or you go to bed." If the child is familiar with this fallacy he may want to respond, "But, father, surely I could *both* eat my dinner *and* go to bed. The alternatives, you see, are not mutually exclusive."

On the other hand, the child might have wanted to call his father's   81
attention to the fallacy by pointing out that the alternatives posed were not jointly exhaustive: "Besides, dad, there are certainly other things to be done. I could watch television, for example, or play with my toys." In either case, the child is detecting the fallacy of black and white.

Fallacies of irrelevance.

In the fallacies of irrelevance there is no connection between the   82
premises and the conclusion. But, even so, we are misled (sometimes intentionally, it would seem) into thinking that there is some connection. The reason that the premises of the argument do not entail the conclusion is that the premises do not "necessitate" the conclusion *at all*. (In the case of the fallacies of petitio the premises did necessitate the conclusion— since they asserted the same thing—but they did not effectively settle the controversy, and did not do so because, in one way or another, they assumed as true the very conclusion which they pretended to entail *with-out* already having assumed themselves.) But, after all, arguments are advanced in order to *effectively* settle some controversy. If, as is the case with the fallacies of irrelevance, the conclusions are irrelevant to the premises, then such arguments can hardly settle any controversies effectively.

1. The first variety of the fallacies of irrelevance is the argument *ad*   83
hominem. One commits *ad hominem* when one argues against a thesis by slandering the character of the person who advances it. If someone were to argue as follows, he would be arguing *ad hominem:*

Senator Toten says that we should use nuclear weapons on our enemy. But he must be mistaken. He cannot be trusted to give good advice to the American people because he was, as everyone knows already, divorced twice, and his own colleagues on the Senate Foreign Relations Committee agree that he is rude and abrupt.

Even though Toten is rude, divorced, and abrupt, that seems quite *irrelevant* to the conclusion that his thesis about the use of nuclear weapons must be mistaken.

The above example is the *abusive* form of *ad hominem*. Another form   *84* is exemplified in the following:

You of all people, coming from Montana, a great hunting state, should certainly be against gun control.

Here the speaker is giving a reason why his adversary on the issue of gun control *should* accept his conclusion, namely, that gun control is bad. He offers no really germane evidence why gun control is bad; he merely implies that there would be something "wrong" with anyone from a hunting state being for gun control. This variety is called the *circumstantial* form of *ad hominem*.

The *tu quoque* form of *ad hominem* occurs when someone argues that   *85* because his opponent has done things equally as bad as he is now doing, therefore, the things he is now doing are *not* so bad, after all. For example:

Student #1: You cheated on that Philosophy exam. That's bad.
Student #2: Ha! You cheated on your chemistry test; and what's more, you have stolen books from the library more than once.

One would certainly think that the fact that Student #1 has done some bad things of his own bears no relation whatever to the conclusion (which is here implied) that Student #2 is thus not blameable for cheating on his Philosophy exam.

2. *Ad populum* is the fallacy of appealing to popular sentiments or   *86* prejudices as constituting proof of some conclusion. Thus if I argue that the President cannot have been mistaken in ordering some action or other because most of the people agreed with him, I am committing *ad populum*. It was, after all, a popular prejudice for a long time that the earth was flat. But we think that just because many people believed that, it hardly follows that the earth really *was* flat.

3. *Ad misericordiam* occurs when one appeals to sympathy in order to   *87* "prove" one's point. When charged with having beaten, robbed, and then murdered a defenseless woman, a defendant might respond, "But, your

honor, I am a man with an unemployable wife and six hungry children."
Clearly, this fact—even if true—does not support the conclusion that
the man is not guilty.

4. A favorite fallacy committed by debaters on various issues is *ad*   88
ignorantiam. The argument consists in negatively proving a conclusion
by showing that its opposite is absurd or false, or, sometimes, merely
unprovable.

> A: I have some doubts that there is an international Communist
> conspiracy seeking to subvert and destroy the peoples of the
> free world.
> B: You can't prove that there is no such conspiracy.
> (Implied conclusion: Therefore, there is one.)

Often one is tempted to support some conclusion by appealing to some   89
authority who also endorses that conclusion. What often happens in
practice, of course, is that the person appealed to as an authority is in
some way *unqualified*. When this is the case, then his testimony in support of the conclusion is not relevant (in the way that it would be if he
were qualified). There is more than one way to be thus unqualified. Two
of the most common are unqualified by reason of not being an authority
on the subject at issue at all, and by reason of suspecting the "authority's" motivations. An example of the first sort is where someone argues
that his views on foreign policy must be true because a famous biochem-
ist agrees with him. An example of the second sort occurs when someone
says, for example:

> Yes, this would be the best place to build the new freeway. This
> is so because Sam Sellright (the local realtor, who stands to make a
> good deal of money on various transactions if the freeway is built
> where our speaker proposes), who should know about these things,
> says so.

Appeal to unqualified authority is called the fallacy of *ad vericundiam*.

Inductive fallacies. David Hume pointed out that the conclusion of an   90
inductive argument may be untrue, regardless of how many supporting
observations (premises) there are. It is logically possible, said Hume, that
there are cases unobserved in which the generalization does not hold.
This is undeniably true. To illustrate the point, I would recall the chicken
story. This is the story of the chicken who reasoned inductively that because the farmer's wife had fed it every day in the past, that, therefore,

"All days on which the farmer's wife comes out into the barnyard are days on which I will be fed by her." The chicken had a rather impressive amount of data in his premises, moreover: on 99 out of 99 days, this very thing happened. But, of course, the chicken turns out to have been naive about the nature of inductive argument. On the one-hundredth day, the chicken, not understanding the nature of good induction, races out of the barn when he sees the farmer's wife come out of the back door of the farmhouse, fully expecting that she will, as per all the evidence to date, merely feed him. She does not. Instead, she grabs his neck and wrings it. Had the chicken read Hume, he would have learned not only that inductive arguments do not provide certainty in their conclusions, but also that some inductions are, for various reasons, not as good as others.

There are characteristic fallacies in induction, just as in deduction. 91 They are of two sorts; first, the pure inductive fallacies, in which the sample which constitutes the premises of the induction is not representative of the entire class. The second kind of inductive fallacy is a causal fallacy, i.e., the conclusion of the inductive argument hastily asserts that something is the "cause" of something else.

Pure inductive fallacies.

In the pure inductive fallacies there is an unrepresentative sample of 92 empirical data which is offered in support of the conclusion. The sample can be unrepresentative in two ways. In one case the sample is not large enough; in the other, the sample is not varied enough. Suppose, for example, that one wished to construct an inductive argument which would serve as a prediction of the results of an election for mayor of a large city. Suppose then that the sampler solicits voter responses from each of the first ten people that he meets. And, suppose, further, that he draws an inductive conclusion on the basis of that sample to the effect that Candidate X is going to win the election for mayor, arguing that 8 out of the 10 people asked reported that X was their choice. The conclusion would be a generalization of the following sort: *"All* the votes will exhibit the ratio observed in the sample, namely 8/10 for Candidate X." Surely, we could object to this induction that the sample is just not *large* enough. We might say things like, "In a city of 100,000 people, one cannot claim to know how the majority is going to vote merely on the basis of 10 responses." Had the interviewer asked 1,500 or 2,000 voters their opinions, then we might tend to regard the conclusion ("X will win the election by 3 to 2") as being sufficiently large.

But another kind of fault could be found regarding this sampling. 93 Namely, we could object to the inductive conclusion about X's winning on the grounds that the sample is not *varied* enough. Suppose that the sampler had responded to our original criticism by interviewing 2,500 people. Would *that* sample then be automatically considered reliable? Not at all. Suppose, for example, that all of the 2,500 were of the same political affiliation, Democrats, same religion, Catholic, and same or nearly the same socioeconomic bracket—$8,000 to 15,000 annual income. Then our objection to the sample would be not that it is not large enough (it is likely that, if properly done in other relevant respects, 2,500 out of 100,000 is a reasonably large sample) but rather that the sample does not reflect the different kinds of groups within the population. We know that large metropolitan populations are not homogeneous. Those who were of modest means or even poor, those of the opposite political affiliation, and different religions were entirely ignored. But we have good reason to believe that precisely those kinds of differences are most important in explaining how people vote; and, thus, we will look askance at inductions based on evidence which ignores differences such as these.

Causal fallacy: post hoc, ergo propter hoc.

Suppose that someone were to claim that a certain professor, well   94
known as an important Marxist scholar, has, by appearing before various student groups in various countries of the world, "caused" student riots occurring some time after his appearance. This is so, the complainant asserts, because after the professor has been the certain places riots have occurred there. Therefore, he concludes, the professor is the cause of these riots. But the mere fact that one object occurs *after* another does not guarantee that it was *caused* by it. Sometimes, it is; but not always. One is only entitled to make the causal claim *after* one has done detailed investigation in a scientific manner—this manner usually involves the use of Mill's "methods." To make a causal claim without having done the necessary scientific research may be to commit the fallacy of *post hoc, ergo propter hoc.*

In the case of the professor, it may be that students in France, Ger-   95
many, and America, are concerned about social problems enough that, even without him, there would be riots. In any case, it is *post hoc* to continue to argue that he is the cause of the riots, because it is clear that if the professor were to go to a country where there was apathy about the course of world affairs, then surely there would be no rioting even though he were there. On the other hand, if we could find a place—and there are many such places—where there are student riots and he has not been present, then this fact too tends to invalidate the hasty causal claim about his being their cause. If the suspected cause is present, but the expected effect fails to materialize, or if the effect occurs even when the suspected

cause is not present, then we no longer have grounds to claim that the two are causally related.

QUESTIONS AND EXERCISES

Vocabulary

Make a list of the logical terms used in this essay and be able to define each briefly.

Exercises

The examples below contain material on inductive fallacies. The student should attempt to locate the fallacy, explain the kind of fallacy it is, remembering that some examples are susceptible of more than one interpretation. The student should try to render the most *plausible* meaning from each example; without assuming any particular context for the argument. Often the arguments are enthymemes, that is, one or more of the parts of the argument is unexpressed. In such cases, the student must, of course, render the suppressed statement explicit before he can assess the argument for a fallacy.

1. "The Duke yet lives that Henry shall depose." (*Henry VI*)
2. Our Army is a strong army; of that we can be sure. The First Division is, by common consent, very strong. The Second Division is also quite strong. While the First Division was destroying the enemy in the east, the Second Division was winning easily in the north. Now that the First and Second are together, we will be equally strong and we can expect further victories.
3. European students are very good students. Hans Unwissend, a German student, wants to be admitted to the University. I suppose we should allow him in; after all, Europeans are quite good students.
4. I want my money back that I paid for this season ticket to the Tiger's home games. The Tigers had orange and black uniforms last season; but now they have changed to green. Therefore, because it is no longer the same team, I want my money back.
5. If that baby cries in this courtroom once more, I must hold him in contempt. The law says that anyone who is noisy in the court must be held in contempt.
6. People sometimes defend the use of marijuana on the grounds that it does not produce addiction. This is false, however, because the use of marijuana does cause addiction.
7. A: I know of no responsible politician in this country who defends the war.

B: Congressman Streit supports the war.

A: Well, then, Congressman Streit is not responsible.

B: Why do you say that? Streit has a commendable record.

A: That may be, but anyone who supports the war is not responsible.

8. Why is it, I wonder, that the very same people who condemn police violence at the same time condone the violence of social protestors?

9. Either we attack the enemy now and utterly destroy him, or else the enemy will attack our country and destroy us. We surely do not want the latter alternative; and, therefore, we must make war on our enemy's country.

10. "What continually astounds me about the Fulbrights and the McGoverns is their consummate gall in attempting to dictate presidential policy. It was Richard Nixon who was elected to the White House, not the George McGovern who couldn't even get nominated by his own party. And although J. William Fulbright wants to be Secretary of State so bad he can taste it, even the liberal-minded John F. Kennedy wouldn't give him the job." (William Randolph Hearst, Jr., in *The Los Angeles Herald-Examiner,* Sun. March 23, 1969)

11. A: I must say that I am opposed to a strike by the meat cutter's union.

    B: I cannot believe my ears — you, of all people. You used to be a meat cutter yourself, don't forget. Surely all meat cutters — old or new — should favor the strike.

12. The young people accuse us of the older generation of many faults: they say we tolerate war and racism, that we are dishonest in business, and hypocritical in our sexual attitudes. Well, I would just remind young people that they are not without their vices: they smoke pot, avoid serving in the armed forces, and often are wholly uninterested in gainful employment.

13. Can you prove that God does not exist? Of course you can't. Some of the greatest minds of the ages have tried to show that God does not exist, and they failed. Thus, God does exist.

14. The theory of evolution must be true. We prepared a detailed questionnaire, and most of the people who responded agreed that the theory is true.

15. For a class project in Sociology, we were required to ask people if they would vote to retain or abolish the first ten amendments to the Constitution. I asked people all over the United States this question: my father here in Chicago, a retired Navy officer living in Nome, Alaska, a surfer in Miami, Fla., a Senator from Nebraska, and half a dozen other people. All told, 7 of the 10 people asked, reported that they would vote for abolition; I generalized in my paper for So-

ciology, therefore, that 70% of the American population prefers to do away with the Bill of Rights.

16. The boycott of California table grapes is receiving very little support. We interviewed a very large number—5,000 in all—of grape ranch owners, and all of the 5,000 are opposing the boycott.

Topics and Assignments for Composition

1. Give an example of one of the types of fallacies listed above.
2. In a paragraph discuss the difference between formal and informal fallacies.
3. Discuss the part fallacies play in our every-day lives.
4. Analyze some short, well-known speech or essay and point out some of the fallacies present.
5. Read the following excerpt from Plato's *Apology*. Write an essay in which you analyze Socrates' argument. Is it fallacious? Why? If it is not fallacious, what makes it valid? If it is a valid argument, why was Socrates found guilty? If it is a fallacious argument, why was it not effective? You need not answer the questions in the order listed; you should, however, include all of them in your essay.

Well, Athenians, this and the like of this is all the defense which I have to offer. Yet a word more. Perhaps there may be some one who is offended at me, when he calls to mind how he himself on a similar, or even less serious occasion, prayed and entreated the judges with many tears, and how he produced his children in court, which was a moving spectacle, together with a host of relations and friends; whereas I, who am probably in danger of my life, will do none of these things. The contrast may occur to his mind, and he may set against me, and vote in anger because he is displeased at me on this account. Now if there be such a person among you—mind, I do not say there is—to him I may fairly reply: My friend, I am a man, and like other men, a creature of flesh and blood, and not "of wood and stone," as Homer says; and I have a family, yes, and sons, O Athenians, three in number, one almost a man, and two other who are still young; and yet I will not bring any of them hither in order to petition you for an acquittal. And why not? Not from any self-assertion or want of respect for you. Whether I am or am not afraid of death is another question, of which I will not speak. But, having regard to public opinion, I feel that such conduct would be discreditable to myself, and to you, and to the whole state.

Max Black

Principles of Really Sound Thinking

. . . There are two major principles of really sound thinking: *1*
         A. Think only as a last resource.
         B. Trust your feelings.

Think Only as a Last Resource

The really sound thinker knows thinking to be an uncomfortable, dis-   *2*
turbing, and anti-social occupation. Consider the attitude of Rodin's
statue "The Thinker." This is not the favorite posture of a successful
executive or a regular guy.

Modern life fortunately provides a number of defenses against the early   *3*
onslaught of thinking. The radio is always close at hand — use it. The company of others, preferably of the opposite sex, is to be strongly recommended. If the irritation is too severe, one may retreat to bed until restored to a healthier frame of mind.

It has to be confessed, however, that complete protection against think-   *4*
ing still remains to be achieved:

> But men at whiles are sober
> And think by fits and starts
> And if they think, they fasten
> Their hands upon their hearts.
>   — A. E. Housman

Conscientious adherence to the next principle will go far to palliate   *5*
the discomforts of unavoidable and involuntary thinking.

Reprinted by permission of *Science,* from *Scientific Monthly,* Vol. 66, pp.
232–234, March 1948.

Trust Your Feelings

The logic texts have created the fiction of Logical Man, coldly calcu-   6
lating the probabilities of alternative hypotheses, willfully blind to human sentiment and passion. Do you want to be this kind of philosophical
monster, interminably vacillating between conflicting conclusions? Of
course not. In any matter of serious concern, you will *feel* strongly that
a certain conclusion *must* be right. This is the clue to success in really
sound thinking. Let yourself go—think in technicolor.

Suppose you are worried about the possibility of war with Russia. You   7
will notice in yourself a tendency to think of Stalin as a bloodthirsty
ruffian, dripping with the gore of murdered innocents. Dwell upon the
notion—let your blood pressure rise. In a short time you *feel* strongly
enough to be able to stop *thinking* altogether. In really sound thinking, it
is the conclusion that counts, not the premises. Trusting your feelings
will quickly provide you with satisfying, heart-warming conclusions.

The two principles of really sound thinking can be illustrated by the   8
following maxims, widely accepted by successful practitioners.

1. *If you must stick to the point, be sure it's blunt.* The natural human
reaction to contact with a sharp point is violent motion in reverse. Such
animal wisdom is deeply significant. It's the dead butterfly that stays on
the point. Cultivate judicious irrelevance.

Example: Does John Smith deserve a raise in salary?

Blunted point: Doesn't everybody deserve a raise?

Really sound reasoning: Of course they do! Who is John Smith to be
favored at the expense of everybody else?

2. *What's in it for me?* Remember that a really sound thinker is practical. And what can be more practical than concern for one's own interests?
The chief advantage of this maxim is the strong light it throws upon the
truth of many a debatable proposition.

Example: Should educational facilities be improved in the South?

Really sound reasoning: What's in it for me? Nothing—I don't live in
the South.

Conclusion: NO. (Notice the directness and incisiveness of the
method.)

3. *It all depends on who says it.* Men are easier to classify than arguments—attend to the man, not the argument. (For classifying the speaker,
see principle B above.)

Example: Should Congress be reorganized?

Really sound reasoning: Who says so? X? Oh—he ran for the Congress three times unsuccessfully.

Conclusion: You can't trust *him.*

4. *A million people can't be wrong.* It would clearly be undemocratic, not to say snobbish, to think otherwise. We can't all be Gallups, but we have a ready fund of popular wisdom to hand in the form of proverbs. Make frequent use of such axioms as "Human nature never changes," and "An ounce of experience is worth a peck of talk," and, especially, "It will all be the same in a thousand years." The last is particularly consoling.

Example: Can we prevent another war?

R. s. r.: I've *seen* men fighting. You'll never change human nature. After all, it will all be the same in a thousand years.

This method can be usefully supplemented by the use of identical propositions, such as "East is East, West is West," "Business is Business," "A man's a man for a' that." These are best introduced by the words "after all." Even a logician can hardly dispute the truth of such tautologies.

5. *The exception proves the rule.* Corollary: The more exceptions, the better the rule. This popular maxim hardly needs recommendation. It has the great advantage of allowing us to make simple generalizations in an intolerably complex world. (See also Maxim 8 below.)

Example: You say women are no good at physics. What about Madame Curie?

R. s. r.: The exception prove the rule! (Absolutely conclusive, as r. s. r. should be.)

6. *It's all right in theory but it won't work in practice.* We might almost say: *Because* it's right in theory, it won't work in practice. This maxim is very useful in puncturing the pretentions of experts.

Example: Should we support the United Nations?

R. s. r.: (You know what!)

7. *Consistency is the hobgoblin of little minds.* None of the great thinkers from Socrates to Korzybski have been consistent. Who are you to improve upon their practice? The sciences are notoriously full of unresolved contradictions. If scientists don't care, why should you?

Example: You say that we ought to work for universal free trade, but insist on raising American tariffs.

R. s. r.: I contradict myself? Very well, I contradict myself.

8. *Truth is always pure and simple.* Notice the purity and simplicity of this maxim. Oscar Wilde denied its truth, and see what happened to him (compare Maxim 3). Anything too complicated for translation into Basic English is unworthy the attention of a really sound thinker. The truth must be incapable of shocking the Johnston (formerly Hays) Office. In any case, truth is too precious to be lightly squandered. It is better to hold it a closely guarded hostage far back in reserve.

Example: Is there anything in psychoanalysis?

R. s. r.: Of course not. Why, I can't even understand it. And it isn't fit to print.

9. *Take care of the sound and the sense will take care of itself.* This is perhaps the most important of all the maxims of really sound thinking. "There is a great advantage in names" (Mark van Doren). Be sure you get the greatest benefit out of the names you use.

If you trust your feelings as you should (principle B above), you should have little trouble in finding the right name. Thus, the *Management Review* lately recommended the use of "Income Account" instead of "Profit and Loss Account," "Earnings" instead of "Profits," "Reinvested in the Business" instead of "Added to Surplus." You get the idea?

Example: On being questioned about the implications of a legislative program no really sound thinker would say, "I don't know." This is better: "It is totally unreasonable to expect a blueprint which answers every question which can arise day after tomorrow in this distraught earth, when no man knows for twenty minutes at a time what is going to happen" (Senator Vandenberg, quoted in the *New York Times,* April 18, 1947).

10. *Never argue with a man who is wrong.* Corollary for married ladies: Never argue with a husband. For the purposes of this maxim, a man who is wrong is easily identified as one who (a) is an unsound thinker, (b) refuses to see that you are right, or (c) has an unwholesome look (see Maxim 3 above).

The careful reader will have noticed that the reasoning used in the above exposition of the principles of really sound thinking provides numerous further illustrations of the principles discussed.   9

QUESTIONS AND EXERCISES

Vocabulary

1. Define or explain each of the following terms:

palliate (5)	corollary (8.5)
hypotheses (6)	maxim (8.5)
irrelevance (8.1)	hobgoblin (8.7)
incisiveness (8.2)	

2. Identify the name or explain the allusion in each of the terms below:

Rodin (2)	Socrates (8.7)
Housman (4)	Korzybski (8.7)
Gallups (8.4)	Hays Office (8.8)
Madame Curie (8.5)	Senator Vandenberg (8.9)

Rhetoric

3. Why is it evident that the entire essay is an example of irony?
4. To be effective, an extended example of irony should not have breaks in the point of view. Are there any confusing inconsistencies in this essay?
5. Discuss the relationship of irony to humor. What evidence of humor do you find in this essay? Are any examples that you have found also examples of irony?
6. What effect does the enumeration of the maxims have upon the irony?

Theme

7. What is the thesis of this essay, in positive, non-ironic terms?
8. To whom would this essay appeal most? Make a list (hierarchic order: appeal to most to appeal to least).
9. Explain paragraph 9.
10. Bring to class examples of the principles explained in this essay. Sources you might use are newspaper editorials, political speeches, government policy, news conferences with experts, and articles in popular magazines.

Topics and Assignments for Composition

1. Write a few maxims of your own; imitate the ironic point of view.
2. In a paragraph, summarize in a non-ironic way the implied thesis of this essay.
3. Write an essay maintaining an ironic point of view used by Black. You may also wish to read "A Modest Proposal" by Jonathan Swift before you write.

Samuel Johnson

Roarers, Whisperers, and Moderators

It is impossible to mingle in conversation without observing the difficulty with which a new name makes its way into the world. The first appearance of excellence unites multitudes against it; unexpected opposition rises up on every side; the celebrated and the obscure join in the confederacy; subtilty furnishes arms to impudence, and invention leads on credulity. 1

The strength and unanimity of this alliance is not easily conceived. It might be expected that no man should suffer his heart to be inflamed with malice, but by injuries; that none should busy himself in contesting the pretensions of another, but when some right of his own was involved in the question; that at least hostilities commenced without cause, should quickly cease; that the armies of malignity should soon disperse, when no common interest could be found to hold them together; and that the attack upon a rising character should be left to those who had something to hope or fear from the event. 2

The hazards of those that aspire to eminence would be much diminished if they had none but acknowledged rivals to encounter. Their enemies would then be few, and what is of yet greater importance, would be known. But what caution is sufficient to ward off the blows of invisible assailants, or what force can stand against unintermitted attacks, and a continual succession of enemies? Yet such is the state of the world, that no sooner can any man emerge from the crowd, and fix the eyes of the publick upon him, than he stands as a mark to the arrows of lurking calumny, and receives, in the tumult of hostility, from distant and from nameless hands, wounds not always easy to be cured. 3

It is probable that the onset against the candidates for renown, is originally incited by those who imagine themselves in danger of suffering by their success; but when war is once declared, volunteers flock to the standard, multitudes follow the camp only for want of employment, and flying squadrons are dispersed to every part, so pleased with an oppor- 4 tunity of mischief that they toil without prospect of praise, and pillage without hope of profit.

When any man has endeavoured to deserve distinction, he will be   5
surprised to hear himself censured where he could not expect to have been named; he will find the utmost acrimony of malice among those whom he never could have offended.

As there are to be found in the service of envy men of every diversity   6
of temper and degree of understanding, calumny is diffused by all arts and methods of propagation. Nothing is too gross or too refined, too cruel or too trifling to be practised; very little regard is had to the rules of honourable hostility, but every weapon is accounted lawful; and those that cannot make a thrust at life are content to keep themselves in play with petty malevolence, to teaze with feeble blows and impotent disturbance.

But as the industry of observation has divided the most miscellaneous   7
and confused assemblages into proper classes, and ranged the insects of the summer, that torment us with their drones or stings, by their several tribes; the persecutors of merit, notwithstanding their numbers, may be likewise commodiously distinguished into Roarers, Whisperers, and Moderators.

The Roarer is an enemy rather terrible than dangerous. He has no other   8
qualification for a champion of controversy than a hardened front and strong voice. Having seldom so much desire to confute as to silence, he depends rather upon vociferation than argument, and has very little care to adjust one part of his accusation to another, to preserve decency in his language, or probability in his narratives. He has always a store of reproachful epithets and contemptuous appellations, ready to be produced as occasion may require, which by constant use he pours out with resistless volubility. If the wealth of a trader is mentioned, he without hesitation devotes him to bankruptcy; if the beauty and elegance of a lady be commended, he wonders how the town can fall in love with rustick deformity; if a new performance of genius happens to be celebrated, he pronounces the writer a hopeless ideot, without knowledge of books or life, and without the understanding by which it must be acquired. His exaggerations are generally without effect upon those whom he compels to hear them; and though it will sometimes happen that the timorous are awed by his violence, and the credulous mistake his confidence for knowledge, yet the opinions which he endeavours to suppress soon recover their former strength, as the trees that bend to the tempest erect themselves again when its force is past.

The Whisperer is more dangerous. He easily gains attention by a soft   9
address, and excites curiosity by an air of importance. As secrets are not to be made cheap by promiscuous publication, he calls a select audience

about him, and gratifies their vanity with an appearance of trust by com-
municating his intelligence in a low voice. Of the trader he can tell that
though he seems to manage an extensive commerce, and talks in high
terms of the funds, yet his wealth is not equal to his reputation; he has
lately suffered much by an expensive project, and had a greater share than
is acknowledged in the rich ship that perished by the storm. Of the beauty
he has little to say, but that they who see her in a morning do not discover
all these graces which are admired in the park. Of the writer he affirms
with great certainty, that though the excellence of the work be incontest-
able, he can claim but a small part of the reputation; that he owed most of
the images and sentiments to a secret friend; and that the accuracy and
equality of the stile was produced by the successive correction of the
chief criticks of the age.

As every one is pleased with imagining that he knows something not   10
yet commonly divulged, secret history easily gains credit; but it is for the
most part believed only while it circulates in whispers, and when once
it is openly told, is openly confuted.

The most pernicious enemy is the man of Moderation. Without in-   11
terest in the question, or any motive but honest curiosity, this impartial
and zealous enquirer after truth, is ready to hear either side, and always
disposed to kind interpretations and favourable opinions. He has heard
the trader's affairs reported with great variation, and after a diligent comparison of the evidence, concludes it probable that the splendid superstructure of business being originally built upon a narrow basis, has lately
been found to totter; but between dilatory payment and bankruptcy there
is a great distance; many merchants have supported themselves by expedients for a time, without any final injury to their creditors; and what
is lost by one adventure may be recovered by another. He believes that
a young lady pleased with admiration, and desirous to make perfect what
is already excellent, may heighten her charms by artificial improvements,
but surely most of her beauties must be genuine, and who can say that
he is wholly what he endeavours to appear? The author he knows to be
a man of diligence, who perhaps does not sparkle with the fire of *Homer,*
but has the judgment to discover his own deficiencies, and to supply them
by the help of others; and in his opinion modesty is a quality so amiable
and rare, that it ought to find a patron wherever it appears, and may justly
be preferred by the publick suffrage to petulant wit and ostentatious
literature.

He who thus discovers failings with unwillingness, and extenuates the   12
faults which cannot be denied, puts an end at once to doubt or vindication; his hearers repose upon his candour and veracity, and admit the
charge without allowing the excuse.

Such are the arts by which the envious, the idle, the peevish, and the   *13*
thoughtless, obstruct that worth which they cannot equal, and by artifices
thus easy, sordid, and detestable, is industry defeated, beauty blasted,
and genius depressed.

QUESTIONS AND EXERCISES

Vocabulary

1. Define or explain each of the following terms:

    calumny (3)   appellation (8)
    censured (5)   promiscuous (9)
    acrimony (5)   pernicious (11)
    vociferation (8)   dilatory (11)
    epithets (8)

2. Point out several examples of archaic spellings.
3. Comment on the range and level of Johnson's vocabulary. What
   other of Johnson's achievements may have a causal relationship
   here?

Rhetoric

4. Analyze one of Johnson's long sentences. Note examples of items in
   a series, parallel structure, and subordination.
5. Note the tight structural organization of the essay. How are the
   "Roarers, Whisperers, and Moderators" ranked in order of annoyance? Is this a dramatic classification?
6. Paragraphs 1-5 function as a preamble. Today's short essay would
   more likely start with paragraph 6. What does this fact have to do
   with the styles of each age?
7. Bacon, Addison, Steele, Johnson, Lamb, Dickens, Mill, Ruskin, and
   Huxley have all influenced the English essay. What qualities of style
   did Johnson have that are still noticeable in today's essay?
8. Comment on the grammar and style of the last sentence of the essay.
9. Find examples of wit or humor in the essay. What kind of humor is it?
10. Johnson wrote during the neo-classical age. What elements of style
    did he share with his age?

Theme

11. What was Johnson's target?
12. How deep was Johnson's attack?
13. What do you think was Johnson's attitude toward human nature?

14. Johnson was a practical man opposed to the wild, disordered romantics of his day. If he was writing today, with whom would he identify (rebels, establishment, angry brigade)?

Topics and Assignments for Composition

1. Write an analysis of the style of Johnson's essay.
2. Write an essay analyzing the assumptions of the essay.
3. Write a short, highly organized essay imitating Johnson's pattern; however, choose your own target.
4. Pope, one of Johnson's contemporaries, wrote, "Whatever is, is right." Write an essay showing why or why not Johnson would have agreed with this slogan.

Hans Selye

Personality Types

Sketches of personality types tend to become caricatures or idealized *1*
portraits if you have strong feelings about your subject. I cannot help
being prejudiced toward certain types of scientists, I might as well admit
it. Some types I love and admire, others I hate and despise, so let me
start by bringing out through exaggeration the features that I dislike most
in them. Then, I shall draw idealized portraits of the perfect chief and
perfect disciple. None of these characters exist in a pure state, but it
would take a Tolstoi or a Dostoevski to picture scientific personalities
as they really are. These sketches of the repulsive and the divine in the
scientists I knew, are the best I can offer to remind us of what to avoid
and what to emulate. (Just between us, in myself I can discern at least
traces of all these types.)

The Doers

1. The fact collector. He is interested only in the discovery of new *2*
facts. As long as they have not been previously published, all findings are
equally interesting (and equally meaningless) to him, because he does not
try to evaluate them; any attempt at evaluation strikes him as objection-
able blabber.

This type is usually a good observer and very conscientious about his *3*
work, but he completely lacks imagination. He keeps regular hours, but
rarely has any inducement to work overtime. His teachers or colleagues
feel compelled to suggest that he should try a dynamic analysis of his
findings, but their remarks invariably fall upon deaf ears. For example,
he may spend years on a meticulous examination of the microscopic
structure of the tiny pineal gland in all animal species to which he can

gain access, without ever attempting to perform a pinealectomy or to prepare a pineal extract in order to find out what this organ is good for. He may conscientiously determine the effect of every newly synthesized steroid hormone upon the preputial gland without ever examining any other effects of these compounds or showing any interest in the function of this gland.

Fact Collectors may find things that are subsequently useful to others — still, I am glad that this type rarely occurs in pure form.   4

2. *The gadgeteer.* This kind is closely related to the preceding one.   5
He constantly tries to improve apparatus or techniques and becomes so interested in their perfection that he never gets to use them. Like the Fact Collector, he considers material for discovery as an end in itself. However, the Gadgeteer is much more original, imaginative and emotionally involved in his work; he rarely limits his activity to regular hours.

The Thinkers

1. *The bookworm.* This is the purest form of theoretician. He reads   6
voraciously and may accumulate encyclopedic knowledge. The Bookworm is usually very intelligent and shows a great disposition for philosophy, mathematics or statistics; he is well informed about the most complex theoretic aspects of biochemistry and biophysics. Owing to the hours spent in the library, the Bookworm is awkward with his hands in the lab, so he rarely uses them, which makes them still more awkward. He must know everything about his field before starting an experiment and then he decides not to do it after all, because it has been done before or would not reveal anything.

"He who can does. He who cannot, teaches" [George Bernard Shaw].   7
The Bookworm likes to teach and teaches well. His lessons are highly informative but impersonal. Like the superannuated ballet dancer, he can teach his art to others without being able to perform it any more — the difference being that the Bookworm never was able to perform. He is implacable at examinations, which he uses largely to show off his own knowledge. His superb memory and experience in the construction of indexes and files, often combined with a talent for the clear expression of his views, may become a formidable tool in committee work. The Bookworm agrees to sit on many committees and to do much teaching as welcome excuses for his failure in the laboratory.

2. *The classifier.* As a child, he used to collect stamps, matchbox   8
covers, butterflies or plants, which he arranged in albums. As a scientist, he may still collect butterflies or plants for Linnaean systematization, or he may classify scientific literature, steroid hormones, pharmacologic

actions, anything that lends itself to the dispelling of confusion by bringing like items together. The Classifier is closely related to the Fact Collector, but likes only closely related facts that fit into a series. To a certain extent he is a theorist, since he assumes something inherently common in the groups he creates; but he rarely goes on to analyze the nature of this commonness. Instead, he labels his groups, which satisfies his need in this respect. Among the medical specialities, dermatology has been most intensely subjected to the work of Classifiers. Following the example of zoologic, botanical, and microbiologic terminologies, innumerable minor variants of skin diseases have received scholarly Greco-Latin designations (often embodying the names of the baptizers).

Classifiers have had a great share in the creation of modern science.   *9* As we shall see, the identification of natural units and their classification into a system is the first step in theory formation. The Classifier has a true scientific soul; he derives pleasure from the contemplation of lawfulness in nature, although he rarely explores further after he has succeeded in putting similar things together. His greatest dangers are the arrangement of items according to irrelevant characteristics, and a plethora of neologisms, sometimes aggravated by egocentric eponymism.

3. The analyst. As a boy, he took his wrist watch apart (although he   *10* could not put it together again) because he just had to know what made it tick. Later, as a scientist, he continued to display the same type of curiosity. One of the purest variants of this personality is the analytical chemist, who spends all his time in the search for components, without giving much thought to the manufacture of new compounds by synthesis. In medicine, the Analyst likes anatomy, histology and analytical biochemistry. (As these Notes show, he may even become curious about what makes himself and his friends tick, and feel the urge to analyze the scientific mentality.)

Some analytical work is an indispensable prerequisite for all classifica-   *11* tion and synthesis; hence, no investigation can have a broad scope without it. The danger lies in forgetting that the only purpose in taking things apart is to find out how they are put together — preferably with improvements.

4. The synthetist. As a child, he liked to build cardhouses, or bridges   *12* and towers out of putty and matches. In science, his synthetic talent depends largely upon certain manual and intellectual skills. The gift for synthesis shows up well in the most varied fields: synthetic chemistry, instrumentation, theory construction, or plastic surgery. The Synthetist is the highest type of scientist, because analysis and classification are only preambles for synthesis. His greatest danger is that he may forget to ask himself whether the thing he tries to put together is really worth having. Synthesis, like all other skills, may become an aim in itself and never get past the card house stage.

The Emotionalists

1. The big boss. As a child, he was the captain of the team—the win-   *13*
ning team. Later he went into science because it has "class." He knew he could win at this game too, and he was right, for he is the born "Fuehrer." His main aim is success, success in anything, success for its own sake. His distorted mind is directed by a monumental inferiority complex, which he despises, and he must hide behind a self-certain, iron façade. His deep wounds were acquired early in childhood. They may have been caused by abject poverty, the ugliness of his features, or social ostracism of his family because of race, religion, alcohol or crime. In any case he was determined to get out from down under; he would show them that, in this big tavern of a world, he can lick anyone at his own game. He might have made almost the same career in business, politics, or the army —but circumstances got him into the "science racket" and, being an opportunist, he wasn't going to miss his chance.

During his early days, as a research assistant, he published some quite   *14*
creditable work in association with others, but it never became very clear how much of it was done by himself.

He had many love affairs which he always terminated quite brutally,   *15*
and finally he "married well," thereby improving his social and financial position. Being an excellent politician, committee man, and organizer, it did not take him long to become chief of a research department.

Even now, his greatest asset is string-pulling and making others do his   *16*
work. His shifty eyes never look straight at you, except to give an order which he knows will be obeyed. Despite his egocentric cruelty, he is hearty, in a condescendingly back-slapping way. He is easily on first-name terms, even with his subordinates, and loves to use jargon. His expressions are hypererudite or vulgar, depending upon the occasion; he uses them with equal ease to play the role of the remote Olympian or the democratic "good guy," as required by the circumstances. He has a prima-donna complex and is essentially a narcissist, very proud of his "vision for what is important in science," although this extroverted, self-centered, cast-iron mind refuses to understand the real values beneath the surface. By skillful participation on the advisory boards of granting agencies and at the dinner tables of millionaires, he succeeds in attracting a great deal of money to his university. Thereby, he manages to enlarge his department and staff to a point where he can keep informed about their work just sufficiently to report on it (though not always correctly) at meet-

ings with "important people." He no longer has time for the lab, but after all, he did just as well as the best among the eggheads, the ivory-tower dreamers, when it came to the tangible status symbols of research. He is satisfied. But, during the rare moments of introspection—when he is tired or slightly drunk—he wonders . . . he wishes he had . . . but no, all he needs is a rest.

As you may gather, I don't like this type very much, but don't under-   17
rate him; one or the other variant of him will have power over you throughout your life.

2. *The eager beaver.* He is so anxious to get there fast that he has no   18
time to think about where he really wants to go. Being an opportunist and a compulsive worker, he explores questions, not because they interest him particularly, but because he happens to have everything needed for a quick solution. When he is young, he hurries to get on the next rung of the career ladder, because there is still such a long stretch to the top — and when he is on top, he hurries because there is so little time left. Actually, he likes speed for its own sake, as the sportsman does.

These young men in a hurry do not love Nature, but merely rape her.   19
They may possess her body as much as we do—but not her spirit.

3. *The cold fish.* He is the ostentatiously unemotional skeptic. With his   20
blank face he murmurs the mottoes of his breed: "Take it easy"; "This is not likely to work"; "You didn't prove your point and there is really no way to prove it"; "You aren't the first to find this." His social life is guided by the code: "Ask no favors, do no favors." And at the end of his course we find the epitaph: "No hits, no runs, no errors."

4. *The desiccated-laboratory-female.* She is the bitter, hostile, bossy   21
and unimaginative female counterpart of the Cold Fish. Usually a technician, she rarely gets past the B.Sc., or at most, the M.Sc. degree, but she may be a Ph.D., less commonly an M.D. In any event, she assumes a dominant position in her own group, has very little understanding of human frailties among her subordinates and almost invariably falls in love with her immediate boss. She may be very useful in performing exacting, dull jobs herself and in enforcing discipline upon others, but tends to create more tension and dissatisfaction than the results warrant. Some women make excellent scientists, but this type never does.

5. *The narcissist.* The embodiment of pure egocentricity, he stands in   22
constant awe of his own talents and is ready for any sacrifice to promote their fulfillment. Each time he performs an operation he relates, to everyone within reach, the incredible complications that have arisen and how they were all successfully overcome. Each time he makes a new (or not so new), significant (or not so significant) observation, he enumerates all the far-reaching consequences this discovery may have upon the prog-

ress of science. Sometimes he takes pains to emphasize the great intricacy and originality of his train of thought and the almost insuperable technical difficulties that had to be mastered to make his observation possible. But, curiously, at other times he derives just as much pleasure from having done it all with the greatest of ease, or even by sheer accident. To the Narcissist, the conquest of obstacles and the stroke of luck are equally eloquent witnesses of his greatness. Since he is not unintelligent, he sometimes senses the danger of inviting derision, if not hostility, by what others may consider obnoxiously ostentatious vanity, but this does not faze him. He merely suggests, with a contented smile, that his apparent immodesty is only make-believe, or a charming exaggeration for fun – but of course, facts are facts, and we are allowed to read between the lines of his modest remarks.

The self-assured Narcissist goes no further, but there are two insecure   23
variants of this type who constantly scan the horizon for possible threats to their prestige and honor:

(a) The *mimosa type* responds to most stimuli by freezing in his tracks and assuming the pouting countenance of complete indifference. He often feels boycotted or left out of things and complains, "Nobody ever tells ME anything."

(b) The cantankerous *toreador type* creates emergencies on purpose so that he may exhibit the manly courage with which he can meet them. "No one is going to tell ME what to do," he says, kicking up a terrible row whenever he thinks someone might question his authority.

6. *The aggressive-arguer.* In school he was the smart aleck who knew   24
it all, and in the research laboratory he remains insufferably cocksure. In scientific arguments, he is interested mainly in being right and defends his point by special pleading, using misleading argument or even straight bluff. This is a dangerous variant of the Narcissist; he can singlehandedly create tensions which destroy the harmony of even the most congenial group.

7. *The credit-shark.* His main preoccupation is with getting his name   25
on as many papers as possible. In the lab, he constantly irritates his colleagues by suggesting that whatever they are doing was actually stimulated by his own earlier remarks. He may be brutally blunt about this if he thinks he is right, or he will take great care to camouflage his assertions in an air of self-evidence, if he knows he is bluffing. For example, he may exclaim with enthusiasm: "As I was saying just the other day, this is exactly the kind of work you should be doing," or "This is a beautiful confirmation of my thesis that. . . ." At the autopsy table, he hurries to a colleague's animals, so that he may be first to point out anatomic changes that anyone would have observed in due course. In papers, he writes long

legalistic introductions to prove that, although what he is about to describe has been seen by many others, he is the first to describe and interpret it quite the right way, and his contribution is what really counts.

8. The saint. Truly chaste in thought, word and deed, he is the Knight   26
of the Holy Grail. As a boy scout, he vowed to do not one, but ten good
deeds a day. Later, he went into medicine only because of its humani-
tarian goals. At first, the Saint studied tropical medicine, because he
planned to practice in a leprosarium; but upon reading Sinclair Lewis'
"Arrowsmith," he came to the conclusion that in the laboratory he could
do even more for his fellow man. He does not play the role of the Saint,
he really is one. And although his self-effacing altruism represents a terrible handicap to his efficiency in the lab, I lack the courage to draw the
caricature of such a truly likeable and respectable person. The qualifications of the Saint would have suited him better for the leprosarium than
for the laboratory. He should not have chosen the life of an investigator,
but the desecration of icons is in bad taste, even if they do not render
special services. In any event, he is only one in a million, so let us keep
his image untarnished as a symbol of purity, beyond the reach of our
worldly critique.

9. The saintly one. He imitates the real Saint. With an ostentatiously   27
modest, sanctimonious bearing, he strikes the attitude of the "knight in
shining armor" when he speaks about his aims in medicine. His smile is
benign and self-righteous; it suggests tolerance and compassion for his
colleagues who just do not have a properly developed sense of right and
wrong. This type is almost as rarely found in laboratories as the true Saint.

10. The goody-goody. In grade school he was the teacher's pet; in   28
medical school, he asked the professor, "What are we responsible for at
examinations?" After he got married, he became a conscientious bread-
winner, but his work as a scientist suffers severely from his sincere desire
to give his wife the attention she deserves. He lives mainly for her and for
his children and is willing to do (or renounce) anything for their happiness. Despite the superficial resemblance, he is quite unlike the Saint
who, on the contrary, sacrifices the family to his moral ideals. The Goody-
Goody may be quite intelligent, but his insipid innocence, his complete
lack of imagination and initiative disqualify him for meaningful scientific
research, and he tends to use his self-imposed restrictions as an excuse
for inefficiency. He is willing to sacrifice his career for that of his children,
who must receive all the privileges that he never had; the Goody-Goody
does not feel that in the succession of generations he is the one whose
work should bear fruit. His desires are honorable, but he forgets that he
could have fulfilled them better had he chosen another walk of life.

The basic defects of the preceding ten personality types are excessive   29 self-effacement or egocentricity and exhibitionism which over-shadow all other forms of scientific motivation. These personality traits, whether morally good or bad, are sterilizing because they focus attention upon the investigator rather than the investigation. Both the Saint and the Narcissist, to take extreme opposites, are more preoccupied with the value of their own conduct than with the progress of knowledge. We may admire or despise them, but their place is not in the laboratory.

The Ideals

1. Faust: the ideal teacher and chief. The pure philosopher-scientist   *30*
has a religious reverence for Nature, but is humbly aware of man's limited power to explore its secrets. He has a profound and compassionate understanding for human frailties, but his kindness does not mislead him into unwarranted tolerance for lack of discipline, superficiality of work, or any other form of behavior incompatible with his calling. His somewhat romantic attitude toward research exhibits sentiment, but no sentimentality. His main assets are: an enthusiasm for the possibilities of research rather than for his own possibilities; respect for the interests of others; a great capacity for singling out important facts; a keen power of observation; lack of blinding prejudice toward man and scientific data; an iron-cast self-discipline, as well as great originality and imagination, combined with scrupulous attention to detail both in laboratory technique and in the logical evaluation of results.

He is neither broken by failure, nor corrupted by victory. Having de-   *31*
cided early in life what he considers to be worth living for, he follows a steady course uninhibited by remorse, temptation, fear or even success. Despite the infinite complications of his work, he remains a simple and real person; no amount of adulation can turn him into a "distinguished personage."

2. Famulus: the ideal pupil and assistant. I left him to the last for, like   *32*
his master, he is the perfect blend of all other types, but in addition he represents the Future. Famulus combines some of the Saint's austere idealism with just enough of each kind of sinful lust to give him the worldliness and healthy appetite needed for an eager and efficient exploration of the world in and around us. The ideal junior basic scientist differs from his teacher and chief only in that we meet him at an earlier point in his course—when he is still less mellowed by experience. His mind is not as mature as that of his spiritual father, still not necessarily richer in youthful vigor. Daring and perseverance in strenuous tasks are qualities we associate with the vigor and strength of youth. Yet, young Famulus may be more cautious and preoccupied with his own security than old Faust, and

his less trained mind may not be as resistant to the stress of prolonged abstract thinking. But his body stands up much better to the exigencies of the lab; his eyesight is keener, his movements more certain; he can stand at the work bench for hours without fatigue, and, most important of all, he has so much more time ahead to make his dreams come true. That is why Famulus is really the most important of our personages. But I need not explain him to you, young man. You know him well already. For you want to be he as much as I want to be Faust, though neither of us can ever succeed. Ideals are not created to be attained, but to point the way. It is good to see clearly in whose image we should try, as best we can, to create ourselves.

Epilogue

None of these prototypes exist in pure form; their characteristics over- *33* lap and many other personality traits may be so dominant in certain individuals as to justify the listing of innumerable additional types. Here, I have tried to sketch only the type of people whom I have met most often, or who left the most profound impressions upon me—good or bad.

If we now look back upon our list, we see that some scientists are pre- *34* dominantly doers, others thinkers, and yet others, the emotionalists, so intensely preoccupied with themselves that their interest in Nature takes second place.

The ideal scientist is not, and perhaps even should not be free of char- *35* acteristics distasteful to the average citizen. Society sanctions the motives that are best for the majority, and scientists are a very small minority. Men are not created equal and should not try to be alike. The splendid musculature of the athlete is admired but not coveted by his wife; the scientist's passion for objectivity would be no asset to the nonobjective painter.

In my long career, I have met no outstanding scientist who was en- *36* tirely free of egotism or vanity, and in the single-minded pursuit of their aims, few of them spent as much time with their families or gave as much attention to political problems as the average good citizen should. To my mind, the highest qualities of mankind are a warmhearted attitude toward our kin, and particularly compassion for all who suffer from disease, poverty or oppression. Yet, each of us needs different, additional motivations and skills to contribute his best in the service of his fellow man. My purpose here is not to sit in judgment over good and bad, but merely to identify the basic qualifications that characterize the scientists I know. Such an analysis can help each of us select and reject what does or does not fit his personality. All I can do is to dissect and characterize the parts that I have learned to see, but the reader of these Notes will have to do the selecting and rejecting himself, in consonance with his own needs and abilities.

QUESTIONS AND EXERCISES

Vocabulary

1. Define or explain the following terms:

caricatures (1)	frailties (21)
blabber (2)	narcissist (22)
pinealectomy (3)	derision (22)
steroid (3)	mimosa (23)
voraciously (6)	leprosarium (26)
ostracism (13)	altruism (26)
egocentric (16)	icons (26)
hypererudite (16)	sanctimonious (27)
prima donna (16)	insipid (28)
ostentatiously (20)	Faust (30)
epitaph (20)	adulation (31)
desiccated (21)	Famulus (32)

Rhetoric

2. Selye bases his entire discussion of "Personality Types" on classification. Outline the selection. Why is it easy to outline?
3. Discuss the nature of the names that he gives to the various types. How is this selection like an allegory?
4. What is the advantage of having each division begin with a title or a number?

Theme

5. According to the author, what personality types should not go into research?
6. Why does Selye say that he recognizes some of the bad traits of each type in himself?
7. Scientists are supposed to be objective. How do Selye's classifications tend to refute this claim of total objectivity?
8. What is the purpose of caricature? Is it a form of satire? Compare verbal caricature to graphic caricature.

Topics and Assignments for Composition

1. In one sentence summarize the type who should not go into the laboratory to do research.
2. In one paragraph summarize the ideal scientist. You may wish to use short direct quotations from Selye's essay.
3. Selye used the word "icon." Why is this essay iconoclastic? Write a paragraph defending it as iconoclastic or maintaining the opposite position.
4. Write an essay in which you set up a classification similar to the one in the essay about an area with which you are familiar. For example, you may classify: students, teachers, life guards, girls on the beach, watchdogs, politicians, etc.

Aldous Huxley

Who Are You?

The most striking fact about human beings is that, in many respects, *1*
they are very unlike one another. Their bodies vary enormously in size
and shape. Their modes of thought and speech and feeling are startlingly
different. Startlingly different, too, are their reactions to even such basic
things as food, sex, money, and power. Between the most highly gifted
and those of least ability, and between persons endowed with one particular kind of talent or temperament and persons endowed with another
kind, the gulfs are so wide as to be bridgeable only by the most enlightened charity.

These are facts which from time immemorial have been recognized, *2*
described in plays and stories, commented on in proverbs, aphorisms,
and poems. And yet, in spite of their obviousness and their enormous
practical importance, these facts are still, to a very great extent, outside
the pale of systematic thought.

The first and indispensable condition of systematic thought is classifi- *3*
cation. For the purposes of pure and applied science, the best classification is comprehensive, covering as many of the indefinitely numerous
facts as it is possible for thought to cover without becoming confused,
and yet is simple enough to be readily understood and used without being
so simple as to be untrue to the essentially complex nature of reality. The
categories under which it classifies things and events are easily recognizable, lend themselves to being expressed in quantitative terms, and
can be shown experimentally to be meaningful for our specifically human
purposes.

Up to the present, all the systems in terms of which men have at- *4*
tempted to think about human differences have been unsatisfactory.
Some, for example, have conspicuously failed to cover more than a part
of the relevant facts. This is especially true of psychology and sociology

Reprinted with the permission of Mrs. Aldous Huxley.

as commonly taught and practised at the present time. How many of even the best of our psychologists talk, write, think, and act as though the human body, with its innate constitution and its acquired habits, were something that, in an analysis of mental states, could safely be ignored! And even when they do admit, rather reluctantly, that the mind always trails its carcass behind it, they have little or nothing to tell us about the ways in which mental and physical characteristics are related.

Sociologists deal with abstractions even more phantasmally bodiless. For example, they will carry out laborious researches into the problems of marriage. But when we read the results, we are flabbergasted to find that the one factor never taken into account by the researchers is who the men and women under investigation actually *are*. We are told every detail about their social and economic background; nothing at all about their inherited psychophysical constitution.   5

There are other classificatory systems which claim to be comprehensive, but in which the indispensable process of simplification has been carried so far that they are no longer true to the facts. The interpretation of all human activity in terms of economics is a case in point. Another type of oversimplification is to be found in such theories as those of Helvetius in the eighteenth century and of certain Behaviorists in the twentieth — theories which profess to account for everything that men do or are in terms of environment, education, or conditioned reflexes. At the other extreme of oversimplification we find some of the more rabid Eugenists, who attribute all the observable differences between human beings to hereditary factors, and refuse to admit that environmental influences may also play a part.   6

It may be remarked in passing that most of the hypotheses and classification systems we use in our everyday thinking are grossly oversimplified and therefore grossly untrue to a reality which is intrinsically complex. Popular theories about such things as morals, politics, economics, and religion are generally of the either-or, A-causes-B variety. But in any real-life situation there are almost always more than two valid and workable alternatives and invariably more than one determining cause. That is why the utterances of speech-making politicians can never, in the very nature of things, be true. In half an hour's yelling from a platform it is intellectually impossible for even the most scrupulous man to tell the delicately complex truth about any of the major issues of political or economic life.   7

We come now to the classification systems which attempt to cover the whole ground, but which have proved scientifically unsatisfactory because (though founded, as they often are, upon profound insights into the nature of human reality) they have made use of categories which could   8 not be expressed in quantitative terms. Thus, for several thousands of years, the Hindus have been classifying human beings within the framework of four main psycho-physico-social categories. Because the caste system in India has become petrified into a rigidity that is untrue to the facts of life and therefore often unjust, the whole idea of caste is repellent to Western minds. And yet that special branch of applied psychology which deals with vocational guidance is concerned precisely with assigning individuals to their proper place in the natural caste system. The work of the specialists in "human engineering" has made it quite clear that individuals belong congenitally to one kind of caste, and that they hurt themselves and their society if, by some mistake, they get enrolled in another caste. Some time in the next century or two the empirical findings of the vocational guidance experts will be linked up with a satisfactory method of analyzing the total psycho-physical organism. When that happens, society will be in a position to reorganize itself on the basis of a rejuvenated and thoroughly beneficent, because thoroughly realistic, caste system.

In the West, for more than two thousand years, men were content with   9
a classification system devised by the Greek physician, Hippocrates. His theory was that one's innate psycho-physical constitution was determined by the relative predominance within one's body of one or other of the four "humors"—blood, phlegm, black bile, and yellow bile. (We still describe temperaments as "sanguine" or "phlegmatic"; we still talk of "choler" and "melancholia.") Humoral pathology persisted into the nineteenth century. Diseases were attributed to a derangement of the normal balance of the individual's humors, and treatment was directed to restoring the equilibrium. This relating of disease to inherited constitution was essentially realistic, and one of the things that modern medicine most urgently needs is a new and sounder version of the Hippocratic hypothesis—a classification of human differences in terms of which the physician may interpret the merely mechanical findings of his diagnostic instruments.

Finally we come to those classification systems which are unsatisfac-   10
tory because the categories they make use of, although susceptible of being expressed in quantitative terms, have not, in practice, turned out to be particularly meaningful. Thus the anthropometrists have measured innumerable skulls, determined the coloring of innumerable heads of hair and pairs of eyes, but have told us very little of genuinely scientific or practical value about human beings. Why? Because, as a matter of empirical fact, these records and measurements could not be related in any significant way to human behavior.

And, not content with telling us very little by means of a colossal vol-   11 ume of statistics, the anthropometrists proceeded to confuse the whole issue by trying to think about human differences in terms of fixed racial types—the Nordic, the Alpine, the Mediterranean, and so forth. But the most obvious fact about all the existing groups of human beings, at any rate in Europe and America, is that each one of them exhibits a large number of individual variations. In certain areas, it is true, a single closely related set of such variations may be more common than in other areas. It is upon this fact that the whole theory of racial types has been built up —a system of classification which has proved extremely unfruitful as an instrument of pure and applied science, and, in the hands of the Nazi ideologists, extremely fruitful as an instrument of discrimination and persecution.

II

So much, then, for the classification systems which have proved to be   12
unsatisfactory. Does there exist a more adequate system? This is a question which it is now possible, I think, to answer with a decided yes. A classification system more adequate to the facts and more potentially fruitful than any other devised hitherto has been formulated by Dr. W. H. Sheldon in two recently published volumes, *The Varieties of Human Physique* and *The Varieties of Temperament*.

Sheldon's classification system is the fruit of nearly fifteen years of re-   13
search, during which he and his collaborators have made, measured, and arranged in order many thousands of standardized photographs of the male body, taken from in front, from behind, and in profile. A careful study of these photographs revealed that the most basic (first order) classification system in terms of which the continuous variations of human physique could adequately be described was based upon the discrimination of three factors, present to a varying degree in every individual. To these three factors Sheldon has given the names of *endomorphy, mesomorphy,* and *ectomorphy*.

Endomorphy is the factor which, when predominant, expresses itself   14
in a tendency for anabolism to predominate over catabolism, which often results in soft and comfortable roundness of physique. At school the extreme endomorph is called Slob or Fatty. By middle life he or she may be so enormously heavy as to be practically incapable of walking. The endomorphic physique is dominated by its digestive tract. Autopsies show that the endomorphic gut is often more than twice as long and weighs more than twice as much as the intestine of a person in whom there is an extreme predominance of the ectomorphic constituent.

Predominant mesomorphy expresses itself in a physique that is hard   15 and muscular. The body is built around strong heavy bones and is dominated by its extraordinarily powerful muscles. In youth, the extreme mesomorph tends to look older than his years, and his skin, instead of being soft, smooth, and unwrinkled, like that of the endomorph, is coarse and leathery, tans easily, and sets in deep folds and creases at a comparatively early age. It is from the ranks of extreme mesomorphs that successful boxers, football players, military leaders, and the central figures of the more heroic comic strips are drawn.

The extreme ectomorph is neither comfortably round nor compactly   *16*
hard. His is a linear physique with slender bones, stringy unemphatic muscles, a short and thin-walled gut. The ectomorph is a lightweight, has little muscular strength, needs to eat at frequent intervals, is often quick and highly sensitive. The ratio of skin surface to body mass is higher than in endomorphs or mesomorphs, and he is thus more vulnerable to outside influences, because more extensively in contact with them. His body is built, not around the endomorph's massively efficient intestine, not around the mesomorph's big bones and muscles, but around a relatively predominant and unprotected nervous system.

Endomorphy, mesomorphy, and ectomorphy occur, as constituting   *17*
components, in every human individual. In most persons the three components are combined fairly evenly, or at least harmoniously. Extreme and unbalanced predominance of any one factor is relatively uncommon.

For example, less than ten boys out of every hundred are sufficiently   *18*
mesomorphic to engage with even moderate success in the more strenuous forms of athletics, requiring great strength and physical endurance. Hence the almost criminal folly of encouraging all boys, whatever their hereditary make-up, to develop athletic ambitions. By doing this, educators condemn large numbers of their pupils to an unnecessary disappointment and frustration, plant the seed of neurosis among the unsuccessful, and foster a conspicuous bumptiousness and self-conceit in the extreme mesomorph. A rational policy with regard to athletics would be to tell all boys the simple truth, which is that very few of them can expect to excel in the more violent sports, that such excellence depends primarily on a particular inheritance of size and shape, and that persons of other shapes and sizes not suited to athletic proficiency have as good a right to realize their own *natural* capacities as the extreme mesomorph and can contribute at least as much to society.

In order to calculate the relative amounts of each component in the   *19*
total individual mixture, Sheldon divides the body into five regions and proceeds to make a number of measurements in each zone. The records of these measurements are then subjected to certain mathematical procedures, which yield a three-digit formula. This formula expresses the

amount of endomorphy, mesomorphy, and ectomorphy present within the organism, as measured on a seven-point scale of values. Thus the formula 7–1–1 indicates that the individual under consideration exhibits endomorphy in its highest possible degree, combined with the lowest degree of mesomorphy and ectomorphy. In practice, he would probably be extremely fat, gluttonous and comfort-loving, without drive or energy, almost sexless, and pathetically dependent on other people. How different from the well-balanced 4–4–4, the formidably powerful and aggressive 3–7–1, the thin, nervous, "introverted" 1–2–7!

The relationships between the components are such that only a certain   *20* number of the mathematically possible combinations can occur in nature. Thus it is obviously impossible for a human being to be a 7–1–7, or a 7–7–7, or a 1–7–7; for nobody can be simultaneously extremely round and soft and extremely hard and compact or extremely narrow, small-gutted, and stringy-muscled. Sheldon and his collaborators have found that, in terms of their seven-point scale of values for three components, seventy-six varieties of human physique can be clearly recognized. If a value scale of more than seven points were used, the number would of course be correspondingly greater. But they have found empirically that the seven-point scale provides an instrument of analysis sufficiently precise for most practical purposes.

The three-digit formula given by an analysis of the basic components   *21* tells some of the story, but not all. It needs to be supplemented by additional information in respect to three secondary components present in all individuals—the factor of *dysplasia* or disharmony; the factor of *gynandromorphy,* or the possession of characteristics typical of the opposite sex; and the factor of *texture,* whether fine or coarse, aesthetically pleasing or the reverse.

Dysplasia occurs when one region or feature of the body is more or   *22* less markedly in disharmony with the rest of the physique. We are all familiar, for example, with the big, barrel-chested man whose legs or arms taper off to an absurdly slender inefficiency. And who has not had to listen to the despairing complaints of the ladies to whom ironic nature has given an elegantly ectomorphic torso, with hips and thighs of the most amply endomorphic scale? Such disharmonies are significant and must be observed and measured, for they provide many clues to the explorers of human personality.

All persons exhibit characteristics of the opposite sex, some to a very   *23* slight degree, others more or less conspicuously. Again, the variations are significant. And the same is true of the factor of texture. Of two individuals having the same fundamental pattern one may be markedly fine-textured, the other markedly coarse-textured. The difference is one which

cannot be neglected. That is why the basic formula is always supplemented by other descriptive qualifications expressing the amount of
dysplasia, gynandromorphy, and fineness of texture observed in the individual under analysis.

III

So much for the varieties of physique and the methods by which they   24
can be classified and measured. Inevitably two questions now propound
themselves. First, is it possible for an individual to modify his basic
physical pattern? Is there any system of dieting, hormone therapy, or
exercise by means of which, say, a 1-1-7 can be transformed into a
7-1-1 or a 3-4-3? The answer would seem to be no. An individual's
basic formula cannot be modified. True, an endomorph may be undernourished to the point of looking like a thing of skin and bones. But this
particular thing of skin and bones will be measurably quite unlike the
thing of skin and bones which is an undernourished, or even tolerably well
nourished ectomorph. Our fundamental physical pattern is something
given and unalterable, something we can make the best of but can never
hope to change.

The second question which naturally occurs to us is this: how closely   25
is our fundamental psychological pattern related to our physical pattern?
That such a relationship exists is a subject upon which every dramatist
and storyteller, every observant student of men and women, has always
been agreed. No writer in his senses would dream of associating the
character of Pickwick with the body of Scrooge. And when the comic-
strip artist wants to portray an athletic hero, he gives him the physique
of Flash Gordon, not of Rosie's Beau. Further, men have always clearly
recognized that individuals of one psycho-physical type tend to misunder-
stand and even dislike individuals whose basic psycho-physical pattern
is different from their own. Here are the words which Shakespeare puts
into the mouth of Julius Caesar:

> Let me have men about me that are fat;
> Sleek-headed men and such as sleep o'nights:
> Yond Cassius has a lean and hungry look;
> He thinks too much: such men are dangerous.

Translated into Sheldon's terminology, this means that the mesomorph
is one kind of animal, the ectomorph another; and that their mutual in-
comprehension very often leads to suspicion and downright antipathy.

In a general way all this has been perfectly well known for the past   26
several thousand years. But it has been known only in an intuitive, empirical way. No organized scientific thinking about the subject has been
possible hitherto, because (in spite of some valuable work done in Europe
and America) nobody had worked out a satisfactory classification system
for describing temperamental differences.

Modern chemistry classifies matter in terms of a system of ninety-two   27
first-order elements. In earlier times, men tried to do their thinking about
matter in terms of only four elements—earth, air, fire, and water. But
earth, air, and water are not first-order elements, but elaborate combinations of such elements; while fire is not an element at all, but something
that happens to all kinds of matter under certain conditions of tempera-
ture. In terms of so inadequate a classification system it was impossible
for scientific thought to go very far.

The problem of psychological analysis is identical in principle with that   28
of the analysis of matter. The psychologist's business is to discover first-
order elements, in terms of which the facts of human difference may be
classified and measured. The failure of psychology—and it has conspicuously failed to become the fruitful Science of Man which ideally it should
be—is due to the fact that it has done its analysis of human differences in
terms of entities that were not first-order elements, but combinations of
elements. Sheldon's great contribution to psychology consists in this:
that he has isolated a number of genuine first-order elements of the basic
psychological pattern which we call temperament, and has demonstrated
their close correlation with the individual's basic physical pattern.

What follows is a summing up—necessarily rather crude and oversim-   29
plified—of the conclusions to which his research has led.

Endomorphy, mesomorphy, and ectomorphy are correlated very   30
closely with specific patterns of temperament—endomorphy with the
temperamental pattern to which Sheldon gives the name of *viscerotonia,*
mesomorphy with *somatotonia,* and ectomorphy with *cerebrotonia.*
Close and prolonged observation of many subjects, combined with an
adaptation of the technique known as factor-analysis, resulted in the
isolation of sixty descriptive or determinative traits—twenty for each of
the main, first-order components of temperament. From these sixty, I
select a smaller number of the more striking and easily recognizable
traits.

Conspicuous among the elements of the viscerotonic pattern of tem-   31
perament are relaxation in posture and movement, slow reaction, profound sleep, love of physical comfort, and love of food. With this love of
food for its own sake goes a great love of eating in company, an almost
religious feeling for the social meal as a kind of sacrament. Another con-

spicuous viscerotonic trait is love of polite ceremony, with which goes a love of company, together with indiscriminate amiability and marked dependence on, and desire for, the affection and approval of other people. The viscerotonic does not inhibit his emotions, but tends to give expression to them as they arise, so that nobody is ever in doubt as to what he feels.

Somatotonia, the temperament associated with the hard and powerful mesomorphic physique, is a patterning of very different elements. The somatotonic individual stands and moves in an assertive way, loves physical adventure, enjoys risk and loves to take a chance. He feels a strong need for physical exercise, which he hugely enjoys and often makes a fetish of, just as the viscerotonic enjoys and makes a fetish of eating. When in trouble, he seeks relief in physical action, whereas the viscerotonic turns in the same circumstances to people and the cerebrotonic retires, like a wounded animal, into solitude. The somatotonic is essentially energetic and quick to action. Procrastination is unknown to him; for he is neither excessively relaxed and comfort-loving, like the viscerotonic, nor inhibited and 'sicklied o'er with the pale cast of thought,' like the cerebrotonic. The social manner of the somatotonic is uninhibited and direct. The voice is normally unrestrained, and he coughs, laughs, snores and, when passion breaks through his veneer of civilization, speaks loudly. He is physically courageous in combat and enjoys every kind of competitive activity. *32*

From a sociological point of view, the most significant of the somatotonic traits is the lust for power. The individual who is high in somatotonia loves to dominate, and since he is (when somatotonia is extreme) congenitally insensitive to other people's feelings, since he lacks the indiscriminate amiability and tolerance of viscerotonia and is devoid of cerebrotonic squeamishness, he can easily become a ruthless bully and tyrant. The somatotonic individual is always an extrovert in the sense that his attention is firmly fixed upon external reality, to such an extent that he is necessarily unaware of what is going on in the deeper levels of his own mind. *33*

It should be noted that somatotonic extroversion is quite different from the extroversion of the viscerotonic; for while the latter is continually spilling the emotional beans and turning for support and affection to his fellows, the former tends to be insensitive to other people, feels little need to confide his emotions, and pursues his trampling course through external reality with an effortless callousness. For him the period of youth is the flower of life; he hates to grow old and often makes desperate efforts, even in advanced middle age, to live as actively as he did at twenty. *34*

The viscerotonic, on the other hand, is orientated toward childhood – his own and that of his offspring. He is the great family man. The cerebrotonic, on the other hand, looks forward, even in youth, to the tranquillity and the wisdom which, he hopes or imagines, are associated with old age.

With cerebrotonia we pass from the world of Flash Gordon to that of *35* Hamlet. The cerebrotonic is the over-alert, over-sensitive introvert, who is more concerned with the inner universe of his own thoughts and feelings and imagination than with the external world to which, in their different ways, the viscerotonic and the somatotonic pay their primary attention and allegiance. In posture and movements, the cerebrotonic person is tense and restrained. His reactions may be unduly rapid and his physiological responses uncomfortably intense. It is the cerebrotonic who suffers from nervous indigestion, who gets stage fright and feels nauseated with mere shyness, who suffers from the various skin eruptions often associated with emotional disturbances.

Extreme cerebrotonics have none of the viscerotonic love of company; *36* on the contrary, they have a passion for privacy, hate to make themselves conspicuous, and have none of the exhibitionistic tendencies displayed both by somatotonics and viscerotonics. In company they tend to be shy and unpredictably moody. When they are with strangers they fidget, their glances are shifting, sometimes furtive; their facial expression is apt to change frequently and rapidly. (For all these reasons no extreme cerebrotonic has ever been a good actor or actress.) Their normal manner is inhibited and restrained and when it comes to the expression of feelings they are outwardly so inhibited that viscerotonics suspect them of being heartless. (On their side, cerebrotonics tend to feel a strong repugnance for the viscerotonic's emotional gush and florid ceremoniousness.)

With self-conscious general restraint goes a marked restraint of voice *37* and of all noise in general. To be compelled to raise the voice, as when speaking to the deaf, is, for the cerebrotonic, sheer torture. And it is also torture for him to have to endure noise made by other people. One of the best recipes for an unhappy marriage is to combine a high degree of noise-hating cerebrotonia with a high degree of loud-speaking, loud-laughing, loud-snoring and, in general, noise-making somatotonia. Cerebrotonics are extremely sensitive to pain, sleep poorly, and suffer from chronic fatigue; nevertheless they often live to a ripe old age – provided always that they do not permit themselves to be forced by the pressure of somatotonic public opinion into taking too much violent exercise. They do not easily form habits and are extremely bad at adapting themselves to an active routine, such as military life. They tend to look younger than their age and preserve a kind of youthful intensity of appearance far into

middle life. Alcohol, which increases the relaxed amiability of viscerotonics and heightens the aggressiveness of the somatotonic, merely depresses the cerebrotonic and makes him feel thoroughly ill.

To determine the degree of viscerotonia, somatotonia, and cerebrotonia   38
present in any given individual, Sheldon makes use of specially designed
interviews, supplemented by a medical history and, where possible, by
observation over a considerable period. The sixty traits are then assessed
on a seven-point scale, in which *one* represents the minimum manifestation and *seven* the most extreme.

How do these temperamental assessments compare with the corre-   39
sponding physical assessments of endomorphy, mesomorphy, and ectomorphy? The answer is that there is a high positive correlation. In some
persons the correlation is complete, and the three-digit formula for temperament is identical with the three-digit formula for physique. More
frequently, however, there is a slight deviation, as when a *four* in physical
endomorphy is correlated with a *three* or a *five* in temperamental viscerotonia. When there is a deviation, it is seldom of more than one point in
any of the three components. Occasionally, however, the discrepancy
between physique and temperament may be as much as two points; when
this happens, the individual is under very considerable strain and has
much difficulty in adapting himself to life. Deviations of more than two
points do not seem to occur in the normal population, but are not uncommon among the insane.

The discrepancies between physique and temperament are probably   40
due, in the main, to what the French philosopher, Jules de Gaultier, has
called "bovarism." Mme. Bovary, the heroine of Flaubert's novel, was a
young woman who consistently tried to be what in fact she was not. To
a greater or less degree we are all bovarists, engaged from earliest childhood in the process of building up what the psychologists call a *persona,*
to suit the tastes of the society surrounding us. The sort of *persona* we
try to build up depends very largely upon our environment, physical and
mental. Thus, in pioneering days, every Westerner tried to bovarize himself into the likeness of an Indian fighter. This was necessary, partly because people had to be tough, wary, and extroverted if they were to survive under frontier conditions, partly because local public opinion
condemned and despised the introverted, the tender-minded, the aesthetes, and the abstract thinkers. Sheldon's researches show exactly how
far bovarism can go without risk of compromising the individual's sanity;
and the highly significant fact is that the borderline between normal and
abnormal is reached pretty quickly. Hence the enormous psychological
dangers inherent in such dogmatic and intolerant philosophies of life as
Puritanism or Militarism—philosophies which exert an unrelenting pres-

sure on those subjected to their influence, forcing a majority to try to change their fundamental psycho-physical constitution, to become something other than what they basically are.

Here a word of warning is necessary. Knowledge of an individual's 41 constitutional make-up is not the same as complete knowledge of his character. Persons with the same temperamental formula may behave in very different ways and exhibit very different characters. Temperamentally similar individuals can make dissimilar uses of their constitutional endowments. It all depends on circumstances, upbringing, and the exercise of free will. Of three men with the same high degree of somatotonia one may become a suavely efficient executive, another a professional soldier of the explosive, blood-and-guts variety, and the third a ruthless gangster. But each in his own way will be aggressive and power-loving, daring and energetic, extroverted and insensitive to other people's feelings. And no amount of training, no effort of the will, will serve to transform them into relaxed and indiscriminately amiable viscerotonics, or into inhibited, hyper-attentional, and introverted cerebrotonics.

We are now in a position to consider a few of the things that constitu- 42 tional analysis and appraisal can do for us. First and most important, it makes it possible for us to know who we and other people really are—of what psychological and bodily elements we and they are composed. Having determined the statics of physique and the closely related dynamics of temperament, we can begin to think in a genuinely intelligent and fruitful way about the environment and the individual's reaction to it. Moreover, to understand is to forgive; and when we realize that the people who are different from us did not get that way out of wickedness or perversity, when we understand that many of the profoundest of such differences are constitutional and that constitution cannot be changed, only made the best of, we may perhaps learn to be more tolerant, more intelligently charitable than we are at present.

Passing from the general to the particular, we find that constitutional 43 appraisal has many important practical applications. In medicine, for example, the constitutional approach will undoubtedly prove helpful both in diagnosis and prognosis, in cure and prevention. To some extent, it is true, all physicians make use of the constitutional approach, and have been doing so for twenty-five centuries at least; but considering the importance of the subject, very little systematic research has been undertaken along these lines.

Education can never in the nature of things be one hundred per cent 44 efficient. Teaching is an art and, in every field, bad artists vastly outnumber good ones. Great educators are almost as rare as great painters and composers. The best we can hope to do is to improve the system within which teachers of average ability do their work. In this improvement of the system, constitutional analysis is likely to prove extremely helpful. Ideally, there should be several educational systems, one adapted to each of the main varieties of human beings. Of the progressive education which in recent years has largely ousted from our schools the formal, suppressive type of training that was at one time universal, Dr. Sheldon makes the following significant remark. "This vigorous progressive education is actually as suppressive as was Christian education at its darkest. It suppresses the third instead of the second component. It is as suppressive to a young cerebrotonic to press him to join in the dance or in the swim, and to make noise and mix and socialize, as it is suppressive to a young somatotonic to make him sit still."

In the fields of history, sociology, and religion, the concepts of constitutional analysis may turn out to be extremely fruitful. From the constitutional point of view, civilization may be defined as a complex of devices for restraining extreme somatotonics from destroying society by their reckless aggressiveness. Of the great world religions one, Confucianism, has been pre-eminently viscerotonic; it has sought to tame somatotonia by inculcating ceremonious good manners, general amiability, and the cult of the family. Most of the other world religions—Buddhism, the higher forms of Hinduism, and, until recent years, Christianity—have been predominantly cerebrotonic. (The figure of Christ in traditional Christian art is almost always that of a man with a high degree of ectomorphy and therefore of cerebrotonia.) These cerebrotonic religions have tried to keep somatotonics in order by teaching them the virtues of self-restraint, humility, and sensitiveness. At the same time they tried to sublimate somatotonic aggressiveness, or to direct it into channels thought to be desirable, such as crusades and wars of religion. On their side, the somatotonics have often succeeded in modifying the cerebrotonic philosophies and institutions of the prevailing religion. For example, no cerebrotonic or viscerotonic would ever have thought of talking about the Church Militant.

IV

In recent years there has been, in Sheldon's phrase, a great Somatotonic Revolution, directed against the dominance of cerebrotonic values as embodied in traditional Christianity. Thus, for traditional Christianity, it was axiomatic that the life of contemplation was superior to the life of action. Today the overwhelming majority even of Christians accept without question the primacy of action.

For traditional Christianity the important thing was the development of the right state of mind about the environment. Today, the important thing is not the state of the mind, but the state of the environment. We believe that men and women will be happy when they are surrounded with the right kind of gadgets. Our forefathers believed that they would be happy if they achieved what one of the greatest of Christian saints called "a holy indifference" to their material surroundings. The change is from a cerebrotonic point of view to the point of view of a somatotonic extrovert.

The Somatotonic Revolution has been greatly accelerated by techno- *48* logical advances. These have served to turn men's attention outward, and have encouraged the belief in a material apocalypse, a progress toward a mechanized New Jerusalem. Such beliefs have been carefully fostered by the writers of advertising copy—the most influential of all authors because they are the only ones whose works are read every day by every member of the population. In a world peopled by cerebrotonics, living an inward-turning life in a state of holy, or even unholy, indifference to their material surroundings, mass production would be doomed. That is why advertisers consistently support the Somatotonic Revolution.

It is hardly necessary to add that total war is another potent factor in *49* creating and sustaining the Somatotonic Revolution. Nazi education, which was specifically education for war, aimed at encouraging the manifestations of somatotonia in those most richly endowed with it, and making the rest of the population feel ashamed of its tendencies towards relaxed amiability or restrained and inward-looking sensitivity. During the war the enemies of Nazism have had to borrow from the Nazi educational philosophy. All over the world millions of young men and even young women are now being educated to be tough, and to admire toughness beyond every other moral quality. Never has somatotonia been so widely or so systematically encouraged as at the present time. Indeed, most societies in the past systematically discouraged somatotonia, because they did not wish to be destroyed by the unrestrained aggressiveness of their most active minority. What will be the result of the present worldwide reversal of what hitherto has been an almost universal social policy? Time alone will show.

QUESTIONS AND EXERCISES

Vocabulary

1. Define or explain the following terms:

immemorial (2)	ectomorphy (13)
aphorisms (2)	anabolism (14)
pale (2)	catabolism (14)

innate (4)	gynandromorphy (21)
flabbergasted (5)	*dysplasia* (21)
pathology (9)	viscerotonia (30)
anthropometrists (10)	somatotonia (30)
empirical (10)	cerebrotonia (30)
endomorphy (13)	fetish (32)
mesomorphy (13)	

2. Identify by ideas, works, or other import:

Helvetius (6)	Mme. Bovary (40)
Behaviorists (6)	bovarism (40)
Hippocrates (9)	Confucianism (45)
Sheldon (12)	Buddhism (45)
Pickwick (25)	Hinduism (45)
Scrooge (25)	Nazi (49)
Flash Gordon (25)	

Rhetoric

3. What pattern of organization does Huxley use? Make a label for each of the five major divisions. Example: Part I—History of Past Theories.
4. What makes it easy to follow Huxley's shifts from one topic to another?
5. Comment on Huxley's use of figurative language in the following quotations:

   "passion breaks through his veneer of civilization" (32)

   "With cerebrotonia we pass from the world of Flash Gordon to that of Hamlet" (35)
6. Find other figures of speech or rhetorical devices.
7. Comment on the definition of classification in paragraph 3.
8. According to the author, what are the dangers of Puritanism and militarism?
9. Into what categories (viscerotonic, somatotonic, cerebrotonic) does Huxley place each of the following?

   Confucianism

   Buddhism

   Christianity
10. What does Huxley have in mind when he speaks of the Somatotonic Revolution?

Topics and Assignments for Composition

1. In a sentence for each, define the following terms:

endomorphy
mesomorphy
ectomorphy

2. In a paragraph appropriately developed, discuss Sheldon's theory of bodily types.

3. Using Sheldon's theory, analyze some historical figures and either accept or reject the validity of his theory based upon the figures you have chosen.

4. In an essay develop a classification of your own about human nature and in a manner similar to Huxley's apply your theory to specific examples.

5. In a well-developed essay comment on this quotation from the essay: "A rational policy with regards to athletics would be to tell all boys the simple truth, which is that very few of them can expect to excel in the more violent sports, that such excellence depends primarily on a particular inheritance of size and shape, and that persons of other shapes and sizes not suited to athletic proficiency have as good a right to realize their own *natural* capacities as the extreme mesomorph and can contribute at least as much to society."

Robert Brinckerhoff

Freudianism, Behaviorism, and Humanism

It is widely believed nowadays that third-force psychology is "humanistic," whereas the older, and still generally more influential, behavioristic and Freudian theories are antihumanistic. According to Professor Matson, an ardent supporter of third-force psychology, there are three essential reasons for this. The first deals with methods of treatment, that is, with therapeutic procedures, and the second and third are theoretical in nature. *1*

Regarding the first point, Dr. Matson believes that an "emphasis upon the human person, upon the individual in his wholeness and uniqueness, is a central feature of the 'psychology of humanism.'" The therapeutic relationship must become an "authentic" encounter between individuals. This relationship, probably best characterized by Buber in his discussion of I-and-Thou, demands that the doctor drop his "protected professional superiority" and reach out to the other person as an equal in search of mutual understanding. In this kind of intimate sharing the patient is helped to become more fully himself. *2*

I have no particular quarrel with this change in therapeutic technique. It seems obviously more humanistic than the detached objectivity of orthodox Freudian procedure. It is important to note, however, that there is no fundamental reason why Freudians can't adopt this more humanistic role. Indeed, I suspect we would find most of the best analysts of all schools achieving a relationship that approaches Buber's I-Thou. There is no necessary contradiction between theory and practice. One can hold to orthodox Freudian theory (or for that matter, behaviorism) *3*

This article first appeared in THE HUMANIST, March/April 1971 and is reprinted by permission of the publisher.

and still adopt the method of therapy characteristic of third-force psychology.

The second and third arguments that Matson advances for equating   *4*
humanism with third-force psychology are much more significant. The
"good guys" (third-force psychologists) believe, first, in the "freedom"
of man and, second, of course, in the inherent goodness of man.

Both Freudian and behavioristic models of human development are   *5*
based on deterministic premises. Men may be free to do as they please,
but their choices are governed by impulse or habit — by internal and often
unconscious drives, or by environmental influences (rewards and punishment). We can do as we will, but the will itself is determined by a combination of biological and environmental factors. Because we can do as
we will, men *feel* free. Those forces, biological and environmental, that
make us want to act as we do are the determining conditions of behavior.
All of science, and psychology should not be ruled out, is founded upon
the belief that behavior, whether at the atomic level or human, is determined by antecedent conditions.

To claim that men are free, as Matson does, means either that men can   *6*
do as they choose or that our inclinations to behave — our motives,
wishes, and desires — are themselves free, that is, undetermined by antecedent conditions. If Matson means only that people are usually free to
do as they choose, then I believe that this is obviously the case and not
inconsistent with determinism. If, on the other hand, Matson is asserting
that our inclinations to behave are undetermined by antecedent conditions, then it seems that we are dealing with a resurrected and still
mysterious ghost in the machine for which there is neither evidence nor
justification, on pragmatic grounds, that further scientific inquiry would
be useful.

Finally, Matson links the large-scale revival of the belief in man's   *7*
aggressiveness (from Freud's concept of the death instinct to Lorenz's
book *On Aggression*) to a widespread failure of nerve. It is not altogether
clear what Matson takes to be the nature of man. His belief in "the capacity of the ordinary human being to lead his *own* life, to go his *own* way
and to grow his *own* way, to be himself and to know himself and to become more himself" [emphasis mine] is all rather vague. The implication,
I take it, is that man is loving, productive, and responsible by nature;
so what we must do is simply to allow man to realize himself. The new
world is at hand: Allow man the "freedom to be himself" and all the
cherished values of Western civilization will finally be realized in man's
self-actualization. This is, at any rate — even if somewhat overstated — a
central theme of most who refer to themselves as third-force psychologists. I believe it to be dangerously naive.

Careful observation of childhood behavior should convince even the   8
most steadfast optimist that the human animal, like his relatives on the
lower rungs of the evolutionary ladder, is aggressive in his quest for satisfaction. Furthermore, all historical and anthropological evidence points
to the fact that cultures everywhere, in order to secure their survival,
have erected social conventions in order to control sexual and aggressive
drives. As Erikson has pointed out in his discussion of the life cycle,
each positive side of a given state of growth has its negative counterpart,
which remains alongside the positive throughout life. "The idea that at
any stage a goodness is achieved which is impervious to new conflicts
within and changes without is a projection on child development of that
success ideology which so dangerously pervades our private and public
daydreams and can make us inept in the face of a heightened struggle for
a meaningful existence in our time" (*Identity and the Life Cycle,* International Universities Press, New York, 1967, p. 61).

Even Skinner faces the problem more squarely than third-force psy-   9
chologists. In his utopian novel, *Walden Two,* he writes, "each of us is
engaged in a pitched battle with the rest of mankind . . . each of us has
interests which conflict with the interests of everybody else. That's our
original sin and it can't be helped" (*Walden Two,* Macmillan, Toronto,
Ontario, 1948, p. 104). Such a resolute facing of the problem seems not
to be a failure of nerve, but a necessary beginning, if we are actually to
make progress in attaining a society that helps to foster the creative potential of each of its members.

Recently, I think, there has been all too much divisive rhetoric among   10
our competing psychological systems. One cause for such division appears to be such mistaken claims as Matson's that reserve the title "humanist" for third-force psychologists exclusively.

"Humanistic psychology," we are told, "tries to tell it not like it is,   11
but like it ought to be." I, and most other humanists I suppose, have no
essential quarrel with how Matson and his friends think it ought to be.
But very often it seems third-force psychologists work the naturalistic
fallacy in reverse: From how it *ought* to be they tend to assume how it
is. Not only *ought* man be good, but man *is* good—and anyone contra-
dicting this pillar of humanistic belief is not only antihumanist but is
suffering a failure of nerve as well.

On the contrary, I believe that if we have any hope of realizing our   12
humanist ideals, we must not fail to take a careful look at the darker side
of man's nature and at the struggle that this view entails for all men of
good will. Erikson (Op. cit., p. 61) shows us, more clearly than most,
that "only in the light of man's inner division and social antagonism is a

belief in his essential resourcefulness and creativity justifiable and productive."

QUESTIONS AND EXERCISES

Vocabulary

1. Define or explain each of the following terms:
   humanistic (1)   orthodox (3)
   behavioristic (1)   pragmatic (6)
   Freudian (1)

Rhetoric

2. Explain the following allusions:
   Buber and "I-and-Thou" (2)   Erikson (8)
   "ghost in the machine" (6)   Skinner (9)
   Lorenz (7)
3. How are references noted in this essay?
4. Comment on the effectiveness of the organization of material.
5. What are some of the transitional devices used to link and distinguish paragraphs?
6. Find and identify a figure of speech.

Theme

7. What does the "freedom of man" mean in paragraph 4?
8. What is meant by the "inherent goodness of man" in paragraph 4?
9. What is the difference between man *feeling* free and the behavioral condition of man?
10. Who are the "third-force" psychologists? What can you infer about their premises from the essay?
11. What is the fallacy mentioned in paragraph 11?
12. What is the concept of the "noble savage"? What is its significance for this essay?

Topics and Assignments for Composition

1. In a short paragraph for each, summarize the main doctrine of each of the following:
   Freudianism
   Behaviorism
   Humanism
2. Write an essay on another current doctrine about the nature of man (existentialism, objectivism) and relate it to humanism.

3. Read a novel that analyzes the nature of man (*Walden Two, Lord of the Flies*) and show the underlying psychological and philosophical premises in it.
4. Research one of the conflicts alluded to in the essay and report the nature and current status of the controversy.

Rubin Carson

The Transcendental, Ecological, Proletarian, Romantic, Radical Chic, Unisexual, Hot Pants, Paramilitary, Nude Los Angeles Woman

In case you haven't noticed—*FASHION IS DEAD!!* No longer can   *1*
a Now Woman sit passively back in her milk bath and allow the senior
editors of *Vogue* to dictate. She must rise up and dress according to WHO
she is. . . . It's far worse for the New Los Angeles Woman. Because of
our being 157.8 cities in search of one city, *location* is where it's at. Not
only must she dress according to WHO she is, she must dress according
to WHERE she lives.

To bring some order out of local chaos, I'm going to carefully divide   *2*
the map of our megalopolis and demonstrate how a few typical Los Angeles Women might dress according to WHO and WHERE they are.

Malibu Beach Transcendental

Be a fading ex-starlet living off your ex-hubby's ex-TV residuals. Study   *3*
Yoga at Santa Monica High Extension but know at least three rock stars
who've taken personally from the Maharishi Mahesh Yogi. THINK
DIAPHANOUS! Cast yourself in your own sepia-tone Indian movie
and be seen wrapped only in silk paisley saris (which are actually Singer
Center mill ends). Don't stand in direct sunlight so that *nobody* notices
you're wearing a flannel body stocking for warmth . . . . MYSTIC DO-
YOUR-THING TOUCH: Tattooed dot on forehead indicating "per-

Reprinted by permission of the author.

petual virgin." FUN ANKLET: Zircon band with motto, "Up the cosmos."

Claremont-Redlands Ecology

You are a concerned faculty wife who *never* shaves her legs. Have the latest phosphate count of detergents on the tip of your tongue and force the kiddies to wear puffy mukluks so as not to kill floor termites . . . . Be seen only in 14th century Venetian outfits that make you seem perpetually on the way to the Renaissance Faire. Affect colors that editorialize: (a) Fire-Blackened Sagebrush; (b) Smog Greige; or (c) Freeway Earthslide Brown. NEEDLEPOINT DESIGN FOR REUSABLE PAPER HANDBAG: Oil-saturated seagull.   *4*

Westwood Proletariat

Take Poly Sci at UCLA and tolerate the Establishment. Accept your father's monthly check but cash it in Culver City so that none of your fellow activists will recognize you . . . . Be ready for an Instant Poverty March by wearing overalls and workshirts to all daytime classes. You *could* buy all your clothes at Army-Navy Surplus but get them instead at an image Protest Products Boutique (they'll honor daddy's Master Charge). ATTACK-OF-WHIMSY TOUCH: Peter Max hard-hat. DECAL MOTTO FOR LUNCH PAIL: "Realpolitik is a gas."   *5*

Pasadena Early-'40s Romantic

Be an ex-Tournament of Roses Queen who thinks like Doris Day talks . . . . *EVENING* is your time. Acquire a photo of Pat Nixon's high school graduation gown and have it copied in imaginatively off-beige moiré. Wear it to the monthly Ronald Reagan Film Festival at the Pasadena Art Museum; afterwards, throw on Ramona-style shawl and mantilla for spontaneous stopover at Bob's Big Boy for "those were the days" order of french fries. JUNE ALLYSON TOUCH: Lace breakaway dickie. FUN EARRINGS: Pair of Limoges Agnew golf balls.   *6*

Beverly Hills Radical Chic

You are a psychiatrist's wife who throws weekly ACLU Brunchoramas and does soul handshake . . . . Join a Black Experience Encounter Group   *7* so that you can get the courage to fire the upstairs live-in and replace her with a cleaning service. Wear a haute funk "natural" to Chasen's but change to your regular Dynel Wiglet for private socializing. Affect the Afro "brillo look" in all your hostess maxi-pajamas and dramatize with slave fetters and ankle irons you purchased at MGM auction. MOTTO FOR FETISH-PENDANT: "Sammy Davis converted for our sins." PRACTICAL BRACELET ENGRAVING: Phone number of caterer who does emergency rumaki airdrops.

Hollywood Unisexual

As a Women's Lib buff, you spend your lunch hours going limp in   8
front of Frederick's of Hollywood (early massage parlor styles for Sex Objects) . . . . Although all the other executive secretaries wear minis, you do your daily thing by wearing oversize jeans and Clint Eastwood cowboy jackets. Break the "horse wranglers" image by periodically wearing Gloria Steinem non-prescription specs and single Gay Liberation Front official earring. SOCKO APPLIQUE FOR BACK OF LEATHER JACKET: "Sappho deserved a Fulbright." MILITANT TOUCH: Two stainless steel hairpins for males trying to get fresh in elevator.

Van Nuys Hot Pants

Listen to the YOUNG SOUND! but be a grandmother who's had   9
everything tucked, lifted and siliconed prior to the first hot flash. Consider quitting Weight Watchers . . . . Wear See-through hot pants (over support hose) when you market at Gelson's and toss on two rows of cartridge belts for dramatic entrance into DuPar's. Discuss taking Tie Dye kerchief course at Everywoman's Village but meanwhile wear the one the Family Dropout sent you on Mother's Day from his artichoke commune. EXISTENTIAL HAIR TOUCH: Two shell barrettes saying HERE and NOW. MOTTO FOR HELL'S ANGEL VEST: "Let it all hang out."

Orange County Paramilitary

Live in a Newport Beach marina and be saving for your own PT boat.   10
Try to (but *don't*) be soft on anything! . . . Attend John Wayne-narrated "Back to mainland China" NOW wedding at Knott's Berry Farm chapel and *really* experience it. Sit on the right side of the altar and wear: (a) crushed velvet Green Beret (b) denim colonel's cape with Minute Man

Red piping (c) Mace-proof cavalry boots. Carry a beaded parasol which looks like and *is* a fencing foil. MOTTO FOR FIELD OVERNIGHT BAG: "Damn the Ping-Pong balls—full speed ahead!" ORNAMENT FOR BOOTS: Goldwater buttons.

Topanga Canyon Nude

Get a Ralph Nader-approved zircon for the navel and carry a big   *11* stick (in case the zoning commission comes after you).

QUESTIONS AND EXERCISES

Vocabulary

1. Define or explain each of the following terms: all of the terms in the title.
   megalopolis (2)
   rumaki (7)

Rhetoric

2. Discuss the level of usage of the vocabulary of this article.
3. How is the essay organized?
4. Find examples of eccentric punctuation and capitalization.
5. What current vogue words and phrases are noticeable?
6. What elements of satire do you find?
7. Are the types satirized easily recognizable?
8. Why is the article a caricature?

Theme

9. Who is the target of the essay?
10. What are some of the assumptions the author makes?
11. What does the essay accomplish?
12. What are some of the advantages of humor? The disadvantages?
13. Compare this essay to other satires you have read.
14. What are the favorite targets of satirists?

Topics and Assignments for Composition

1. Take one of the types sketched by Carson and write a longer description of it.
2. Analyze the style and nature of satire in this essay.
3. Choose two satirists and compare their styles and humor.

Student Example

Three Faces of Youth

The turbulent late 1960s will undoubtedly be remembered as the era of Vietnam, Black Power, street violence, the moon shots, and the Youth Revolt. The attitudes, behavior, philosophy, and morals of American youth have been discussed, probed, analyzed, and inspected almost to the point of total exhaustion. It is said that the current generation of American youth, and youth of the rest of the Western world as well, has rejected the moral, social, political, cultural, and ethical beliefs of their parents and of their societies. They are said to disdain the life styles, goals, and principles which their elders revere, to laugh at ideals for which wars have been fought. The hippies, the anti-war, anti-draft crusades, the so-called sexual revolution, the increasing use of drugs, the clothes and styles, the campus revolts, and the widespread hatred of the Establishment are among the many examples cited to prove that the young are indeed headed in a new direction, away from established standards and concepts. While this evaluation is partially true, it must be realized that the young cannot be analyzed and dismissed so simply and smugly. There are divisions and differences within the ranks of the young which form as deep a chasm as does any real or imagined Generation Gap.

Basically, today's youth (this term now includes anyone of junior high, high school, or college age, as well as those in their still-hip twenties) fall into three major categories: the Iconoclasts, the Traditionalists, and the Confused. The Iconoclasts have come to symbolize their entire generation while in reality they represent nothing but themselves and their varied individual ideas, many of which have been adopted and adapted from adults. Iconoclasts by no means constitute a unified, cohesive group. They range from twelve-year-old pot smokers to sixteen-year-old groupies to twenty-five-year-old campus agitators. Though the possibility of a national revolution and takeover by the Iconoclasts has been suggested by newspapers, magazines, television, songs, and movies such as "Zabriskie Point," this idea must be placed in the realm of total fantasy.

It is ludicrous to imagine affluent teeny-boppers, stoned hippies, and angry SDSers marching along arm-in-arm to invade the capital, perhaps arguing over who should provide the revolution's theme-song, the Partridge Family, the Who, or the Steve Miller Blues Band. Clearly, the threat of the Iconoclasts has been overemphasized in this context.

Despite their diversity in ages and interests, Iconoclasts do share one common characteristic: they are rebels, political, moral, or social. They have rejected one or more of society's rules and have substituted their individual preferences and beliefs. They are obviously not going to take over the country, much as they might like to, but they have succeeded in shaking it up badly. Some Iconoclasts are actively working for change in society, some have dropped out completely, and still others want to live within society, but to have the freedom to do what they wish with their lives. Their futures will probably be as varied as they are. Some will die, some will go to jail, some will go straight, and others will find a niche in society in which they are able to rebel and still survive.

The second group, Traditionalists, are probably equally or more prevalent than Iconoclasts. Traditionalists are the young people whom our political and religious leaders praise and hold up as examples. They support the existing structure, particularly traditional moral standards, often with great fervor. They are disgusted by the actions of their more trend-setting contemporaries and dedicate themselves to the cause of counteracting the Iconoclasts' power and influence. They are usually more religious, more patriotic, and more conservative in appearance, taste, and behavior than others of their generation. Most of them will become conservative, respectable adults and will lead morally acceptable, if not model, lives, at least on the surface.

The most common yet most enigmatic portion of today's youth are the Confused. These individuals exhibit characteristics of both Traditionalists and Iconoclasts without developing their own philosophy and attitudes. Like Traditionalists and Iconoclasts, the Confused are subjected to a constant barrage of information, attitudes, and answers from home, school, public authorities, friends, acquaintances, and the mass media. But unlike Traditionalists and Iconoclasts, who are usually able to disregard that which does not coincide with their particular ideas, the Confused are influenced by anything and everything with which they come in contact, which results in division of loyalty, hypocrisy, and even split personality.

A confused teenager, for example, may smoke pot for enjoyment or because his friends do; yet at the same time he may feel guilty, still adhering to the societal belief that pot smoking is morally wrong. This distinguishes him from the Iconoclast, who feels no guilt, only apprehension about getting caught, and from the Traditionalist, who would never do such a thing in the first place. The Confused youth may agree that military service is necessary, but he may question the morality of Vietnam and militarism, thus placing himself in a position of agonizing doubt and uncertainty. In this situation, the Iconoclast would refuse to be inducted while the Traditionalist would serve willingly.

Youth has always been and still is a time of uncertainty, but it is the Confused who feel this uncertainty most strongly. Iconoclasts, while often unsure and purposeless, are secure in the belief that their rebellion, whatever form it may take, is valid, meaningful, and justified. Traditionalists, while often bewildered by their society and themselves, are firm and contented in their support of authority. The Confused, on the other hand, have no basic ideology or sustaining belief. They shift with the wind, always wondering and watching others. Clearly, American youth is not headed in one particular direction but in three — three sometimes coinciding, sometimes overlapping but distinctly different directions.

Part Seven:

Analysis and Process

Joseph C. Pattison

How to Write an "F" Paper: Fresh Advice for Students of Freshman English

Writing an "F" paper is admittedly not an easy task, but one can learn to do it by grasp of the principles to use. The thirteen below, if practiced at all diligently, should lead any student to that fortune in his writing.

Obscure the ideas:

1. Select a topic that is big enough to let you wander around the main idea without ever being forced to state it precisely. If an assigned topic has been limited for you, take a detour that will allow you to amble away from it for a while.

2. Pad! Pad! Pad! Do not develop your ideas. Simply restate them in safe, spongy generalizations to avoid the need to find evidence to support what you say. Always point out repetition with the phrase, "As previously noted. . . ." Better yet, repeat word-for-word at least one or two of your statements.

3. Disorganize your discussion. For example, if you are using the time order to present your material, keep the reader alert by making a jump from the past to the present only to spring back into the past preparatory to a leap into the future preceding a return hop into the present just before the finish of the point about the past. Devise comparable stratagems to use with such other principles for organizing a discussion as space, contrast, cause-effect, and climax.

4. Begin a new paragraph every sentence or two.

"How to Write An 'F' Paper" by Joseph C. Pattison, *College English*, October 1963. Reprinted with permission of the National Council of Teachers of English and Joseph C. Pattison.

By generous use of white space, make the reader aware that he is look-ing at a page blank of sustained thought.

Like this.

Mangle the sentences:

5. Fill all the areas of your sentences with deadwood. Incidentally, "the area of" will deaden almost any sentence, and it is particularly flat when displayed prominently at the beginning of a sentence.

6. Using fragments and run-on or comma-spliced sentences. Do not use a main subject and a main verb, for the reader will get the complete thought too easily. Just toss him part of the idea at a time, as in "Using fragments. . . ." To gain sentence variety, throw in an occasional run-on sentence thus the reader will have to read slowly and carefully to get the idea.

7. Your sentence order invert for statement of the least important matters. That will force the reader to be attentive to understand even the simplest points you make.

8. You, in the introduction, body, and conclusion of your paper, to show that you can contrive ornate, graceful sentences, should use in-volution. Frequent separation of subjects from verbs by insertion of involved phrases and clauses will prove that you know what can be done to a sentence.

Slovenize the diction:

9. Add the popular "-wise" and "-ize" endings to words. Say, "Time-wise, it is fastest to go by U.S. 40," rather than simply, "It is fastest to go by U.S. 40." Choose "circularize" in preference to "circulate." Prac-tice will smartenize your style.

10. Use vague words in place of precise ones. From the start, establish vagueness of tone by saying, "The thing is . . ." instead of, "The issue is. . . ." Make the reader be imaginative throughout his reading of your paper.

11. Employ lengthy Latinate locutions wherever possible. Shun the sim-plicity of style that comes from apt use of short, old, familiar words, espe-cially those of Anglo-Saxon origin. Show that you can get the *maximum* (L.), not merely the *most* (AS.), from every word choice you make.

12. Inject humor into your writing by using the wrong word occasionally. Write "then" when you mean "than" or "to" when you mean "too." Every reader likes a laugh.

13. Find a "tried and true" phrase to use to clinch a point. It will have a comfortably folksy sound for the reader. Best of all, since you want to

end in a conversational and friendly way, sprinkle your conclusion with clichés. "Put a little frosting on the cake," as the saying goes.

Well, too ensconce this whole business in a nutshell, you, above all,   2
an erudite discourse on nothing in the field of your topic should pen.
Thereby gaining the reader's credence in what you say.

Suggestion-wise, one last thing: file-ize this list for handy reference the   3
next time you a paper write.

QUESTIONS AND EXERCISES

Vocabulary

1. Define or explain each of the following terms:
   involution (1.8)   ensconce (2)
   contrive (1.8)   erudite (2)
   slovenize (1.9)   credence (2)
   cliché (1.13)

Rhetoric

2. Explain the technique of humor utilized in this essay.
3. Explain the use of language in the last two paragraphs.
4. What are vogue words? Give examples.
5. What is irony? Illustrate.
6. What is a parody?

Theme

7. What audience do you think appreciates this type of writing most?
8. How effective is advice given in this fashion? Explain.
9. What other essays have you read that utilize the techniques used in this essay?

Topics and Assignments for Composition

1. Write a few sentence-long directions in imitation of the ones in this essay.
   Example: Always utilize redundancy; if a thing is worth saying once, it is worth repeating.
2. Put some of the advice into positive, non-ironic language.
3. Write an imitation of this essay, duplicating the tone and pattern.

Richard K. Redfern

A Brief Lexicon of Jargon for Those Who Want to Speak and Write Verbosely and Vaguely

Area

The first rule about using *area* is simple. Put *area* at the start or end of 1 hundreds of words and phrases. *The area of* is often useful when you want to add three words to a sentence without changing its meaning.

Instead of	*Say or write*
civil rights	the area of civil rights
in spelling and pronunciation	in the area of spelling and pro- nunciation
problems, topics	problem areas, topic areas
major subjects	major subject (*or* subject-matter) areas

Second, particularly in speech, use *area* as an all-purpose synonym. 2 After mentioning scheduled improvements in class-rooms and offices, use *area* for later references to this idea. A few minutes later, in talking about the courses to be offered next term, use *area* to refer to required courses, to electives, and to both required and elective courses. Soon you can keep three or four *area's* going and thus keep your audience alert by making them guess which idea you have in mind, especially if you insert, once or twice, a neatly disguised geographical use of *area:* "Graduate student response in this area is gratifying."

"A Brief Lexicon of Jargon" by Richard K. Redfern, *College English,* May 1967. Reprinted with the permission of the National Council of Teachers of English and Richard K. Redfern.

Field

If the temptation arises to say "clothing executive," "publishing execu-   *3*
tive," and the like, resist it firmly. Say and write "executive in the clothing field" and "executive in the field of publishing." Note that *the field
of* (like *the area of*) qualifies as jargon because it adds length, usually
without changing the meaning, as in "from the field of literature as a
whole" and "prowess in the field of academic achievement" (which is
five words longer than the "academic prowess" of plain English). With
practice you can combine *field* with *area, level,* and other standbys:

In the sportswear field, this is one area which is growing. (Translation from context: Ski sweaters are selling well.)

[The magazine is] a valuable source of continuing information for
educators at all levels and for everyone concerned with this field. (Plain
English: The magazine is a valuable source of information for anyone
interested in education.)

A master of jargon can produce a sentence so vague that it can be   *4*
dropped into dozens of other articles and books: "At what levels is coverage of the field important?" Even in context (a scholarly book about the
teaching of English), it is hard to attach meaning to *that* sentence!

In Terms of

A sure sign of the ability to speak and write jargon is the redundant use   *5*
of *in terms of.* If you are a beginner, use the phrase instead of prepositions
such as *in* ("The faculty has been divided in terms of opinions and attitudes") and *of* ("We think in terms of elementary, secondary, and higher
education"). Then move on to sentences in which you waste more than
two words:

Instead of	*Say or write*
The Campus School expects to have three fourth grades.	In terms of the future, the Campus School expects to have three fourth grades. (5 extra words)
I'm glad that we got the response we wanted.	I'm glad that there was a response to that in terms of what we wanted. (6 extra words)

Emulate the masters of jargon. They have the courage to abandon the   *6*
effort to shape a thought clearly:

A field trip should be defined in terms of where you are.

They are trying to get under way some small and large construction in terms of unemployment.

When we think in terms of muscles, we don't always think in terms of eyes.

Level

Although *level* should be well known through overuse, unobservant   7
young instructors may need a review of some of its uses, especially if they are anxious to speak and write *on the level of* jargon. (Note the redundancy of the italicized words.)

Instead of	*Say or write*
She teaches fifth grade.	She teaches on the fifth grade level. (3 extra words)
Readers will find more than one meaning.	It can be read on more than one level of meaning. (4 extra words)
My students	The writers on my level of concern (5 extra words)

Long Forms

When the shorter of two similar forms is adequate, choose the longer;   8
e.g., say *analyzation* (for *analysis*), *orientate* (for *orient*), *origination* (for *origin*), *summarization* (for *summary*). Besides using an unnecessary syllable or two, the long form can make your audience peevish when they know the word has not won acceptance or, at least, uneasy ("Is that a new word that I ought to know?"). If someone asks why you use *notate* instead of *note* (as in "Please notate in the space below your preference . . ."), fabricate an elaborate distinction. Not having a dictionary in his pocket, your questioner will be too polite to argue.

With practice, you will have the confidence to enter unfamiliar terri-   9
tory. Instead of the standard forms *(confirm, interpret, penalty, register,* and *scrutiny),* try *confirmate, interpretate, penalization, registrate,* and *scrutinization.*

Vogue Words

You have little chance of making a name for yourself as a user of jargon   10
unless you sprinkle your speech and writing with vogue words and phrases, both the older fashions (e.g., *aspect, background, field, level,*

situation) and the newer (e.g., *escalate, relate to, share with; facility, involvement; limited, minimal*). An old favorite adds the aroma of the cliché, while a newly fashionable term proves that you are up-to-date. Another advantage of vogue words is that some of them are euphemisms. By using *limited,* for example, you show your disdain for the directness and clarity of *small,* as in "a man with a limited education" and "a limited enrollment in a very large room."

Unfortunately, some vogue expressions are shorter than standard   *11*
English, but their obscurity does much to offset the defect of brevity.

Instead of	*Say or write*
The children live in a camp and have both classes and recreation out-doors.	The children live in a camp-type situation.
She reads, writes, and speaks German and has had four years of Latin.	She has a good foreign-language background.
Many hospitals now let a man stay with his wife during labor.	The trend is to let the father have more involvement.

A final word to novices: dozens of words and phrases have been   *12*
omitted from this brief lexicon, but try to spot them yourselves. Practice steadily, always keeping in mind that the fundamentals of jargon — verbosity and needless vagueness — are best adorned by pretentiousness. Soon, if you feel the impulse to say, for example, that an office has one secretary and some part-time help, you will write "Administrative clerical aids implement the organizational function." Eventually you can produce sentences which mean anything or possibly nothing: "We should leave this aspect of the definition relatively operational" or "This condition is similar in regard to other instances also."

QUESTIONS AND EXERCISES

Vocabulary

1. Define or explain each of the following terms:

lexicon (title)	emulate (6)
jargon (title)	peevish (8)
verbosely (title)	escalate (10)
prowess (3)	cliché (10)
redundant (5)	euphemisms (10)

Rhetoric

2. What is the main tone of the essay? Where is the first evidence of this?
3. What are some of the advantages of irony? What are the disadvantages?
4. Find evidences of humor in this selection. What kind of humor is it?
5. What is the difference between "lexicon" and "dictionary?"

Theme

6. Who is most likely to appreciate this essay?
7. Who is most guilty of using jargon?
8. When is jargon justified?
9. What is the difference between vogue words and slang?
10. Where does one find the answers to problems of diction?

Topics and Assignments for Composition

1. Make your own Lexicon of Slang and Jargon.
2. Summarize your dictionary's commentary on levels of usage, slang, jargon, etc.
3. Write an essay emulating the tone and point of view of "A Brief Lexicon of Jargon."
4. Write an essay entitled "In Defense of Jargon."

Kenneth L. Pike

No Empty Universe

Some scholars are curiously uninformed about Biblical Christianity. *1*
They think that Christians are so egocentric that they think that the whole
universe contains only man-plus-God (who in turn exists for man). But,
these scholars argue, if we *really* understood the laws of probability we
would see that it is overwhelmingly certain that there *must* be other
galaxies like this one, other planets like this one, therefore concatena-
tions of forces which led to atoms, heavy proteins, and living organisms,
and even creatures comparable to those of earth. How stupid we must be,
they imply—how egocentric—to assume that we alone are sentient in this
vast world of the stars!

It interests me, on the other hand, to note the man-tied imagination of *2*
many writers of science fiction. Often, when trying to create weird imaginary beings the best they can do is to suggest a metal manlike Martian
with antennae sticking out of its cranium. This represents only a very
small change from ears—merely receptors for waves known to us. There
is really no basic difference.

Few people that I meet, however, seem to have been curious enough *3*
to think seriously about the most extraordinary beings (just one kind
among many) which Christianity or Judaism mentions—the seraphim.
Six wings (Isaiah 6:2). "With twain he covered his face." I wonder why?
As a symbol of the holiness of God? "With twain he covered his feet."
Why? As a symbol of modesty? And with two of them, only, he flew—
through what kind of air?

In Ezekiel, the first chapter, there is a further extraordinary set of *4*
creatures. Out of the midst of the brightness, out of the fire, out of this
major energy source (as if there were a birthplace of atomic might right
there) came four creatures. They had the likeness of a man. Four faces.

From STIR-CHANGE-CREATE by Kenneth L. Pike. Reprinted by permission of William B. Eerdmans Publishing Co.

Why? I have no idea – although various people have proposed speculative answers to such questions. Four wings. Why? And their feet were straight feet, like the sole of a calf's foot. They sparkled. They had the hands of a man under their wings, and faces in their wings. They didn't turn when they went. Is this why they had wings on all sides? Their four faces were different. One was like a man. One was like a lion. One like an ox, and one like an eagle. (If this is by chance a simple metaphor, *what* is it a metaphor *of*?)

They went straight forward. They didn't turn as they went. Were these "creatures"? They ran. They returned. And their appearance was like a flash of lightning. You couldn't see them, they were so fast. (I wonder if they went faster than the speed of light. I don't see how God can control things unless He can act fantastically faster than the speed of light. How would He ever catch up to a star? Or an angel? The speed of light must be a limiting factor of our world culture – it can have nothing whatever to do with limits on God.) And the creatures had "wheels." They were curious wheels; they didn't go round and round. They are hierarchically ordered – wheels within wheels. They had eyes round about. They could see in any direction without turning. Is this metaphor?

To me as linguist, two points are of special interest. Where the spirit of the creatures wants to go, they go. Is that thought control? Teleportation? In addition, there was a lot of noise around them. Did they have their loudspeakers on – for communication signals the author could neither recognize nor translate? Some of the Scriptural creatures were obviously able to interact with the communication devices of our culture. There was the angel who went up before the parents of Samson in a flame of fire (Judges 13). Gabriel was able to recognize Mary's fear (Luke 1:30).

What I am trying to point out is that the Scriptures, whether taken in full literalness or in metaphor, by no means allow belief in an empty universe.

Does the universe look the same from an "angel's-eye view," from the perspective of a sinless creature in God's presence? Apparently not. In I Peter 1:12 one of the most extraordinary Scriptures is found. It refers to these heavenly powers and says that unto them "it was revealed that not unto themselves, but unto us they did minister the things, which are now reported unto you by them that have preached the gospel unto you with the Holy Ghost sent down from heaven" – that is, the Gospel and the cross – "which things the angels desire to look into." Perhaps, if they don't themselves need redemption, these creatures want to study *us,* as in a play (I Corinthians 4:9), to see about the cross.

Egocentricity is scientifically unavoidable. No science can operate, no mathematical formula serve, without a starting point where the observer takes his real or his pretended stand. Language cannot operate without *some* bench mark in reference to which it can retain coherent orientation as it surveys the scene. Nor can man, whether physicist or theologian. It is the nontheist — not the inheritors of the Judeo-Christian tradition — who elevates the useful but arbitrary humanity bench mark into the status of eternal psychological center, when he makes man — instead of the person of God — the absolute measure of all things meaningful and moral.

As linguist, also, I speculate on the kind of *lingua franca* which some   *10* day in heaven will link us all — human, non-human, seraphim, and God — in one communication network, but with roots of our past, and every tongue (cf. Revelation 5:9) contributing to the preservation of our identity and individuality.

QUESTIONS AND EXERCISES

Vocabulary

1. Define or explain each of the following terms:

egocentric (1)	hierarchically (5)
concatenations (1)	linguist (6)
sentient (1)	teleportation (6)
seraphim (3)	*lingua franca* (10)

Rhetoric

2. There are several biblical allusions in this essay. Explain what the numbers mean in Isaiah 6:2 and Peter 1:12.
3. Attempt to answer the question at the end of paragraph 4. Is it an actual question or a rhetorical one?
4. Pike uses the term "bench mark" several times. Explain the literal and the figurative meanings of the term.
5. For many readers theological allusions are difficult to follow. Comment on the organization and the lucidity of this essay, considering it contains such allusions.

Theme

6. What is the central thesis of this essay?
7. What are some of the logical arguments presented?
8. What premises are assumed by Pike?
9. Analyze the arguments within the parentheses in paragraph 5.
10. What criticism does Pike make of science fiction writers?
11. What criticism does he make of nontheists in paragraph 9?
12. What are some current conflicts between theology and science?

13. In informal and private discussion sessions, what topics generate the most emotional reactions?

Topics and Assignments for Composition

1. Write an analysis of Pike's intellectual stance.
2. "Theologians are becoming scientific and scientists are becoming more theological." Explain and defend or attack this statement.
3. Discuss the importance of symbol and metaphor in religious and philosophical positions.
4. Research and report on the relationship between linguistics and Bible study and between linguistics and science.

Joan W. Moore and Ralph Guzman

The Mexican-Americans:
New Wind from the Southwest

For Americans, the word "minority" evokes the images of a people   *1*
with iong-standing grievances. It implies a moral claim on American
society and, probably, a potential for political action and civil disruption.
Here at the moment "minority" means Negro, but American society contains at least one other population, rigorously a minority, that is rarely
thought of when the word comes up.

Four million Mexican-Americans in five Southwestern states bear   *2*
important grievances and problems. They represent a major political
potential. Recently they have shown signs of a capacity for civil disruption. It is ironic that the Mexican struggle for the simplest of the heritages
of American life should occur in the Southwest, for the Western states
are outspoken in praise (if not in practice) of free-swinging tolerance.
Today a new purposefulness is appearing in the forgotten ghettos of the
Southwest. The new hope lies in a discovery by the Mexican of himself
as a minority. He is even accepting the image of himself as a national
problem – disfranchised, poor, badly educated and excluded from the
national dialogue. This acceptance is a remarkable victory for a new
leadership that now seeks goals on the national level. It is the first sign
that the stereotype of the Mexican-Americans as rural and as foreign is
breaking down and it makes possible a start toward fuller political participation.

Evidence of this vital change has been growing for several years. The   *3*
election in Crystal City, Tex., whereby for a time the Mexicans won control of the city government attracted national attention. Most significant,

"The Mexican-Americans: New Wind From the Southwest" by Joan W. Moore
and Ralph Guzman. In *The Nation*, May 30, 1966 and reprinted with permission.

however, was the fact that Mexicans and interested Anglo organizations came to Crystal City — and stayed — until the Mexicans had won.

Earlier this year, the Delano, Calif., grape workers' strike became *4* front-page news in *The New York Times*. This pleased the Mexicans, of course, but the real significance lies in Cesar Chavez's careful engineering of the strike on a national scale, using — after the manner of Selma — a full range of interested religious and civil rights groups. A national boycott was widely publicized, political leaders from the governor of California on down were involved, often against their will. And, in time, Schenley Industries acted according to a national rather than a Kern County policy.

A less widely known event, but one even more important to the Mexi- *5* cans, climaxed a long and frustrating relationship with federal equal rights groups. The present Equal Employment Opportunities Commission is headed by Franklin D. Roosevelt, Jr., a man who promised the Mexicans "personal" attention to their employment problems in the Southwest. But not only was there no action on this promise; the commission failed even to give a single Mexican a voice in policy — either among the commissioners or on the staff. Last March, the commission called still another in a long series of meetings to "discuss" the problem. But the new Mexican-American leaders were tired of meetings and promises. At Albuquerque they walked out of the meeting and proceeded to organize themselves into a committee to deal directly with President Johnson. This dramatic bypassing of a federal agency stems from a completely new definition of the "Mexican problem" by the Mexican leaders. The men and women at Albuquerque considered themselves quite able to speak for all the Mexicans in five states — and on a national level.

The fifty-odd rebels making up that committee are relatively young, *6* few older than the late 40's. Nearly all are native-born Americans, but it is significant that few of them hold any elected office. It is still almost impossible to elect Mexican-Americans to public office in most parts of the Southwest. There are among them no paid representatives of Mexican organizations, and that is a handicap, because the time for equal rights leadership must be stolen from business, scholarship and the professions.

Most important of all, this group is closely tied together by long and *7* close cooperation; as a "network," it has existed for years. What is new is the climate that now allows it to present Mexican problems on a national level. A long process of internal change within the Mexican population is now making itself felt on the surface of American life.

Among the changes is a weakening of the traditional pattern of political *8* isolation. The question, "Why should I become an American citizen?"

was common among the older immigrant generation. "I can't wear my naturalization papers. People still treat me as Mexican." But the rate of naturalization has been increasing, particularly in far Western segments of the Mexican population and in urban areas. A little-noticed provision of the Walters-McCarran Act of 1950 gave legal residents of foreign birth who were 50 years of age or over the privilege of qualifying for naturalization in their native language. Organized groups like the Community Service Organization (CSO) speeded the already increasing rate of naturalization when they established Spanish classes in U.S. citizenship. Further, the older and sometimes more embittered generation is being replaced by a younger population which accepts American citizenship as a normal fact of life. Both the steady jobs that this once transient population found during World War II and the new habit of living for many years in a single city have accelerated the rate of naturalization. As one might expect, each year the ties, real or imagined, with Mexico and "Mexican culture" grew fainter. Parades celebrating Mexican national holidays increasingly function like New York's St. Patrick's Day celebration—a field day for politicians.

Mexicans are learning to live with the full range of modern institutions   9
in large cities. Schools, welfare bureaucracies, labor unions, police and an elaborate public health system have all required adaptation. All of them disturbed and disrupted the highly localistic Mexican communities. Traditional spokesmen were replaced by younger leaders who drew their authority from the local community rather than from Anglo politicians. With the new ways of life came new reasons for uniting the community. Police brutality, for example, is still an ugly and immediate reality to many Mexicans. An urbanized community meant that immigration agents could more easily locate illegal immigrants. And no matter how harmless, youthful Mexican gangs became permanently identified in the Anglo mind with juvenile delinquency. These and other conflicts sharpened the need for organized Mexican voting. In California, the Community Service Organization (supported by Saul Alinsky's Industrial Areas Foundation) set up the machinery for mass registration drives.

The larger society is also changing, however slowly. Not only is Amer-   10
ica generally more liberal; large-scale migration to the West has brought in a young, well-educated populace only faintly acquainted with Southwestern patterns of intolerance. Again the changes occur most rapidly in large cities. Studies of Mexican segregation in California show that even today some of the smaller cities ghettoize Mexicans as rigidly as Southern communities segregate the Negroes.

The new leaders have built this growing consciousness of identity   11
despite the handicap of an enormously diverse population. However pos-

sible it may be to imagine an average Negro or an average Japanese-American, it is obviously ridiculous to postulate a typical Mexican-American. At one extreme, nearly 1 million Texas Mexicans live at an economic level not much above that of their ancestors in the aftermath of their defeat in the war with the United States. Most of these are concentrated in south Texas, a sort of Appalachia (AP-uh-LACH-uh) that runs through thirty counties along the lower Gulf Coast and the Rio Grande valley. Here the Mexican is largely rural, nearly illiterate and lives in part according to the Mexican colonial class system, in part by the plantation system of the South. Further north and west, the "Spanish" of New Mexico and Colorado are very different. Many claim unmixed ancestry from early Spanish settlers to escape the "Mexican" stigma; some, in fact, adopt the racial prejudices of the Anglos, discriminating against new arrivals from Mexico and, generally, against anyone of dark complexion. While California Mexicans appear to be more militant in their demands, they are also less specific about their goals. Texans, on the other hand, appear more specific about goals but less militant in tactics. In the far West, and particularly in the booming industrial cities of California, a better-educated, better-fed, but a not necessarily politically more mature group has appeared since World War II. Many are migrants from other parts of the Southwest. This group supplies most of the Young Turks among the California Mexican leadership.

In past years this very diversity of population has prevented effective *12* national expression of Mexican hopes. Even now at least one respected and well-informed Mexican theorist believes that this minority cannot be organized nationally. Many who are identified with the new leadership persist in thinking otherwise, even in the teeth of several failures to consolidate existing Mexican organizations or to build a single pressure group.

Very recently (and most unexpectedly) the new leadership has picked *13* up some important support. It comes as a strange by-product of the new federal poverty legislation. For the first time in American history, impoverished groups can get direct assistance from the federal government and by-pass the local power establishment. Moreover, help is given not to qualified and needy individuals but to qualified and needy groups. The result in thousands of Mexican communities has been electrifying. Local poverty programs are giving Mexicans a high degree of self-consciousness. And the immediate result of nearly every poverty program in nearly every community is social conflict. Sometimes the Anglo power structure must be fought in order to get the assistance, as is happening in south Texas. Sometimes the spoils must be divided with other minorities.

This latter cause of friction is of increasing importance. Mexicans are *14* now being forced, willy-nilly, to join forces in order to compete with Negroes. In Los Angeles, as a notable example, the Negro rioting in Watts was particularly resented by many Mexicans because the Mexicans got no rewards for *not* rioting. After the riots new job-training programs, new schools, new hospitals, new job opportunities seemed to pour into Watts. There were few such benefits for East Los Angeles where the Mexicans live, and the lesson is not lost on the leadership. Albert Pena of Texas comments: "Last year at the President's meeting on civil rights there were 3,000 delegates. But there were only eight of us Latin Americans. Our problems were not discussed — only Negro problems. We were told consistently, 'The trouble with you is, you don't make enough noise, you don't demonstrate, you don't raise Cain enough.' "

Many Mexican leaders hope for a Negro-Mexican coalition. Many fear   15
that the militancy of the Negro will leave the Mexican without a fair share of programs stemming from the war on poverty. Others fear that irresponsible voices will distort the nature of the competition between the Negro poor and the unemployed Mexican and thereby inflame passions and cause conflict. Others insist that the problem of competition is less among the people on the community level and more among the professionals who compete for appointive positions and political advantage. Minority coalitions have never done well in the Southwest. Nonetheless the new Mexican leader studies Negro civil rights technique with a degree of attention approaching the Pentagon's study of Chinese guerrillas. Mexican and Negro objectives are the same: to squeeze as much money and help as possible out of the federal government.

In contrasting Negro and Mexican techniques it must be remembered   16
that the Negro drive for civil rights is based at least partially on a mass movement with mass organizations. Mexican leadership as yet rests on the frailest of rank-and-file participation. The new wave of regional solidarity may yet produce such a mass movement, but even the most optimistic of the new leaders believe it to be far in the future. Perhaps some dramatic touch is needed. The Mexican population was sharply reduced by mass repatriations on two separate occasions: in the 1930s at least 100,000 persons were removed to Mexico, and again in 1955 more than 1 million persons were rounded up in Operation Wetback. These events, traumatic to the Mexicans, are little known by the general public. Sympathy for minorities in the United States seems to flourish in a climate of well-publicized persecution. Anti-Semitism became nearly extinct after Hitler. The Mexicans have not profited from the drama inherent in the Puerto Ricans' sudden invasion of New York. There have been no Emancipation Proclamations. Few ballad singers or novelists

(there have been one or two exceptions) speak to the nation—and to the world—on behalf of the Mexican.

Mexicans, still largely confined to one region of the United States, are   17
hard to see and hard to understand. Until very recently, they have escaped the attention of academic students of race relations. Even the West's widespread and undeserved reputation for racial tolerance has helped to obscure its Mexican population, which has not found effective ways to communicate its complaints.

It is likely that this passivity is ending. In a sense, it ended for the   18
Mexican leaders after the walkout at Albuquerque. Now it is also ending in hundreds of communities through the mechanism of the war against poverty. In time a new militancy may sweep away both regional differences and political isolation. The new techniques of the Albuquerque protest and of Cesar Chavez suit the temper of the Mexican population. Recently, Dr. Hector Garcia, the founder of the Mexican G.I. Forum in San Antonio, warned the White House of the new temper. He said (and this is remarkable for a Mexican whose home is in Texas) that Mexicans were prepared to march in the streets if that were necessary to reach their goals. Dr. George Sanchez puts it all in Spanish. *No queremos que nos den atole con el dedo.* (We don't want to be fed mush with a finger.)

QUESTIONS AND EXERCISES

Vocabulary

1. Define or explain each of the following terms:
   disfranchised (2)   Anglo (3)
   stereotype (2)
2. Explain the allusion in each of the following terms:
   ghettos (2)   willy-nilly (14)
   Selma (4)   raise Cain (14)
   Appalachia (11)   Operation Wetback (16)
   Young Turks (11)
3. Discuss the formation of the verb from the noun form by adding the suffix "ize" as in "ghettoize" in paragraph 10.

Rhetoric

4. What is the tone of this essay?
5. Is much use made of figurative language? If so, list the examples and identify them.
6. Paragraph variety is often used to give emphasis to points the writer wishes to highlight. What emphases do you find in this essay?

Theme

7. What is the main purpose of this essay? Do you find it difficult to answer this question? If so, why?
8. Compare the struggles of the Mexican-American to the struggles of other American minorities to gain equality. What advantages have the Mexican-Americans had? What characteristics have held them back?

Topics and Assignments for Composition

1. In one sentence tell what the new wind from the Southwest is.
2. In a short essay analyze the plight of the American Indian.
3. In an essay develop a theory of the origin of various stereotypes that are prevalent in American life. Identify the stereotypes and try to establish the cause of the concepts.
4. In an essay discuss the psychological cause of prejudice.

Jan Ehrenwald

The Occult

We live at a time when theologians have pronounced – somewhat pre-   *1*
maturely, I believe – the death of God. We live at a time when Bible
scholars, followed by historians and sociologists, have proceeded to de-
mythologize myths and when large segments of American youth are re-
sorting to mysticism, drugs, and the occult in order to escape the malaise
of what can be described as the myth-deprivation of modern man. The
numbers of these young people are difficult to estimate. Some are found
among the hippies or "street people." Others are merely the alienated
and disenchanted of our time, moving in and out of one or another cultist
group – lost souls in search of themselves and of a purpose in life or, failing this, of grass, acid, or speed. Is there no other antidote for their
malaise?

Throughout history one of the traditional remedies for alienation or   *2*
disenchantment has been to fall back on primitive beliefs, magic, witchcraft, or sorcery in times of crisis. Preliterate man, unable to deal with the
forces of nature, devised a variety of compulsive rituals, charms, and
incantations in an effort to ward off disaster. The religious believer sought
salvation through submission to or identification with the divinity. Myths
– the collective daydreams of mankind – were spiritual flights of fancy
which served the same purpose through the myth-maker's identification
with various heroes, titans, or demigods.

Needless to say, established religion frowned on such devices. De-   *3*
posed pagan idols, turned into fallen angels or devils, were relegated into
the netherworld of the unconscious, together with man's repudiated instinctual drives. Alternatively, they eked out a precarious existence in
the lunatic fringe of our culture. In the end, they were demoted to the
status of comic figures in folklore and fairy tale.

From *Today's Education*, Vol. 60, No. 6, September 1971. Reprinted by permission of the author and publisher.

Despite all this, the underground river of magic mentality has never *4* ceased to flow. In the Middle Ages, it surfaced in the form of witchcraft and the belief in demons, Christian style. In the fifteenth century, these practices drew the fire (in more than one sense) of such fanatical witch-burners as the Dominican monks Kramer and Sprenger and their ilk. Prominent figures of the Renaissance and the Reformation were equally determined to root out these vestiges of the pagan heritage. One of the last reverberations of the witch craze was felt in America in 1692, when 19 or 20 men and women were put to death in Salem, Massachusetts.

Closer inspection of these events reveals two paradoxical features. *5* First, the forces which mobilized against the purported witches, warlocks, and sorcerers were not always the champions of bigotry and obscurantism they are usually made out to be. Some were prominent scholars, statesmen, and patrons of the arts who considered themselves defenders of reason against unreason and crusaders of Christian enlightenment against a threatening throwback to pagan superstition and idolatry.

Secondly, there is evidence that some of the charges made against vic- *6* tims of the witch-hunts had some basis in fact.

For example, there are reports that Agnes Simpson, one of the *7* "witches" of North Berwick, who was condemned to death for her practices, could whisper to King James I the exact words he had spoken to his 15-year-old queen on their bridal night in Oslo. There is a similar story of alleged telepathy between Joan of Arc and King Charles VII of France, and some of her voices and visions reportedly contained elements of truth. Soeur Jeanne, one of the hysterical nuns of Loudun who was accused of witchcraft, apparently "read" the thoughts of one of her inquisitors.

Similarly, documents of the Salem witch trials indicate that some of *8* the accused may have indeed been "guilty" of what would be described today as telepathy, clairvoyance, or physical phenomena.

After a century and a half—with the resurgence in Western Europe of *9* witchcraft during the Thirty Years' War and with the advent of Mesmerism, phrenology, and other fads—the underground river surfaced once more in the United States. This time it lacked the external trappings of witchcraft and rapidly gained momentum under the heading of spiritualism.

It all started in about 1850 with the Fox sisters in Hydesville, New *10* York, who were disturbed by (or produced) such mysterious physical manifestations as noises or knocks of purportedly unknown origin in their home. Spiritualism spread like wildfire over the country and soon also became popular in Europe.

Despite repeated exposures of fraudulent practices by the Fox sisters *11* and many European practitioners of the occult, spiritualism became a fad in the British Isles and all over the Continent. Not until the 1880's did serious investigators of the English Society for Psychical Research turn their attention to the problem, giving "respectability" to the study of trance mediumship, telepathy, and related phenomena. In this way, psychical research, subsequently called parapsychology, ultimately emerged as a new, albeit controversial, branch of the behavioral sciences.

The origin of psychical research from the magic arts is unmistakable, *12* much as astronomy can be traced back to astrology. The major concern of psychical research has, in fact, remained much the same as that of the magic arts, though its language and methodology have undergone considerable change over the years.

The magician was replaced by the experimenter; the witches, by trance *13* mediums, psychics, or sensitives. The notions of thought reading, action at a distance, prophecy, and divination became known as ESP, PK (psychokinesis), precognition, or the noncommittal term *psi phenomena,* which is aimed at moving the aura of the occult surrounding it. Still, broad segments of the scientific community and the educated public remain unconvinced.

In an intriguing replay of history, the forces of progress and enlighten- *14* ment seem to be lining up once more against the irrational—against what Freud described as the "return of the repressed." Significantly, it is the confused, alienated "now generation" rather than their elders that tends to ally itself with the witches.

Psychical researchers (or their subjects) are no longer burned at the *15* stake and their lives and limbs are no longer in jeopardy. The age-old struggle between primitive mentality and "enlightened" reason is being acted out by less fanatical means. But there is one major casualty in the battle: Together with some lingering archaic fallacies, many of Western man's traditional values, religious beliefs, and tribal loyalties have fallen victim to the new rationalistic purge. What is left behind in the wake of his demythologizing zeal is a spiritual vacuum and the malaise of myth-deprivation enveloping large segments of our alienated youth.

This group of problem children and young adults have lost their illu- *16* sions on virtually all fronts. Sex has been stripped of its mystery. With the advent of new techniques of contraception—and the careless disregard of the still extant dangers of VD—yesterday's sexual taboos are being brushed aside.

Radical criticism from the left and the right, aided by recurrent exposés *17* by the mass media, have led many young people to believe that big business, financial institutions, the police, the military, the churches and synagogues are all enemies of the people. Indeed, large numbers of young people hold the same view regarding schools, colleges, and universities. Teachers, high school principals, deans, and college presidents are assigned the roles of evil parent figures and turned into scapegoats upon whom the rebellious young can vent their hostility.

(I have the sneaking suspicion that even the brilliant author of *The Greening of America* does the same thing with the bugaboo of the Corporate State. Yet the actual sources of Charles Reich's grievances – or, for that matter, of at least some of Portnoy's complaints – are all around us: the ravages of the environment, social unrest, racial strife, urban decay, and, above all, the bloodletting of an interminable war and the destruction wrought by a relentless and dehumanizing war machine.) *18*

It is at this point that those despairing of their ability to cope with reality by revolutionary action, social engineering, or some other pragmatic means, are turning to untried, unorthodox, faddist expedients. Like primitive man of a past era, they proceed by trial and error, and it is anyone's guess whether or not they will learn from experience. Some hope that an exotic cult, esoteric doctrine, eccentric diet, or outlandish costume will do the trick. Some seek refuge in sundry Utopian experiments with communal living derived from such models as those given in *Walden* or in Skinner's *Walden Two*. *19*

Others resort to magic – or at least make-believe magic practices. They play at reviving a new, dehydrated twentieth century brand of witchcraft to make up for their failure in coping with the outside world. Those who have reached the limits of their capacity to deal with the pressures of their instinctual drives – especially their repressed violence – turn to drugs. Through chemical means these people hope to obtain relief from their frustrations and to regain, as a fringe benefit, so to speak, their lost illusions of omnipotence. *20*

Psychoanalysts talk about two major avenues for man's adaptation to his environment: *alloplastic* (trying to change things in the outside world) or *autoplastic* (adapting passively to the environment). *21*

Our contemporary drug culture can be thought of as a third way of adaptation – the *chemoplastic*. It is an attempt at creating a new, hallucinatory, psychic reality in the hope of attaining instant salvation, transcendental insight, or ecstasy. The drug user numbs himself to painful external stimuli. He tries to shut out the "bad vibrations" of daily living, even at the price of losing his grip on life. In some cases, such practices amount to virtual suicide in installments, if not to mass suicide among some of our ghetto youth, reminiscent of the suicidal behavior of the lemmings on the Arctic wastes. One may conjecture that, by the same token, the ceremonial use of peyote or the sacred mushroom was respon- *22* sible for the mysterious disappearance of certain pre-Columbian Mayan tribes from the stage of history.

The recent reemergence of spiritualism and astrology and the faddist use of Yoga practices, palmistry, and the I Ching (oracular sayings of Chinese wisdom) are more innocuous features of the contemporary scene. They too express youth's groping attempts to escape frustrations and existential anxieties by essentially magic means. They are resorted to by the helpless and perplexed, who hope to attain superior knowledge, mystic enlightenment, omnipotence, and omniscience "without even trying." *23*

Astrology in particular may seem to serve a useful purpose in this quest. If the world is perplexing, if one's own motivations are faltering, if tribal traditions, religious doctrine, or moral principles can no longer be relied upon as dependable guides for conduct, is it not better to leave the making of decisions in the laps of the gods – or to shift the burden to the constellations of the stars? *24*

The modern primitive, having lost faith in tradition, religion, parental authority, his own personal judgment, and his psychoanalyst or marriage counselor, consults his horoscope, the I Ching, or the Tarot (fortune-telling) Cards. Since God has been pronounced dead or is presumed to be playing with dice, the search is on for some other principle of order and lawfulness without which even the most alienated hippie cannot exist. *25*

That none of these devices is likely to live up to one's expectations is another matter. You cannot use ready-made metaphysical nostrums loaned from a foreign culture or a different age to solve your present-day existential problems. Nor can new myths be expected to grow on the barren soil of frustration and alienation. *26*

If this is true, has modern man maneuvered himself into a blind alley? Are we bent to continue on our course of trial and error in matters moral and spiritual, while managing our technological juggernaut according to the most up-to-date principles of computerized engineering and cost accounting? Is it the return of magic and myth that threatens our survival or does the threat lie in a malignant growth of rationalism, of a soulless, demythologized science and technology? The question is too big to go into in the present context. But who says that it must be viewed in terms of mutually exclusive alternatives? *27*

Magic, the underground river, may well carry the seeds of new spiritual beginnings among its flotsam and jetsam. I hinted that parapsychology, its latterday successor, has managed to scoop up several grains of truth in its nets. *28*

The possibilities of thought and action at a distance of mind over mat- *29* ter, of mastery over the electrical activity of the brain cortex and, perhaps, ultimate control over our vegetative nervous system and bodily functions open up a new dimension of freedom to Western man. These possibilities are certainly no longer will-o'-the-wisp dreams pursued by witches, shamans, or witch doctors. They have become the distinct goals of hard-nosed men of science.

It may well be that new myths will be spawned from such pursuits in 30 the fringes of our culture which have not yet been identified, labeled, and catalogued by analytic thought. Nevertheless—or rather for that very reason—they may hold the promise of revitalizing our tired efforts at coping with the human situation.

QUESTIONS AND EXERCISES

Vocabulary

1. Define or explain each of the following terms:

malaise (1)	parapsychology (11)
alienation (2)	psychokinesis (13)
netherworld (3)	scapegoats (17)
eked (3)	pragmatic (19)
ilk (4)	esoteric (19)
paradoxical (5)	alloplastic (21)
Mesmerism (9)	autoplastic (21)
phrenology (9)	chemoplastic (22)
spiritualism (9)	nostrums (26)

Rhetoric

2. Dr. Ehrenwald uses direct and indirect allusions extensively. In paragraph 18 he alludes directly to Charles Reich to make a point. In the same paragraph explain the allusion to "Portnoy's complaints."

3. Comment on the extensive use of the rhetorical question. Check paragraph 27 as an example of this practice.

4. What does the average length of paragraphs do for the style of this essay?

5. How are transitions between paragraphs made?

6. What is the tone of the essay? To what audience is Dr. Ehrenwald writing?

7. Find the figures of speech in paragraphs 27 and 28. Are they effective?

8. What does Dr. Ehrenwald's use of figures of speech to explain his meaning suggest about the value of figurative language?

Theme

9. What is the main idea of the essay?
10. Comment on the legitimacy of the analysis of the current interest of the occult.
11. What optimistic note does Dr. Ehrenwald strike?
12. What do you think is the future of parapsychology?

Topics and Assignments for Composition

1. In a short paragraph show the relationship between the occult and religion.
2. In a short essay defend parapsychology.
3. Develop your own thesis to explain the current interest in the occult. Write a short essay establishing this causal relationship.
4. Research one aspect of the occult and write a report of your investigation.

Melvin Maddocks

The Limitations of Language

In J. M. G. Le Clézio's novel *The Flood,* the anti-hero is a young man   *1*
suffering from a unique malady. Words—the deluge of daily words—have
overloaded his circuits. Even when he is strolling down the street, mind-
ing his own business, his poor brain jerks under the impact of instructions
(WALK—DON'T WALK), threats (TRESPASSERS WILL BE PROSECUTED), and
newsstand alarms (PLANE CRASH AT TEL AVIV). Finally, Le Clézio's
Everyman goes numb—nature's last defense. Spoken words become
mere sounds, a meaningless buzz in the ears. The most urgent printed
words—a poem by Baudelaire, a proclamation of war—have no more
profound effect than the advice he reads (without really reading) on a
book of matches: PLEASE CLOSE COVER BEFORE STRIKING.

If one must give a name to Le Clézio's disease, perhaps semantic   *2*
aphasia will do. Semantic aphasia is that numbness of ear, mind and heart
—that tone deafness to the very meaning of language—which results from
the habitual and prolonged abuse of words. As an isolated phenomenon,
it can be amusing if not downright irritating. But when it becomes epidemic, it signals a disastrous decline in the skills of communication, to
that mumbling low point where language does almost the opposite of
what it was created for. With frightening perversity—the evidence mounts
daily—words now seem to cut off and isolate, to cause more misunder-
standings than they prevent.

Semantic aphasia is the monstrous insensitivity that allows generals to   *3*
call war "pacification," unions leaders to describe strikes or slowdowns
as "job actions," and politicians to applaud even moderately progressive
programs as "revolutions." Semantic aphasia is also the near-pathological
blitheness that permits three different advertisers in the same women's
magazine to call a wig and two dress lines "liberated."

So far, so familiar. Whenever the ravishing of the English language   *4* comes up for perfunctory headshaking, politicians, journalists, and ad writers almost invariably get cast as Three Horsemen of the Apocalypse. The perennially identified culprits are guilty as charged, God knows. At their worst—and how often they are!—they seem to address the world through a bad PA system. Does it matter what they actually say? They capture your attention, right? They are word manipulators—the carnival barkers of life who misuse language to pitch and con and make the quick kill.

So let's hear all the old boos, all the dirty sneers. Paste a sticker proclaiming STAMP OUT AGNEWSPEAK on every bumper. Take the ribbons out of the typewriters of all reporters and rewritemen. Force six packs a day on the guy who wrote "Winston tastes good *like* . . ." Would that the cure for semantic aphasia were that simple.   5

What about, for example, the aphasics of the counterculture? The ad   6 writer may dingdong catch phrases like Pavlov's bells in order to produce saliva. The Movement propagandist rings his chimes ("Fascist!" "Pig!" "Honky!" "Male chauvinist!") to produce spit. More stammer than grammar, as Dwight Macdonald put it, the counterculture makes inarticulateness an ideal, debasing words into clenched fists ("Right on!") and exclamation points ("Oh, wow!"). Semantic aphasia on the right, semantic aphasia on the left. Between the excesses of square and hip rhetoric the language is in the way of being torn apart.

The semantic aphasia examined so far might be diagnosed as a hys-   7 terical compulsion to simplify. Whether pushing fluoride toothpaste or Women's Lib, the rhetoric tends to begin, rather than end, at an extreme. But there is a second, quite different variety of the disease: overcomplication. It damages the language less spectacularly but no less fatally than oversimplification. Its practitioners are commonly known as specialists. Instead of unjustified clarity they offer unjustified obscurity. Whether his discipline is biophysics or medieval Latin, the specialist jealously guards trade secrets by writing and speaking a private jargon that bears only marginal resemblances to English. Cult words encrust his sentences like barnacles, slowing progress, affecting the steering. And the awful truth is that everybody is a specialist at something.

If the oversimplifier fakes being a poet, the overcomplicator fakes being   8 a scientist. Perhaps it is unfair to pick on economists rather than anybody else—except that they are, after all, talking about money. And as often as not it turns out to be our money. Here is a master clarifier-by-smokescreen discussing the recruiting possibilities of a volunteer army if wages, military (W_m) are nudged seductively in the direction of wages, civilian (W_c): "However, when one considers that a military aversion factor must be added to W_c or subtracted from W_m, assuming average aversion is positive, and that only a portion of military wages are perceived, the wage ratio is certainly less than unity and our observations could easily lie on the increasing elasticity segment of the supply curve." All clear, everyone?

The ultimate criticism of the overcomplicator is not that he fuzzes but   9
that he fudges. If the cardinal sin of the oversimplifier is to inflate the trivial, the cardinal sin of the overcomplicator is to flatten the magnificent — or just pretend that it is not there. In the vocabulary of the '70s, there is an adequate language for fanaticism, but none for ordinary, quiet conviction. And there are almost no words left to express the concerns of honor, duty or piety.

For the noble idea leveled with a thud, see your nearest modern Bible.   10
"Vanity of vanities, saith the Preacher . . ." In one new version his words become, "A vapor of vapors! Thinnest of vapors! All is vapor!" — turning the most passionate cry in the literature of nihilism into a spiritual weather report. The new rendition may be a more literal expression of the Hebrew original, but at what a cost in grace and power.

Who will protect the language from all those oversimplifiers and over-   11
complicators who kill meaning with shouts or smother it with cautious mumbles? In theory, certain professions should serve as a sort of palace guard sworn to defend the mother tongue with their lives. Alas, the enemy is within the gates. Educators talk gobbledygook about "non-abrasive systems intervention" and "low structure-low consideration teaching style." Another profession guilty of non-defense is lexicography. With proud humility today's dictionary editor abdicates even as arbiter, refusing to recognize any standards but usage. If enough people misuse disinterested as a synonym for uninterested, Webster's will honor it as a synonym. If enough people say infer when they mean imply, then that becomes its meaning in the eyes of a dictionary editor.

Con Edison can be fined for contaminating the Hudson. Legislation   12
can force Detroit to clean up automobile exhausts. What can one do to punish the semantic aphasics for polluting their native language? None of man's specialities of self-destruction — despoliation of the environment, overpopulation, even war — appear more ingrained than his gift for fouling his mother tongue. Yet nobody dies of semantic aphasia, and by and large it gets complained about with a low-priority tut-tut.

The reason we rate semantic aphasia so low — somewhere between   13
athlete's foot and the common cold on the scale of national perils — is that we don't understand the deeper implications of the disease. In his classic essay, *Politics and the English Language,* George Orwell pointed out what should be obvious — that sloppy language makes for sloppy thought. Emerson went so far as to suggest that bad rhetoric meant bad men.

Semantic aphasia, both men recognized, kills after all. "And the Lord said: 'Go to, let us go down, and there confound their language, that they may not understand one another's speech.'" Is there a more ominous curse in the Bible? It breathes hard upon us at this time of frantic change, when old purposes slip out from under the words that used to cover them, leaving the words like tombstones over empty graves.

How, then, does one rescue language? How are words repaired, put *14* back in shape, restored to accuracy and eloquence, made faithful again to the commands of the mind and the heart? There is, sadly enough, no easy answer. Sincerity is of little help to clichés, even in a suicide note, as Aldous Huxley once remarked. Read, if you can, the Latinized techno-pieties of most ecologists. Good intentions are not likely to produce another Shakespeare or a Bible translation equivalent to that produced by King James' bench of learned men. They wrote when English was young, vital and untutored. English in 1971 is an old, overworked language, freshened sporadically only by foreign borrowings or the flickering, vulgar piquancy of slang. All of us — from the admen with their jingles to the tin-eared scholars with their jargon — are victims as well as victimizers of the language we have inherited.

Concerning aphasia, the sole source of optimism is the logic of neces- *15* sity. No matter how carelessly or how viciously man abuses the language he has inherited, he simply cannot live without it. Even Woodstock Nation cannot survive on an oral diet of grunts and expletives. Mankind craves definition as he craves lost innocence. He simply does not know what his life means until he says it. Until the day he dies he will grapple with mystery by trying to find the word for it. "The limits of my language," Ludwig Wittgenstein observed, "are the limits of my world." Man's purifying motive is that he cannot let go of the Adam urge to name things — and finally, out of his unbearable solitude, to pronounce to others his own identity.

QUESTIONS AND EXERCISES

Vocabulary

1. Define or explain each of the following terms:

malady (1)	biophysics (7)
semantic (2)	gobbledygook (11)
aphasia (2)	

Rhetoric

2. What is the obvious difficulty one encounters when writing about language?

3. In paragraph 3 the process of forming euphemisms is described. Find other examples of euphemism that are common in the language. What is the effect of using dysphemisms (words that give a negative connotation to a topic that may normally have a favorable connotation)?
4. What kind of sentence introduces paragraph 4? How is such a sentence justified?
5. What rhetorical device introduces paragraph 6?
6. What is the current status of some of the counter-culture terms found in paragraph 6? What does this suggest about the nature of slang?
7. How is paragraph 8 developed?
8. What rhetorical devices are used in paragraphs 13 and 14?
9. How effective are the transitions between paragraphs 8 and 9 and between paragraphs 12 and 13?

Theme

10. Discuss the assumptions about language implied in the essay. How does such an attitude compare with most theories held by linguists and lexicographers?
11. Whom does Maddocks attack in his essay?
12. What is the effect of linking Wittgenstein (an analytical philosopher) and Adam? Is such a sweeping inclusion prepared for in the essay?
13. What is Maddocks's main thesis?
14. Who determines the meaning of words?
15. Why is Maddocks hostile toward dictionary editors, educators, and current usage?
16. How deep do you think this essay is? Justify your answer with evidence from the essay. You may wish to compare this essay with Gove's "Preface to WEBSTER'S THIRD" for another attitude toward language. Who is the "better" authority?

Topics and Assignments for Composition

1. Write an essay showing the relationship between language and thought.
2. Research the differences between prescriptive and descriptive approaches toward English usage. Write an objective report of your findings.
3. Compile a short dictionary of current slang words giving their literal equivalents.
4. Choose an aspect of language (imagery, figurative language, grammar) and develop a central idea about it. Write an essay developing your idea and giving examples.

Eugene Rabinowitch

Student Rebellion: The Aimless Revolution?

Revolutions have been motivated in the past by large-scale social, national, or religious injustices; they were uprisings of major groups — often the majority of a nation — born of despair of ever obtaining the redress of grievances by nonviolent means. They have been strongly influenced, if not directly inspired, by ideological leadership, and committed to a concrete — if often unrealistic — program of change. *1*

An unprecedented phenomenon of our time is widespread revolutionary violence in the prosperous industrial West, originating with non-oppressed comparatively well-to-do groups — particularly the young — with no major economic grievances, and not motivated by any coherent social and political program. *2*

In America, this new — and, on the face of it, implausible — type of rebellion has acquired a certain rationality by association with the black people's drive for political and economic equality. Thus, rioting students of Columbia University asked for a stop to the construction of a gymnasium in Morningside Park — an area that could provide additional recreational facilities for the residents of Harlem. Obviously, this aim, however laudable, was not the basic reason for the revolt! German students in Berlin and Munich, French students in Nanterre and Paris, or students of 28 Italian universities, had other and even more legitimate grievances — overcrowding of lecture halls, inanity of examinations, lack of student representation in academic administration, and so forth — but none was convincing enough to justify the volume and intensity of the upheaval. In Paris, some students raised red flags of communism; others, black flags of anarchy; some displayed caricatures of President Johnson as a "war criminal." But obviously, the true motivation of their uprising *3*

Reprinted with permission from the September 1968 issue of the *Bulletin of the Atomic Scientists*.

was not indignation over the war in Vietnam, or belief in the ideology of communism (in its Western, Far Eastern, or Latin American version), or enthusiasm for the tenets of anarchism!

The student riots, whether they occurred in New York, Paris, Berlin, Rome, or Belgrade, with all their specific local overtones, were, I believe, expressions of the general discontent of youth with contemporary society, and with the university as it now exists — even though this society is committed to providing them with secure jobs, and this university to making these jobs good-paying and socially respectable.   4

No doubt, the riots and sit-ins were led, in New York as well as in Paris or Berlin, by small groups of "professional malcontents," which exist in all societies at all times; but the wide resonance of their actions among the large academic constituencies, including many of the young faculty, does not permit dismissing them as the handiwork of small, unrepresentative groups. Whence, then, this widespread and violent discontent? The Russian has an expression: "getting crazy from too much fat." Is this what is happening to economically secure youth, cradled in the lap of rich industrial civilization?   5

I do not believe so. The students, while free of immediate worry for their personal economic future, do not feel that they live in a secure and satisfying environment. Prospects of profitable employment do not compensate for a widespread alienation from the contemporary society — the feeling of being lost in an immense, impersonal, inhuman, mechanical society, with no individual challenge and no personal involvement in sight. And even the prosperity and security of the life offered to them in the white, industrialized communities of Europe and America is, they know, deceptive. In fact, never in the past was the future of all men so obviously and extremely insecure as it is now; and traditional learning, dispensed by the universities, does not suggest how to overcome this danger. Some among those who study science and technology can at least hope that new scientific discoveries and new technological processes will permit technological short-cuts ("fixes," Alvin Weinberg of Oak Ridge National Laboratory calls them), curing society ills without an active, conscious involvement of the people themselves. Students in law, philosophy, and social science must have a stronger feeling of how irrelevant the education they are offered is to the revolutionary changes and dangers society is facing.   6

The Intellectual Rebels

Intellectual rebels of today seem largely unaware of the fact (or deliberately ignore it?) that the main problems of contemporary society are those   7 created by the scientific and technological revolution. They cannot be solved by ignoring this origin and retaining the framework of pre-scientific concepts and institutions. These problems call for concerted, imaginative application of forces released by science and technology to the advancement of human needs; and this requires radical adaptation of traditional social and political institutions to the realities of the scientific age.

The *racial crisis* in America is, in essence, the consequence of the mechanization of agriculture (which has caused millions of agricultural workers and share-croppers to move from the rural South to the industrial North), and of the automation of industry (which is rapidly putting and end to the need for unskilled, menial labor in the city). The *overpopulation* crisis on the underdeveloped continents is caused by rapid reduction of infant mortality, resulting from application of elementary hygiene to birth and rearing of children, uncompensated by a corresponding reduction in birth rate. The trouble is exacerbated by the spread of electronic communications, leading to an awareness, by peoples living in the remotest corners of the world, of the gulf between their way of life and that of advanced industrial societies, and the consequent impatience to close it—the so-called "revolution of rising expectations." 8

Finally, the greatest danger to mankind is undoubtedly that of all engulfing, nuclear war between major technological nations—a danger that is unquestionably a product of the scientific revolution (or rather, of pre-scientific, traditional forms of international existence continuing into the scientific age). 9

Many intellectual rebels seem to seek answers to the evils of the technological society in a return to less organized, more individualistic ways of economic and political life in a "direct," "participating" democracy. Their attitudes are reminiscent of Jean-Jacques Rousseau's or Henry Thoreau's attacks on industrial civilization at its beginnings. In a television interview, Norman Mailer, who took part in the "siege" of the Pentagon, voiced the "anti-technological" bias of the participants in this action. The product of the New Left, Professor Herbert Marcuse, displays a similar attitude. The decreased interest of high school graduates in Europe and in America in the study of science and engineering—which, they say, is "posing more problems than solving them"—reflects the same disillusion. 10

Servan-Schreiber, a leading French publicist, in an interview in *Life* magazine represented the rebellious French students as fighters for the cause of the technological revolution against the rigid, pre-scientific political and social establishment that still rules France and several other European countries. He hopes that the "uprising of 20-year-olds" will cause the leadership in Europe to pass from the old generation, typified by 11 the General, to Servan-Schreiber's own generation of the "40-year-olds." France and Europe will then join, he believes, the great technological revolution inaugurated in America—a view Servan-Schreiber had brilliantly presented before *le de American*. But it is difficult to see in this interpretation of the student riots in France more than wishful thinking by one who aspires to turn a destructive movement with an anti-technological undertone onto the path of constructive technological progress.

A not unrelated development had been noticeable in art, long before it   *12* spread to the political and social arena. The history of art in the twentieth century is one of gradual destruction of conventional forms, and dissolution of rational content—as if these had been ties, holding the free human spirit in bondage to some alien tyranny. A similar spirit seems to pervade now the attitude of youth to social and political institutions. But what is justifiable as experiment, and, perhaps, ultimately creative in art, can be deadly in economic and political life. Playful destruction could become, in this irreversibly advancing world, a threat to the very survival of man. This survival is inexorably tied to rational adaptation of the human species to its new technological habitat. There can be nothing more futile than trying to destroy this habitat, because it seems uninviting and cold. It would be an intellectual imitation of the fabled behavior of lemmings!

Even more than at the time of the Luddites, rebellion against technol-   *13* ogy is now foolish, futile, and dangerous. All-out constructive utilization of the potentialities of science and technology is needed to assure the mere survival on earth of six billion men and women (and so many there will be a quarter century from now!)—not to speak of giving them a better life. Even now, technological society could not operate without enormous, highly organized—and highly productive—units. Whether these units be government-owned, as in the East, or privately-owned, as in the West, makes no fundamental difference. (This is why rebellious students denounce the communist establishment of the Soviet Union in the same breath with which they denounce the capitalist establishment of the United States.)

Even larger investment of capital and manpower, in enterprises re-   *14* quiring still more elaborate, complex, and disciplined organization on a continent-wide if not world-wide scale, will be needed for technological progress in the future: for example, for nuclear (particularly thermonuclear) power generation, or manufacture of light metals from sea water or igneous rocks; for the conversion of sprawling, traffic-choked, slum-infested cities into pleasantly habitable clusters of communities; for the cleansing of air and water, polluted and poisoned by industry and transport; and for maintenance of adequate land and air communications over continents and oceans—not to speak of navigation in space.

Man in the Technological Age

What is needed under these conditions, is not the objectively impos-   *15*
sible retreat from our mechanized automated, technological civilization,
but rapid adaptation of all political and social organization to the requirements of this civilization, permitting its intelligent application to serve
human needs. A way must be found to direct the immense creative and
productive capacities of science and technology toward making the earth
a satisfactory habitat for the hosts of human beings who have only too
well fulfilled the biblical injunction to "multiply and fill the earth." It is
within a highly organized technological society, and not on its ruins, that
mechanisms for the protection of individual freedom, for the stimulation
of individual creativity, and for safeguarding individual privacy, will have
to be found. This is not a matter of preference (many will sigh for the
emotionally and spiritually more satisfying life of the pre-technological
past!), but of the inescapable logic of the cultural and social evolution of
the species. A difficult evolutionary challenge; but it cannot be avoided.
The only alternative to meeting it successfully is for *Homo sapiens* to
join the innumerable species discarded in the course of evolution because
they were unable to adapt themselves to a changed habitat. That in the
present case man himself, and not external events, has been responsible
for reshaping his habitat, does not make the change less irreversible, or
the challenge less inescapable. Hope lies in the fact that adaptation to the
new habitat can be achieved by an intelligent effort, and does not depend
on the infinitely slower mechanism of genetic mutation and selection.

The most obvious barrier in the path of mankind's adaptation to life in   *16*
the technological age is the perpetuation into this age of the self-sufficient,
self-contained units – nations and states – which consider the pursuit of
their interests the legitimate paramount purpose of their existence, and
which call, in the pursuit of this aim, for unquestioned life-and-death
allegiance of their members. This self-centered behavior inescapably
leads to conflicts of interest between nations. Wars had been the universally accepted means to resolve such conflicts in the past; but the
scientific revolution has made war unsuitable as the *ultima ratio* of kings
(or as "continuation of politics by other means"). But despite widespread
awareness of this change, even among ruling elites and military leaders,
the traditional behavior of nation-states has not changed substantially.

An inevitable consequence of this failure to adapt to the new realities   *17*
of national existence is the continuation of the arms race, which has
ceased to be a competition in preparation for *winning* the next war (and
thus achieving some economic or political aims of the nation) and has
become an absurd and ruinous exercise in so-called "deterrence," with

nightmarish excesses such as the race to develop biological war agents, and multibillion dollar extravagances such as the race to build antiballistic missile systems.

Mankind's adaptation to the scientific-technological age calls for ending this senseless race, and redirecting the economic and human resources of technological society to constructive aims.   *18*

The Student Rapport

The youth is bound to feel that the fragmented society their parents are passing on to them—nations engaged in a $100 billion arms races, including the development of ABMs and of nuclear striking forces "aimed in all directions" (*tous azimuts* the French call it), islands of poverty in the midst of plenty, of urban decay, and of inadequate education—is anything but secure and rational. But students everywhere fail to direct their protest at the true source of this insecurity and irrationality—the worldwide "establishment" of national states. Instead, they rebel against weaknesses or faults of their individual societies and establishments. They seek the source of injustice and tension in the specific economic or political system prevailing in their (or other) nations—be it capitalism or communism, democracy or dictatorship—or even in the very existence of organized society, as anarchists do. They fail to see the main source of trouble in the pre-scientific state of international anarchy and conflicts, once justified by limitations of natural wealth (making fighting between classes and nations for a greater share of this wealth inevitable), but now made obsolete by man's new, immense capacity to create wealth by constructive technological effort.   *19*

The threat to survival of the coming generations of Americans, Russians, French, or Chinese, lies not in the deficiencies of their respective political and economic systems, but in the continued existence of all of them as self-centered, "sovereign" units, applying their greatest efforts to combatting each other. We have seen libertarian systems such as the American, or socialistic ones such as the Russian, dragged first reluctantly, and then with growing abandon, onto the dead-end path of national aggrandizement, once naively supposed to be associated only with militaristic empires or greedy capitalists.   *20*

If youth were rebelling against national insulation and isolation; if it were clamoring for transfer of responsibility, power, and influence from national to international organizations, such as the United Nations or the World Court; if they were rallying to the support of international organization of workers, scholars, or churches; if they were calling for acceptance of greater responsibility by the rich nations for the economic   *21* advancement of the poor ones, then they would be fighting in alliance with the evolutionary forces of our time, toward the emergence of a new order, in which the survival of mankind, if not assured, would be at least not impossible. But there is, at least as yet, no sign of rallying of youth to meet this crucial challenge.

Trying to smash the contemporary technological civilization in the hope (voiced by some student leaders in Europe and America), that in the very process of this destruction more satisfactory institutions and more humane ways of living will emerge, offers no hope. It is a sentimental counterrevolution, rather than the desperately needed rational revolution. 22

It is notoriously easier to rebel against the immediate authority than against a remote, impersonal power. In the Polish national epic, Mickiewicz' *Pan Tadeusz,* a speaker suggests to a gathering of rural Polish nobility that, instead of planning an insurrection against the Czar in support of Napoleon's invasion of Russia, they should each start fighting their own local enemies: "Thus," he argued, "the Commonwealth will rise and flourish." It is easy for students to rebel in Paris against de Gaulle and his obtuse educational authorities; in New York against Columbia's conservative President Grayson Kirk and the rough city police; in Rome against the archaic academic structure of Italy. It is much more difficult to fight the worldwide establishment of national sovereignties. And yet, only such a movement could mark a turning point in human history, and lead mankind out of the dead end of ruinous competition and senseless preparation for suicidal war. 23

The remarkable coincidence of student riots in the United States, Germany, France, Italy, Yugoslavia, Spain, Latin America, and Asia shows that there is enough rapport among the youth of all continents to make a concerted, constructive action—of which visionaries have so often dreamed in the past—more than an idle dream now. 24

QUESTIONS AND EXERCISES

Vocabulary

1. Define or explain each of the following terms:

redress (1)	inexorably (12)
inanity (3)	habitat (12)
caricature (3)	igneous (14)
tenets (3)	*Homo sapiens* (15)
resonance (5)	*ultima ratio* (16)
alienation (6)	humane (22)
exacerbated (8)	obtuse (23)

2. Identify or explain the importance of the following people or terms:

Rousseau (10)   Servan-Schreiber (11)
Thoreau (10)   behavior of lemmings (12)
Marcuse (10)   Luddites (13)
Mailer (10)

Rhetoric

3. What level of diction is maintained in this essay?
4. There are very few examples of imagery and figurative language. What is the resultant tone?
5. Find a figure of speech in paragraph 5.
6. What is the function of the first sentence in paragraph 6?
7. What is the average length of the sentences in this essay? What effect does this length have on the style?
8. Why is the argument from analogy presented in paragraph 15?

Theme

9. Why is the student rebellion an aimless revolution?
10. In the opinion of the writer, what is the cause of the main problems of contemporary society? How can they be solved?
11. What is the real threat to the world today?
12. Why do students in law, philosophy, and social sciences feel that their education is irrelevant to the revolutionary changes and dangers society is facing? Do you agree with the writer?
13. Explain the statement, "It is notoriously easier to rebel against the immediate authority than against a remote, impersonal power." Give an illustration of this claim from a rebellion with which you are familiar.
14. Is the writer optimistic about the potential of the students to bring about a change if they realize their real enemies?

Topics and Assignments for Composition

1. Summarize the thesis of this essay in one sentence.
2. Write a one-paragraph analysis of the style of the essay.
3. Write an essay in which you make an analysis of a contemporary social, political, or religious movement. Develop a thesis about it in a manner similar to "Student Rebellion: The Aimless Revolution?"

John Taylor

The Shadow of the Mind

The manner in which the brain determines behaviour is one of the most *1* exciting and challenging problems in science today. It involves an increasing number of scientists from an ever-widening range of disciplines: physiologists, psychologists, biochemists, anatomists, physicists, engineers, and mathematicians. The results being obtained are gradually allowing the basic questions of brain structure and function to be unravelled, though there are still many parts of this vast jigsaw puzzle which have to be obtained and put into place before the grand picture will be complete. Structures of basic importance in perception, memory, attention and consciousness, emotional states and sleep have tentatively been recognised, and their detailed mode of operation is being elucidated; the knowledge so gained is being put to practical use in the treatment of mental illness. At the same time attempts to build machines which can act intelligently are proceeding with increasing success, as the reports at the recent conference on artificial intelligence, held at Imperial College, London, have described.

There are numerous ethical problems which are natural concomitants *2* of this vigorous research programme and which are presently under discussion and inquiry. An example of this was the controversy last year over the results of Professor Arthur Jensen on intelligence and heredity. While such questions may not always get a completely satisfactory discussion they are indubitably exposed to some degree of critique by society. There is, however, a deeper and far more important aspect of brain research which raises the deepest ethical problems of all, but which has received only desultory consideration so far. This is concerned with the nature of mind and, in particular, of free will. In this article I want to

This article first appeared in NEW SCIENTIST, the weekly review of science and technology, 128 Long Acre, London WC 2. Reprinted by permission of the publisher.

discuss some of these questions and outline what I consider to be their deeper ethical implications. In particular I want to show that the scientists who work in this area carry a very great responsibility to society.

It is accepted by "hard-nosed" scientists and by nearly all laymen that   *3*
it will never be possible to discover the inner content of mental sensations by analysing physical processes, be they rates of firing of neurons, concentrations of certain chemicals in certain paths of the brain, or detailed behaviour patterns of response in the situation of interest. In other words, it is held that mental sensations cannot be measured, while a scientific description is only complete when it has been suitably quantified. This impasse would appear to be modified by the success being obtained in controlling mental states by suitable physical manipulation of the brain. The mind appears now to be a near-powerless "epiphenomenon" of the physical brain. But it still has the subjective quality which will never allow the scientist to get at its subjective content. Or will it? Might it not just be that hard-nosed scientists and laymen alike have had drummed into them since childhood that mind and matter are evidently different so that one cannot possibly explain the other?

There have been tentative suggestions, in the last few years, that cause   *4*
one to suspect the thesis that matter can never explain mind. These have led to what I propose to call the "relational theory" of mind, which allows a description of mind to be given purely in terms of the physical states of the brain and leads to a breakdown of the completely subjective nature of mental states. This relational theory of mind arises naturally in answer to the question as to what can be constructed of a non-physical nature from a set of measurements of physical quantities. The response to this is that it is the set of *relations* between these quantities, in other words whether one of them is larger or smaller than another. This set of relations or comparisons is not, itself, a set of numbers, but is constructed directly from them. If we consider the need for forming such a set of relations between the current rates of firing of neurons in the brain, both with each other and with those at past times, for the efficient working of a large and complicated brain such as that of man, then we would expect such a comparison to have come about.

This comparison process would determine which incoming information   *5*
is of most importance to be attended to immediately by the animal; storage of the results of reactions to such information would add further to the complexity of the set of relations in that brain. It would evidently be inefficient for all past states of all neurons in the brain to be related to on-going states, and coding of such information would evidently occur. Evidence for coding of incoming sensory information has been found in

a number of animals, as has strong indication that the limbic and reticular formations in the brain are involved in this process of comparison.

I am suggesting, then, that mental sensations have their non-physical character in that they are composed of relationships with other ongoing sensations as well as past sensations. It is this process of comparison which gives content to the mind; the blueness of the sky which can be experienced on a clear day has become so due to the countless past experiences of it. Just after birth an infant will have a rather "thin" or "empty" mind, having little to compare ongoing experiences with. To an adult a completely new experience will have little "mental" content, though it is very unlikely that such an experience can ever be obtained. The subjective content of a mental experience will thus be given by determining, objectively, the set of relations involved in this experience; they will show, for example, how blue the sky actually appeared. However, even with an efficient coding system reducing the amount of information being related to a minimum, there will still most likely be an enormous number of relations giving the detailed structure of a mental event. For a long time it is not to be expected that subjective states of humans will give up their secrets to the inquisitive probe of the brain researcher. However, simpler animals will undoubtedly be analysable along these lines; if they have a relational mechanism similar to that being discovered in higher vertebrates then undoubtedly they will have a mind, at least along the lines being discussed here.

How can this physical theory of the mind be proved or disproved? I said earlier that there is some evidence for a relational mechanism in the brain, as well as a strong but non-rigorous argument for the need for such a mechanism in higher animals, so giving an explicit model as to how mind has arisen by evolution from simpler animals. However, none of this is watertight. In order to validate this relational theory of mind it will be necessary to show that the detailed structure and function of the brain is just that of a comparison machine. In the absence of other models of the mind, this would appear to be the general goal towards which the brain research should direct itself. Its realisation is evidently some way off, though a time scale of decades might be realistic for its achievement.

I said earlier that I wished to consider free will along with the mind. If the sequence of mental events are merely epiphenomena then free will would be purely an illusion. In particular if the relational theory of mind outlined above is validated then certainly there is no place for free will. However it has been suggested that there must be a logical loophole in the determinist's net, and since this seems to have influenced a large number of brain researchers, I will briefly describe it before I refute it.

The thesis, as presented by Donald Mackay of Keele is that it is impossible to make a prediction of the future state of a person's brain (or mind) which is independent of whether or not the person is informed of this prediction beforehand. This is because, according to Mackay, "(the) prediction, to be successful, must allow for any relevant effect its formulation and communication will have on the subject's brain; but these effects could not all in general be calculated unless the prediction itself were already known, so that in general the exact calculation can never be completed." These remarks have been modified slightly in more recent discussions to take account of the subject's belief in the truth of the predictions ("The bankruptcy of determinism," New Scientist, vol 47, p 24), but the basic problem remains unchanged. It is essentially one of self-consistency, as Landsburg and Evans have also noted recently in the British Journal for the Philosophy of Science (vol 21, p 343). That is, the predication of A's brain state one hour hence must be so chosen that it will be correct if he learns about it half an hour from now and tries, cussedly enough, to prevent it from coming true. This type of self-consistency problem arises in many parts of physics, and corresponds to a non-linear fixed point problem. There are pathological cases where such problems have no solution, though naturally they cannot correspond to any physical situation. Careful analysis of the general manner of development of brain states from earlier ones shows that we have no pathology here: such self-consistent predictions of A's future brain state, given that he is told the prediction before it occurs, are always possible. Thus here is no logical loophole in the determinist's net.

It is still of great interest to ask how it is that free will has had such a good innings. Where has the illusion of free will (if so it is) arisen from? One possible source of it, which is a great determinant of behaviour in simpler animals, is that caused by spontaneous firing of neurons. This phenomenon arises at synapses between neurons and comes about from the spontaneous release of packets of the transmitter substance. Even though each separate packet may be below the threshold required for firing the subsequent cell, the convergence of a large number of neurons may well cause the spontaneous firing of their common receptor. This is, in fact, very important in insects, where for example, spontaneously firing circuits cause the male praying mantis' copulatory behaviour after its head has been removed; the head contains circuits which completely inhibit this spontaneous behaviour. The effect of convergence of tens of thousands of neurons in the cortex and lower brain structures may well produce spontaneous effects which generate the illusion of free will. In particular one can conjecture that the reticular formation of the brain stem, due to its highly interconnected structure, may have a strong component of such spontaneous character; when higher organisation circuits are at a deadlock as to what action to take, this spontaneous behaviour may take over and random action be chosen.

So far I've described a completely physical model of the mind and brain   *10* which has some supporting evidence. The validation of this, or a comparable model would seem to be the overall aim of brain research. What about the ethical implications of such a goal? One of these is that of the diminished responsibility of criminals. There are, indeed, well known cases of criminals whose violent acts could only be explained by brain pathology. In some cases it has even been found that brain surgery can cause them to become acceptable members of society with little modification other than destruction of their anti-social drive. Thus sexual offenders in Germany have been treated by unilateral destruction of their sex centres in the hypothalamus. These operations are allowed in German law as an alternative to imprisonment. Cases where there is no obvious pathology of brain function are more difficult to treat, but a thoroughgoing determinism can only allow incarceration of criminals to be regarded as on the same level as the isolation of patients with infectious diseases; cure of such social deviants must be regarded as one of the priorities of applied brain research.

But more important than this is that the success of such a programme   *11* of brain research as I have outlined above will cause a complete destruction of many people's understanding of their place in the world, as well as undermining the traditional institutions of society. While such a possibility has been with us ever since man began to think about himself, it has only been recently that the possibility has become a probability. The success of the model I have briefly outlined above would undoubtedly achieve this. Brain researchers must realise that, each in his own way, they are contributing to this success, and must take some of the responsibility for it when it is accomplished. This responsibility includes the need to inform society precisely what the general goal of brain research is. To say that such a model has not yet been proved and that determinism may be wrong after all appears to be shirking this responsibility, since there is no demonstration that it is incorrect, but only increasing evidence in its favour.

In a matter as important as this any scientist worth his humanity has to   *12* be prepared to act before everything is cut and dried. It may be very dangerous to wait until then; the need is to start to prepare people now to live in a deterministic world, so that the transition can be moderate and not too abrupt. Unless care is taken, the shadow of the mind may be strong enough to destroy society when the light of truth is brought to bear on it.

QUESTIONS AND EXERCISES

Vocabulary

1. Define or explain each of the following terms:

   concomitants (2)   explicit (7)
   epiphenomenon (3)   pathological (8)
   limbic (5)   synapses (9)
   reticular (5)   deviants (10)

2. Notice examples of British spellings in the essay of words like "recognised," "programme," and "realise."

Rhetoric

3. Although this essay is a rather formal, technical one, figurative language is used to make points clear. What is the meaning of "hard-nosed scientist" and "have had drummed into them" in paragraph 3?

4. In the first paragraph we find a sentence ending, ". . . though there are still many parts of this vast jigsaw puzzle which have to be obtained and put into place before the grand picture will be complete." Comment on the figure of speech contained in the excerpt.

5. What is a "thin" or "empty" mind? Why does Taylor put the two words into quotation marks?

6. Is "watertight" in paragraph 7 literal or figurative?

7. In paragraph 12 explain the meaning of "cut and dried"? Is this a literal, figurative, or a dead metaphor?

8. Explain what is the "shadow of the mind." Notice how rhetoric and meaning blend in the final sentence of the essay: "Unless care is taken, the shadow of the mind may be strong enough to destroy society when the light of truth is brought to bear on it."

9. Why is the last sentence in paragraph 11 difficult to understand?

Theme

10. What is the conflict between free will and determinism? Which side, according to Taylor, is likely to win?

11. Why must scientists prepare people for the conclusions of their research?

12. What were the "good innings" of free will?

13. What disciplines are involved in the understanding of this essay?

14. Professor Taylor's specialties are mathematics and theoretical physics. How would you account for his academic versatility?

15. Comment on the analogies made from the lower to higher animals, especially the praying mantis example.

16. Do humans need to hold on to the concept of free will even though

scientists may eventually demonstrate its deficiencies? Have there been analogous losses in the past? What have been the resultant rationalizations?

Topics and Assignments for Composition

1. Summarize the thesis of this essay.
2. Write a short analysis of the logic in paragraph 8.
3. Write an essay in which you argue the case of either determinism or free will.

Adrian Dove

Soul Story

It was a stormy Monday morning in Watts early last year when Willie *1*
Lee Jackson, a high school graduate of average learning ability, and a
black, applied for a routine assembly-line job. After meeting all of the
other requirements, he enthusiastically took the written exam — a widely
used personnel test devised in 1942. It's supposed to be a "culture-free"
measure of intelligence. But because Jackson didn't know the meaning
of "R.S.V.P." and had trouble with proverbs like "Many a good cow hath
a bad calf," he got a jacket hung on him; he was labeled a "hard-core unemployed."

I was then on a special committee on testing which had been trying to *2*
locate a "culture-free" intelligence test. Some of us felt that the measurable aspects of intelligence are so interwoven with culture that the only
fair way was to devise separate tests for separate cultures — and I had just
finished writing such a test, with a bias in favor of the ghetto dweller,
when I heard about Jackson's getting done in. Jackson took the test and
passed it strong, but the white middle-class employers on our committee
didn't. They commented: If suddenly tomorrow everyone had to pass
such a test, based on the ghetto culture, there would be an outcry from
the "culturally disadvantaged" non-ghetto dwellers complaining of discrimination and cultural bias. The charge would be justified. Yet in personnel offices all over the country, many intelligent black people are being
rejected because they haven't been raised in the white culture.

The day after I gave Jackson my test, a group of us — all black — went *3*
back to the employer who'd refused Jackson, and we ran it down to him
like it was — showed him exactly what he had done and how biased his
test was — but he didn't understand. The irony is that this employer (we'll
call him Harvey Butler), who hath rejected Jackson and cast him upon
the midden, considered this a just act and himself a just man. He is one

of his city's leading liberal businessmen, well-known for his sincere participation in, and contribution to, all the civil-rights and fair-employment programs around.

All Butler did was take us on a trip: *4*

"I would really like to find a way not to reject this kind of black applicant, but I can't throw out test scores, and I won't segregate my testing just because you say they have a separate culture. I always thought we had joined this fight so that we could promote integration. Don't you think we all should integrate into one culture?"   *5*

Which one, I wanted to know? Italian-American? Swedish-American? Irish-American? I told him, integration is *not* the real goal. It may become a healthy byproduct, but what we want is equality.   *6*

Cultural pluralism is what this country's all about. And it was only conscious recognition of the blessings of Irish-American culture, spurred by "Irish-power" moves in Boston, which overcame discrimination against that ethnic group and ultimately produced a President Kennedy for all of the people. "You say you want to integrate," I said, "but Willie Lee Jackson can hardly integrate if he's kept outside the factory because you refuse to acknowledge his intelligence and his culture."   *7*

Butler tapped his pipe on the edge of his desk. He allowed as how maybe all that made some sense—for the Irish and even the Mexican-Americans—but he just couldn't imagine what this black culture could be. He wanted to ask in a hip way, so he said, "Sock it to me," or something like that. And I began to tell him—not all of it, but part of it—in a big black voice. The gist of what I told him went something like this.   *8*

Black is our mind color, and Afro-American is our culture and language. Afro-American, popularly known as Soul, is an evolving culture that is indigenous to this land, but it's separate, too.   *9*

Indigenous, because we are not cultural Africans any more. The 22 million black men in this country could not move en masse to any nation in Africa and find complete cultural compatibility in terms of food, religion, what-have-you.   *10*

Separate, because we are not white Americans, and 22 million black men could not move, in small groups even, into the suburbs and resorts of this nation and find cultural compatibility, not to mention physical safety. No black man doubts this who.has tried to buy a home in Glendale, Calif., to play tennis at a Chevy Chase, Md., country club or, being really daring, to just go for a evening stroll through Cicero, Ill.   *11*

Nevertheless, some individual black men have gone back and are making it in African cultures. Others have moved into the white world and have become very popular participants. But it seems safe to say that the great majority of black men in the U.S.A. are not into either extreme.   *12*

Instead, they are seeking to develop and understand their own black culture. And that's Soul.

We know that the Soul culture is evolving and is not yet complete because we do not control all of our own institutions. We do control our language, customs and traditions—and three of our institutions: family, religion and art. We do not yet, however, exercise local control of our institutions of commerce, education and government.   *13*

Soul is love, and it's fed by the Southern farm and the big-city ghetto.   *14*
It's being flexible, and it's being spontaneous. The Soul brother is likely to be a bit more sensitive and frank. He's cool, too—he judges things by what he sees, not just by what the credentials say. Where black people meet, you find a special warmth you don't catch other places—Soul brothers can communicate by using only the essence of a message—straight to the point—results are more important than procedures.

When a brother has a car that's falling apart, dying right there on him,   *15*
and he's got no training in fixing cars—but he turns a screw here and puts a rubber band on there, and the car runs: that car is running on Soulforce.

When a welfare mother who never got past the fifth grade stands up at   *16*
a public meeting and outthinks a welfare director and puts him down so he knows it and everybody else knows it: that takes Soul.

It's many things, and it's everything that happens in the black experi-   *17*
ence, in church, nightclub or university. It's un-Soulful to try and define Soul, so here are some examples.

Take words. Language, as noted, is one element of the black man's life   *18*
that is within control of the black community itself. Here are some samples of the Afro-American vocabulary:

Big juice—A big-time white racketeer, believed to enjoy police protection.

Blow—The message of a person's conversation; what he said that particular time. Synonym: *rap.*

Burn—To improvise superlatively, in music or in life. The phrase "Burn, baby," was shouted at singers and orators long before the riot in Watts. During the riot, it became a pun.

Burner—The tops in his field, whatever his field is.

Changes, going through some—Having difficulties; regularly on the receiving end of bad news.

Chest, trying to get some—Looking for a fight.

Dap—Impeccably attired. Synonym: *clean.*

Down—Something so good it's out of sight, the best ever.

Dozens, playing the—A contest to see which young brother can remember or make up the greatest number of obscene, rhymed couplets reflecting on the opponent's parents. Sometimes called "signifying" or "mamma talk." Sometimes done with finger-snapping accompaniment. Though it may start in fun, it often attracts a crowd of admirers, and it can easily end in a fight. Not approved by parents.

Dues—Those unpleasant things which somehow, some day, are supposed to become blessings in disguise. Summed up by the saying, "If it ain't good to you, it must be good for you."

For days—Forever and until eternity.

Fox—Beautiful female.

Gig—A job. Synonyms: *slave, hustle.*

Hog—Any large automobile.

Heavy—An extremely intelligent person. But with a slight change in inflection, an extremely stupid person.

Hummer—A nothing person or event.

Jive—An unreliable person. A persuasive talker, quick to make commitments but prone to lie and make excuses for not delivering. Always late but always with an excuse.

Lame—A socially backward, clumsy person. Synonym: *square.*

Main man—A woman's boyfriend; a man's closest friend. Feminine form: *main squeeze.*

Member—An Afro-American, or Soul brother.

Pig—A frightened, sadistic and corrupt individual who happens to be a policeman. He may be white or black, but most blacks are adjudged not qualified.

Set—A close gathering, usually good.

Together—A person or event near perfection. Synonym: *ready* ("We made this down set in Vegas last week, and it was together.")

Twisted—To do time in the penitentiary. Someone who says he twisted behind a hummer means, he did the time but he didn't do the crime.

Whale—To run very fast, think very clearly or be in any way a righteous burner.

There's something special about these words—many deal with law and order. It seems that only in the black ghetto does there remain a living laboratory for properly defining words like "riot" and "violence."   *19*

We are taught by American history professors that if a frustrated group of people (not a "mob," of course) attacks property in 1773, it is not "violence" but a Boston Tea Party. If the authorities react truculently and in another "party" three years later two citizens are killed, it is not a "riot" but a Boston Massacre and just cause for some kind of declaration, particularly if the murderous officials are set free with a verdict of "justifiable homicide."   *20*

The moderate Tories might have triumphed in the United States (as in   *21*

Canada) and changed revolution into evolution if the colonizer had recognized the colony's determination to preserve and adapt all institutions to the reality of local control. America is today at the same crossroads Britain faced then. The big question is whether the next stage will be revolution or evolution.

Then there is the church. White Christianity was the only black institution that was allowed on this continent during slavery (aside from freedmen, the black family as an institution was almost totally destroyed by slave sales and forced "breeding" practices). So it happens that the white Jesus is very big in the ghetto.   22

Many sensitive black men over the years have lamented the fact that we are one of the few peoples in the history of the world who worship an anthropomorphic god who bears no resemblance to them. Some men have tried to do something about it. Malcolm X abandoned the white Jesus, looked to the East and found Allah. The Rev. Albert Cleague of Detroit has taught his expanding congregation that Jesus was not white but swarthy or black. And there are other, more conventional stirrings among black clergymen seeking to define black Christianity, to come to terms with the white church institution.   23

Yet the church, white God and all, has still been vital to the development of the Soul culture. In many small Southern towns there was no place else to go — nothing else to do but go to church and pray, and sing.   24

If you were down, you could find comfort in singing "Somebody Need You, Jesus Come By Here." If you were happy and wanted to let everybody know, you could sing "I'm on My Way." And there were even hymns and spirituals that could go either way, like "Where Shall I Be When I Hear That Trumpet Sound?"   25

The extremes of sorrow and joy were something outside the ken of the white church, and the way we express ourselves in the black church, in the singing and the preaching, the all-out givingness of the congregation and the minister, are also at the heart of Soul.   26

And the church has given black people more than just songs and sermons. It was the rock from which Dr. Martin Luther King rose to lead the black man into meaningful confrontations with repression and gave him new cause for pride in himself and his people. Adam Clayton Powell, too, a much-maligned hero, was catapulted from pulpit to Congress via the civil-rights struggle.   27

The church is as the roots of another very dynamite man, the Rev. Jesse Jackson, a product of Dr. King's Southern Christian Leadership Conference. Jackson is the director of Operation Breadbasket, an ex-   28 citing black-equality movement in Chicago. (Actually, I didn't tell Harvey Butler about this because it hasn't started yet—but I would have.)

Every Saturday morning on Chicago's South Side, Operation Bread-   29
basket holds a combination religious service, concert and civil-rights meeting. Some 3,000 people, mostly black but some white, hear speakers call for economic and political action against discrimination; parole officers sharing the same emotions as their parolees: the Blackstone Rangers, one of Chicago's most outlaw teen-age gangs, mixing with mainstream blacks and professional people and laborers; the music goes all the way from spirituals to the latest jazz. After service the participants march out to bolster Operation Breadbasket's civil-rights program by picketing some 40 stores of a supermarket chain that hasn't hired black managers.

Religion and music and civil rights and pride in being black—the   30
Chicago meetings are stone Soul.

The word "Soul" comes out of the church, of course, but jazz and blues   31
brought it out for the world. Soul music embraces a wide variety, from seditty M.J.Q. (Modern Jazz Quartet) pieces to Bobby Bland's squala sound, and it all has the distinct feeling.

I remember going to an integrated party recently. The hi-fi was playing,   32
and Ben Branch was burning on his tenor sax. Then he started a new number, which was actually a spiritual that Dr. King had been requesting of Branch at the moment when he was murdered. Without exception, all the brothers and sisters at the party began to sing or hum "Precious Lord, Please Hold My Hand . . ." The whites thought it was just a new jazz tune.

For the brother, music is important. He can be moved by Soul music   33
for days. At a theater where, say, Soul Brother Number One, rhythm-and-blues singer James Brown, is into his act, performer and audience are not separate from each other. They're together, they feel as one, and the music is made up to fit the mood right then and there. You know this moment will never happen again.

But you don't have to be at a theater to feel it. I do a lot of traveling,   34
and wherever I go, if my day has been foul, I can turn on my transistor radio and everything's mellow. Soul music and the black press are my first links to the whole world where I can feel part of something special.

Jazz is what many people think of when Soul music is mentioned, and   35
it is a big part of it. The jazz of Basie (Count), Monk (Thelonious), Miles (Davis) and (Sonny) Stitt has gone from finger-poppin' to cool and back to burnin' again. It keeps changing, partly because when it moves outside it gets captured and changed by the white culture, and then we have to

go and develop another new thing. (The same process happens in dancing, too. In the ghetto the African Twist and Funky Broadway and Bugaloo are giving way to the Tighten-Up and the Four Corners and a new calisthenic called the L.A. Shuffle.)

But there is other Soul music, too, like the Negro National Anthem. *36* When I was a child in Texas our *de facto* segregated school day would start with "The Negro National Anthem," a beautiful tune by James Weldon Johnson, and it united black children everywhere. It is not sung by students in *de facto* segregated schools today, but it has been preserved in some churches, and now it is making a comeback as a record, using its first line as a title: "Lift Ev'ry Voice and Sing . . ."

Whatever style it is, Soul music is another gift from our culture to all of *37* America. Unlike the more rigid and formalized classical music, Soul music is relevant to this time, this place and these people.

There is much more to Soul, but I didn't have time to tell Harvey Butler *38* everything. Food, as I say. Plenty of super-sophisticated whites already know about chitlings — "Soul food restaurants" have sprung up in places like Hollywood and lower Manhattan. So black people started calling chitlings ruffle steaks, out of the need of black privacy; now whites are picking up that term and the ghetto has started calling them wrinkles. Of course, privacy is only part of it. We know that when ruffle steaks become a gourmet dish, the price goes up.

It's all a little funny, because Soul food was originally nothing more *39* than leftovers. When the slaveholder down on that old Southern plantation ate turnips, slave got greens. When it was ham or bacon for the big house, slave got innards to make chitlings or the hard end of the nose to make snout (pronounced "snoot") or the tips of the feet to make trotters.

Soul food traveled in a shopping bag on the train with the big move *40* from farm to city and from South to North. The black man found all kinds of fancy new food in the new places, but it wasn't what he liked. It wasn't strong-flavored and it didn't fill you up the way Soul food does. It still doesn't.

A part of Soul involves appearance. Although hair-straightening for- *41* tunately seems on the way out (the hair styles called conks, or do's or processes), and the do-rag brother is giving way to the natural man, who wears a bush or an Afro, both styles are part of our culture. New clothing styles from New Breed and other stores blend the African and American cultures into "our own thing." The bright colors are more suited to a dark skin, but some whites are buying these fashions to wear with their Afro wigs.

About this time a guard came by to lock up the empty building, and we *42* noticed it was 8 P.M. So I told Harvey Butler we'd stop our lecture, but there was just one more point to make.

One really important thing our culture needs, I told him, in order to   *43* develop in a responsible way, is an honorable source of income for the male head of a household. People like Willie Lee Jackson, for instance, who didn't know about R.S.V.P.

"O.K., O.K.," Butler said. "I didn't know all these things about black   *44* culture. Tell you what I'll do. I'll hire Willie Lee Jackson, even though he failed in my white middle-class test. What do you think of that?"

And I answered him in a big, black, warm voice: "You're only gonna   *45* hire *one*?"

Test of Tests

The test devised by Adrian Dove to prove to his colleagues that no personnel test can be culture-free attracted considerable interest outside his Los Angeles office. Dove had hopes that it might be incorporated into tests for policemen and welfare workers operating in ghetto areas of California. But he gave up his hope, he says, after two years of futile effort – and moved to Washington.

Two of the questions on the "Dove Counterbalance General Intelligence Test" were:

1. Down South today, for the average Soul Brother who is picking cotton (in season) from sunup until sundown, what is the average earning (take home) for one full day?

(a) $.75, (b) $1.65, (c) $3.50, (d) $5, (e) $12.

2. If a dude is up-tight with a woman who gets state aid, what does he mean when he talks about "mother's day"?

(a) second Sunday in May, (b) third Sunday in June, (c) fourth Monday of every month, (d) the beginning and middle of every month.

The answers are: 1. (d); 2. (d)

QUESTIONS AND EXERCISES

Vocabulary

1. Define or explain each of the following terms:

ghetto (2)	truculently (20)
ethnic (7)	anthropomorphic (23)
Soul (9)	ken (26)
indigenous (9)	chitlings (38)

en masse (10)   gourmet (38)
impeccably (18)

2. Discuss the level of usage of each of the following:

"he got a jacket hung on him" (1)   "sock it to me" (8)
"ran it down to him like it was" (3)   "making it" (12)
"who hath rejected Jackson and cast him   "He's cool" (14)
    upon the midden" (3)   "puts him down" (16)
"he allowed as how" (8)   "lawandorder" (19)
"in a hip way" (8)   "our own thing" (41)

Rhetoric

3. How is the entire essay unified?
4. What tone do you feel the author is trying to maintain? What evidence do you have?
5. This essay has many elements of organization: narrative, example and illustration, and definition. Which is the dominant one?
6. Why does Dove use so many of the current idioms?

Theme

7. Explain this sentence: "Black is our mind color, and Afro-American is our culture and language." (9)
8. Explain the use of black and Afro-American vs. Negro and colored.
9. In paragraph 18 there are definitions of some Afro-American vocabulary. Add other words that should be here and define them.

Topics and Assignments for Composition

1. In one sentence define "Soul."
2. Develop a paragraph by one rhetorical technique and in the paragraph define "Soul."
3. Write a short essay in which you develop a definition of "Soul," "black," and "Afro-American."
4. Write an essay in which you compare and contrast the use of the terms "Soul" vs. "Square," "Black" vs. "Negro," and "Afro-American" vs. "American."
5. Develop a vocabulary list of some aspect of contemporary slang. Give your definitions and synonyms.
6. Write an essay in which you develop an extended definition of a contemporary, popular idea or vogue word like "soul," "charisma," or "mystique."

Student Example

Thorns under the Flowers

The psychedelic revolution was created by and in turn created social and psychological change. But if drugs like acid and mescaline have increased the consciousness, sharpened the awareness, deepened the insight of many, they have led others further and further into the shadowy realms of confusion, delusion, terror, and eventual madness. Or rather, the victims have ventured, consciously or unconsciously, into this territory themselves through over-indulging and ignoring their physical and emotional tolerance limits, or becoming too psychologically dependent on psychedelics to provide them with vision and direction. Consequently, there are many acid casualties around: the unluckier ones in jail or hospitals; others still wandering, stoned and confused, searching for Nirvana, or else straight and unhappy, having experienced only emptiness in one world and terror in the other.

People with a sufficient understanding of themselves, the desire to overcome the tyranny of physical and material preoccupations, and some source of emotional security have probably benefited most from psychedelic excursions. They had enough common sense to know when they were physically or emotionally unfit to take acid; they respected the drug, realizing its potential dangers as well as its positive aspects; and they have probably emerged from their acid experiences with a greater insight into themselves, a new understanding of their relation to the external world, and greatly heightened peace and happiness. Others, lacking the qualities needed to handle and profit from sudden confrontation with the secrets of their sub- or semi-conscious minds, freaked at what was revealed to them. The results were terror and paranoia-filled trips often followed by periods of depression, confusion, anxiety, and fear deeper and more difficult to shake than that produced by any previous psychological upsets.

But some bad trips still provided valued insights. Of the many acid users who weren't psychologically prepared for the revelations and experiences they encountered, those who employed their straighter virtues of caution, moderation, and common sense, came out relatively unscathed, their frightening experiences balanced by their enlightening ones.

However, the unfortunate victims are more numerous. The most disturbing casualties are those whose disillusionment has led them to a desire for guidance so frantic that they will grasp at anything which offers security and direction. This may be one factor explaining the recent popularity of various occult religious groups and communes. Fortunately, people like Charles Manson's pathetic zombies are still rare, but there are numerous other, less extreme, examples to be found everywhere. "Rolling Stone" recently ran a series on Mel Lyman, leader of several communes on both the East and West Coasts. Lyman, as Manson and most other cultist leaders do to one degree or another, proclaims himself to be God. His followers display a slavish devotion to him, seemingly typical of this trend toward the adoption of weird and scary Christ/Satan/father figures to whom disciples surrender every scrap of individualism in order to achieve the meaning, wholeness, and godliness of their leader, to effectively realize and embody his maxim that Life is Love is Death is Life. . . . Like the Jesus cult (but more frightening and sinister because many of them engage in expressly evil deeds) these communes reflect their members' unfulfilled longings to be dominated and possessed. The cults also reflect the willingness of many to reject everything in order to reach a state of freedom (through a sort of slavery) and peace.

The connection between acid and these cults is that not only are many of their members acid casualties, but one of the most obvious effects of acid is that it can create the need for these kinds of groups. Acid tends to produce ego-shedding, self-transcending experiences that can lead one to sublimate oneself to the first "savior" and spiritual guide who appears, complete with promises about attaining the desired knowledge, transcendent unity, and bliss—provided there is total subjugation to his will, of course. Thus any fanatic who is fairly eloquent, charismatic, and sensitive or shrewd enough to spot and then exploit the longings for meaningfulness, fulfillment, and belonging in the more desperate refugees of psychedelia can now apparently establish himself as leader of a self-devised cult composed of sad and frightened victims.

This development is probably the worst aftereffect of the acid phenomenon, the sickest and most tortuous route the psychedelic journey has taken so far. There is no one clear-cut villain. One can only observe that in an atmosphere of callousness, exploitation, fear, and confusion, elements that a portion of our present society thrives on, the psychedelic vision is bound to become twisted and warped, tangled in the evil and cruelty from which it is trying to liberate itself.

Part Eight:

Reports and Abstracts

Philip B. Gove

Preface to Webster's Third New International Dictionary

WEBSTER'S THIRD NEW INTERNATIONAL DICTIONARY is a completely   *1*
new work, redesigned, restyled, and reset. Every line of it is new. This
latest unabridged Merriam-Webster is the eighth in a series which has its
beginning in Noah Webster's *American Dictionary of the English Language,* 1828. On Webster's death in 1843 the unsold copies and publishing rights of his dictionary were acquired by George and Charles Merriam, who in 1847 brought out a revision edited by Noah Webster's
son-in-law, Professor Chauncey A. Goodrich of Yale College. The 1847
edition became the first Merriam-Webster unabridged dictionary. G. & C.
Merriam Company now offers WEBSTER'S THIRD NEW INTERNATIONAL
DICTIONARY to the English-speaking world as a prime linguistic aid to
interpreting the culture and civilization of today, as the first edition served
the America of 1828.

As the number of students in school and college jumps to ever-increas-   *2*
ing heights, the quantity of printed matter necessary to their education
increases too. Not only are more words used more often with these increases; words must be used more economically and more efficiently
both in school and out. More and more do people undertaking a new job,
practicing a new hobby, or developing a new interest turn to how-to
pamphlets, manuals, and books for both elementary instruction and advanced guidance. Where formerly they had time to learn by doing, they
now need to begin by reading and understanding what has been recorded.
A quick grasp of the meanings of words becomes necessary if one is to
be successful. A dictionary opens the way to both formal learning and to
the daily self-instruction that modern living requires. It is the key also

to the daily newspaper and to a vast number of other periodicals that demand our attention. This edition has been prepared with a constant regard for the needs of the high school and college student, the technician, and the periodical reader, as well as of the scholar and professional. It undertakes to provide for the changes in public interest in all classes of words as manifested by what people want to read, discuss, and study. The dictionary more than ever is the indispensable instrument of understanding and progress.

G. & C. Merriam Company have produced this THIRD NEW INTER-   *3*
NATIONAL at a cost of over $3,500,000. The budgetary and technical planning underlying its production has been directed and coordinated since 1953 by the Company's president, Mr. Gordon J. Gallan. His activity, understanding, and cooperation have contributed indispensably to its editorial completion and have made possible the maintenance of a Merriam-Webster permanent office staff constituted according to need. This staff is in effect a faculty which specializes in different branches of knowledge much as a small college faculty does. Listed among the resident editors are a mathematician, a physicist, a chemist, a botanist, a biologist, a philosopher, a political scientist, a comparative religionist, a classicist, a historian, and a librarian as well as philologists, linguists, etymologists, and phoneticians whose speciality is the English language itself. Their academic affiliations and their degrees can be seen one by one in the "Merriam-Webster Editorial Staff" that follows this preface. Besides the office staff over two hundred other scholars and specialists have served as outside consultants in supplementary reviewing, revising, and submitting new definitions in subjects in which they are authorities. The range and experience of this special knowledge appear in the listing of their names alphabetically after the editorial staff.

In conformity with the principle that a definition, to be adequate, must   *4*
be written only after an analysis of usage, the definitions in this edition are based chiefly on examples of usage collected since publication of the preceding edition. Members of the editorial staff began in 1936 a systematic reading of books, magazines, newspapers, pamphlets, catalogs, and learned journals. By the time of going to press the collection contained just under 4,500,000 such new examples of recorded usage, to be added to more than 1,665,000 citations already in the files for previous editions. Further, the citations in the indispensable many-volume *Oxford English Dictionary,* the new citations in Sir William Craigie's four-volume *Dictionary of American English* and Mitford M. Mathews' two-volume *Dictionary of Americanisms,* neither of which was available to the editors of the preceding edition, and the uncounted citations in dozens of concordances to the Bible and to works of English and American writers

and in numerous books of quotations push the citation background for the definitions in this dictionary to over ten million. This figure does not include freely consulted text matter in the office library of reference books. Nor does it include thousands of textbooks in the private and academic libraries of the editors and consultants, nor books consulted in the Springfield City Library whose librarians have generously given the editorial staff ready and frequent access to its large and valuable word-hoard.

While dictionaries of special subjects, glossaries, indexes, and check-   5
lists are collected and examined to verify the existence of special words, no word has been entered in this dictionary merely on the authority of another dictionary, special or general, and no definition in this dictionary has been derived from any other dictionary (except, of course, Merriam-Webster predecessors). Learned and industrial organizations have created numerous committees of nomenclature to collect, define, and standardize the terminology in their fields. Some of the staff editors serve as advisory members of such committees. Nevertheless prescriptive and canonical definitions have not been taken over nor have recommendations been followed unless confirmed by independent investigation of usage borne out by genuine citations.

The primary objective of precise, sharp defining has been met through   6
development of a new dictionary style based upon completely analytical one-phrase definitions throughout the book. Since the headword in a definition is intended to be modified only by structural elements restrictive in some degree and essential to each other, the use of commas either to separate or to group has been severely limited, chiefly to units in apposition or in series. The new defining pattern does not provide for a predication which conveys further expository comment. Instead of encyclopedic treatment at one place of a group of related terms, each term is defined at its own place in the alphabet. Every phrase in lowercase roman type following a heavy black colon and running to the next heavy colon or to a divisional number or letter is a complete definition of one sense of the word to which it is attached. Defining by synonym is carefully avoided by putting all unqualified or undifferentiated terms in small capital letters. Such a term in small capitals should not be considered a definition but a cross-reference to a definition of equivalent meaning that can be substituted for the small capitals.

A large number of verbal illustrations mostly from the mid-twentieth   7
century has been woven into the defining pattern with a view to contributing considerably to the user's interest and understanding by showing a word used in context. The illustration is often a brief combination of words that has actually been used in writing and when this is so the illustration is attributed to its author or source. More than 14,000 different

authors are quoted for their use of words or for the structural pattern of their words but not for their opinions or sentiments.

A number of other features are (1) the recognition and separate entry (with part-of-speech label) of verb-plus-adverb compounds (as *run down*) that function like one-word verbs in every way except for having a separable suffix, (2) the recognition (by using the label *n* for noun) that substantive open compounds (as *clothes moth*) belong in the same class as nouns written solid or hyphened, (3) the recognition (by using the label *often attrib*) of nouns that often function as adjectives but otherwise do not behave like the class of adjectives, (4) the indication (by inserting suffix-symbols, as -s or -ES, ED/-ING/-S or -ES, -ER/-EST) of the inflectional forms of nouns, verbs, adjectives, and adverbs at which the forms are not written out in full, (5) the recognition (by beginning entries with a lowercase letter and by inserting either the label *cap, usu cap, often cap,* or *sometimes cap*) that words vary considerably according to circumstances and environment, (6) the recognition (by not using at all the status label *colloquial*) that it is impossible to know whether a word out of context is colloquial or not, and (7) the incorporation of abbreviations alphabetically in the main vocabulary. 8

In continuation of Merriam-Webster policy the editors of this new edition have held steadfastly to the cardinal virtues of dictionary making: accuracy, clearness, and comprehensiveness. Whenever these qualities are at odds with each other, accuracy is put first and foremost, for without accuracy there could be no appeal to WEBSTER'S THIRD NEW INTERNATIONAL as an authority. Accuracy in addition to requiring freedom from error and conformity to truth requires a dictionary to state meanings in which words are in fact used, not to give editorial opinion on what their meanings should be. 9

In the editorial striving for clearness the editors have tried to make the definitions as readable as possible. Even so, the terminology of many subjects contains words that can be adequately and clearly explained only to those who have passed through preliminary stages of initiation, just as a knowledge of algebra is prerequisite for trigonometry. A dictionary demands of its user much understanding and no one person can understand all of it. Therefore there is no limit to the possibilities for clarification. Somewhat paradoxically a user of the dictionary benefits in proportion to his effort and knowledge, and his contribution is an essential part of the process of understanding even though it may involve only a willingness to look up a few additional words. 10

Comprehensiveness requires maximum coverage with a minimum of compromise. The basic aim is nothing less than coverage of the current vocabulary of standard written and spoken English. At the same time the 11 scientific and technical vocabulary has been considerably expanded to keep pace with progress especially in physical science (as in electronics, nuclear physics, statistics, and soil science), in technology (as in rocketry, communications, automation, and synthetics), in medicine, and in the experimental phases of natural science. Therefore space has been found not only for new terms but also for new uses of old terms, for English like other living languages is in a metabolic process of constant change. The changes affect not only word stock but meaning, syntax, morphology, and pronunciation.

The demands for space have made necessary a fresh judgment on the *12* claims of many parts of the old vocabulary. This dictionary is the result of a highly selective process in which discarding material of insubstantial or evanescent quality has gone hand in hand with adding terms that have obtained a place in the language. It confines itself strictly to generic words and their functions, forms, sounds, and meanings as distinguished from proper names that are not generic. Selection is guided by usefulness, and usefulness is determined by the degree to which terms most likely to be looked for are included. Many obsolete and comparatively useless or obscure words have been omitted. These include in general words that had become obsolete before 1755 unless found in well-known major works of a few major writers.

In definitions of words of many meanings the earliest ascertainable *13* meaning is given first. Meanings of later derivation are arranged in the order shown to be most probable by dated evidence and semantic development. This arrangement applies alike to all meanings whether standard, technical, scientific, historical, or obsolete. No definitions are grouped alphabetically by subject labels. In fact this edition uses very few subject labels. It depends upon the definition for incorporating necessary subject orientation.

The pronunciation editor is Mr. Edward Artin. This edition shows as *14* far as possible the pronunciations prevailing in general cultivated conversational usage, both informal and formal, throughout the English-speaking world. It does not attempt to dictate what that usage should be. It shows a wide variety of acceptable pronunciations based on a large file of transcriptions made by attentive listening to actual educated speech in all fields and in all parts of the country—the speech of those expecting to be completely understood by their hearers. The facility with which such speech can be checked today by television, radio, and recordings has made it possible to show more representative and more realistic pronunciations than in the past.

To this end the Merriam-Webster pronunciation key has been revised. *15* Many of the symbols of preceding editions have been retained, some with slight alteration, a few substitutions have been made, and some symbols that have outlived their usefulness have been dropped altogether. It is still fundamentally a diacritical key that makes use of many of the conventions of English spelling and is based on the principles that every distinct significant sound should have a distinct symbol to represent it and that no sound should be represented in more than one way. The elimination of symbols for all nonsignificant differences in sound makes it possible for transcriptions to convey to speakers in different parts of the English-speaking world sounds proper to their own speech. The new pronunciation alphabet is designed to represent clearly the standard speech of educated Americans.

It should be clearly understood that in striving to show realistic pronunciations definite limitations are fixed by the very nature of a dictionary. Each word must be isolated and considered apart from its place in connected spoken discourse. It is impracticable to show in a dictionary many kinds of variations—rising or falling pitch, syllabic emphasis or lack of emphasis, contradiction or prolongation of sounds—to which the pronunciation of a word is susceptible under the influence of other words temporarily associated with it. Some of these variations are discussed under several headings in "Guide to Pronunciation," which contains also several paragraphs on the subject of correctness in pronunciation.

The etymologist for this edition is Dr. Charles R. Sleeth. In the etymologies the aim has been to retrace step by step the line of transmission by which the words have come down to modern English from the language in which they are first recorded. The present work adheres in this respect to the sound general principles governing the presentation of word histories in previous editions and indeed applies them with a consistency that has not previously been attained. With particular care it traces back to Middle English every word which is recorded in Middle English; also it carefully distinguishes the age of borrowings from French by giving the source language as Old French if the word came into English before 1300, as Middle French if it came into English between 1300 and 1600, and as French only if it came into English in the seventeenth century or later.

The etymologies fall into four general groups based on the origins of English words. Native words (as *hound*) that have been in the language as long as it has existed are traced first through Middle English to Old English and then to Germanic languages other than English and to Indo-European languages other than Germanic. Old and well-established borrowings (as *chief, add,* and *dialect*) that have been in English since medieval or Renaissance times and comes from languages, usually French, Latin, or often indirectly Greek, which belong, like English, to the Indo-European language family are traced back through their immediate source to their ultimate source in as much detail as native words. Many more recent borrowings (as *éclair, anile, hubris, sforzando, lariat, dachshund, smorgasbord, galore, muzhik,* and *karma*) are incorporated into the network of Indo-European etymology more thoroughly than in earlier dictionaries by going beyond the immediate source to either a list of cognates or a cross-reference to another entry. Borrowings (as *bushido, tepee, sheikh, sampan,* and *taboo*) from non-Indo-European languages are traced to the immediate source and analyzed into their parts if in the source language they are compounds or derivatives.

In the modern technical vocabulary of the sciences it is difficult if not *19* impossible to adhere strictly to the principle of tracing step by step the line of transmission of a word, because such vocabulary has expanded rapidly in numerous fields and has been transmitted freely across language boundaries. Very few works of reference give full or systematic information about the language of origin of technical terms in any one field, and consequently it is impossible for the etymological staff of a general dictionary to garner and present such information about the technical terms of all fields. The present work attempts a new solution of this problem by introducing the label ISV (for International Scientific Vocabulary), for use in the etymology of such words when their language of origin is not positively ascertainable but they are known to be current in at least one language other than English. Examples of the use of ISV and further details about it are given in "Explanatory Notes," 7.6. Some ISV words (like *haploid*) have been created by taking a word with a rather general and simple meaning from one of the languages of antiquity, usually, Latin or Greek, and conferring upon it a very specific and complicated meaning for the purposes of modern scientific discourse. More typically, however, ISV words are compounds or derivatives, made up of constituents that can be found entered in their own alphabetical position with their own ulterior etymology, again generally involving Latin or Greek. In either case an ISV etymology as given in the present work incorporates the word into the system of Indo-European etymology as well as if the immediate source language were known and stated. At the same time, use of ISV avoids the often untenable implication that the word in question was coined in English, and recognizes that the word as such is a product of the modern world and gets only its raw materials, so to speak, from antiquity.

The scheme of biological classification used has been concerted in *20* consultation between Dr. Mairé Weir Kay, staff biologist, and specialists in the several divisions of taxonomy. It is planned to coordinate in the broadest way with current professional usage and specifically avoids undue reliance on any single school or system. The total taxonomic coverage is far more extensive than this characterization might imply and is designed to include and link with the preferred scheme both historically important though now disused terminology and the more important terms pertinent to divergent schools or professional thought (as in the question of whether the leguminous plants constitute one or several families).

Words that are believed to be trademarks have been investigated in the *21* files of the United States Patent Office. No investigation has been made of common law trademark rights in any word since such investigation is impracticable. Those that have current registrations are shown with an initial capital and are also identified as trademarks. The inclusion of any word in this dictionary is not, however, an expression of the publishers' opinion on whether or not it is subject to proprietary rights. Indeed, no definition in this dictionary is to be regarded as affecting the validity of any trademark.

This dictionary has a vocabulary of over 450,000 words. It would have *22* been easy to make the vocabulary larger although the book, in the format of the preceding edition, could hardly hold any more pages or be any thicker. By itself, the number of entries is, however, not of first importance. The number of words available is always far in excess of and for a one-volume dictionary many times the number that can possibly be included. To make all the changes mentioned only to come out with the same number of pages and the same number of vocabulary entries as in the preceding edition would allow little or no opportunity for new words and new senses. The compactness and legibility of Times Roman, a typeface new to Merriam-Webster dictionaries, have made possible more words to a line and more lines to a column than in the preceding edition, and a larger size page makes a better proportioned book.

The preparation of this edition has absorbed 757 editor-years. This *23* figure does not include the time of typists, photocopiers, and clerical assistants or the time of over 200 consultants. The book appears, like its predecessor, after more than ten years of active full-time preparation. It is hardly necessary to observe that no one editor could harmonize all the diverse and disparate matter by reading and criticizing every line or even determine and keep firm control over editorial policy, nor could an editorial board of fixed membership. Instead the editor in chief has used his editors one by one and has delegated multiple responsibilities to them individually as occasion required. In this way members of the Merriam-Webster staff have been grouped and regrouped to form hundreds of task forces performing simultaneously thousands of missions. The editor can say with gratitude and relief that the accomplishment is not a one-man dictionary. "What individual," asks Noah Webster in his preface, "is competent to trace to their source, and define in all their various applications, popular, scientific, and technical, sixty or seventy thousand words!"

WEBSTER'S THIRD NEW INTERNATIONAL DICTIONARY is a collabora- 24
tive effort. Without the cooperation of the scholarly, scientific, and technical world, the specialized guidance of our outside consultants, and the ingenuity of the compositors and printers, G. & C. Merriam Company and its permanent editorial staff could not have brought the work to its successful culmination. Those most deeply involved with overall responsibility deserve special mention here. Three associate editors, Mr. Artin, Dr. Kay, and Dr. Sleeth, have already been named in this preface. Among others who have shared large responsibilities are these associate editors: Miss Anne M. Driscoll, Dr. Philip H. Goepp, Mr. Hubert P. Kelsey, Dr. Howard G. Rhoads, and Dr. H. Bosley Woolf; two assistant editors, Miss Ervina E. Foss and Mrs. Laverne W. King; and the departmental secretary, Mrs. Christine M. Mullen.

It is now fairly clear that before the twentieth century is over every 25
community of the world will have learned how to communicate with all the rest of humanity. In this process of intercommunication the English language has already become the most important language on earth. This new Merriam-Webster unabridged is the record of this language as it is written and spoken. It is offered with confidence that it will supply in full measure that information on the general language which is required for accurate, clear, and comprehensive understanding of the vocabulary of today's society.

PHILIP B. GOVE

Springfield, Mass.
June 1, 1961

QUESTIONS AND EXERCISES

Vocabulary

1. Define or explain each of the following terms:

philologists (3)	syntax (11)
phoneticians (3)	morphology (11)
etymologists (3)	evanescent (12)
concordances (4)	generic (12)
canonical (5)	diacritical (15)
nomenclature (5)	taxonomy (20)
predication (6)	divergent (20)
verbal illustration (7)	leguminous (20)
substantive (8)	

Rhetoric

2. Discuss the logic of the presentation. Begin with a list of general subjects covered.
3. Make an analysis of one of the long sentences in this selection. Choose a sentence that has over 50 words in it. What kind of sentence is it? Why does it have to be that long?
4. Did you find it necessary to read any phrase several times to understand it? Find the phrase and explain the difficulty.

Discussion

5. Discuss the assumptions and implications in this sentence: "In conformity with the principle that a definition, to be adequate, must be written only after an analysis of usage, the definitions in this edition are based chiefly on examples of usage collected since publication of the preceding edition."
6. Discuss the way pronunciation of words was established.
7. How many words does the dictionary include? Are these all the words in the language?
8. Why did the editors omit the status label "colloquial"?
9. Is the general philosophy of WEBSTER'S THIRD prescriptive or descriptive? Explain and defend your answer.

Topics and Assignments for Composition

1. Find a definition in WEBSTER'S THIRD and compare it with the same definition in WEBSTER'S SECOND. List both and make a one-sentence analytical commentary.
2. Look up the pronunciation of several words with which you have had trouble. After you have looked them up, in a paragraph discuss the problems of learning pronunciation from a dictionary.
3. Read Wilson Follett's "Sabotage in Springfield" and Bergen Evans' "But What's a Dictionary For?" Write an essay in which you compare and contrast the two writers' opinions toward WEBSTER'S THIRD NEW INTERNATIONAL DICTIONARY.
4. In an essay compare WEBSTER'S THIRD NEW INTERNATIONAL DICTIONARY to the *Oxford English Dictionary*.

Elizabeth McGough

Body Language . . . It Tells on You

When you walk into a room full of people, you communicate with
everyone there without ever saying a word. *Kinesics,* or body language,
sends the message. Faster than words, it conveys much of what you
really think or feel. 1

For example, if you join a group without offering the customary polite
looks and acknowledging glances – sort of look off into space – you are
likely to set a somewhat hostile scene. Some may think that you consider
yourself superior. 2

Sue hates to be noticed, is extremely shy and "pulled in." She avoids
looking at people and withholds the expected little smiles and gestures
of greeting. Yet she wonders why she feels unwelcome. Simple. Her
body language communicates unfriendliness. 3

Warm greetings, like laughter, tend to create a bond. Cool greetings
evoke cold or even hostile response. Body language flashes the message
without words – loud and clear. 4

Body language varies from culture to culture and between ethnic
groups. Kinesics, according to anthropologists, is the study of this nonverbal communication. This rather young science has only made the
scene within the last two decades, but already it has revealed some
amazing clues to our hidden thoughts and attitudes. 5

The way we meet someone's eyes and look away tells many things, for
example. When an American boy and girl look searchingly into each
other's eyes, emotions are turned on. 6

"He makes me feel so uncomfortable," Jean giggles, after Steve's gaze
seems to hold her eyes. Americans are guarded about how, and for how
long, eyes meet. Normal eye contacts last about one second before some- 7

From AMERICAN YOUTH Magazine March/April 1971. Reprinted by
special permission of AMERICAN YOUTH Magazine.

one looks away. Holding a gaze longer than usual often tips the relationship to a warmer one. Avoiding direct eye contact in certain circumstances says you have something to hide. The eyes admit that your body
doesn't know how to lie.

Our eyes act like conversational traffic signals, controlling how talking   *8*
time is shared. Eye behavior in a conversation might go something like
this: As Jean talks, she looks away briefly during hesitations while she
organizes her thoughts. She glances at Steve from time to time for feedback, to make sure he is attentive. Steve holds his gaze longer when eyes
meet, nods to show attention. This tells Jean she can go on talking. A
raised eyebrow might indicate doubt, or a question, or a request to repeat
a message. A pause, combined with a rather long glance by the speaker,
signals to the listener that it is his turn to talk. Watch a couple of conversations sometime, and see if it isn't so.

Eyes can challenge, too. A student meets the teacher's eyes, holding   *9*
the gaze longer than necessary. This presents a subtle test of authority or,
occasionally, outright defiance.

Eye talk is emphasized by the eyebrows. Kinesics experts tell us the   *10*
eyebrows have a repertoire of more than 20 positions. They tend to
qualify the spoken word in their fleeting movements. Men "talk" with
eyebrows more than women do.

Dr. Sue-Ellen Jacobs, anthropologist at Sacramento State College,   *11*
points out that you can also look for facial clues, or *kinemes,* during conversations. You can tell a favorable reaction to what is said, she says, or
you can catch a look of scorn or disbelief, however brief. A look of scorn
might be only a slight compressing of the lips and furrowing of the eyebrows, but it says a great deal.

Other signals: A girl tilts her head sideways and says, in body lan-   *12*
guage, "You interest me." In a mixed group, both boys and girls show
more grooming gestures, particularly with the hair, twisting and combing
it (anxiety, uneasiness) more than they would if they were grouped with
only their own sex.

The feeling of being liked or disliked frequently boils down to that old   *13*
saw, "It's not what he said, but how he said it." Such a message comes
through in spite of the choice of words. Psychologists consider the
formula for total message impact to be 7 percent verbal (choice of words),
38 percent vocal (tone), and 55 percent body language.

Can you tell how people feel about each other, via body language?   *14*
Psychologists say you can. Experiments involving men with other men
showed that posture can indicate like or dislike.

The least relaxed man, with tense hands, rigid posture, says in effect, *15* "I dislike you and feel threatened, or intimidated."

The man who appears most relaxed, body twisted, perhaps, leaning far *16* back in the chair and to one side, says, "I don't like you, but feel no intimidation." Superior feelings may be present.

A moderately relaxed body posture, slumped forward slightly says, *17* "I like the person I am with."

Try this little game with yourself the next time you are involved in a *18* group rap session that turns into a heated discussion. Sort out the two sides of the argument. Most of the "pros" will sit with crossed legs. The "cons" will have outstretched legs and folded arms. The middle-of-the-roaders might try a combined posture. An abrupt shift in position can signal a person is changing sides. He is saying, "I disagree with you" to the present speaker.

With some effort, you can profit by some of the things scientists have *19* learned about kinesics. For example, when you are interviewed for a job, if you assume an elaborately nonchalant position during the interview, arm thrown around the back of the chair, you have all but struck out. An employer doesn't want an unconcerned employee. Your nonchalance may be a cover-up for being uptight, but it may come across in body language as "I don't care."

Your arms and legs also can betray you in countless ways. Many of us *20* can successfully control facial expressions, but that finger tapping, the foot or leg jiggling reveal anxiety or stress. They're tattletale movements.

Kinesics investigators have some interesting theories about leadership *21* qualities and the use of body language. In a recent study on leadership, several high school boys were singled out in their peer group. In 15 recorded situations, three boys were found to be heavy vocalizers and accounted for more than 70 percent of the conversation. But only one of the three had real leadership qualities. He initiated more conversation and thought trends than any other boy.

However, another boy in the group, who was observed to have high *22* leadership qualities, had one of the lowest word counts. He originated conversations at an average rate and spoke only 16 per cent of the words. His leadership, however, was a kinesic one. He was kinesically more mature, and though he talked relatively little, he held the reputation of being a good conversationalist. He was a good listener and did not trans-mit negative signals—leg shuffling and foot jiggling, for example.

You may never be fully aware of what you communicate through body *23* language. On the other hand, if you make an effort to discover what others see, you might even be able to find out things you've been hiding from yourself.

QUESTIONS AND EXERCISES

Vocabulary

1. Define or explain each of the following terms:
kinesics (1)	feedback (8)
anthropologists (5)	*kinemes* (11)

Rhetoric

2. This short essay contains many concise, almost textbook examples of basic punctuation patterns. Notice the use of commas, quotation marks, colons, and dashes. How is the problem of the use of numbers solved?
3. There is almost a complete absence of figurative language. What quality does this lack impart to the essay?
4. Comment on the length and development of paragraphs.
5. What is the principal method of development used by the author?

Theme

6. How is the substance of the article substantiated?
7. How would one go about setting up an experiment to support some of the claims made in the essay?
8. What is the relationship between the unconscious and body language?
9. Find other examples of body language in everyday behavior.
10. Find examples of body language in literature. Does this suggest that fiction writers have read psychology books?
11. Are there theories that link physical appearances with psychological types? With moral qualities?

Topics and Assignments for Composition

1. Summarize the thesis of the essay.
2. Write a narrative that includes an example of body language.
3. Write about a personal experience in which, in retrospect, you realized that your body gave more information about your thoughts than you were then aware of.
4. Research the scientific literature on body language and write an objective report summarizing the findings.

Dexter K. Strong

Hair: The Long and the Short of It

The length of a man's hair and beard has become, in the minds of many,   *1*
one of the major issues of our time. This fact crept up on me gradually.
Schoolmasters such as myself have for years been responsible for seeing
to it that the young get their hair cut. A father's determination to keep his
son's hair neatly trimmed is legendary, and usually begins early, when he
has to overcome Mother's reluctance about that first trip to the barbershop. Currently, however, the subject of long hair and beards is causing
more than gentle family arguments. It is a hotter issue between generations than ever before in *my* lifetime, and wherever the topic is discussed
it raises blood pressures to alarming levels. It is likely to lead from discussions of style and discipline to frantic condemnations of draft-evasion,
homosexuality, and LSD.

Even the newspapers fan the flames. Periodically, front pages carry the   *2*
story of, say, a Stanford coach barring a runner from a track meet, or a
principal excluding a long-haired boy from school.

Perhaps reasonable men should be above such a hullaballoo over hair,   *3*
but my guess is that when any of us first encountered, on Piccadilly or on
University Way, a six-foot man with hair down to his shoulders, we ourselves had some strong feelings on the subject—feelings that were unlikely to be changed by argument.

If we did react that way, we were normal. Through all of history, men's   *4*
beards and hair have had such profound significance—superstitious,
political, military, religious, social, and psychological—as to set men,
from time to time, at each other's throats. Most American males over,
say, thirty have their hair trimmed whenever they get around to it, without any fuss, but not a Cavalier—not with those Roundheads breathing
down his neck. We all know what Delilah did to Samson. We may never

From "Hair: The Long and the Short of It," *Seattle Magazine* 4 (October
1967): 44-48, 59. Reprinted by permission of the publisher and the author.

have sworn by the beard of the Prophet, but millions have, and have thought, to boot, that all beardless men were either unbelievers or slaves. Some of us can even remember the passing of the Chinaman's queue with the revolution of 1911. High blood pressure on the subject obviously did not begin with the Beatles.

Take, for example, the war in which David managed to have Uriah   5 killed. The result of the war, David's acquisition of a wife, is far better remembered than what started the war in the first place. In an attempt to reach an understanding with the Ammonites, David had sent his peace emissaries to their new king, Hanun. "Wherefore," according to II Samuel XI, 4, "Hanun took David's servants, and shaved off one half of their beards, and cut off their garments in the middle, even to their buttocks, and sent them away." And note what happened when David heard of this indignity: "The men were greatly ashamed. And the king said, 'Tarry at Jericho until your beards be grown, and then return.' " Apparently the men's lack of pants was a consideration not worth comment. In any case, 33,000 Syrians, hired by the Ammonites, were soon trying to stand off David's hosts led by Joab.

This was no isolated incident. Except when in mourning, the Jews   6 considered shaving, or even trimming the corners of the beard, a sin of the Gentiles, and in some orthodox circles, the beard continues to play an important role today. The Assyrians, too, sported beards – big square ones – and even managed to give them an aggressive forward tilt. The Egyptians, on the other hand, though they used false beards at times, loathed hair, and according to Herodotus, regarded the bearded Greeks as barbarians.

The classical Greeks were bearded, and they pictured most of their   7 gods the same way. Indeed, the beard was so common among the Greeks that Herodotus assumed that the beardless Scythians suffered some disease that made them look like women. There is speculation that the Scythians may even have given rise to the legend of the Amazons.

Certainly the Greeks did not take their beards lightly. Diogenes had a   8 great deal to say on the subject, all of it insulting. When approached by a clean-shaven man one day, Diogenes shouted at him to take off his clothes to prove his sex and refused to say another word to him unless – and until – he did so. Today, anyone choosing to adopt Diogenes's belligerent tactics on University Way would probably find himself shouting not at a hairless man, but at a man with too *much* hair.

Alexander the Great changed everything for the Greeks by requiring   9 his soldiers to shave off their beards, lest, according to one contemporary commentator, the Persians use them as handles. Perhaps he was just reacting against his father, Philip, a believer in beards. According to Plutarch, Philip once appointed a man to a judgeship who was later found to have dyed his hair and beard. The king summarily removed him saying, "I could not think that one that was faithless in his hair could be trusty in his deeds."

The Romans, too, went through cycles of facial hair styles, though   10
they were fairly consistent in wearing the hair of their head short and in brushing it out in all directions from the crown—a style that has frequently been imitated in modern times. Up to about 300 B.C. the Romans were bearded, then they took to beardlessness until the time of Hadrian, who grew a beard to hide some kind of facial disfiguration.

As with other ancient peoples, young Romans were likely to let their   11
hair grow and then to sacrifice the first cuttings to a god. Also obvious among the Romans was a theory of opposites: During periods when shaving was in style, slaves were required to grow beards, but when beards were in fashion, they had to shave on orders of their bearded masters. Similarly, growing a beard in clean-shaven times was a sign of mourning, just as taking off a beard expressed mourning if beards were in style.

The establishment of the Christian church simply added fuel to the   12
flames of dissension, no matter which way the styles were going. The church not only issued meticulous regulations on the shape of the tonsure for priests, but also tried, time and again, to regulate the length of hair and beards for *all* men.

At one point, the church decreed that part of a man's ears and eyes   13
should be visible. Saint Wolstan, when Bishop of Worcester, even stated officially that long hair on men was "highly immoral, criminal and beastly." In the mid-ninth century, the Greek church was beardless, the Roman church, bearded. In Rome a clean face was once mentioned as a grievance in an edict of excommunication. Yet, in 1105, the Bishop of Amiens announced at Christmastime that he would refuse communion to anyone *wearing* a beard.

Mahomet was just as specific, though perhaps more consistent. He   14
dyed his own beard red and instructed his followers to trim theirs in such a way as to differentiate them from the Jews. Slaves in Islam were beardless and so were idolaters. One bard's story of the Crusades—there were folksingers in those days, too—gives Richard Coeur de Lion's recipe for serving up a Saracen's head: Remove the hair "off hed, off berd, and eke off lyppe." This was obviously as cruel a fate as the bard could dream up for a Moslem, even more dreadful than decapitation.

Excitement over hair styles reached a new peak when first long hair,   15 and then wigs, came into fashion in the seventeenth century. Many considered the new style scandalous, and, of course, there were rules against it. The General Court of Massachusetts forbade long hair "if uncomely or prejudical to the common good," and Harvard did not permit its boys "to wear Long Haire, Lockes, Foretops, Curlings, Crispings, Partings, or Powdering of Ye Haire."

In 1653, Thomas Hall, B.D., of Kingsnorton, published a book entitled *The Loathsomeness of Long Haire: or a Treatise Wherein you have the Question stated, many Arguments against it produced, and most material Arguments for it repelled and answered, with the current judgment of Divines both old and new against it. With an Appendix against Painting, Spots, Naked Breasts, etc.* The full title not only makes the author's thesis clear – though he does muddy things up a bit there at the end – but also shows how strongly he feels on the subject.   16

In his text, the author specifies five ways to tell if a man's hair *is* too long, and No. 4 is most revealing: Hair is too long "when it is scandalous and offensive, when it is so long that the godly are thereby grieved, the weak offended and the wicked hardened." He also strikes a familiar note in his contention that long hair "is the trick of youth and the badge of proud hearts. . . . Indeed it is a foreign trick . . . and therefore unlawful . . . which God condemns."   17

Hall was no less jaundiced about wigs and stated a man "may not wear the long haire of another, be it of a man, a woman, or it may be of some harlot, who is now in Hell lamenting there the abuse of that excrement." But despite his title and his firm position against long hair and wigs, Thomas Hall was in favor of beards and considered them "a signe of manhood given by God to distinguish the Male from the Female sex." A student of this subject, not to mention a protagonist, has to be able to turn on a dime.   18

Despite the Reverend Mr. Hall and the divine support he invoked, men stopped wearing beards and started wearing long hair, and they soon took to wigs as well. Pepys tells us of his gradual conversion to the new style. In March of 1663, he tried on two or three wigs at his barber's, but had "no stomach for it." In October, with his wife's help, he selected one and wore it to church the following month, surprised to find that no one "cast their eyes" upon him. By 1665 he had cut off his own hair – periwigs were such a convenience – and in 1667 he records that he bought a new wig for four pounds, ten shillings, "and made a great show."   19

Once wigs were established, the tumult died down and many predictable things happened. The wigmakers' guild separated from the barber-surgeons' and set up on its own. Peruke-makers petitioned the king to require all adults to wear wigs, but were denied. The ultimate sign of wig   20 acceptance came when men who didn't wear wigs, like George III in his early years and George Washington throughout his adult life, wore their hair to make it *look* as if they did.

Then as now, fathers and sons disagreed sharply on hair styles. Lord   *21*
Chesterfield, for instance, wrote to his son in 1748:

> I can by no means agree to your cutting off your hair. I am very sure that your headaches do not proceed from thence. . . . Your own hair is at your age an ornament, and a wig, however well made, [is] such a disguise that I will on no account whatever have you cut off your hair. Nature did not give it to you for nothing, still less to cause you the headache. . . .

With the advent of wigs, hair styles became particularly associated   *22*
with class and calling. Men of law wore the clerical, or tie, peruke; army and navy officers sported a brigadier or possibly a great fox-ear, with a cluster of curls at the temple; men of business were characterized by a full-bottomed, or moderate, tie; elegants, back from Italy, built high toupees on top of a club wig and, along with this total headdress, were called macaronis; and coachmen were said to wear theirs in imitation of the curled hair of a water dog.

Apparently wigs even became a factor in government. Horace Walpole   *23*
said of Lord Sandwich: "I could have no hope of getting at his ear, for he has put on such a first-rate tie that nothing without the lungs of a boatswain can ever think to penetrate the thickness of his curls." The false-hair fashion, moreover, was responsible for the eighteenth century equivalent of singing commercials. A sign over a shop in London read:

> Oh Absalom! Oh Absalom!
> Oh Absalom! my son,
> If thou hadst worn a periwig,
> Thou hadst not been undone.

And in Paris:

> Passans, contemplex la douleur
> D'Absalom pendu par la nuque;
> Il eut évité ce malheur
> S'il avait porté perruque.

The passing of wigs and long hair caused just as much fuss as their   *24*
introduction, and while they may not actually have been an issue in the French Revolution, short hair did become fashionable in France in the

1790's. Like the queue in China, the earlier, longer style became associated with the pre-revolutionary regime.

In England and America the change to short hair began about 1783. 25 Though more gradual than in France, it was no less painful. Sometimes the transition was just physically difficult. A well-known, left-profile portrait of John Adams, for example, shows him with a half-wig behind — a kind of tail-piece — to supplement his front hair as it gradually grew out. As late as 1799, Dr. Randolph, Bishop of Oxford, encountered such scandalized opposition when he began to wear his own hair that he reverted to his wig for services of divine worship.

Pigtails came off the British army between 1804 and 1808 by official 26 order, and as far as is known, without incident. But in the U.S. Army, one Lieutenant Colonel, Thomas Butler, refused to obey a similar order of 1801 and clung to his pigtail. For his stubbornness, the army court-martialed and convicted him, imprisoned him, released him (still with his pigtail on) tried him again — and then let him die, unshorn, of yellow fever before condemning him a second time.

In one profession, the law, the wig stayed on, but not without a fight. 27 Lord Eldon, made Chief Justice of Common Pleas in 1799, did not like his powdered bush wig. Needled by his wife, he asked George III for a special dispensation on account of headaches. King George, with little sympathy for either the baron or baroness, replied tartly: "I will have no innovations in my time" — and made his decision stick.

During the nineteenth century, hair styles did not cause much excite- 28 ment in either England or America, but there was a lot of fuss about beards and whiskers. The previous century had been one of the few beardless epochs in western history, and the return of these adornments sent blood pressure up to predictable heights.

There had been some advance indications of what would happen when 29 beards returned. In the late eighteenth century, a New Jersey Quaker named Joshua Evans grew a beard. To be sure, he was a bit odd in other ways: He was a vegetarian, wore suits made of undyed wool, and had fundamental objections to the use of leather. It was the beard, though, that aroused his fellow Friends.

One day they visited him in formal delegation, but "left him with a 30 beard on, much as they found him, none having power, or a razor, to cut it off." Foiled in this attempt, his associates took to avoiding him in meeting and denying him a license to travel as a minister. Evans made a spirited defense, and, what's more, he triumphed — *but it took him fourteen years.* He later admitted that his beard was useful in his profession, "many being induced . . . to come to hear me on account of my singular appearance."

The very strength and depth of the anti-beard feeling, and the length of   *31*
time that Western man had gone beardless actually influenced the return
of beards. Certainly the first general crop, those of the French romantics,
were symbols of revolt. Young France considered the vast expanse of
white cravat then in style a mark of reactionary, classical tastes. Their
scorn was profound. Any white linen marked a man as *"un profane, un
retardataire, un hottentot, un epicier, un bourgeois, un philistin—pour
tout dire en un mot—un classique." So* the young romantics used vast
black cravats, or beards, in place of the white expanse.

The same element of revolt does not appear to have accompanied   *32*
beards back to England and America. Their proponents, drawing with
dignity on natural and divine law, on the rules of good health, and on
appeals to men's virility, overcame all attacks. As early as 1847, a book
appeared entitled *Beard Shaving and the Common Use of the Razor, an
Unnatural, Irrational, Unmanly, Ungodly and Fatal Fashion Among
Christians.* Some time in the 1850's, an article in the *London Methodist
Quarterly Review* expressed concern over the amount of bronchitic infection among ministers of the gospel; this unhappy condition, wrote the
author, was attributable to the ministers' disregard of "hygienic law." The
cure: Grow a beard to keep your chest warm.

Others wrote not so much with caution as with male bravado: *33*

> Deprive the lion of his mane, the cock of his comb, the peacock of
> the emerald plumage of his tail, the ram and deer of their horns, and
> they are not only displeasing to the eye, but they lose much of their
> power and vigor. . . . Only fashion forces the Englishman to shave off
> those appendages which give the male countenance the true mascu-
> line character indicative of energy, bold daring, and decision.

From the 1860's through the 1890's whiskers and beards were every-   *34*
where. This is made clear by Brady's photographs of Civil War generals
and pictures of the Presidential cabinets of the 1870's, not to mention the
Presidents themselves. Lincoln was clean-shaven during the election of
1860, but grew a beard before his inauguration. Andrew Johnson was
clean-shaven—but, of course, he was very nearly impeached. Grant,
Hayes, Garfield, and Harrison wore beards, Arthur wore whiskers, and
Cleveland a mustache. Even after the beard disappeared in the 1890's,
the mustache stayed on with both T. R. and Taft. McKinley was clean-
shaven but it was not until Woodrow Wilson that the clean-shaven line
was reestablished.

One of the happy aspects of the era was the variety of styles that men   *35*
evolved in their beards, mustaches, and whiskers. There were Imperials,

Dundrearies, and Piccadilly Weepers; there was the Uncle Sam; Horace Greeley himself wore a Saucer, or Trencher, though out West, where he was pointing; John Muir wore a Nokomis and common men tended to the Square, the Swallowtail or the Miners' beard. There were Mutton Chops and Breakwaters (Disraeli developed a Breakwater); there were Burnsides and Sideburns, Van Dykes, Billees and Goatees, and Horseshoes and Walruses (commonly known as Soupstrainers). Those of us who belong to the gray-flanneled generation can only vaguely grasp what we are missing.

When beards made their exit, beginning in the 1890's, there was almost   *36* as much excitement as when they made their entrance fifty years before, largely because the first to adopt the new style were the young English aesthetes. No record exists of what Benjamin Harrison had to say about Oscar Wilde—perhaps this is fortunate—but no doubt he could get as much venom and disgust into a phrase like "that beardless so-and-so" as a 1967 personnel manager can put into "these blankety-blank bearded beatniks."

Harrison, however, lost and the young aesthetes won. By 1903, one   *37* writer could state: "I never saw a man wearing a Van Dyke beard who was not selfish, sinister, and pompous as a peacock."

Though beards were *passé* by the turn of the century, the health-and-   *38* hair dispute continued. In 1904, *Harper's* carried an article pointing out that mustaches picked up coffee and gravy, but it was the scientists, now deep in the study of germs, who really came charging to the fore. The first official tally was made by a German (naturally), who reported that the average beard contained two million misanthropic microbes. The French approached the subject with more flair. In 1907, a scientist in Paris arranged and carried out a public experiment—medical journals please note. He guided two men, one bearded and one clean-shaven, through the streets and stores of the capital for about an hour. Waiting for them were two young ladies whose lips had been carefully sterilized. The bearded man kissed one young lady, the clean-shaven man the other. Immediately, a sterile brush was passed over each pair of female lips, and then each brush was placed in a separate solution of agar-agar and left for four days.

The results were sensational. The culture from the lips of the girl kissed   *39* by the clean-shaven man contained only a few harmless yeast germs, but the other culture, according to the official report, "literally swarmed with malignant microbes, tubercle bacillus, diphtheria and putrefactious germs, minute bits of food, hair from a spider's leg, and other odds and ends."

Science affected men's hair styles for more realistic reasons when the   *40* louse was discovered to carry typhus. Soldiers in World War I all had their heads shaved close, and that style has become traditional for the military. Short hair has persisted in civilian life as well, and although a few toothbrush mustaches appeared in the 1920's, not to mention a variety of haircut styles since then among the young (pompadours, crew cuts, butches, Princetons, flattops, and ducktails), the years up to and past World War II have been short-haired, unwhiskered, and beardless.

Now all hell seems to have broken loose again. It is too soon to say   *41* whether a new cycle of style is upon us. Certainly hackles and blood pressures are up, and, in the past, these symptoms have often heralded a major change.

What is all the excitement about anyway?   *42*

To discover that men have been getting just as excited, off and on, for   *43* thousands of years, puts the matter in perspective but hardly answers the question. The Freudians think they have the answer. (Personally, I am inclined to guffaw over some of the more extreme applications of Freudian theory, but I try to restrain myself because I know just enough to concede that the guffaw itself may be highly revealing.)

In his book, *The Unconscious Significance of Hair,* published in 1951,   *44* Charles Berg points out that there is plenty of evidence, both clinical and anthropological, to associate hairiness with virility and libidinal development. That the appearance of facial hair coincides with the passage from childhood to manhood is clear enough to me, and I can even follow some of Berg's comments on the folklore of the subject—though I am several laps behind when he gets through with the legend of Rapunzel.

Our attitude toward hair, like all other behavior, says Berg, is an ex-   *45* pression of various opposed tensions of the unconscious conflict within us.

> When we attend, preserve or love our hair, we are expressing in displaced form our appreciation of and pleasure in our sexuality. When we remove, cut or control our hair we are giving expression to reaction formations against the . . . libido.

As for beards specifically, Berg considers them either a mark of mas-   *46* culine aggression or an attempt to compensate for unconscious feelings of anonymity. "They may also be," Berg goes on, "a gesture of rebellion against, or emancipation from, the castrating trammels of convention."

If the Freudians are right, then we have a pattern and code-book to   *47* help us understand all the bitterness, vituperation, sarcasm, pride, pleasure, shame, and name-calling that have so often accompanied changes in the way men wear their hair and beards.

In a more general way, however, other factors are surely involved.   *48* Custom, for one thing is important. If, in our lifetime, shoulder-length hair has been for girls, then shoulder-length hair on boys seems effeminate — despite the certainty that Abraham, Diogenes, D'Artagnan, and George Washington would all have heartily and manfully disagreed.

Our sense of conformity also plays a part. Some of us men probably   *49* have grown beards when cruising or camping, but we have always shaved before turning up at church, at the office, or at the Rainier Club. If Jim Owens goes off to the Rose Bowl with a planeload of young men, all of whom are beardless and have their hair neatly trimmed, then this becomes the pattern; and a coach who turns up with a halfback who has grown a beard is bound to feel he has lost face in more senses than one.

More important, we are again in a period when hair styles have in-   *50* creasingly become associated with other, more urgent issues. If some of the vocal demands for a more meaningful and more relevant curriculum come from bearded young men, then we find some of our lifetime assumptions about a liberal education challenged, and beards, by association, themselves become a challenge — perhaps even a threat.

To a strong supporter of the war in Vietnam who sees hairy objectors   *51* carrying placards, long hair and beards are for the doves, Freud or no Freud: *What are these damned fringies up to, smoking pot and making a religion out of LSD? By George, these fellows who grow beards and avoid barbers are upsetting everything! Why aren't they out there fighting? What do they mean by taking psychedelic trips and wearing necklaces and telling us how to run the world? Who the hell do they think they are anyway?*

So there we are, right back where we started, confusing hair with war   *52* and peace, belief and unbelief, suppression and freedom, traditionalism and revolt. In all our angry uncertainty, though, we may rest quietly assured of this: Hair styles, like the tides, will keep on changing, and life's vital issues will continue to be hopelessly intertwined with what goes on — or does not go on — in the barbershop.

QUESTIONS AND EXERCISES

Vocabulary

1. Define or explain each of the following terms:

queue (4)	*passé* (38)
tonsure (12)	misanthropic (38)
idolaters (14)	putrefactions (39)
aesthetes (36)	libidinal (44)

2. Comment on the reasons for some of the archaic spellings.
3. Identify the allusions:

Cavalier (4)	Diogenes (8)

Samson and Delilah (4)	Alexander the Great (9)
Prophet (4)	Mahomet (14)
David (5)	Saracen (14)
Jericho (5)	Wilde (36)
Amazons (7)	Freudians (43)

4. List the names of types of beards. (35)
5. List a few names of hair styles. (40)

Rhetoric

6. What figure is each of the following:
   ". . . added fuel to the flames of dissension . . ." (12)
   ". . . he has to be able to turn on a dime . . ." (18)
   ". . . had 'no stomach for it' . ." (19)
   ". . . 'castrating trammels of convention' . . ." (46)
7. Comment on the analogy in paragraph 33.
8. What are the dominant methods by which Strong develops his paragraphs?
9. How does Strong create interest in his subject?
10. What transitional devices does he use?

Theme

11. What is the purpose of the essay?
12. What becomes evident about the relationships that people of all cultures and eras have established between appearance and reality?
13. How do we now establish causal relationships?
14. What tentative thesis does Strong make at the end of his analysis? Is his conclusion inductive or deductive?

Topics and Assignments for Composition

1. Analyze the ways in which Strong develops his paragraphs.
2. What are the implicit conclusions one may infer from the importance people place on appearance. Write an essay explaining and defending your thesis.
3. Write an essay similar to Strong's about another of man's conventions.
4. Choose one of the theories in the essay and conduct research to extend, prove, reject, or modify the theory. Write an academic treatment of your subject.

Edward J. Moody

Urban Witches

Every Friday evening just before midnight, a group of men and women   *1*
gathers at a home in San Francisco; and there, under the guidance of their
high priest, a sorcerer or magus sometimes called the "Black Pope of
Satanism," they study and practice the ancient art of black magic. Precisely at midnight they begin to perform Satanic rituals that apparently
differ little from those allegedly performed by European Satanists and
witches at least as early as the seventh century. By the dim and flickering
light of black candles, hooded figures perform their rites upon the traditional Satanic altar—the naked body of a beautiful young witch—calling
forth the mysterious powers of darkness to do their bidding. Beneath the
emblem of Baphomet, the horned god, they engage in indulgences of flesh
and sense for whose performance their forebears suffered death and torture at the hands of earlier Christian zealots.

Many of these men and women are, by day, respected and responsible   *2*
citizens. Their nocturnal or covert practice of the black art would, if exposed, make them liable to ridicule, censure, and even punishment. Even
though we live in an "enlightened" age, witches are still made a focus of
a community's aggression and anxiety. They are denounced from the
pulpit, prosecuted to the limit of the law, and subjected to extralegal
harrassment by the fearful and ignorant.

Why then do the Satanists persist? Why do they take these risks? What   *3*
benefits do they derive from membership in a Satanic church, what rewards are earned from the practice of witchcraft? What indulgences are
enjoyed that they could not as easily find in one of the more socially acceptable arenas of pleasure available in our "permissive" society?

The nearly universal allegation of witchcraft in the various cultures of   *4*

From CONFORMITY AND CONFLICT: Readings in Cultural Anthropology, James P. Spradley and David W. McCurdy, pages 280-290. Copyright
© 1971 by Little, Brown and Company (Inc.). Reprinted by permission.

the world has excited the interest of social scientists for years and the volume of writing on the topic is staggering. Most accounts of witchcraft, however, share the common failing of having been written from the point of view of those who do not themselves practice the black art. Few, if any, modern authors have had contact with witches, black magicians, or sorcerers, relying instead on either the anguished statements of medieval victims of inquisition torture, or other types of secondhand "hearsay" evidence for their data. To further confuse the issue, authoritative and respected ethnologists have reported that black magic and witchcraft constitute an imaginary offense because it is impossible—that because witches cannot do what they are supposed to do, they are nonexistent.

Witches and Magicians

But the witches live. In 1965 while carrying out other research in San   5
Francisco, California, I heard rumors of a Satanic cult which planned to given an All-Hallows Eve blessing to a local chamber of horrors. I made contact with the group through its founder and high priest and thus began over two years of participant-observation as a member of a contemporary black magic group. As a member of this group I interacted with my fellow members in both ritual and secular settings. The following description is based on the data gathered at that time.

The witches and black magicians who were members of the group   6
came from a variety of social class backgrounds. All shades of political opinion were represented from Communist to American Nazi. Many exhibited behavior identified in American culture as "pathological," such as homosexuality, sadomasochism, and transvestism. Of the many characteristics that emerged from psychological tests, extensive observations, and interviews, the most common trait, exhibited by nearly all Satanic novices, was a high level of general anxiety related to low self-esteem and a feeling of inadequacy. This syndrome appears to be related to intense interpersonal conflicts in the nuclear family during socialization. Eighty-five percent of the group, the administrative and magical hierarchy of the church, reported that their childhood homes were split by alcoholism, divorce, or some other serious problem. Their adult lives were in turn marked by admitted failure in love, business, sexual, or social relationships. Before entering the group each member appeared to have been battered by failure in one or more of the areas mentioned, rejected or isolated by a society frightened by his increasingly bizarre and unpredictable behavior, and forced into a continuing struggle to comprehend or give meaning to his life situation.

Almost all members, prior to joining the group, had made some pre-   7 vious attempt to gain control over the mysterious forces operating around them. In order to give their environment some structure, in order to make it predictable and thus less anxiety-provoking, they dabbled in astrology, the Tarot, spiritualism, or other occult sciences, but continued failure in their everyday lives drove them from the passive and fatalistic stance of the astrologer to consideration of the active and manipulative role of sorcerer or witch. In articles in magazines such as *Astrology* and *Fate,* the potential Satanist comes into direct contact with magic, both white and black. Troubled by lack of power and control, the pre-Satanist is frequently introduced to the concept of magic by advertisements which promise "Occult power . . . now . . . for those who want to make real progress in understanding and working the forces that rule our Physical Cosmos . . . a self-study course in the practice of Magic." Or, Ophiel will teach you how to "become a power in your town, job, club, etc.," how to "create a familiar [a personal magic spirit servant] to help you through life," how to "control and dominate others." "The Secret Way" is offered free of charge, and the Esoteric Society offers to teach one how herbs, roots, oils, and rituals may be used, through "white magic," to obtain love, money, power, or a peaceful home. They will also teach one self-confidence and how to banish "unwanted forces." The reader is invited to join the Brotherhood of the White Temple, Inc.; the Monastery of the Seven Rays (specializing in sexual magic); the Radiant School; and numerous other groups that promise to reveal the secrets of success in business, sex, love, and life—the very secrets the potential or pre-Satanist feels have eluded him. Before joining the group, the pre-Satanist usually begins to perform magic ceremonies and rituals whose descriptions he receives for a fee from one of the various groups noted above, from magical wholesale houses, or from occult book clubs. These practices reinforce his "magical world view," and at the same time bring him in contact with other practitioners of the magical arts, both white and black.

Although most of the mail-order magic groups profess to practice "white" magic—benevolent magic designed only to benefit those involved and never aggressive or selfish, only altruistic—as opposed to "black," malevolent, or selfish magic, even white magic rituals require ingredients that are rare enough so they can be bought only at certain specialty stores. These stores, usually known to the public as candle shops although some now call themselves occult art supply houses, provide not only the raw materials—oils, incenses, candles, herbs, parchments, etc.—for the magical workings, but serve as meeting places for those interested in the occult. A request for some specific magic ingredient such as "John the Conqueror oil," "Money-come" powder, "crossing" powder, or black candles usually leads to a conversation about the magical arts and often to introductions to other female witches and male warlocks. The realization that there are others who privately practice magic, white or black, supports the novice magician in his new-found interest in magical manipulation. The presence of other witches and magicians in his vicinity serves as additional proof that the problems he has personally experienced may indeed be caused by witchcraft, for the pre-Satanist has now met, firsthand, witches and warlocks who previously were only shadowy figures, and if there are a few known witches, who knows how many there might be practicing secretly?

Many witches and magicians never go beyond the private practice of white or black magic, or at most engage in a form of magic "recipe" swapping. The individual who does join a formal group practicing magic may become affiliated with such a group in one of several ways. In some cases he has been practicing black magic with scant success. Perhaps he has gone no further than astrology or reading the designs on the ancient Tarot cards, a type of socially acceptable magic which the leader of the Satanic church disparagingly calls "god in sport clothes." But the potential Satanist has come to think of the cosmos as being ordered, and ordered according to magical—that is, imperceptible—principles. He is prompted by his sense of alienation and social inadequacy to try to gain control of the strange forces that he feels influence or control him and, hearing of a Satanic church, he comes to learn magic. *9*

Others join because of anxiety and inadequacy of a slightly different nature. They may be homosexual, nymphomaniac, sadist, or masochist. They usually have some relatively blatant behavioral abnormality which, though they personally may not feel it wrong, is socially maladaptive and therefore disruptive. As in many "primitive" societies, magic and witchcraft provide both the "disturbed" persons and, in some cases, the community at large with a ready and consistent explanation for those "forces" or impulses which they themselves have experienced. Seeking control, or freedom, the social deviants come ultimately to the acknowledged expert in magic of all kinds, the head of the Satanic church, to have their demons exorcised, the spells lifted, and their own powers restored. *10*

Others whose problems are less acute come because they have been brought, in the larger religious context, to think of themselves as "evil." If their struggle against "evil" has been to no avail, many of the individuals in question take this to mean that the power of "evil" is greater than the power of "good"—that "God is dead"—and so on. In their search for a source of strength and security, rather than continue their vain struggle with that "evil" force against which they know themselves to be powerless, they seek instead to identify themselves with evil, to join the "winning" side. They identify with Satan—etymologically the *11* "opposition" — and become "followers of the left-hand path," "walkers in darkness."

Finally, there are, of course, those who come seeking thrills or titilla- *12* tion, lured by rumors of beautiful naked witches, saturnalian orgies, and other strange occurrences. Few of these are admitted into the group.

Black Magic

For the novice, initial contact with the Satanists is reassuring. Those *13* assisting the "Prince of Darkness" who heads the church are usually officers in the church, long-term members who have risen from the rank and file to positions of trust and authority. They are well-dressed, pleasant persons who exude an aura of confidence and adequacy. Rather than hav- ing the appearance of wild-eyed fanatics or lunatics, the Satanists look like members of the middle-class, but successful middle-class. The Prince of Darkness himself is a powerfully built and striking individual with a shaven head and black, well-trimmed beard. Sitting among the imple- ments of magic, surrounded by books that contain the "secrets of the centuries," he affirms for those present what they already know: that there is a secret to power and success which can and must be learned, and that secret is black magic.

All magic is black magic according to the Satanists. There is no al- *14* truistic or white magic. Each magician intends to benefit from his magical manipulation, even those workings performed at someone else's behest. To claim to be performing magic only for the benefit of others is either hypocrisy — the cardinal sin in Satanic belief — or naiveté, another serious shortcoming. As defined by the Satanists, magic itself is a surprisingly common-sense kind of phenomenon: "the change in situations or events in accordance with one's will, which would, using normally accepted methods, be unchangeable." Magic can be divided into two categories: ritual (ceremonial) and nonritual (manipulative).

Ritual, or "the greater magic," is performed in a specified ritual area *15* and at a specific time. It is an emotional, not an intellectual act. Although the Satanists spend a great deal of time intellectualizing and rationalizing magic power, they state specifically that "any and all intellectual activity must take place *before* the ceremony, not during it."

The "lesser magic," nonritual (manipulative) magic, is, in contrast, a *16* type of transactional manipulation based upon a heightened awareness of the various processes of behavior operative in interaction with others, a Satanic "games people play." The Satanist in ritual interaction is taught to analyze and utilize the motivations and behavioral Achilles' heels of others for his own purposes. If the person with whom one is interacting has masochistic tendencies, for example, the Satanist is taught to adopt the role of sadist, to "indulge" the other's desires, to be dominant, forceful, and even cruel in interaction with him.

Both the greater and the lesser magic is predicated upon a more general *17* "magical" world view in which all elements of the "natural world" are animate, have unique and distinctive vibrations that influence the way they relate to other natural phenomena. Men, too, have vibrations, the principal difference between men and inanimate objects being that men can alter their pattern of vibrations, sometimes consciously and at will. It is the manipulation and the modification of these vibrations, forces, or powers that is the basis of all magic. There are "natural magicians," untrained and unwitting manipulators of magic power. Some, for example, resonate in harmony with growing things; these are people said to have a "green thumb," gardeners who can make anything grow. Others resonate on the frequency of money and have the "Midas touch" which turns their every endeavor into a profit-making venture. Still others are "love magnets"; they automatically attract others to them, fascinate and charm even though they may be physically plain themselves. If one is a "natural magician," he does some of these things unconsciously, intuitively, but because of the intellectual nature of our modern world, most people have lost their sensitivity to these faint vibrations. Such individuals may, if they become witches, magicians or Satanists, regain contact with that lost world just as tribal shamans are able to regain contact with another older world where men communicated with animals and understood their ways. It is this resensitization to the vibrations of the cosmos that is the essence of magical training. It takes place best in the "intellectual decompression chamber" of magical ritual, for it is basically a "subjective" and "non-scientific" phenomenon.

Those who have become members of the inner circle learn to make *18* use of black magic, both greater and lesser, in obtaining goals which are the antithesis of Christian dogma. The seven deadly sins of Christian teaching—greed, pride, envy, anger, gluttony, lust, and sloth—are depicted as Satanic virtues. Envy and greed are, in the Satanic theology, natural in man and the motivating forces behind ambition. Lust is necessary for the preservation of the species and not a Satanic sin. Anger is the force of self-preservation. Instead of denying natural instincts the Satanist learns to glory in them and turn them into power.

Satanists recognize that the form of their ritual, its meanings and its *19* functions are largely determined by the wider society and its culture. The novitiate in the Satanic cult is taught, for example, that the meaning of the word "Satan" etymologically is "the opposition," or "he who opposes," and that Satanism itself arose out of opposition to the demeaning and stultifying institutions of Christianity. The cult recognizes that had there been no Christianity there would be no Satanism, at least not in the form it presently takes, and it maintains that much of the Satanic ritual and belief is structured by the form and content of Christian belief and can be understood only in that larger religious context. The Satanists choose black as their color, not white, precisely because white is the symbol of purity and transcendence chosen by Christianity, and black therefore has come to symbolize the profane earthy indulgences central to Satanic theodicy. Satanists say that their gods are those of the earth, not the sky; that their cult is interested in making the sacred profane, in contrast to the Judeo-Christian cults which seek to make the profane sacred. Satanism cannot, in other words, be understood as an isolated phenomenon, but must be seen in a larger context.

The Satanic belief system, not surprisingly, is the antithesis of Christianity. Their theory of the universe, their cosmology, is based upon the notion that the desired end state is a return to a pagan awareness of the mystical forces inhabiting the earth, a return to an awareness of their humanity. This is in sharp contrast to the transcendental goals of traditional Christianity. The power associated with the pantheon of gods is also reversed: Satan's power is waxing; God's, if he still lives, waning. The myths of the Satanic church purport to tell the true story of the rise of Christianity and the fall of paganism, and there is a reversal here too. Christ is depicted as an early "con man" who tricked an anxious and powerless group of individuals into believing a lie. He is typified as "pallid incompetence hanging on a tree." Satanic novices are taught that early church fathers deliberately picked on those aspects of human desire that were most natural and made them sins, in order to use the inevitable transgressions as a means of controlling the populace, promising them salvation in return for obedience. And finally, their substantive belief, the very delimitation of what is sacred and what is profane, is the antithesis of Christian belief. The Satanist is taught to "be natural; to revel in pleasure and in self-gratification. To emphasize indulgence and power in this life."

The opposition of Satanists to Christianity may be seen most clearly in the various rituals of greater magic. Although there are many different types of rituals all aimed at achieving the virtues that are the inverted sins of the Christian, we shall examine briefly only two of these: blasphemy and the invocation of destruction. By far the most famous of Satanic institutions, the Black Mass and other forms of ritual blasphemy serve a very real and necessary function for the new Satanist. In many cases the exhortations and teachings of his Satanic colleagues are not sufficient to alleviate the sense of guilt and anxiety he feels when engaging in behavior forbidden by Judeo-Christian tradition. The novice may still cower before the charismatic power of Christian symbols; he may still feel guilty, still experience anxiety and fear in their presence. It is here that the blasphemies come into play, and they take many forms depending on the needs of the individuals involved.

A particular blasphemy may involve the most sacred Christian rituals   22
and objects. In the traditional Black Mass powerful Christian symbols such as the crucifix are handled brutally. Some Black Masses use urine or menstrual flow in place of the traditional wine in an attempt to evoke disgust and aversion to the ritual. If an individual can be conditioned to respond to a given stimulus, such as the communion wafer or wine, with disgust rather than fear, that stimulus's power to cause anxiety is diminished. Sexuality is also used. A young man who feared priests and nuns was deliberately involved in a scene in which two witches dressed as nuns interacted with him sexually; his former neurotic fear was replaced by a mildly erotic curiosity even in the presence of real nuns. The naked altar—a beautiful young witch—introduces another deliberate note of sexuality into a formerly awe-inspiring scene.

By far the most frequently used blasphemy involves laughter. Awe-   23
inspiring or fear-producing institutions are made the object of ridicule. The blasphemous rituals, although still greater magic, are frequently extremely informal. To the outsider they would not seem to have any structure; the behavior being exhibited might appear to be a charade, or a party game. The Satanists decide ahead of time the institution to be ridiculed and frequently it is a Christian ritual. I have seen a group of Satanists do a parody of the Christmas manger scene, or dress in clerical garb while performing a satire of priestly sexual behavior. The target of blasphemy depends upon the needs of the various Satanists. If the group feels it is necessary for the well-being of one member, they will gladly, even gleefully, blaspheme anything from psychiatry to psychedelics.

In the invocation of destruction black magic reaches its peak. In some   24
cases an individual's sense of inadequacy is experienced as victimization, a sense of powerlessness before the demands of stronger and more ruthless men. The Satanic Bible, in contrast to Christian belief, teaches the fearful novice that "Satan represents vengeance instead of turning the other cheek." In the Third Chapter of the Book of Satan, the reader is exhorted to "hate your enemies with a whole heart, and if a man smite you on one cheek, SMASH him on the other . . . he who turns the other cheek is a cowardly dog."

One of the most frequently used rituals in such a situation is the Con-   25 juration of Destruction, or Curse. Contrary to popular belief, black magicians are not indiscriminately aggressive. An individual must have harmed or hurt a member of the church before he is likely to be cursed. Even then the curse is laid with care, for cursing a more powerful magician may cause one's curse to be turned against oneself. If, in the judgment of the high priest and the congregation, a member has been unjustly used by a non-Satanist, even if the offender is an unaffiliated witch or magician, at the appropriate time in the ritual the member wronged may step forward and, with the aid and support of the entire congregation, ritually curse the transgressor. The name of the intended "sacrifice" is usually written on parchment made of the skin of unborn lamb and burned in the altar flame while the member himself speaks the curse; he may use the standard curse or, if he so desires, prepare a more powerful, individualistic one. In the curse he gives vent to his hostility and commands the legions of hell to torment and sacrifice his victim in a variety of horrible ways. Or, if the Satanist so desires, the High Priest will recite the curse for him, the entire group adding their power to the invocation by spirited responses.

The incidence of harmful results from cursing is low in the church of   26
Satan because of two factors: first, one does not curse other members of the church for fear that their superior magic might turn the curse back upon its user; second, victims outside the congregation either do not believe in the power of black magic or do not recognize the esoteric symbols that should indicate to them they are being cursed.

On only one occasion was I able to see the effect of a curse on a "vic-   27
tim." A member attempted to use the church and its members for publicity purposes without their permission. When the leader of the group refused to go along with the scheme, the man quit – an action that would normally have brought no recrimination – and began to slander the church by spreading malicious lies throughout San Francisco social circles. Even though he was warned several times to stop his lies, the man persisted; so the group decided to level the most serious of all curses at him, and a ritual death rune was cast.

Casting a death rune, the most serious form of greater magic, goes   28
considerably beyond the usual curse designed to cause only discomfort or unhappiness, but not to kill. The sole purpose of the death rune is to cause the total destruction of the victim. The transgressor's name is written in blood (to the Satanist, blood is power – the very power of life) on special parchment, along with a number of traditional symbols of ceremonial magic. In a single-minded ritual of great intensity and ferocity, the emotional level is raised to a peak at which point the entire congregation

joins in ritually destroying the victim of the curse. In the case in question, there was an orgy of aggression. The lamb's-wool figurine representing the victim was stabbed by all members of the congregation, hacked to pieces with a sword, shot with a small calibre pistol, and then burned.

A copy of the death rune was sent to the man in question, and every *29* day thereafter an official death certificate was made out in his name and mailed to him. After a period of weeks during which the "victim" maintained to all who would listen that he "did not believe in all that nonsense," he entered the hospital with a bleeding ulcer. Upon recovery he left San Francisco permanently.

In fairness, I must add that the "victim" of the curse had previously *30* had an ulcer, was struggling with a failing business, and seemed hypertense when I knew him. His knowledge of the "curse" may have hastened the culmination of his difficulties. The Satanic church, however, claimed it as a successful working, a victory for black magic, and word of it spread among the adherents of occult subculture, enhancing the reputation of the group.

Conclusion

Contemporary America is presently undergoing a witchcraft revival. *31* On all levels, from teenagers to octogenarians, interest in, or fear of, witchcraft has increased dramatically over the past two years. It is hardly possible to pass a popular magazine rack without seeing an article about the revival of the black arts. Covens and cults multiply, as does the number of exorcisms and reconsecrations. England, France, Germany, and a host of other countries all report a rebirth of the black art. Why? Those who eventually become Satanists are attempting to cope with the everyday problems of life, with the here and now, rather than with some transcendental afterlife. In an increasingly complex world which they do not fully understand, an anxiety-provoking world, they seek out a group dedicated to those mysterious powers that the sufferers have felt moving them. Fearful of what one witch calls "the dark powers we all feel moving deep within us," they come seeking either *release* or *control*. They give various names to the problems they bring, but all, anxious and afraid, come to the Satanic cult seeking help in solving problems beyond their meager abilities. Whatever their problem — bewitchment, business failure, sexual impotence, or demonic possession — the Satanists, in the ways I have mentioned and many more, *can* and *do* help them. Witchcraft, the witches point out, "is the most practical of all beliefs. According to its devotees, its results are obvious and instantaneous. No task is too high or too lowly for the witch." Above all, the beliefs and practices provide the witch and the warlock with a sense of power, a feeling of control, and an explanation for personal failure, inadequacy, and other difficulties.

Moreover, a seeker's acceptance into the Inner Circle provides a major *32* boost for his self-esteem; he has, for the first time, been accepted into a group as an individual despite his problems and abnormalities. Once within the Inner Circle that support continues. The Satanic group is, according to the cultural standards of his society, amoral, and the Satanist frequently finds himself lauded and rewarded for the very impulses and behavior that once brought shame and doubt.

Each Satanist is taught, and not without reason, that the exposure of *33* his secret identity, of the fact that he is a powerful and adequate black magician, means trouble from a fearful society. Therefore, in keeping with the precepts of lesser magic, he learns to transform himself magically by day (for purposes of manipulation) into a bank clerk, a businessman, or even a college professor. He wears the guise and plays the role expected by society in order to manipulate the situation to his own advantage, to reach his desired goals. Members of society at large, aware only of his "normal" role behavior and unaware of the secret person within, respond to him positively instead of punishing him or isolating him. Then, in the evening, in the sanctity of his home, or when surrounded by his fellow magicians, he reverts to his "true" role, that of Satanic priest, and becomes himself once again. Inadequate and anxious persons, guilty because of socially disapproved impulses, are accepted by the Satanists and taught that the impulses they feel are natural and normal, but must be contained within certain spatial and temporal boundaries—the walls of the ritual chamber, the confines of the Inner Circle.

QUESTIONS AND EXERCISES

Vocabulary

1. Define or explain each of the following terms:

Satanism (1)	altruistic (14)
zealots (1)	naiveté (14)
hearsay (4)	shamans (17)
pathological (6)	antithesis (18)
sadomasochism (6)	novitiate (19)
transvestism (6)	charismatic (21)
syndrome (6)	blasphemy (22)
a familiar (7)	parody (23)
esoteric (7)	death rune (27)

warlocks (8)	octogenarians (31)
nymphomaniac (10)	covens (31)
exorcised (10)	

Rhetoric

2. What is the rhetorical function of paragraph 3?
3. What is the meaning of euphemisms like "opposition," "followers of the left-hand path," "walkers in darkness," and "Prince of Darkness"?
4. What is the allusion in paragraph 16?
5. Explain the allusions and figurative expressions found in paragraph 17.
6. Explain the use of "waxing" and "waning" in paragraph 20.
7. Of what value is the section beginning with paragraph 31?

Theme

8. Is all magic black magic?
9. Comment on how the seven deadly sins of Christianity become the Satanic virtues.
10. Why, according to the Satanists, is Christianity the cause of Satanism? How does Christian dogma accept this allegation?
11. Explain the meaning of paragraph 21 in the symbiotic relationship between Christianity and Satanism.
12. What names and forms would Satanism take in a non-Christian culture?
13. How are sex and laughter used to further Satanism at the expense of Christianity?
14. How is it possible to blaspheme psychiatry and psychedelics? Literally? Figuratively?
15. Explain the meaning of the curse in paragraph 25.
16. Explain the psychological import of paragraph 32.
17. In what way does the author of the essay put himself above the material he is investigating? What tool allows him such a perspective?
18. Could Moody make an analogous analysis of Christianity? What initial barriers would he have to overcome?

Topics and Assignments for Composition

1. Using the various definitions and explanations found in the essay, write a summary of the essay (note especially the conclusion).
2. Write a cause and effect relationship between a given culture and the nature of that culture's "black magic."

3. Write a paper commenting on Moody's analysis of the cause of today's rampant interest in witchcraft, the supernatural, and black and white magic.
4. Research some aspect of the essay to substantiate or to reject some of the factual elements Moody mentions.
5. Write a paper in which you develop a thesis concerning the importance of witchcraft in literature. (See the works of Hawthorne, Hershey, Mann, Chaucer, Shakespeare, Goethe, Marlowe, etc.)

Donald W. Hastings and Glenn M. Vernon

Ambiguous Language as a Strategy for Individual Action

While all behavior has a structured (normative) dimension, it also has an unstructured (anomic) dimension.[1] Lack of consensus with respect to specific areas of activity (situational ambiguity) forces interactants to seek a basis of agreement which permits interaction to proceed. For individuals within T groups, sensitivity groups, and learning groups the experience of confronting ambiguity is common although it is not restricted to these situations.[2] Research involving such groups has sensitized us to one frequently used technique which provides structure in "unknown territory" and appears to merit further study.

This technique is to confront situational ambiguity with verbal ambiguity. In ambiguous situations, individuals come to realize that the use of specialized, specific vocabularies is somewhat futile.[3] Accordingly,

[1] For a discussion of various conceptions of groups which focuses on the degree of structure, *see* Golembiewski (1962).

[2] For a discussion of the orientation phase of problem-solving groups in the pattern of question, answer, and positive or negative evaluation, *see* Bales (1955).

[3] For a discussion of "anticipatory socialization" to specific groups by individuals who may or may not be members, *see* Merton (1957, pp. 225-386 and Shibutani (1961, pp. 249-279).

For a particularly insightful discussion of this phenomenon as interwoven in the first three stages of five which typify the life cycle of the group (i.e., the encounter, testing of boundaries and modeling roles, negotiating an indigenous normative system, production, and separation), *see* Mills (1964, pp. 42-83) and Slater (1966, pp. 7-23).

use may be made of verbal behavior involving idiomatic or ambiguous expressions such as "you know," "you see," "you understand, don't you," and "you realize that, don't you." Such behavior might be called probing, feed-forward, sounding out, or a "beachhead device."

Habitual modes of behavior[4] including speech often persist well after conditions which initiated and sustained them cease to exist. Stinchcombe (1968) suggested that such social phenomena "tend to be causes of themselves—once established, they tend to maintain themselves. This gives rise to an infinite self-replicating causal loop, which preserves social effects of historical causes" (p. 8). Idiomatic expressions are of such a nature. Such expressions are ambiguous through overuse and misuse. It is, however, precisely in ambiguity that idiomatic expression gains its greatest utility as a mechanism for aiding the individual in his adjustment to an unstructured situation. That stimulus ambiguity frequently leads to conformity is well documented by social-psychological research (*see* Walker & Heyns, 1967).   3

With the use of ambiguous idiomatic expressions the speaker communicates to his audience that a personal decision tentatively has been reached, the content of which may or may not be clear since the meaning of the symbol is unclear. To the audience, however, it appears that at least one member of the group has started to provide structure. This use of an idiomatic expression, then, constitutes a subtle appeal to the authority of prior experiences of the audience, suggesting that at least minimal agreement has been reached with reference to the immediate point under discussion. If the use of the expression goes unchallenged, both the speaker and his audience share the belief that a common point of understanding has developed at least with reference to the matter under discussion. Whether or not agreement actually exists, the belief that it exists and is shared, contributes to stability of interaction.   4

In unstructured situations, without a storehouse of prior expectations upon which to draw, individuals may become particularly sensitive to the behavior of others, looking for cues as to what behavior can be appropriately introduced into the situation.[5] Use of ambiguous terms permits the user to entertain the possibility, in effect, of moving in different directions, without specific commitment to any. He knows this but others may not. (On the other hand, he may be unaware of this consequence of his behavior and merely habitually utilize this speech technique.) Decisions as to the mode of action to which to commit himself, then, can be made   5

---

[4] It should be noted that it is difficult to assess whether or not this is "displacement behavior," "probing tactic," or a function of an individual's verbal facility.

[5] For an insightful presentation at the other end of the continuum—how silence is used to destroy structure—*see* Kranes (1964).

after obtaining and assessing the reactions of other members of the audience. Such a commitment carries with it, at this point, the implication that this action was intended from the beginning.

Such a pattern of speech behavior is protective or "face-saving" for   6
speaker and audience in that many areas of activity can be evaluated tentatively by the interactants without any individual's placing himself in the position of being considered dogmatically committed to one particular position. In effect, neither speaker nor any member of the audience can be held clearly responsible for initiating the definition of the situation. Further, no single individual is likely to bear the full force of criticism if the initial interpretation is rejected or its meaning is modified. In short, we contend that the individual may be viewed as staking out a symbolic beachhead position with language ambiguous or vague enough to permit his withdrawal if others do not rally around the established position. Such action makes possible the mutual clarification and exploration of areas for group activity which would not be possible without some common idiomatic starting point.

Another way in which vagueness facilitates harmonious interaction is   7
suggested by Quine (1964):

> Vagueness is an aid in coping with the linearity of discourse. An expositor finds that an understanding of some matter A is necessary preparation for an understanding of B, and yet that A cannot itself be expounded in correct detail without, conversely, noting certain exceptions and distinctions which require prior understanding of B. Vagueness, then, to the rescue. The expositor states A vaguely, proceeds to B, and afterwards touches up A, without even having to call upon his reader to learn and unlearn any outright falsehood in the preliminary statement of A (p. 127).

This sounding-out process may be used in other types of interaction   8
such as formal negotiations between labor and management or between formal organizations on issues such as merger possibilities. In this case the procedure is a strategy deliberately chosen by one participant prior to the interaction. In T-Group interaction, the use of such a procedure is of a more crescive nature dictated more by immediate situational factors than by prior decisions to specifically do so.

Somewhat the same function is served by the use of analogies with   9
ambiguous meaning. Expressions such as "let's get the ball rolling" or "let's get down to brass tacks" appear to be useful in efforts to define the production goals of a group. Langer (1942) points out that all discourse involves a context which is well known to the speaker and the listener

and, in addition, a novel element. To express the latter, the speaker will utilize a metaphor or analogy if precise descriptive terms do not already exist. The context tells the listener that the analogy is not to be taken at face value.

The study of idiomatic or ambiguous expressions exploring what *10* Garfinkel (1964) calls background factors which are "seen without being noticed" seems to be of merit.

References

Bales, R. F. "The Equilibrium Problem of Small Groups." In A. P. Hare, E. F. Borgatta, & R. F. Bales (eds.), *Small Groups: Studies in Social Interaction*. New York: Knopf, 1955. Pp. 424-456.

Garfinkel, H. "Studies in the Routine Grounds of Everyday Activities." *Social Problems*, II, Winter 1964, 225-250.

Golembiewski, R. T. *The Small Group: An Analysis of Research Concepts and Operations*. Chicago: The University of Chicago Press, 1962.

Kranes, D. *One Act Play performed at Playwright's Laboratory*. New Haven, Conn.: Yale University Press, 1964.

Langer, S. *Philosophy in a New Key*. New York: Penguin Books, Inc., 1942.

Merton, R. K. *Social Theory and Social Structure*. Glencoe, Ill.: Free Press, 1957.

Mills, T. M. *Group Transformation: An Analysis of a Learning Group*. Englewood Cliffs, N.J.: Prentice-Hall, 1964.

Quine, W. V. *Word and Object*. Cambridge, Mass.: Massachusetts Institute of Technology (Paperback), 1964.

Shibutani, T. *Society and Personality: An Interactionist Approach to Social Psychology*. Englewood Cliffs, N.J.: Prentice-Hall, 1961.

Slater, P. E. *Microcosm: Structural, Psychological, and Religious Evolution in Groups*. New York: Wiley, 1966.

Stinchcombe, A. *Constructing Social Theories*. New York: Harcourt, Brace & World, 1968.

Walker, E. L., & Heyns, R. W. *An Anatomy for Conformity*. Belmont, Calif.: Brooks/Cole Publishing Co., 1967.

QUESTIONS AND EXERCISES

Vocabulary

1. Define or explain each of the following terms:

normative (1)   analogies (9)
anomic (1)   idiomatic (10)
T-Groups (1)

Rhetoric

2. What is the function of the following expressions:
   "you know" (2)
   "you see" (2)
   "you understand, don't you" (2)
   "you realize that, don't you" (2)
   "let's get the ball rolling" (9)
   "let's get down to brass tacks" (9)
3. What is the level of diction in this essay?
4. With few exceptions ("staking out a symbolic beachhead", paragraph 6) there is almost no figurative language or imagery used in the composition. What does this lack do to the "readability" of the essay? Is the style appropriate for the purpose?
5. Point out phrases of professional jargon in the article. For whom was this report intended?
6. Comment on the individuals found in the references. How are the footnotes handled?
7. Evaluate the essay as a brief research report.

Theme

8. Summarize the thesis of the report.
9. Comment on the extent of the evidence. How does the bibliography contribute to the support of the thesis?
10. With what aspect of human behavior does sociology deal?
11. Quine and Langer have written primarily about philosophy. Several of the writers are psychologists. What do these two facts suggest about the complexity of language and about the study of language?

Topics and Assignments for Composition

1. Translate the thesis of this essay into everyday English.
2. Develop a concise thesis about some aspect of language and write an essay attempting to argue your theory.
3. Read one of the authors in the references and use your research to support or to attack the thesis of this essay.

Part Nine:

Arguments and Persuasion

John Milton

In Defense of Books
from Areopagitica

I deny not, but that it is of greatest concernment in the Church and 1
Commonwealth, to have a vigilant eye how books demean themselves as
well as men; and thereafter to confine, imprison, and do sharpest justice
on them as malefactors. For books are not absolutely dead things, but do
contain a potency of life in them to be as active as that soul was whose
progeny they are; nay, they do preserve as in a vial the purest efficacy and
extraction of that living intellect that bred them. I know they are as lively,
and as vigorously productive, as those fabulous dragon's teeth; and being
sown up and down, may chance to spring up armed men. And yet, on the
other hand, unless wariness be used, as good almost kill a man as kill a
good book. Who kills a man kills a reasonable creature, God's image; but
he who destroys a good book, kills reason itself, kills the image of God,
as it were in the eye. Many a man lives a burden to the earth; but a good
book is the precious life-blood of a master-spirit, embalmed and treasured
up on purpose to a life beyond life. 'Tis true, no age can restore a life,
whereof perhaps there is no great loss; and revolutions of ages do not oft
recover the loss of a rejected truth, for the want of which whole nations
fare the worse.

We should be wary therefore what persecution we raise against the 2
living labors of public men, how we spill that seasoned life of man, preserved and stored up in books; since we see a kind of homicide may be
thus committed, sometimes a martyrdom, and if it extend to the whole
impression, a kind of massacre; whereof the execution ends not in the
slaying of an elemental life, but strikes at that ethereal and fifth essence,
the breath of reason itself, slays an immortality rather than a life.

QUESTIONS AND EXERCISES

Vocabulary

1. Define or explain each of the following terms:
   demean (1)   vial (1)
   malefactors (1)   efficacy (1)
   progeny (1)   ethereal (2)
2. Explain the allusion to "fabulous dragon's teeth."
3. Explain the meaning and origin of "Areopagitica."

Rhetoric

4. Analyze paragraph 2. Comment on the grammar, punctuation, and style. How does it compare to contemporary styles?
5. What analogy does Milton set up?
6. Find a simile in the excerpt.

Theme

7. Make an outline of Milton's argument.
8. Milton is considered a great English writer; he was also a Puritan and an official in the Commonwealth. Do you find his argument surprising in light of your previous knowledge about the Puritans?
9. What is meant by the "fifth essence"?

Topics and Assignments for Composition

1. Write an imitation of one of Milton's longer sentences. Notice how important "coordination" and "subordination" of ideas become.
2. Make a report on one of Milton's other essays. Give his pattern of argument and an evaluation of the validity of the reasoning.
3. Write a short essay of the general pattern of Milton in which you defend an idea or action. Examples:
   In Defense of Loafing
   In Defense of War
   In Defense of Freedom

Celia Hubbard

Missing the Yellow Submarine

Religion is where you find it, and it isn't strange that today, when   *1*
authentic religious experience is so noticeably absent from the old familiar
places, it should be popping up in new and off-beat ones. The voice of the
prophet and mystic is heard in the land, but the voice does not belong to
the Fulton Sheens, the Billy Grahams or Norman Vincent Peales. It belongs to the young folk singers, poets, playwrights, media-makers.

On the album cover of David Steinberg's record, "The Incredible   *2*
Shrinking God," we read, "When ancestral kings corrupted their captains, and the Church blessed both captains and kings, the court jester
got laughs simply by sniffing the troubled air, implying that the stink in the
herring begins in its head. In our times, it isn't surprising to find men and
women crowding the night clubs in hopes of seeing someone sniff the air.
In such times clowns become witnesses."

Such "clowns" as the Beatles, Bob Dylan, Simon and Garfunkel,   *3*
Leonard Cohen, the young authors of "Hair," and many more, are continually sniffing the troubled air. Today night club entertainers *are* preachers, protest *is* ritual, ceremonial, and folksingers *are* prophets and theologians for the Now generation. Speed kills and so does the Establishment.
The young question their relationship to the structures of established
society. Some reject it, some withdraw, others seek to change it. All feel
more or less alienated; they are disturbed by the status quo, bogged down
under the pharisaical bourgeois baggage. And in reacting, they have
started what amounts to their own spiritual revolution.

The qualities and values most prized by this generation of young   *4*
people are very similar. What does it mean in the fullest sense to be a
human being? The innerspace odyssey begins in a personal search for
self and/or God, an intensification of personal and interpersonal experience, authentic and meaningful relationships, not hung up with personal

Reprinted with permission of Commonweal Publishing Company, Inc.

guilt in such a way as to make intimacy, openness and love impossible. Flexibility in an ever-changing environment, honesty, non-violence and brotherhood are basic beliefs. There is a strong back-to-the-tribe or ahead-to-the-tribe à la McLuhan feeling which seeks to create small intimate groups of people who can come together as equals in an atmosphere of openness, trust and mutual respect and take active part in making the decisions that affect their lives.

The capacity for identification, involvement and collaboration makes   5
these young groups in practice, as well as theory, unselfconsciously and genuinely interracial and international. The "I-believe-so-I-am" creed makes for a closer identification with the alien, the deprived, the non-white, even the peasant in Vietnam. The current Broadway production "Hair," a tribal love-rock musical, celebrates exuberantly what it's all about. It is searingly anti-war, anti-dishonesty, pro-life, pro-love, pro-sex, pro-joy, pro-music, pro-color and pro-fantasy. In this multi-media manifesto of tribal religiosity, the actors fairly fling themselves upon the audience in order to put the point across. To see, touch and know things as they are and to expand these experiences into a fused cosmic brotherhood is the point. People as people are very much a part of this whole loving, touching, swaying, dancing, singing, sexing, hairy community. When someone complained that he couldn't follow the show's story line, a member of the cast answered, "Man, we're not asking you to follow anything, just dig what's going on. That's what it's all about. Opening up your mind."

If you can't dig and groove you are likely to miss the yellow submarine   6
altogether these days. George Harrison of the Beatles says, "God is a good vibration. God's in so many ways, just in everything and everyone, but particularly, I think, in art forms where people just do things. This is being maybe pretentious to some people, saying our music is an art form. But it is if we dig doing it, and lots of people dig what we're doing . . . so it's really that every moment's important and just to dig it all and by digging it all you're naturally harmonizing with it, which is a form of appreciation of God." To groove means to yield youself to the flow of the activity around you, and this includes the ability to receive clashing stimuli simultaneously, a sensory bombardment which is intentional and not undisciplined. Grooving requires a lot of personal freedom and self-assurance and the younger you are, the easier it is!

It is little wonder that young travelers into inner space are not taking   7
their trip with Jesus, in that leaky old spaceship, the Christian Church, but turning on to the wise men coming from the East, as well as such local Western gurus as McLuhan, Ginsberg, Fuller, Mailer, Cage, Brown.

The Christian Church, especially the Roman Catholic, has been so pre-   8 occupied with its institutionalism that it has failed to notice that the world is operating on another wave-length altogether; there exists so much repressive concern for dogma and authority that any mystical flights and direct religious experiences which are a valid part of the Church's tradition have all but been stifled. It is small wonder that youths who ceremonially burn money and draftcards, and sometimes themselves, aren't about to buy a dogmatic, hierarchically structured religious system, where money, the law and absolute power, authority have become God. The endless face-saving pronouncements and continual chewing on the old bones of papal infallibility, birth control and priestly celibacy have turned Christendom into Boredom; the strain on credibility increases and increases. Actions speak louder than words, especially abstract ambiguous words, and the do-nothing-Church becomes more and more irrelevant, if not almost immoral by its inactivity and uninvolvement in the world's great crisis situations. Its attitude toward freedom and the individual is archaic, and modern psychology, sociology and anthropology make this more of an embarrassment daily. The new wave of Pentecostals may quench the thirst of those longing for signs and wonders, and the emotionally charismatic touch may help leaven the heaviness and humorlessness of the Church scene; but only "may."

Small groups and student communities have a chance to cheer on the   9
weary pilgrim if they are given freedom and a sympathetic ministry which is "with it." The teach-preach Catholic overkill, however, is a real threat to establishing any real rapport with the younger generation. At a Mass for students in Boston, it was thought preferable to change the lyrics of Bob Dylan's "Blowin' in the Wind" to ones with doggerel references to precious blood and Jesus saves. This, if not downright dishonest, is clearly lacking trust in the Spirit blowing where it will.

However, the Spirit will blow where it wills and at the moment it seems   10
to be purposefully circumnavigating the institutional Church, perhaps distrustful of ecclesiastics over 30. But signs of hope are bursting out over the younger scene. Never has a generation been so determined and fearless in its criticism of society, its wars and failures; never has a generation affirmed the individual so idealistically. The potential for truth and goodness and an authentic holiness is enormous.

QUESTIONS AND EXERCISES

Vocabulary

1. Define or explain the following terms:

    alienated (3)   dogmatic (8)

hung up (4)   hierarchically (8)
exuberantly (5)   charismatic (8)
multi-media (5)   leaven (8)
gurus (7)

2. Explain the importance of the following people or ideas:

Fulton Sheen (1)   Ginsberg (7)
Billy Graham (1)   Fuller (7)
Norman Vincent Peale (1)   Mailer (7)
Establishment (3)   Cage (7)
speed kills (3)   Brown (7)
Now generation (3)   Pentecostals (8)
pharisaical (3)   Bob Dylan (9)
bourgeois (3)   doggerel (9)
odyssey (4)   rapport (9)
à la McLuhan (4)

3. Explain the meaning of the following terms and put a usage label on each (use one of the current college level dictionaries to obtain the level of usage).

hung up (4)   groove (6)
dig (5)   is "with it" (9)

Rhetoric

4. Explain the allusion in the sentence "The voice of the prophet and mystic is heard in the land." (1)
5. Identify the use of analogy in paragraphs 2 and 3.
6. What is the tone of this essay? What elements contribute to this tone?
7. Several sentences make use of repetition. For example, "It is searingly anti-war, anti-dishonesty, pro-life, pro-love, pro-sex, pro-joy, pro-music, pro-color, and pro-fantasy." What is the effect of such repetition?
8. What evidence not mentioned thus far is there of a witty irreverent attitude manifesting itself in a facile, witty, irreverent style?
9. Explain the analogy in paragraph 7.

Theme

10. Criticism of a society, institution, or a segment of either may come from within or without. What is the case in this essay?
11. Explain the significance of the title. Why, like poetry, is it a cryptic title?
12. What is the relationship of the churches of today to the youth of today? Can you generalize?
13. In paragraph 3 the claim is made that "Today night club entertainers

are preachers, protest *is* ritual, ceremonial, and folksingers *are* prophets and theologians for the Now generation." Comment.

Topics and Assignments for Composition

1. State the thesis of this essay in one well-constructed sentence.
2. Analyze the style of this essay. Include such ingredients as diction,
   allusions, figurative language, and tone.
3. Analyze a contemporary institution in relation to a current problem.
   Be sure to have a thesis that comments on the relationship.

John Donne

Meditation XVII
from Devotions Upon
Emergent Occasions

Perchance he for whom this bell tolls may be so ill, as that he knows not it tolls for him; and perchance I may think myself so much better than I am, as that they who are about me, and see my state, may have caused it to toll for me, and I know not that. The church is catholic, universal, so are all her actions; all that she does belongs to all. When she baptizes a child, that action concerns me; for that child is thereby connected to that head which is my head too, and ingrafted into that body whereof I am a member. And when she buries a man, that action concerns me: all mankind is of one author, and is one volume; when one man dies, one chapter is not torn out of the book, but translated into a better language; and every chapter must be so translated; God employs several translators; some pieces are translated by age, some by sickness, some by war, some by justice; but God's hand is in every translation, and his hand shall bind up all our scattered leaves again for that library where every book shall lie open to one another. As therefore the bell that rings to a sermon calls not upon the preacher only, but upon the congregation to come, so this bell calls us all; but how much more me, who am brought so near the door by this sickness. There was a contention as far as a suit (in which both piety and dignity, religion and estimation, were mingled), which of the religious orders should ring to prayers first in the morning; and it was determined, that they should ring first that rose earliest. If we understand aright the dignity of this bell that tolls for our evening prayer, we would be glad to make it ours by rising early, in that application, that it might be ours as well as his, whose indeed it is. The bell doth toll for him that thinks it doth; and though it intermit again, yet from that minute that that occasion wrought upon him, he is united to God. Who casts not up his eye to the sun when it rises? but who takes off his eye from a comet when that breaks out? Who bends not his ear to any bell which upon any occasion rings? but who can remove it from that bell which is passing a piece of himself out of this world? No man is an island, entire of itself; every man is a piece of the continent, a part of the main. If a clod be washed away by the sea, Europe is the less, as well as if a promontory were, as well as if a manor of thy friend's or of thine own were: any man's death diminishes me, because I am involved in mankind, and therefore never send to know for whom the bell tolls; it tolls for thee. Neither can we call this a begging of misery, or a borrowing of misery, as though we were not miserable enough of ourselves, but must fetch in more from the next house, in taking upon us the misery of our neighbors. Truly it were an excusable covetousness if we did, for affliction is a treasure, and scarce any man hath enough of it. No man hath affliction enough that is not matured and ripened by it, and made fit for God by that affliction. If a man carry treasure in bullion, or in a wedge of gold, and have none coined into current money, his treasure will not defray him as he travels. Tribulation is a treasure in the nature of it, but it is not current money in the use of it, except we get nearer and nearer our home, Heaven, by it. Another man may be sick too, and sick to death, and this affliction may lie in his bowels, as gold in a mine, and be of no use to him; but this bell, that tells me of his affliction, digs out and applies that gold to me: if by this consideration of another's danger I take mine own into contemplation, and so secure my self, by making my recourse to my God, who is our only security.

QUESTIONS AND EXERCISES

Vocabulary

1. Define or explain each of the following terms:
   catholic   covetousness
   promontory   tribulation
2. Find words that have archaic spelling.

Rhetoric

3. This meditation is developed by three analogies. Identify them. Which is the most famous one?
4. Find a simile in this selection.
5. Who used a short excerpt from this essay for the title of his famous novel? Explain the relevancy of the allusion.

Theme

6. In literal language state the meaning of the analogy beginning "No man is an island . . ."

7. What aspect contributes most to the persuasiveness of the argument: the logic or the figurative language?
8. Is the polemic thrust deductive or inductive?

Topics and Assignments for Composition

1. Compose an analogy reflecting one of your ideas about a human trait.
2. Compare the style of John Donne to that of Sir Francis Bacon.
3. Write a short book review of *For Whom the Bell Tolls* in which you compare the theme of the book with Donne's essay.
4. Write a short imitation of John Donne's Meditation XVII in which you maintain one of two tones: a) serious emulation, or b) a parody for humor.

Jonathan Swift

A Modest Proposal for Preventing the Children of poor People in Ireland, from being a Burden to their Parents or Country; and for making them beneficial to the Publick

It is a melancholly Object to those, who walk through this great Town,   *1*
or travel in the Country; when they see the *Streets*, the *Roads*, and
Cabbins-doors crowded with *Beggars* of the Female Sex, followed by
three, four, or six Children, *all in Rags*, and importuning every Passenger
for an Alms. These *Mothers*, instead of being able to work for their honest
Livelyhood, are forced to employ all their Time in stroling to beg Sustenance for their *helpless Infants;* who, as they grow up, either turn
Thieves for want of Work; or leave their *dear Native Country, to fight for
the Pretender in* Spain; or sell themselves to the *Barbadoes*.

I think it is agreed by all Parties, that this prodigious Number of Chil-   *2*
dren in the Arms, or on the Backs, or at the *Heels* of their *Mothers*, and
frequently of their *Fathers*, is *in the present deplorable State of the Kingdom*, a very great additional Grievance; and therefore, whoever could
find out a fair, cheap, and easy Method of making these Children sound
and useful Members of the Commonwealth; would deserve so well of the
Publick, as to have his Statue set up for a Preserver of the Nation.

But my Intention is very far from being confined to provide only for   *3*
the Children of *professed Beggars:* It is of a much greater Extent, and
shall take in the whole Number of Infants at a certain Age, who are born
of Parents, in effect as little able to support them, as those who demand
our Charity in the Streets.

As to my own Part, having turned my Thoughts for many Years, upon **4** this important Subject; and maturely weighed the several *Schemes of other Projectors,* I have always found them grosly mistaken in their Computation. It is true, a Child *just dropt from its Dam,* may be supported by her Milk, for a Solar Year with little other Nourishment; at most not above the Value of two Shillings; which the Mother may certainly get, or the Value in *Scraps,* by her lawful Occupation of *Begging:* And, it is exactly at one Year old, that I propose to provide for them in such a Manner, as, instead of being a Charge upon their *Parents,* or the *Parish,* or *wanting Food and Raiment* for the rest of their Lives; they shall, on the contrary, contribute to the Feeding, and partly to the Cloathing, of many Thousands.

There is likewise another great Advantage in my *Scheme,* that it will **5** prevent those *voluntary Abortions,* and that horrid Practice of *Women murdering their Bastard Children;* alas! too frequent among us; sacrificing the *poor innocent Babes,* I doubt, more to avoid the Expence than the Shame; which would move Tears and Pity in the most Savage and inhuman Breast.

The Number of Souls in *Ireland* being usually reckoned one Million **6** and a half; of these I calculate there may be about Two Hundred Thousand Couples whose Wives are Breeders; from which Number I subtract thirty thousand Couples, who are able to maintain their own Children; although I apprehend there cannot be so many, under *the present Distresses of the Kingdom;* but this being granted, there will remain an Hundred and Seventy Thousand Breeders. I again subtract Fifty Thousand, for those Women who miscarry, or whose Children die by Accident, or Disease, within the Year. There only remain an Hundred and Twenty Thousand Children of poor Parents, annually born: The Question therefore is, How this Number shall be reared, and provided for? Which, as I have already said, under the present Situation of Affairs, is utterly impossible, by all the Methods hitherto proposed: For we can *neither employ them in Handicraft* or *Agriculture;* we neither build Houses, (I mean in the Country) nor cultivate Land: They can very seldom pick up a Livelyhood *by Stealing* until they arrive at six Years old; except where they are of towardly Parts; although, I confess, they learn the Rudiments much earlier; during which Time, they can, however, be properly looked upon only as *Probationers;* as I have been informed by a principal Gentleman in the County of *Cavan,* who protested to me, that he never knew above one or two Instances under the Age of six, even in a Part of the Kingdom *so renowned for the quickest Proficiency in that Art.*

I am assured by our Merchants, that a Boy or a Girl before twelve **7**

Years old, is no saleable Commodity; and even when they come to this Age, they will not yield above Three Pounds, or Three Pounds and half a Crown at most, on the Exchange; which cannot turn to Account either to the Parents or Kingdom; the Charge of Nutriment and Rags, having been at least four Times that Value.

I shall now therefore humbly propose my own Thoughts; which I hope will not be liable to the least Objection.   8

I have been assured by a very knowing *American* of my Acquaintance in *London;* that a young healthy Child, well nursed, is, at a Year old, a most delicious, nourishing, and wholesome Food; whether *Stewed, Roasted, Baked,* or *Boiled;* and, I make no doubt, that it will equally serve in a *Fricasie,* or *Ragoust.*   9

I do therefore humbly offer it to *publick Consideration,* that of the Hundred and Twenty thousand Children, already computed, Twenty thousand may be reserved for Breed; whereof only one Fourth Part to be Males; which is more than we allow to *Sheep, black Cattle,* or *Swine;* and my Reason is, that these Children are seldom the Fruits of Marriage, *a Circumstance not much regarded by our Savages;* therefore, *one Male* will be sufficient to serve *four Females.* That the remaining Hundred thousand, may, at a Year old, be offered in Sale to the *Persons of Quality* and *Fortune,* through the Kingdom; always advising the Mother to let them suck plentifully in the last Month, so as to render them plump, and fat for a good Table. A Child will make two Dishes at an Entertainment for Friends; and when the Family dines alone, the fore or hind Quarter will make a reasonable Dish; and seasoned with a little Pepper or Salt, will be very good Boiled on the fourth Day, especially in *Winter.*   10

I have reckoned upon a Medium, that a Child just born will weigh Twelve Pounds; and in a solar Year, if tolerably nursed, encreaseth to twenty eight Pounds.   11

I grant this Food will be somewhat dear, and therefore very *proper for Landlords;* who, as they have already devoured most of the Parents, seem to have the best Title to the Children.   12

Infants Flesh will be in Season throughout the Year; but more plentiful in *March,* and a little before and after: For we are told by a grave Author, an eminent *French* Physician, that *Fish being a prolifick Dyet,* there are more Children born in *Roman Catholick Countries* about Nine Months after *Lent,* than at any other Season: Therefore reckoning a Year after *Lent,* the Markets will be more glutted than usual; because the Number of *Popish Infants,* is, at least, three to one in this Kingdom; and therefore it will have one other Collateral Advantage, by lessening the Number of *Papists* among us.   13

I have already computed the Charge of nursing a Beggar's Child (in   14 which List I reckon all *Cottagers, Labourers,* and Four fifths of the *Farmers*) to be about two Shillings *per Annum,* Rags included; and I believe, no Gentleman would repine to give Ten Shillings for the *Carcase of a good fat child;* which, as I have said, will make four Dishes of excellent nutritive Meat, when he hath only some particular Friend, or his own Family, to dine with him. Thus the Squire will learn to be a good Landlord, and grow popular among his Tenants; the Mother will have Eight Shillings net Profit, and be fit for Work until she produceth another Child.

Those who are more thrifty *(as I must confess the Times require)* may   15
flay the Carcase; the Skin of which, artificially dressed, will make admirable *Gloves for Ladies,* and *Summer Boots for fine Gentlemen.*

As to our City of *Dublin;* Shambles may be appointed for this Purpose,   16
in the most convenient Parts of it; and Butchers we may be assured will not be wanting; although I rather recommend buying the Children alive, and dressing them hot from the Knife, as we do *roasting Pigs.*

A very worthy Person, *a true Lover of his Country,* and whose Virtues   17
I highly esteem, was lately pleased, in discoursing on this Matter, to offer a Refinement upon my Scheme. He said, that many Gentlemen of this Kingdom, having of late destroyed their Deer; he conceived, that the Want of Venison might be well supplied by the Bodies of young Lads and Maidens, not exceeding fourteen Years of Age, nor under twelve; so great a Number of both Sexes in every County being now ready to starve, for Want of Work and Service: And these to be disposed of by their Parents, if alive, or otherwise by their nearest Relations. But with due Deference to so excellent a Friend, and so deserving a Patriot, I cannot be altogether in his Sentiments. For as to the Males, my *American* Acquaintance assured me from frequent Experience, that their Flesh was generally tough and lean, like that of our School-boys, by continual Exercise; and their Taste disagreeable; and to fatten them would not answer the Charge. Then, as to the Females, it would, I think, with humble Submission, *be a Loss to the Publick,* because they soon would become Breeders themselves: And besides it is not improbable, that some scrupulous People might be apt to censure such a Practice (although indeed very unjustly) as a little bordering upon Cruelty; which, I confess, hath always been with me the strongest Objection against any Project, how well soever intended.

But in order to justify my Friend; he confessed, that this Expedient   18
was put into his Head by the famous *Salmanaazor,* a Native of the Island *Formosa,* who came from thence to *London,* above twenty Years ago, and in Conversation told my Friend, that in his Country, when any young Person happened to be put to Death, the Executioner sold the Carcase to *Persons of Quality,* as a prime Dainty; and that, in his Time, the Body

of a plump Girl of fifteen, who was crucified for an Attempt to poison the Emperor, was sold to his Imperial *Majesty's prime Minister of State,* and other great *Mandarines* of the Court, *in Joints from the Gibbet,* at Four hundred Crowns. Neither indeed can I deny, that if the same Use were made of several plump young Girls in this Town, who, without one single Groat to their Fortunes, cannot stir Abroad without a Chair, and appear at a *Play-house,* and *Assemblies* in foreign Fineries, which they never will pay for; the Kingdom would not be the worse.

Some Persons of a desponding Spirit are in great Concern about that *19* vast Number of poor People, who are Aged, Diseased, or Maimed; and I have been desired to employ my Thoughts what Course may be taken, to ease the Nation of so grievous an Incumbrance. But I am not in the least Pain upon that Matter; because it is very well known, that they are every Day *dying,* and *rotting,* by *Cold* and *Famine,* and *Filth,* and *Vermin,* as fast as can be reasonably expected. And as to the younger Labourers, they are now in almost as hopeful a Condition: They cannot get Work, and consequently pine away for Want of Nourishment, to a Degree, that if at any Time they are accidentally hired to common Labour, they have not Strength to perform it; and thus the Country, and themselves, are in a fair Way of being soon delivered from the Evils to come.

I have too long digressed; and therefore shall return to my Subject. I *20* think the Advantages by the Proposal which I have made, are obvious, and many, as well as of the highest Importance.

For, *First,* as I have already observed, it would greatly lessen *the Num-* *21* *ber of Papists,* with whom we are yearly over-run; being the principal Breeders of the Nation, as well as our most dangerous Enemies; and who stay at home on Purpose, with a Design *to deliver the Kingdom to the Pretender;* hoping to take their Advantage by the Absence *of so many good Protestants,* who have chosen rather to leave their Country, then stay at home, and pay Tithes against their Conscience, to an idolatrous *Episcopal Curate.*

Secondly, The poorer Tenants will have something valuable of their *22* own; which, by Law, may be made liable to Distress, and help to pay their Landlord's Rent; their Corn and Cattle being already seized, and *Money a Thing unknown.*

Thirdly, Whereas the Maintenance of an Hundred Thousand Children, *23* from two Years old, and upwards, cannot be computed at less than ten Shillings a Piece *per Annum,* the Nation's Stock will be thereby encreased Fifty Thousand Pounds *per Annum;* besides the Profit of a new Dish, introduced to the Tables of all *Gentlemen of Fortune* in the Kingdom, who have any Refinement in Taste; and the Money will circulate among our selves, the Goods being entirely of our own Growth and Manufacture.

Fourthly, The constant Breeders, besides the Gain of Eight Shillings *24* *Sterling per Annum,* by the Sale of their Children, will be rid of the Charge of maintaining them after the first Year.

Fifthly, This Food would likewise bring great *Custom to Taverns,* *25* where the Vintners will certainly be so prudent, as to procure the best Receipts for dressing it to Perfection; and consequently, have their Houses frequented by all the *fine Gentlemen,* who justly value themselves upon their Knowledge in good Eating; and a skilful Cook, who understands how to oblige his Guests, will contrive to make it as expensive as they please.

Sixthly, This would be a great Inducement to Marriage, which all wise *26* Nations have either encouraged by Rewards, or enforced by Laws and Penalties. It would encrease the Care and Tenderness of Mothers towards their Children, when they were sure of a Settlement for Life, to the poor Babes, provided in some Sort by the Publick, to their annual Profit instead of Expence. We should soon see an honest Emulation among the married Women, *which of them could bring the fattest Child to the Market.* Men would become as *fond* of their Wives, during the Time of their Pregnancy, as they are now of their *Mares* in Foal, their *Cows* in Calf, or *Sows* when they are ready to farrow; nor offer to beat or kick them, (as it is too *frequent* a Practice) for fear of a Miscarriage.

Many other Advantages might be enumerated. For Instance, the Addi- *27* tion of some Thousand Carcasses in our Exportation of barrelled Beef: The Propagation of *Swines Flesh,* and Improvement in the Art of making good *Bacon;* so much wanted among us by the great Destruction of *Pigs,* too frequent at our Tables, and are no way comparable in Taste, or Magnificence, to a well-grown fat yearly Child; which, roasted whole, will make a considerable Figure at a *Lord Mayor's Feast,* or any other publick Entertainment. But this, and many others, I omit; being studious of Brevity.

Supposing that one Thousand Families in this City, would be constant *28* Customers for Infants Flesh; besides others who might have it at *merry Meetings,* particularly at *Weddings* and *Christenings;* I compute that *Dublin* would take off, annually, about Twenty Thousand Carcasses; and the rest of the Kingdom (where probably they will be sold somewhat cheaper) the remaining Eighty Thousand.

I can think of no one Objection, that will possibly be raised against this *29* Proposal; unless it should be urged, that the Number of People will be thereby much lessened in the Kingdom. This I freely own; and it was indeed one principal Design in offering it to the World. I desire the Reader will observe, that I calculate my Remedy *for this one individual Kingdom of* IRELAND, *and for no other that ever was, is, or I think ever can be upon Earth.* Therefore, let no Man talk to me of other Expedients: *Of taxing our Absentees at five Shillings a Pound: Of using neither Cloaths, nor Houshold Furniture; except what is of our own Growth and Manufacture: Of utterly rejecting the Materials and Instruments that promote foreign Luxury: Of curing the Expensiveness of Pride, Vanity, Idleness, and Gaming in our Women: Of introducing a Vein of Parsimony, Prudence and Temperance: Of learning to love our Country; wherein we differ even from* LAPLANDERS, *and the Inhabitants of* TOPINAMBOO: *Of quitting our Animosities, and Factions; nor act any longer like the* Jews, *who were murdering one another at the very Moment their City was taken: Of being a little cautious not to sell our Country and Consciences for nothing: Of teaching Landlords to have, at least, one Degree of Mercy towards their Tenants.* Lastly, *Of putting a Spirit of Honesty, Industry, and Skill into our Shop-keepers; who, if a Resolution could now be taken to buy only our native Goods, would immediately unite to cheat and exact upon us in the Price, the Measure, and the Goodness; nor could ever yet be brought to make one fair Proposal of just Dealing, though often and earnestly invited to it.*

Therefore I repeat; let no Man talk to me of these and the like Expedients; till he hath, at least, a Glimpse of Hope, that there will ever be some hearty and sincere Attempt to put *them in Practice.*   *30*

But, as to my self; having been wearied out for many Years with offering vain, idle, visionary Thoughts; and at length utterly despairing of Success, I fortunately fell upon this Proposal; which, as it is wholly new, so it hath something *solid* and *real,* of no Expence, and little Trouble, full in our own Power; and whereby we can incur no Danger in *disobliging* ENGLAND: For, this Kind of Commodity will not bear Exportation; the Flesh being of too tender a Consistence, to admit a long Continuance in Salt; *although, perhaps, I could name a Country, which would be glad to eat up our whole Nation without it.*   *31*

After all, I am not so violently bent upon my own Opinion, as to reject any Offer proposed by wise Men, which shall be found equally innocent, cheap, easy, and effectual. But before something of that Kind shall be advanced, in Contradiction to my Scheme, and offering a better; I desire the Author, or Authors, will be pleased maturely to consider two Points. *First,* As Things now stand, how they will be able to find Food and Raiment, for a Hundred Thousand useless Mouths and Backs? And *secondly,* There being a round Million of Creatures in human Figure, throughout this Kingdom; whose whole Subsistence, put into a common   *32*

Stock, would leave them in Debt two Millions of Pounds *Sterling;* adding those, who are Beggars by Profession, to the Bulk of Farmers, Cottagers, and Labourers, with their Wives and Children, who are Beggars in Effect; I desire those Politicians, who dislike my Overture, and may perhaps be so bold to attempt an Answer, that they will first ask the Parents of these Mortals, Whether they would not, at this Day, think it a great Happiness to have been sold for Food at a Year old, in the Manner I prescribe; and thereby have avoided such a perpetual Scene of Misfortunes, as they have since gone through; by the *Oppression of Landlords;* the Impossibility of paying Rent, without Money or Trade; the Want of common Sustenance, with neither House nor Cloaths, to cover them from the Inclemencies of the Weather; and the most inevitable Prospect of intailing the like, or greater Miseries upon their Breed for ever.

I profess, in the Sincerity of my Heart, that I have not the least personal Interest, in endeavouring to promote this necessary Work; having no other Motive than the *publick Good of my Country, by advancing our Trade, providing for Infants, relieving the Poor, and giving some Pleasure to the Rich.* I have no Children, by which I can propose to get a single Penny; the youngest being nine Years old, and my Wife past Childbearing. *33*

QUESTIONS AND EXERCISES

Vocabulary

1. Define or explain each of the following:
   importuning (1)   idolatrous (21)
   prodigious (2)   emulation (26)

Rhetoric

2. The language shows obvious signs of the period in which the essay was written. Point out a few differences in spelling and diction from today's practice.
3. Explain the profusion of words beginning with capitals.
4. Irony, sarcasm, and satire require a very controlled tone. Does Swift manage to keep a consistent tone and point of view?
5. Explain the impact of the word "modest" in the title.
6. How does Swift manage to present the real conditions of Ireland in his tract?
7. During the past few years humor labeled "sick" or "black" has become commonplace. Does Swift's essay fit this genre?
8. Explain the many allusions to foreign lands.

9. What is the effect of Swift's analogy between infants and animals raised for slaughter?
10. Is there a point at which the essay becomes too painful to read? Could such a point defeat the purpose of the essay?
11. Outline the pattern of the essay. Compare its form to a non-ironic essay of its time. Why is the similarity important to the success of Swift's essay?

Theme

12. What is the discrepancy between the stated purpose and the actual purpose of the essay? Is this irony?
13. What are the dangers of attempting to make a serious point by using irony?
14. Who are the landlords mentioned in paragraph 12?
15. In view of the current struggle in Northern Ireland, comment on the allusions to "Popish infants" and to "Papists" in the essay.
16. What are some of the implicit beliefs of the English and of the Irish that emerge from the essay?
17. On which side do Swift's sympathies lie?
18. What audience was Swift trying to reach?

Topics and Assignments for Composition

1. In a paragraph, show the relationship between irony and humor.
2. In a paragraph explain how satire may be achieved.
3. Choose a serious, contemporary problem and write a short imitation of Swift's "A Modest Proposal."
4. Research other essays patterned after Swift's. Write a report in which you illustrate how the imitators copied the original.
5. Write a satirical essay using contemporary trends in humor, irony, and wit.

Karla Hurtik

One-Track Liberation?

Anyone who has stopped to consider it would have to admit that *1*
women have been and are being treated very unfairly in terms of legis-
lated inequality and cultural tradition. Demands for equal pay, education,
and job opportunities; an end to hiring and promotion discrimination;
more political power and representation; the status of independent,
autonomous being men automatically enjoy; free day-care nurseries,
birth control, and abortion on request are valid and necessary. For years
Liberationists have pointed out the political, economic, and social realities of sexual inequality and discrimination that have been so built into
the system and taken for granted that they have passed almost unnoticed
until recently. Legal absurdities (such as women being forbidden the
jurisdiction over their own bodies to enable them to get rid of unborn,
unwanted children legally) can be altered, stiff though the opposition is.
But, drawbacks to educational and professional advancement are more
vague and subtle, more difficult to uproot. And, of course, the archetypical
social roles of women as mother, wife, sex object, brainless menial
worker, capable but always subordinate secretary, patient nurse or
teacher, are most entrenched and still present genuine obstacles to feminine progress and individual choice.

Women have suffered very real and acute injustices which have in the *2*
past decade been brought more and more into the open, discussed,
lamented, and resisted. Militant feminism, which vanished with the granting of the vote, has reappeared in modern and powerful form. Like the
causes of other oppressed and newly militant minorities—the Blacks,
Chicanos, American Indians—Women's Lib, given a big publicity boost
from the media, became topical and trendy. But despite the value, necessity, and integrity of the movement, despite the fact that I agree com-

Reprinted by permission of the author.

pletely with its goals, I can't work up much enthusiasm for it. My reasons fall into three general areas.

First, in many ways the Women's Lib movement seems too Establishment-oriented, too concerned with achieving equality and status within the existing system. Although most of the active Women's Libbers are radicals, or at least strong liberals who are concerned with developing alternative structures and social roles, they are working within a society which has been based on the accepted inferior position of certain groups, including women. The whole system will have to be overhauled before anything concrete can be accomplished. Granted, changes can be made from within in a sort of Trojan Horse style, infiltrate and conquer, but it seems pointless to aim at achieving equality under the *status quo* and operating under its dictates. Thus, even if women become company directors, military and government officials, stockbrokers, college presidents, lawyers, doctors, airline pilots, engineers, and diplomats by the thousands, I can't see that this would bring about beneficial social change. There would be a great increase in status, power, money, and opportunity for the women involved, and by virtue of their example, for women in general. The institutions concerned would, of course, change, but at the same time most of them are probably capable of absorbing women and still continuing in basically the same direction. Thus, equality under the present system, or some mutant form of it, would undoubtedly increase personal status, but would it dramatically alter or improve the system itself? What is the point of gaining parity with capitalistic, imperialistic, chauvinistic men in institutions which they have created and maintained? Who *wants* equality in these areas?

Perhaps equality within the system is the first step to a new way of life, a necessary stage in the development of liberation for everyone, but it seems dubious. In an admittedly exaggerated example, striving for equality might lead to women being given more power to tell others what to do (as they have already in the roles of housewife and mother), more chance to be drafted or draft others, to exert physical and financial power, to hold the guns and drop the napalm, to lead what they should be trying to change. In demanding equality, are women fighting the system or fighting to join it, to get more out of it?

Second, in terms of the injustices currently being perpetrated: poverty, repression of political dissidents, drug laws, the draft, and so on, Women's Lib, by itself, simply doesn't seem that important. Nevertheless it *is* important taken in the context of these other injustices. The attempt to restrict women to a few confining social roles and particularly to repress those who are working toward societal alternatives, is part of the blueprint for controlling potentially dangerous segments of the population whose values and goals may undermine basic political, economic, and social patterns. Thus, black, brown, and white revolutionaries, anarchists and freaks must be controlled and eliminated if necessary. Women who get too far out of line present a similar danger. Therefore, in a sense, it is all one fight and should be fought with some kind of unity. And although there are significant differences among revolutionaries of all kinds, and countless variations in approach, attitudes, lifestyle, and degree of involvement, all are united against repression, and all are in favor of greater freedom, flexibility, and choice. Though probably too diverse and spontaneous (virtues which unfortunately impede effectiveness) to present a truly united front against their common enemy, these flexible groups do realize the necessity of cooperation

But Women's Lib, though linked with and in part spawned by, these 6 groups, seems to me too segregated and self-centered to achieve this goal. To me it can only be valid in terms of an overall alternative culture, where individual freedom and community cooperation, an open atmosphere in which sex, like race, is unimportant, are vital components. Naturally a beleaguered group must stick together and develop group identity and pride, but this group cohesiveness must not become an end in itself. It is simply a means to liberation.

Men are just as shackled as women, forced to fight wars they don't 7 believe in or become outlaws, to do work they find meaningless in order to survive, and they are equally subject to confining sexual roles. Certainly men oppress women; some consciously and on principle, as they shoot and jail blacks and as they hound young white dropouts; others as poor whites oppress blacks, in ignorance and fear. True, women do not dominate the power structure and can't be held as responsible for the brutalities and injustices committed as some men can. Nevertheless, they have openly and tacitly supported the system as much as men have, sending their sons off to war and signing petitions against black families moving next door. Women are not special, nor are they blameless; nor are they as a group superior or inferior to men. They are individuals. And they should work and fight for change as individuals, with like-minded allies.

Finally, there is my difficult to explain but very tangible reaction 8 against the exclusivity of Women's Lib, the attitude of communion against men, of self-righteousness and superiority which so many Women's Libbers exude. There is no denying that sexism and male chauvinism, the movement's catch-words, are real and that they form tough barriers and cause frustration, bitterness, and anger. But, if one accepts the argument that women are not unique, nor is their cause, this emphasis on man as the villain is not viable. Individual men discriminate against women, think them inferior, and treat them as enslaving and comforting mothers, dowdy house objects, sexual objects to be leered at, and subordinates to give orders to; but it is our society and culture which are most at fault. And women are as much to blame as men in perpetuating and acting out these roles.

There is nothing wrong with wanting to have a home and children, to   9
cook and clean, or to be attractive. It is the attitudes behind these roles, the feelings of inferiority, confinement, possessiveness, lack of identity and personal value that society has instilled which are oppressive. There is nothing wrong, as the most militant Libbers seem to suggest, in emphasizing, even exploiting, one's femaleness, unless it is because one has no other distinct and valuable qualities. But the roles one wishes to assume should be based on freedom of choice and exploration, not on the guidelines of a sexually rigid society nor on those of certain women who claim to be liberated and thus know everything.

Thus my main objection to the Women's Lib movement is that standing   10
alone it lacks context, perspective, and meaning. It must join with those groups which are working toward an alternative culture in which everyone can choose his or her roles without restriction. There is also something rather frightening about the more extreme members of the movement as it presently exists. They are just a bit too shrill, hysterical, and witch-like. I've no wish to join the complacent mass of Middle Americans like Julie Eisenhower, who thinks them "strident," but it seems likely that many of these women have included their neuroses in the movement to such an extent that it becomes so wound up with emotion as to be almost a parody. Injustice and frustration are emotional subjects, and cool rationalism is a much-used weapon of the defenders of the *status quo;* but the feeling remains that the more extreme fringes of the movement hold a neurotic type of woman, seizing on any hint of sexism to feed her feelings of inferiority. These feelings have no doubt been instilled by a sexist society, but I feel little identification with or compassion for those obsessed with the trivia of exploitation and repression (being called honey or Miss by an unenlightened chauvinist) at the expense of the movement's substance. The purpose of Women's Lib is surely to promote the idea of women as individuals instead of objects, but is the movement itself not stereotyping and segregating women? Is running around in frenzied bands sticking "this ad exploits women" on sexist advertising in any way preferable to joining other rebels and outcasts in a united effort to resist, or replace the forces behind that advertising? After all, the fight for woman's freedom can only be a part of the fight for human freedom as a whole or it becomes distorted and meaningless. Women are only people.

QUESTIONS AND EXERCISES

Vocabulary

1. Define or explain each of the following terms:

   Chicanos (2)   beleaguered (6)
   Trojan Horse (3)   chauvinism (8)
   mutant (3)

Rhetoric

2. Find examples of words or phrases that a college level dictionary labels as nonstandard.
3. Are there any phrases that could be called slanted language? What do they do for the tone of the essay?
4. Comment on the transitional and introductory devices in paragraphs 3, 5, and 8. What help are they in the organization of the essay?

Theme

5. Why is the author against the Women's Liberation movement?
6. Is there a constructive alternative offered?
7. What difficulties for argumentation are present when one agrees with an adversary's goals but rejects his methods?

Topics and Assignments for Composition

1. Defend Women's Liberation against the charges made in this essay.
2. Write an essay in which you defend the goals of a movement but attack the means used to gain them.
3. Write an essay in which you analyze the difficulties inherent in any attempt to defend a position which is primarily a value judgment. Suggest approaches that may gain acceptance of such a value judgment by one who is initially opposed.

McGeorge Bundy

The Corrosiveness of Prejudice

The most deep-seated and destructive of all the causes of the Negro problem is still the prejudice of the white man. This is not a new proposition—it was Myrdal's central finding a generation ago, and Styron has just reaffirmed it in a major work of art. The social scientist and the artist do not say that prejudice is the only source of our trouble, and neither do I: the catalog of such sources is very long, and provides much opportunity for fierce self-criticism to whites who do *not* have prejudice and indeed to Negroes themselves. Still it is the white man's fears and hates that must have first place. . . .

Prejudice is a subtle and insidious vice. It can consume those who think themselves immune to it. It can masquerade as kindness, sympathy, and even support. The cause of the American Negro has nourished the self-righteousness of generations of white men who never troubled to understand how destructive it can be to make the uplifting of others the means of one's own self-esteem.

Prejudice, of course, is not a novelty among Americans. We have managed to be narrow-minded about one another since 1607 in the South and 1620 in the North. The combination of fear and contempt has exercised its potent charms on one social group after another; it is no respecter of religion or race. But I think we make a mistake when we attempt to compare the white/black relation with those between the Yankees and the Irish, or the WASPs and the Jews, or any other of the dozens of conflict-laden relations that have marked our social history. This one is so much deeper and bigger that it has a different order of meaning.

Yet the answer has to be the same here as in every other case: that prejudice must be overcome. Men *are* brothers, with all that brotherhood implies in terms of rights and claims. And if I do not feel that way, then

Reprinted with permission of the Ford Foundation and *CTA Journal*.

I am guilty of an offense against the fundamental principles of the open society; in this sense there is no right to prejudice.

This first commandment is harder for some among us than for others. No man is the best judge of his own behavior in such matters, and reasonable men should be wary of hasty judgment on others. Yet the deep corrosiveness of white prejudice requires honest recognition, for as long as it persists it will be the most powerful single enemy of the very Negro progress which will in the end do most to end it.

A dialogue has developed between some Negroes and some whites in these last years on "black nationalism" as against "integration." I do not hold with those who suppose that it is for the Negro alone to discuss his own purposes: no group in our society can properly claim such immunity from outside comment.

Yet in offering these comments I recognize that Negroes have the same rights as the rest of us to make their own decisions about what they will do and with whom they will associate. That much said, it seems to me the plainest of facts that the destiny of the Negro in America is to be both Negro and American, and that as he makes progress he is likely to do what the rest of us do: he will take pride in his particular group at the same time that he insists on full membership in the society as a whole.

There can be paradox and even conflict in this double assertion, but the black man, like white groups before him, will make it just the same. How can he not? Can he really give up all that attaches him to his kind of people on his kind of terms? Who can deny the right of young black students to have a part of their lives kept black? And who can be surprised that many of them exercise that right?

Yet apartness will not be enough. The drive toward integration is at least equally authentic, and the individual who deliberately limits his associations to "his own kind"—for whatever reason—limits his life as an individual. Moreover the Negro, like everyone else, has a right—an obligation—to play his part in the society as a whole, and in that wider society the great opportunities can never be reserved for one kind only. Much too slowly still, but with steadily increasing speed, American Negroes will take their share of leadership in the general institutions of society. They will not thereby cease to be black, and not for a long time will any proud Negro forget the need to serve his people's cause along with his own individual interests. But none of us who are white should suppose that Negroes will really choose to stand aside from American life as a whole. They will insist, instead, on integration. There is only one bar and bench, only one system of government, only one national marketplace, and only one community of scholars. Our great general institutions

—unions and universities, businesses and bureaucracies—will have to be open to all.

Where Negroes take public power—as they will, more and more—they 10 will face the same tension between the interest of their own people and the interest of all that other leaders from minority groups have faced in their first moments of victory. The choices thus forced will inevitably cause some resentment on both sides. For a Negro to prefer a Negro, or to refuse to prefer him, can each cause trouble; it has been so in cases where the heritage of bitterness was less. Such public tension will parallel the internal tension that Negroes will experience at the intersecting edges of their need for apartness and their need for membership in the whole. There is no reason to believe that Negroes will be less fair than others as they come to make such choices.

The Problem Must Be Solved

The American Negro will have to have much more economic and 11 political power than he has today before the rest of us will have any reason to believe that he has more than his fair share. (As it has for the rest of us, equality for the Negro will mean a share of privilege as well as a share of power.)

Our society is going to solve this problem. The white man will outgrow 12 his prejudices and the Negro will strengthen both his sense of identity and his membership in the whole of society. This is the only possible final outcome. All the rest is temporary. It is a colossal task, of course, because the inheritance of neglect and injustice is enormous. But it will happen. No one can tell how long it will take, and it will happen faster in some parts of our land and life than in others.

Already there is less prejudice than there was; in spite of noisy rejec- 13 tions at each extreme, black men and white men are learning to know each other better and to work together more honestly than before. Abrasions at the edges of this process should not blind us to the fact that the national direction is right, though the pace is badly wrong. There is more self-respect and determination among Negroes and more awareness among whites than we would have found in earlier decades. . . .

Progress against prejudice will grow in speed as the next generation 14 moves on stage. I believe that before the present college generation begins to lose patience with its college-age children this problem will be more behind us than ahead. For I believe the young today, both white and black, are learning to regard as natural the equality which many of the rest of us see only as logical. What we see as a legal right they tend to see as a human reality. They have begun to live on the far side of prejudice, and they will decide.

It Will Require Great Effort

From the three conclusions I have outlined above I draw a fourth: that *15* the preachers of hate who seem so much the men of the moment are in fact merely spume on the wave of the past. They sometimes seem to dominate the television screens, and that is not altogether the fault of the broadcasters. Throughout our history we have given excessive attention to wild men, taking them too readily at their own valuation, and assuming too easily that the few who really do intend to live by hate are the real leaders. Yet no one who has dealt honestly with legitimately militant black leaders will confuse their properly angry words with any conspiracy to commit general violence, and no one who loves this country can believe that the ultimate instinct of its white majority is that of the backlash. Certainly we have been, at times, a violent people, but we have never made a religion of violence, or even a politics. The country of Abraham Lincoln is not going to become a no man's land for an apocalyptic contest between white and black fanatics. It is inevitably going to right these ancient wrongs, and this time by peaceful means.

The mode by which the inevitable comes to pass is effort. There is *16* nothing automatic about any part of the American Dream. Those of us who want peaceful progress toward equality will have to work for it. All Americans, black and white, North and South, must show new initiative, and accept new responsibility.

QUESTIONS AND EXERCISES

Vocabulary

1. Define or explain each of the following terms:

   insidious (2)   apocalyptic (15)
   paradox (8)

2. Identify or explain the allusion in each of the following terms:

   corrosiveness (title)   1607 in the South (3)
   Myrdal (1)   1620 in the North (3)
   Styron (1)   WASPS (3)

Rhetoric

3. The first sentence in paragraph 15 is a transitional one connecting the

first fourteen paragraphs to the last two. Comment on other transitional devices between other paragraphs.

4. Does Bundy use much figurative language? Find evidence to support your answer.
5. What is the tone of this essay? What, in general, is the relationship between tone and style?
6. How does Bundy handle the terms "Negro," "Afro-American," and "black"?

Theme

7. What new insights does Bundy offer for the problem of prejudice?
8. What do you think is the main purpose of this essay?
9. Even though there are no new plans or solutions offered, is there a value in having the same things said not by the rebels or blacks but by a member of the establishment?
10. Bundy says, "I believe that before the present college generation begins to lose patience with its college-age children this problem will be more behind us than ahead." Do you agree?

Topics and Assignments for Composition

1. In one sentence explain the corrosiveness of prejudice.
2. In one paragraph discuss one of the following:
   a. Comment on Bundy's analysis of current race relationships in the United States.
   b. Comment on his predictions for the future.
3. Write an essay discussing some aspect of prejudice.

John D. Rockefeller, III

The Youth Revolution: A Positive Response

I am very much aware of the purposes and ideals of the Society for the 1
Family of Man. And I am also very much aware of the most distinguished
persons who have received your award in the past. For these reasons, I
am deeply and humbly grateful for this honor.

There is of course a great deal of familial strife in the Family of Man. 2
One of the strengths of this Society is a healthy sense of realism in its concern for complex human problems. There is recognition that merely utter-
ing lofty ideals is not enough; one must confront the problems directly.

In this spirit, I would like to explore with you a problem that has special 3
relevance to the concept of the Family of Man. For lack of a better term,
it has been called the youth revolution. For some months past, I have
been embarked on the adventure of trying to understand the world of the
young. My trip was not fueled by LSD, but it had its psychedelic moments. I even attended a performance of "Hair" — and I enjoyed it, especially the music. In my encounters with student activists, I found that
I have a chronological problem, being somewhat past the age of 30. And
for some reason, they also tend to see me as a member of the Establishment.

Although I am sure the students went away thinking of me as more 4
square than groovy, I did feel that we communicated well. When you are
really interested in them, young people will not only talk — they will also
listen. Similarly, I met with a number of older persons and found the discussions with them equally productive.

When I started on my trip, I assumed that I would end up by directing 5
my remarks to the young. And I worried about this because I did not

want to seem paternalistic or to preach. I need not have worried because I quickly came to the conclusion that my thoughts on this subject would be best addressed to that large minority group of persons over the age of 40, my fellow members of the older generation.

Today's youth revolution puzzles many of us. We wonder if it is really 6 new and distinctively different. After all, there is nothing new about youthful idealism and youthful protest. Every generation has had its gap. But it seems to me unmistakably clear that we are experiencing something much more than the age-old rebelliousness of youth. The ferment of today is deep and intense. Although the activists are a minority of young people, it is a larger and more vocal minority than ever before. The youth revolt is a worldwide phenomenon, occurring not only in the United States, but in a dozen other countries such as France, Mexico, Japan and Czechoslovakia. There is a tenacity that was lacking in the past. Young people do not seem to be merely getting something out of their systems. Perhaps it is too early to tell, but I do not believe they will slip easily into the comforts of suburbia and the career, leaving behind their idealism and impulse for change.

How do we explain this phenomenon as it is occurring in the United 7 States? There are many theories and no entirely satisfactory answers. The young people of today were born after the depression and under a nuclear shadow. In an age of affluence and potential Armageddon, they are less concerned about material security and more concerned about basic human values. They feel that time is running out on the great problems—war, racial injustice, poverty. They dislike the impersonalism of large organizations and of rapid technological change. Because of the influence of the mass media and the freedoms of our society young people today learn faster and mature earlier. They become quickly aware—and deeply resentful—of the differences between what older people say and what they do.

In short, the very accomplishments of our generation—in technology, 8 communications, affluence—have served to focus the attention of the young on what we have failed to accomplish.

I want to confess frankly that when I started my inquiry, I was biased. 9 My instincts told me that very much of what young people are doing and saying today basically makes sense and is good. I found this to be even more true than I had thought.

At the same time I do not ignore the disturbing elements of the youth 10 revolution. There are the far-left extremists who say that present society must be destroyed. Their challenge must be met. There are the truly alienated, the loners and drops-outs. They must be helped. There is the use of dangerous drugs. This must be stopped. Too often, while fighting for their beliefs, young people disregard the basic human values and rights which they are espousing. They frequently lack compassion. They are often contemptuous of those who do not fully agree with them. While crying out to be heard, they will shout down a speaker.

Yes, there is much to irritate and disturb the older generation. But I submit that we have let ourselves be distracted by the colorful fringes to the point where we miss the central meaning of today's youthful protest. I am convinced that not only is there tremendous vitality here, but there is also great potential for good if we can only understand and respond positively. I believe this becomes evident if we examine how the youth revolution is manifested in three of the basic institutions of our society.   *11*

There is, first of all, the legal framework of society and its attendant issues of violence, social protest, justice, and respect for the law. A major factor distinguishing the current revolt from the past is the skill of young people in the tactics of social protest. They act in ways that would have been hard to imagine for the rebels of my generation. They have learned well from the civil rights movement of the 1950s and the Vietnam protest of the 1960s.   *12*

Yet, for the most part young people attempt to work within normal channels to present their grievances and establish a dialogue. They have tried to work through the political system, with their support of Senator McCarthy as the best example. It is they who have made the Peace Corps, VISTA, and the Teachers Corps more than slogans. Many young people are preparing for long-term efforts to change society. For example, the law students of today are concerned less about trusts and estates and corporate law and more about how just the laws are, how poor people and black people can get a better break before the law.   *13*

But even as the majority of young people work constructively for change, it remains a fact that severe provocation and even violence have increased as forms of social protest. The protestors are fired by their sense of moral righteousness. They feel they have learned from experience that it is necessary to be loud and demonstrative to get results. It is this behavior that compels attention and strikes fear for the very stability of American society.   *14*

The nature of our response is crucial, for it has everything to do with whether there will continue to be violence and whether violence will pay.   *15*

We must understand that social protest has an honorable history and has a rightful place in any enlightened society. We have only to remember that it was social protest that brought this nation into being.   *16*

At the same time we must recognize that respect for law and the maintenance of order are essential for the protection of everyone in our society. Young people — anyone — who break the law as a form of protest   *17* must be prepared to pay the penalty and hope for ultimate vindication.

But if we stop here we will have failed. The concept of law and order   18
is meaningless without justice. We must be ready to re-examine our assumptions—and our laws. To do so, we must open channels of communication. We must have dialogue. If we do not—if we think the only answer
is to suppress dissent—then the responsibility for violence hangs as
heavily on us as it does on those who protest.

Many persons feel today that another of our fundamental institutions—   19
the family—is in trouble. Much has been written and said about the permissive nature of the American family, which allegedly is responsible for
many of the ills of today's youth. Yet criticism of American parents'
"overpermissiveness" has been part of our society since the 17th century
Puritans. In his penetrating study of our country early in the 19th century, De Tocqueville comments about the domination of youth and their
lack of respect for their elders. Even the authoritarian Victorian age was
beset with youthful rebellion.

The family provides a framework and a set of guidelines for a child's   20
growth and development toward adulthood. It is the parents' responsibility to give the child love, freely and warmly shared, and discipline,
fairly but firmly administered, which in turn means time, attention and interest devoted to the child. In this way, family life plays a major role in
determining the stability of the child, and the depth and solidarity of his
values.

I cannot stress too strongly my belief that children learn much more   21
from what their parents do than from what they say. Many young people
state that while their parents talk about love, integrity, freedom, and fair
play, their actions are heavily oriented toward materialistic security, comfort and status. They repeatedly point out that they are not rejecting their
parents themselves, but rather what they see as the hypocrisy of their
parents' double-standard approach to important social values.

Again, it seems to me that the nature of our response is crucial. If I am   22
right that the ferment of youth is potentially of enormous benefit to society, then we might ask: Would we really rather have apathetic and
obedient copies of ourselves? More importantly, we might take the criti-
cisms of young people seriously and re-examine some of our basic assumptions. This of course is not easy. We are used to our children listening to us, not our listening to them. Everyone likes to think that he has
done reasonably well in life so that it comes as a shock to find our children
believing differently. Change can be very difficult and threatening, especially when the pressure comes from the young. The temptation is to
tune them out; it takes much more courage to listen.

When we turn to the third of our basic institutions—the church—we   23 encounter a deep irony. Young people today are committed to values of love, human dignity, individual rights, and trust in one's fellowman. These are precisely the values of our Judeo-Christian heritage. The church has been their proponent for centuries. And yet no institution in our society is today suffering more from the sheer indifference of the young. By and large, they have dismissed the church as archaic, ineffective, and even irrelevant.

One young man told me: "There's a genuine religious revival going on, but the church is missing out on it." Another said: "The church could fill a great need in our society, if it would focus less on the divine and more on how to apply Christian teaching to today's world." *24*

The problem again is that the young people perceive hypocrisy. They know the values the church upholds, but they see too little in the way of action and results. Religion to many of them is Sunday morning tedium instead of a guiding force and an inspiration. *25*

Once again, we must examine our own behavior, we of the older generation. The church is not some impersonal edifice, although all too often it seems that way. The church is what we have made it. Its dilemma is that while its mission should be the righting of wrongs and the active pursuit of the great Judeo-Christian values, we have instead made it for the most part a force for the status quo. *26*

By and large, we are much more conservative as elders of the church than we are as parents. The minister who would remain a minister all too often must please a conservative laity, those who support the church financially. The result is that the church loses some of the finest members of the younger generation. *27*

If we have made this situation, we can also change it. Any dramatic reversal seems improbable. But the young people will come back gradually if the church becomes a place for searching inquiry, for social action, if more of the clergy become involved in today's problems and if the laity support them—and become involved too. *28*

There are common threads that run through all of these basic institutions of our society. The problem is not in our legal system, or the family, or the church. The problem lies in ourselves as people. The crucial issue is not the revolt of youth but the nature of our response to it. *29*

Broadly speaking, it seems to me that there are three possible responses. One is backlash and suppression. We caught frightening glimpses of what this would be like in Chicago and Mexico City. If we choose this route, the only victors will be the small fringe of extremists who want to see our society destroyed. They are playing one of the oldest of political games, that of the provocateur. They *want* a backlash because they know that repression starts a vicious circle that inevitably leads to greater and *30* greater explosions. If we are foolish enough to fall into this trap, then we will deserve what happens to us.

A much more likely response is apathy or muted hostility. We are re-   *31* sentful over the ingratitude and brashness of the young. We think if we cover our eyes and stop our ears their noise and fervor will go away. They don't understand how really complex everything is, we say. Being older, we believe we are wiser. We know idealism is tempered by time and that realism sets in. Soon the young activists will pass the magic age of 30 and eventually they will be stepping into our vacant shoes. We secretly enjoy thinking about what a tough time they will have explaining to their children why they did not solve all the problems of the world.

This response, or lack of response, basically avoids the issue or yields   *32* grudgingly in a kind of tokenism. It is not working very well, and if I am right that the youth revolt of today is something much more than the normal rebelliousness of the young, then it will not work at all in the long run. We will find ourselves constantly pushed toward the brink of back-lash.

The greater tragedy will be the opportunity we will have lost. For we   *33* know all too well that time *is* running out on the great problems the world faces. It seems to me that we have a choice. By suppression or apathy, we can make the youth revolution into yet another problem—in which case the burden will become crushing. Or we can respond in positive ways so that the energy and idealism of youth can be a constructive force in helping to solve the world's great problems.

This is the third possible response. It is simply to be responsive—to   *34* trust our young people, to listen to them, to understand them, to let them know that we care deeply about them.

Instead of worrying about how to suppress the youth revolution we of   *35* the older generation should be worrying about how to sustain it. The student activists are in many ways the elite of our young people. They perform a service in shaking us out of our complacency. We badly need their ability and fervor in these troubled and difficult times.

In my judgment, the key to sustaining the energy and idealism of youth   *36* is more direct and effective action on the problems about which young people are concerned—the problems of our cities, of our environment, of racial injustice, of irrelevant and outmoded teachings, of overpopulation, of poverty, of war.

To achieve such action we of the older generation must re-examine our   *37* attitudes, our assumptions and our goals. We must take as seriously as do the young the great Judeo-Christian values of our heritage. We must be as dedicated as they in fighting injustices and improving our laws. We must have a sense of responsibility individually and collectively for resolving the massive problems of our society.

And secondly, we must revitalize our existing institutions whether they *38* be in education, government, religion, business or politics. They must be made more relevant to today's problems, have a greater sense of mission. At the same time, in support of the initiative of the young, new programs and institutions must be developed which can be effective in areas of pressing social need. Fresh approaches to meeting today's problems are essential.

A unique opportunity is before us to bring together our age and experi- *39* ence and money and organization with the energy and idealism and social consciousness of the young. Working together, almost anything is possible.

If we follow this course each of us will be involved personally and posi- *40* tively in the great drama of our times rather than feeling ourselves to be weary and impotent victims of imponderable forces. The antidote to despair is to be involved, to be imbued with the same spirit that fires the imagination and the efforts of the young. There is a VISTA slogan which captures this spirit: "If you're not part of the solution, you're part of the problem."

QUESTIONS AND EXERCISES

Vocabulary

1. Define or identify the following terms:

psychedelic (3)	tedium (25)
tenacity (6)	status quo (26)
alienated (10)	laity (27)
espousing (10)	provocateur (30)
dialogue (13)	tokenism (32)
vindication (17)	antidote (40)
hypocrisy (25)	impotent (40)

2. Identify or explain the allusions of the following terms:

"Hair" (3)	VISTA (13)
"Establishment" (3)	Puritans (19)
Armageddon (7)	de Tocqueville (19)

Rhetoric

3. Find examples of figurative language. What does figurative language or the lack of it do for tone?

4. Discuss the following metaphor: "We will find ourselves constantly

pushed toward the brink of backlash." Is this a mixed metaphor? Why?

5. What is the method of development used to organize most of the paragraphs?

6. Most of the paragraphs are quite short. What does this brevity do for the style of the essay?

Theme

7. What is the main point of the essay?

8. What special difficulties do you think Mr. Rockefeller has in establishing his thesis?

9. What words would you find pertinent to describe the ideological position of Mr. Rockefeller? In the speech he rejects the far left and the backlash far right. What does he advocate?

10. Do you think that his suggestions will solve the problems? That is, will dialogue, after all is said, have any efficacy in solving the race problem?

11. It is possible that the images of the protestors and rebels have become as stereotyped as the stereotypes of the establishment. Is it any more valid to call rebels idealistic than to call all over the age of 30 materialistic cynics?

Topics and Assignments for Composition

1. Summarize the problem that Mr. Rockefeller is analyzing.

2. In a paragraph present the highlights of his proposed solution.

3. Write an essay discussing the youth revolution with a different audience in mind from the one Mr. Rockefeller had in this one. Have in mind one of the following:

>Student rebels (white)
>Student rebels (black)
>A conservative political group
>A doctrinaire left-wing group
>A conservative religious group

Robert Kasanoff

Right to Lie?

There does, and ought to, exist a right to lie. Not in the self-contra- *1*
dictory or nonsensical sense that is sometimes said to be a right to revolution or, as Hobbes suggested, a right not to go voluntarily to one's own
execution. Rather, there is a right to lie in the plain and ordinary sense
that in appropriate circumstances the state, particularly the democratic
state, ought to encourage or at least protect lying.

For the purposes of the law of fraud, lying is generally held to be a *2*
deliberate falsification of an existing state of facts, but such a view is far
too narrow. Blackstone's definition is: "a variance between oath and belief," or, as applied to everyday conditions, a variance between statement
and belief. If there is a variance between what the speaker says and his
inner thoughts most of us will simply take him to be lying.

Each of us has been taught that lying is erosive to discourse, disruptive *3*
to sound personal relations, and anathema to the proper conduct of public
business. In practice, however, the right to lie is the ordinary man's political and religious asylum. It is the risk-venturer's source of credit. It is at
the heart of that central institution of political democracy, the secret
ballot. The practical function of the secrecy of the ballot is to permit the
labor-union member to be a closet Republican and the Union League
Club member to be a secret socialist.

That lying is useful and necessary to discourse and helpful to sound *4*
personal relations can hardly be doubted. To maintain a position in which
one does not believe in order to test one's own ideas and those of the
other participants in the dialectic is surely one of the oldest intellectual
devices. It is, of course, robbed of its vitality if one discloses that it is
only an exercise. Indeed, despite its rigor, legal argument enjoys a poor
reputation and is widely thought to be shallow precisely because of the
fact that the arguers are not arguing from conviction.

Reprinted from *The Center Magazine* by permission of the publisher.

In serious intellectual development there come times of change and   5
shift. Very frequently a formerly held idea crumbles long before its re-
placement has taken shape, and in order to form a new idea it is necessary
to maintain the old one, even though belief in it is lacking. Most men in
such circumstances are unable to declare themselves totally adrift, and
continue to profess the old idea until the new shore is clearly in sight.

A rule of *caveat emptor* in intellectual matters is a good one; and to   6
rely upon the fact that, as a condition of discourse, all participants are
telling the truth as they know it is risky and leads to much too great a
reliance on the signature and much too little attention to the signal.

In personal relationships, the love affair must surely and obviously be   7
the prime proof for the utility of lying. One sage has observed that the
three most commonly employed lies are: "It's in the mail," "Let's have
lunch," and "I love you."

Within the psychological structure, dreams offer an interesting example   8
of how lying is worked into man's nature. The truth of what's going on in
the unconscious would awaken us and it is therefore disguised and mis-
represented, i.e. lied about, by the use of symbols and disguises, thus
making sleep possible and life bearable.

All of this, it may be objected, is whimsical enough in its place, but   9
when it comes to dealing with the government it is only right and proper
that in every instance when called upon to state the facts to the government or to the voters, the citizen ought to do just that. However, it is perfectly clear that many publicly announced standards are unrealistic, and
that what the government wants is a conventional and customary answer
and not the truth. Learned Hand may be cited as an authority for this
contention. A college teacher of French and German named Schmidt
sought to become an American citizen and necessarily had to demonstrate that he was "of good moral character." He swore, however, that
"Now and then I engaged in an act of sexual intercourse with women.
These women have been single and divorced women. As to the frequency
of these acts, I can only state that they occurred now and then. My last
such act took place about half a year ago with an unmarried woman."
Learned Hand found that he "was in every way qualified as a citizen,
except that, in a moment of what may have been unnecessary frankness,
he verified an affidavit . . ." (containing the above-quoted passage).

Judge Hand's remarks may be read in two ways: the first is that the   10
exception to qualification to be a citizen is the man's sexual activity as
disclosed; the second and equally plausible reading is that the exception
to the man's qualification to be a citizen is that he was so unnecessarily
candid that he revealed himself to be lacking in a correct understanding

of democratic institutions, failing to distinguish when the government wants to hear the truth and when it wants to hear the conventional pieties.

The adjudication of pornography is another rich vein where perjury *11* serves to harmonize changing social standards. Works that are plainly pornographic are found to have redeeming social importance by a variety of academics. What in many, if not all, cases they really think is that it is not a bad thing for people to read dirty books. Pornography in the literal sense, the writing of a whore, was pulled into the light of day, by professors and others treating it as a document of social conditions, in the *Fanny Hill* case.

Many important questions of social policy are being resolved by the *12* courts against the interests of privacy, individual freedom, and individual integrity simply because it is not generally thought good rhetoric to invoke the right to lie. Centralized computer-bank storage of information on individuals is frequently attacked on the ground that it permits too much snooping into private matters. One of the strong arguments to be made against it is that it makes it harder for someone to lie. One is reminded of the story of the Englishman who bet his friend that he could, without leaving the club where they were both staying, cause the Archbishop of Canterbury to disappear. The following day the Archbishop disappeared in mysterious circumstances, and when the loser paid the bet he asked how the disappearance was accomplished. The reply was, "I sent him a telegram reading 'ALL IS DISCOVERED. FLEE! A FRIEND.'"

All of the notions of fairness and justice contained in paying one's debt *13* to society, overcoming the past, making a new life, and starting fresh rely in part, at least, on the ability to lie successfully. As surely as a democratic society must efficiently detect spies and punish criminals it must give to its citizens the right to hold unorthodox or unpopular views, to keep the delicate and intimate details of their private lives closed except as they choose to reveal them. It must protect the ability of citizens to live different lives during the course of one lifetime. In order to do so the state must recognize and protect the right to lie.

QUESTIONS AND EXERCISES

Vocabulary

1. Define or explain each of the following terms:

erosive (3)	pornography (11)
anathema (3)	perjury (11)
dialectic (4)	academics (11)

pieties (10)   unorthodox (13)
adjudication (11)

2. Identify or explain the allusions in the following terms:
   Hobbes (1)   *caveat emptor* (5)
   Blackstone (2)   Learned Hand (9)
   Union Club League (3)

Rhetoric

3. How is lying defined in this essay?
4. Analyze the structure of the first sentence in paragraph 4.
5. Identify and comment on the appropriateness of the metaphor at the end of paragraph 5.
6. Paragraph 6 is developed by analogy. Explain the similarities of the two items compared.
7. Kasanoff develops many of his points by using anecdotes, illustrations, and examples. What rhetorical advantage do these methods have?
8. Describe the tone of the essay. What elements contribute to this tone?

Theme

9. How does the author attempt to prove his thesis? What are the assumptions around which the evidence is formed?
10. Does the author make clear the instances when one should not lie?
11. On what occasions is lying now accepted?
12. What makes this essay unusual?
13. Is there any evidence of irony in the essay?

Topics and Assignments for Composition

1. Kasanoff sharpens his argument immediately. His first sentence allows no vacillation. Write five such argumentative opening sentences advocating some position.
2. Write a paragraph attacking or defending Kasanoff's position.
3. Write an essay defending an unpopular side of a controversial subject. Try to emulate Kasanoff's pattern.

Robert M. Hutchins

Limits of Dissent

Much of the talk about law and order goes on in a world of genteel   *1*
fantasy. That world is one in which all the channels of communication are
open to everybody. It is one in which all laws are ordinances of reason
directed to the common good, in which the law is easily discovered and
understood and justly and humanely enforced. It is one in which representative government represents all the people and in which the legislative process is truly deliberative. It is one in which all governmental
officers at every level are alert and attentive, eager to seek out injustice
and to rectify it. It is one in which the rights set forth in the First Amendment can be readily and effectively exercised by every citizen. It is one
in which political parties offer a significant choice of persons and programs and in which the voter can feel, when he is casting his ballot, that
he is having some slight effect on the course of history.

In such a world dissenters would have little reason for taking to the   *2*
streets and none at all for breaking the law.

In his recent book, *Concerning Dissent and Civil Disobedience,* Justice   *3*
Abe Fortas, a wise and experienced judge and one of the ablest lawyers
of his generation, accounts in the following way for the social revolution
of our time: "How wonderful it is that freedom's instruments—the rights
to speak, to publish, to protest, to assemble peaceably and to participate
in the electoral process—have so demonstrated their power and vitality!
These are our alternatives to violence. . . ."

Mr. Justice Fortas wrote these words with the report of the National   *4*
Advisory Commission on Civil Disorders before him. That report is a
detailed recital, in 581 pages of fine print, of the failure of freedom's instruments. There were evidently no effective alternatives to violence.
The Commission finds that the violence it describes resulted from the

Reprinted from *The Center Magazine* by permission of the publisher.

"frustrations of powerlessness," that is, from the inability of the Negro to move the society at a reasonable rate by means of the First Amendment and the electoral process. The present level of popular concern about minorities and the young would not have been reached if the dissenters had remained, as Mr. Justice Fortas says they must, within the law. The Civil Rights Act of 1968 would not have been passed without the push given Congress by Watts, Detroit, and Newark. The few changes that have been passed without the push given the country would not have taken place if the conduct of protesting students at such places as Berkeley and Columbia had always been perfectly legal.

The limits of dissent cannot be the limits set by law, because nobody   5
knows what the law is, and while the Supreme Court sits nobody will. What was illegal yesterday is lawful today, because the Court changes its composition or its mind. The only way to find out whether an ordinance, regulation, or statute is Constitutional is to violate it and see what happens. *Stare decisis* does not apply in Constitutional cases, and not a term passes in which the Court does not overrule previous holdings, some of them very recent. Where the object of the infraction is to test the constitutionality of the law in question, and no illegal violence is done by the defendants, they should not be held to have passed the limits of dissent.

Since it is in the best interests of the community to promote the exer-   6
cise of First Amendment rights, and not merely to tolerate it, the presumption must be against any official action, ordinance, regulation, or statute tending to restrict it. The prosecution should bear a heavy burden of proof that the defendants were not provoked by an excessive display of force, that they did not act in self-defense, and that what they did endangered human life.

There are laws and laws. Those designed for the convenience of the   7
public should not prevail against the First Amendment. The best analogy is the strike. What used to be regarded as a major crime is now a normal means of obtaining what the strikes regard as economic justice. The charge of "disruption" is often brought, and always fails. The highest paid laborers in the world, the airplane pilots, may tie up a vast country, simply to get more money, and there will not be a peep about law and order. People will complain, but even if they are stranded in a distant airport they will not say the strikers are subversive. Negroes or young people marching down the street because it is the only method of making a point about freedom and justice, on television or in the newspapers, are likely to be attacked by the police as a threat to the foundations of society.

We ought to try harder to make freedom's instruments work. At the   8
moment the cry for law and order has a hollow and hypocritical sound.

QUESTIONS AND EXERCISES

Vocabulary

1. Define or explain each of the following terms:
   genteel (1)   *stare decisis* (5)
   rectify (1)   hypocritical (8)

Rhetoric

2. Which paragraph is a transitional paragraph?
3. Explain the meaning of, "There are laws and laws." (7)
4. Describe the analogy in paragraph 7.

Theme

5. What is the function of paragraph 1?
6. What has been the value of dissent?
7. What argument does Hutchins use to support his claim that the limits of dissent cannot be set by law?
8. Hutchins mentions the First Amendment several times. Why is it relevant here?
9. What is Hutchins' opinion of the phrase, "law and order"?

Topics and Assignments for Composition

1. State Hutchins' thesis in one sentence.
2. In one paragraph analyze the meaning and logic of the First Amendment.
3. Write an essay on your concept of the limits of dissent.
4. Pick one of the other amendments and analyze it in the light of 20th century problems and conditions.

Philip Wylie

Generation of Zeros

Newspapers recently reported that a leading educator was advocating 1
the local abandonment of marks and grades in school and high school.
His cause was an extension to its absolute of what has been, for more
than a generation, the basic philosophy of our educators – education must
avoid traumatizing the pupil, must spare tot and teen-ager alike; any experience that might tend to hurt feelings gives a sense of inferiority.

Innumerable schools already move students on, without reference to 2
effort or capability. Such automatic promotion is presumed to prevent
the trauma that used to occur when a poor or lazy student was kept back
a grade. Yet, these educators still maintain that they are preparing youth
for adult life.

Grown-up life is, still, a life of ruthless competition where promotion 3
depends on the equivalent of marks. And these are accorded by business,
industry and the professions – publicly and without the slightest consideration of potential trauma. The man who makes it to a corporation presidency is *never* one who was sheltered from competition and spared the
spiritual blow of constant comparative rating with his associates. Nor
was he the man who went up the ladder with what would have been a
D-minus grade at every rung. In sum, education by the philosophy now
inbred into teaching is utterly unsuitable as preparation for real life in a
real world because it is, basically, *nothing education.*

Another and even darker thought is likely to follow – a growing realiza- 4
tion that much of all we consume, do, think and believe is, in one way or
another, *also* a "nothing." Wherever one looks for the evidence, the evidence can be found without too much difficulty.

The generation, now adult, that by and large wasn't taught how to read 5
is an example. Perforce, it has recourse to that illiterate form of so-called

communication, TV. *Nothing readers* are, in consequence, know-noth-ings, or near to it.

Again, in the current campus uproar, the anti-Vietnam demonstrations, the undergraduate opposition to the draft and so on, one perceives how nothing-teaching has created nothing thinkers. For, in all this passionate protest, there is virtually no intimation, even in the loud negatives, of what these young people are *for*. The simple truth of the intent of Com-munism is either unknown to them or beyond their understanding. ₆

They claim to want freedom — yet they libel the very men who are now dying to save their own. They want equality and even go into the South to face possible martyrdom in the effort to win Negro enfranchisement. Yet they reserve the right to judge who's equal *to them*. All persons who oppose their "right" to ordain what their professors shall teach, or their "right" to take drugs if they wish, or to parade, strike, riot, burn draft cards and stop troop trains, are held to be far from equal. They are squares. To be anti-square, without considering the problems, ideas, efforts and attainments of squares is, I think, to be a *nothing citizen* and near to a *nothing person*. ₇

Art generally runs ahead of human conditions. Art shares one property: creativity. And creativity implies what genuine art achieves — some new value, perception, insight or direction that, then, becomes the general possession. So art is prophetic; art that arises from denial cannot be called creative. But, even before the First World War, many painters had be-come enamoured of what will certainly be termed, if mankind lasts long enough to regain some sanity, *nothing art*. ₈

Today, of course, many major art forms plainly produce nihility. Yet leading critics, art judges, museum directors and gallery owners have created entire languages to accord the stuff their loftiest praise — nothing languages, of course, explaining why a blow-up of a tin-can label (Pop) is terrific, why mere optical illusion (Op) is worth a fortune per doodle and, lately, why a half-burned mattress, a dirty and paint-bloodied quilt or some heap of plastic chips glued together at random is also Art, as much as anything the Florentines ever did. ₉

In music, the solemn farce has become a similar religion. I remember when George Antheil's "Ballet Mécanique" had its Manhattan premiere. I was there. Besides an orchestra, the composition required synchronized pianos — 13, as I recall — some airplane engines with attached propellers, going full blast at one point, and doorbells, too. Many in the audience laughed at the concert. Some booed. But certain high-brow critics under-took, even then, to find a way of talking that would dignify that cacopho-nous travesty. Nowadays, of course, music that isn't — *nothing music* — has become a cult. ₁₀

Let's examine *people themselves* in the light of this lust for nothing- *11*
ness. The reduction of man's sense of his own worth is often set forth as
an effect of our civilization. Crowded living-space diminished his sense
of private dignity. Repetitive chores at assembly lines, desks or machine-
controls reduce him to a seemingly petty object. Instead of resisting these
pressures, man seems to be growing ever more willing, in America at
least, to abet his own shrinkage. Made to feel less, he wants to become
less still.

His version of the "new morality" shows how he goes about that sickly *12*
deed. The "new" morality relates to sex and followed the sexual revolution undertaken with the century's turn. It assumes that once truth and
decency replace the venerable doctrine of "evil," sex and its consumma-
tion would heighten the value men placed on themselves. The assumption
was logical since the old dogma demeaned and besmirched man's sense
of self.

But people are not using this new enlightenment as the "new moralists" *13*
intended. On the contrary, many tend to employ the newly revealed
"truth" as a means to achieving private pleasure, without reference to
any human value. Wives are swapped. Clubs for such trading and for
other mass sex "games" abound. The only rule is that the players must not
become concerned with any partner as a person. They must purge themselves of *humanity* ·

This is reflected, too, in contemporary dances, where each one of any *14*
pair stands apart from the other and performs his exercises, however
erotic, with no physical touch—depersonalized and wholly self-immersed.
Such behavior cannot be called "nothing sex"—but it is sex by persons
who make themselves into nothing much—nonpersons shorn of their very
identity.

Another evidence of the self-reduction of mankind is noninvolvement. *15*
The first instance to receive national attention concerned a horror in
Kew Gardens, New York. There, a woman was twice attacked by stab-
bing and spent an hour crawling in the lighted streets begging for help. No
one came to help. No one even called the police—not even anonymously.
Afterward, investigators found 38 people who had watched the event—
not one had made any effort to aid the woman who was being slowly
murdered.

From many American cities, innumerable examples of exactly that sort *16*
of behavior have since been cited. And, always, those who could have
aided but merely watched, explained that they "didn't want to become
involved." Since, to remain human, humanity must be and remain *involved* with itself, such persons are sub-human, nothing people.

There is an even more astonishing example of this national trend—a   *17*
growing group of theologians are developing a theology (sic!) on the
premise that "God is dead." Being professional religious men they hold,
or some do, anyhow, a second premise of the cunning sort typical of
dogmatists: that "God" could be "resurrected"—presumably by following *them.*

The fact that even a few "theologians" can take up such a monstrously   *18*
incongruous idea shows how hardput and how diminished *they* are in
their search for a gimmick that might explain and suit the nothingness of
the times. Now, *I* believe man's potential is nearly or truly infinite, supposing he gives himself time to approach that state—or infinite time to
achieve it. But if man's potential is even near infinite, it includes the
potential to destroy his species. Lately, we have acquired the means for
that—and found ourselves in a scary new situation. Are we, perhaps,
dedicating our lives and love and energy to nothingness, to diminishing
ourselves as an unconscious means of easing the blow, should something
slip and man's extirpation follow? The less we value ourselves, as individuals and as a species, the less would be the loss.

That *may* be the motivation of the nothing-seekers.   *19*

In any event, many Americans in high places are very disturbed about   *20*
the poor "condition" of the citizens. Of them, one group attributes the
phenomenon to materialism—a passion for acquiring things and gauging
importance by relative piles of possessions, tends to diminish everybody,
as human beings. But materialism has always been man's main folly and
other civilizations have been more dedicated to things, and more ruthless
in their collection, than we.

It is odd, furthermore, that another group of American "analysts" and   *21*
"thinkers" ascribe their worry about manifestly poor public attitudes to
the *lack* of things—to the failure of our society to spread enough of everything among everybody.

None of them seems to see, however, what I have tried to make evi-   *22*
dent, here. Prior societies of a materialist caste have, after all, valued real
things. People have not, till now, accepted ersatz products and substitute
acts save when the corresponding reality was unavailable. We seem,
rather, to be trying to dematerialize—to be non-involved—when there *is*
no alternative for involvement short of the abandonment of any claim to
being human.

And if that's right, or if any similar evasion of reality *as a defense* is   *23*
our motive, where will it leave us if the bombs never fall—if whatever
situation we are trying to prepare for and cope with, by a massive shrinking toward zero, doesn't occur?

A nation, I suggest, so tremendously engaged in becoming nothing   *24*
people—a nation motivated by unconscious fear—can hardly hope to
create a Great Society, the precondition of which is a great citizenry.

Such a nation can hardly hope at all, in fact: Hope—like faith—is   *25*
founded on something, however frail, and not on nothing.

Anybody who would study his fellow Americans to discern how much   *26*
of nothing enters into their being and doing will find my sketchy samples
sound, if merely a scratch on the surface. So, I think this hitherto unnoticed orientation-toward-nothing needs watching, needs further documentation and also deep contemplation. It may not be too late, though the
reason for so much self-swindle may be more complex and obscure than
I've suggested. Whatever it be, it needs seeking.

Perhaps, however, it *is* too late. Too late to restore something to our-   *27*
selves in order that we as a people may reverse the trend and become
something, eventually. A dubious prospect.

For the scrutiny needs what we are running short of—*Entity. Identity.*   *28*
Presence. And perhaps we already have become terrified of our own
selves—and don't know it.

Correct?   *29*

Or wouldn't you know?   *30*

QUESTIONS AND EXERCISES

Vocabulary

1. Define or explain each of the following terms:

traumatizing (1)	dogma (12)
perforce (5)	demeaned (12)
libel (7)	besmirched (12)
enfranchisement (7)	erotic (14)
enamoured (8)	*sic* (17)
nihility (9)	incongruous (18)
cacophonous (10)	extirpation (18)
travesty (10)	ersatz (22)
consummation (12)	

Rhetoric

2. Philip Wylie uses many figures of speech and rhetorical devices to
   develop his essay. The psychologists have a term "gestalt" that may
   be used to describe Wylie's style: no one figure or device makes the
   style what it is but the total effect seems to be stronger than the sum
   of all these devices and figures. Describe Wylie's style.

3. How many different words does Wylie use that have negative denotations and connotations?
4. Find examples of the following:
     alliteration: paragraph 1 = tot and teenager
     metaphor: paragraph 3 =
     irony: paragraph 9 =
     oxymoron: paragraph 10 =
     invective: paragraph 10 =
     alliteration: paragraph 11 =
     irony: paragraph 30 = (explain)
5. What gives this essay unity and coherence?
6. What effect does the length of paragraphs have on the style?
7. What general areas of contemporary life are analyzed as contributing to the development of "nothing people"?

Theme

8. Does Wylie adequately define his terms? Give some of his definitions.
9. What philosophy makes use of the term "nothingness"? Does Wylie mention it?
10. What evidence does Wylie offer for the state of affairs?
11. Challenge or defend Wylie's position in a specific area with which you are familiar: education, art, music, religion, sex.
12. What does Wylie mean in paragraph 28 by the words: "Entity," "Identity," "Presence"?
13. Do you think that "Grown-up life is, still, a life of ruthless competition . . ." in paragraph 3 is an accurate statement in view of price-fixing, fixed rates for phony competitive bidding, wage-controls, monopolies, etc.?
14. To what other areas do you think you could apply the term "nothing"? For example: nothing-heroes, nothing-books, nothing-sports.

Topics and Assignments for Composition

1. Describe Wylie's generalization about contemporary American life.
2. In a paragraph discuss Wylie's style; give illustrations and examples to support your thesis.
3. Write a similar essay about the shortcomings in our culture. Maintain the same tone throughout your essay.
4. Attack or defend some aspect of Wylie's evidence or reasoning.

Mervyn Cadwallader

Marriage as a Wretched Institution

Our society expects us all to get married. With only rare exceptions we   1
all do just that. Getting married is a rather complicated business. It involves mastering certain complex hustling and courtship games, the
rituals and the ceremonies that celebrate the act of marriage, and finally
the difficult requirements of domestic life with a husband or wife. It is an
enormously elaborate round of activity, much more so than finding a job,
and yet while many resolutely remain unemployed, few remain unmarried.

Now all this would not be particularly remarkable if there were no   2
question about the advantages, the joys, and the rewards of married life,
but most Americans, even young Americans, know or have heard that
marriage is a hazardous affair. Of course, for all the increase in divorce,
there are still young marriages that work, unions made by young men and
women intelligent or fortunate enough to find the kind of mates they want,
who know that they want children and how to love them when they come,
or who find the artful blend between giving and receiving. It is not these
marriages that concern us here, and that is not the trend in America today.
We are concerned with the increasing number of others who, with mixed
intentions and varied illusions, grope or fling themselves into married
disaster. They talk solemnly and sincerely about working to make their
marriage succeed, but they are very aware of the countless marriages they
have seen fail. But young people in particular do not seem to be able to
relate the awesome divorce statistics to the probability of failure of their
own marriage. And they rush into it, in increasing numbers, without any
clear idea of the reality that underlies the myth.

Parents, teachers, and concerned adults all counsel against premature   3
marriage. But they rarely speak the truth about marriage as it really is in

modern middle-class America. The truth as I see it is that contemporary marriage is a wretched institution. It spells the end of voluntary affection, of love freely given and joyously received. Beautiful romances are transmuted into dull marriages, and eventually the relationship becomes constricting, corrosive, grinding, and destructive. The beautiful love affair becomes a bitter contract.

The basic reason for this sad state of affairs is that marriage was not designed to bear the burdens now being asked of it by the urban American middle class. It is an institution that evolved over centuries to meet some very specific functional needs of a nonindustrial society. Romantic love was viewed as tragic, or merely irrelevant. Today it is the titillating prelude to domestic tragedy, or, perhaps more frequently, to domestic grotesqueries that are only pathetic.   4

Marriage was not designed as a mechanism for providing friendship, erotic experience, romantic love, personal fulfillment, continuous lay psychotherapy, or recreation. The Western European family was not designed to carry a lifelong load of highly emotional romantic freight. Given its present structure, it simply has to fail when asked to do so. The very idea of an irrevocable contract obligating the parties concerned to a lifetime of romantic effort is utterly absurd.   5

Other pressures of the present era have tended to overburden marriage with expectations it cannot fulfill. Industrialized, urbanized America is a society which has lost the sense of community. Our ties to our society, to the bustling multitudes that make up this dazzling kaleidoscope of contemporary America, are as formal and as superficial as they are numerous. We all search for community, and yet we know that the search is futile. Cut off from the support and satisfactions that flow from community, the confused and searching young American can do little but place all of his bets on creating a community in microcosm, his own marriage.   6

And so the ideal we struggle to reach in our love relationship is that of complete candor, total honesty. Out there all is phony, but within the romantic family there are to be no dishonest games, no hypocrisy, no misunderstanding. Here we have a painful paradox, for I submit that total exposure is probably always mutually destructive in the long run. What starts out as a tender coming together to share one's whole person with the beloved is transmuted by too much togetherness into attack and counterattack, doubt, disillusionment, and ambivalence. The moment the once-upon-a-time lover catches a glimpse of his own hatred, something precious and fragile is shattered. And soon another brave marriage will end.   7

The purposes of marriage have changed radically, yet we cling desperately to the outmoded structures of the past. Adult Americans behave as   8 though the more obvious the contradiction between the old and the new, the more sentimental and irrational should be their advice to young people who are going steady or are engaged. Our schools, both high schools and colleges, teach sentimental rubbish in their marriage and family courses. The texts make much of a posture of hard-nosed objectivity that is neither objective nor hard-nosed. The basic structure of Western marriage is never questioned, alternatives are not proposed or discussed. Instead, the prospective young bride and bridegroom are offered housekeeping advice and told to work hard at making their marriage succeed. The chapter on sex, complete with ugly diagrams of the male and female genitals, is probably wedged in between a chapter on budgets and life insurance. The message is that if your marriage fails, you have been weighed in the domestic balance and found wanting. Perhaps you did not master the fifth position for sexual intercourse, or maybe you brought cheap term life rather than a preferred policy with income protection and retirement benefits. If taught honestly, these courses would alert the teenager and young adult to the realities of matrimonial life in the United States and try to advise them on how to survive marriage if they insist on that hazardous venture.

But teen-agers and young adults do insist upon it in greater and greater   9
numbers with each passing year. And one of the reasons they do get married with such astonishing certainty is because they find themselves immersed in a culture that is preoccupied with and schizophrenic about sex. Advertising, entertainment, and fashion are all designed to produce and then to exploit sexual tension. Sexually aroused at an early age and asked to postpone marriage until they become adults, they have no recourse but to fill the intervening years with courtship rituals and games that are supposed to be sexy but sexless. Dating is expected to culminate in going steady, and that is the beginning of the end. The dating game hinges on an important exchange. The male wants sexual intimacy, and the female wants social commitment. The game involves bartering sex for security amid the sweet and heady agitations of a romantic entanglement. Once the game reaches the going-steady stage, marriage is virtually inevitable. The teen-ager finds himself driven into a corner, and the one way to legitimize his sex play and assuage the guilt is to plan marriage.

Another reason for the upsurge in young marriages is the real cultural   10
break between teen-agers and adults in our society. This is a recent phenomenon. In my generation there was no teen culture. Adolescents wanted to become adults as soon as possible. The teen-age years were a time of impatient waiting, as teen-age boys tried to dress and act like little men. Adolescents sang the adults' songs ("South of the Border,"

"The Music Goes Round and Round," "Mairzy Doats"—notice I didn't say anything about the quality of the music), saw their movies, listened to their radios, and waited confidently to be allowed in. We had no money, and so there was no teen-age market. There was nothing to do then but get it over with. The boundary line was sharp, and you crossed it when you took your first serious job, when you passed the employment test.

Now there is a very definite adolescent culture, which is in many ways *11* hostile to the dreary culture of the adult world. In its most extreme form ir borrows from the beats and turns the middle-class value system inside out. The hip teen-ager on Macdougal Street or Telegraph Avenue can buy a costume and go to a freak show. It's fun to be an Indian, a prankster, a beat, or a swinging troubadour. He can get stoned. That particular trip leads to instant mysticism.

Even in less extreme forms, teen culture is weighted against the adult *12* world of responsibility. I recently asked a roomful of eighteen-year-olds to tell me what an adult is. Their deliberate answer, after hours of discussion, was that an adult is someone who no longer plays, who is no longer playful. Is Bob Dylan an adult? No, never! Of course they did not want to remain children, or teens, or adolescents; but they did want to remain youthful, playful, free of squares, and free of responsibility. The teen-ager wants to be old enough to drive, drink, screw, and travel. He does not want to get pushed into square maturity. He wants to drag the main, be a surf bum, a ski bum, or dream of being a bum. He doesn't want to go to Vietnam, or to IBM, or to buy a split-level house in Knotty Pines Estates.

This swing away from responsibility quite predictably produces friction *13* between the adolescent and his parents. The clash of cultures is likely to drive the adolescent from the home, to persuade him to leave the dead world of his parents and strike out on his own. And here we find the central paradox of young marriages. For the only way the young person can escape from his parents is to assume many of the responsibilities that he so reviles in the lifestyle of his parents. He needs a job and an apartment. And he needs some kind of emotional substitute, some means of filling the emotional vacuum that leaving home has caused. And so he goes steady, and sooner rather than later, gets married to a girl with similar inclinations.

When he does this, he crosses the dividing line between the cultures. *14* Though he seldom realizes it at the time, he has taken the first step to adulthood. Our society does not have a conventional "rite of passage." In Africa the Masai adolescent takes a lion test. He becomes an adult the first time he kills a lion with a spear. Our adolescents take the domesticity test. When they get married they have to come to terms with the system in one way or another. Some brave individuals continue to fight it. But most simply capitulate.

The cool adolescent finishing school or starting college has a skeptical *15* view of virtually every institutional sector of his society. He knows that government is corrupt, the military dehumanizing, the corporations rapacious, the churches organized hypocrisy, and the schools dishonest. But the one area that seems to be exempt from his cynicism is romantic love and marriage. When I talk to teen-agers about marriage, that cool skepticism turns to sentimental dreams right out of *Ladies' Home Journal* or the hard-hitting pages of *Readers' Digest*. They all mouth the same vapid platitudes about finding happiness through sharing and personal fulfillment through giving (each is to give 51 percent). They have all heard about divorce, and most of them have been touched by it in some way or another. Yet they insist that their marriage will be different.

So, clutching their illusions, young girls with ecstatic screams of joy *16* lead their awkward brooding boys through the portals of the church into the land of the Mustang, Apartment 24, Macy's, Sears, and the ubiquitous drive-in. They have become members in good standing of the adult world.

The end of most of these sentimental marriages is quite predictable. *17* They progress, in most cases, to varying stages of marital ennui, depending on the ability of the couple to adjust to reality; most common are (1) a lackluster standoff, (2) a bitter business carried on for the children, church, or neighbors, or (3) separation and divorce, followed by another search to find the right person.

Divorce rates have been rising in all Western countries. In many coun- *18* tries the rates are rising even faster than in the United States. In 1910 the divorce rate for the United States was 87 per 1000 marriages. In 1965 the rate had risen to an estimated figure of well over 300 per 1000 in many parts of the country. At the present time some 40 percent of all brides are between the ages of fifteen and eighteen; half of these marriages break up within five years. As our population becomes younger and the age of marriage continues to drop, the divorce rate will rise to significantly higher levels.

What do we do, what can we do, about this wretched and disappointing *19* institution? In terms of the immediate generation, the answer probably is, not much. Even when subjected to the enormous strains I have described, the habits, customs, traditions, and taboos that make up our courtship and marriage cycle are uncommonly resistant to change. Here and there creative and courageous individuals can and do work out their own unique solutions to the problem of marriage. Most of us simply suffer without understanding and thrash around blindly in an attempt to reduce the acute pain of a romance gone sour. In times, all of these individual actions will show up as a trend away from the old and toward the new, and the bulk of sluggish moderates in the population will slowly come to accept this trend as part of social evolution. Clearly, in middle-class America, the trend is ever toward more romantic courtship and marriage, earlier pre-marital sexual intercourse, earlier first marriages, more extramarital affairs, earlier first divorces, more frequent divorces and remarriages. The trend is away from stable lifelong monogamous relationships toward some form of polygamous male-female relationship. Perhaps we should identify it as serial or consecutive polygamy, simply because Americans in significant numbers are going to have more than one husband or more than one wife. Attitudes and laws that make multiple marriages (in sequence, of course) difficult for the romantic and sentimental among us are archaic obstacles that one learns to circumvent with the aid of weary judges and clever attorneys.

Now, the absurdity of much of this lies in the fact that we pretend that *20* marriages of short duration must be contracted for life. Why not permit a flexible contract perhaps for one to two or more years, with periodic options to renew? If a couple grew disenchanted with their life together, they would not feel trapped for life. They would not have to carry about the stigma of marital failure, like the mark of Cain on their foreheads. Instead of a declaration of war, they could simply let their contract lapse, and while still friendly, be free to continue their romantic quest. Sexualized romanticism is now so fundamental to American life—and is bound to become even more so—that marriage will simply have to accommodate itself to it in one way or another. For a great proportion of us it already has.

What of the children in a society that is moving inexorably toward con- *21* secutive plural marriages? Under present arrangements in which marriages are ostensibly lifetime contracts and then are dissolved through hypocritical collusions or messy battles in court, the children do suffer. Marriage and divorce turn lovers into enemies, and the child is left to thread his way through the emotional wreckage of his parents' lives. Financial support of the children, mere subsistence, is not really a problem in a society as affluent as ours. Enduring emotional support of children by loving, healthy, and friendly adults is a serious problem in America, and it is a desperately urgent problem in many families where divorce is unthinkable. If the bitter and poisonous denouement of divorce could be avoided by a frank acceptance of short-term marriages, both adults and children would benefit. Any time husbands and wives and ex-husbands and ex-wives treat each other decently, generously, and respectfully, their children will benefit.

The braver and more critical among our teen-agers and youthful adults   22
will still ask, But if the institution is so bad, why get married at all? This
is a tough one to deal with. The social pressures pushing any couple who
live together into marriage are difficult to ignore even by the most resolute
rebel. It can be done, and many should be encouraged to carry out their
own creative experiments in living together in a relationship that is wholly
voluntary. If the demands of society to conform seem overwhelming, the
couple should know that simply to be defined by others as married will
elicit married-like behavior in themselves, and that is precisely what they
want to avoid.

How do you marry and yet live like gentle lovers, or at least like friendly   23
roommates? Quite frankly, I do not know the answer to that question.

QUESTIONS AND EXERCISES

Vocabulary

1. Define or explain each of the following terms:

   hustling (1)   vapid (15)
   awesome (2)   platitudes (15)
   wretched (3)   ubiquitous (16)
   titillating (4)   ennui (17)
   grotesqueries (4)   taboos (19)
   pathetic (4)   monogamous (19)
   kaleidoscope (6)   polygamy (19)
   microcosm (6)   stigma (20)
   paradox (7)   inexorably (21)
   ambivalence (7)   collusions (21)
   schizophrenic (9)   affluent (21)
   reviles (13)   denouement (21)
   rapacious (15)   elicit (22)
   cynicism (15)

2. Explain or identify the allusion implied in each of the following terms:

   Macdougal Street (11)   "rite of passage" (14)
   Telegraph Avenue (11)   Masai (14)
   Bob Dylan (12)   "land of the Mustang" (16)
   surf bum (12)   mark of Cain (20)
   ski bum (12)

3. Discuss the connotations of the following terms used by the author:

   awesome   dreary culture of the adult world
   wretched   hip teen-ager
   love affair   stoned

romantic love	instant mysticism
phony	split-level house in Knotty Pines Estates
sentimental rubbish	cool adolescent

Rhetoric

4. Notice the author's deliberate attempts to provide links in form and meaning between paragraphs.

And so . . . (7)	Even in less . . . (12)
But . . . (9)	This swing . . . (13)
Another reason . . . (10)	When he does this . . . (14)
Now there . . . (11)	

   Find other examples.

5. Find examples of clichés. Distinguish between clichés used seriously and clichés used for ironic effect.
6. Explain the paradox in paragraph 13.
7. Comment on the author's point of view in the statement, "He knows that government is corrupt, the military dehumanizing, the corporations rapacious, the churches organized hypocrisy, and the schools dishonest." (15) What tone is he trying to achieve?
8. What is the irony in "the hard-hitting pages of *Readers' Digest*" (15)?
9. Is there a change in the point of view and tone in the paragraph? If so, what evidence is there of the change?
10. What kind of definition is found in paragraph 12?

Theme

11. Comment on the goals of teen-agers as explained in paragraph 12.
12. Discuss the cultural gap between adults and teenagers. Put the current situation into historical perspective. Do you agree with Cadwallader's facts? With his interpretations? With his evaluations?
13. Does Cadwallader offer at least a partial solution? Discuss it. Does it fit the problems he presents?
14. What does the last paragraph tell about the author?

Topics and Assignments for Composition

1. In one sentence describe the myth about marriage. In another sentence describe the reality.
2. In a paragraph analyze one of the following concerns that are either assumed or implied in the essay:
   validity of generalizations
   nature of generation gap
   sociological accuracy of analysis

omitted items for purposes of simplification

ambivalence of point of view

3. Write a theme in which you describe courses in "sex education" or "marriage and the family" and comment on the validity of Cadwallader's charge against them.

4. Pick an institution in American life and write an essay about it. State your thesis in a manner similar to Cadwallader's.

Ashley Montagu

The Natural Superiority of Women

Oh, no! I can hear it said, *not* superior. Equal, partners, complementary, different, but *not* superior. I can even foresee that men will mostly smile, while women, alarmed, will rise to the defense of men — women always have, and always will. I hope that what I shall have to say in this article will make them even more willing to do so, for men need their help more than they as yet, mostly, consciously realize.

1

Women superior to men? This is a new idea. There have been people who have cogently, but apparently not convincingly, argued that women were as good as men, but I do not recall anyone who has publicly provided the evidence or even argued that women were better than or superior to men. How, indeed, could one argue such a case in the face of all the evidence to the contrary? Is it not a fact that by far the largest number of geniuses, great painters, poets, philosophers, scientists, etc., etc., have been men, and that women have made, by comparison, a very poor showing? Clearly the superiority is with men. Where are the Leonardos, the Michelangelos, the Shakespeares, the Donnes, the Galileos, the Whiteheads, the Kants, the Bachs, *et al.,* of the feminine sex? In fields in which women have excelled, in poetry and the novel, how many poets and novelists of the really first rank have there been? Haven't well-bred young women been educated for centuries in music? And how many among them have been great composers or instrumentalists? Composers — none of the first rank. Instrumentalists — well, in the recent period there have been such accomplished artists as Myra Hess and Wanda Landowska. Possibly there is a clue here to the answer to the question asked. May it not be that women are just about to emerge from the period of subjection during which they were the "niggers" of the masculine world?

2

The Royal Society of London has at last opened its doors and admitted

3

women to the highest honor which it is in the power of the English scientific world to bestow—the Fellowship of the Royal Society. I well remember that when I was a youth—less than a quarter of a century ago—it was considered inconceivable that any woman would ever have brains enough to attain great distinction in science. Mme. Curie was an exception. But the half dozen women Fellows of the Royal Society in England are not. Nor is Lise Meitner. And Mme. Curie no longer remains the only woman to share in the Nobel Prize award for science. There is Marie Curie's daughter, Irene Joliot-Curie, and there is Gerty Cori (1947) for physiology and medicine. Nobel prizes in literature have gone to Selma Lagerlof, Grazia Deledda, Sigrid Undset, Pearl Buck, and Gabriela Mistral. As an artist Mary Cassatt (1845–1926) was every bit as good as her great French friends Degas and Manet considered her to be, but it has taken the rest of the world another fifty years grudgingly to admit it. Among contemporaries Georgia O'Keeffe can hold her own with the best.

It is not, however, going to be any part of this article to show that women are about to emerge as superior scientists, musicians, painters, or the like. I believe that in these fields they may emerge as equally good, and possibly not in as large numbers as men, largely because the motivations and aspirations of most women will continue to be directed elsewhere. But what must be pointed out is that women are, in fact, just beginning to emerge from the period of subjection when they were treated in a manner not unlike that which is still meted out to the Negro in the Western world. The women of the nineteenth century were the "niggers" of the male-dominated world. All the traits that are mythically attributed to the Negro at the present time were for many generations saddled upon women. Women had smaller brains than men and less intelligence, they were more emotional and unstable, in a crisis you could always rely upon them to swoon or become otherwise helpless, they were weak and sickly creatures, they had little judgment and less sense, could not be relied upon to handle money, and as for the world outside, there they could be employed only at the most menial and routine tasks. 4

The biggest dent in this series of myths was made by World War I, when women were for the first time called upon to replace men in occupations which were formerly the exclusive preserve of men. They became bus drivers, conductors, factory workers, farm workers, laborers, supervisors, executive officers, and a great many other things at which many had believed they could never work. At first it was said that they didn't do as well as men, then it was grudgingly admitted that they weren't so bad, and by the time the war was over many employers were reluctant to exchange their women employees for men! But the truth was out— women could do as well as men in most of the fields which had been con- 5 sidered forever closed to them because of their alleged natural incapacities, and in many fields, particularly where delicate precision work was involved, they had proved themselves superior to men. From 1918 to 1939 the period for women was one essentially of consolidation of gains, so that by the time that World War II broke out there was no hesitation on the part of anyone in calling upon women to serve in the civilian roles of men and in many cases also in the armed services.

But women have a long way to go before they reach full emancipation — emancipation from the myths from which they themselves suffer. It is, of course, untrue that women have smaller brains than men. The fact is that in proportion to body weight they have larger brains then men; but this fact is in itself of no importance because within the limits of normal variation of brain size and weight there exists no relation between these factors and intelligence. Women have been conditioned to believe that they are inferior to men, and they have assumed that what everyone believes is a fact of nature; and as men occupy the superior positions in almost all societies, this superiority is taken to be a natural one. "Woman's place is in the home" and man's place is in the counting house and on the board of directors. "Women should not meddle in men's affairs." And yet the world does move. Some women have become Members of Parliament and even attained Cabinet rank. In the United States they have even gotten as far as the Senate. They have participated in peace conferences, but it is still inconceivable to most persons that there should ever be a woman Prime Minister or President. And yet that day, too, will come. *Eppure si muove* [nevertheless it moves]! 6

Woman has successfully passed through the abolition period, the abolition of her thralldom to man; she has now to pass successfully through the period of emancipation, the freeing of herself from the myth of inferiority, and the realization of her potentialities to the fullest. 7

And now for the evidence which proves the superiority of woman to man. But first, one word in explanation of the use of the word "superiority." The word is used in its common sense as being of better quality than, or of higher nature or character. Let us begin at the very beginning. What about the structure of the sexes? Does one show any superiority over the other? The answer is a resounding "Yes!" And I should like this "Yes" to resound all over the world, for no one has made anything of this key fact which lies at the base of all the differences between the sexes and the superiority of the female to the male. I refer to the chromosomal structure of the sexes. The chromosomes, those small cellular bodies which contain the hereditary particles, the genes, which so substantially influence one's development and fate as an organism, provide us with our basic facts. 8

In the sex cells there are twenty-four chromosomes, but only one of   9
these is a sex chromosome. There are two kinds of sex chromosomes,
X and Y. Half the sperm cells carry X and half carry Y chromosomes.
All the female ova are made up of X-chromosomes. When an X-bearing
sperm fertilizes an ovum the offspring is always female. When a Y-bear-
ing chromosome fertilizes an ovum the offspring is always male. And this
is what makes the difference between the sexes. So what? Well, the sad
fact is that the Y-chromosome is but an iota, the merest bit of a remnant
of an X-chromosome; it is a crippled X-chromosome. The X-chromosomes are fully developed structures; the Y-chromosome is the merest
comma. It is as if in the evolution of sex a particle one day broke away
from an X-chromosome, and thereafter in relation to X-chromosomes
could produce only an incomplete female — the creature we now call the
male! It is to this original chromosomal deficiency that all the various
troubles to which the male falls heir can be traced.

In the first place the chromosomal deficiency of the male determines   10
his incapacity to have babies. This has always been a sore point with men,
though consciously they would be the last to admit it, although in some
primitive societies, as among the Australian aborigines, it is the male who
conceives a child by dreaming it, and then telling his wife. In this way a
child is eventually born to them, the wife being merely the incubator who
hatches the egg placed there through the grace of her husband.

The fact that men cannot have babies and suckle them nor remain in   11
association with their children as closely as the wife has an enormous
effect upon their subsequent psychological development. Omitting altogether from consideration the psychologic influences exercised by the
differences in the hormonal secretions of the sexes, one can safely say
that the mother-child relationship confers enormous benefits upon the
mother which are not nearly so substantially operative in the necessary
absence of such a relationship between father and child. The maternaliz-
ing influences of being a mother in addition to the fact of being a woman
has from the very beginning of the human species — about a million years
ago — made the female the more humane of the sexes. The love of a
mother for her child is the basic patent and the model for *all* human relationships. Indeed, to the extent to which men approximate in their relationships with their fellow men to the love of the mother for her child, to
that extent do they move more closely to the attainment of perfect human
relations. The mother-child relationship is a dependent-interdependent
one. The interstimulation between mother and child is something which
the father misses, and to that extent suffers from the want of. In short, the
female in the mother-child relationship has the advantage of having to be

more considerate, more self-sacrificing, more cooperative, and more altruistic than usually falls to the lot of the male.

The female thus acquires, in addition to whatever natural biological   *12*
advantages she starts with, a competence in social understanding which
is usually denied the male. This, I take it, is one of the reasons why
women are usually so much more able to perceive the nuances and pick
up the subliminal signs in human behavior which almost invariably pass
men by. It was, I believe, George Jean Nathan who called woman's intuition merely man's transparency. With all due deference to Mr. Nathan
and sympathy for his lot as a mere male, I would suggest that man's
opacity would be nearer the mark. It is because women have had to be so
unselfish and forbearing and self-sacrificing and maternal that they possess a deeper understanding than men of what it is to be human. What is
so frequently termed feminine indecision, the inability of women to make
up their minds, is in fact an inverse reflection of the trigger-thinking of
men. Every salesgirl prefers the male customer because women take time
to think about what they are buying, and the male usually hasn't the sense
enough to do so. Women don't think in terms of "Yes" or "No." Life
isn't as simple as all that — except to males. Men tend to think in terms of
the all-or-none principle, in terms of black and white.

By comparison with the deep involvement of women in living, men   *13*
appear to be only superficially so. Compare the love of a male for a female
with the love of the female for the male. It is the difference between a
rivulet and a great deep ocean. Women love the human race; men are, on
the whole, hostile to it. Men act as if they haven't been adequately loved,
as if they had been frustrated and rendered hostile, and becoming aggressive they say that aggressiveness is natural and women are inferior in this
respect because they tend to be gentle and unaggressive! But it is precisely in this capacity to love and unaggressiveness that the superiority
of women to men is demonstrated, for whether it be natural to be loving
and cooperative or not, so far as the human species is concerned, its
evolutionary destiny, its very survival is more closely tied to this capacity
for love and cooperation than with any other. So that unless men learn
from women how to be more loving and cooperative they will go on
making the kind of mess of the world which they have so effectively
achieved thus far.

And this is, of course, where women can realize their power for good   *14*
in the world, and make their greatest gains. *It is the function of women to
teach men how to be human.* Women must not permit themselves to be
deviated from this function by those who tell them that their place is in
the home in subservient relation to men. It is, indeed, in the home that

the foundations of the kind of world in which we live are laid, and in this sense it will always remain true that the hand that rocks the cradle is the hand that rules the world. And it is in this sense that women must assume the job of making men who will know how to make a world fit for human beings to live in. The greatest single step forward in this direction will be made when women consciously assume this task—the task of teaching their children to be like themselves, loving and cooperative.

As for geniuses, I think that almost everyone will agree that there have   *15* been more geniuses for being human among women than there have among men. This, after all, is the true genius of women, and it is because we have not valued the qualities for being human anywhere nearly as highly as we have valued those for accomplishment in the arts and sciences that we have out-of-focusedly almost forgotten them. Surely, the most valuable quality in any human being is his capacity for being loving and cooperative. We have been placing our emphases on the wrong values —it is time we recognized what every man and every woman at the very least subconsciously knows—the value of being loving, and the value of those who can teach this better than anyone else.

Physically and psychically women are by far the superiors of men. The   *16* old chestnut about women being more emotional than men has been forever destroyed by the facts of two great wars. Women under blockade, heavy bombardment, concentration camp confinement, and similar rigors withstand them vastly more successfully than men. The psychiatric casualties of civilian populations under such conditions are mostly masculine, and there are more men in our mental hospitals than there are women. The steady hand at the helm is the hand that has had the practice at rocking the cradle. Because of their greater size and weight men are physically more powerful than women—which is not the same thing as saying that they are stronger. A man of the same size and weight as a woman of comparable background and occupational status would probably not be any more powerful than a woman. As far as constitutional strength is concerned women are stronger than men. Many diseases from which men suffer can be shown to be largely influenced by their relation to the male Y-chromosome. From fertilization on more males die than females. Deaths from almost all causes are more frequent in males at all ages. Though women are more frequently ill than men, they recover from illness more easily and more frequently than men.

Women, in short, are fundamentally more resistant than men. With the   *17* exception of the organ systems subserving the functions of reproduction women suffer much less frequently than men from the serious disorders which affect mankind. With the exception of India women everywhere live longer than men. For example, the expectation of life of the female child of white parentage in the United States at the present time is over seventy-one years, whereas for the male it is only sixty-five and a half years. Women are both biologically stronger and emotionally better shock absorbers than men. The myth of masculine superiority once played such havoc with the facts that in the nineteenth century it was frequently denied by psychiatrists that the superior male could ever suffer from hysteria. Today it is fairly well known that males suffer from hysteria and hysteriform conditions with a preponderance over the female of seven to one! Epilepsy is much more frequent in males, and stuttering has an incidence of eight males to one female.

At least four disorders are now definitely known to be due to genes carried in the Y-chromosomes, and hence are disorders which can appear only in males. They are barklike skin (ichthyosis hystix gravior), dense hairy growth on the ears (hypertrichosis), nonpainful hard lesions of the hands and feet (keratoma dissapatum), and a form of webbing of the toes. It is, however, probable that the disadvantages accruing to the male are not so much due to what is in the Y-chromosome as to what is wanting in it. This is well shown in such serious disorders as hemophilia or bleeder's disease. Hemophilia is inherited as a single sex-linked recessive gene. The gene, or hereditary particle, determining hemophilia is linked to the X-chromosome. When, then, an X-chromosome which carries the hemophilia gene is transmitted to a female it is highly improbable that it will encounter another X-chromosome carrying such a gene; hence, while not impossible, hemophilia has never been described in a female. Females are the most usual transmitters of the hemophilia gene, but it is only the males who are affected, and they are affected because they don't have any properties in their Y-chromosome capable of suppressing the action of the hemophilia gene. The mechanism of and the explanation for (red-green) color blindness is the same. About 8 per cent of all white males are color blind, but only half of one per cent of females are so affected.

Need one go on? Here, in fact, we have the explanation of the greater constitutional strength of the female as compared with the male. This may not be, and probably is not, the complete explanation of the physical inferiorities of the male as compared with the female, but it is certainly physiologically the most demonstrable and least questionable one. To the unbiased student of the facts there can no longer remain any doubt of the constitutional superiority of the female. I hope that I have removed any remaining doubts about her psychological superiority where psychological superiority most counts, namely, in a human being's capacity for loving other human beings.

I think we have overemphasized the value of intellectual qualities and grossly underemphasized the value of the qualities of humanity which women possess to such a high degree. I hope I shall not be taken for an anti-intellectual when I say that intellect without humanity is not good enough, and that what the world is suffering from at the present time is not so much an overabundance of intellect as an insufficiency of humanity. Consider men like Lenin, Stalin, and Hitler. These are the extreme cases. What these men lacked was the capacity to love. What they possessed in so eminent a degree was the capacity to hate. It is not for nothing that the Bolsheviks attempted to abolish the family and masculinize women, while the Nazis made informers of children against their parents and put the state so much before the family that it became a behemoth which has well-nigh destroyed everyone who was victimized by it.

What the world stands so much in need of at the present time, and what   21
it will continue to need if it is to endure and increase in happiness, is more of the maternal spirit and less of the masculine. We need more persons who will love and less who will hate, and we need to understand how we can produce them; for if we don't try to understand how we may do so we shall continue to flounder in the morass of misunderstanding which frustrated love creates. For frustrated love, the frustration of the tendencies to love with which the infant is born, constitutes hostility. Hatred is love frustrated. This is what too many men suffer from and an insufficient number of women recognize, or at least too many women behave as if they didn't recognize it. What most women have learned to recognize is that the much-bruited superiority of the male isn't all that it's cracked up to be. The male doesn't seem to be as wise and as steady as they were taught to believe. But there appears to be a conspiracy of silence on this subject. Perhaps women feel that men ought to be maintained in the illusion of their superiority because it might not be good for them or the world to learn the truth. In this sense this article, perhaps, should have been entitled, "What Every Woman Knows." But I'm not sure that every woman knows it. What I am sure of is that many women don't appear to know it, and that there are even many women who are horrified at the thought that anyone can entertain the idea that women are anything but inferior to men. This sort of childishness does no one any good. The world is in a mess. Men, without any assistance from women, have created it, and they have created it not because they have been failed by women, but because men have never really given women a chance to serve them as they are best equipped to do—by teaching men how to love their fellow men.

Women must cease supporting men for the wrong reasons in the wrong   22
sort of way, and thus cease causing men to marry them for the wrong reasons, too. "That's what a man wants in a wife, mostly," says Mrs. Poyser (in *Adam Bede*), "he wants to make sure o' one fool as 'ull tell

him he's wise." Well, it's time that men learned the truth, and perhaps they are likely to take it more gracefully from another male than from their unacknowledged betters. It is equally important that women learn the truth, too, for it is to them that the most important part, the more fundamental part, of the task of remaking the world will fall, for the world will be remade only by remaking, or rather helping, human beings to realize themselves more fully in terms of what their mothers have to give them. Without adequate mothers life becomes inadequate, nasty, and unsatisfactory, and Mother Earth becomes a battlefield on which fathers slay their young and are themselves slain.

Men have had a long run for their money in running the affairs of the 23 world. It is time that women realized that men will continue to run the world for some time yet, and that they can best assist them to run it more humanely by teaching them, when young, what humanity means. Men will thus not feel that they are being demoted, but rather that their potentialities for good are so much more increased, and what is more important, instead of feeling hostile toward women they will for the first time learn to appreciate them at their proper worth. There is an old Spanish proverb which has it that a good wife is the workmanship of a good husband. Maybe. But of one thing we can be certain: a good husband is the workmanship of a good mother. The best of all ways in which men can help themselves is to help women realize themselves. This way both sexes will come for the first time fully into their own, and the world of mankind may then look forward to a happier history than it has thus far enjoyed.

QUESTIONS AND EXERCISES

Vocabulary

1. Define or explain each of the following terms:

cogently (2)	subliminal (12)
"niggers" (4)	opacity (12)
thralldom (7)	preponderance (17)
chromosomes (8)	havoc (17)
iota (9)	accruing (18)
aborigines (10)	hemophilia (18)
humane (11)	behemoth (20)
altruistic (11)	morass (21)
nuances (12)	much-bruited (21)

2. Explain the allusion or identify the individual.

Leonardo (2)	Georgia O'Keeffe (3)
Michelangelo (2)	George Jean Nathan (12)

Galileo (2)   "the old chestnut" (16)
Whitehead (2)   Lenin (20)
Donne (2)   Stalin (20)
Mme. Curie (3)   Hitler (20)

Rhetoric

3. What function do the numerous allusions perform in this essay?
4. Find a paragraph developed by analogy.
5. What tone does Montagu wish to maintain in his presentation? Why?
6. Discuss Montagu's idioms. For example, how effective are expressions like the following?

    ". . . that it's cracked up to be" (21)

    ". . . have had a long run for their money" (23)
7. What is the purpose of the question at the beginning of paragraph 19?

Theme

8. What is the major thesis of Montagu's essay?
9. Outline the pattern of proof used to support the main thesis.
10. What obstacles does Montagu have to overcome to establish his point?
11. Discuss the historical relationships between men and women in view of Montagu's claims.
12. Where does Montagu's argument shift from facts to speculation? For example, what kind of argument is found in paragraph 20?
13. Find a scientist whose writing substantiates Montagu's chromosome theory.
14. Discuss the concept of superiority: man vs. woman, race vs. race, culture vs. culture, etc. What are the problems in establishing the superiority of one thing over another?

Topics and Assignments for Composition

1. In one sentence give a summary of Montagu's theory.
2. In one paragraph discuss the persuasive points of the argument. In another paragraph present the objections that remain.
3. Write an essay in which you present an argument much in the manner of Ashley Montagu. Find a thesis that allows you to present the superiority of one entity over another.

Thomas Hobbes

Of the Natural Condition of Mankind as Concerning Their Felicity and Misery

Nature hath made men so equal in the faculties of body and mind as *1* that, though there be found one man sometimes manifestly stronger in body or of quicker mind than another, yet when all is reckoned together the difference between man and man is not so considerable as that one man can thereupon claim to himself any benefit, to which another may not pretend as well as he. For as the strength of body, the weakest has strength enough to kill the strongest, either by secret machination, or by confederacy with others that are in the same danger with himself.

And as to the faculties of the mind — setting aside the arts grounded *2* upon words, and especially that skill of proceeding upon general and infallible rules, called science; which very few have, and but in few things; as being not a native faculty, born with us; nor attained, as prudence, while we look after somewhat else — I find yet a greater equality amongst men than that of strength. For prudence is but experience, which equal time equally bestows on all men, in those things they equally apply themselves unto. That which may perhaps make such equality incredible is but a vain conceit of one's own wisdom, which almost all men think they have in a greater degree than the vulgar — that is, than all men but themselves and a few others, whom by fame, or for concurring with themselves, they approve. For such is the nature of men, that howsoever they may acknowledge many others to be more witty, or more eloquent, or more learned, yet they will hardly believe there be many so wise as themselves; for they see their own wit at hand, and other men's at a distance. But this proveth rather that men are in that point equal, than unequal. For there is not ordinarily a greater sign of the equal distribution of anything than that every man is contented with his share.

From this equality of ability ariseth equality of hope in the attaining of   *3*
our ends. And therefore if any two men desire the same thing, which
nevertheless they cannot both enjoy, they become enemies; and in the
way to their end (which is principally their own conservation, and sometimes their delectation only) endeavor to destroy or subdue one another.
And from hence it comes to pass that where an invader hath no more to
fear than another man's single power; if one plant, sow, build, or possess
a convenient seat, others may probably be expected to come prepared
with forces united, to dispossess and deprive him, not only of the fruit of
his labor, but also of his life or liberty. And the invader again is in the like
danger of another.

And from this diffidence of one another, there is no way for any man to   *4*
secure himself so reasonable as anticipation; that is, by force or wiles to
master the persons of all men he can, so long, till he see no other power
great enough to endanger him, and this is no more than his own conservation requireth, and is generally allowed. Also because there be some, that
taking pleasure in contemplating their own power in the acts of conquest,
which they pursue farther than their security requires; if others that
otherwise would be glad to be at ease within modest bounds, should not
by invasion increase their power, they would not be able long time, by
standing only on their defense, to subsist. And by consequence, such
augmentation of dominion over men being necessary to a man's conservation, it ought to be allowed him.

Again, men have no pleasure, but on the contrary a great deal of grief,   *5*
in keeping company, where there is no power able to overawe them all.
For every man looketh that his companion should value him at the same
rate he sets upon himself; and upon all signs of contempt, or undervaluing,
naturally endeavors, as far as he dares (which amongst them that have no
common power to keep them in quiet, is far enough to make them destroy
each other), to extort a greater value from his contemners by damage, and
from others by the example.

So that in the nature of man, we find three principal causes of quarrel.   *6*
First, competition; second, diffidence; thirdly, glory.

The first maketh men invade for gain; the second, for safety; and the   *7*
third, for reputation. The first use violence to make themselves masters
of other men's persons, wives, children, and cattle; the second, to defend
them; the third, for trifles, as a word, a smile, a different opinion, and any
other sign of undervalue, either direct in their persons, or by reflection in
their kindred, their friends, their nation, their profession, or their name.

Hereby it is manifest that during the time men live without a common   *8*
power to keep them all in awe, they are in that condition which is called
war; and such a war as is of every man against every man. For war con-

sisteth not in battle only, or the act of fighting, but in a tract of time wherein the will to contend by battle is sufficiently known, and therefore the notion of time is to be considered in the nature of war, as it is in the nature of weather. For as the nature of foul weather lieth not in a shower or two of rain, but in an inclination thereto of many days together; so the nature of war consistenth not in actual fighting, but in the known disposition thereto, during all the time there is no assurance to the contrary. All other time is peace.

Whatsoever therefore is consequent to a time of war, where every man   9 is enemy to every man; the same is consequent to the time wherein men live without other security than what their own strength and their own invention shall furnish them withal. In such condition there is no place for industry, because the fruit thereof is uncertain, and consequently no culture of the earth; no navigation, nor use of the commodities that may be imported by sea; no commodious building; no instruments of moving, and removing, such things as require much force; no knowledge of the face of the earth; no account of time; no arts; no letters; no society; and which is worst of all, continual fear, and danger of violent death; and the life of man, solitary, poor, nasty, brutish, and short.

It may seem strange to some man that has not well weighed these   10 things, that nature should thus dissociate, and render men apt to invade and destroy one another; and he may therefore, not trusting to this inference, made from the passions, desire perhaps to have the same confirmed by experience. Let him therefore consider with himself, when taking a journey, he arms himself and seeks to go well accompanied; when going to sleep, he locks his doors; when even in his house he locks his chests; and this when he knows there be laws, and public officers, armed, to revenge all injuries shall be done him; what opinion he has of his fellow subjects, when he rides armed; of his fellow citizens, when he locks his doors; and of his children, and servants, when he locks his chests. Does he not there as much accuse mankind by his actions, as I do by my words? But neither of us accuse man's nature in it. The desires and other passions of man are in themselves no sin. No more are the actions that proceed from those passions, till they know a law that forbids them, which, till laws be made, they cannot know, nor can any law be made, till they have agreed upon the person that shall make it.

It may peradventure be thought there was never such a time nor con-   11 dition of war as this; and I believe it was never generally so, over all the world; but there are many places where they live so now. For the savage people in many places of America, except the government of small families, the concord whereof dependeth on natural lust, have no government at all and live at this day in that brutish manner, as I said before. Howsoever, it may be perceived what manner of life there would be, where there were no common power to fear; by the manner of life which men that have formerly lived under a peaceful government use to degenerate into in a civil war.

But though there had never been any time wherein particular men were   *12* in a condition of war one against another; yet in all times, kings and persons of sovereign authority, because of their independency, are in continual jealousies, and in the state and posture of gladiators; having their weapons pointing, and their eyes fixed on one another; that is, their forts, garrisons, and guns upon the frontiers of their kingdoms; and continual spies upon their neighbors; which is a posture of war. But because they uphold thereby the industry of their subjects, there does not follow from it that misery which accompanies the liberty of particular men.

To this war of every man against every man, this also is consequent: *13* that nothing can be unjust. The notions of right and wrong, justice and injustice, have there no place. Where there is no common power, there is no law; where no law, no injustice. Force and fraud are in war the two cardinal virtues. Justice and injustice are none of the faculties neither of the body nor mind. If they were, they might be in a man that were alone in the world, as well as his senses and passions. They are qualities that relate to men in society, not in solitude. It is consequent also to the same conditions that there be no propriety, no dominion, no *mine* and *thine* distinct; but only that to be every man's, that he can get; and for so long as he can keep it. And thus much for the ill conditions which may by mere nature is actually placed in; though with a possibility to come out of it, consisting partly in the passions, partly in his reason.

The passions that incline men to peace are fear of death, desire of such   *14* things as are necessary to commodious living, and a hope by their industry to obtain them. And reason suggesteth convenient articles of peace, upon which men may be drawn to agreement. These articles are they which otherwise are called the Laws of Nature whereof I shall speak more particularly in the two following chapters.

QUESTIONS AND EXERCISES

Vocabulary

1. Define or explain each of the following terms:
   machination (1)   diffidence (4)
   conceit (2)   peradventure (11)
2. The label of Modern English is put on writing after 1500. Hobbes' *Leviathan* (from which this essay was taken) was written in 1651.

This is supposed to be Modern English and yet it has an archaic flavor to it. Why?

Rhetoric

3. Like Sir Francis Bacon, Hobbes' style is characterized by rhetorical devices. The sentences are often carefully wrought and balanced. Pick out two sentences that illustrate this careful construction.
4. Notice the organization of paragraphs 6 and 7. Paragraph 6 was a tripart classification of causes of quarrel, and paragraph 7 is organized according to this classification, with examples and illustrations.
5. In paragraph 9 Hobbes gives voluminous, concrete examples in style that reflects the style of our own era: ". . . no account of time; no arts; no letters; no society; and what is worst of all, continual fear, and danger of violent death; and the life of man, solitary, poor, nasty, brutish, and short." Find similar examples.
6. Notice the caustic wit in paragraph 2. There are two excellent examples of sarcasm and irony. Find and explain them.

Theme

7. Compare the styles of Bacon and Hobbes.
8. Hobbes has been called a man of ideas; among other things his philosophy has been labelled materialistic, skeptical rationalism, mechanistic, iconoclastic, atheistic, and cynical. From this essay discuss what you think to be Hobbes' assumptions about human nature.
9. What are the implications of Hobbes' view of the natural condition of mankind as far as the type of government that he would advocate?
10. In what ways does Hobbes believe that all men are created equal?

Topics and Assignments for Composition

1. Imitate Hobbes' style by writing a long sentence about the nature of man. Example:

    Hobbes: To this war of every man against every man, this also is consequent: that nothing can be unjust.

    Imitation: To this struggle of every man against every man for property, it follows: there is no right or wrong in the pursuit of territory.

2. Write a paragraph imitating one of Hobbes' argumentative paragraphs. Use contemporary diction.
3. In an organized essay answer all or a portion of Hobbes' thesis about the nature of man.

W. T. Stace

Man Against Darkness

I

The Catholic bishops of America recently issued a statement in which   *1*
they said that the chaotic and bewildered state of the modern world is due
to man's loss of faith, his abandonment of God and religion. For my part
I believe in no religion at all. Yet I entirely agree with the bishops. It is
no doubt an oversimplification to speak of *the* cause of so complex a state
of affairs as the tortured condition of the world today. Its causes are
doubtless multitudinous. Yet allowing for some element of oversimplification, I say that the bishops' assertion is substantially true.

M. Jean-Paul Sartre, the French existentialist philosopher, labels him-   *2*
self an atheist. Yet his views seem to me plainly to support the statement
of the bishops. So long as there was believed to be a God in the sky, he
says, men could regard him as the source of their moral ideals. The universe, created and governed by a fatherly God, was a friendly habitation
for man. We could be sure that, however great the evil in the world, good
in the end would triumph and the forces of evil would be routed. With the
disappearance of God from the sky all this has changed. Since the world
is not ruled by a spiritual being, but rather by blind forces, there cannot
be any ideals, moral or otherwise, in the universe outside us. Our ideals,
therefore, must proceed only from our own minds; they are our own inventions. Thus the world which surrounds us is nothing but an immense
spiritual emptiness. It is a dead universe. We do not live in a universe
which is on the side of our values. It is completely indifferent to them.

Years ago Mr. Bertrand Russell, in his essay *A Free Man's Worship*,   *3*
said much the same thing.

Such in outline, but even more purposeless, more void of meaning,
is the world which Science presents for our belief. Amid such a

world, if anywhere, our ideals henceforward must find a home. . . . Blind to good and evil, reckless of destruction, omnipotent matter rolls on its relentless way; for man, condemned today to lose his dearest, tomorrow himself to pass through the gate of darkness, it remains only to cherish, ere yet the blow falls, the lofty thoughts that ennoble his little day; . . . to worship at the shrine his own hands have built; . . . to sustain alone, a weary but unyielding Atlas, the world that his own ideals have fashioned despite the trampling march of unconscious power.

It is true that Mr. Russell's personal attitude to the disappearance of   4
religion is quite different from either that of M. Sartre or the bishops or myself. The bishops think it a calamity. So do I. M. Sartre finds it "very distressing." And he berates as shallow the attitude of those who think that without God the world can go on just the same as before, as if nothing had happened. This creates for mankind, he thinks, a terrible crisis. And in this I agree with him. Mr. Russell, on the other hand, seems to believe that religion has done more harm than good in the world, and that its disappearance will be a blessing. But his picture of the world, and of the modern mind, is the same as that of M. Sartre. He stresses the *purposelessness* of the universe, the facts that man's ideals are his own creations, that the universe outside him in no way supports them, that man is alone and friendless in the world.

Mr. Russell notes that it is science which has produced this situation.   5
There is no doubt that this is correct. But the way in which it has come about is not generally understood. There is a popular belief that some particular scientific discoveries or theories, such as the Darwinian theory of evolution, or the views of geologists about the age of the earth, or a series of such discoveries, have done the damage. It would be foolish to deny that these discoveries have had a great effect in undermining religious dogmas. But this account does not at all go to the root of the matter. Religion can probably outlive any scientific discoveries which could be made. It can accommodate itself to them. The root cause of the decay of faith has not been any particular discovery of science, but rather the general spirit of science and certain basic assumptions upon which modern science, from the seventeenth century onwards, has proceeded.

II

It was Galileo and Newton—notwithstanding that Newton himself was   6
a deeply religious man—who destroyed the old comfortable picture of a friendly universe governed by spiritual values. And this was effected, not

by Newton's discovery of the law of gravitation nor by any of Galileo's brilliant investigations, but by the general picture of the world which these men and others of their time made the basis of the science, not only of their own day, but of all succeeding generations down to the present. That is why the century immediately following Newton, the eighteenth century, was notoriously an age of religious skepticism. Skepticism did not have to wait for the discoveries of Darwin and the geologists in the nineteenth century. It flooded the world immediately after the age of the rise of science.

Neither the Copernican hypothesis nor any of Newton's or Galileo's   7 particular discoveries were the real causes. Religious faith might well have accommodated itself to the new astronomy. The real turning point between the medieval age of faith and the modern age of unfaith came when the scientists of the seventeenth century turned their backs upon what used to be called "final causes." The final cause of a thing or event meant the purpose which is was supposed to serve in the universe, its cosmic purpose. What lay back of this was the presupposition that there is a cosmic order or plan and that everything which exists could in the last analysis be explained in terms of its place in this cosmic plan, that is, in terms of its purpose.

Plato and Aristotle believed this, and so did the whole medieval Chris-   8 tian world. For instance, if it were true that the sun and the moon were created and exist for the purpose of giving light to man, then this fact would explain why the sun and the moon exist. We might not be able to discover the purpose of everything, but everything must have a purpose. Belief in final causes thus amounted to a belief that the world is governed by purposes, presumably the purposes of some overruling mind. This belief was not the invention of Christianity. It was basic to the whole of Western civilization, whether in the ancient pagan world or in Christendom, from the time of Socrates to the rise of science in the seventeenth century.

The founders of modern science—for instance, Galileo, Kepler, and   9 Newton—were mostly pious men who did not doubt God's purposes. Nevertheless they took the revolutionary step of consciously and deliberately expelling the idea of purpose as controlling nature from their new science of nature. They did this on the ground that inquiry into purposes is useless for what science aims at: namely, the prediction and control of events. To predict an eclipse, what you have to know is not its purpose but its causes. Hence science from the seventeenth century onwards became exclusively an inquiry into causes. The conception of purpose in the world was ignored and frowned on. This, though silent and almost unnoticed, was the greatest revolution in human history, far outweighing in

importance any of the political revolutions whose thunder has reverberated through the world.

For it came about in this way that for the past three hundred years   *10*
there has been growing up in men's minds, dominated as they are by science, a new imaginative picture of the world. The world, according to
this new picture, is purposeless, senseless, meaningless. Nature is nothing
but matter in motion. The motions of matter are governed, not by any
purpose, but by blind forces and laws. Nature on this view, says Whitehead—to whose writings I am indebted in this part of my paper—is
"merely the hurrying of material, endlessly, meaninglessly." You can
draw a sharp line across the history of Europe dividing it into two epochs
of very unequal length. The line passes through the lifetime of Galileo.
European man before Galileo—whether ancient pagan or more recent
Christian—thought of the world as controlled by plan and purpose. After
Galileo European man thinks of it as utterly purposeless. This is the great
revolution of which I spoke.

It is this which has killed religion. Religion could survive the discover-   *11*
ies that the sun, not the earth, is the center; that men are descended from
simian ancestors; that the earth is hundreds of millions of years old. These
discoveries may render out of date some of the details of older theological
dogmas, may force their restatement in new intellectual frameworks. But
they do not touch the essence of the religious vision itself, which is the
faith that there is plan and purpose in the world, that the world is a moral
order, that in the end all things are for the best. This faith may express
itself through many different itellectual dogmas, those of Christianity, of
Hinduism, of Islam. All and any of these intellectual dogmas may be
destroyed without destroying the essential religious spirit. But that spirit
cannot survive destruction of belief in a plan and purpose of the world,
for that is the very heart of it. Religion can get on with any sort of astronomy, geology, biology, physics. But it cannot get on with a purposeless
and meaningless universe.

If the scheme of things is purposeless and meaningless, then the life of   *12*
man is purposeless and meaningless too. Everything is futile, all effort
is in the end worthless. A man may, of course, still pursue disconnected
ends, money, fame, art, science, and may gain pleasure from them. But
his life is hollow at the center. Hence the dissatisfied, disillusioned, restless spirit of modern man.

The picture of a meaningless world, and a meaningless human life, is,   *13*
I think, the basic theme of much modern art and literature. Certainly it
is the basic theme of modern philosophy. According to the most characteristic philosophies of the modern period from Hume in the eighteenth
century to the so-called positivists of today, the world is just what it is,

and that is the end of all inquiry. There is no reason for its being what it is. Everything might just as well have been quite different, and there would have been no reason for that either. When you have stated what things are, what things the world contains, there is nothing more which could be said, even by an omniscient being. To ask any question about *why* things are thus, or what purpose their being so serves, is to ask a senseless question, because they serve no purpose at all. For instance, there is for modern philosophy no such thing as the ancient problem of evil. For this once famous question presupposes that pain and misery, though they seem so inexplicable and irrational to us, must ultimately subserve some rational purpose, must have their places in the cosmic plan. But this is nonsense. There is no such overruling rationality in the universe. Belief in the ultimate irrationality of everything is the quintessence of what is called the modern mind.

It is true that, parallel with the philosophies which are typical of the   *14* modern mind, preaching the meaninglessness of the world, there has run a line of idealistic philosophies whose contention is that the world is after all spiritual in nature and that moral ideals and values are inherent in its structure. But most of these idealisms were simply philosophical expressions of romanticism, which was itself no more than an unsuccessful counterattack of the religious against the scientific view of things. They perished, along with romanticism in literature and art, about the beginning of the present century, though of course they still have a few adherents.

At the bottom these idealistic systems of thought were rationalizations   *15* of man's wishful thinking. They were born of the refusal of men to admit the cosmic darkness. They were comforting illusions within the warm glow of which the more tender-minded intellectuals sought to shelter themselves from the icy winds of the universe. They lasted a little while. But they are shattered now, and we return once more to the vision of a purposeless world.

III

Along with the ruin of the religious vision there went the ruin of moral   *16* principles and indeed of all values. If there is a cosmic purpose, if there is in the nature of things a drive towards goodness, then our moral systems will derive their validity from this. But if our moral rules do not proceed from something outside us in the nature of the universe—whether we say it is God or simply the universe itself—then they must be our own inventions. Thus it came to be believed that moral rules must be merely an expression of our own likes and dislikes. But likes and dislikes are notoriously variable. What pleases one man, people, or culture displeases another. Therefore morals are wholly relative.

This obvious conclusion from the idea of purposeless world made its   *17*
appearance in Europe immediately after the rise of science, for instance in the philosophy of Hobbes. Hobbes saw at once that if there is no purpose in the world there are no values either. "Good and evil," he writes, "are names that signify our appetites and aversions; which in different tempers, customs, and doctrines of men are different. . . . Every man calleth that which pleaseth him, good; and that which displeaseth him, evil."

This doctrine of the relativity of morals, though it has recently re-   *18*
ceived an impetus from the studies of anthropologists, was thus really implicit in the whole scientific mentality. It is disastrous for morals because it destroys their entire traditional foundation. That is why philosophers who see the danger signals, from the time at least of Kant, have been trying to give to morals a new foundation, that is, a secular or nonreligious foundation. This attempt may very well be intellectually successful. Such a foundation, independent of the religious view of the world, might well be found. But the question is whether it can ever be a *practical* success, that is, whether apart from its logical validity and its influence with intellectuals, it can ever replace among the masses of men the lost religious foundation. On that question hangs perhaps the future of civilization. But meanwhile disaster is overtaking us.

The widespread belief in "ethical relativity" among philosophers, psy-   *19*
chologists, ethnologists, and sociologists is the theoretical counterpart of the repudiation of principle which we see all around us, especially in international affairs, the field in which morals have always had the weakest foothold. No one any longer effectively believes in moral principles except as the private prejudices either of individual men or of nations or cultures. This is the inevitable consequence of the doctrine of ethical relativity, which in turn is the inevitable consequence of believing in a purposeless world.

Another characteristic of our spiritual state is loss of belief in the   *20*
freedom of the will. This also is a fruit of the scientific spirit, though not of any particular scientific discovery. Science has been built up on the basis of determinism, which is the belief that every event is completely determined by a chain of causes and is therefore theoretically predictable beforehand. It is true that recent physics seems to challenge this. But so far as its practical consequences are concerned, the damage has long ago been done. A man's actions, it was argued, are as much events in the natural world as is an eclipse of the sun. It follows that men's actions are as theoretically predictable as an eclipse. But if it is certain now that

John Smith will murder Joseph Jones at 2.15 P.M. on January 1, 1963, what possible meaning can it have to say that when that time comes John Smith will be *free* to choose whether he will commit the murder or not? And if he is not free, how can he be held responsible?

It is true that the whole of this argument can be shown by a competent   21
philosopher to be a tissue of fallacies — or at least I claim that it can. But the point is that the analysis required to show this is much too subtle to be understood by the average entirely unphilosophical man. Because of this, the argument against free will is generally swallowed whole by the unphilosophical. Hence the thought that man is not free, that he is the helpless plaything of forces over which he has no control, has deeply penetrated the modern mind. We hear of economic determinism, cultural determinism, historical determinism. We are not responsible for what we do because our glands control us, or because we are the products of environment or heredity. Not moral self-control, but the doctor, the psychiatrist, the educationist, must save us from doing evil. Pills and injections in the future are to do what Christ and the prophets have failed to do. Of course I do not mean to deny that doctors and educationists can and must help. And I do not mean in any way to belittle their efforts. But I do wish to draw attention to the weakening of moral controls, the greater or less repudiation of personal responsibility which, in the popular thinking of the day, result from these tendencies of thought.

IV

What, then, is to be done? Where are we to look for salvation from the   22
evils of our time? All the remedies I have seen suggested so far are, in my opinion, useless. Let us look at some of them.

Philosophers and intellectuals generally can, I believe, genuinely do   23
something to help. But it is extremely little. What philosophers can do is to show that neither the relativity of morals nor the denial of free will really follows from the grounds which have been supposed to support them. They can also try to discover a genuine secular basis for morals to replace the religious basis which has disappeared. Some of us are trying to do these things. But in the first place philosophers unfortunately are not agreed about these matters, and their disputes are utterly confusing to the non-philosophers. And in the second place their influence is practically negligible because their analyses necessarily take place on a level on which the masses are totally unable to follow them.

The bishops, of course, propose as remedy a return to belief in God   24
and in the doctrines of the Christian religion. Others think that a new

religion is what is needed. Those who make these proposals fail to realize that the crisis in man's spiritual condition is something unique in history for which there is no sort of analogy in the past. They are thinking perhaps of the collapse of the ancient Greek and Roman religions. The vacuum then created was easily filled by Christianity, and it might have been filled by Mithraism if Christianity had not appeared. By analogy they think that Christianity might now be replaced by a new religion, or even that Christianity itself, if revivified, might bring back health to men's lives.

But I believe that there is no analogy at all between our present state *25* and that of the European peoples at the time of the fall of paganism. Men had at that time lost their belief only in particular dogmas, particular embodiments of the religious view of the world. It had no doubt become incredible that Zeus and the other gods were living on the top of Mount Olympus. You could go to the top and find no trace of them. But the imaginative picture of a world governed by purpose, a world driving towards the good—which is the inner spirit of religion—had at that time received no serious shock. It had merely to re-embody itself in new dogmas, those of Christianity or some other religion. Religion itself was not dead in the world, only a particular form of it.

But now the situation is quite different. It is not merely that particular *26* dogmas, like that of the virgin birth, are unacceptable to the modern mind. That is true, but it constitutes a very superficial diagnosis of the present situation of religion. Modern skepticism is of a wholly different order from that of the intellectuals of the ancient world. It has attacked and destroyed not merely the outward forms of the religious spirit, its particularized dogmas, but the very essence of that spirit itself, belief in a meaningful and purposeful world. For the founding of a new religion a new Jesus Christ or Buddha would have to appear, in itself a most unlikely event and one for which in any case we cannot afford to sit and wait. But even if a new prophet and a new religion did appear, we may predict that they would fail in the modern world. No one for long would believe in them, for modern men have lost the vision, basic to all religion, of an ordered plan and purpose of the world. They have before their minds the picture of a purposeless universe, and such a world-picture must be fatal to any religion at all, not merely to Christianity.

We must not be misled by occasional appearances of a revival of the *27* religious spirit. Men, we are told, in their disgust and disillusionment at the emptiness of their lives, are turning once more to religion, or are searching for a new message. It may be so. We must expect such wishful yearnings of the spirit. We must expect men to wish back again the light that is gone, and to try to bring it back. But however they may wish and try, the light will not shine again,—not at least in the civilization to which we belong.

Another remedy commonly proposed is that we should turn to science   28
itself, or the scientific spirit, for our salvation. Mr. Russell and Professor Dewey both make this proposal, though in somewhat different ways. Professor Dewey seems to believe that discoveries in sociology, the application of scientific method to social and political problems, will rescue us. This seems to me utterly naïve. It is not likely that science, which is basically the cause of our spiritual troubles, is likely also to produce the cure for them. Also it lies in the nature of science that, though it can teach us the best means for achieving our ends, it can never tell us what ends to pursue. It cannot give us any ideals. And our trouble is about ideals and ends, not about the means for reaching them.

V

No civilization can live without ideals, or to put it in another way,   29
without a firm faith in moral ideas. Our ideals and moral ideas have in the past been rooted in religion. But the religious basis of our ideals has been undermined, and the superstructure of ideals is plainly tottering. None of the commonly suggested remedies on examination seems likely to succeed. It would therefore look as if the early death of our civilization were inevitable.

Of course we know that it is perfectly possible for individual men, very   30
highly educated men, philosophers, scientists, intellectuals in general, to live moral lives without any religious convictions. But the question is whether a whole civilization, a whole family of peoples, composed almost entirely of relatively uneducated men and women, can do this.

It follows, of course, that if we could make the vast majority of men as   31
highly educated as the very few are now, we might save the situation. And we are already moving slowly in that direction through the techniques of mass education. But the critical question seems to concern the time-lag. Perhaps in a few hundred years most of the population will, at the present rate, be sufficiently highly educated and civilized to combine high ideals with an absence of religion. But long before we reach any such stage, the collapse of our civilization may have come about. How are we to live through the intervening period?

I am sure that the first thing we have to do is to face the truth, however   32
bleak it may be, and then next we have to learn to live with it. Let me say a word about each of these two points. What I am urging as regards the first is complete honesty. Those who wish to resurrect Christian dogmas

are not, of course, consciously dishonest. But they have that kind of un-conscious dishonesty which consists in lulling oneself with opiates and dreams. Those who talk of a new religion are merely hoping for a new opiate. Both alike refuse to face the truth that there is, in the universe outside man, no spirituality, no regard for values, no friend in the sky, no help or comfort for man of any sort. To be perfectly honest in the admission of this fact, not to seek shelter in new or old illusions, not to indulge in wishful dreams about this matter, this is the first thing we shall have to do.

I do not urge this course out of any special regard for the sancity of truth in the abstract. It is not self-evident to me that truth is the supreme value to which all else must be sacrificed. Might not the discoverer of a truth which would be fatal to mankind be justified in suppressing it, even in teaching men a falsehood? Is truth more valuable than goodness and bounty and happiness? To think so is to invent yet another absolute, another religious delusion in which Truth with a capital T is substituted for God. The reason why we must now boldly and honestly face the truth that the universe is non-spiritual and indifferent to goodness, beauty, happiness, or truth is not that it would be wicked to suppress it, but sim-ply that it is too late to do so, so that in the end we cannot do anything else but face it. Yet we stand on the brink, dreading the icy plunge. We need courage. We need honesty.

Now about the other point, the necessity of learning to live with the truth. This means learning to live virtuously and happily, or at least con-tentedly, without illusions. And this is going to be extremely difficult be-cause what we have now begun dimly to perceive is that human life in the past, or at least human happiness, has almost wholly depended upon illusions. It has been said that man lives by truth, and that the truth will make us free. Nearly the opposite seems to me to be the case. Mankind has managed to live only by means of lies, and the truth may very well destroy us. If one were a Bergsonian one might believe that nature de-liberately puts illusions into our souls in order to induce us to go on living.

The illusions by which men have lived seem to be of two kinds. First, there is what one may perhaps call the Great Illusion—I mean the re-ligious illusion that the universe is moral and good, that it follows a wise and noble plan, that it is gradually generating some supreme value, that goodness is bound to triumph in it. Secondly, there is a whole host of minor illusions on which human happiness nourishes itself. How much of human happiness notoriously comes from the illusions of the lover about his beloved? Then again we work and strive because of the illusions con-nected with fame, glory, power, or money. Banners of all kinds, flags, emblems, insignia, ceremonials, and rituals are invariably symbols of some illusion or other. The British Empire, the connection between mother country and dominions, is partly kept going by illusions surrounding the notion of kingship. Or think of the vast amount of human happiness which is derived from the illusion of supposing that if some nonsense syllable, such as "sir" or "count" or "lord" is pronounced in conjunction with our names, we belong to a superior order of people.

There is plenty of evidence that human happiness is almost wholly   36 based upon illusions of one kind or another. But the scientific spirit, or the spirit of truth, is the enemy of illusions and therefore the enemy of human happiness. That is why it is going to be so difficult to live with the truth.

There is no reason why we should have to give up the host of minor   37 illusions which render life supportable. There is no reason why the lover should be scientific about the loved one. Even the illusions of fame and glory may persist. But without the Great Illusion, the illusion of a good, kindly and purposeful universe, we shall *have* to learn to live. And to ask this is really no more than to ask that we become genuinely civilized beings and not merely sham civilized beings.

I can best explain the difference by a reminiscence. I remember a   38 fellow student in my college days, an ardent Christian, who told me that if he did not believe in a future life, in heaven and hell, he would rape, murder, steal, and be a drunkard. That is what I call being a sham civilized being. On the other hand, not only could a Huxley, a John Stuart Mill, a David Hume, live great and fine lives without any religion, but a great many others of us, quite obscure persons, can at least live decent lives without it.

To be genuinely civilized means to be able to walk straightly and to   39 live honorably without the props and crutches of one or another of the childish dreams which have so far supported men. That such a life is likely to be ecstatically happy I will not claim. But that it can be lived in quiet content, accepting resignedly what cannot be helped, not expecting the impossible, and thankful for small mercies, this I would maintain. That it will be difficult for men in general to learn this lesson I do not deny. But that it will be impossible I would not admit since so many have learned it already.

Man has not yet grown up. He is not adult. Like a child he cries for   40 the moon and lives in a world of fantasies. And the race as a whole has perhaps reached the great crisis of its life. Can it grow up as a race in the same sense as individual men grow up? Can man put away childish things and adolescent dreams? Can he grasp the real world as it actually is, stark and bleak, without its romantic or religious halo, and still retain his ideals, striving for great ends and noble achievements? If he can, all may yet be well. If he cannot, he will probably sink back into the savagery and brutality from which he came, taking a humble place once more among the lower animals.

QUESTIONS AND EXERCISES

Vocabulary

1. Define or explain the following terms:

   chaotic (1)   positivists (13)
   multitudinous (1)   omniscient (13)
   existentialist (2)   quintessence (13)
   omnipotent (3)   rationalizations (15)
   berates (4)   ethnologists (19)
   dogmas (5)   fallacies (21)
   skepticism (6)   paganism (25)
   reverberated (9)   opiates (32)
   simian (11)

2. Identify or explain the allusion:

   Sartre (2)   Islam (11)
   Russell (3)   Hume (13)
   Galileo (6)   Hobbes (17)
   Newton (6)   Kant (18)
   Darwin (6)   Mithraism (24)
   Copernican hypothesis (7)   Zeus (25)
   Plato (8)   Dewey (28)
   Aristotle (8)   Bergsonian (34)
   Kepler (9)   Huxley (38)
   Whitehead (10)   Mill (38)
   Hinduism (11)

Rhetoric

3. How many main divisions are there in this essay?
4. Stace often uses the word "this" to link paragraphs, as in paragraphs 5, 10, 11, 15, 18, 21, and 33. Find another technique that he also uses to link paragraphs.
5. Find an entire paragraph that functions as a transition between divisions of the essay.
6. Find the transitional sentence in paragraph 11.
7. Stace uses figurative language sparingly but effectively. Find and identify two examples of figurative language in paragraph 15, and one in paragraph 33.
8. Discuss the development of paragraph 35.

Theme

9. Summarize the main idea of each division.
10. What is the thesis of the entire essay?
11. In Stace's opinion, what killed religion?
12. Discuss the logic in paragraphs 19 and 20.
13. Comment on the claim found in paragraph 36 that "human happiness is almost wholly based upon illusions of one kind or another."
14. Explain the meaning of the claims in paragraph 40 that "Man has not yet grown up. He is not adult."
15. Discuss the distinction between the "Great Illusion" and the "minor illusion" in paragraph 35.

Topics and Assignments for Composition

1. In one sentence describe Stace's philosophical position.
2. In a paragraph make a classification of the scientists and philosophers Stace refers to in the essay. Try to make several categories to encompass them.
3. In a paragraph discuss the differences between Stace's and Russell's attitudes toward religion.
4. Write an essay in which you accept or reject Stace's thesis as expressed in this essay.
5. Write an essay outlining the current conflict between science and religion.

Charles E. Wyzanski, Jr.

On Civil Disobedience

Disobedience is a long step beyond dissent. In this country, at least in theory, no one denies the right of any person to differ with the government, or his right to express that difference in speech, in the press, by petition, or in an assembly.   *1*

But civil disobedience, by definition, involves a deliberate and punishable breach of a legal duty. However much they differ in other respects, both passive and violent resisters intentionally violate the law. So, in general, it is unnecessary in considering the moral qualities of disobedience to spend much time in determining what is the correct construction of the law. By hypothesis the law has been broken, and broken knowingly.   *2*

The virtual exclusion of legal topics makes it possible to discuss the mortality of resistance to the Vietnam War without answering the question whether the President as Commander in Chief under the Constitution, or as the Chief Executive authorized by the Congress or otherwise has power to send to Vietnam armed forces regularly enlisted or conscripted, or whether the Constitution gives power to draft men to serve in a conflict not covered by a formal declaration of war, or whether there is any rule of international or domestic law which inhibits the President or the Congress or the armed forces either from conducting in Vietnam any operations whatsoever or any particular operations, or from using any specific methods of fighting or injuring other persons, military or civilian.   *3*

There cannot be an issue of civil disobedience unless there is a conscious choice to violate not merely a governmental policy but a technically valid law or order. Only such laws and orders as are ultimately   *4* held valid under our Constitution are subject to genuine civil disobedience.

Of course, until the Supreme Court has spoken, a person may not   5
know whether a particular law or order is valid. If because he believes
the law is invalid under the Constitution he refuses to obey it until the
order has been upheld, he is not in the strictest sense engaged in civil
disobedience. Thus many of the recent refusals of Negroes to obey
segregation orders of local authorities, though they are popularly referred to as examples of civil disobedience, have been, in fact, nothing
more than challenges to laws believed to be and often found to be unconstitutional.

If it turns out that the Supreme Court should hold that the government   6
lacks power to order the induction of men into military training and
service for the Vietnam War, then one who had refused to obey the induction order would not have been guilty of civil disobedience. He
would merely have been vindicating his constitutional rights.

But if, as I suppose the majority of informed lawyers expect, the   7
Supreme Court, at least during the continuation of hostilities, does not
hold an induction order void on the ground of lack of legislative or
executive power, then one who continues willfully to disobey is engaged
in civil disobedience. The same would be true of one who, on the ground
that the funds were used for war, refused to pay taxes, or who in protesting war deliberately injured another's person or property, or who
went beyond argument and persuasion to advocate resistance to lawful
orders.

There are many people who have asserted that a man always has an   8
undeniable moral claim to disobey any law to which he is conscientiously opposed. Antigone, Thoreau, and Gandhi are cited. It is contended that resistance to the law is the proper response to the still small
voice of conscience.

That extreme position seems untenable. Every time that a law is dis-   9
obeyed by even a man whose motive is solely ethical, in the sense that
it is responsive to a deep moral conviction, there are unfortunate consequences. He himself becomes more prone to disobey laws for which he
has no profound repugnance. He sets an example for others who may
not have his pure motives. He weakens the fabric of society.

Those disadvantages are so serious that in *Principia Ethica* G. E.   10
Moore, the English philosopher who set the tone for twentieth-century
thought on ethics, concluded that in most instances civil disobedience is
immoral. A dramatic precursor of Moore was Socrates. He swallowed
hemlock pursuant to an arbitrary Athenian decree rather than refuse

obedience to the laws of the city-state which had formed and protected him.

However, it is not here suggested that disobedience is always morally *11* wrong, or that it is never ethically proper for a man to organize opposition to an immoral law even before the state brings its command directly to his door.

There are situations when it seems plainly moral for a man to disobey *12* an evil law promulgated by a government which is entirely lacking in ethical character. If a man has lost confidence in the integrity of his society, or if he fears that unless he acts forthwith there will not come a later day when he can effectively protest, or if (in terms reminiscent of Burke's metaphor) he seeks to terminate the partnership of the American dead, the American living, and the as yet unborn Americans, then there is much justification for his disobedience.

The gangster state operated by the Nazis presented such a picture to *13* many conscientious men. But no unprejudiced observer is likely to see the American government in its involvement in Vietnam as in a posture comparable with that of the Nazi regime. Nor is there reason to suppose that men must act now or forever be silenced. We are not moving either torrentially or glacially toward despotism.

It is, of course, conceivable that if men resist forthwith, they may *14* forestall grave consequences. It is certain that many, many Americans and Asians will lose their lives if the war continues. It is possible that if fighting is not promptly stopped, the scale will increase dramatically, and at worst, might produce a holocaust of worldwide dimensions.

But what is by no means assured is that resistance would avert those *15* consequences. Historical prediction is clouded by ambiguities. Political developments move to a heterogeneity of ends. No one can tell whether, as the resisters would hope, they, by rallying widespread support, would prove that in a democracy substantial segments of public opinion have the residual power to terminate or veto a war, or, as less implicated observers fear, the resisters, by provoking the responsive passions of the belligerent, would set the stage for a revival of a virulent McCarthyism, an administrative system of impressment into the armed forces, and the establishment of a despotic tyranny bent on impairing traditional civil liberties and civic rights.

Most thoughtful men have always been aware how dangerous it is to *16* go beyond persuasion and to defy the law by either peaceful or violent resistance. If the effort is successful, as with the Revolution of the American colonists, then history accepts the claims of the victors that they acted morally. But if the effort not merely fails but produces a horrible reaction, then history is likely to ask whether there were not other courses that could have been more wisely followed.

To illustrate how perplexing is the problem, nothing is more illumi-   17
nating than the struggle in America in the 1850s and 1860s over the slavery question. Abraham Lincoln thought laws enforcing slavery were immoral. Yet he declared he would endure, and thus aid the enforcement of, slavery in the Southern states if that would preserve the Union. His position was shared by two great jurists of my state who were his contemporaries: Lemuel Shaw, Chief Justice of Massachusetts, and Benjamin Robbins Curtis, Associate Justice of the Supreme Court of the United States, both of whom enforced the Fugitive Slave Law.

But Lincoln's position was challenged by, among others, two men   18
whom the city of Boston has honored by statues erected after their death — Wendell Phillips and William Lloyd Garrison, each of whom disobeyed the Fugitive Slave Law and wrote approvingly of the murderous violence of John Brown. What should give us even greater pause is that Oliver Wendell Holmes, Jr., the future Justice, in effect adhered to the Abolitionist cause when he joined the small group of Abolitionists who, during the winter of 1860–1861, made themselves responsible for securing the physical safety of Wendell Phillips against the threats of the Boston mobs, a protection which the Boston police seemed unlikely to provide. The details are set forth in Professor Mark Howe's discriminating biography of Holmes.

If it was morally right to break the laws supporting slavery even when   19
it cost the nation its unity and helped precipitate what, despite W. H. Seward, may not have been an "irrepressible conflict," one cannot be so certain that it is morally wrong to resist the war in Vietnam if one deeply believes its purposes or methods are wicked.

At any rate the Lincolnian analogy has not the final authority that it   20
may seem to have on cursory inspection. In 1860 and 1861 our country was in immediate grave peril. Lincoln adhered to the ancient Roman maxim that the safety of the people is the highest law. But that maxim has no obvious application today. Even the most ardent supporters of our role in Vietnam would hardly aver that the threat they see in Communism or Asian nationalism is one of such immediacy as existed when the Civil War erupted. Perhaps there are long-term dangers from the Asian and other Communist powers, but one may wonder if Mr. Justice Holmes would have regarded them as either "clear" or "present." Would not President Lincoln have invoked our recollection not of 1860 or 1861 but rather of 1863 when, the battle of Antietam having made a change of policy practical, he issued the Emancipation proclamation?

In support of the moral right of resistance, another, if cognate, point   21 must be made, however uncongenial it is to me both temperamentally and officially. A man may conscientiously believe that his deepest obligation is to do his utmost to eradicate an evil, to stand athwart a wicked action, forcefully to promote reform, or to establish a new social or legal or religious order. Luther and Lenin serve as archetypes. They share to some degree the view Vanzetti on the eve of his electrocution expressed to his lawyer Thompson: "that, as he read history, every great cause for the benefit of humanity had to fight for its existence against entrenched power and wrong."

Perceptive observers may support Vanzetti's social theorem. Anguished souls may yield to its persuasiveness. Effective men may make that vision once again prove its reality.   22

Yet the fierce passion which moves men to rebel is often, not always, dangerously mixed with vanity, self-righteousness, and blindness to possible, nay probable, consequences far different from those sought. The voice of reason urges, in Cromwellian terms, "I beseech you, in the bowels of Christ, think it possible you may be mistaken."   23

Violent disorder once set in motion may spawn tyranny, not freedom. Rebellion may fail to gain its contemplated support, and as surely as in other human relations, result in "the expense of spirit in a waste of shame."   24

Or, what is far harder to bear, the rebellion may in form succeed but in substance impose a new oppressive yoke, a nihilistic world regime, of chaos instead of a community of nations. The wager on a finer, purer, more fraternal world order may be disastrously lost. Before one places all one's strength behind the rebel's cause, he should have not only naïve faith but that invincible insight which warrants martyrdom.   25

For men of conscience there remains a less risky but not less worthy moral choice. Each of us may bide his time until he personally is faced with an order requiring him as an individual to do a wrongful act. Such patience, fortitude, and resolution find illustration in the career of Sir Thomas More. He did not rush in to protest the Act of Henry VIII's Parliament requiring Englishmen to take an oath of supremacy attesting to the King's, instead of the Pope's, headship of the English Church. Only when an attempt was made to force him to subscribe to the oath did he resist. In present circumstances the parallel to not resisting the Act of Supremacy before it has been personally applied is to await at the very least an induction order before resisting. Indeed, since, when inducted, one does not know if he will be sent to Vietnam, or if sent, will be called upon directly to do what he regards as an immoral act, it may well be that resistance at the moment of induction is premature.   26

This waiting until an issue is squarely presented to an individual and   27 cannot further be avoided will not be a course appealing to those who have a burning desire to intervene affirmatively to save this nation's honor and the lives of its citizens and citizens of other lands. It seems at first blush a not very heroic attitude. But heroism sometimes lies in withholding action until it is compelled, and using the interval to discern competing interests, to ascertain their values, and to seek to strike a balance that marshals the claims not only of the accountant and of others in his society, but of men of distant lands and times.

Such restraint will in no way run counter to the rules applied in the   28
judgment of the Nuremberg Tribunal. That judgment recognized that no one may properly be charged with a crime unless he personally participated in it by doing the wrong or by purposefully aiding, abetting, and furthering the wrong. As the Nuremberg verdicts show, merely to fight in an aggressive war is no crime. What is a crime is personally to fight by foul means.

Those who look upon Sir Thomas More as one of the noblest exem-   29
plars of the human spirit reflecting the impact of the love of God may find a delayed civil disobedience the response most likely to give peace of mind and to evidence moral courage.

QUESTIONS AND EXERCISES

Vocabulary

1. Define or explain each of the following terms:

hypothesis (2)	maxim (20)
untenable (9)	cognate (21)
precursor (10)	eradicate (21)
hemlock (10)	archetype (21)
promulgated (12)	theorem (22)
torrentially (13)	nihilistic (25)
heterogeneity (15)	exemplars (29)
virulent (15)	

2. Identify or explain the allusion in each of the following:

Antigone (8)	Luther (21)
Thoreau (8)	Lenin (21)
Gandhi (8)	Vanzetti (21)
Socrates (10)	Cromwellian (23)
Burke (12)	Sir Thomas More (26)
McCarthyism (15)	Nuremberg Tribunal (28)
Abolitionist (18)	

Rhetoric

3. Why is paragraph 2 developed by definition?
4. What figure of speech is, "He weakens the fabric of society."? (9)
5. Explain the literal meaning of "We are not moving either torrentially or glacially toward despotism."
6. How appropriate is the metaphor, "Violent disorder once set in motion may spawn tyranny, not freedom."?
7. What function does the title serve? Does its allusion to Thoreau's "On The Duty of Civil Disobedience" help in organizing the essay?

Theme

8. What is Judge Wyzanski's position on civil disobedience?
9. How do his views compare to Thoreau's position?
10. What is the main danger of civil disobedience according to Judge Wyzanski?
11. Do you think the hundred years of history between Thoreau and today would bring Thoreau's position closer to Judge Wyzanski's position?
12. Discuss the relationships between law, morality, ethics, and justice.

Topics and Assignments for Composition

1. In a sentence state the main danger of civil disobedience.
2. In a paragraph analyze one of the examples Judge Wyzanski uses to illustrate his argument.
3. Write an essay expressing your own ideas on civil disobedience.
4. Analyze the possibility of civil disobedience in a totalitarian society. You may wish to comment on Gandhi's passive resistance against the British. How would such a resistance fare under Hitler, Stalin, or Mao? What would Thoreau do in Imperial Russia? In Russia today? What would happen to him?

Paul Ehrlich

Eco-Catastrophe

I

The end of the ocean came late in the summer of 1979, and it came *1*
even more rapidly than the biologists had expected. There had been
signs for more than a decade, commencing with the discovery in 1968
that DDT slows down photosynthesis in marine plant life. It was announced in a short paper in the technical journal, *Science,* but to ecologists it smacked of doomsday. They knew that all life in the sea depends on photosynthesis, the chemical process by which green plants
bind the sun's energy and make it available to living things. And they
knew that DDT and similar chlorinated hydrocarbons had polluted the
entire surface of the earth, including the sea.

But that was only the first of many signs. There had been the final gasp *2*
of the whaling industry in 1973, and the end of the Peruvian anchovy
fishery in 1975. Indeed, a score of other fisheries had disappeared quietly
from overexploitation and various eco-catastrophes by 1977. The term
eco-catastrophe was coined by a California ecologist in 1969 to describe
the most spectacular of man's attacks on the systems which sustain his
life. He drew his inspiration from the Santa Barbara offshore oil disaster
of that year, and from the news which spread among naturalists that virtually all of the Golden State's seashore bird life was doomed because
of chlorinated hydrocarbon interference with its reproduction. Eco-
catastrophes in the sea became increasingly common in the early 1970's.
Mysterious "blooms" of previously rare microorganisms began to appear
in offshore waters. Red tides—killer outbreaks of a minute single-celled
plant—returned to the Florida Gulf coast and were sometimes accompanied by tides of other exotic hues.

It was clear by 1975 that the entire ecology of the ocean was changing. *3*

A few types of phytoplankton were becoming resistant to chlorinated hydrocarbons and were gaining the upper hand. Changes in the phytoplankton community led inevitably to changes in the community of zooplankton, the tiny animals which eat the phytoplankton. These changes were passed on up the chains of life in the ocean to the herring, plaice, cod and tuna. As the diversity of life in the ocean diminished, its stability also decreased.

Other changes had taken place by 1975. Most ocean fishes that re- *4* turned to fresh water to breed, like the salmon, had become extinct, their breeding streams so dammed up and polluted that their powerful homing instinct only resulted in suicide. Many fishes and shellfishes that bred in restricted areas along the coasts followed them as onshore pollution escalated.

By 1977 the annual yield of fish from the sea was down to thirty mil- *5* lion metric tons, less than one-half the per capita catch of a decade earlier. This helped malnutrition to escalate sharply in a world where an estimated fifty million people per year were already dying of starvation. The United Nations attempted to get all chlorinated hydrocarbon insecticides banned on a worldwide basis, but the move was defeated by the United States. This opposition was generated primarily by the American petrochemical industry, operating hand in glove with its subsidiary, the United States Department of Agriculture. Together they persuaded the government to oppose the U.N. move—which was not difficult since most Americans believed that Russia and China were more in need of fish products than was the United States. The United Nations also attempted to get fishing nations to adopt strict and enforced catch limits to preserve dwindling stocks. This move was blocked by Russia, who, with the most modern electronic equipment, was in the best position to glean what was left in the sea. It was, curiously, on the very day in 1977 when the Soviet Union announced its refusal that another ominous article appeared in *Science*. It announced that incident solar radiation had been so reduced by worldwide air pollution that serious effects on the world's vegetation could be expected.

II

Apparently it was a combination of ecosystem destabilization, sun- *6* light reduction, and a rapid escalation in chlorinated hydrocarbon pollution from massive Thanodrin applications which triggered the ultimate catastrophe. Seventeen huge Soviet-financed Thanodrin plants were operating in underdeveloped countries by 1978. They had been part of a massive Russian "aid offensive" designed to fill the gap caused by the collapse of America's ballyhooed "Green Revolution."

It became apparent in the early 70's that the Green Revolution was   7
more talk than substance. Distribution of high yield "miracle" grain
seeds had caused temporary local spurts in agricultural production. Simultaneously, excellent weather had produced record harvests. The combination permitted bureaucrats, especially in the United States Department of Agriculture and the Agency for International Development
(AID), to reverse their previous pessimism and indulge in an outburst of
optimistic propaganda about staving off famine. They raved about the
approaching transformation of agriculture in the underdeveloped countries (UDCs). The reason for the propaganda reversal was never made
clear. Most historians agree that a combination of utter ignorance of
ecology, a desire to justify past errors, and pressure from agro-industry
(which was eager to sell pesticides, fertilizers, and farm machinery to the
UDCs and agencies helping the UDCs) was behind the campaign. Whatever the motivation, the results were clear. Many concerned people,
lacking the expertise to see through the Green Revolution drivel, relaxed. The population-food crisis was "solved."

But reality was not long in showing itself. Local famine persisted in   8
northern India even after good weather brought an end to the ghastly
Bihar famine of the mid-60's. East Pakistan was next, followed by a
resurgence of general famine in northern India. Other foci of famine
rapidly developed in Indonesia, the Philippines, Malawi, the Congo,
Egypt, Colombia, Ecuador, Honduras, the Dominican Republic, and
Mexico.

Everywhere hard realities destroyed the illusion of the Green Revo-   9
lution. Yields dropped as the progressive farmers who had first accepted
the new seeds found that their higher yields brought lower prices—
effective demand (hunger plus cash) was not sufficient in poor countries
to keep prices up. Less progressive farmers, observing this, refused to
make the extra effort required to cultivate the "miracle" grains. Transport
systems proved inadequate to bring the necessary fertilizer to the fields
where the new and extremely fertilizer-sensitive grains were being
grown. The same systems were also inadequate to move produce to
markets. Fertilizer plants were not built fast enough, and most of the
underdeveloped countries could not scrape together funds to purchase
supplies, even on concessional terms. Finally, the inevitable happened,
and pests began to reduce yields in even the most carefully cultivated
fields. Among the first were the famous "miracle rats" which invaded
Philippine "miracle rice" fields in early 1969. They were quickly followed by many insects and viruses, thriving on the relatively pest-sus-
ceptible new grains, encouraged by the vast and dense plantings, and
rapidly acquiring resistance to the chemicals used against them. As

chaos spread until even the most obtuse agriculturists and economists realized that the Green Revolution had turned brown, the Russians stepped in.

In retrospect it seems incredible that the Russians, with the American   *10* mistakes known to them, could launch an even more incompetent program of aid to the underdeveloped world. Indeed, in the early 1970's there were cynics in the United States who claimed that outdoing the stupidity of American foreign aid would be physically impossible. Those critics were, however, unaware that the Russians had been busily destroying their own environment for many years. The virtual disappearance of sturgeon from Russian rivers caused a great shortage of caviar by 1970. A standard joke among Russian scientists at that time was that they had created an artificial caviar which was indistinguishable from the real thing—except by taste. At any rate the Soviet Union, observing with interest the progressive deterioration of relations between the UDCs and the United States, came up with a solution. It had recently developed what it claimed was the ideal insecticide, a highly lethal chlorinated hydrocarbon complexed with a special agent for penetrating the external skeletal armor of insects. Announcing that the new pesticide, called Thanodrin, would truly produce a Green Revolution, the Soviets entered into negotiations with various UDCs for the construction of massive Thanodrin factories. The USSR would bear all the costs; all it wanted in return were certain trade and military concessions.

It is interesting now, with the perspective of years, to examine in some   *11* detail the reasons why the UDCs welcomed the Thanodrin plan with such open arms. Government officials in these countries ignored the protests of their own scientists that Thanodrin would not solve the problems which plagued them. The governments now knew that the basic cause of their problems was over-population, and that these problems had been exacerbated by the dullness, daydreaming, and cupidity endemic to all governments. They knew that only population control and limited development aimed primarily at agriculture could have spared them the horrors they now faced. They knew it, but they were not about to admit it. How much easier it was simply to accuse the Americans of failing to give them proper aid; how much simpler to accept the Russian panacea.

And then there was the general worsening of relations between the   *12* United States and the UDCs. Many things had contributed to this. The situation in America in the first half of the 1970's deserves our close scrutiny. Being more dependent on imports for raw materials than the Soviet Union, the United States had, in the early 1970's, adopted more and more heavy-handed policies in order to insure continuing supplies. Military adventures in Asia and Latin America had further lessened the international credibility of the United States as a great defender of free-dom—an image which had begun to deteriorate rapidly during the point-less and fruitless Viet-Nam conflict. At home, acceptance of the carefully manufactured image lessened dramatically, as even the more romantic and chauvinistic citizens began to understand the role of the military and the industrial system in what John Kenneth Galbraith had aptly named "The New Industrial State."

At home in the USA the early 70's were traumatic times. Racial vio-   *13*
lence grew and the habitability of the cities diminished, as nothing sub-stantial was done to ameliorate either racial inequities or urban blight. Welfare rolls grew as automation and general technological progress forced more and more people into the category of "unemployable." Si-multaneously a taxpayers' revolt occurred. Although there was not enough money to build the schools, roads, water systems, sewage sys-tems, jails, hospitals, urban transit lines, and all the other amenities needed to support a burgeoning population, Americans refused to tax themselves more heavily. Starting in Youngstown, Ohio in 1969 and followed closely by Richmond, California, community after community was forced to close its schools or curtail educational operations for lack of funds. Water supplies, already marginal in quality and quantity in many places by 1970, deteriorated quickly. Water rationing occurred in 1723 municipalities in the summer of 1974, and hepatitis and epidemic dysentery rates climbed about 500 per cent between 1970–1974.

III

Air pollution continued to be the most obvious manifestation of en-   *14*
vironmental deterioration. It was, by 1972, quite literally in the eyes of all Americans. The year 1973 saw not only the New York and Los Angeles smog disasters, but also the publication of the Surgeon Gen-eral's massive report on air pollution and health. The public had been partially prepared for the worst by the publicity given to the U.N. pollu-tion conference held in 1972. Deaths in the late 60's caused by smog were well known to scientists, but the public had ignored them because they mostly involved early demise of the old and sick rather than people dropping dead on the freeways. But suddenly our citizens were faced with nearly 200,000 corpses and massive documentation that they could be the next to die from respiratory disease. They were not ready for that scale of disaster. After all, the U.N. conference had not predicted that accumulated air pollution would make the planet uninhabitable until almost 1990. The population was terrorized as TV screens became filled

with scenes of horror from the disaster areas. Especially vivid was NBC's coverage of hundreds of unattended people choking out their lives outside of New York's hospitals. Terms like nitrogen oxide, acute bronchitis, and cardiac arrest began to have real meaning for most Americans.

The ultimate horror was the announcement that chlorinated hydro- *15* carbons were now a major constituent of air pollution in all American cities. Autopsies of smog disaster victims revealed an average chlorinated hydrocarbon load in fatty tissue equivalent to 26 parts per million of DDT. In October, 1973, the Department of Health, Education and Welfare announced studies which showed unequivocally that increasing death rates from hypertension, cirrhosis of the liver, liver cancer, and a series of other diseases had resulted from the chlorinated hydrocarbon load. They estimated that Americans born since 1946 (when DDT usage began) now had a life expectancy of only 49 years, and predicted that if current patterns continued, this expectancy would reach 42 years by 1980, when it might level out. Plunging insurance stocks triggered a stock market panic. The president of . . . a major pesticide producer went on television to "publicly eat a teaspoonful of DDT" (it was really powdered milk) and announce that HEW had been infiltrated by Communists. Other giants of the petro-chemical industry, attempting to dispute the indisputable evidence, launched a massive pressure campaign on Congress to force HEW to "get out of agriculture's business." They were aided by the agro-chemical journals, which had decades of experience in misleading the public about the benefits and dangers of pesticides. But by now the public realized that it had been duped. The Nobel Prize for medicine and physiology was given to Drs. J. L. Radomski and W. B. Deichmann, who in the late 1960's had pioneered in the documentation of the long-term lethal effects of chlorinated hydrocarbons. A Presidential Commission with unimpeachable credentials directly accused the agro-chemical complex of "condemning many millions of Americans to an early death." The year 1973 was the year in which Americans finally came to understand the direct threat to their existence posed by environmental deterioration.

And 1973 was also the year in which most people finally compre- *16* hended the indirect threat. Even the president of Union Oil Company and several other industrialists publicly stated their concern over the reduction of bird populations which had resulted from pollution by DDT and other chlorinated hydrocarbons. Insect populations boomed because they were resistant to most pesticides and had been freed, by the incompetent use of those pesticides, from most of their natural enemies. Rodents swarmed over crops, multiplying rapidly in the absence of predatory birds. The effect of pests on the wheat crop was especially disastrous in the summer of 1973, since that was also the year of the great drought. Most of us can remember the shock which greeted the announcement by atmospheric physicists that the shift of the jet stream which had caused the drought was probably permanent. It signalled the birth of the Midwestern desert. Man's air-polluting activities had by then caused gross changes in climatic patterns. The news, of course, played hell with commodity and stock markets. Food prices skyrocketed, as savings were poured into hoarded canned goods. Official assurances that food supplies would remain ample fell on deaf ears, and even the government showed signs of nervousness when California migrant field workers went on strike again in protest against the continued use of pesticides by growers. The strike burgeoned into farm burning and riots. The workers, calling themselves "The Walking Dead," demanded immediate compensation for their shortened lives, and crash research programs to attempt to lengthen them.

It was in the same speech in which President Edward Kennedy, after   *17* much delay, finally declared a national emergency and called out the National Guard to harvest California's crops, that the first mention of population control was made. Kennedy pointed out that the United States would no longer be able to offer any food aid to other nations and was likely to suffer food shortages herself. He suggested that, in view of the manifest failure of the Green Revolution, the only hope of the UDCs lay in population control. His statement, you will recall, created an uproar in the underdeveloped countries. Newspaper editorials accused the United States of wishing to prevent small countries from becoming large nations and thus threatening American hegemony. Politicians asserted that President Kennedy was a "creature of the giant drug combine" that wished to shove its pills down every woman's throat.

Among Americans, religious opposition to population control was very   *18* slight. Industry in general also backed the idea. Increasing poverty in the UDCs was both destroying markets and threatening supplies of raw materials. The seriousness of the raw material situation had been brought home during the Congressional Hard Resources hearings in 1971. The exposure of the ignorance of the cornucopian economists had been quite a spectacle—a spectacle brought into virtually every American's home in living color. Few would forget the distinguished geologist from the University of California who suggested that economists be legally required to learn at least the most elementary facts of geology. Fewer still would forget that an equally distinguished Harvard economist added that they might be required to learn some economics, too. The overall message was clear: America's resource situation was bad and bound to get worse. The hearings had led to a bill requiring the Departments of State, Interior, and Commerce to set up a joint resource procurement council with the express purpose of "insuring that proper consideration of American resource needs be an integral part of American foreign policy."

Suddenly the United States discovered that it had a national consensus: population control was the only possible salvation of the underdeveloped world. But that same consensus led to heated debate. How could the UDCs be persuaded to limit their populations, and should not the United States lead the way by limiting its own? Members of the intellectual community wanted America to set an example. They pointed out that the United States was in the midst of a new baby boom: her birth rate, well over twenty per thousand per year, and her growth rate of over one per cent per annum were among the very highest of the developed countries. They detailed the deterioration of the American physical and psychic environments, the growing health threats, the impending food shortages, and the insufficiency of funds for desperately needed public works. They contended that the nation was clearly unable or unwilling to properly care for the people it already had. What possible reason could there be, they queried, for adding any more? Besides, who would listen to requests by the United States for population control when that nation did not control her own profligate reproduction?

Those who opposed population controls for the U.S. were equally vociferous. The military-industrial complex, with its all-too-human mixture of ignorance and avarice, still saw strength and prosperity in numbers. Baby food magnates, already worried by the growing nitrate pollution of their products, saw their market disappearing. Steel manufacturers saw a decrease in aggregate demand and slippage for that holy of holies, the Gross National Product. And military men saw, in the growing population-food-environment crisis, a serious threat to their carefully nurtured Cold War. In the end, of course, economic arguments held sway, and the "inalienable right of every American couple to determine the size of its family," a freedom invented for the occasion in the early 70's, was not compromised.

The population control bill, which was passed by Congress early in 1974, was quite a document, nevertheless. On the domestic front, it authorized an increase from 100 to 150 million dollars in funds for "family planning" activities. This was made possible by a general feeling in the country that the growing army on welfare needed family planning. But the gist of the bill was a series of measures designed to impress the need for population control on the UDCs. All American aid to countries with overpopulation problems was required by law to consist in part of population control assistance. In order to receive any assistance each nation was required not only to accept the population control aid, but also to match it according to a complex formula. "Overpopulation" itself was defined by a formula based on U.N. statistics, and the UDCs were required not only to accept aid, but also to show progress in reducing birth rates. Every five years the status of the aid program for each nation was to be reevaluated.

The reaction to the announcement of this program dwarfed the response to President Kennedy's speech. A coalition of UDCs attempted to get the U.N. General Assembly to condemn the United States as a "genetic aggressor." Most damaging of all to the American cause was the famous "25 Indians and a dog" speech by Mr. Shankarnarayan, Indian Ambassador to the U.N. Shankarnarayan pointed out that for several decades the United States, with less than six per cent of the people of the world, had consumed roughly fifty per cent of the raw materials used every year. He described vividly America's contribution to worldwide environmental deterioration, and he scathingly denounced the miserly record of United States foreign aid as "unworthy of a fourth-rate power, let alone the most powerful nation on earth." 22

It was the climax of his speech, however, which most historians claim once and for all destroyed the image of the United States. Shankarnarayan informed the assembly that the average American family dog was fed more animal protein per week than the average Indian got in a month. "How do you justify taking fish from protein-starved Peruvians and feeding them to your animals?" he asked. "I contend," he concluded, "that the birth of an American baby is a greater disaster for the world than that of 25 Indian babies." When the applause had died away, Mr. Sorensen, the American representative, made a speech which said essentially that "other countries look after their own self-interest, too." When the vote came, the United States was condemned. 23

IV

This condemnation set the tone of U.S.-UDC relations at the time the Russian Thanodrin proposal was made. The proposal seemed to offer the masses in the UDCs an opportunity to save themselves and humiliate the United States at the same time; and in human affairs, as we all know, biological realities could never interfere with such an opportunity. The scientists were silenced, the politicians said yes, the Thanodrin plants were built, and the results were what any beginning ecology student could have predicted. At first Thanodrin seemed to offer excellent control of many pests. True, there was a rash of human fatalities from improper 24 use of the lethal chemical, but as Russian technical advisors were prone to note, these were more than compensated for by increased yields. Thanodrin use skyrocketed throughout the underdeveloped world. The Mikoyan design group developed a dependable, cheap, agricultural aircraft which the Soviets donated to the effort in large numbers. MIG sprayers became even more common in UDCs than MIG interceptors.

Then the troubles began. Insect strains with cuticles resistant to   25
Thanodrin penetration began to appear. And as streams, rivers, fish culture ponds and onshore waters became rich in Thanodrin, more fisheries began to disappear. Bird populations were decimated. The sequence of events was standard for broadcast use of a synthetic pesticide: great success at first, followed by removal of natural enemies and development of resistance by the pest. Populations of crop-eating insects in areas treated with Thanodrin made steady comebacks and soon became more abundant than ever. Yields plunged while farmers in their desperation increased the Thanodrin dose and shortened the time between treatments. Death from Thanodrin poisoning became common. The first violent incident occurred in the Canete Valley of Peru, where farmers had suffered a similar chlorinated hydrocarbon disaster in the mid-50's. A Russian advisor serving as an agricultural pilot was assaulted and killed by a mob of enraged farmers in January, 1978. Trouble spread rapidly during 1978, especially after the word got out that two years earlier Russia herself had banned the use of Thanodrin at home because of its serious effects on ecological systems. Suddenly Russia, and not the United States, was the *bête noir* in the UDCs. "Thanodrin parties" became epidemic, with farmers, in their ignorance, dumping carloads of Thanodrin concentrate into the sea. Russian advisors fled, and four of the Thanodrin plants were leveled to the ground. Destruction of the plants in Rio and Calcutta led to hundreds of thousands of gallons of Thanodrin concentrate being dumped directly into the sea.

Mr. Shankarnarayan again rose to address the U.N., but this time it   26
was Mr. Potemkin, representative of the Soviet Union, who was on the hot seat. Mr. Potemkin heard his nation described as the greatest mass killer of all time as Shankarnarayan predicted at least thirty million deaths from crop failure due to overdependence on Thanodrin. Russia was accused of "chemical aggression," and the General Assembly, after a weak reply by Potemkin, passed a vote of censure.

It was in January, 1979, that huge blooms of a previously unknown   27
variety of diatom were reported off the coast of Peru. The blooms were accompanied by a massive die-off of sea life and of the pathetic reminder of the birds which had once feasted on the anchovies of the area. Almost

immediately another huge bloom was reported in the Indian ocean, centering around the Seychelles, and then a third in the South Atlantic off the African coast. Both of these were accompanied by spectacular die-offs of marine animals. Even more ominous were growing reports of fish and bird kills at oceanic points where there were no spectacular blooms. Biologists were soon able to explain the phenomena: the diatom had evolved an enzyme which broke down Thanodrin; that enzyme also produced a breakdown product which interfered with the transmission of nerve impulses, and was therefore lethal to animals. Unfortunately, the biologists could suggest no way of repressing the poisonous diatom bloom in time. By September, 1979, all important animal life in the sea was extinct. Large areas of coastline had to be evacuated, as windrows of dead fish created a monumental stench.

But stench was the least of man's problems. Japan and China were   28 faced with almost instant starvation from a total loss of the seafood on which they were so dependent. Both blamed Russia for their situation and demanded immediate mass shipments of food. Russia had none to send. On October 13, Chinese armies attacked Russia on a broad front. . . .

V

A pretty grim scenario. Unfortunately, we're a long way into it already.   29 Everything mentioned as happening before 1970 has actually occurred; much of the rest is based on projections of trends already appearing. Evidence that pesticides have long-term lethal effects on human beings has started to accumulate, and recently Robert Finch, Secretary of the Department of Health, Education and Welfare, expressed his extreme apprehension about the pesticide situation. Simultaneously the petro-chemical industry continues its unconscionable poison-peddling. For instance, Shell Chemical has been carrying on a high-pressure campaign to sell the insecticide Azodrin to farmers as a killer of cotton pests. They continue their program even though they know that Azodrin is not only ineffective, but often *increases* the pest density. They have covered themselves nicely in an advertisement which states, "Even if an over-powering migration [sic] develops, the flexibility of Azodrin lets you regain control fast. Just increase the dosage according to label recommendations." It's a great game—get people to apply the poison and kill the natural enemies of the pests. Then blame the increased pests on "migration" and sell even more pesticide!

Right now fisheries are being wiped out by overexploitation, made   30 easy by modern electronic equipment. The companies producing the equipment know this. They even boast in advertising that only their equipment will keep fishermen in business until the final kill. Profits must obviously be maximized in the short run. Indeed, Western society is in the process of completing the rape and murder of the planet for economic gain. And, sadly, most of the rest of the world is eager for the opportunity to emulate our behavior. But the underdeveloped peoples will be denied that opportunity — the days of plunder are drawing inexorably to a close.

Most of the people who are going to die in the greatest cataclysm in *31* the history of man have already been born. More than three and a half billion people already populate our moribund globe, and about half of them are hungry. Some ten to twenty million will starve to death *this* year. In spite of this, the population of the earth will increase by seventy million souls in 1969. For mankind has artificially lowered the death rate of the human population, while in general birth rates have remained high. With the input side of the population system in high gear and the output side slowed down, our fragile planet has filled with people at an incredible rate. It took several million years for the population to reach a total of two billion people in 1930, *while a second two billion will have been added by 1975!* By that time some experts feel that food shortages will have escalated the present level of world hunger and starvation into famines of unbelievable proportions. Other experts, more optimistic, think the ultimate food-population collision will not occur until the decade of the 1980's. Of course, more massive famine may be avoided if other events cause a prior rise in the human death rate.

Both worldwide plague and thermonuclear war are made more probable *32* as population growth continues. These, along with famine, make up the trio of potential "death rate solutions" to the population problem — solutions in which the birth rate — death rate imbalance is redressed by a rise in the death rate rather than by a lowering of the birth rate. Make no mistake about it, *the imbalance will be redressed.* The shape of the population growth curve is one familiar to the biologist. It is the outbreak part of an outbreak-crash sequence. A population grows more rapidly in the presence of abundant resources, finally runs out of food or some other necessity, and crashes to a low level or extinction. Man is not only running out of food, he is also destroying the life support systems of the Spaceship Earth. The situation was recently summarized very succinctly: "It is the top of the ninth inning. Man, always a threat at the plate, has been hitting Nature hard. It is important to remember, however, that NATURE BATS LAST."

QUESTIONS AND EXERCISES

Vocabulary

1. Define or explain each of the following terms:

   photosynthesis (1)   endemic (11)
   ecologists (1)   panacea (11)
   eco-catastrophe (2)   chauvinistic (12)
   phytoplankton (3)   ameliorate (13)
   zooplankton (3)   hegemony (17)
   drivel (7)   *bête noire* (25)
   exacerbated (11)   diatom (27)
   cupidity (11)   moribund (31)

Rhetoric

2. What figure of speech is "chains of life" in paragraph 3?
3. In what ways is this essay indebted to *1984* and *Brave New World?*
4. What is the irony in the statement in paragraph 5, "This opposition was generated primarily by the American petrochemical industry, operating hand in glove with its subsidiary, the United States Department of Agriculture."? What other figure of speech is involved?
5. What is the allusion to the "Green Revolution" found in paragraphs 6 and 7?
6. What figure of speech is found at the end of paragraph 9?
7. What humor is there in paragraph 10?
8. The argument is based on a scenario that is a type of science-fiction narrative. What is the balance of science and fiction?

Theme

9. Do you agree that the military-industrial complex is a mixture of greed and avarice?
10. Summarize the predictions made in "Eco-Catastrophe."
11. What are the chances that man will avoid the end predicted by Ehrlich?
12. Are there any optimistic notes?
13. Describe the villains and show the nature of their greed and avarice.
14. What can be done to prevent the disaster?
15. Compare the future predicted in "Eco-Catastrophe" with the futures forecast in other works like *1984, Brave New World,* and *Walden Two.* Which is the disaster of your choice?

Topics and Assignments for Composition

1. Summarize the thesis of the essay.

2. Compare or contrast the narrative technique with other science-fiction works you have read.
3. Write a narrative similar to Ehrlich's to indicate what you think will happen within the next couple of decades.
4. Research the scientific aspects of Ehrlich's presentation and report the results of your findings.
5. Write an open letter to the leaders of your government indicating what they should do to prevent the catastrophe.

A. J. Ayer

The Elimination of Metaphysics

The traditional disputes of philosophers are, for the most part, as un- *1*
warranted as they are fruitful. The surest way to end them is to establish
beyond question what should be the purpose and method of a philosophical enquiry. And this is by no means so difficult a task as the history
of philosophy would lead one to suppose. For if there are any questions
which science leaves it to philosophy to answer, a straightforward process
of elimination must lead to their discovery.

We may begin by criticising the metaphysical thesis that philosophy *2*
affords us knowledge of a reality transcending the world of science and
common sense. Later on, when we come to define metaphysics and
account for its existence, we shall find that it is possible to be a metaphysician without believing in a transcendent reality; for we shall see
that many metaphysical utterances are due to the commission of logical
errors, rather than to a conscious desire on the part of their authors to
go beyond the limits of experience. But it is convenient for us to take the
case of those who believe that it is possible to have knowledge of a
transcendent reality as a starting-point for our discussion. The arguments which we use to refute them will subsequently be found to apply
to the whole of metaphysics.

One way of attacking a metaphysician who claimed to have knowl- *3*
edge of a reality which transcended the phenomenal world would be to
enquire from what premises his propositions were deduced. Must he not
begin, as other men do, with the evidence of his senses? And if so, what
valid process of reasoning can possibly lead him to the conception of a
transcendent reality? Surely from empirical premises nothing whatsoever
concerning the properties, or even the existence, of anything super-
empirical can legitimately be inferred. But this objection would be met

From *Language Truth and Logic* by Alfred Jules Ayer. Dover Publications,
Inc., New York. Reprinted through the permission of the publisher.

by a denial on the part of the metaphysician that his assertions were ultimately based on the evidence of his senses. He would say that he was
endowed with a faculty of intellectual intuition which enabled him to
know facts that could not be known through sense-experience. And even
if it could be shown that he was relying on empirical premises, and that
his venture into a non-empirical world was therefore logically unjustified, it would not follow that the assertions which he made concerning
this non-empirical world could not be true. For the fact that a conclusion
does not follow from its putative premise is not sufficient to show that it
is false. Consequently one cannot overthrow a system of transcendent
metaphysics merely by criticising the way in which it comes into being.
What is required is rather a criticism of the nature of the actual statements which compromise it. And this is the line of argument which we
shall, in fact, pursue. For we shall maintain that no statement which
refers to a "reality" transcending the limits of all possible sense-experience can possibly have any literal significance; from which it must follow
that the labours of those who have striven to describe such a reality have
all been devoted to the production of nonsense.

It may be suggested that this is a proposition which has already been   *4*
proved by Kant. But although Kant also condemned transcendent metaphysics, he did so on different grounds. For he said that the human
understanding was so constituted that it lost itself in contradictions when
it ventured out beyond the limits of possible experience and attempted to
deal with things in themselves. And thus he made the impossibility of a
transcendent metaphysic not, as we do, a matter of logic, but a matter of
fact. He asserted, not that our minds could not conceivably have had the
power of penetrating beyond the phenomenal world, but merely that they
were in fact devoid of it. And this leads the critic to ask how, if it is possible to know only what lies within the bounds of sense-experience, the
author can be justified in asserting that real things do exist beyond, and
how he can tell what are the boundaries beyond which the human understanding may not venture, unless he succeeds in passing them himself. As Wittgenstein says, "in order to draw a limit to thinking, we should
have to think both sides of this limit," a truth to which Bradley gives a
special twist in maintaining that the man who is ready to prove that metaphysics is impossible is a brother metaphysician with a rival theory of
his own.

Whatever force these objections may have against the Kantian doc-   *5*
trine, they have none whatsoever against the thesis that I am about to
set forth. It cannot here be said that the author is himself overstepping
the barrier he maintains to be impassable. For the fruitlessness of
attempting to transcend the limits of possible sense-experience will be

deduced, not from a psychological hypothesis concerning the actual constitution of the human mind, but from the rule which determines the literal
significance of language. Our charge against the metaphysician is not that
he attempts to employ the understanding in a field where it cannot profit-
ably venture, but that he produces sentences which fail to conform to the
conditions under which alone a sentence can be literally significant. Nor
are we ourselves obliged to talk nonsense in order to show that all sentences of a certain type are necessarily devoid of literal significance. We
need only formulate the criterion which enables us to test whether a sentence expresses a genuine proposition about a matter of fact, and then
point out that the sentences under consideration fail to satisfy it. And
this we shall now proceed to do. We shall first of all formulate the criterion in somewhat vague terms, and then give the explanations which
are necessary to render it precise.

The criterion which we use to test the genuineness of apparent state-   6
ments of fact is the criterion of verifiability. We say that a sentence is
factually significant to any given person, if, and only if, he knows how to
verify the proposition which it purports to express—that is, if he knows
what observations would lead him, under certain conditions, to accept
the proposition as being true, or reject it as being false. If, on the other
hand, the putative proposition is of such a character that the assumption
of its truth, or falsehood, is consistent with any assumption whatsoever
concerning the nature of his future experience, then, as far as he is concerned, it is, if not a tautology, a mere pseudo-proposition. The sentence
expressing it may be emotionally significant to him; but it is not literally
significant. And with regard to questions the procedure is the same. We
enquire in every case what observations would lead us to answer the
question, one way or the other; and, if none can be discovered, we must
conclude that the sentence under consideration does not, as far as we are
concerned, express a genuine question, however strongly its grammatical
appearance may suggest that it does.

As to the validity of the verification principle, in the form in which we   7
have stated it, a demonstration will be given in the course of this book.
For it will be shown that all propositions which have factual content are
empirical hypotheses; and that the function of an empirical hypothesis is
to provide a rule for the anticipation of experience. And this means that
every empirical hypothesis must be relevant to some actual, or possible,
experience, so that a statement which is not relevant to any experience is
not an empirical hypothesis, and accordingly has no factual content. But
this is precisely what the principle of verifiability asserts.

It should be mentioned here that the fact that the utterances of the   8
metaphysician are nonsensical does not follow simply from the fact that

they are devoid of factual content. It follows from that fact, together with the fact that they are not *a priori* propositions. And in assuming that they are not *a priori* propositions, we are once again anticipating the conclusions of a later chapter in this book. For it will be shown there that *a priori* propositions, which have always been attractive to philosophers on account of their certainty, owe this certainty to the fact that they are tautologies. We may accordingly define a metaphysical sentence as a sentence which purports to express a genuine proposition, but does, in fact, express neither a tautology nor an empirical hypothesis. And as tautologies and empirical hypotheses form the entire class of significant propositions, we are justified in concluding that all metaphysical assertions are nonsensical. Our next task is to show how they come to be made.

The use of the term "substance," to which we have already referred,   9
provides us with a good example of the way in which metaphysics mostly comes to be written. It happens to be the case that we cannot, in our language, refer to the sensible properties of a thing without introducing a word or phrase which appears to stand for the thing itself as opposed to anything which may be said about it. And, as a result of this, those who are infected by the primitive superstition that to every name a single real entity must correspond assume that it is necessary to distinguish logically between the thing itself and any, or all, of its sensible properties. And so they employ the term "substance" to refer to the thing itself. But from the fact that we happen to employ a single word to refer to a thing, and make that word the grammatical subject of the sentences in which we refer to the sensible appearances of the thing, it does not by any means follow that the thing itself is a "simple entity," or that it cannot be defined in terms of the totality of its appearances. It is true that in talking of "its" appearances we appear to distinguish the thing from the appearances, but that is simply an accident of linguistic usage. Logical analysis shows that what makes these "appearances" the "appearances of" the same thing is not their relationship to an entity other than themselves, but their relationship to one another. The metaphysician fails to see this because he is misled by a superficial grammatical feature of his language.

A simpler and clearer instance of the way in which a consideration of   10
grammar leads to metaphysics is the case of the metaphysical concept of Being. The origin of our temptation to raise questions about Being, which no conceivable experience would enable us to answer, lies in the fact that, in our language, sentences which express existential propositions and sentences which express attributive propositions may be of the same grammatical form. For instance, the sentences "Martyrs exist" and "Martyrs suffer" both consist of a noun followed by an intransitive verb, and

the fact that they have grammatically the same appearance leads one to assume that they are of the same logical type. It is seen that in the proposition "Martyrs suffer," the members of a certain species are credited with a certain attribute, and it is sometimes assumed that the same thing is true of such a proposition as "Martyrs exist." If this were actually the case, it would, indeed, be as legitimate to speculate about the Being of martyrs as it is to speculate about their suffering. But, as Kant pointed out, existence is not an attribute. For, when we ascribe an attribute to a thing, we covertly assert that it exists: so that if existence were itself an attribute, it would follow that all positive existential propositions were tautologies, and all negative existential propositions self-contradictory; and this is not the case. So that those who raise questions about Being which are based on the assumption that existence is an attribute are guilty of following grammar beyond the boundaries of sense.

A similar mistake has been made in connection with such propositions   *11* as "Unicorns are fictitious." Here again the fact that there is a superficial grammatical resemblance between the English sentences "Dogs are faithful" and "Unicorns are fictitious," and between the corresponding sentences in other languages, creates the assumption that they are of the same logical type. Dogs must exist in order to have the property of being faithful, and so it is held that unless unicorns in some way existed they could not have the property of being fictitious. But, as it is plainly self-contradictory to say that fictitious objects exist, the device is adopted of saying that they are real in some non-empirical sense – that they have a mode of real being which is different from the mode of being of existent things. But since there is no way of testing whether an object is real in this sense, as there is for testing whether it is real in the ordinary sense, the assertion that fictitious objects have a special non-empirical mode of real being is devoid of all literal significance. It comes to be made as a result of the assumption that being fictitious is an attribute. And this is a fallacy of the same order as the fallacy of supposing that existence is an attribute, and it can be exposed in the same way.

In general, the postulation of real nonexistent entities results from the   *12* superstition, just now referred to, that, to every word or phrase that can be the grammatical subject of a sentence, there must somewhere be a real entity corresponding. For as there is no place in the empirical world for many of these "entities," a special non-empirical world is invoked to house them. To this error must be attributed, not only the utterances of a Heidegger, who bases his metaphysic on the assumption that "Nothing" is a name which is used to denote something peculiarly mysterious, but also the prevalence of such problems as those concerning the reality of propositions and universals whose senselessness, though less obvious, is no less complete.

These few examples afford a sufficient indication of the way in which   *13* most metaphysical assertions come to be formulated. They show how easy it is to write sentences which are literally nonsensical without seeing that they are nonsensical. And thus we see that the view that a number of the traditional "problems of philosophy" are metaphysical, and consequently fictitious, does not involve any incredible assumptions about the psychology of philosophers.

Among those who recognize that if philosophy is to be accounted a   *14* genuine branch of knowledge it must be defined in such a way as to distinguish it from metaphysics, it is fashionable to speak of the metaphysician as a kind of misplaced poet. As his statements have no literal meaning, they are not subject to any criteria of truth or falsehood: but they may still serve to express, or arouse, emotion, and thus be subject to ethical or aesthetic standards. And it is suggested that they may have considerable value, as means of moral inspiration, or even as works of art. In this way, an attempt is made to compensate the metaphysician for his extrusion from philosophy.

I am afraid that this compensation is hardly in accordance with his   *15* deserts. The view that the metaphysician is to be reckoned among the poets appears to rest on the assumption that both talk nonsense. But this assumption is false. In the vast majority of cases the sentences which are produced by poets do have literal meaning. The difference between the man who uses language scientifically and the man who uses it emotively is not that the one produces sentences which are incapable of arousing emotion, and the other sentences which have no sense, but that the one is primarily concerned with the expression of true propositions, the other with the creation of a work of art. Thus, if a work of science contains true and important propositions, its value as a work of science will hardly be diminished by the fact that they are inelegantly expressed. And similarly, a work of art is not necessarily the worse for the fact that all the propositions comprising it are literally false. But to say that many literary works are largely composed of falsehoods, is not to say that they are composed of pseudo-propositions. It is, in fact, very rare for a literary artist to produce sentences which have no literal meaning. And where this does occur, the sentences are carefully chosen for their rhythm and balance. If the author writes nonsense, it is because he considers it most suitable for bringing about the effects for which his writing is designed.

The metaphysician, on the other hand, does not intend to write non-   *16* sense. He lapses into it through being deceived by grammar, or through committing errors of reasoning, such as that which leads to the view that the sensible world is unreal. But it is not the mark of a poet simply to make mistakes of this sort. There are some, indeed, who would see in the fact that the metaphysician's utterances are senseless a reason against the view that they have aesthetic value. And, without going so far as this, we may safely say that it does not constitute a reason for it.

It is true, however, that although the greater part of metaphysics is   *17* merely the embodiment of humdrum errors, there remain a number of metaphysical passages which are the work of genuine mystical feeling; and they may more plausibly be held to have moral or aesthetic value. But, as far as we are concerned, the distinction between the kind of metaphysics that is produced by a philosopher who has been duped by grammar, and the kind that is produced by a mystic who is trying to express the inexpressible, is of no great importance: what is important to us is to realise that even the utterances of the metaphysician who is attempting to expound a vision are literally senseless; so that henceforth we may pursue our philosophical researches with as little regard for them as for the more inglorious kind of metaphysics which comes from a failure to understand the workings of our language.

QUESTIONS AND EXERCISES

Vocabulary

1. Define or explain the following terms:

metaphysics (title)	linguistic (9)
transcending (2)	covertly (10)
phenomenal (3)	postulation (12)
empirical (3)	entities (12)
verifiability (6)	extrusion (14)
putative (6)	humdrum (17)
tautology (6)	mystical (17)
pseudo-proposition (6)	duped (17)
a priori (8)	

2. Explain or identify the following people:

Kant (4)	Bradley (4)
Wittgenstein (4)	Heidegger (12)

Rhetoric

3. What is the tone of this essay?
4. Why are there very few examples of figurative language in this essay?
5. At what level audience is the author aiming his argument?

6. Describe the basic pattern of organization.
7. Why are very few transitional devices needed to maintain continuity and coherence?

Theme

8. Distinguish between philosophy and metaphysics as Ayer uses the term.
9. How does Ayer use the term "nonsense"?
10. Why is verifiability important in philosophy?
11. What is a tautology? What part do tautologies play in philosophy?
12. What is the implication of the claim that ". . . tautologies and empirical hypothesis form the entire class of significant propositions, we are justified in concluding that all metaphysical assertions are nonsensical."
13. Why does grammar lead metaphysicians to make nonsensical claims?
14. Distinguish between metaphysicians and poets. Do you think that they both talk nonsense?
15. Are mystical experiences also nonsense? What kind of propositions do religious philosophers make?

Topics and Assignments for Composition

1. Write five sentences that are tautologies. Example: All male siblings are brothers.
2. Write five sentences that are empirical propositions. Example: Doctors earn more money on the average per year than do professors.
3. Write five metaphysical sentences. Example: The really important things in life are revealed by transcendental meditation.
4. Choose a philosopher with whose works you are familiar and find a significant quotation of his and analyze it in the light of Ayer's discussion.
5. Analyze your personal philosophy and evaluate it according to Ayer's essay.
6. Write an expository essay on either logical positivism or logical analysis.

Shirley Chisholm

Needed: Equal Educational Opportunity for All

A democratic society depends upon the intelligence and wisdom of *1* the mass of people to keep the country moving. A government of the people, by the people, and for the people necessarily depends upon the people's judgment to make decisions that affect the growth of the country. In America, we have delegated to institutions of higher education the responsibility to train the minds of those who will make scientific and medical discoveries; who will give us an intellectual basis for law, order, and justice; and who will propagate an appreciation for the arts — thus, supplying us with cultural training.

While the fulfillment of these responsibilities remain the central pur- *2* pose of institutions of higher education, American society casts another, less theoretical responsibility upon institutions of higher learning — that of granting "union cards" for upward social mobility. The slogan, "education is the key to success," is interpreted, in the United States, to mean that graduation from college opens up job possibilities at a salary range which is above that of the average American. Indeed, this very practical consideration of what one can do with a college degree — usually referred to as a college education — too often interferes with the more esoteric concern of how one's mind is strengthened by studying a particular curriculum at school.

It is the mundane and practical consideration of acquiring a college *3* degree for the purpose of upward mobility which is inescapably on the minds of minority groups in their demand for equal participation in the mainstream of American society. Higher education is the key to this goal;

Reprinted from *School & Society,* April 1972 with permission from the publisher.

and institutions of higher learning must address themselves to a relatively new constituency.

Toward this end, there must be universal acceptance of the premise   *4*
that higher education is the right of every American who has demonstrated the ability of potential for doing academic work at the college level. Many Americans have come to accept this in theory, but few have become directly involved in seeking ways of implementation. The municipal government of New York City, in conjunction with the Board of Education, has taken a bold step in practically applying the theory. New York City now has a policy of open admissions, where high school graduates who are residents of the city are guaranteed admission to one of the colleges in the city's college system upon application. The program was devised after the demands of blacks from Bedford-Stuyvesant and Harlem and of Puerto Ricans from the Bronx, but it has proved to be as valuable to the white residents of Queens and Staten Island as it has to minorities from ghettoes.

Neither the quality of education offered nor respect for the integrity   *5*
of a college diploma has been impaired by the institution of open enrollment. It is certainly a program worthy of implementation throughout the country, and one which is absolutely necessary for allowing the economically disadvantaged to assume their right of education. But, at this point, our nation lacks the commitment to invest the proper resources in higher education.

Resources from the government and private sources are mandatory,   *6*
for open enrollment as well as any other program designed to open college doors to minorities places an extra financial burden upon the institutions. Thus, institutions of higher education must be given plenty of financial assistance if they are to fulfill the new obligations of allowing minorities and the poor access to higher education—toward the ultimate end of entrance into the mainstream of American society.

Will we have the courage and commitment to stop utilizing our re-   *7*
sources on warfare and to work on the intellectual and economic development of the American people? Will we desist from practices that deprive minorities and women of the opportunity to participate fully in our society? These are questions which the great majority of Americans will have to answer; and higher education must do the same.

There must be a willingness on the part of college administrators to   *8*
propose policies on admission that will take into consideration the obligation of higher education to address itself to the needs of minorities, women, and the poor. There also must be steps taken to make sure that the course of study effectively treats the contributions of minorities to

the growth and development of American society and that courses are offered which will educate college students to the abuses and inequalities in our system and which will urge their involvement in activities designed to promote equality of rights for all Americans.

Such education should be part of the curriculum in any democratic society; and it does not involve, in my view, the institutions, themselves, in social activity. Rather, it presents the students with the opportunity to apply certain theories to practical situations, which is in keeping with the notion that the only valuable education is one which promotes an understanding of what is necessary in order for human beings to make a contribution to the growth, prosperity, and durability of an orderly society.   9

QUESTIONS AND EXERCISES

Vocabulary

1. Define or explain each of the following terms:
   "union cards" (2)
   mundane (3)
   ghettoes (4)
   mandatory (6)

Rhetoric

2. What elements of style are apparent in Chisholm's essay?
3. Explain the absence of figurative language. At what audience is this essay aimed?
4. Analyze the grammatical structure of the sentences in paragraph 2.
5. Find the figure of speech in paragraph 3. In paragraph 6.

Theme

6. What is the concept of open enrollment referred to in paragraph 5?
7. In what paragraph is the thesis of the essay stated? What is the thesis?
8. What are the barriers to the achievement of the goals outlined in the essay?
9. Why does Chisholm link the minorities and the poor with women in paragraphs 7 and 8?
10. Is there another thesis presented in paragraphs 8 and 9? Why is it there?

Topics and Assignments for Composition

1. Analyze the relationship of clichés and meaning in the essay.

2. In a short essay comment on the ideas expressed in the essay; consider the reasoning, the audience addressed, and the effectiveness of expression.
3. Write an essay of personal reaction to any of the ideas presented in Chisholm's essay.

Student Example

The Los Angelization of the World:
A Cultural Tragedy

In his film "Weekend," Jean-Luc Godard symbolized the end of the world as an immense traffic jam. The best symbol for the total Los Angelization of the world might be a huge global parking lot, divided by interminable freeways and clusters of gas stations, car dealers, race tracks, car washes, used car lots, drive-in restaurants, drive-in theaters, drive-in banks, drive-in supermarkets, and junkyards. While Los Angelization has not yet reached this point, even in Los Angeles, the above scene is not as far-fetched as one might believe. Much of the world is rapidly becoming Americanized while America is becoming Los Angelized. This in itself is not necesarily bad; Los Angeles in many ways represents a break from the patterns and traditions of the decaying East and the dull Middle West. But as a culture, Los Angeles is barren. The common assumption that Los Angelization means progress is not particularly valid; it can be just as easily argued that Los Angelization means cultural chaos and retrogression.

In addition to being the epitome of the dehumanized Car Culture, Los Angeles is a prime example of the Non-City. It is composed of a group of sprawling cities, communities, and neighborhoods, surrounded, connected, and divided by miles of freeway. The tourist in Los Angeles cannot stroll through the heart of the city as he can in backward, not totally Los Angelized places such as London and Paris. If he wishes to capture the unique Los Angeles atmosphere, he must get into a car and drive somewhere, anywhere. If the symbol of Los Angeles is the car, then the heart of Los Angeles is the freeway.

Physically, then, Los Angelization represents the triumph of the automobile and its accouterments, such as air pollution, freeways, and gas stations. The social manifestations of Los Angelization are even more disturbing. Because of the elements of mobility, modernity, and swift change present in Los Angeles culture, there is also an element of confusion, of cultural schizophrenia. One basic characteristic of Los Angeles culture is the emotional adherence to the ideals of Youth, Affluence, and Fun. These ideals, of course, are common throughout America and the rest of the Western world, but in Los Angeles culture they have been accepted and promoted to an overwhelming degree.

The California youth cult is a good example of this. It was in Los Angeles that the surfer—bronzed god—California blond stereotype was created a few years ago, developing a huge market for "baggies" and Clairol. More recently, the fads, fashions, and antics of teenyboppers, hippies, and youth in general have been publicized, commercialized, and promoted to the extent that they have been adopted by adults and by the envious, admiring young people of Akron, Saigon, and Katmandu. To be Los Angelized means to be "with it" at all times.

The excessive commercialism is, of course, a reflection of affluence. People have the money to wear the latest styles, buy the newest products, and indulge in the most popular fads and activities.

In a general sense, Los Angeles is a "have" culture. The affluent and those on the brink of affluence are constantly looking for something new, exciting, and different to buy or to do. The acquiring of material objects and the pursuit of Fun often seem to result in boredom and frustration. This is particularly true in relation to the young, who, with their insatiable appetites for excitement and gratification, often go to extremes in their search; the widespread use of dangerous drugs is a typical example of this. Basically, Los Angeles is a culture in which the norms of affluence and prosperity have led to frustration and alienation, to a confused and sometimes overly hedonistic society. Films such as "Divorce American Style" and "The Graduate," both set in Los Angeles, depicted a super-affluent but soulless environment.

The other face of the schizophrenic Los Angeles culture is a repressive, neo-Puritan one. For example, though there is an atmosphere of overall youth worship, there is seemingly a hatred of the young themselves, characterized by curfew laws and police surveillance and harassment. There is a tendency to isolate nonaffluent minority groups in their little freeway-enclosed ghettos and to ignore them until they start trouble, at which time the police are called in. There is the ridiculous "topless and bottomless" controversy, in which the police make token arrests to accommodate "outraged public morality." There are the periodic "clean-up drives," in which bare feet, discotheques, and long-haired youth are subject to special harassment until it is decided that the hippie problem is once again under control.

All of the characteristics of Los Angeles culture are now becoming typical of the rest of the country as well, but there is something about Los Angeles which makes it special. It is an undisputed leader, a city which is setting the pattern for much of the world's future. Many social scientists feel that within the next twenty years, most of the Western world and much of the American-influenced non-Western world will come to resemble Los Angeles, both visually and culturally. Los Angelization will bring technological advancement and increased affluence, but millions of people from Bali to Andorra, as they sit in their Mustangs at the nearest Jack-in-the-Box, and as they drive across twelve-lane freeways to their suburban homes and alienated children, will perhaps wonder just what cultural progress has been made.

Part Ten:
Reviews

George Frazier

A Sense of Style

He was seventeen years old, acted like he was about twelve, and he   *1*
was the most terrific liar you ever saw in your life. Four prep schools had
found it a privilege to get along without him and once, after he had offered
an operation on his clavichord as an excuse for his continence, a call
girl had dismissed him as a crum-bum. He was really kind of impossible —
enormously lovable, of course, but kind of impossible just the same —
and the only wonder is how he ever managed to stay out of a mental institution as long as he did. And yet, for all the frailties of his flesh, all
the aberrations of his brain, he was the sharpest and fussiest observer of
other people's social behavior to have come along in the two-hundred-
odd years since Philip Dormer Stanhope, the fourth Earl of Chesterfield,
wrote his 421st, and last, letter to his son.

They make such an odd couple, those two — Holden Caulfield of *The*   *2*
Catcher in the Rye and that suave cynical old peer of the realm who was
accused of teaching his son "the morals of a whore and the manners of a
dancing master"; the one so profuse with his "goddams" as he races
through that saddest and funniest of all odysseys, wearing his red hunting
hat and wondering where the ducks go when the lagoon in Central Park
freezes over, the other so polished in his phrasing, so proper with his
"your humble servants." And yet they had a thing in common, this
oddest of all odd couples — they both cared about the social graces, both
were obsessed by a man's sense of style. And, perhaps not too surprisingly, both were destined to be misunderstood, Holden Caulfield
ending up as an image of the antic and milord as literature's most ma-
ligned correspondent.

As for the odium that Chesterfield's memory has had to endure these   *3*
two centuries, the blame for that can be traced to old Sam Johnson and
his calumny about the letters teaching the morals of a whore and so

forth. Naturally, this is unfortunate, but what, after all, is to be expected of a pair of gabby old aunties like the doctor and that toady of a Boswell, gossipy, spiteful, and looking for all the world as if they were in drag, the Gertrude Stein and Alice B. Toklas of their time? Eventually, of course, Johnson got around to acknowledging that milord's manner was "exquisitely elegant," but by then the harm had been done and the good interred with Chesterfield's bones.

But Holden Caulfield's case is not quite the same, for we misunder- *4*
stand *him,* not out of animosity, but affection. We love him so much, so to speak, we can't see straight. He could be the nastiest, most miserable little son of a bitch on two feet, but we would be the last to know it, for we are too captive to his charm, too enchanted by his imagery, too incredulous at his imaginings, too transfixed by the inflections of his voice. And, naturally, he is always saying such funny things, such marvelous, preposterous things—one minute, "What really knocks me out is a book that, when you're all done reading it, you wish the author that wrote it was a terrific friend of yours and you could call him up on the phone whenever you felt like it," and the next minute, "Sensitive. That killed me. That guy Morrow was about as sensitive as a goddam toilet seat"; on this page, "I hate actors. They never act like people," on that page, "I'm quite illiterate, but I read a lot."

And so on and on, so wittily or poignantly or perceptively that we are *5*
absolutely enthralled—so completely so, in fact, that we hate, we positively loathe, we simply cannot stand the sight of any stupid bastard who doesn't share our commitment to Caulfield. And damned well we should, too, for who needs those kinds of people? After all, this boy—well, there has never been anyone else in American fiction quite so captivating, or not at least since Huck Finn. But we are too enchanted to notice that this is more than merely a funny boy. This is also a very bright boy, and, more than that, a social arbiter more acute than anyone since Chesterfield. No one, not even milord himself, has ever been so outraged by the awful.

If there's one thing depresses Holden Caulfield—it makes him so de- *6*
pressed he can't stand it, for Chrissake!—it is all the pathetic people who simply do not know any better, all the people with no sense of style. And the world we live in is teeming with such people—the well-meaning, but ignorant, the poor souls who watch the "Miss America" contest on TV and take it seriously; people who eat a slice of toast without breaking it into pieces; people who drive white cars; people, in short, who just do not know any better. And then, of course, there are the unforgivables, the truly terrible people who tug at your sleeve to emphasize a point, discuss

unattractive things at the dinner table, pick their teeth in public, and talk with their mouths full. God, those people are awful!

As it happens, Holden Caulfield's opprobrium was not directed at any 7 of those people, nor at women who almost put out your eye with their umbrellas, either, but he did not want for occasions of indignation. Naturally, he did not entirely ignore the obvious—people who pick their noses, who say "grand"—but it is a measure of his expertise in such matters, his fastidiousness, that he concentrates upon the awful that is esoteric, the awful, if you will, that is, in a reverse way, "in," like, for instance, men who try to conceal their baldness ("those bald guys that comb all their hair over from the side to cover up the baldness. I'd rather be bald than do that"), secret slobs (the boy who "always *looked* all right . . . but you should've seen the razor he shaved himself with"), and cheap luggage. If there's one thing that Holden Caulfield can't stand, for Chrissake, one thing that depresses him, it's cheap luggage. "It sounds terrible to say it," he admits, "but I can even get to hate somebody, just *looking* at them, if they have cheap suitcases with them."

These are the people for whom Holden Caulfield reserves his most 8 withering contempt—these people, and people who dance with little kids ("I don't like people that dance with little kids, because most of the time it looks terrible. I mean if you're out at a restaurant somewhere and you see some old guy take his little kid out on the dance floor. Usually they keep yanking the kid's dress up in back by mistake, and the kid can't dance worth a damn *any*way"), and people, really appalling people like the three women he met in the bar of his hotel one night ("They were so ignorant, and they had those sad, fancy hats on and all. And that business about getting up early to see the first show at Radio City Music Hall depressed me. If somebody, some girl in an awful-looking hat, for instance, comes all the way to New York—from Seattle, *Wash*ington, for God's sake—and ends up getting up early in the morning to see the goddam first show at Radio City Music Hall, it makes me so depressed I can't stand it").

But it is part of Caulfield's sense of style, as it was of Chesterfield's, 9 that he is ever observant of *noblesse oblige,* that his castigation is never directed toward conditions beyond a person's control. Chesterfield's bequests to his servants were addressed to "unfortunate friends, my equals by nature, and my inferiors only by the difference of our fortunes," and once, in a letter to his son, he said, "Are you better born, as silly people call it, than the servant who wipes your shoes? Not in the least; he had a father and mother, and they had fathers and mothers." Holden Caulfield may be so depressed by black-and-white shoes and suits with padded shoulders that he can't stand it, but his real scorn is directed less toward a man who would wear them than toward a headmaster "who'd be charming as hell" except if some boy's father should turn up in such an outfit. In the catechism according to Caulfield, the most mortal of all sins is phoniness, for to be phony is to be without any style at all.

This is why *The Catcher in the Rye* is the text for the time of youth. It   *10* seems so ironic that Holden Caulfield, who was such a penetrating judge of style in other people, should have been so unaware of what a stylesetter he was himself, peppering the parlance of youth with his impudent idioms, serving as a model for the intransigent, providing a platform even for a John Lennon. "Jesus was all right but his disciples were thick and ordinary," Lennon observed last August. "It's them twisting it that ruins it for me."

Fifteen years before, Holden Caulfield had put it this way, "I like Jesus   *11* and all, but I don't care too much for most of the other stuff in the Bible. Take the Disciples, for instance. They annoy the hell out of me, if you want to know the truth. They were all right after Jesus was dead and all, but while He was alive, they were about as much use to Him as a hole in the head. All they did was keep letting Him down. I like almost anybody in the Bible better than the Disciples."

QUESTIONS AND EXERCISES

Vocabulary

1. Define or explain the meaning of the following terms:

continence (1)	enthralled (5)
aberration (1)	opprobrium (7)
cynical (2)	expertise (7)
odysseys (2)	fastidiousness (7)
odium (3)	esoteric (7)
calumny (3)	catechism (9)
animosity (4)	ironic (10)
incredulous (4)	parlance (10)
preposterous (4)	intransigent (10)
poignantly (5)	

2. Identify or explain the allusion in each of these items:

Earl of Chesterfield (1)	Gertrude Stein (3)
"the doctor" (3)	Alice B. Toklas (3)
Boswell (3)	*noblesse oblige* (9)
"in drag" (3)	John Lennon (10)

Rhetoric

3. What is the tone of this essay?
4. What is the purpose of the comparison of Holden Caulfield to Lord Chesterfield? How effective is this analogy?
5. How does the author manage to capture the style of Holden Caulfield?
6. Comment on the level of diction of some of the expressions. What justifies their use in this essay?
7. Define how "style" is used in this essay.

Theme

8. What is the main purpose or theme of this essay? Do you find any ambivalence in the focus?
9. What are some of the targets of Holden's scorn?
10. Do you think Frazier shares the same views? Support your answer with specific evidence from the text.
11. How are John Lennon and Holden Caulfield compared?
12. What books are the current college and sophisticated high school students reading (unassigned reading)?

Topics and Assignments for Composition

1. In a well-developed sentence summarize the main idea that Frazier presents in this essay.
2. In a paragraph discuss the comparisons that Frazier develops in "A Sense of Style."
3. Write a book review of a contemporary novel in which you take an unusual tone or point of view. Use some of the techniques used by Frazier: extensive quotations, comparisons, and allusions.
4. Write a parody of a portion of a well-known popular novel. A parody usually is used for gentle satire, but it does point out eccentricities and excesses of the style of the original. Read a few parodies of well-known authors before you try yours. J. D. Salinger is one of the favorite targets of parodies.

Herbert Gold

Richard Brautigan Mystifies Gently

Who is Richard Brautigan? What is he? A minigeneration of college *1*
kids has been burning to find the answer to this question: and so, perhaps, has Richard Brautigan. His fantastic popularity suggests, among
other matters, the answer to a whole host of questions about hippie,
post-modern, flower-child, California, new-poetics, San Francisco, North
Beach writing. Those are questions you haven't asked? Never mind;
those are the questions you might ask if you are considering this poet
who, along with his elder brethren, Lawrence Ferlinghetti and Alan Ginsberg, has persevered from beatness unto hipness and on into the 70s.

Rod McKuen takes care of the groupie children of This-is-my-beloved. *2*

Michael McClure keeps the ravenous and witty descendants of the *3*
Marquis De Sade in leather and meat.

Gary Snyder lurks in the East, coming on gently. *4*

But Richard Brautigan is really popular. And respectable. And whim- *5*
sical. And children can give his books to their parents without either
condescension or being accused of a dirty, rotten, hostile, oedipal act.
He writes poems, stories, and novels of great simple charm, and appeals
to complex motives.

What are the questions? (See Paragraph One.) *6*

Is it necessary to be deep? Answer: No. *7*

Is it necessary to tell the truth? Answer: No. *8*

Is it necessary to arouse, rabble-rouse, or carouse? Answer: No. *9*

Then what need a poet do to be a spokesman and leader in these *10*
TIMES? Answer, in a paragraph all by itself:

Make magic. Brautigan mystifies gently. Brautigan paints reality so *11*
that you no longer see it, and paints unreality so that it becomes real. He
is a portable coffee jag. It is no wonder that his latest book, "Revenge
of the Lawn," is dedicated to his friend, the novelist Don Carpenter, who

Reprinted by permission of the author.

preaches hypoglycemia with the passion others have spent on the steam engine and the armored car. The stories send a fellow floating.

What do they mean? They ask you to find meanings below the reverie   *12* line, where you listen to soft rock, where you lie awake in the morning after sleeping too much, where you pour that third cup or maybe the fourth.

They make a simple point: Nice to be home. Sorry Dad's dead. Glad   *13* to be in love. Too late for some people. What a long day.

But that sounds like Sherwood Anderson, and this is not Sherwood   *14* Anderson agony time. You have the feeling that Brautigan nodded his yellow hair and mustache over a glass of dark brown liquid, wetting his pencil in his teeth, on his tongue, without breaking off the point, and scribbled in notebook, and by the time the waiter at Enrico's came with the next glass of brown liquid (not coffee), the story was done.

Nightcrawlers in San Francisco see Richard Brautigan groupies   *15* harassing him at his labors, and admire his patience, the patience of the only surviving Confederate general from Big Sur, as he gently fends them off, or, if they are serious and pretty and lissome, fends them into the chair beside him. He sits silently. He listens. He writes another story.

Everyone will have favorites among these savantly wilted little tales.   *16* "Coffee" is about lost love, tender, regretful, winningly self-pitying, a glorious little devotion to a girl whose morning clothes don't yet bend to her body. Nor will she let the hero bend to her body anymore.

Many of these stories tell about inexplicable girls who look deep and   *17* are not. "The Betrayed Kingdom" is about a princess of the last season of the Beat Generation, and she gets men to drive her home, and it's a long way across bridges, and they end up sleeping on a blanket on the floor, anyway.

And there are childhood strophes and stories little longer than haikus,   *18* oh, maybe five or six times 17 syllables, and stories about sitting around. At his best, Brautigan provides a cool Platonic form of intimacy. The content is abstract. But the breath of coffee and wine, whisper and touch, is reassuring.

Once upon a time I contributed to the publication of "Please Plant   *19* This Book," a book of seeds wrapped in envelopes with poems by Richard Brautigan on them. I suppose this makes me one of his publishers, but I think I can be honest about his work anyway. At its best, it's lovely. At its second-best, it reads as if somebody is listening to Richard Brautigan all the time, and feels cute today. At its weakest, it makes an admirer want to say: Richard, you're in touch with the mystery, but don't sell it off. Get in touch with the other pasts and futures, too.

The time has come when even Joan Baez gets a dose of coolness from   *20* the young public. As Consciousness III enters the remainder phase, and the kids are marking each other down, Brautigan's sweet whimsy faces a hard season. From the audience which has treasured him in a paroxysm of embraces, surely; but also from himself, that most essential critic and audience.

The man who uses words like prophecy must speak to the uplifted   *21*
faces, and drip more than honey on them.

"She stared at them, not saying anything for a while." That's a quota-   *22*
tion from one of these stories.

Now remain silent, and then speak, Richard.   *23*

QUESTIONS AND EXERCISES

Vocabulary

1. Define or explain each of the following terms.
   oedipal act (5)   strophes (18)
   hypoglycemia (11)   paroxysm (20)
   groupies (15)

Rhetoric

2. Identify the following names alluded to:
   Lawrence Ferlinghetti (1)   Marquis De Sade (3)
   Alan Ginsberg (1)   Gary Snyder (4)
   Rod McKuen (2)   Sherwood Anderson (14)
   Michael McClure (3)   Joan Baez (20)
3. Why does Gold use many names in his review?
4. What is the tone of the review? Do you think Gold is condescending (a term he uses in paragraph 5)?
5. Does Gold give much information about *Revenge of the Lawn, Stories 1962–70?*
6. How does Gold's indirect approach fit his topic?

Theme

7. What is Gold's attitude toward Brautigan?
8. Do you want to know more about Brautigan after reading this review? Why?
9. What is the function of a review?
10. How does Gold indicate his qualifications to review this book to readers who may not be familiar with him?

Topics and Assignments for Composition

1. Write a short review of a book without giving the characters, setting,

and plot. Make extensive comparisons, contrasts, and allusions to other works.
2. Find another review of *Revenge of the Lawn, Stories 1962–70* and make a comparison with Gold's review.
3. Write a short essay setting forth what a book review should be and do.

Ronald Hilton

Ten Commandments for the New Behavioral Science — A Case Study

Political History Of Latin America by Ronald M. Glassman

Perhaps the most remarkable phenomenon in academe during the last decade has been the explosion of the behavioral sciences. The Ford Foundation lit the match; that should have been sufficient warning. It was assumed that the behavioral sciences would help society to solve its problems. University administrators, for whom there is no more potent argument than money and the fashions which attract it, were easily convinced. Those of us who are sympathetic to the social sciences and feel the need for academic renewal welcomed the newcomers. Then everything went sour.

Academic programs which represented decades of devoted work were neglected or wrecked. The social science departments throughout the country became havens for all kinds of idealists and misfits who were looking for a refuge within a refuge (the university) from which to launch their attacks on society. They incited physical violence on the university administrations which had encouraged them, and then turned on their departmental mentors, accusing them of irrelevance. More serious perhaps than these surface eruptions is the effect the behavioral sciences have had on scholarship. That is the subject of this review, since the book here examined provides us with a case study. Here are the characteristics of the new learning.

1. Take a limited subject but make it appear that it is of immense importance. Choose an appropriate, or rather inappropriate title: this book is certainly not a political history of Latin America. The first part deals with medieval Spain, the second with the quasi-feudal society of colonial America, the third with the origin of Latin American cities. A more exact

title would have been "Some considerations about the transfer of characteristics of medieval Iberian society to the New World."

2. Claim that your work brings new insights into social problems. The author asserts: "This kind of analysis has never been extended in depth to any of the underdeveloped countries, although some rudimentary attempts have been made in studying the Middle East and Africa. . . . No attempt to apply this model to Latin America has been made at all." In reality the book tells us little that a competent historian does not know already.

3. Invoke the name of Max Weber, as a Soviet Marxist invokes those of Marx and Lenin. This proves that you are orthodox and respectable. The name of Weber appears three times on the first page of the Foreword.

4. Show that you belong to a scientific elite by using strange words even though there is a more common synonym. If these words were used by Weber, so much the better. "Charismatic" used to be an esoteric term, but now it is common coin. So our author repeatedly uses "kingship" instead of "king," "monarchy" or "government." Why "legist" instead of "jurist," "lawmaker" or "lawyer"? If a person withdraws into his own private world, this is "retreatism." Throw in words like "surrogate" and "clan" whenever possible. What on earth is "dereified"? My dictionaries don't give it, and my sociology colleagues at Stanford don't know it. Although "charismatic" has lost its charisma, try it in exotic combinations like "law charisma" or "clan-charismatic." Combinations like "clan-heritable" are favored.

5. Prove your expertise by writing an English which is not only cumbersome but positively unpleasant to anyone who has a sense of style. In his acknowledgments the author thanks two colleagues who made the book more readable. Yet the style is still utterly lacking in "charisma."

6. Claim that you have a model that will bring order into a confused mass of facts. In this book the model is not clear, and after struggling through some 300 pages, the reader is left in a state of obfuscation, longing for an old-fashioned book which is well organized and in which ideas are expressed lucidly.

7. Don't bother too much about facts. At the recent annual meeting of the International Studies Association, a behavioral scientist pontificated: "Models without facts are no vice, facts without models are no virtue." It sounded as if he were reading from the Little Red Book of the Behavioral Scientist. The author of this book asserts airily that "the empirical data on Latin America have been available for almost a century—they are easily obtainable." Having thus dismissed the problem of "empirical data," he proceeds to make one mistake after another.

A whole review could be filled with the factual errors in the book; to mention but one, the author thinks that Havana was the seat of a vice-royalty. Anyone with experience in the field should know how extremely difficult it is to assemble facts about the political history of Latin America. Since the Hispanic American Report disappeared, we have had no good source for contemporary Latin America, and the situation is worse regarding other areas. Our ignorance of the facts is one reason why we make such mistakes in foreign policy. It is much easier to play with models. If an old-fashioned scholar stresses the extreme difficulty of checking and assembling facts, this is dismissed as "busy work" unworthy of a creative scholar. This, incidentally, is the rationale of the lazy and essentially mediocre students who wish to reduce classes to muddled, uninformative bull-sessions.

8. Since old-fashioned scholarship is "out," the author tells us at the *11* beginning of his bibliography that he will not list many books specifically on Latin America. He does list a number of them, but he seems to have depended largely on Jean Mariéjol's "The Spain of Ferdinand and Isabella" (in the English translation), Eyler N. Simpson's "The Ejido: Mexico's Way Out" (which is out of date—1937—and frequently wrong), and two books by George M. McBride, "The Land Systems of Mexico" (1923) and "Chile, Land and Society" (1936). McBride's studies were good for their time, but they are quite inadequate for present needs. From these four books, the author quotes frequently verbatim. There is no mention of the vast periodical literature without which it is impossible to write the political history of Latin America.

9. Acquiring the necessary linguistic mastery to study a foreign area *12* takes a lifetime. As a defense mechanism, belittle the study of languages or say you have satisfied the requirement by taking an N.D.E.A.-sponsored summer course. A study of the political history of Latin America would require a detailed study of books, articles and newspapers at least in Spanish and Portuguese. The bibliography does not list a single item in any foreign language. A favorite insult of the behavioral scientists is to call old-fashioned scholars "culture-bound." Who in reality could be more culture-bound than the student of a foreign area who relies essentially on sources in English?

10. If the scholarly study of foreign languages is "out," a display of *13* mathematics is "in." Here our author disappoints us; this book contains absolutely no mathematics. Yet it is impossible to write the political history of Latin America without statistics, and while the use of mathematical formulae by behavioral scientists is often dust in the reader's eyes, some of the most important work in the Latin-American field today is being done in the compilation of historical statistics by scholars like Woodrow Borah and Sherburne F. Cook of Berkeley, James W. Wilkie

of U.C.L.A., and Frederic Mauro of the University of Paris-Nanterre. Any substantial political history of Latin America should contain at least some reference to this work.

Such are the Ten Commandments for the new behavioral scientist. *14* And while the behavioral scientists are engaging in their games (game theory being very much "in" and also more fun than the despised empirical facts), our young men are dying in Vietnam and Western civilization is beset by corruption within and a battering from without. This is not 1985, it is 1453.

QUESTIONS AND EXERCISES
Vocabulary

1. Define or explain each of these terms:

élite (6)	obfuscation (8)
charismatic (6)	pontificated (9)
esoteric (6)	rationale (10)
surrogate (6)	verbatim (11)
dereified (6)	linguistic (12)
expertise (7)	empirical (14)

2. Identify each of the following:

Max Weber (5)   N.D.E.A. (12)
Marx and Lenin (5)

3. Why does the reviewer use quotation marks around "busy work," "out," and "in"?

Rhetoric

4. Explain the allusion to the Ten Commandments.
5. Find examples of irony in the review.
6. Discuss the tone that results from the mixture of serious analysis and ironic commentary.
7. What is the purpose of paragraph 14?
8. Discuss the advantages and disadvantages of the organization of the review.

Theme

9. Discuss the readers that are likely to read this review; at what level is the reviewer aiming?
10. Summarize the traits that Hilton admires.
11. Assuming that one is not an expert in the discipline under discussion, which side do you think one would choose, the reviewer's or the au-

thor's? Does the use of irony constitute an unfair technique in reviewing books?

12. What facts does the reviewer emphasize to make his points?
13. Find implications of philosophical differences between the reviewer and the author of the book.

Topics and Assignments for Composition

1. Write a paragraph analyzing some aspect of the figurative language used by the reviewer.
2. Analyze the attack on the behavioral sciences presented in paragraphs 1 and 2 specifically, and in the rest of the review generally.
3. Analyze the use of the Ten Commandments in the review. Discuss their appropriateness and efficacy as a method of organization and commentary.
4. Write a review of a scholarly book or article and emulate some of the salient techniques used in this review.

Stefan Kanfer

Holden Today: Still in the Rye

In the summer of 1951, a modest 277-page book was published. Its author: the little-known short-story writer J.D. Salinger. Its narrator: Holden Caulfield, a 16-year-old whose picaresque journey took him from Pencey Prep (the third private school from which he had been dismissed) to his home in New York City three days later. The Catcher in the Rye *became a prodigious bestseller, transfiguring the emotional landscape, the mores and insights of an entire generation. It gave Salinger an abrupt prominence throughout America, Europe, Asia and Africa, and triggered what Critic George Steiner resentfully labeled "the Salinger industry"—a furious parsing of the author's fragile corpus.*

But as Salinger's last story, Hapworth, *noted, quoting Proust: "A cathedral, a wave in a storm, a dancer's leap never turn out to be as high as we had hoped." The tide has gone out; the factories of the Salinger industry have experienced vast layoffs; the author himself has not communicated with his readers for seven years. And Holden Caulfield—has his voice been muted by his creator's silence? What happens to a prodigy two decades after his debut, when he is pushing 40? An admirer can only hazard a guess:*

If you really want to hear about it, with the stylistic tics and all, the *1* what-ever-happened-to-Soames-Forsyte kind of crap, you'll have to look elsewhere. When I was a cynosure I spake as a cynosure, and when I grew up I gave the vocabulary to the parodists. Actuarially speaking, a generation has grown since I first appeared. Gazing at that boy with the red hunting cap on the old Signet paperback, I wonder: What would he think of me today? But then that gray-and-white snapshot in *your* high school yearbook—what is that youth to you? Would you have anything to say to each other now?

Anyway, when we last left me, I was in a California institution for the   2
emotionally disturbed. In ascending order I was suffering from 1) under-
weight, 2) pneumonia, 3) debilitation, and 4) terminal sanctity. The first
three were cured handily. My brother D.B. kept driving over from Hollywood with sandwiches and books; the books were supposed to cure
No. 4. Perhaps they did.

Maybe you were one of those who felt that after all the maundering I   3
would wind up exactly like my father—that all along I was a conformist
manqué. You were right. Boy, were you right! For a while. A long while.
At first I bought the whole shot. My head got straight; I went to Columbia—after I said I would never go to any of those phony Ivy schools
—and even tried a year of law school. I wore a Tattersall vest. I even
wore a *hat,* for God's sake. Not a red hunting cap, I mean a *hat.* A
whaddyacall it. A fedora. My father used to rate me like a New York pollution inspector: good, acceptable, unhealthy. I became a Good Boy.

It shouldn't surprise you. In those days I was always being compared   4
to Huckleberry Finn. You know how he ended? According to Mark
Twain, as a "justice of the peace in a remote village in Montana, and was
a good citizen and greatly respected." If you get slipped a Finn like that,
what can you reasonably expect of *me?*

I married right out of college. Old Sally Hayes, of course. Even though   5
I said, "I didn't even *like* her much," I also admitted, "I felt like I was in
love with her and wanted to marry her. I swear to God I'm crazy. I admit
it." We horsed around in an apartment in the East Village that had a fire-
place and what she called "tons of charm." My father got me a job in a
public relations company. I built images, including my own, and took to
preceding all my sentences with "Actually."

You remember Mr. Antolini talking to me? Just before I went to sleep   6
and woke up with him touching my hair and making me jump about a
thousand feet? He said: "I have a feeling that you're riding for some kind
of terrible, terrible fall . . . It may be the kind where at the age of 30 you
sit in some bar hating everybody who comes in looking as if he might
have played football in college. Then again, you may pick up just enough
education to hate people who say, 'It's a secret between he and I.' Or
you may end up in some business office, throwing paper clips at the nearest stenographer." I chose all three. I hated jocks, grimaced at grocery
stores with signs selling APPLE'S, and I threw paper clips at stenogra-
phers. Then I threw myself. The old Caulfield Charm. I couldn't believe
what was happening to me. But then I could never believe what happened
to me—in life or in lit.

Of all the lorn, adolescent souls kicking around the bestseller list, why   7
did *I* make the existential leap to Required Reading? I was writing a mad

letter, not a petition. How did it acquire so many signers? I mean not just kids, but critics. Because I think they felt, as I did, that uncertainty was the American state of mind. Old Gertrude Stein on her deathbed sighed, "What is the answer?" And topped it with "What is the question?" You could go to literary distinction with that kind of exit line, and in a sense, that is where Salinger took me.

In a senescent epoch, even the young are senile. America in the '50s 8 was undergoing adolescence. Again. I was its sudden, unbidden spokesyouth. But surely there have been free alterations since 1951. Nonfiction is in the bucket seat and drives mankind. By now I should be a literary footnote. But no: the paperback sold more than 3,000,000 copies between 1953 and 1964. And even *more* between then and now. How do you figure *that?* I mean, those glancing insights, those adolescent knighterrantries, aren't they old news? Haven't our tastes altered 180 degrees?

Probably not. Inside every man (all right, *and* every woman) there is a 9 poet who died young. The youth who read me grow younger each day. You *had* to read *The Catcher in the Rye* at Andover, for instance. And the new audience is never very different from the old Holden. They may not know the words, but they can hum along with the malady. My distress is theirs. They, too, long for the role of adolescent savior. They, too, are aware of the imminent death in life. As far as the sexual explosion is concerned, I suspect a lot of what you've heard is just noise. "Sex is something I really don't understand too hot," I said. It still remains a mystery to the adolescent. I have no cure, only consolation: someone has passed this way before.

Yet there is something more important, more durable about *The* 10 *Catcher in the Rye.* In the interstices of the memoir were seedling predictions, just waiting for the rain. And it came, it came. Take my love/hate for movies. Wouldn't you know that *College English* would run a piece, without irony, suggesting that my name, "one suspects"—*one* maybe, two never—"is an amalgam of the last names of Movie Stars William Holden and Joan Caulfield." Yeah, well . . . And yet my obsessive cinematic fantasies were really everyone's hang-up with nostalgia, camp and collective memory. Remember me camping it up with my roommate Stradlater: "I'm the goddam Governor's son . . . He doesn't want me to be a tap dancer. He wants me to go to Oxford. But it's in my goddam blood, tap-dancing." Movies made all of us. That's why we don't know how to *really* feel about them. Half the time I'm still crazy about them; the other half I'm very grateful Salinger never sold me to Hollywood. (Can't you see the movie of *Catcher,* with Warren Beatty, probably, all cut up inside, haunted-looking because the director wouldn't let him eat for two days before filming?)

As for my deep animus toward "athletic bastards who stick together,"   *11*
see Bouton, Meggyesy, *et al.* And as for my hatred of those teachers who
overinstruct but undernourish, yelling "digression!" in Oral Expression
every time a student gets interesting, the romantic critiques of Kozol and
Herndon have left me winded.

My distaste for mechanization, my preference for the four-footed over   *12*
the four-wheeled ("A horse is at least *human,* for God's sake") —
well, that has become a contagion by now. As has that yearning for
Thoreauesque communal living in New England: "We'll stay in these
cabin camps and stuff like that till the dough runs out . . . We could live
somewhere with a brook and all and . . . I could chop all our own wood in
the wintertime and all."

Obsession with vulgarity and physical decay? Look around. The book-   *13*
stores, the grind houses. That's not even sex, it's cold cuts. And the
shlock stores are shlockier. I saw a brass statue of a guy rolling a stone
up a hill. Underneath it was a label: "That's life." The myth of Sisyphus
became a piece of shoddy merch.

And yet . . . and yet . . . Somehow, I have a feeling *all* things have not   *14*
deteriorated. Some unexpected people have awakened to the voices of
their children, who have turned out to be — surprise! — the holders of
moral strength. Innocence is no longer suspect. Sally Hayes called me a
sacrilegious atheist because I thought Jesus would have puked at the
Radio City Music Hall Christmas stage show. I said, "The thing Jesus
really would've liked would be the guy that plays the kettle drums in the
orchestra." Well, maybe that humanizing is behind *some* of the Jesus
Revolution. Anyway, he would have liked the drummer at *Superstar.* Not
the show, though. And I see I'm not the only one to wonder about the
ducks in Central Park. Now they're worried about species I never even
heard of.

Antolini once advised me: "Many, many men have been just as trou-   *15*
bled morally and spiritually as you are right now. Happily, some of them
kept records of their troubles. You'll learn from them — if you want to."
I wanted to. I read Wilhelm Stekel, who authored my favorite vaudeville
bill, *Wandering Mania, Dipsomania, Pyromania and Other Allied Impul-
sive Acts.* And I read George Orwell, who let me know that I was not
the first adolescent to be obsessed with excrement (he compared *his*
Pencey to a "tightrope over a cesspool"). I read Albert Camus' *Notebooks* and stumbled on a paragraph that illumined, I think, the Salinger
myth: "I withdrew from the world not because I had enemies, but because I had friends. Not because they did me an ill turn, as is customary,
but because they thought me better than I am. It was a lie I could not
endure."

Among the lies *I* could not endure was me. My wife Sally shared my 16
sentiments, and one day, when I committed my ultimate indiscretion
(other husbands bring home lipstick on their collars; I brought home my
secretary), I found the apartment empty. No books, no furniture, no
Sally. No future.

That initiated my second suicidal period, during which I came into the 17
office at 11, canceled my account at Brooks Brothers, and began dressing
in Sweet-Orr corduroys. I once called my employer at midnight with two
questions that had long intrigued me: "What is a runcible spoon?" and
"Do you think Geppetto was a good father?" My employer told me that
he was weary of my Rare, Quixotic Gestures. So, frankly, was I.

I tried total withdrawal in Europe, but the Europeans put me in my 18
place, which was America. As Zooey Glass said, "I was *born* here. I
went to *school* here. I've been *run over* here . . . I have no business in
Europe." I lived in New England for a while, à la Salinger. But unless
you're a writer or a turtleback painter or something, you want *somebody*
to talk to. Or else you feel like calling up dead authors all the time.

My father induced me to emerge from my shell by coercing a client to 19
sign me on as an assistant golf pro. I was once good enough, remember, to
appear in a golf movie (but I didn't). It worked for two years. Then one
day I *list*ened to the guys I was instructing. One of them was saying
"cost per thousand"; the other was saying "tax-free municipals." Both
of them said "*act*ually" a lot. I realized that I was working in a conference
room with Zoysia grass. Few sights have been as beautiful as my five iron
arcing over the Hudson and settling among the carp and the effluents.

I returned to New York and began again, this time with a girl who re- 20
minded me of old Jane Gallagher. She had the same kind of mucklemouth,
and when she played checkers she kept all her kings in the back row too.
She taught remedial reading to kids and remedial living to me. We have
two daughters, Esmé and Phoebe. I know the rustle of little souls tossing
in beds, and I no longer have to press my ear to the wire fence at the
schoolyard to hear great dialogues of children who wonder, too, about
Geppetto. Besides, I am at the schoolyard all day. Having tried a series
of futile desk jobs, I realized I was not built to dwell in modules. The
school at which I teach used to be as snobbish and phony as Pencey or
Whooton. But one day they remembered where they were—93rd Street
—and changed. I teach writing and history and Oral Expression, and the
kids and I digress all day long.

There I stand in the rye of the inner city, with my arms open. The pay 21
is lousy and the hours are long and the demands are unending. At night
the streets are dangerous; during the day the air is dirty. It is a hassle
getting to and from anywhere. We are all well. I push the stone up the hill

and down it falls. Holden S. Caulfield. Holden Sisyphus Caulfield. Camus, that nightingale who thought he was an owl, was right. At the end of *The Myth of Sisyphus,* he says, watching the old boy toil up and down forever, "We must imagine him happy." Happy. That kills me. It really does.

QUESTIONS AND EXERCISES

Vocabulary

1. Define or explain each of the following terms:

    cynosure (1)   imminent (9)
    parodists (1)   interstices (10)
    maundering (3)   animus (11)
    manqué (3)   schlock (13)
    lorn (7)   merch (13)
    senescent (8)   effluents (19)
    malady (9)

Rhetoric

2. This essay obviously parodies the style of *The Catcher in the Rye.* How does it differ from most parodies?
3. Make a short list of some of the elements of style that Kanfer emulates.
4. The essay abounds with allusions. List a few of them and show how they add to the meaning.
5. What are some of the limitations of parody?
6. Select words and phrases that may be labeled nonstandard by a college level dictionary.

Theme

7. What is Kanfer's purpose in this essay?
8. What aspects of the generation gap are evident in this essay?
9. Ostensibly Kanfer is writing about Holden; are there explicit or implicit clues that he is also writing about himself?
10. What are some of the problems that Holden faced in his adolescence, and how do those same problems manifest themselves today? Are some patterns built into the maturation process no matter what changes are made in customs and environment?
11. Holden faced adolescence, sex, parents, teachers, schools, peers, children, women, athletes, etc. in his tribulations. How have these items changed for today's youth. Are there new foils that have replaced some of the old ones?

12. Show the special relationship between style and meaning in this essay. Like irony, parody carries a built-in meaning to the essay from the work being parodied.

13. This essay is a form of book review. Explain what it does to and for *The Catcher in the Rye.*

Topics and Assignments for Composition

1. Write a definition of parody and relate it to humor.
2. Choose a different book that made a strong impression on you and write an essay imitating Kanfer's approach.
3. Write an essay about the seemingly universal problem of youth's initiation into the mature world.
4. Compare *The Catcher in the Rye* with *Huckleberry Finn.*

Student Example

The Use and Significance of Dark/Light Imagery in Joseph Conrad's Heart of Darkness

Conrad uses much visual imagery throughout *Heart of Darkness* to illustrate his basic points. The dark/light or black/white imagery is perhaps most apparent and effective in contributing to the theme of the story. It appears constantly, so much that it almost becomes routine, but this imagery plays a significant role in the presentation of Conrad's ideas.

The story begins in London, surrounded by "mournful gloom." This sets the scene for the continuing use of dark/light imagery. It is dusk; the brilliant light is giving way to the somber gloom. This description, combined with Marlow's discussion of the darkness of Britain in Roman times, serves as foreshadowing and also indicates that even the most civilized city in the world has been, and perhaps still is, a place of darkness. Marlow then begins the story of his meeting with Kurtz, saying that this experience "seemed somehow to throw a kind of light on everything about me." Thus, light, symbolizing truth, is presented for the first time in the story. Marlow explains that, to him, the Congo had ceased to be a "white patch . . . to dream gloriously over" and had become a place of darkness.

The women in Brussels knitting black wool and Marlow's predecessor, killed in a dispute over two black hens, are presented as omens of impending doom. As Marlow travels down the coast of Africa, the brilliant sun contrasts with the darkness of the land. He sees black natives with "the whites of their eyeballs glistening." This seems to represent their natural state of simple truth. They are working hard and are sweating; they are natural and real. Marlow, disembarking, is told of a man who has recently hanged himself. He asks why and is told that the sun was too much for the man. Sunlight, of course, is truth.

Marlow soon witnesses the rapacious behavior of the whites and the suffering of the blacks. He watches a black man die and notices "a kind of blind, white flicker in the depths of the orbs, which died out slowly." This is similar to the other reference to the whiteness in black men's eyes. The white men Marlow meets are without exception greedy and insensitive.

Darkness is mentioned again when Marlow meets the manager of the Central Station, who warns Marlow that toughness is necessary in the Congo. The manager then "sealed the utterance with that smile of his, as though it had been a door opening into a darkness he had in his keeping." While still at the Central Station, Marlow sees a sketch of a blindfolded woman carrying a lighted torch. The sketch, drawn by Kurtz, which seems to depict the role of, or attitude toward, women, may also represent the author's belief that truth or illumination is not making much headway in the darkness.

Conrad makes many allusions to the darkness, blackness, and wildness of the jungle. When he overhears the manager talking with his uncle, the uncle makes a gesture toward the forest, a gesture which "seemed to beckon with a dishonoring flourish before the sunlit face of the land a treacherous appeal to the lurking death, to the hidden evil, to the profound darkness at its heart." In contrast, Marlow finds an old book on seamanship which he describes as luminous. The book is a small bit of brightness in the dark.

The imagery continues as Marlow travels upriver to the Inner Station. The night is described as blinding — perhaps an allution to the overwhelming reality of man's savagery. In the morning, there is an even more blinding white fog, which may be another symbol of blindness in the search for truth. Another interesting symbol is lightening, used in describing the impact of Kurtz's phrase, "Exterminate the brutes." Marlow calls this a "flash of lightening in a serene sky." It hints at the truth about Kurtz and man.

When Marlow reaches the Inner Station, Conrad uses more dark/light imagery. The shrunken heads on the wooden knobs are black. Marlow does not want to know about the ceremonies involved in approaching Kurtz; he feels that these ceremonies would be worse than the shrunken heads which are "pure, uncomplicated savagery . . . a positive relief, being something that had a right to exist — obviously — in the sunshine." This form of savagery, Conrad is saying, is more honest and natural, therefore less dark. One of the most clearly symbolic passages is found when Marlow is talking to the Russian. They stand in dazzling sunlight, while Kurtz's house is in the gloom. Marlow soon realizes that he is in the midst of "the darkness of an impenetrable night" as is Kurtz. The fires accompanying the unspeakable rites illuminate the darkness surrounding the Inner Station, but the truth they reveal is a dark one. When Kurtz is dying in darkness, there is a candle a few feet from him, representing the truth. At his death, the somber veil is swept away and the truth is revealed to Kurtz about himself. Marlow, too, gains a measure of understanding and enlightenment, symbolized by his frequent references to candles and lamps contrasted with the darkness outside.

When Marlow returns to civilization, he meets Kurtz's fiancee. The dark/light imagery is used continuously throughout their conversation. She first appears in the sunlight, an indication of her nature and character. Of course, as Marlow points out, "sunlight can be made to lie, too," but she is obviously genuine. Marlow thinks constantly of Kurtz's darkness, and as dusk falls, the darkness within Marlow grows as he faces the problem of what to tell the woman about Kurtz. The darkness grows; the room becomes shadowy with light still surrounding the fiancee. Marlow sees her, Kurtz, and Kurtz's black mistress all together in the darkness. The story ends in London, again in somber darkness.

Throughout *Heart of Darkness* black is used to represent evil and confusion, while white generally represents truth, civilization, and illumination. Physical darkness, or the darkness of a country, meant to represent savagery, is always related to mental or intellectual darkness, man's groping for truth. Lightness is the realization of truth, a clear view of oneself. The entire meaning of the imagery, however, is not quite this simple. There are many complexities and contradictions. Conrad shows the white men as black-hearted, while the black man, though by no means perfect, is shown to be purer and more natural, much closer, perhaps to the truth. The next question is the nature of the truth. To some, the white truth, everything connected with civilized order and decency, is reality and truth. There also exists a dark or black truth or reality, that of a man as a savage. Conrad, through skillful use of imagery, presents both of these concepts of reality and shows that they are equally valid. Man has elements of both black and white in his nature. He must realize and cope with it, without totally yielding to the dark side, as Kurtz does, but without being blinded by the fantasies of the white side, as Kurtz's fiancee is.

Part Eleven:

Letters and Miscellany

Frederick S. Perls

An Editorial: I Am What I Am — No Instant Joy

I want to talk about the present development of humanistic psychol-   *1*
ogy. It took us a long time to debunk the whole Freudian crap, and now
we are entering a new and more dangerous phase. We are entering the
phase of the turner-onners: turn on to instant cure, instant joy, instant
sensory-awareness. We are entering the phase of the quacks and the con-
men, who think if you get some breakthrough, you are cured—disregarding any growth requirements, disregarding any of the real potential, the
inborn genius in all of you. If this is becoming a faddism, it is as dangerous to psychology as the year-decade-century-long lying on the couch. At
least the damage we suffered under psychoanalysis does little to the patient except for making him deader and deader. This is not as obnoxious
as this quick-quick-quick thing. The psychoanalysts at least bring good
will with them. I must say I am *very* concerned with what's going on
right now.

One of the objections I have against anyone calling himself a Gestalt   *2*
Therapist is that he uses technique. A technique is a gimmick. A gimmick should be used only in the extreme case. We've got enough people
running around collecting gimmicks, more gimmicks, and abusing them.
These techniques, these tools, are quite useful in some seminar on sensory awareness or joy, just to give you some idea that you are still alive,
that the myth that the American is a corpse is not true, that he *can* be
alive. But the sad fact is that this jazzing-up more often becomes a dangerous substitute activity, another phony therapy that *prevents* growth.

Now the problem is not so much with the turner-onners but with the   *3*
whole American culture. We have made a 180-degree turn from puritanism and moralism to hedonism. Suddenly everything has to be fun, pleas-

ure, and any sincere involvement, any really *being here,* is discouraged.

> A thousand plastic flowers
> Don't make a desert bloom
> A thousand empty faces
> Don't fill an empty room.

In Gestalt Therapy, we are working for something else. We are here to promote the growth process and develop the human potential. We do not talk of instant joy, instant sensory awareness, instant cure. The growth process is a process that takes time. We can't just snap our fingers and say, "Come on, let's be gay! Let's do this!" You can turn on if you want to with LSD and jazz it up, but that has nothing to do with the sincere work of that approach to psychiatry which I call Gestalt Therapy. In therapy, we have not only to get through the role-playing. We also have to fill in the holes in the personality to make the person whole and complete again. And again, as before, this can't be done by the turner-onners. In Gestalt Therapy we have a better way, but it is no magic short-cut. You don't have to be on a couch or in a Zendo for twenty or thirty years, but you have to invest yourself, and it takes time to grow.

The conditioners also start out with a false assumption. Their basic premise that behavior is "law" is a lot of crap. That is: we learn to breathe, to eat, we learn to walk. "Life is nothing but whatever conditions into which it has been born." *If,* in the behaviorist reorganization of our behavior, we get a modification towards better self-support, and throw away all the artificial social roles we have learned, then I am on the side of the behaviorists. The stopping block seems to be anxiety. Always anxiety. Of course you are anxious if you have to learn a new way of behavior, and the psychiatrists usually are afraid of anxiety. They don't know what anxiety *is.* Anxiety is the excitement, the *élan vital* which we carry with us, and which becomes stagnated if we are unsure about the role we have to play. If we don't know if we will get applause or tomatoes, we hesitate, so the heart begins to race and all the excitement can't flow into activity, and we have stage fright. So the formula of anxiety is very simple: anxiety is the gap between the *now* and the *then.* If you are in the now, you can't be anxious, because the excitement flows immediately into ongoing spontaneous activity. If you are in the now, you are creative, you are inventive. If you have your senses ready, if you have your eyes and ears open, like every small child, you find a solution.

A release to spontaneity, to the support of our total personality—yes, yes, yes. The pseudo-spontaneity of the turner-onners as they become hedonistic—just, let's do something, let's take LSD, let's have instant joy, instant sensory-awareness—*No.* So between the Scylla of conditioning and the Charybdis of turning on, there is something—a person that is real, a person that takes a stand.

As you know, there is a rebellion on in the United States. We discover   7
that producing things, and living for things, and the exchange of things, is not the ultimate meaning of life. We discover that the meaning of life is that it is to be lived, and it is not to be traded and conceptualized and squeezed into a pattern of systems. We realize that manipulation and control are not the ultimate joy of life.

But we must also realize that so far we only have a rebellion. We don't   8
have a revolution yet. There is still much of substance missing. There is a race on between fascism and humanism. At this moment it seems to me that the race is about lost to the fascists. And the wild hedonistic, unrealistic, jazz-it-up, turner-onners have nothing to do with humanism. It is protest, it's a rebelliousness, which is fine as such, but it's not an end. I've got plenty of contact with the youngsters of our generation who are in despair. They see all the militarism and the atomic bomb in the background. They want to get something out of life. They want to become real and exist. If there is any chance of interrupting the rise and fall of the United States, it's up to our youth and it's up to you in supporting this youth. To be able to do this, there is only one way through: to become real, to learn to take a stand, to develop one's center, to understand the basis of existentialism: a rose is a rose is a rose. I am what I am, and at this moment I cannot possibly be different from what I am. I give you the Gestalt prayer, maybe as a direction. The prayer in Gestalt Therapy is:

> I do my thing, and you do your thing.
> I am not in this world to live up to your expectations
> And you are not in this world to live up to mine.
> You are you and I am I,
> And if by chance we find each other, it's beautiful.
> If not, it can't be helped.

QUESTIONS AND EXERCISES

Vocabulary

1. Define or explain each of the following terms:

humanistic (1)	*élan vital* (5)
Gestalt (2)	hedonistic (6)
Zendo (4)	existentialism (8)
behaviorist (5)	

Rhetoric

2. Explain the following allusions:
   "the whole Freudian crap"
   "Gestalt Therapist"
   "role-playing"
   "between the Scylla . . . and the Charybdis . . ."
3. Are there discordant elements in the levels of diction?
4. What elements of style tend to give the essay a breezy, almost flippant tone?

Theme

5. How does Perls manage to cover so very much ground? What does he assume about his readers?
6. Perls alludes to many ideological controversies. What are the issues between the following camps:
   humanistic psychology vs. quacks and con-men
   Freudians vs. Gestalt Therapy
   fascism vs. humanism
   existentialism vs. behaviorism
7. With which camp do you tend to identify? How do these labels fit the overall philosophy one may hold?
8. What implications for religion do these conflicts entail?
9. What are the political implications?

Topics and Assignments for Composition

1. Write a preamble to the philosophy of life you hold.
2. Write an essay in which you take a position on one of the controversies listed in question 6.
3. Write an essay showing the influence of psychology on some aspect of life today.
4. Research the current conflicts concerning psychiatric therapies and write a report of your conclusions.

Henry F. Ottinger

In Short, Why Did the Class Fail?

Much of what I'm about to say does not apply to all of you; some of it *1*
might. To use a cliché, if the shoe fits, wear it. And, if any further justification is needed, I'll say that I have suffered through reading a lot of
trash that you've written this semester, so you can suffer through some
of mine—with the added benefit, a benefit apparently dear to some of
you, that you won't have to read it. You just have to absorb it.

As you know, I began the semester in a way that departed from the *2*
manner in which I had taught composition classes in the past. Much of
my attitude at that time was influenced by Farber's book, *The Student as
Nigger*. On the first day of class, I read to you the following:

> School is where you let the dying society put its trip on you. Our
> schools may seem useful: to make children into doctors, sociolo-
> gists, engineers—to discover things. But they're poisonous as well.
> They exploit and enslave students; they petrify society; they make
> democracy unlikely. And it's not *what* you're taught that does the
> harm but *how* you're taught. Our schools teach you by pushing you
> around, by stealing your will and your sense of power, by making
> timid, apathetic slaves of you—authority addicts.

Well, that sounded like a breath of fresh air, way back in February— *3*
and I suggested that we try to break the mold, that we could write papers
on any subject we wanted, that we could spend class time discussing
things, either "the burning issues of the day," or otherwise. You seemed
to agree and we spent time agreeing together that indeed Farber had *the*
word and we would do what we could to break the mold.

As you know, things went from initial ecstasy to final catastrophe. And *4*
recently, I fell back—no, you forced me back—into assigning general

Reprinted by permission of the author.

topics. As a result of that action – and a lot of other factors I will mention – this semester has been the worst I have ever taught. I fact, I even debated with myself whether or not to go on teaching next year. But in some ways, the semester was valuable because I learned something, if you didn't.

Let me share with you some of the things I learned: and keep in mind   5
that this does not apply to *all* of you, but it does apply to the majority.

I learned that all this bull about "getting it together," or "working to-   6
gether," (be it for peace or a grade), is just that – bull. The 1950s were labeled by pop sociologists as "the silent generation": I assure you they have nothing on you. Ten years ago the people around the fountains wore saddle shoes, chinos, and had crewcuts. Now they're barefoot, wear army fatigues, and have long hair. Big revelation: it's the same bunch of people – only the superficial appearances have changed. Generally, this class has been the most silent, reticent, paranoid bunch of people in a group I have ever experienced. If you are indicative of the generation that's supposed to change things, good luck. Change is predicated on, among other things, communication between people, "which in your case," as the poem "Naming of Parts" goes, "you have not got."

You had an opportunity to exchange ideas, (which, it often turned out,   7
"you have not got,") and you were too embarrassed to do so.

You had an opportunity to find out about each other – you didn't. (Or,   8
perhaps you found out some of the same things I did: if so, congratulations; the semester has not been a waste for you.)

You had an opportunity to find out something about yourselves. This,   9
by the way, is the crux of education. And, as far as I can see, you found out very little. Perhaps by the end of this hot air, you may have an inkling of what one person thinks "yourself" is.

You had an opportunity to explore ideas – on your own – and didn't.   10
Most of the papers hashed over the usual cliché-ridden topics: abortion, the SST, the population explosion; one person went so far as to churn out a masterpiece on the pros and cons of fraternities, a topic that was really hot back around 1956. In short, there was little attempt at being fresh, original, or creative.

You had an opportunity to learn how to write – and I must admit that   11
a few of you now can do that. Let me mention a few points by way of amplification:

1) At the outset of the semester, I told you that you could bring rough drafts by my office and I'd go over them. For the most part, the "A" and "B" students were the only ones who showed up. There was, of course, a great rush in the past couple of weeks by some who were *beginning* to sweat out their grades.

2) I also told you at the beginning of the semester, and several times throughout the semester, that you should correct your papers before handing them back in, yet 90% of the returned themes have not a mark of yours on them. Don't think this doesn't figure in the final grade.

So much for the writing part.

Most of all, you had the opportunity to be free—to be free from the usual absurdities of a composition class where topics are assigned, thesis statements are submitted, and so on. You also had freedom of thought, as long as it was confined to the standards of formal English. You had the opportunity to be free—to be responsible to yourselves—and you succeeded in proving to me and to yourselves that Freedom is Slavery, a line from *1984* which I hope, for the sake of all of us, isn't prophetic.   *12*

But you protest! (Oh, how I have wished you would), "We're incapable of handling all this freedom at once—you see, Mr. Ottinger, we've been conditioned; we're not used to all of this!" Well, I read that in Farber too, and it's bull. Rats and dogs are conditioned, and are usually incapable of breaking that conditioning. Human beings can break conditioning, if it's to their advantage. But here, it's too good an excuse to say, "I'm conditioned," Obviously, then, it's to your advantage *not* to break out of the mold.   *13*

And now, the Big Question: *Why* is it to your advantage not to break out of the mold? In short, why did the class fail? It failed because, as Dostoevski's "Underground Man" pointed out, thinking causes pain. And, like good little utilitarians, you want to avoid pain. No, it's so much easier to come up with instant esthetics, instant solutions, instant salvation through instant mysticism or intuition: instant thoughts. After all, instant things, like breakfasts and TV dinners, are easily digestible—and easily regurgitated—and not terribly nourishing, by the way.   *14*

Along this same line, one of the more atrociously nauseating remarks I have heard this semester is: "Gosh, college is no fun," or, when an idea is presented, "It doesn't turn me on." Who in the hell said college was *supposed* to be fun? That idea went out with fraternities, again back in the 50s. In fact, it went out long before that. Granted, "fun" is a two-way street. What's fun to one may not be fun to someone else. But, if you don't find learning fun, you're in the wrong place. If you don't find discovering something you didn't previously know about (be it either a GNP in Economics 51, or Kaolinite in Geology, or ribonucleic acid in Botany,) you're in the wrong place. If you don't believe that knowledge for its own sake is a valid and valuable goal, then you're in the wrong place, and you'd do much better in a vocational school, studying how to be a plumber or a beautician.   *15*

And if you don't believe, along with Ezra Pound, that "Real education   *16* must ultimately be limited to men who INSIST on knowing," you are definitely in the wrong place. You are merely clutter.

Granted there are problems within the University itself — serious problems — that despite what you may think, show some sign of possible solution. One step they could take (but probably won't) is to limit enrollment, and keep the forty-five percent of you out who don't belong here, because it's no fun. In fact, we would do well to adopt an idea of Robert Hutchins, since a college degree has become so worthless in recent years, especially at M.U. Hutchins suggests that a B.A. should be issued to each child at birth, since most people (students included), seem to think a degree is some kind of birthright. We could also issue, at age 21, a book full of cliché phrases that could be dropped at appropriate places: the office, the cocktail or pot party — even scribbled on john walls. Then, some people would be happy — after all, you wouldn't have to go through this non-fun place, and take all these non-fun courses, from all these non-fun instructors. And, you'd have four years to do something *meaningful, significant, relevant,* and, of course, *fun.*   *17*

Well, it's time, I suppose, to bring this to a halt, and let you go over to the Commons, or wherever. As to the next to the last comment, I invite you to listen to the lyrics of the Beatles' "Nowhere Man," and, if it fits, take it to heart.   *18*

Last, I will bid a good-bye (until the final) and say that if at any time some sly hint, or clue, or (God forbid!) a half-truth slipped out of my unconscious and slid out the corner of my mouth, and, pardon the expression, "turned one of you on," then we have not failed, you and I.   *19*

And to all of you, this: I love you for what you might be; I'm deeply disturbed by what you are.   *20*

See you at the final.   *21*

QUESTIONS AND EXERCISES

Vocabulary

1. Define or explain each of the following terms:

    paranoid (6)   esthetics (14)
    utilitarians (14)

Rhetoric

2. What is the dominant tone of this essay?
3. Obviously Ottinger is a college professor. How does he use clichés? Why?

4. There is sarcasm in several paragraphs, notably in paragraph 17. What are the advantages and disadvantages of using sarcasm?
5. Are there any elements of diction that could be labeled nonstandard? Why are they used in this essay? What does their use suggest about what is right and wrong in the levels of usage?
6. "Style is the man" is a literary cliché. What is Ottinger's style? What does it show about him?

Theme

7. What is the central purpose of Ottinger's essay?
8. Why are there difficulties in his presentation? Notice that he several times makes clear that he does not mean *all* of the students. What are the dangers of generalizations?
9. Who is to blame for the failure of the class? Does the author accept a part of the blame?
10. How will he structure his next class? Is his experience typical?
11. Is Ottinger an idealist, cynic, humanist, behaviorist, pedant, intellectual snob, or _____? Justify your response from the specifics in his essay.
12. What class procedure or atmosphere is most conducive to learning?
13. What is the future of education in general and of college in particular?

Topics and Assignments for Composition

1. Write a rebuttal essay to Ottinger's. Imagine that your audience is composed of instructors who teach freshman courses.
2. Choose just one aspect of Ottinger's essay and expand it into a self-contained unit either supporting or attacking Ottinger's generalizations.
3. Write an essay on changing life styles and try to develop some cause and effect relationships.

John F. Kennedy

Inaugural Address

Fellow citizens:

We observe today not a victory of party but a celebration of freedom— 1
symbolizing an end as well as a beginning—signifying renewal as well as
change. For I have sworn before you and Almighty God the same solemn
oath our forebears prescribed nearly a century and three-quarters ago.

The world is very different now. For man holds in his mortal hands the 2
power to abolish all forms of human poverty and all forms of human life.
And yet the same revolutionary beliefs for which our forebears fought are
still at issue around the globe—the belief that the rights of man come not
from the generosity of the state but from the hand of God.

We dare not forget today that we are the heirs of that first revolution. 3
Let the word go forth from this time and place, to friend and foe alike, that
the torch has been passed to a new generation of Americans—born in this
century, tempered by war, disciplined by a hard and bitter peace, proud
of our ancient heritage—and unwilling to witness or permit the slow un-
doing of those human rights to which we are committed today at home
and around the world.

Let every nation know, whether it wishes us well or ill, that we shall 4
pay any price, bear any burden, meet any hardship, support any friend,
oppose any foe to assure the survival and the success of liberty.

This much we pledge—and more. 5

To those old allies whose cultural and spiritual origins we share, we 6
pledge the loyalty of faithful friends. United, there is little we cannot do
in a host of cooperative ventures. Divided, there is little we can do—for
we dare not meet a powerful challenge at odds and split asunder.

To those new states whom we welcome to the ranks of the free, we 7
pledge our word that one form of colonial control shall not have passed
away merely to be replaced by a far more iron tyranny. We shall not always expect to find them supporting our view. But we shall always hope
to find them strongly supporting their own freedom—and to remember

that, in the past, those who foolishly sought power by riding the back of the tiger ended up inside.

To those peoples in the huts and villages of half the globe struggling to   8
break the bonds of mass misery, we pledge our best efforts to help them help themselves, for whatever period is required—not because the Communists may be doing it, not because we seek their votes, but because it is right. If a free society cannot help the many who are poor, it cannot save the few who are rich.

To our sister republics south of our border, we offer a special pledge—   9
to convert our good words into good deeds—in a new alliance for progress —to assist free men and free governments in casting off the chains of poverty. But this peaceful revolution of hope cannot become the prey of hostile powers. Let all our neighbors know that we shall join with them to oppose aggression or subversion anywhere in the Americas. And let every other power know that this hemisphere intends to remain the master of its own house.

To that world assembly of sovereign states, the United Nations, our   10
last best hope in an age where the instruments of war have far outpaced the instruments of peace, we renew our pledge of support—to prevent it from becoming merely a forum for invective—to strengthen its shield of the new and the weak—and to enlarge the area in which its writ may run.

Finally, to those nations who would make themselves our adversary,   11
we offer not a pledge but a request: that both sides begin anew the quest for peace, before the dark powers of destruction unleashed by science engulf all humanity in planned or accidental self-destruction.

We dare not tempt them with weakness. For only when our arms are   12
sufficient beyond doubt can we be certain beyond doubt that they will never be employed.

But neither can two great and powerful groups of nations take comfort   13
from our present course—both sides overburdened by the cost of modern weapons, both rightly alarmed by the steady spread of the deadly atom, yet both racing to alter that uncertain balance of terror that stays the hand of mankind's final war.

So let us begin anew—remembering on both sides that civility is not a   14
sign of weakness, and sincerity is always subject to proof. Let us never negotiate out of fear. But let us never fear to negotiate.

Let both sides explore what problems unite us instead of belaboring   15
those problems which divide us.

Let both sides, for the first time, formulate serious and precise pro-   16
posals for the inspection and control of arms—and bring the absolute power to destroy other nations under the absolute control of all nations.

Let both sides seek to invoke the wonders of science instead of its ter-   17 rors. Together let us explore the stars, conquer the deserts, eradicate disease, tap the ocean depths and encourage the arts and commerce.

Let both sides unite to heed in all corners of the earth the command of Isaiah—to "undo the heavy burdens . . . [and] let the oppressed go free." 18

And if a beach-head of cooperation may push back the jungle of suspicion, let both sides join in creating a new endeavor, not a new balance of power, but a new world of law, where the strong are just and the weak secure and the peace preserved. 19

All this will not be finished in the first 100 days. Nor will it be finished in the first 1,000, nor in the life of this Administration, nor even perhaps in our lifetime on this planet. But let us begin. 20

In your hands, my fellow citizens, more than mine, will rest the final success or failure of our course. Since this country was founded, each generation of Americans has been summoned to give testimony to its national loyalty. The graves of young Americans who answered the call to service surround the globe. 21

Now the trumpet summons us again—not as a call to bear arms, though arms we need—not as a call to battle, though embattled we are—but a call to bear the burden of a long twilight struggle year in and year out, "rejoicing in hope, patient in tribulation"—a struggle against the common enemies of man: tyranny, poverty, disease and war itself. 22

Can we forge against these enemies a grand and global alliance, north and south, east and west, that can assure a more fruitful life for all mankind? Will you join in that historic effort? 23

In the long history of the world, only a few generations have been granted the role of defending freedom in its hour of maximum danger. I do not shrink from this responsibility—I welcome it. I do not believe that any of us would exchange places with any other people or any other generation. The energy, the faith, the devotion which we bring to this endeavor will light our country and all who serve it—and the glow from that fire can truly light the world. 24

And so, my fellow Americans: ask not what your country can do for you—ask what you can do for your country. 25

My fellow citizens of the world: ask not what America will do for you, but what together we can do for the freedom of man. 26

Finally, whether you are citizens of America or citizens of the world, ask of us here the same high standards of strength and sacrifice which we ask of you. With a good conscience our only sure reward, with history the final judge of our deeds, let us go forth to lead the land we love, asking His blessing and His help, but knowing that here on earth God's work must truly be our own. 27

QUESTIONS AND EXERCISES

Vocabulary

1. Define or explain each of the following terms:

   invective (10)   invoke (17)
   writ (10)   eradicate (17)
   civility (14)   tribulation (22)

Rhetoric

2. Much of the impact of President Kennedy's speech lay in its rhetorical devices and figures of speech. Identify the figures of speech in paragraphs 9, 19, and 22.
3. What rhetorical device is used in paragraphs 3, 4, and 17?
4. Explain the technique used in paragraphs 14 and 25.
5. Find and explain two uses of allusion.
6. What are the advantages of figurative language over literal prose?

Theme

7. What were some of the problems that President Kennedy faced at the start of his administration?
8. What steps does he suggest to meet these problems?
9. How has history dealt with President Kennedy thus far?

Topics and Assignments for Composition

1. Copy five particularly effective sentences in the speech. Write an imitation of each sentence.
2. In a paragraph analyze one aspect of Kennedy's style.
3. There is a saying that style is the man. Compare Kennedy the man to his style.
4. Write an essay comparing the Kennedy inaugural address to the inaugural address of President Nixon or any of the other famous inaugural addresses of the past.

Dwight D. Eisenhower

The Dangers of a Military-Industrial Complex

Three days from now, after half a century in the service of our country, *1*
I shall lay down the responsibilities of office as, in traditional and solemn
ceremony, the authority of the Presidency is vested in my successor.

This evening I come to you with a message of leavetaking and farewell, *2*
and to share a few final thoughts with you, my countrymen.

Like every other citizen, I wish the new President, and all who will *3*
labor with him, Godspeed. I pray that the coming years will be blessed
with peace and prosperity for all.

Our people expect their President and the Congress to find essential *4*
agreement on issues of great moment, the wise resolution of which will
better shape the future of the nation.

My own relations with the Congress, which began on a remote and *5*
tenuous basis when, long ago, a member of the Senate appointed me to
West Point, have since ranged to the intimate during the war and immediate post-war period, and finally to the mutually interdependent during
these past eight years.

In this final relationship, the Congress and the Administration have, on *6*
most vital issues, cooperated well, to serve the nation's good rather than
mere partisanship, and so have assured that the business of the nation
should go forward. So my official relationship with the Congress ends in a
feeling, on my part, of gratitude that we have been able to do so much
together.

We now stand ten years past the midpoint of a century that has wit- *7*
nessed four major wars among great nations—three of these involved our
own country.

Despite these holocausts America is today the strongest, the most in- *8*
fluential and most productive nation in the world. Understandably proud

of this pre-eminence, we yet realize that America's leadership and prestige depend, not merely upon our unmatched material progress, riches
and military strength, but of how we use our power in the interests of
world peace and human betterment.

Throughout America's adventure in free government, our basic pur-   9
poses have been to keep the peace; to foster progress in human achievement, and to enhance liberty, dignity and integrity among peoples and
among nations.

To strive for less would be unworthy of a free and religious people.   10

Any failure traceable to arrogance or our lack of comprehension or   11
readiness to sacrifice would inflict upon us grievous hurt, both at home
and abroad.

Crises there will continue to be. In meeting them, whether foreign or   12
domestic, great or small, there is a recurring temptation to feel that some
spectacular and costly action could become the miraculous solution to
all current difficulties. A huge increase in newer elements of our defenses; development of unrealistic programs to cure every ill in agriculture; a dramatic expansion in basic and applied research—these and many
other possibilities, each possibly promising in itself, may be suggested as
the only way to the road we wish to travel.

But each proposal must be weighed in the light of a broader considera-   13
tion; the need to maintain balance in and among national programs—
balance between the private and the public economy, balance between
the cost and hoped for advantages—balance between the clearly necessary and the comfortably desirable; balance between our essential requirements as a nation and the duties imposed by the nation upon the
individual; balance between actions of the moment and the national welfare of the future. Good judgment seeks balance and progress; lack of it
eventually finds imbalance and frustration.

The record of many decades stands as proof that our people and their   14
Government have, in the main, understood these truths and have responded to them well in the face of threat and stress.

But threats, new in kind or degree, constantly arise. Of these, I mention   15
two only.

A vital element in keeping the peace is our military establishment. Our   16
arms must be mighty, ready for instant action, so that no potential aggressor may be tempted to risk his own destruction.

Our military organization today bears little relation to that known of   17
any of my predecessors in peacetime—or, indeed, by the fighting men of
World War II or Korea.

Until the latest of our world conflicts, the United States had no arma-   18 ments industry. American makers of plowshares could, with time and as required, make swords as well.

But we can no longer risk emergency improvisation of national defense. *19* We have been compelled to create a permanent armaments industry of vast proportions. Added to this, three and a half million men and women are directly engaged in the defense establishment. We annually spend on military security alone more than the net income of all United States corporations.

Now this conjunction of an immense military establishment and a large *20* arms industry is new in the American experience. The total influence— economic, political, even spiritual—is felt in every city, every state house, every office of the Federal Government. We recognize the imperative need for this development. Yet we must not fail to comprehend its grave implications. Our toil, resources and livelihood are all involved; so is the very structure of our society.

In the councils of Government, we must guard against the acquisition *21* of unwarranted influence, whether sought or unsought, by the military-industrial complex. The potential for the disastrous rise of misplaced power exists and will persist.

We must never let the weight of this combination endanger our liber- *22* ties or democratic processes. We should take nothing for granted. Only an alert and knowledgeable citizenry can compel the proper meshing of the huge industrial and military machinery of defense with our peaceful methods and goals, so that security and liberty may prosper together.

Akin to, and largely responsible for the sweeping changes in our indus- *23* trial-military posture has been the technological revolution during recent decades.

In this revolution research has become central. It also becomes more *24* formalized, complex and costly. A steadily increasing share is conducted for, by, or at the direction of the Federal Government.

Today the solitary inventor, tinkering in his shop, has been over- *25* shadowed by task forces of scientists, in laboratories and testing fields. In the same fashion, the free university, historically the fountainhead of free ideas and scientific discovery, has experienced a revolution in the conduct of research. Partly because of the huge costs involved, a Government contract becomes virtually a substitute for intellectual curiosity.

For every old blackboard there are now hundreds of new electronic *26* computers.

The prospect of domination of the nation's scholars by Federal em- *27* ployment, project allocations and the power of money is ever present, and is gravely to be regarded.

Yet, in holding scientific research and discovery in respect, as we *28* should, we must also be alert to the equal and opposite danger that public policy could itself become the captive of a scientific-technological elite.

It is the task of statesmanship to mold, to balance, and to integrate   29
these and other forces, new and old, within the principles of our democratic system — ever aiming toward the supreme goals of our free society.

Another factor in maintaining balance involves the element of time.   30
As we peer into society's future, we — you and I, and our Government — must avoid the impulse to live only for today, plundering, for our own ease and convenience, the precious resources of tomorrow.

We cannot mortgage the material assets of our grandchildren without   31
risking the loss also of their political and spiritual heritage. We want democracy to survive for all generations to come, not to become the insolvent phantom of tomorrow.

During the long lane of the history yet to be written America knows   32
that this world of ours, ever growing smaller, must avoid becoming a community of dreadful fear and hate, and be, instead, a proud confederation of mutual trust and respect.

Such a confederation must be one of equals. The weakest must come to   33
the conference table with the same confidence as do we, protected as we are by our moral, economic and military strength. That table, though scarred by many past frustrations, cannot be abandoned for the certain agony of the battlefield.

Disarmament, with mutual honor and confidence, is a continuing imperative. Together we must learn how to compose differences — not with   34
arms, but with intellect and decent purpose. Because this need is so sharp and apparent, I confess that I lay down my official responsibilities in this field with a definite sense of disappointment. As one who has witnessed the horror and the lingering sadness of war, as one who knows that another war could utterly destroy this civilization which has been so slowly and painfully built over thousands of years, I wish I could say tonight that a lasting peace is in sight.

Happily, I can say that war has been avoided. Steady progress toward   35
our ultimate goal has been made. But so much remains to be done. As a private citizen, I shall never cease to do what little I can to help the world advance along that road.

So, in this, my last good night to you as your President, I thank you for   36
the many opportunities you have given me for public service in war and in peace.

I trust that in you — that, in that service, you find some things worthy.   37
As for the rest of it, I know you will find ways to improve performance in the future.

You and I — my fellow citizens — need to be strong in our faith that all   38 nations, under God, will reach the goal of peace with justice. May we be ever unswerving in devotion to principle, confident but humble with power, diligent in pursuit of the nation's great goals.

To all the peoples of the world, I once more give expression to America's prayerful and continuing aspiration: *39*

We pray that peoples of all faiths, all races, all nations, may have their   *40* great human needs satisfied; that those now denied opportunity shall come to enjoy it to the full; that all who yearn for freedom may experience its spiritual blessings, those who have freedom will understand, also, its heavy responsibility; that all who are insensitive to the needs of others, will learn charity, and that the sources—scourges of poverty, disease and ignorance—will be made to disappear from the earth; and that in the goodness of time, all peoples will come to live together in a peace guaranteed by the binding force of mutual respect and love.

Now, on Friday noon, I am to become a private citizen. I am proud to   *41* do so. I look forward to it.

Thank you, and, good night.   *42*

QUESTIONS AND EXERCISES

Vocabulary

1. Define or explain each of the following terms:
   tenuous (5)   grievous (11)
   holocaust (8)

Rhetoric

2. What elements unite the speech?
3. How does General Eisenhower organize his remarks?
4. Comment on the length of the paragraphs.
5. What rhetorical devices can you identify in this selection?

Theme

6. General Eisenhower makes an historical, factual analysis of the state of the nation as he is leaving the presidency. What general advice does he give his audience?
7. What specific threats does he see to the nation's welfare?
8. Why did Eisenhower appeal to such a broad spectrum of the American population?
9. Has the U.S. government heeded General Eisenhower's warning?

Topics and Assignments for Composition

1. Write a thesis statement incorporating General Eisenhower's main idea so that your sentence might be used in a more formally structured essay rather than in a speech.
2. Using the evidence in the speech, write a paragraph in which you describe General Eisenhower's political philosophy.
3. Analyze today's military-industrial complex and compare its status to the situation existing in General Eisenhower's analysis.
4. In a short essay analyze General Eisenhower's prose style.

Malcolm X

Letter from Mecca

I have reflected since that the letter I finally sat down to compose had
been subconsciously shaping itself in my mind.

The *color-blindness* of the Muslim world's religious society and the
color-blindness of the Muslim world's human society: these two influences had each day been making a greater impact, and an increasing
persuasion against my previous way of thinking.

The first letter was, of course, to my wife, Betty. I never had a moment's question that Betty, after initial amazement, would change her
thinking to join mine. I had known a thousand reassurances that Betty's
faith in me was total. I knew that she would see what I had seen—that
in the land of Muhammad and the land of Abraham, I had been blessed by
Allah with a new insight into the true religion of Islam, and a better understanding of America's entire racial dilemma.

After the letter to my wife, I wrote next essentially the same letter to
my sister Ella. And I knew where Ella would stand. She had been saving
to make the pilgrimage to Mecca herself.

I wrote to Dr. Shawarbi, whose belief in my sincerity had enabled me
to get a passport to Mecca.

All through the night, I copied similar long letters for others who were
very close to me. Among them was Elijah Muhammad's son Wallace
Muhammad, who had expressed to me his conviction that the only possible salvation for the Nation of Islam would be its accepting and project-
ing a better understanding of Orthodox Islam.

And I wrote to my loyal assistants at my newly formed Muslim
Mosque, Inc. in Harlem, with a note appended, asking that my letter be
duplicated and distributed to the press.

I knew that when my letter became public knowledge back in America, many would be astounded – loved ones, friends, and enemies alike. And no less astounded would be millions whom I did not know – who had gained during my twelve years with Elijah Muhammad a "hate" image of Malcolm X.

Even I was myself astounded. But there was precedent in my life for 9 this letter. My whole life had been a chronology of – *changes*.

Here is why I wrote . . . from my heart: 10

"Never have I witnessed such sincere hospitality and the overwhelm- 11 ing spirit of true brotherhood as is practiced by people of all colors and races here in this Ancient Holy Land, the home of Abraham, Muhammad, and all the other prophets of the Holy Scriptures. For the past week, I have been utterly speechless and spellbound by the graciousness I see displayed all around me by people *of all colors.*

"I have been blessed to visit the Holy City of Mecca. I have made 12 my seven circuits around the Ka'ba, led by a young *Mutawaf* named Muhammad. I drank water from the well of Zem Zem. I ran seven times back and forth between the hills of Mt. Al-Safa and Al-Marwah. I have prayed in the ancient city of Mina, and I have prayed on Mt. Arafat.

"There were tens of thousands of pilgrims, from all over the world. 13 They were of all colors, from blue-eyed blonds to black-skinned Africans. But we were all participating in the same ritual, displaying a spirit of unity and brotherhood that my experiences in America had led me to believe never could exist between the white and the non-white.

"America needs to understand Islam, because this is the one religion 14 that erases from its society the race problem. Throughout my travels in the Muslim world, I have met, talked to, and even eaten with people who in America would have been considered 'white' – but the 'white' attitude was removed from their minds by the religion of Islam. I have never before seen *sincere* and *true* brotherhood practiced by all colors together, irrespective of their color.

"You may be shocked by these words coming from me. But on this 15 pilgrimage, what I have seen, and experienced, has forced me to *re- arrange* much of my thought-patterns previously held, and to *toss aside* some of my previous conclusions. This was not too difficult for me. Despite my firm convictions, I have been always a man who tries to face facts, and to accept the reality of life as new experience and new knowl- edge unfolds it. I have always kept an open mind, which is necessary to the flexibility that must go hand in hand with every form of intelligent search for truth.

"During the past eleven days here in the Muslim world, I have eaten 16 from the same plate, drunk from the same glass, and slept in the same bed (or on the same rug) – while praying to the *same God* – with fellow Muslims, whose eyes were the bluest of blue, whose hair was the blondest of blond, and whose skin was the whitest of white. And in the *words* and in the *actions* and in the *deeds* of the 'white' Muslims, I felt the same sincerity that I felt among the black African Muslims of Nigeria, Sudan, and Ghana.

"We were *truly* all the same (brothers) – because their belief in one   17
God had removed the 'white' from their *minds,* the 'white' from their *behavior,* and the 'white' from their *attitude.*

"I could see from this, that perhaps if white Americans could accept   18
the Oneness of God, then perhaps, too, they could accept *in reality* the Oneness of Man – and cease to measure, and hinder, and harm others in terms of their 'differences' in color.

"With racism plaguing America like an incurable cancer, the so-called   19
'Christian' white American heart should be more receptive to a proven solution to such a destructive problem. Perhaps it could be in time to save America from imminent disaster – the same destruction brought upon Germany by racism that eventually destroyed the Germans themselves.

"Each hour here in the Holy Land enables me to have greater spiritual   20
insights into what is happening in America between black and white. The American Negro never can be blamed for his racial animosities – he is only reacting to four hundred years of the conscious racism of the American whites. But as racism leads America up the suicide path, I do believe, from the experiences that I have had with them, that the whites of the younger generation, in the colleges and universities, will see the handwriting on the wall and many of them will turn to the *spiritual* path of *truth* – the *only* way left to America to ward off the disaster that racism inevitably must lead to.

"Never have I been so highly honored. Never have I been made to feel   21
more humble and unworthy. Who would believe the blessings that have been heaped upon an *American Negro?* A few nights ago, a man who would be called in America a 'white' man, a United Nations diplomat, an ambassador, a companion of kings, gave me *his* hotel suite, *his* bed. By this man, His Excellency Prince Faisal, who rules this Holy Land, was made aware of my presence here in Jedda. The very next morning, Prince Faisal's son, in person, informed me that by the will and decree of his esteemed father, I was to be a State Guest.

"The Deputy Chief of Protocol himself took me before the Hajj Court.   22
His Holiness Sheikh Muhammad Harkon himself okayed my visit to Mecca. His Holiness gave me two books on Islam, with his personal seal and autograph, and he told me that he prayed that I would be a

successful preacher of Islam in America. A car, a driver, and a guide, have been placed at my disposal, making it possible for me to travel about this Holy Land almost at will. The government provides air-conditioned quarters and servants in each city that I visit. Never would I have even thought of dreaming that I would ever be a recipient of such honors — honors that in America would be bestowed upon a King — not a Negro.

"All praise is due to Allah, the Lord of all the Worlds.   23

"Sincerely,

"*El-Hajj Malik El-Shabazz*
"*(Malcolm X)*"

QUESTIONS AND EXERCISES

Vocabulary

1. Define or explain the purpose of allusion to each of the following terms:

   Muslim (2)   Elijah Muhammad (6)
   Muhammad (3)   Mt. Arafat (12)
   Abraham (3)   imminent (19)
   Islam (3)   Protocol (22)
   Mecca (4)

Rhetoric

2. What two events is Malcolm X developing in his chronology? Which is more important?
3. Explain the figurative use of language in paragraph 17. Why is figurative language often a shorter way to explain an idea than literal prose?
4. Comment on the originality of the figures of speech in paragraphs 19 and 20.

Theme

5. What experiences made such an impact on Malcolm X?
6. Explain the importance of paragraph 14.
7. On the "love"/"hate" continuum, in which direction was Malcolm X moving in this letter?
8. What previously held thought-patterns was Malcolm X in the process of re-arranging?
9. In paragraph 20 Malcolm X offers an analysis of the race problem

in America. What is his suggested solution? What will happen if this path is not taken?

10. Discuss the various black movements mentioned by Malcolm X and their interrelationship.
11. What happened to Malcolm X?
12. Bring the history of the black movement up to date.

Topics and Assignments for Composition

1. Pick out one sentence from the selection that reflects Malcolm X's emphasis upon spiritual awakening or insieht.
2. Write a definition of "satori." Illustrate your definition with examples from Malcolm X's letter.
3. Write an analysis and classification of the various black organizations that have developed during the past ten years.
4. Write a letter outlining a spiritual awakening or satori. Imitate some of the methods of development used by Malcolm X (example, illustration, description.)

Douglas M. Davis

An Interview with Peter De Vries
Westport, Connecticut, July 1966

Which of your novels do you rate the highest? 1

I've never read any of them. Would I if I hadn't written them? It's a 2
tantalizing question: whether, if the stuff weren't one's own, it would be
one's dish of tea. But I sincerely trust some are not as good as others,
because, as Max Beerbohm said, only mediocrity is always at its best.
Of course, humorists are not forgiven these lapses the way serious writers
are.

Then you don't regard yourself as a serious writer? One occasionally 3
finds you quoted in the reverse.

Oh, I never said any such thing. Doesn't it sound out of character? I 4
certainly hope so, because it sounds like the remark of an ass. I don't
mess with terms like that anyway. Such distinctions have very little validity in literature. Nobody has been funnier than Faulkner, nor has anyone a better grasp of the human predicament than Mark Twain. And
didn't Yeats say Hamlet and Lear are gay? Frost said of this basic principle of playfulness (in discussing Edwin Arlington Robinson, of all people), "If it is with outer seriousness, it must be with inner humor. If it
is with outer humor, it must be with inner seriousness. Neither one alone
without the other under it will do." Any comic worth his salt knows this
instinctively, even without being able to put it in Charlie Chaplin's
words: "If what you're doing is funny, don't be funny doing it." Any
attempt to isolate the "serious" from whatever you want to call its opposite is like trying to put asunder what God hath joined together. The
reverse is equally foredoomed. There's a kind of hilarious frustration

"An Interview with Peter De Vries" by Douglas M. Davis, *College English*,
April 1967. Reprinted with the permission of the National Council of Teachers
of English and Douglas M. Davis.

about it, like working one of those puzzles where you no more than get one pellet into its hole than the other rolls out again.

But speaking for myself—not about myself—I'd rather offer the reader   5
an honest surfboard ride than pack him into a diving bell and then lower him into what turns out to be three feet of water. As many so-called "serious" writers do.

But there seems to be a clear movement in your novels away from the   6
farce and fun of The Tunnel of Love, *for example, toward a more bitter-sweet kind of comedy (tragicomedy, if you will). Is this conscious or simply one result of maturation?*

If middle age is the term you're groping for, help yourself. Yes, there is   7
an inevitable darkening, or sobering, that comes with the increasing realization that life is a tragedy, which entails, however, no need to banish gaiety. Painters know that there is nothing like black to bring out the best in other colors—the pinks and whites and oranges. It makes them dance. Still, my aim generally is refreshment, and anybody looking for nourishment is on his own, and perfectly welcome. I have recently read a couple of serious-type articles about what I am actually up to, and I can only conclude that my stuff is really over my head.

Which of the three terms most often used to describe your novels—   8
comedy, satire, or humor—suits you the best?

You're forgetting another name they're called—farce. So we have four,   9
and our work cut out for us.

I think the distinction between humor and satire is clearer than that be-   10
tween either and farce—which I take to mean the *degree* of absurdity, which can be present in anything, including tragedy. (You will note the term "tragi-farce" used nowadays more than "tragi-comedy." Because of existentialists shooting for the upper-case Absurd, you know, which regards the universe as meaningless and life as a joke, and hence no laughing matter.) I would say, very roughly, that the difference between satire and humor is that the satirist shoots to kill while the humorist brings his prey back alive—often to release him again for another chance. Swift destroyed the human race, Thurber enables it to go on. Humor is more charitable, and, like charity, suffereth long and is kind. Well, I don't think I shoot to kill. If I did I'd been dead long ago myself, since, like most humorists, I'm my own best butt. I don't think I have enough lemon in me to be a satirist. What I like to show is something perfectly plain: that we're all absurd variations of one another. A humorist does not so much laugh at mankind as invite mankind to laugh at itself. Anyhow, the wisest thing for me to do is eschew Wisdom and stay lower-case.

You have not commented about comedy. Where would you put that?   11

At the summit, I suppose. Anthony Powell would typify that high *12* estate, and I must say I was surprised to hear that he disclaimed the term "comic" as a description of him as a writer. He says what he is trying to write is simply the naturalistic novel. Of course, there is high comedy and low, and the higher you go the less loudly they laugh. I had a student at a university recently tell me, or at least clearly imply, that while he admitted he laughed aloud at what I wrote, he missed in it the more cerebral comedy of more intellectual novelists, the appreciative smile, the flicker of inner perception.

What did you tell him? *13*

I could only tell him what the comedian told his critics in *Through the* *14* *Fields of Clover:* "Rolling 'em in the ailes is good enough for me."

What is the major difference between your kind of writer and the kind *15* *represented by, say, Norman Mailer?*

Humorists are more easily housebroken. *16*

You rarely use "normal" names for your characters. A few that recur *17* *to me are Mopworth, Mackerel, Sweetie Appleyard, Cotton Marvel, Bushrod. Even the hero of your most "serious" novel,* The Blood of the Lamb, *was named Don Wanderhope. Why is this? Few modern humorists indulge this convention, which was native to nineteenth-century writers such as Dickens.*

I simply like names that have some thematic or connotative reference. *18* I like the challenge of making up names that sound exactly like the characters themselves. It's hard to do. I set myself a difficult task in *Reuben, Reuben,* for example: A name that would sound exactly like one of the old Scottish clans and yet represent the man. "McGland" was the answer.

Why do you use suburbia as the background for most of your novels? *19*

It's what I know best. I'm a regionalist, like Thomas Hardy. And I love *20* those yokels who get off the same bar car at the same time every night and have never swum in anything but a pool in their own backyard. It's really a new provincialism.

But you obviously like suburbia, as your 15 years in Westport prove. *21*

I enjoy it because it gives me as much of the country as I can get with- *22* out taking a sleeper to the city. I can look out of my window here and drink in the trees. I also have a part-time job that takes me to New York and allows me to drink in Fifth Avenue.

What do you think of suburbia's many critics—the people who claim *23* *that modern suburbia is an artificial growth, made up of people without roots, and largely a matriarchy from 9 to 5. You know how the line goes.*

Has the average city dweller deeper roots? Who lives on the old home- 24
stead any more? And where are the New York and Chicago fathers between 9 and 5? I don't see any difference in this regard between the
suburbs and the urbs.

One of the recurrent figures of fun in your books is the man who tries 25
to commit adultery but never brings it off—due either to an attack of con-
science or bad luck. Why? Do you consider such unfortunates funny or
pitiable?

All I can afford to consider is that failure is funny, while success is 26
not. There is no comic mileage in peace and harmony, any more than
there is drama in it.

Yet you are fascinated by the subject of adultery. You don't consider 27
it immoral, do you?

Now you are asking me how long a piece of string is. The answer in any 28
case must always hang on elements unspecified in the question. What is
important is who is doing what and to whom, and I mean that in the most
serious moral sense. Is there a victim, real or potential? And even that
can't be answered in the abstract, only with the closest reference to the
parties concerned. There are good husbands and wives who are not physically loyal, and there are mates faithful unto death who kill each other
daily. Give us the former any time. But isn't adultery one of the lesser
causes of divorce? I don't mean officially, I mean actually. In any event,
I suppose civilized society as we know it in the modern world represents
a slow approach to Bertrand Russell's summation of the matter many
years ago—that marriage should be regarded as permanent if at all possible even though it ought not to exclude other relations. But that is an ideal
that may ask an awful lot of an innocent person. There are a lot of bad
reasons for being good and a lot of good reasons for being bad—also
fortunately, a lot of good reasons for being good. Marriage remains still
the most satisfactory framework for the sexual emotions.

You have probably made more fun of sex in marriage than any writer 29
I know. But Mary McCarthy recently said that she felt it immoral to
write or joke about "normal" sex. How do you feel about that?

Poking fun at sex is not the same as having fun *with* it—which is what I 30
would say I do. To equate the two would give you a pretty sizeable tradition of bawdy literature to explain, with Shakespeare in the thick of it.
What is worth noting about this tradition, by the way, is the absence of
women from it. They will not write bawdily though they will write eroti-
cally, even though in real life they are basically just as bawdy as men. I
am not talking about risqué stories, but about the more vital reality of
enjoying, or realizing, the comedy inherent in, or possible to, the sexual

relationship, which at its fullest has laughter in it as well as ecstasy and poetry and tenderness. I recently read an authority, a psychologist or something, who said that women as a whole are more ready than men to laugh in love-making, and I have a friend, a practised amorist, who confirms this. Yet women are temperamentally reluctant to reflect this on paper, which is perhaps as it should be. One would not expect even an emancipated woman novelist to write like J. P. Donleavy. But the thing I'm trying to say is that the sanctity of sex, in which I devoutly believe, does not preclude laughter, either in it or for that matter, at it. There is surely more ribaldry in a decent marriage than in a public smoking car. Which I think discredits Freud's theory that bawdy humor is always vicarious, a substitute for the real thing, made necessary by repression. But I don't mean to sound prim.

What about the so-called Ordeal of Modern Woman, which seems to interest you? Do you care to comment on that?   31

The term is really a misstatement. It should be the Modern Ordeal of Woman, for it is but an acute inflammation of chronic woe. Shaw put his finger on its eternal core when he said, in I think *Back to Methuselah*, that woman resents the burden of creation being so unequally divided. I think that's only half the story; she further resents the fact that the life she produced is organized by the sex that didn't. The urge to correct this manifests itself on those petty levels familiar to us as the nag, the battle-ax, the back seat driver, but on the worthier levels we see her spreading her wings in art, government, business. Woman today is educated for, and dreams of, the latter—to find herself oftener on the local zoning board than in the halls of Congress, her picture staring back at her from the bedroom wall oftener than hanging in a national gallery. Now those odds are the same as for a man, but her disillusionment has been parlayed into an Ordeal from which man is excluded, and with a powerful lobby of journalists and anthropologists putting her case for her. Isn't it about time this lobby were dissolved and woman recognized a general human Ordeal, with her husband as full partner, as trapped in an office when he wants to write as she in a kitchen when she wants to paint? I just thought I'd mention it. What we need is not any submission of one to the other but both to the hard facts of life—or we shall soon see a counterlobby demanding equal rights for men—I should say equal wrongs for men—and then the jig will be up. It is nearly up now, I'm afraid. There is so much sand in the matrimonial gears that the old machine can hardly function any more, and a fresh crop each spring from Radcliffe and Bennington, swinging briefcases and paint boxes, can hardly be expected to ease matters. Well, the problem of the sexes seems to be that of plain co-   32 existence, which makes it the same as for the great political powers: not to let rivalry become enmity. I would advise all newlyweds to make a sampler of that and hang it over the kitchen sink. That way the husband will see it as often as the wife.

Do you sympathize with Freud and his followers in any way, despite all the shafts you've directed at them?   33

I think you have to judge Freud in the light of the validity of his two   34
discoveries—the importance of the unconscious and of sex in our lives. Both of these are corroborated by human experience. The collateral absurdities of psychoanalysis result from its determination to interpret absolutely everything in the light of them.

Do you think there is any truth in the oft heard charge that the New   35
Yorker *isn't as funny as it once was?*

I think that's the old nostalgia trick we play on ourselves. Glorifying   36
the old days by remembering the peaks and forgetting the stretches of valley between. The hymnists of the good old days of the *New Yorker* should be sat down and be made to go through *all* of the decade hankered for, say the thirties, issue for issue and word for word. Then let them decide whether there wasn't so much dross in them thar hills as now, or as much gold in these as there.

For all that, many believe the tone of the New Yorker's *humor has*   37
changed. With you as an exception, of course, it seems to be far less frank and gay than in the great days of Thurber, Benchley, Parker, and Perelman.

I would like to say two things about that. One, you can't blame a maga-   38
zine for a momentary dearth of prose clowns. All this harping or carping about the *New Yorker* is in a way a kind of tribute to it, because it shows where people look for the new humorists and where they'll most likely turn up. And that's all pure happenstance—when any new one comes along. When the accidents of nerves and glands and environmental torment that go into the making of a humorist combine in a man, he will write humor. He is not produced by fiat of Ross or Shawn, and it will do you no good to keep yelling "Louder and funnier" while you're waiting. The second thing is this: If there are fewer comics today, or if they seem less funny, the serious writers are more so. There is more wit and comedy in, say, Cheever and Updike and Salinger than there was in a comparable clutch of "serious" fiction writers in the good old days. And there was a lot in the best of Liebling, too. So that precious commodity hasn't disappeared from the store—it's just on another shelf. And I hope customers are still getting their money's worth.

Well, just for the record, how do you feel about the modern world?   39

I'll answer that by taking down *A Tale of Two Cities* and reading you   40

the opening line: "It was the best of time, it was the worst of times . . . "
And it always has been.

QUESTIONS AND EXERCISES

Vocabulary

1. Define or explain each of the following terms:

   tantalizing (2)   amorist (30)
   absurdity (10)   vicarious (30)
   Absurd (10)   parlayed (32)
   existentialist (10)   enmity (32)
   eschew (10)   sampler (32)
   naturalistic (12)   corroborated (34)
   cerebral (12)   collateral (34)
   connotative (18)   hymnist (36)
   yokels (20)   dross (36)
   matriarchy (23)   dearth (38)
   urbs (24)   carping (38)
   bawdy (30)   happenstance (38)
   risqué (30)

2. Identify or explain the allusion involved in each of the following items:

   Max Beerbohm (2)   J. P. Donleavy (30)
   Faulkner (4)   Shaw (32)
   Yeats (4)   Benchley (37)
   Edwin Arlington Robinson (4) Parker (37)
   Charlie Chaplin (4)   Perelman (37)
   Swift (10)   Ross or Shawn (38)
   Thurber (10)   Cheever (38)
   Anthony Powell (12)   Updike (38)
   Norman Mailer (15)   Salinger (38)
   Thomas Hardy (20)   Liebling (38)
   Bertrand Russell (28)   *A Tale of Two Cities* (40)
   Mary McCarthy (29)

Rhetoric

3. This interview suggests that the essay has undergone changes. Writers feel that the interview is a more direct presentation of another person's views and ideas. What technological factors have made the interview a growing "genre"? What pertinency has Marshal McLuhan's theory that the "medium is the message" to the interview technique?

4. This interview abounds with figurative language, wit, and rhetoric devices. Find examples of the following:

    simile   pun
    metaphor   euphemism
    analogy   wit

5. Classification may be used to explain, but it may also be used to comment on something. Explain the purpose in paragraph 32.

6. De Vries utilizes analogies to prove his points. Why do analogies suggest a greater degree of proof than do metaphors?

7. It is difficult to define wit. Freud's analysis of wit often misses the point. Explain the wit in the following items, if indeed you find them witty: "Ordeal of Modern Woman" becomes "Modern Ordeal of Woman" (31) (32)

    "and a fresh crop each spring from Radcliffe and Bennington, swinging briefcases and paint boxes" (32)

    "the suburbs and urbs" (24)

    "There are a lot of bad reasons for being good and a lot of good reasons for being bad—also fortunately, a lot of good reasons for being good." (28)

8. In the course of the interview De Vries makes several definitions. Find the definitions of the following terms and comment on the nature of the definition used:

    satire   absurd
    humorist   farce

9. Several of De Vries' statements are aphoristic, as for example, "not to let rivalry become enmity." (32) Find several other such examples.

Theme

10. What is De Vries' comment on the modern world?

11. According to De Vries, what makes a humorist (38)?

12. Discuss the differences in meaning of the following terms: comedy, satire, humor, and farce.

13. Distinguish the philosophical differences between the concepts of humor of the existentialists and the Freudians. What is De Vries' position?

Topics and Assignments for Composition

1. In one sentence for each, write your own definitions of each of the following:

    humor   wit
    satire

2. Much of Plato's philosophy was written in the pattern of a dialogue. Write a short paragraph in which you discuss the difference between a dialogue and an interview.
3. Conduct a short interview and write it in the pattern used by Davis.
4. Write an essay in which you evaluate the advantages and disadvantages of the interview form and in which you suggest its future in expository writing.

John C. Pollard

An Open Letter to New Students on the Subject of Substances, Both Natural and Synthetic, That Have the Property of Getting You in Trouble, of Various Sorts

Dear Freshman,

Some weeks ago I was asked to write an article, or perhaps "paper" is *1* the correct professional term, about the use and abuse of drugs and such substances. This paper was to be included in a booklet with other items of wisdom to make your advent to the University as smooth and painless as possible. "Heck" I said to myself, or something like that, what can I tell these people that they don't already know? Why should they listen to me? Why should they expect me to be any more or less truthful than the "authorities" have been in the past on this subject? So I decided against a paper. A letter instead. Then I can write as I talk.

Not that giving you my credentials is likely to make that much differ- *2* ence, but I think you are entitled to them—and if you've read so far, you must be sort of interested. Some years ago—just about the time Timothy Leary was stirring things up with his LSD "research" at Harvard, a group of us here were also conducting some experiments. Several of us at Michigan, at the Mental Health Research Institute, were studying isolation stress and the production of hallucinations. And later we studied the relationship between LSD* and creativity. In these experiments we used several hallucinogenic substances besides LSD 25. If you are curious as to the results and can stand to read rather dull "scientific" reports, I will

Reprinted with permission of the author and *The Michigan Alumnus.*

* Never seen it? Look on the cover of the Sergeant Pepper album.

give you the references. Unlike Dr. Leary's research, ours was "official." That is, we had not only University approval, but since the government was paying the expenses, we had government approval through the National Institute of Mental Health. During the inception of these experiments it was necessary for the researchers to use themselves as subjects. Not only would it have been impossible to know what questions were pertinent under the "drugged" state, but it would also have been impossible to know what testing a subject would be capable of, unless we had tried the substance ourselves. Furthermore, these chemicals were even more unknown then, than they are now and it is the time honored medical tradition that a researcher does not ask a subject to do what he would not do himself. So, to put it plainly, some eight years ago I was a subject in my own experiments. I have taken LSD and similar substances.

At this point I have probably turned off a large section of your parents, who like one mischievous gentleman of the press, assumed by the foregoing that I'm obviously an acid head with psychedelic gorillas on my back. *Honi soit qui mal y pense.* I *can* tell you this, my experiences weren't a bit like Peter Fonda's. If you're still with me, I have two more points that come under the heading of credentials. Friedenberg said that adults envy the young because "they have not yet wasted their opportunities." Well, I'm not sure I've wasted mine, but simple chronological facts bear witness that youth has many more opportunities than I have, and I do envy that. Finally, in the last several years I have been seeing many "drug" casualties. Those who have scared the heck out of themselves by a "bad trip"; those who have had old and previously handled troubles flare up following drug use. And even a few young people habituated to the use of amphetamines and barbiturates. Even saw a pot head who said blowing pot was so pleasurable he preferred it to work. This guy was a great thinker! *3*

Now, what am I to tell you? Seems to me that if you don't know a lot about drugs after all the battering from the press, movies and television, then you've been living under a rock and I don't know what you are doing at Michigan. You'd better go back. Unfortunately, in this "battery" the press is not always scrupulous about the facts. And sometimes things are presented as facts that are at best "maybe" facts. Take marijuana for instance. Whatever the pharmacological properties of the substance are, I think it would be classified more appropriately as an irritant. A social irritant. It is a botanical, used individually for its real and symbolic effects, the real being the production of a mild intoxication which is usually felt to be pleasureable—the degree of pleasure or displeasure being related to myriad variables such as strength of dose, *4* environment, purpose, and the personality of the user. Let's look at some of these variables more closely. Strength and dose. Cannabis comes in many forms—the weakest is "grass," the leaves and flowering tops of the Indian hemp plant; whose strength varies with the age and origin. So there's the first hazard in the pleasurable experience. You don't know how much you are getting. Environment, I shall consider this with purpose. If marijuana is used because of a dare, to be in, cool, or with it, or it dissolves a few tenuous inhibitions, and then if you can accept that you can only do all or any of these things with the "help" of an intoxicant, then you've accepted yourself as a phony and you've passed that variable. Now what about personality. I think we mislead ourselves in thinking of this as a static absolute thing. Sure there's a pattern to our personalities, but do we always feel the same? How are you on Monday, even if your sign *is* Cancer? Could not this—or any intoxicant stir up heaven knows what in all those factors that have been nicely dormant? Which reminds me, if you go after any substance as an instant analysis, you will be disappointed. But it would appear that pot smoking is pleasurable, and what's wrong with pleasure? Absolutely nothing, except that this way of getting pleasure can be as seductive as a whole rock covered with Hefner sirens. Like the boy said, he preferred it to work. Let me share a personal aside here—I went to school in Europe and used to clutch before exams—at least a week before. Guess what my cop out was? Movies. Beautiful double features. Three hours and fifteen minutes of the worst that Hollywood could produce (you don't even get to see the ones they sent to Europe). And then having escaped unsuccessfully with Rita Hayworth's anatomy substituted for Gray's, feeling ten times more clutched, I went the coffee and midnight oil route. The movies were over; if you'll pardon the pun, there wasn't another joint.

What about the symbolic meaning. The social irritant. Something's   5
happening and you don't know what it is, do you Mr. Jones? says Bob Dylan. Social psychologists will tell you that this generation gap-noncommunication is not new, and historians will make parallels with the anabaptist rebellions. But something is new. The vehicle. Drugs. In the cops and robbers, parents-child, establishment-antiestablishment conflict, one new thing is the vehicle. The chemical metaphor. I don't think either "side" chose it, but there it is in all its twentieth century confusion. Symbolic facts are irrelevant, save one; the fact of illegality.

At this point, some of you are saying "Shouldn't the use of pot be   6
legalized?" I'll gladly answer if you'll pardon the lapse into dialogue, but first could you shape up your question a little? Legalized for whom?

You, me, ten year olds? And you say "pot." Are you referring to that tired old Mexican grass that wanders weakly into—where shall I say?—Chilicote, Iowa? Or are you including red, gold, and hash? If so, we'll have to put our cards on the table as to what we really know about all forms of Cannabis. Which isn't very much. And by legalize do you mean anyone, anyplace, any amount? If you do, you are a lot tougher than I when it comes to sirens. But—you say—you really know that thousands of people smoke it regularly and don't have trouble. The great trouble is that I don't know that, I *suspect* it to be true for many, I *know* it is not true for all, and would you have me legalize something because I suspect it is not very harmful? Not *very* harmful, I shivered then. Is that good enough for you? What will I say, and thus alienate the remainder of your parents—and maybe some of you—is that the laws should be *changed*—the punishments as they now stand are irreconcilable with the few known facts and often related to vindictiveness (as is readily demonstrated by individual interpretation by both police and jurists). I would further suggest that the laws scarcely reflect the wishes of the informed public. I am told that at an international level, one country has requested that there be no modifications of the international laws relating to marijuana because that country could not handle the internal problems that would arise. So that's their problem. I further believe, as I have stated elsewhere, that the execution of the marijuana legislation as it now stands, represents a waste of public money that could well be used for fact-finding research that could replace conjecture and opinion.

But tell me, if there were facts revealed that showed marijuana to be harmful, would you believe it? No! All right then, back to the cops and robbers. Was it not Thomas Jefferson who said "If laws do not change with time, it is like expecting a grown man to wear child's clothing." The laws and the interpretations of the laws will change, but at this moment the sale, possession, and use of marijuana, *or the knowledge of such* is a serious offense covered by both federal and state laws. Laws are rarely changed by violating them.   7

Now I shall turn to LSD 25 (or acid) and similar hallucinogenic substances. A list is dull. How about a unique classification?   8

Class A. Those purchasable in a distinctly furtive and clandestine manner (much like pot is) which will include LSD 25, Psilocybin, DMT, DET, STP, etc.

Class B. Those purchasable with or without trading stamps, at your neighborhood grocery store or hobby shop

Class C. Those growing in the bosky woods of Michigan. (see

natural history books under fungi.) Please note, it's against state law to pick wild flowers and plants.

Class D. Those purchasable without prescription at any drug store.

They all have two things in common. First they can alter your state of consciousness, and secondly they can all be very dangerous, whether or not they are approved of as medicines or even religious sacraments, or even legislatively like alcohol.

But, but—you are saying, "I know plenty of people who have taken   9
hallucinogenic substances, and they seem okay—and you took it, what about *you*?" Well, maybe those friends that *seem* okay are lucky. Maybe I have been too. But even to use the words "seem" and "lucky" makes me cross my fingers because I have seen many who have *not* been lucky and do not seem to be okay. Maybe extended psychotic episodes are rare—but the intoxication by LSD and similar substances is a very profound and often disrupting experience. It can be psychologically very painful and even if a "trip" doesn't result in a long psychotic episode, can we really say the experience was harmless? Suicides have occurred, but how many have died a little, and yet not been listed as casualties? Flashbacks are real. Recurrent hallucinations—sometimes three to six months later—to me appearing to be stress-related. How about a nice hallucination the next time you take an exam. Or try I-94 just west of Detroit at five o'clock. I'll stay home. Unlike marijuana, when you've taken acid, you're on a brain roller coaster and you can't get off. Who said something about a guide? Has *he* been in *your* mind, is he going where you are going? Granted, a hostile, exploiting environment will guarantee you a very painful time—but the opposite does not prevail. (Want evidence? Ask me to give you the U.C.L.A. studies.)

Acid is old hat. *Time, Life, Saturday Evening Post* and The Los   10
Angeles Free Press have told you all about it. Did they mention that it raises your blood pressure, increases heart rate, contracts smooth muscles, (gives girls cramps) reduces dream time, impairs visual focusing, impairs visual motor coordination, increases deep reflexes, alters brain electrical activity, selectively acts on the limbic and arousal brain systems? Oh, yes, and it may damage your genes.

Who said, "And so does coffee"? I said I'd try to give you facts and   11
here they are. There is evidence that damaged chromosomes have appeared in the blood cells of *some* people who have taken LSD. They have not been found in the blood cells of all people who have taken LSD. The damaged chromosomes resemble those found in certain diseases—such as leukemia (cancer of the white cells). There is no record

at this time of anyone developing the disease as a direct result of taking LSD, nor have abnormalities of the (first generation) offspring appeared. But, animal studies, using mice, rats and hamsters have shown fetal abnormalities particularly in the development of the central nervous system. (If you are really interested and would like to see some gruesome pictures, look through "Science" within the last year.) It is nothing more than conjecture, but I suggest that there are susceptible individuals for whom LSD is particularly cyto (cell) toxic, while others may be relatively immune. Which are you?

It is obviously beyond the scope of this letter to go into each hallucino- *12* genic substance even in the brief way that I have discussed LSD. They are all intoxicants—what else could they be? If I repeat myself, forgive me, but I say again, approval or disapproval of a substance really doesn't alter the chemical properties. Just because some people approve of alcohol (do they really, or are they just resigned?) and disapprove of marijuana and LSD, does one become good and the other bad? Maybe in time something could evolve as depicted in The Tenth Victim. Maybe if we really have to have drugs, we will have to make them safer. But no one seems to have developed a cirrhosis-free booze yet, they haven't even filtered out the hangover. Somehow I have a feeling that whatever we seek with drugs is really with us all the time, the trouble is that love, beauty and tranquility sound either corny or commercial—or even worse, phony. Maybe we should make them fashionable again.

I should say something about barbiturates and amphetamine-like drugs. *13* "Speed kills" says the button from Plum Street. And so it can. Methedrine and other amphetamine drugs are stimulants, unwisely used in my opinion, for weight reduction and relief of temporary fatigue and depression. But they are habituating. The "high" is "good." You stayed up all night—felt alert, bright and read twice as many pages. (Contrary to many studies, you even remembered what you read.) Good for you. Now the next time you are down, take another—why not? You didn't sleep—felt a little jittery, classes next day, so take another, try two. That is but a variation on a theme, not common, but common enough. After a few weeks you'll need ten times the initial dose to keep you up. Don't worry about the confusion, irritability, jitters and occasional hallucination. They all go away after you stop—if you do. That is when you've gotten over the withdrawal symptoms.

Barbiturates (sleeping pills)—goof balls, yellow jackets, etc. are not *14* always "downers." They alter your level of consciousness too. The danger again is the confusion and impairment of ability to concentrate. Habituation, which simply means that you have to take more and more, can take place easily, and while the barbiturate toxic state is not as gruesome as with amphetamines, the withdrawal often results in seizures. And of course, an overdose of sleeping pills . . .

In many ways you have been deciding things for yourself for quite *15* some time. If you didn't like what you decided, there are always plenty of people to blame. And those you blame will no doubt return the compliment. If you have arrived as freshmen at college without *some* idea of what is right or wrong for you personally to do, or not to do, then you've pretty well lost out anyway. I'll tell you what I think is good for *me,* but you have to decide about yourself. You know, making up one's mind is a curious expression, but when it comes to the "mind" whose else could really decide about it? Whether you wish to expand it or contract it, it *is* yours. You won't get another one this trip.

QUESTIONS AND EXERCISES

Vocabulary

1. Define or explain each of the following terms:

   hallucinations (2)   dormant (4)
   hallucinogenic (2)   cop out (4)
   turned off (3)   Mexican grass (6)
   acid head (3)   red, gold, and hash (6)
   psychedelic (3)   alienate (6)
   Honi soit qui mal y pense (3)   vindictiveness (6)
   "bad trip" (3)   LSD 25 (8)
   amphetamines (3)   furtive (8)
   barbiturates (3)   clandestine (8)
   pot head (3)   Psilocybin (8)
   blowing pot (3)   DMT (8)
   pharmacological (4)   DET (8)
   myriad (4)   STP (8)
   Cannabis (4)   fungi (8)
   "grass" (4)   psychotic (9)
   tenuous (4)   limbic (10)

2. Identify or explain each of the allusions involved in each of these terms:

   Timothy Leary (2)   Rita Hayworth's anatomy
   psychedelic gorilla on my   substituted for Gray's (4)
      back (3)   Bob Dylan (5)

Peter Fonda (3)   Anabaptist rebellion (5)
Friedenberg (3)   the Tenth Victim (12)
the clutch (4)
whole rock covered with
    Hefner sirens (4)

Rhetoric

3. What is the effect of paragraph 1 on the tone and style of the essay?
4. What is the purpose of paragraph 2?
5. Find an example of irony in paragraph 3.
6. Dr. Pollard's thesis begins in paragraph 4. Is it possible to emulate his pattern of development in a 500-word essay?
7. Paragraph 8 is developed by classification. What are the advantages of this technique?
8. Find several examples of humor in the letter.
9. What figures of speech does Dr. Pollard use?

Theme

10. Psychiatrists use verbal clues to analyze people; by using Dr. Pollard's language, wit, examples, and analyses, make a composite picture of what you see to be his attitude toward college freshmen.
11. With which type of freshman is Dr. Pollard's approach most likely to be effective?
12. Point out any factual flaws in Dr. Pollard's presentation.
13. Are there any logical lapses?
14. Show evidence of Dr. Pollard's semantic sophistication.
15. What are some of his assumptions about values?
16. Assuming you had a personal problem about drugs, sex, beliefs, the draft, or college, to whom would you turn for advice or help?

Topics and Assignments for Composition

1. Make a series of five sentences, not necessarily connected grammatically or logically, in which you summarize five bits of advice overtly or covertly presented in Dr. Pollard's letter.
2. Defend or attack one factual claim in the essay.
3. Write an open letter to one representative of the establishment and answer his exhortations to conduct your life along his precepts.
4. Make up an original essay with a challenging title and thesis. Example: Witch Doctors, Preachers, and Psychiatrists: Brothers Under the Skin, Parents, Teachers, Preachers, and other Fakirs I have Known.

Anonymous

Desiderata

Go placidly amid the noise & haste & remember what peace there may be in silence. As far as possible without surrender be on good terms with all persons. Speak your truth quietly & clearly; and listen to others, even the dull & ignorant; they too have their story. Avoid loud & aggressive persons, they are vexations to the spirit. If you compare yourself with others, you may become vain & bitter; for always there will be greater & lesser persons than yourself. Enjoy your achievements as well as your plans. Keep interested in your own career, however humble; it is a real possession in the changing fortunes of time. Exercise caution in your business affairs; for the world is full of trickery. But let this not blind you to what virtue there is; many persons strive for high ideals; and everywhere life is full of heroism. Be your self. Especially do not feign affection. Neither be cynical about love; for in the face of all aridity & disenchantment it is perennial as the grass. Take kindly the counsel of the years, gracefully surrendering the things of youth. Nurture strength of spirit to shield you in sudden misfortune. But do not distress yourself with imaginings. Many fears are born of fatigue & loneliness. Beyond a wholesome discipline, be gentle with yourself. You are a child of the universe, no less than the trees & the stars; you have a right to be here. And whether or not it is clear to you, no doubt the universe is unfolding as it should. Therefore be at peace with God, whatever you conceive him to be, and whatever your labors & aspirations, in the noisy confusion of life keep peace with your soul. With all its sham, drudgery & broken dreams, it is still a beautiful world. Be careful. Strive to be happy.

Found in Old Saint Paul's Church, Baltimore; Dated 1692.

Student Example

Bopping Down Memory Lane

As past decades have a way of doing, the fifties seem to be in line for a big comeback. In the fast-paced, permissive, sexy, violent sixties, there was no era so totally boring and forgotten as the cold, gray fifties. The twenties, thirties, and forties were distant enough to be remembered with a touch of nostalgia by the older generation, and not remembered at all by the young. Thus, these decades took on an aura of glamour and mystery, their fashions, fads, heroes, and villains assuming a retrospective stylishness and appeal they probably never had in their prime. Bonnie and Clyde, for all their pretensions of glory and fame, were apparently considered minor criminals in their own time; the status of folk heroes accorded them in the sixties would undoubtedly have surprised, though certainly pleased them. In the sixties, these decades were popular by virtue of their distance, strangeness, and irrelevance. In an era of political and social flux, nostalgia, particularly for a period which one dimly remembers or has never known, and is thus untainted by reality, can be a pleasant and comforting diversion.

The fifties, however, were too depressingly recent to receive the same treatment as their predecessors: that which has just passed always seems the most dated and uninteresting. But with the onset of the seventies, a fresh decade with an inevitably new perspective, there may well be a glorious fifties revival in store. The popularity of "The Last Picture Show" may have heralded the new mood. This was an interesting and different film in which the young hero was not once seen taking dope; in fact, he never mentioned it. Sex was secret, embarrassing, and deliciously sinful, not just a routine matter of going to the doctor or drugstore for the monthly supply of pills. Korea was on people's minds, going to the movies on Saturday was the only real form of escapism, hair was short, skirts were long, styles were drab, rock, whose birth was one of the few innovations of the decade, hadn't yet spread. A weird, faraway time, the fifties were so downright drab as to be somehow mysterious and amusing.

The current interest in rock n' roll has greatly renewed interest in seminal fifties rock figures like Chuck Berry, Little Richard, Jerry Lee Lewis, Buddy Holly, the Everly Brothers, the Drifters, and others. Black bluesmen of the fifties and earlier, so ignored and forgotten when rock was blossoming, have been enjoying recognition and revival for some time. White "let's go to the hop" rock is being dug out of the moldy oldie collections; and Don McLean who apparently longs for the simple days of early rock n' roll, remembering the good old days when he was "a lonely teenage broncking buck with a pink carnation and a pickup truck," provides instant nostalgia, especially for those who actually have some vague memories of the fifties.

Marilyn Monroe and James Dean have long been cult figures, and Marlon Brando is re-emerging. There are hundreds of forgotten fifties movies, stars, and television programs which now seem funny and enjoyable as remnants of a past generation. Shows like "Donna Reed" and "Father Knows Best" have high nostalgia value. Designers have recently shown raglan sleeves, tight skirts, high heels, seamed stockings, strapless dresses, pedal pushers, low-cut sweaters, and fifties hair styles and makeup, a sign that the decade is distant enough to be stylish and a source of new inspiration in fashion and fad.

In England, where the fifties were, if anything, duller than in the States, there is a revival of the Teddy Boys—tough, brash, rock n' roll lovers of the swirly greasy pompadours, drainpipe trousers, long velvet jackets (drains and drapes) flourescent socks, and suede shoes, which used to carry razor blades in the toe. In the decade before the Beatles, Teds were a spot of shocking color and bravado on the damp, drab landscape.

Though some of the previously mentioned elements of fifties culture are interesting, unique, and historically significant enough to warrant rediscovery, it's doubtful whether there can be any real heartfelt nostalgia for the complacent postwar decade. Older people might remember it as a time of relative peace and prosperity, free from excess violence or challenge to middlebrow values; a time when racism was tacitly accepted, the young still had some respect for their elders, and the term sexism hadn't yet been coined, let alone discussed. It was a time when America still believed in itself and its values; when everything unpleasant was still swept under the collective carpet. But in that pre-Kennedy, Vietnam, Beatles, Black Power, Pill, Dope, Moonshots, Dropout, Woodstock, Woman's Lib, Ecology era, the same problems and conflicts (or the seeds and roots of them) existed as do today. They were simply not understood or articulated. Many people still believed in the superiority and validity of the American Democracy and Way of Life. Silence, apathy, and contentment in the *status quo* were not even much shaken by the witchhunts instigated by the zealot McCarthy (Joe not Gene). College students were primarily engrossed in beer parties and degrees. Minorities were still acquiescent, too rooted in their differentness, too much accepting and helping to prolong their inferior status, to identify and confront the forces which created and sustained their lower position. Whites still accepted the American dream.

But the fifties was the last decade in which these middle-class values were virtually universally accepted. Black inferiority, the ultimate desirability of material progress, the natural superiority of America and all things American, the necessity of the draft, the value of religion and the double standard in sexual attitudes, the desirability of being conformist, and the belief that change must come slowly and gradually which were the cornerstones of American thinking began to erode during the late fifties.

Thus, the fifties saw the Civil Rights movement demand, with a dignity and politeness which later gave way to long-repressed frustration and rage, equality for blacks. Though in different ways and on different levels, the birth of Civil Rights and rock were developments which shaped and influenced much of what would happen in the next decade. Other challengers of the old order were the Beats, Kerouac, Ginsberg, and others who explored and often questioned America. And the birth of television, despite the fact that it has done nothing but reflect the desires, fantasies, and ideas of middle-class materialist society, created an immediacy of communication that also had an effect on the development of and response to events of the sixties.

The stable, stolid fifties, which drew to a close thirteen years ago, can now be viewed through the mist of time, its fads, fashions, heroes, villains, and preoccupations seen as amusing, endearing, and quaint. The more indistinct a decade becomes, the more it is imbued with nostalgic interest and appeal, and the less relevance to and connection with contemporary reality it retains. Already we are looking back on the advent of the Beatles, the emergence of rock festivals, the flowering of dope, and, in fact, on much that took place in the sixties with a feeling tinged with longing for the glamour and excitement of those bygone times. . . . The cycle goes on.

Glossary

A fortiori: A conclusion that is inferred to be stronger than another conclusion.

A posteriori: A factual statement to be verified by sense experience or empirical data; a type of induction.

A priori: That which precedes. An *a priori* statement is one that is accepted and considered true independently of any factual evidence.

Absolute expression: A statement at the beginning of a sentence not related grammatically to the rest of the sentence. *The game having ended, we went into the club to celebrate.*

Abstract: The idea of things, works, and relationships that may have no concrete reality. Antonym of concrete.

Acronym: A word formed from the initial letters of a phrase or name. CORE, SNAFU, NASA.

Adage: A type of proverb or saying; a truism. *Good fences make good neighbors.*

Ad baculum **argument:** The appeal to force fallacy. A resort to or threat of force rather than the use of reason.

Ad hominem **fallacy:** A "to the man" argument appealing to feelings and prejudices rather than to reason. *Don't listen to the dean; he's a fascist.*

Ad ignorantiam **fallacy:** An appeal to the lack or absence of knowledge. *X is true because it hasn't been proved false, or X is false because it hasn't been proved true.*

Ad misercordiam **fallacy:** An argument based on an appeal to pity. *Please, sir, give me the job; you wouldn't want to see my poor old mother starve.*

Ad populum **fallacy:** An argument that appeals "to the people" or at least to the prejudices of a given group. *All of us here in Center City don't need outside agitators to tell us how to solve our race problems, do we folks?*

Ad verecundiam **argument:** A fallacy appealing to authority but not relevant to the issue under discussion. *I am quite sure that George Washington never intended us to get mixed up with foreign entanglements by joining the United Nations.*

Aesthetic: Dealing with the beautiful or artistic. Aesthetics is a branch of philosophy dealing with the study of the nature of beauty.

Affix: Any prefix, suffix, or root used to form a new word.

Allegory: A story that has symbolic figures representing the accepted truths about human beings in a given culture. The allegorical meaning is in addition to the literal meaning. Allegory may also be called an extended metaphor or analogy. It has the advantage of making abstract concepts like evil or goodness into concrete images.

Alliteration: The repetition of the initial sounds of two or more successive words. Makes prose sound poetic and often clichéd. *Thick and thin; time and tide.*

Allusion: Reference to a person, place, thing, or any entity in history or literature, used for the purpose of comparison, contrast, humor, emotion, or explanation.

Ambiguity: The state of having more than one possible meaning or interpretation; may be inadvertent or deliberate, serious or humorous.

Anachronism: An error in the logic of time; chronologically out of order, for example, having gunpowder in Homer's Greece.

Anacoluthon: A type of incoherence in a sentence. A shift of thought causing the shift. *You need to-aw, do it you own way.*

Anagram: The rearrangement of letters to form a new word or phrase. *Erewhon = nowhere; William Shakespeare = We all make his praise.*

Analects: A miscellaneous collection of passages from one author. *The Analects of Confucius.*

Analogy: An extended comparison of two objects or ideas for the purpose of illustration or argument. The analogy may be merely an extended metaphor, but the analogy is used more overtly as a pattern of argument rather than as a mere figure of speech for rhetorical purposes. One may explain the unknown on the basis of the known. For example, old age may be compared to the autumn of the year. Analogies suggest and clarify but do not prove.

Analysis: A type of expository writing that breaks a complicated whole into its major, logical components for examination.

Anecdote: A short story of an event.

Annotation: An explanation or clarification of the text by the use of marginal notes.

Antiphrasis: A type of irony which uses a word to mean its opposite; a type of sarcasm. *Brutus is an honorable man.*

Antithesis: A contrast of ideas by parallelism or by the direct statement of an opposite idea. *Young men want to be faithful and are not; old men want to be faithless and cannot.*

Antonym: A word having the opposite meaning of another word. *Black-white.*

Aphorism: A short statement giving a general truth. Synonyms: maxim, proverb, saw, epithet, adage, and apothegm. *It is better to have loved and lost than to have never loved at all.*

Apology: A defense of one's view. *He is an apologist for racism.*

Apostrophe: A direct address to someone not present. *Listen, you old people, to the new voices.*

Apothegm: A succinct saying that affirms a commonly accepted truth. An aphorism.

Appendix: Material added to the main part of a book to illuminate, explain, or amplify the text.

Archetype: Any object, situation, or pattern which may serve as a model for another experience. May be compared to a myth or a type of universal truth.

Argument: Writing that attempts to persuade by using logic and evidence. Includes and uses formal logic and material logic and the corresponding patterns of argument. Often formal and material fallacies are part of an argumentative essay Polemics is a synonym.

Article: A type of essay which tries to be less personal and more objective than the informal essay and exposition.

Assonance: The repetition of vowel sounds in succeeding words. *Late-day.*

Assumption: That which is accepted as true to begin a chain of reasoning.

Asymmetry: Not equal in some measurement, non-parallel in construction.

Authority: An expert in a given area; not considered an authority outside his field of specialization.

Autobiography: Writing of a life by the person himself; may include his letters, journals, and memoirs.

Balanced sentence: A sentence that uses parallelism of phrases or clauses to put several ideas in sequence for dramatic or logical emphasis. *I came, I saw, I conquered.*

Barbarism: Any obvious misuse of language; a type of solecism.

Bathos: The act of including sentimentalism, insincerity, triteness, or the commonplace in an otherwise serious essay.

Begging the question: *Petitio principii.* Assumes that which is to be proved. *X is true because X is true.*

Belle-Lettres: Writing that is noted for elegance, ornamentation, and frivolity.

Black and white fallacy: A type of either-or thinking that states if something is false then the opposite must be true.

Body: The main part of the essay that carries the thrust of the evidence and development. The main rhetorical methods of development are consciously used: induction, deduction, narrative, analogy, comparison and contrast, process, and analysis.

Bromide: A term for a cliché, common saying, adage, saw, or proverb.

Caricature: The deliberate distortion of an

already obvious quality for making a comic or satirical commentary. A type of parody or travesty.

Casuistry: A type of misuse of reasoning similar to rationalizing or sophistry.

Categorical syllogism: An Aristotelian type of logical structure that has a major premise, a minor premise, and a conclusion. Four types of categorical propositions are included:

A. Universal-Affirmative: *All men are mortal.*

B. Universal-negative: *No men are mortal.*

C. Particular-Affirmative: *Some men are mortal.*

D. Particular-negative: *Some men are not mortal.*

Major Premise: *All men are mortal.*
Minor Premise: *Socrates is a man.*
Conclusion: *Socrates is mortal.*

Cause and Effect: A method of development of paragraphs and entire essays in which the emphasis is on the analysis of the causal relationship between two events. In some instances the method may be almost indistinguishable from the inductive method of development. Usually the only difference is in the emphasis.

Central purpose: The thesis or controlling idea in an essay.

Chronology, Chronological order: The chronological development utilizes the logic of time. The chronological organization is one that begins with what happens first and continues with the items put into time sequence.

Circumlocution: A euphemism or redundancy by which a direct reference to an unpleasant subject is avoided. Circumlocution leads to wordiness and genteelness.

Classes: Sets, collections, or categories in logic. Membership in classes is an important aspect of classification on the use of deductive logic. Other terms pertaining to classes are the null class, class complement, universe of discourse, and categorical statements.

Classification: A method of exposition which attempts to analyze relationships by using divisions based upon meaningful similarities, for example: highbrow, middlebrow, and lowbrow.

Cliché: An overused, wornout phrase, saying, or expression. *Sadder but wiser we returned home.*

Coherence: The unity between elements of sentences, of paragraphs, and of essays.

The overall organization of any essay.

Colloquial: Speech considered informal, standard usage. WEBSTER'S THIRD has dropped it as a meaningful label for level of usage.

Colloquy: A type of dialogue.

Comparison and contrast: A method of development of paragraphs or entire essays in which the emphasis is upon similarities and differences of ideas.

Compendium: A short, comprehensive collection of information about a given subject. Synonyms: *digest, syllabus, survey, prospectus.*

Complex sentence: A sentence having at least one subordinate clause and one or more main clauses. *When the sun comes out, the day becomes cheerful.*

Compound sentence: A sentence containing two or more independent clauses. *Writing is an individual activity; speaking involves an interaction between the participants.*

Compound-complex sentence: A sentence containing one or more subordinate clauses and two or more main clauses: *Although the student understood the point, he did not let on to the others; he feared their censure.*

Conclusion: A definite ending to an essay rather than an inconclusive fading. A satisfactory conclusion should, of course, fit the rest of the essay in logic, implications, and style.

Concrete: The opposite of abstract; uses specific names, places, events, and references rather than general terms.

Condensation: A shortened version of a work, usually a work of fiction, synonyms: *abridgment, digest, or précis.*

Conditional statement: A statement in the form of *if . . . then . . . If you study, you will pass the course.*

Connotation: A meaning suggested either by context, personal experience, or usage that goes beyond the denotative or explicit meaning.

Consonance: The repetition of final consonant sounds. *Cracks and reeks.*

Conspectus: A synopsis or summary.

Context: The relationship of words to those that precede and follow. Context can shape, influence, or change meaning.

Contrast: A rhetorical device used to highlight the difference between two elements.

Controlling purpose: Also called the statement of purpose, thesis statement, and main idea. The basic purpose of an essay is to state the topic and to prove its thesis.

Coordination: The process of joining words,

phrases, and clauses by conjunctions. Coordination is involved in parallel structure.

Criteria: The standards by which something is judged.

Criticism: The process of evaluating some aspect of literature. Items to be considered for criticism are content, style, and logic. Criticism usually implies evaluation, but analysis may precede evaluation.

Critique: A type of analysis that combines reporting and evaluation.

Cynicism: The philosophy that human conduct is motivated only by self-interest.

Deadwood: Redundant, superfluous expressions. A type of circumlocution and verbosity. *In our contemporary world of ours today . . .*

Deductive reasoning: The logic of applying generalizations and premises to specific instances. Also the name for formal, syllogistic, and symbolic logic.

Definition: An attempt to give verbal equivalents by developing various types of explanations. The main types of definitions: *Formal, lexical, stipulative, persuasive, ostensive, and etymological.*

Denotation: The direct literal meaning of words. The lexical definition without personal or contextual connotations.

Description: A presentation of factual elements of places, persons, and things. May utilize imagery as well as figurative language.

Dialect: A pattern of expression peculiar to a region of the country; may be informal standard usage for that region.

Dialectic: The process of reasoning, rational discourse, or philosophical analysis. Uses question and answer pattern.

Dialogue: A conversation between two or more persons. Originally used primarily in a work of fiction, dialogue now means almost any portrayal of argument or analysis of divergent points of view.

Diatribe: Writing that uses invective for severe criticism.

Diction: Choice of words for best effect of tone, style, meaning, and appropriateness.

Didacticism: Emphasis upon preaching and moralizing.

Digest: A collection of shortened material on a given subject. Synonyms: *abridgment, compendium, summary.*

Dilemma: An argument presenting two alternatives.

Discourse: Any organized presentation put in the form of narration, description, exposition, and argumentation.

Disjunctive syllogism: Either-or syllogism. This corresponds with the black-or-white fallacy. *Either man descended from the apes or he is the child of God.*

Dissertation: A formal treatise or thesis, as for a doctoral degree.

Documentation: The citing of authorities, sources, illustrations, and other materials in footnotes and bibliographies.

Elliptical omission: Leaving out words, phrases, or clauses when the meaning is perfectly clear without them. *I knew as much as he.*

Emotive language: The use of slanted or connotative elements in persuasion or argumentation.

Empathy: The ability to realize the feelings of another. In poetry it may extend to the ability to empathize with inanimate objects and animals.

Emphasis: Deliberate structuring of points to have them receive attention. Techniques used may include: position, repetition, balance, devices, active and passive voice, sentence order, and syntax.

Empirical statement: A statement or proposition which can be verified by sense data, facts, or sense experience.

Enthymeme: A syllogism with one of the premises omitted. *Of course he is pushy, he's from New York, isn't he? (All New Yorkers are pushy.) He is from New York. He is pushy.*

Enumeration: A type of listing in some logical sequence.

Epigram: A witty poem or thought pointed at a specific object or event. A more general epigram becomes a maxim.

Epilogue: A concluding speech or section in a book.

Epistomology: The study of the source of knowledge.

Epithet: A disparaging word, a substitution, or a label of a term for a name. *That old goat, Mr. Smith.*

Epitome: An aperçu, a pointed overview retaining the main idea, theme, or moral of the original.

Equivocation: A fallacy that changes the meaning of terms in the process of an argument.

Essay: A composition on a single, unified topic usually emphasizing the writer's personal views. May range on a continuum from informal to formal, the classification being vague. Originally meant an attempt when the form was developed by Montaigne.

Ethics: The part of philosophy which deals

with the nature and source of value, conduct, right and wrong.

Etymology: The study of the origin of words, tracing the history of their evolution and development.

Euler's circles: A way to represent syllogistic arguments graphically:

A. *All men are mortal.*
B. *Socrates is a man.*
C. *Socrates is mortal.*

Euphemism: A circumlocution for a disagreeable term, used either with delicate genteelness or irony. Synonyms: *Circumlocution, periphrasis.*

Euphony: Pleasant sound. Antonym: *cacophony, harsh sound.*

Evaluation: An aspect of criticism in which general value patterns are applied to specific works or portions of works for the purpose of persuading others to accept the judgment.

Evidence: Proof in reasoning. The nature of the argument determines the nature of proof: *induction = empirical evidence; deduction = logical consistency.* Evidence may thus be empirical, authoritative, or logical.

Example: A method of paragraph development which gives illustrations; specific examples of general ideas being formulated.

Exegesis: A detailed explanation or interpretation of a difficult passage.

Exemplification: The use of examples to explain, to illustrate, and te repeat. May be used as evidence in the formation of a generalization or as illustrations in a deductive pattern.

Existentialism: A philosophical position that holds that existence precedes essence, and consequently emphasis is put upon existence as a basis for all values and essences.

Explanatory exposition: Writing that attempts to objectively present facts, processes, and events.

Expletive: A type of interjection used in speech; a superfluous expression. *You see; As it were.*

Exposition: Any attempt at explanation or interpretation. The greater portion of most essays is composed of exposition.

Extended definition: A rhetorical technique used to develop definitions of abstract words like *justice* and *liberty*.

Extensional meaning: The semantic equivalent of denotation.

Eulogy: Writing that praises in a formal fashion.

Fable: A kind of story told with allegorical intent, having animals represent people as in *Animal Farm* and Aesop's *Fables*.

Fallacy: Any example of faulty logic. The two main types of fallacies are material fallacies and formal fallacies. Material fallacies involve faulty inductive reasoning; formal fallacies involve a violation of the rules of deductive logic.

False analogy: The faulty use of an analogy to prove that there is a reasonable similarity between two items to warrant an extension of assumed similarities to the similarities to be established.

Figurative language: Meaning which goes beyond literal meaning of words, phrases, and sentences for various rhetorical purposes. Figurative language attempts to explain the abstract in terms of the concrete.

Figures of speech: The non-literal uses of the language in order to develop comparisons, exaggerations, understatements, and other emotive expressions. Some of the major figures are metaphor, simile, personification, allusion, synecdoche, metonymy, irony, hyperbole, litotes, alliteration, and onomotopeia.

Formal definition: A definition that has two standard parts: 1. the *genus* or general classification and 2. the *differentiae* or the ways the item differs from others in its class. *A car is a vehicle that moves by its own power.*

Formal English: English used in academic writing and in other professional publications.

Formal logic: The structure and validity of deductive arguments.

Generalization: A conclusion based upon inductive logic. Going from sufficient specifics to a conclusion covering those specifics.

Genetic fallacy: An argument that considers the origin of an idea as the reason for the acceptance or the rejection of the idea.

Genre: A category of literature. Some of the main genres are: tragedy, comedy, epic, lyric, pastoral, novel, short story, and essay.

Gestalt: A doctrine in psychology that considers the whole to be more than the sum of its parts.

Gloss: An explanation in the margin, used

now to mean to explain too briefly as to "gloss over." Today *glossary* is the more familiar form.

Gobbledygook: Double talk, nonsense, redundancy.

Grammar: A study of the rules and principles which are operative in language. The two major approaches of grammar are prescriptive and descriptive. The former attempts to enforce assumed rules about the language; the latter attempts to analyze and describe the language as it actually is.

Harangue: A type of exhortation, a diatribe.

Hasty generalizations: A material fallacy that develops a conclusion upon too few or poorly selected examples.

Hiatus: A break between two vowel sounds; a break in time, a gap; an omission in a chain o' reasoning.

Homographs: Words which are spelled alike but have different pronunciations. *lead = metal; lead = present tense of to lead.*

Homonym: A word sounding like another but having a different meaning. *alter-altar.*

Honorific: Having a favorable connotation, praising. Opposite of pejorative.

Humanism: The philosophical position that makes man the measure of all things and rejects supernaturalism.

Humor: The quality in writing that points out the incongruous, ironic, absurd, ludicrous.

Hyperbole: A figure of speech that uses exaggeration for special effect of irony, humor, or criticism. *I told you a million times that you can not go to the movie.*

Hypothesis: A supposed answer or solution to a problem to test the probability of its truth. An impossible assumption for emphasis. *If you had the world, you would still be poor.*

Hypothetical example: An example that is not real but is assumed for the sake of developing an argument. A conditional example. *If X is true, then Y is also true.*

Hypothetical syllogism: A syllogism that has an if clause as a major premise, the positing or negation as a minor premise, and a conclusion. *If P, then C. P. Therefore C.*

Idealism: A theory in philosophy that holds that only minds or their ideas exist or that true reality transcends material reality.

Idiom: An expression peculiar to one language the meaning of which is not seen from literal meaning of the components. An agreed upon grammatical or syntactical deviation.

Ignoratio elenchi: The fallacy of ignoring the argument by mistaking it or deliberately misunderstanding it; a type of equivocation.

Illustration: A type of example used in exposition; a specific sample.

Image: A re-creation of sense experience developed by using language that tries to describe sense experiences like sight, hearing, smell, and feel.

Imagery: The product of the attempt to represent sense experience by means of language. The main sense impressions are seeing, hearing, smelling, and feeling. Imagery is more sensuous than language that is abstract. Imagery, thus, attempts a more direct re-creation of experience than does abstract language or figurative language.

Implication: The logical consequence of a proved or established thesis.

Implicit: Something that may be understood to be the case even though it has not been directly stated. Usually contrasted with *explicit* which is directly stated. Often topic sentences may be implied. The thesis of an essay may be implicit rather than explicit, as often is the case in irony.

Inductive reasoning: The logic in which generalizations and conclusions are formed by going from specific examples to conclusions based on probability or modality. To lead to a conclusion by means of evidence based upon experience.

Inference: The study of the logical consequences of premises, usually a deductive analysis.

Innuendo: Slanting or hinting of meaning not explicitly stated.

Intensional meaning: The semantic equivalent of connotation.

Interpretation: An explanation of the meaning of a passage of prose.

Introduction: The first element in a tripart organization used by many writers. The other two divisions are the body and the conclusion. There are many approaches to an effective introduction, among them: *thesis statement, anecdote, questions, definitions, startling facts, conclusions.*

Intuition: Unreasoned knowing, hunches, non-analytical, non-supported conclusions; known by transcendent means.

Invalid: Conclusions of an argument that do not logically follow from the premises.

Invective: An abusive speech. Synonyms: *diatribe, vituperations, insults.*

Inverted order: The reversing of the usual order of the elements of the sentence, usually accomplished by placing the verb first in a declarative sentence. *Finally, out came the truth.*

Irish Bull: A type of extended malapropism in which the error consists of a type of contradiction. *Anyone who goes to a psychiatrist should have his head examined.*

Irony: A figure of speech that utilizes subtle tone to make the intended meaning the opposite of the literal one. Irony is often used for the purpose of humor and ridicule and may take many forms: sarcasm, satire, irony of situation, and understatement.

Jargon: Technical language often characterized by circumlocutions and pretensions. A type of dialect.

Key terms: The use of repetition of main ideas or key terms for emphasis and amplification.

Ladder of abstraction: Going from the specific to the abstract. *"Bessie," cow, farm animal, animal, living being, farm commodity, wealth.*

Lampoon: To ridicule with invective and irony.

Lemma: An assumption used to illustrate another assumption.

Levels of usage: The division between standard and nonstandard diction. Standard may include formal, informal, and colloquial. Nonstandard includes illiterate, slang, and localisms.

Lexicon: A collection of words usually of a special activity; a dictionary.

Linguistics: The study that deals with the structure of language. Some topics dealt with are phonetics, graphemics, phonology, phonemes, morphemes, syntax, semantics, semasiology.

Litotes: A figure of speech that states the positive by denying the opposite. A type of understatement. *Not too bad. She was not the smartest girl in the world.*

Logic: Patterns of reasoning usually divided into inductive, deductive, and reductive. Deductive logic is also called formal logic. Inductive logic is also known as material logic. Reductive logic is merely graphic simplification of either.

Logical empiricism: The philosophical outlook that accepts logical analysis as the method of philosophy, and as a consequence accepts as meaningful only logically analytic or empirically verifiable statements. Metaphysics is considered meaningless and value judgments are said to be emotive in nature and origin.

Loose sentence: A sentence which has the meaning or emphasis placed at the beginning of the sentence rather than at the end.

Malapropism: A misuse of words employing words that sound alike but distort meaning. *That certainly is a meretricious idea and should solve our problems.*

Malediction: A cutting remark, opposite of benediction. A curse, diatribe, or imprecation.

Material logic: A determination whether factual propositions are true or false. Closely linked with inductive logic.

Materialism: The philosophical position that holds that matter is the only reality.

Maxim: A short witty bit of advice; an adage or proverb.

Metaphor: A figure of speech in which two items are compared for the purpose of emphasizing a common element of similarity. It is a way to clarify one thing by means of another. *Life's but a walking shadow.*

Metaphysics: "Above" physics. Speculation about matters that lie beyond empirical inquiry. Includes the study of being or ontology.

Metonymy: A figure of speech which uses a related idea for the idea itself. *The pen is mightier than the sword.*

Mixed metaphor: A faulty figure of speech where a comparison combines two valid metaphors into one faulty one. *I was hanging by a thread skating over thin ice.*

Myth: A story used to explain natural phenomena now having the implication of being pure fiction hence a false explanation or belief.

Name calling: Another name for the *ad hominem* fallacy.

Narration: A story or an account of events. Important in fiction but used sparingly in expository prose.

Neologism: A new word formed for a specific purpose.

Non sequitur: "It does not follow" fallacy in which the conclusion does not necessarily follow the premises. *He was the best song-and-dance man; he should be our senator.*

Nonce word: A word to fit a special situation or phenomenon, but quickly falling into disuse.

Nonstandard English: The English that is not accepted as standard usage by the educated and professional community, usually listed as nonstandard by dictionaries.

Ockham's razor: (Occam's) The theory introduced by William of Ockham (c. 1280–1350) which holds that an explanation involving the fewest assumptions is to be preferred to more complicated explanations.

Onomatopoeia: A word that imitates the sound or suggests the sound. *Pop, bang, crack, hiss.*

Order: A system of showing logical relationships. Methods of established order: *alphabetical, numerical, spatial, chronological, logical, hierarchic, classification, comparison and contrast.*

Organization: The conscious attempt to give an essay a pattern that is consistent with the meaning and purpose of the essay. The main principles of organization are: *logic, induction, deduction, chronological, narrative, analogy, comparison and contrast, classification.*

Outlining: A method of ordering material. The major types of outlines are: *topic, sentence, paragraph, and numerical.*

Oversimplification: A fallacy that reduces a complicated argument to simple terms that do not fully reflect the complexity of the issue under consideration.

Overstatement: A type of exaggeration; a hyperbole.

Oxymoron: A type of irony. An apparent contradiction that is a condensed paradox. *A sweet pain. A dark light.*

Palindrome: A word or phrase that reads the same forward or backward. *Civic; Able was I ere I saw Elba.*

Parable: Any narrative having a didactic purpose, as an allegory.

Paradigm: A model or pattern of an argument; a rubric.

Paradox: A figure of speech involving an apparent contradiction which may be true when the meaning is correctly interpreted. *My life closed twice before its close.*

Paragraph: Unity of thought in composition that serves to bind together sentences having some logical relation. One sentence paragraphs are usually used for transition or emphasis.

Parallelism: A rhetorical device in which elements of equal status are put into similar grammatical patterns. *We study to learn, to understand, and to succeed.*

Paraphrase: Restating a passage in different words but keeping essentially the same meaning.

Parenthesis: A remark used to explain, amplify, or elucidate; a parenthetical remark.

Parenthetical expression: A comment or explanation apart from the main theme of discourse.

Parody: An imitation of another literary work by exaggeration of one of the characteristics of the imitated work such as language, style, plot, or content.

Pathetic fallacy: Giving human feelings to inanimate objects. *The cruel sea.*

Pathos: The quality in writing that appeals to feeling or sympathy.

Pejorative: A remark meant to be critical or negative in connotation or denotation. Antonym of honorific.

Periodic sentence: A sentence in which the main emphasis and ideas are placed at the end.

Periphrasis: A type of circumlocution, using more words than necessary; a type of redundancy.

Persiflage: Bantering or frivolous style or attitude.

Personification: A figure of speech in which human qualities are attributed to objects, animals, or abstractions. *The night had many eyes.*

Persuasion: Writing that tries to convince by showing the validity and strength of one's position.

Persuasive definition: A definition slanted in such a way as to be pejorative or honorific. *Patriotism is the last refuge of the scoundrel. Poetry is the record of the best thoughts of the best minds.*

Philology: The study of language, usually on historical principles.

Philosophy: Literally, love of wisdom. The study of reality, aesthetics, ethics, logic, metaphysics, epistomology, ontology, and cosmology.

Platitude: A hollow, worn out expression. A clichéd truism. Empty and hypocritical praise. *The youth of the country are our wealth and our future; we should listen to them because out of the mouths of babes come great truths.*

Pleonasm: A wordy redundancy. *I saw him with my own eyes.*

Point of view: The writer's vantage point; the degree of the author's involvement with his subject. May be expressed in attitudes: *objective, subjective, impersonal, emotional;* or by techniques: *first person, third person, formal and informal tone.* Philosophical, valuative, aesthetic, or semantic beliefs may be involved.

Polemics: An argumentative discourse; writing dealing with controversy.

Portmanteau word: Words made by uniting two words into one, a type of neologism. Smog = smoke + fog; Slithy = lithe + slimy.

Post hoc, ergo propter hoc: "After this, therefore BECAUSE of this." A fallacy that wrongly attributes a cause and effect relationship before one has been proved merely on the basis of chronological order. *When A happens, B follows. Therefore, A causes B.*

Pragmatism: The philosophical theory that an idea is true if it works as expected.

Précis: An accurate summary of the main points of an essay. Synonyms: *compendium, abstract, apercu, digest, survey, and syllabus.*

Predication: The foundation of an argument or proposition. Usually the information that is stated about the subject. Used both in grammar and in logic.

Preface: An introduction to a book which states the necessary preamble. A prolegomenon or prologue.

Premise: An assumption basic to deductive logic. A syllogism has a major premise, a minor premise, and a conclusion. A basis, assumed or proved, for argument or inference.

Prolepsis: A foreshadowing or preparatory summary.

Prolix: A synonym for verbose, wordy, longwinded, redundant, circumlocutory.

Proposition: The main thesis in an essay; the item to be established by argument and evidence.

Prototype: A pattern for future items of the same form or genre.

Proverb: A statement having a truth or wisdom of folk origin. May be poetic or archaic.

Pseudonym: An assumed name by a writer; a *nom de plume.*

Pun: A word that may have two or more meanings because of the similarity of the sound. *One man's Mede is another man's Persian.*

Rationalism: The philosophical position that emphasizes reason as opposed to empiricism, mysticism, or authority. Closely tied to age of reason, neoclassism, deism.

Rationalize: To use reason to justify a position even if the position is not reasonably tenable; a misuse of reason.

Realism: The doctrine that holds objects exist independently of being perceived.

Reasoning: Using logic and rational patterns in inductive and deductive fashion. Any form of rational analysis.

Reductio ad absurdum: The reduction of an argument to such a degree as to show an inconsistency or absurdity. Extending the premises of an argument beyond the intended limits in order to destroy it.

Redundancy: The use of superfluous words.

Repetition: A rhetorical device to indicate emphasis; an unintentional repetition may weaken discourse.

Résumé: Summary of main points.

Review: A commentary on a current book, play, or film. A type of literary criticism.

Rhetoric: The techniques by which ideas, style, and logic are fused into writing. Usually unity, coherence, and emphasis are associated with rhetoric. The purpose of rhetoric is explanation and persuasion.

Rhetorical question: A device used to make a comment when no answer is expected.

Rhythm: The presence of accented and unaccented syllables in words arranged in regular patterns. At certain points prose may take on the sound of poetry and poetry may become prose-like.

Rubric: An established form by which other examples may be judged, a paradigm.

Sarcasm: A type of irony that is cutting and caustic.

Satire: In general, satire is criticism expressed in a continuum from gentle humor to bitter irony. Satire is used primarily in essays, as Swift's *A Modest Proposal.*

Scientific method: The utilization of induction, hypothesis, evidence, checking conclusions by logic, experience, and revision as new evidence forces changes in probability.

Semantics: The study of the meaning of words or the meaning of meaning. Emphasis is upon context, connotation, and changes of meaning.

Semiotic: The study of language that emphasizes signs and symbols.

Simile: A figure of speech that compares two different items by linking them with *like, as,* and *then.*

Skepticism: The philosophical position that stresses uncertainty especially in the realm of knowledge.

Slang: A nonstandard level of usage, usually figurative, to cover new phenomena and to give new means of expression to older phenomena. Some slang vanishes while other slang words or expressions become accepted as standard usage.

Slanted language: The utilization of emotion and connotative words to give a bias to prose. Tone, diction, and context may also be used to slant discourse.

Solecism: A fault in grammar or diction.

Solipsism: The philosophical position that only the self exists and everything else exists only in the mind of the solipsist.

Sorites: An argument that has three or more premises, thus requiring two or more syllogisms to deduce the conclusion.

Spatial development: The logic of a statement is determined by the position of its separate parts.

Spoonerism: A misuse of the language by transposing the beginning of words. *Herbert Hoover—Hoobert Herver.*

Statement of purpose: The thesis or main point of an essay as well as the subject to be developed.

Stereotype: A form of clichéd prejudice that continues inaccurate pictures of people, nations, races, and institutions.

Stipulative definition: A definition fashioned for the purpose of a given essay or an assumed definition to begin a polemic discourse.

Stoicism: The philosophy that emphasizes indifference to pleasure or pain.

Style: The overall effect of the techniques used in composition, including diction, syntax, point of view, imagery, figurative language, rhythm, tone, and rhetorical devices. Style emphasizes the techniques of composition rather than the content.

Style sheet: A sheet of rules and conventions used by newspapers, magazines, and publishing houses outlining usage, diction, punctuation, and other editorial points.

Subordination: Putting minor or supporting ideas into grammatically subordinate constructions to emphasize the main ideas. The most obvious such subordinate constructions are the adjective and adverb clauses in complex sentences.

Summary: A short restatement of a longer work. Synonyms: *précis, compendium, synopsis, abstract, and abridgment.*

Syllogism: A formal argument in deductive logic having a major premise, a minor premise, and a conclusion. *All men are mortal. Socrates is a man. Socrates is mortal.*

Syllogistic arguments: Arguments that may be structured into syllogisms and found valid or invalid by the rules of the categorical syllogism.

Symbol: A sign, figure, image, or other agreed upon emblem that stands for another entity. Usually a specific term is used to represent an abstraction: a flag for the nation, a color for quality. A symbol may connote more than it actually denotes. There are natural symbols like the moon, sea, and earth; arbitrary symbols like flags, crown, and badges; and private symbols used in poetry standing for very complicated private abstractions.

Symbolic logic: The logic that uses symbols to represent statements and shows certain inferences, implications, and conclusions about those statements.

Synecdoche: A figure of speech that uses a part of something to stand for the whole.

Synonym: A word having the same meaning as another word. *firm = resolute.*

Synonymy: A repetition of synonyms: *a sad, rueful, nostalgic memory.*

Syntax: The combination of grammar and rhetoric to make the best use of both in order to write effective, coherent, balanced sentences.

Synthesis: The unifying of opposing elements to make a new whole.

Synthetic statement: A statement that can not be validated by logical analysis but which has some sort of *a priori* "truth."

Tautology: An analytically valid statement that can be established as valid by logical analysis. *All brothers are male siblings.*

Theme: A general word used to mean: composition, essay, subject for an essay, written exercise or central idea.

Theology: The study of God by religious or philosophical means.

Thesis statement: The specific identification of the main idea or purpose of the essay. May also be called controlling purpose or thesis.

Tone: The emotional flavor of the writing. An element of style. Tone may be determined by diction, figurative language, and rhetorical devices. Some possible tones: *serious, mocking, ironic, maudlin, condescending, objective, emotional, sarcastic, humorous, innocent, cynical, and blasé.* Tone may be called the emotional meaning of a work.

Topic sentence: The sentence in a paragraph that summarizes the thesis or main thrust and purpose of the paragraph. It may appear anywhere in the paragraph or it may be implied; usually it is stated at the beginning.

Transition: The linking device between sentences, paragraphs, or sections of a composition that gives unity, coherence, balance, and meaning to the work. Transitional devices are most effective between paragraphs where they aid the shift and flow of ideas. Some transitional devices fall into the following categories:

Time: *soon, later, after*

Place: *here, beyond, near*

Result: *therefore, thus, hence, in this way*

Comparison: *likewise, similarly, in this fashion*

Contrast: *however, still, but, yet, otherwise*

Addition: *also, too, and, and therefore, moreover, finally*

Miscellaneous: *for example, in fact, indeed, moreover.*

Transitional paragraphs: A paragraph that

is used to change tone, conclude a section, introduce a new idea, or to focus an argument. Usually a short paragraph.

Truism: A self-evident truth, usually trite.

Truth: The result of induction, empirically verified.

Tu Quoque: "You're another" fallacy. A type of reverse name calling.
"You're a witch hunter."
"Yes, but you're an anarchist."

Understatement: A deliberate lessening of the significance of emotions, thought, or meaning of a work, leading to a kind of irony. The opposite of exaggeration and hyperbole.

Unity: The coherence of ideas, supporting evidence, style, tone, and purpose of a piece of writing. Unity may be a consideration within sentences, paragraphs, and entire essays. It may be achieved by organization, singleness of purpose, transitional devices, uniformity of language, and point of view.

Universe of discourse: The limits put to a deductive argument in order to define classes and categories.

Validity: Classification of argument that is logical because the premises imply the conclusions.

Venn diagrams: A graphic presentation of the syllogistic or class membership.

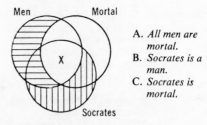

A. *All men are mortal.*
B. *Socrates is a man.*
C. *Socrates is mortal.*

Verbatim: Word for word.

Verisimilitude: A term used in criticism to show the degree of truth-like qualities in a given work.

Vogue word: A word that may have been dormant or not much used in the language until used in a notable fashion by a politically or socially prominent person, causing it to become popular. *Charisma, escalation, mystique.*

Wit: A type of intellectual humor.